PRINCIPLES OF GUIDED MISSILE DESIGN

Editor of the Series

GRAYSON MERRILL, CAPTAIN, U.S.N.

Navy Technical Director, Jupiter Ballistic Missile Project
Bureau of Ordnance

GUIDANCE
  by Arthur S. Locke and collaborators

AERODYNAMICS, PROPULSION, STRUCTURES AND DESIGN PRACTICE
  by E. A. Bonney, M. J. Zucrow, and C. W. Besserer

OPERATIONS RESEARCH, ARMAMENT, LAUNCHING
  by G. Merrill, H. Goldberg, and R. H. Helmholz

SYSTEMS ENGINEERING, RANGE TESTING
  by J. J. Jerger and R. F. Freitag

SPACE FLIGHT
  by K. A. Ehricke

GUIDED MISSILE DESIGNER'S HANDBOOK
  by C. W. Besserer

PRINCIPLES OF
GUIDED MISSILE DESIGN

Edited by
GRAYSON MERRILL, CAPTAIN, U.S.N.

GUID

ARTHUR S. LOCKE
Formerly Consultant
Radar Division
Naval Research Laboratory
Presently Associate Director
Vitro West Orange Laboratory
Vitro Corporation of America

ANCE

In Collaboration with
CHARLES H. DODGE
SAMUEL F. GEORGE
LAURENCE F. GILCHRIST
WILLIAM C. HODGSON
JOHN E. MEADE
JOHN A. SANDERSON
CHARLES F. WHITE
of the Naval Research Laboratory

D. VAN NOSTRAND COMPANY, INC.
PRINCETON, NEW JERSEY · TORONTO · NEW YORK · LONDON

D. VAN NOSTRAND COMPANY, INC.
120 Alexander St., Princeton, New Jersey (*Principal office*)
257 Fourth Avenue, New York 10, New York

D. VAN NOSTRAND COMPANY, LTD.
358, Kensington High Street, London, W.14, England

D. VAN NOSTRAND COMPANY (Canada), LTD.
25 Hollinger Road, Toronto 16, Canada

COPYRIGHT © 1955, BY
D. VAN NOSTRAND COMPANY, INC.

Library of Congress Catalogue Card No. 55-9903

No reproduction in any form of this book, in whole or in part (except for brief quotation in critical articles or reviews), may be made without written authorization from the publishers.

First Printing, September 1955
Reprinted December 1955
September 1956, October 1957

PRINTED IN THE UNITED STATES OF AMERICA

PREFACE

The technology of war has reached its culmination in the guided missile. For thousands of years men have been destroying other men and property with projectile weapons of ever-increasing complexity and power; but these have been uncontrolled after release. Now electromagnetic techniques permit man to guide his weapons in flight and thus to achieve even greater lethality through increased accuracy.

Unfortunately, human progress in morality and law has not been sufficient to rule out war as a chief determinant in our way of life; consequently, preservation of the free world depends, in part, upon mastery of guided missile technology.

This is one of several volumes, collectively entitled *Principles of Guided Missile Design*, which endeavor to set forth the underlying principles of guided missile technology. This volume treats those devices and techniques that are employed to guide missiles and is accordingly entitled "Guidance." Other volumes contain sections entitled "Operations Research," "Systems Engineering," "Structures and Design Practice," "Aerodynamics," "Propulsion," "Armament," "Launching," and "Range Testing."

The purpose of the series as a whole is to give a basis for instruction to graduate students, professional engineers, and technical officers of the armed services so that they can become well grounded in the technology of guided missiles. An engineer who absorbs only this material will not be ready at once to commence the design of a guided missile or of its components. Utilization of the classified literature is essential to this end. However, he should become well fitted to comprehend, evaluate, and utilize the classified literature (which, of course, is protected by security regulations and is generally noninstructional in nature) when and if it is made available to him.

Two unique difficulties arose in the creation of this work. First, it became apparent that the subject embraced such a variety of the basic sciences that no single author could cover it as well as a coordinated group of specialists. Consequently, separate sections have been written by specialists in their fields. Second, great care has been required to avoid disclosure of classified material. The Department of Defense has reviewed this volume and has stated no objection to its open publication.

The "Guidance" section, comprising this volume of the series, was written by Arthur S. Locke and a group of associates of the Naval Research Laboratory. Members of this group have served as consultants to all branches of the military in the solution of specialized problems of research and development relating to missile guidance and to guided missile systems.

Criticism and constructive suggestions are invited. By this means and by keeping abreast of the state of the art we hope to make timely revisions to this volume.

Grateful acknowledgment is made to the persons too numerous to name who assisted in the work and to the Department of Defense whose helpful cooperation made possible a meaningful text without violation of security.

The opinions or assertions contained herein are the private ones of the writers and are not to be construed as official or reflecting the views of the Navy Department or the Naval Establishment at large.

GRAYSON MERRILL
Editor

Johnsville, Pa.

FOREWORD

Discussion of the principles of missile guidance involves so many fields and subfields of science that, in the interest of writing a volume of the required scope within a reasonable time, it was expedient to employ the coordinated writings of a group of specialists rather than the efforts of a single author. The authors associated herein have had many years of experience in team effort, other than in the production of this volume. The majority of the authors have worked together in the research and development of military equipment, both during and subsequent to World War II. The completed work represents, in addition to their individual efforts, the product of the interchange of ideas, discussions, and critical appraisals among the authors. It is therefore difficult to pinpoint specific credit in many instances, the work being truly the result of group effort.

Related to the problem of coordinating the various scientific fields involved in missile guidance was the question of the various mathematical notations used by the different sciences. Notations which are conventionally employed in a specific technical field are used in the sections dealing with that science. In an attempt to avoid ambiguities in those chapters which heavily employ mathematical notation, the notation used in the chapter is given in tabular form at the beginning and within each chapter and, in general, is only exact for that chapter.

Chapters 1, 2, 3, and 4—covering the introduction to and the fundamental problems of missile guidance, the prior and presently available and related arts, terrestrial and celestial reference information, and the transmission of radio waves—were written by Arthur S. Locke. The effect of flame on the transmission of electromagnetic energy was written by William W. Balwanz, of the Radar Division, Naval Research Laboratory.

Chapter 5, covering the emission, transmission, and detection of infrared radiation, was written by Dr. John A. Sanderson, Superintendent, Optics Division, NRL.

Chapter 6, dealing with the mathematical groundwork considered essential in the field, was written by Samuel F. George, Consultant, Radar Division, NRL.

Chapter 7, on servo-system theory, was written by Charles F. White, Consultant, Equipment Research Branch, Radar Division, NRL.

Chapters 8 and 9, dealing with tactical considerations of missile guidance and measurements of missile motion, were written by Arthur S. Locke, subject to the particularly pertinent criticisms of James W. Titus of the Radar Division, NRL.

Chapter 10, covering detection and information gathering, is the result of a joint effort by Laurence F. Gilchrist and Howard Gordon of the Radar Division, NRL. John P. Kirwan, also of the Radar Division, wrote the material on beaconry.

Chapter 11, discussing target considerations in the light of radar employment, was written by John E. Meade, Associate Superintendent, Radar Division, NRL.

Chapter 12, dealing with the analysis of missile flight paths, was written by S. F. George, assisted by C. E. Corum and John P. Barry of the Radar Division, NRL.

Chapters 13, 15, and 20, which respectively have to do with prelaunching and launching, economics, and the systems concept, were written by A. S. Locke.

Chapter 14, which discusses the missile airframe and the derivation of transfer characteristics for it, was written by Charles H. Dodge, Consultant, Radar Division, NRL, and A. S. Locke and draws heavily upon the earlier work of J. W. Titus.

Chapter 16 which deals with the types and sub-types of missile guidance systems was written as a group effort by John C. Ryon, Kelly G. Miles, Ernest W. Peterkin, and William C. Hodgson, under the direction of the latter. All of these authors are of the Radar Division, NRL.

Chapter 17, illustrating the application of servo-system theory to bandwidth studies concerning elements of the guidance system, was written by C. F. White.

Chapter 18, a continuation of the bandwidth studies, but concerned principally with missile guidance system bandwidth, was written by C. H. Dodge, assisted by C. F. White and A. S. Locke.

Chapter 19, concerning analog and digital simulation as applied to missile guidance and discussing other techniques or devices which are employed to assist in the design of missile guidance equipment, is the combined writing of several authors coordinated by A. S. Locke. These are: Dr. Louis Bauer, Project Director of Project Cyclone, Reeves Instrument Co., N.Y.C., who discusses generalities of missile guidance simulation; W. A. McCool of the Mechanics Division, Naval Research Laboratory, who writes about the mechanization of equations for analog computation; D. H. Gridley, directing designer of the NAREC digital computer, of the Applications Research Division, who deals with digital computation; Mr. White, who illustrates the use of conventional aircraft and analog computers as simulators of guided missiles; Paul T. Stine, Radar Division, who reviews telemetry as an aid to missile guidance system design; and Dr. N. L. Walbridge, H. M. Smith, Jr., and L. A. Woodward of the University of

Vermont who write about the use of a ripple tank in the simulation of electromagnetic wave phase-fronts.

Acknowledgments

In addition to the authors, there are many to whom acknowledgment must be made for an active part in the writing of this book. Members of the Department of Defense, and in particular those of the matériel bureaus of the Navy, assisted with suggestions, criticisms, and technical readings. The deepest thanks must be extended to the many officers, officials, and scientists of the Naval Research Laboratory who assisted the authors both by encouragement in the venture and by actual participation in the preparation of this volume. Dr. Robert M. Page, Associate Director of Research for Electronics of the NRL, was of considerable assistance in the initial stages of the work. The continued advice, criticism, and assistance of Peter Waterman, Head of the Equipment Research Branch, Radar Division, NRL, with whom the principal author has worked closely for many years, were essential elements in the development of this book. In addition to his authorship of two of the chapters of this book, Mr. George also had the responsibility of reviewing the mathematical aspects of the other chapters in the book.

The responsibility accepted by Mrs. Arthur S. Locke in typing the majority of the manuscript and assisting in the many mechanical processes of correction and proof reading represents a large personal contribution which is most gratefully acknowledged.

ARTHUR S. LOCKE
Principal Author

CONTENTS

Preface v
Foreword vii

CHAPTER 1 FUNDAMENTAL PROBLEMS OF MISSILE GUIDANCE

1-1	Introduction	1
1-2	Guided Missile	3
1-3	Guided Missile System	4
1-4	Missile Guidance System	4
1-5	Categories of Guided Missiles	4
1-6	Surface-to-Surface Missile Guidance	5
1-7	Surface-to-Air Missile Guidance	8
1-8	Air-to-Surface Missile Guidance	10
1-9	Air-to-Air Missile Guidance	12
1-10	Guided Missiles Against Underwater Targets	14
1-11	Basis for Military Service Requirements	16
1-12	Guidance Phases During Missile Flight . . .	18
1-13	Missile Guidance Fundamentals . . .	19

CHAPTER 2 PRIOR DEVELOPMENTS

2-1	Conventional Weapon Systems . .	22
2-2	Anti-Aircraft Gunfire Control . . .	23
2-3	Surface Gunfire Control . . .	27
2-4	Shipboard Stabilization of Gunfire Control Systems . . .	28
2-5	Parallax Computation . . .	29
2-6	Airborne Gunfire Control Systems . . .	30
2-7	Missile Guidance Systems of World War II . . .	33
2-8	V-1 Guidance System	35
2-9	V-2 Guidance System	36
2-10	German Radio Command Guidance Systems . . .	38
2-11	Glide Bombs	42
2-12	Postwar Missile Guidance Developments . . .	44
2-13	The Viking Rocket	44
2-14	Airborne Navigation	47
2-15	Navigation by Observation and Recognition	47
2-16	Navigation by Triangulation	48
2-17	Navigation by Earth or Space References . . .	51
2-18	Automatic Control of Aircraft . . .	52
2-19	Aircraft Autopilots . . .	52

CHAPTER 3 TERRESTRIAL AND CELESTIAL REFERENCES

3-1	Chart Projections . .	55
3-2	Mercator Projection	57

CONTENTS

3-3	Transverse Mercator Projection	59
3-4	Gnomonic Projection	61
3-5	Polar Charts	61
3-6	Lambert Conformal Projection	61
3-7	Polyconic Projection	63
3-8	Motions of the Earth	64
3-9	Effects of Rotation of the Earth	64
3-10	Shape of the Earth	64
3-11	Effect of Rotation of the Earth on Gravity	65
3-12	The Coriolis Effect	69
3-13	Time	72
3-14	Revolution, Precession and Space Motion of the Earth	73
3-15	Terrestrial Magnetism	74
3-16	Additional Terrestrial References	75
3-17	Celestial References	76
3-18	The Navigational Triangle	78
3-19	Marine and Air Celestial Navigation	82
3-20	Celestial Navigation by Automatic Means	84
3-21	Polar Navigation	86

CHAPTER 4 TRANSMISSION OF RADIO WAVES

4-1	Classification of Radio Frequencies	89
4-2	The Atmosphere	91
4-3	Effect of the Ionosphere on Radio Wave Transmission	92
4-4	Multipath Transmission	94
4-5	Effect of Index of Refraction of Air on Transmission	95
4-6	Polarization of Radio Waves	97
4-7	Reflection of Radio Waves	98
4-8	Dual Path Transmission	99
4-9	Factors Affecting Choice of Polarization	104
4-10	Diffraction of Radio Waves	106
4-11	Typical Field Strength Curves	107
4-12	Absorption of Radio Waves	109
4-13	Scattering of Radio Waves	110
4-14	Attenuation by Condensed Water and Other Forms of Precipitation	111
4-15	Factors Affecting Choice of Frequency	113
4-16	Radomes	113
4-17	Transmission Through a Sheet of Dielectric Material	115
4-18	Effect of Flames on Radio Wave Transmission	119
4-19	Conductivity of a Gaseous Medium with a Free Charge	120
4-20	Absorption in a Gaseous Medium with a Free Charge	121
4-21	Reflection at a Boundary Between Air and a Gaseous Medium with a Free Charge	122
4-22	Experimental and Theoretical Studies	122

CHAPTER 5 EMISSION, TRANSMISSION AND DETECTION OF THE INFRARED

	List of Symbols	126
5-1	Total Radiation	127
5-2	The Spectral Distribution of Radiation	138

5-3	Simplified Forms of the Distribution Law	143
5-4	Detectors of Thermal Radiation	144
5-5	Atmospheric Transmission	157
5-6	Integrated Response of a Detector	166
5-7	Optical Materials	169

CHAPTER 6 MATHEMATICAL GROUNDWORK

	List of Symbols	176
6-1	Linear Networks	177
6-2	The Laplace Transformation	179
6-3	Development of Function-Transform Pairs	180
6-4	Basic Theorems of the Laplace Transformation	182
6-5	The Solution of a Simple I-D Equation	184
6-6	The L^{-1} Transform of Rational Fractions	186
6-7	The Solution of Some Important I-D Equations	188
6-8	The Fourier Transform	192
6-9	The Frequency-Response Function	193
6-10	Simplification by Replacing $\frac{d}{dt}$ by $j\omega$ for Steady State	195
6-11	The Transfer Characteristic of a System	196
6-12	Correlation Functions	197
6-13	Poles, Zeros, and Analytic Functions	199
6-14	Stability in Feedback Systems	200
6-15	Two Methods of Curve Fitting	211
6-16	Brief Discussion of Probability Theory	222

CHAPTER 7 SERVO SYSTEM THEORY

	List of Symbols	230
7-1	Servo System Design Problem	232
7-2	Closed Loop Relationships	234
7-3	Basic Type I Servo System	236
7-4	Improved Type I Servo System	250
7-5	Basic Type II Servo System	255
7-6	Transfer-Function Design Technique	263
7-7	Improvement of System Performance	282
7-8	Interplay of Frequency Response and Transient Response Theory in System Design	289

CHAPTER 8 TACTICAL CONSIDERATIONS

8-1	Target Damage Definitions	293
8-2	Terminology of Errors	296
8-3	Surface-to-Surface Missile Guidance	301
8-4	Surface-to-Air Missile Guidance	308
8-5	Air-to-Surface Missile Guidance	316
8-6	Air-to-Air Missile	320

CHAPTER 9 MEASUREMENTS OF MISSILE MOTION

9-1	Datum Determination	326
9-2	The Gyroscope	327

CONTENTS

9-3	The Vertical Gyroscope	330
9-4	Airborne Magnetic Compasses	335
9-5	The Single Degree of Freedom Mechanical System	337
9-6	Linear Accelerometers	339
9-7	Angular Accelerometers	349
9-8	Rate Gyroscopes	350
9-9	Use of Motion-Measuring Devices	353

CHAPTER 10 DETECTION AND INFORMATION GATHERING

	List of Symbols	356
10-1	Typical Communications Systems	357
10-2	Modes of Intelligence Transmission	357
10-3	Amplitude Modulation—Carrier and Two Sidebands	358
10-4	Amplitude Modulation—Suppressed Carrier, Two Sidebands	358
10-5	Amplitude Modulation—Single Sideband, Suppressed Carrier	359
10-6	Frequency Modulation	360
10-7	Subcarriers	362
10-8	The Nature of Guidance Intelligence	364
10-9	Spectrum of the Primary Carrier	364
10-10	Loran	365
10-11	Basic Concepts in Loran	365
10-12	Identification of Loran Pairs	367
10-13	Service Areas for Loran	368
10-14	Propagation Effects on Loran	369
10-15	Loran System Accuracy	371
10-16	Possible Loran Missile Application	373
10-17	Radar	374
10-18	FM Radar System	377
10-19	Pulsed Radar System Parameters	382
10-20	Radar Antennas	383
10-21	Radar R-F Components	387
10-22	Radar Transmitters	389
10-23	Pulse Modulators	390
10-24	Tracking Radar	392
10-25	The Radar Receiver	393
10-26	Mixers and Local Oscillators	394
10-27	Noise Figure Considerations	395
10-28	I-f Systems	398
10-29	Video Amplifiers and Detectors	399
10-30	Automatic Gain Control	402
10-31	Automatic Range Tracking	408
10-32	Range Units	413
10-33	Angle Error Detectors	415
10-34	Power Sources	419
10-35	Radar Tracking at Low Elevation Angles	422
10-36	Correlation Techniques	424
10-37	Traveling Wave Tubes	426
10-38	Beaconry	428
10-39	Reliable Beacon Range	429
10-40	Beacon Receivers	429
10-41	Beacon Modulators	431

CONTENTS

10-42	Beacon Antenna Considerations	433
10-43	Use of the Beacon in Missile Guidance Systems	433

CHAPTER 11 TARGET CONSIDERATIONS

11-1	Reflection of Radio Waves	435
11-2	Aircraft as Targets	435
11-3	Statistical Characteristics of Aircraft Targets	436
11-4	Determination of Angular Coordinates	437
11-5	Determination of the Range Coordinate	438
11-6	Determination of Tracking Noise	439
11-7	Origin of Target Noise	439
11-8	Analysis of a Two-Element Target	440
11-9	Effects of Amplitude Fluctuation	442
11-10	Large Target Tracking	443
11-11	Low Angle Tracking	444

CHAPTER 12 THE ANALYSIS OF FLIGHT PATHS

	List of Symbols	445
12-1	Line-of-Sight Course (Beam-Rider Missile)	446
12-2	Pure Pursuit Course	459
12-3	Deviated Pursuit Course	468
12-4	Constant-Bearing Course	473
12-5	Proportional Navigation	475

CHAPTER 13 PRELAUNCHING AND LAUNCHING

13-1	Prelaunching Operations, General	479
13-2	Prelaunching Operation, Guidance Equipment	480
13-3	Launching, General	482
13-4	Launching, Surface-to-Surface Missile Guidance	485
13-5	Launching, Surface-to-Air Missile Guidance	486
13-6	Launching, Air-to-Surface Missile Guidance	488
13-7	Launching, Air-to-Air Missile Guidance	489

CHAPTER 14 THE MISSILE AIRFRAME

14-1	Airframe Environment	490
14-2	The Airframe as an Element in Control Loops	492
14-3	Classical Expressions for the Airframe	494
14-4	Derivation of Transfer Functions in Pitch	496
14-5	Effect of Change of Environmental Parameters	507
14-6	Effect of Variation of Stability Parameters	509
14-7	Derivation of Transfer Function in Roll	511
14-8	Experimental Confirmation of the Frequency Response of an Airframe	513
14-9	Use of Airframe Characteristics by the Control Designer	514

CHAPTER 15 ECONOMIC CONSIDERATIONS

15-1	Peacetime Economy *vs* Wartime Economy	516
15-2	Missile Guidance Equipment Research and Development Program	518
15-3	Production and Distribution of Equipment External to the Missile	523

CONTENTS

15-4	Production and Distribution of Missile Borne Guidance Equipment	525
15-5	Maintenance of Shipborne Guidance Equipment	530
15-6	Maintenance of Missile Borne Guidance Equipment	530
15-7	Guided Missile System Costs	530
15-8	Environmental Specifications	532
15-9	Equipment Environmental Research	533
15-10	Environmental Acceptance Tests	534
15-11	Reliability	535

CHAPTER 16 MISSILE GUIDANCE SYSTEMS

	List of Symbols	539
16-1	System Design Considerations	540
16-2	Homing Guidance Systems	541
16-3	Command Guidance Systems	562
16-4	Beam-Rider Guidance Systems	574
16-5	Inertial, Terrestrial and Celestial Reference Guidance Systems	583
16-6	Application of Radio Navigation Techniques to Missile Guidance	595
16-7	Missile Guidance by Acoustic Means	602
16-8	Guidance System Combinations	605

CHAPTER 17 BANDWIDTH STUDIES

	List of Symbols	608
17-1	Tactical Problem	609
17-2	Radar Range Calculations	611
17-3	Missile System	612
17-4	Illuminating Radar and Launcher	613
17-5	Launcher Computer	618
17-6	Stabilization Against Ship Motion	618
17-7	Missile-borne Radar	618
17-8	Interpretation	623

CHAPTER 18 MISSILE GUIDANCE BANDWIDTH STUDIES

18-1	General Discussion	624
18-2	Space Geometry and Kinematic Terms	627
18-3	The Autopilot Loop	630
18-4	Pitch Guidance Loop	637
18-5	Launching Transients	638
18-6	Roll Control	639
18-7	Miss Due to System Limitations	642
18-8	Interpretations	643

CHAPTER 19 SIMULATION, COMPUTATION AND TELEMETRY

19-1	Simulation	644
19-2	Mechanization of Equations	648
19-3	Essentials of Three-Dimensional Guided Missile Simulation	660
19-4	Computers, Analog and Digital	664
19-5	Digital Computers	665
19-6	Simulation of Missile by Conventional Aircraft	672

19-7	The Use of Radio Telemetry as an Aid to Missile Guidance System Design	684
19-8	Radio Wave Propagation Simulation	698
19-9	Discussion	705

CHAPTER 20 THE SYSTEM CONCEPT

20-1	Scope of System Study	709
20-2	The Human as a System Element	710
20-3	Future Missile Guidance Systems	712

INDEX 715

Launching of the Viking Aboard the USS Norton Sound

U. S. Navy Photo

CHAPTER 1

FUNDAMENTAL PROBLEMS OF MISSILE GUIDANCE

1-1 INTRODUCTION

The guided missile is, for the moment, the most recent extension of a series of weapons designed to permit man, with destructive intent, to hit a target, while remaining at a relatively safe distance. It is the logical sequel to the thrown stone, the cast spear, the gun, and the rocket. The fundamental requirements have remained unchanged—despite advances in technology or whether the missile is directed in defense or in attack—namely, to destroy the target and to remain in safety.

Targets have changed, and will continue to change, in specific form and behavior. The basic categories of targets, however, are still the stationary target and the moving target. When it first became important to defend a place or a group of people rather than an individual, specialization in weapons began to develop. The weapons used for attack had to be powerful enough to destroy the protective cover before the defenders could be engaged. Since the defended areas were immovable and the attackers had to come to them, weapons were made mobile. The mobile weapons, in turn, became targets. As conflicts became generalized, the mobility of weapons was extended to many forms on the land and sea and in the air. The basic categories, nevertheless, remain unchanged.

In the case of the stationary target, the intelligence required to bombard it is conventionally derived from known information about its location as referred to the location of the bombardment weapon. The continued increase in the ability of the defenders of a stationary target to retaliate from a distance has necessitated corresponding increases in range of the bombardment weapon. In conventional bombardment by gunfire, the position of the target is determined by sight or by local grid survey transferred in proper coordinates to the aiming point. In general, the errors of gunfire at the target increase with the range of fire. When the range is increased to hundreds of miles, even the most precise aim practicable may result in large errors at the target. When intercontinental ranges are considered, the missile must be endowed with sufficient intelligence to acquire, from terrestrial or celestial references, information to keep it on course to the target.

In the case of the moving target, the intelligence which directs the conventional weapons is usually derived from actual observation of the target and measurement or estimate of its motion. Since the shell or rocket requires a finite time to reach the target, a prediction of the future position of the target must be made and the weapon aimed and fired at that future position. If the target moves slowly and the time of flight of the shell is short, reasonable accuracy may be expected. If the target moves rapidly, to the degree that it can maneuver away from its predicted position within the time of flight of the shell, the probability of its destruction becomes low. Correspondingly, if the target is difficult to observe and its motion cannot be measured accurately, the probability of its destruction decreases. Aircraft targets have continued to increase in velocity and have become more difficult to see. In using guided missiles against moving targets such as aircraft, the missile must be controlled in flight in correspondence to changes in target motion. In guided missiles, for use against either stationary or moving targets, the essential change from conventional weapons is the transposition of all or part of the intelligence and/or control from the aiming point to the missile; and it is with this transposition we are here primarily concerned.

The application of guidance and control within the missile rather than at the aiming point has been attended by many subsidiary problems. The engineering technologies involved, while none are new, are forced into combinations which have not previously existed. The necessity for a common language between engineering specialties has been emphasized, and an appreciation for the better tools of companion professions is being realized. All of the physical sciences are involved to a greater or lesser degree. The missile guidance system is essentially a "series" device, wherein each element must function in order that the system as a whole will operate correctly. This requires not only that coordination must exist among the designers of different elements or components in different professional fields, but also that the development within each of the fields must proceed simultaneously to an equal standard of usability.

The designer of the guidance system has the complex problem of combining many different components into a functional and reliable guided missile. It is necessary that the designer understand what basic intelligence exists in regard to the specific target, how to detect it, and how to communicate the intelligence in a usable manner. The effect of the propulsion device on both the transmission of intelligence and the control of the missile must be recognized. The behavior of the vehicle as it responds to intelligence supplied to it must be thoroughly appreciated. The detailed design of the control mechanisms is within his province. The effect of each element of the system must be analyzed, so that in the final eventuality of use the missile will be brought to the target with predictable accuracy and probability of kill.

The designer of a guidance system is frequently inhibited by component design. Elements of the guidance system may become immutably fixed, forcing undesirable compromises on other elements of the system. Conversely, a necessary component may be deferred in development, only to find that the assumed perfection of this element cannot be obtained and severe compromises of system performances result. The designer of each component of the system must appreciate the part that his own element plays, both as an entity within itself and as a part of the functional whole. The designer of a missile guidance system, however, cannot be concerned only with the design and analysis of a specific system; since there are so many possible system types, he must be prepared also to analyze the effectiveness of his specific design as opposed to other guidance systems.

The purpose of this text is (a) to reduce the problem of missile guidance to its fundamentals and to review prior development and the physical sciences as required by these fundamentals; (b) to show some of the tactical and practical considerations required in component and system design; and (c) to illustrate the design of guidance systems in simple form suitable for synthesis of both components and complete systems. The information collected and the applications shown are intended to be basic in character, i.e., for the purpose of illustrating the interrelationships which must exist between the several engineering fields, rather than to cover completely any of the fields so involved. Experience in complex system design indicates that the major problems result from a lack of appreciation for the overall fundamentals rather than from a lack of knowledge of the details of a specific field of engineering.

1-2 GUIDED MISSILE

A guided missile is defined as a space-traversing unmanned vehicle which carries within itself the means for controlling its flight path.

In addition to this simple definition, there are several conditions which must be kept in mind. Although the American philosophy does not include deliberate suicide on the part of a man who acts as a guidance system, this philosophy is not universal, as evidenced by the Baka bomb of the Japanese. A guided missile is considered to operate only above and not on or under the surface of the earth. Homing torpedoes and guided surface vehicles, such as tanks and boats, may rightfully be considered as guided weapons, but the guidance systems for them will not be considered in this text. The word *missile* is commonly defined as "a weapon, as a spear, arrow, or bullet" and is considered implicitly to involve destructive intent. If, however, in certain guided missiles the warhead, or source of destructive intent, is removed, it may be replaced with a payload of scientific instruments for upper atmosphere or other research. The guidance system may still be required for safety requirements, but the missile is now designated as an upper atmosphere research rocket.

1-3 GUIDED MISSILE SYSTEM

A guided missile system is defined as a combination of a guided missile and its ancillary launching, guidance, test and handling equipment which together accomplish a mission of destruction of the target. The reader is referred to the "Systems Engineering Section" of this series of volumes for a broader treatment of this subject.

1-4 MISSILE GUIDANCE SYSTEM

A missile guidance system is defined as a group of components which measures the position of a guided missile with respect to its target and causes changes in the flight path as required. Some of the system elements may be external to the missile: at the launching site; enroute to the target; or on the target. Normally the missile guidance system includes sensing, computing, directing, stabilizing and servo-control components.

The word *control* is frequently used, loosely or otherwise, as being nearly synonymous with guidance. As herein employed, a control system or device is considered to be a component part of the guidance system. It is most usually employed to designate the elements which actuate the missile or other portions of the system in response to intelligence generated elsewhere.

1-5 CATEGORIES OF GUIDED MISSILES

The most descriptive way to establish guided missile categories for operational and tactical use is by reference to the physical areas of launching and the physical areas containing the target to be destroyed. The physical area of launching inherently discloses the general logistics of the situation and, to some degree, specifies the service branch within which the major tactical interest lies; the physical area of the target discloses the nature of the target threat or the tactical duty of the missile. The reader is referred to the "Operations Research Section" of this series for greater detail. The four general categories of guided missiles are:

        a. Surface-to-surface
        b. Surface-to-air
        c. Air-to-surface
        d. Air-to-air

1-6 SURFACE-TO-SURFACE MISSILE GUIDANCE

The category of surface-to-surface guided missiles includes any missile launched from the surface of the earth, the function of which is to destroy a target also on the surface of the earth. This classification does not differentiate between missiles launched from ships as opposed to land; nor between targets which are stationary as opposed to surface targets which are in motion. The type of guidance, missile, and warhead or any other characteristics are immaterial within the scope of this weapon classification.

If we examine specific surface targets in the light of possible tactical demands, it is possible to draw some general conclusions on guidance system requirements. Surface targets come in infinite variety of sizes but vary little in ability of motion. Let us consider first the stationary target. It may vary from an entire city, or a specific area within a city such as a factory making strategic materials, to a target as small as an entrenchment delaying an infantry advance. The range to the target

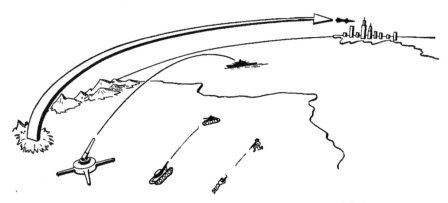

FIG. 1-1 The Size of the Target Tends to Increase with Range.

from the launching point also varies greatly for stationary targets. For destruction of strategic targets or large areas within the borders of an enemy country, the range should be sufficient so that any possible target can be reached from launching positions within our country or from bases controlled by our forces. For destruction of targets which represent opposition to the advance of ground forces, the range would be expected to vary from a few hundred yards for close infantry support to perhaps fifty to two hundred miles for destruction of rear echelon supporting troops, ammunition dumps, or transportation facilities. It will be noted that, as in Fig. 1-1, the size of the target generally increases with range; or, conversely, the absolute accuracy required of the weapon tends to decrease with range.

In order to direct a guided missile or any weapon from the launching or aiming point to the target it is necessary first to know the position of one with respect to the other. The available information varies with the range between them. Targets at close range can be seen or otherwise sensed, and the intelligence as to their location is direct from the aiming point. As the range increases, the positions of the target and the aiming point can be accurately related by triangulation, when both positions can be viewed simultaneously, although direct sight between target and aiming point may be impossible. If an accurate survey of the complete tactical area is available (which is the result of having previously established line-of-sight relationships), the target can be indicated as a position on a geographical grid. This target location permits establishment of coordinates of fire related not directly to the target but established by some feature of, or reference to, the earth.

The accuracy of any weapon system depending upon geographical or other similar references is directly affected by the accuracy of locating both the target and aiming point within the reference framework. For example, suppose a spotter for artillery fire calls for a salvo on a target fixed by grid coordinates. If he is in error in locating the target, and the salvo falls on the grid coordinates he requested, the miss is directly caused by error in estimated target position. Conversely, if the computed aim is based upon an erroneous gun position, a miss results. If the range is increased to the degree that intercontinental distances are considered, then the only relationships which exist must be developed from such terrestrial or celestial references available that indicate the location of the target and the launching position in common terms. The accuracy to which the location of each is known will directly affect the accuracy of the hit.

The guidance system must measure the position of the missile with respect to the target and cause changes in the flight path as required. In the case of the stationary target, if the range is short, the relation between the missile in flight and the target may be measured by direct sight. If the range is too great to establish a direct visual relationship between the missile and the target, the guidance system must continuously relate the position of the missile in flight to the known position of the target. If the missile can be seen and its position measured from a ground station, the position and motion of the missile can be measured either from the ground or in the missile, and the proper flight path to the target can be continuously computed. In a long-range piloted bomber, navigation is by means of visual contact with references on the ground, by radio navigation, by use of terrestrial references such as a compass, or by celestial navigation. The pilot, however, at the end of his flight can then visually detect his target so that the accuracy of his navigation need only be sufficient to bring him to the general area. All of the methods of navigation available to the pilot can conceivably be made available in automatic form to the missile, with the added requirement that accuracy of navigation of the missile may have to be of a higher order to replace the terminal guiding ability of the pilot.

Summarizing the general conclusions which have been developed pertinent to guiding missiles against stationary targets, we find:

a. The size of the target tends to increase with range; or, conversely, the absolute accuracy demanded of the guidance system tends to decrease the range.

b. When the measurement of the position of the missile with respect to the target is dependent upon geographic or other references, the accuracy of locating the target with respect to the reference directly affects the accuracy of the missile's hit.

c. The missile may be guided by establishing its position with respect to the target directly by line-of-sight; or it may be navigated to the target by incorporating some method of automatic navigation.

With regard to moving surface targets, the possible targets on land are tanks, trains, trucks, or other vehicles; and on the sea, surface ships and subsurface craft. All of the surface vehicles have relatively low velocities, as compared to guided missiles, but since motion does exist and the target is relatively small, direct observation of its location and measurement of its motion are required. Against isolated targets, the accuracy needed for destruction does not vary with range. If a group of targets exists, such as a truck or tank depot, or a convoy of trucks, the target becomes a stationary one, since the depot or the road becomes the point at which the missile is aimed. Some of the vehicles, for example tanks and warships, employ protective armor so that, to be destructive, a hit must be direct or nearly so. The accuracy required for a hit on any specific target is also a function of the destructive power of the missile's warhead; obviously, as the radius of destruction is increased, the requirement for accuracy of the hit decreases in order to achieve the same probable amount of destruction at the target.

The following conclusions logically develop, pertinent to guidance systems, with regard to isolated moving targets:

a. Direct observation of location and motion of the target is required from some element of the guidance system.

b. The accuracy required for destruction tends to be high; the need for absolute accuracy at the target does not vary with range.

c. The absolute accuracy required of the guidance system is an inverse function of the destructive power of the warhead.

1-7 SURFACE-TO-AIR MISSILE GUIDANCE

The category of surface-to-air guided missiles includes any guided missile launched from the surface of the earth, the primary function of which is to destroy a target in the air. No differentiation is made between missiles launched from ships as opposed to missiles launched from land; nor is any distinction drawn as to the type of airborne target. The character of the guidance system, warhead, missile, or other characteristics are immaterial within the scope of this weapon category.

Examination of the possible airborne targets in the light of the tactical use of a guided missile indicates some general conclusion on guidance system requirements for surface-to-air missiles. The aircraft targets may be assumed to be other guided missiles and propeller- or jet-driven aircraft of all types. All these targets have high-speed capabilities and all are relatively small in size. The high-speed and maneuvering capability of the target indicates that some element of the missile guidance system must be able to sense the target and to measure continuously the position of the missile with respect to the target. Since the targets are small in size, the guidance system must be accurate in order to effect a target kill. The target is free to maneuver in space, within limits, so that the missile and guidance system must be prepared to accept such maneuvers without intolerable loss in accuracy. The target is not constrained in altitude, except by physical limits of the aircraft type; it may fly at high altitude or it may fly immediately above the ground. The missile guidance system must be at least equally capable of satisfactory performance insofar as altitude is concerned. The target may fly singly or in numbers. The missile guidance system may be forced to isolate one aircraft from among others in order to effect a kill.

The tactical mission of airborne targets is assumed to be the destruction of a location that the surface-to-air missile is defending. The guided missile employed in defense against airborne targets must destroy them before they can release their own weapons, as in Fig. 1-2, or the attack mission will have been successful. Where the surface-to-air missile launcher is located on or at the target to be defended, it is desirable that the range of the guidance system be greater than the range of the weapons employed by the attacking aircraft.

A finite time between sighting a moving target and putting any weapon in use against the target is required. In one of the most simple examples, a man, having detected a moving target, must bring his rifle to his shoulder, aim, mentally compute the lead for target motion, and fire. As a generality, the more complex the weapon system is and the faster the target is moving, the greater is the time required to observe the target, measure its motion, compute the proper interception, and fire the weapon. When its speed is great, the target may travel many miles during the time between sighting it and firing the missile. It is desirable, then, to obtain accurate knowledge of the behavior and identity of an approaching aircraft target as soon as possible. It is equally desirable that such knowledge be supplied to the missile guidance system so that full use may be obtained of the maximum guidance range.

Aircraft targets are inherently small in size and high in speed and maneuverability. Both these characteristics represent factors of difficulty in detecting the target and accurately measuring its motion after it has

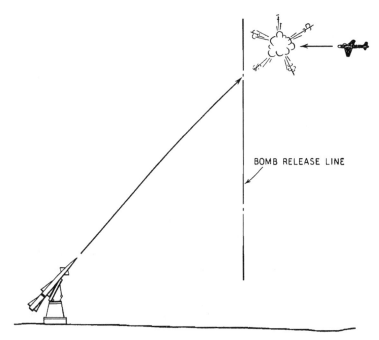

FIG. 1-2 The Guided Missile Must Destroy the Aircraft Before the Aircraft Can Release Its Own Weapon.

been found. The problems of searching for, identifying, and accurately observing an airborne target are not compatible with long-range system operation. Consequently, difficulty may be encountered in the solution of this guidance problem.

Some of the tentative general conclusions which may be reached, pertinent to the surface-to-air guided missile are as follows:

a. Because of the speed and maneuverability of the target, some element of the guidance system must be able to sense the target in order to measure the position of the missile with respect to it.

b. The small size of the target indicates the need for accurate interception by the missile in order to effect a kill.

c. The aircraft target is not necessarily inhibited in altitude; the guidance system should be equally versatile.

d. The target has a high order of performance as to speed and maneuverability; the missile and guidance system should be capable of performance which will effectively combat the target.

e. Targets may exist simultaneously in large numbers. The guidance system may have to isolate a single target to effect a kill.

f. The range required of the guidance system may be partially determined by the weapons carried by the aircraft; it may be partially determined by the tactics of defense.

g. Since the speed of the target is high, the operational time required to put the missile into useful service should be kept at a minimum.

h. The problem of searching for and finding aircraft targets and accurately observing them is important to the interception of airborne targets.

i. Except in extreme tactical circumstances, the target must be identified as friend or foe before any action against it is taken.

1-8 AIR-TO-SURFACE MISSILE GUIDANCE

The category of air-to-surface guided missiles includes any guided missile launched from an aircraft against any target on the surface of the earth. No differentiation is made as to the type of aircraft from which the missile is launched nor as to the type of target against which it is employed. The character of the guidance system, warhead, missile, or other characteristics of the weapon system are immaterial within the scope of the weapon classification.

If we again examine surface targets and consider them in the light of possible tactical use of an air-launched missile, some deductions may be made, of general character, pertinent to the guidance system for such a missile. Surface targets are both stationary and moving. The stationary targets are highly variable in size and, therefore, to some degree, in the accuracy required of the guidance system. The aircraft that serves as the missile launching platform is in rapid motion. Although mobile surface targets move slowly as compared to missile-carrying aircraft or missiles, motion of the surface target is not negligible in the problem when the time of flight is appreciable. The primary reason for employing aircraft as a long-range bombardment weapon is to put an observer in a location where the target may be seen, as in Fig. 1-3, and hence increase the accuracy of the bombardment despite the long range involved. The mobility of the aircraft makes it possible to seek out for destruction mobile targets and small stationary targets that otherwise cannot be reduced.

Every effort is made to make surface targets difficult to observe from the air. Stationary targets are hidden; mobile targets are camouflaged. Targets are painted or otherwise covered to make them indistinguishable from their background. When observation is made by electronic means, suitable countermeasures are employed.

Summarizing some general deductions pertinent to guidance systems for the air-to-surface missile, we find:

a. Some portion of the guidance system will be required to observe the target.

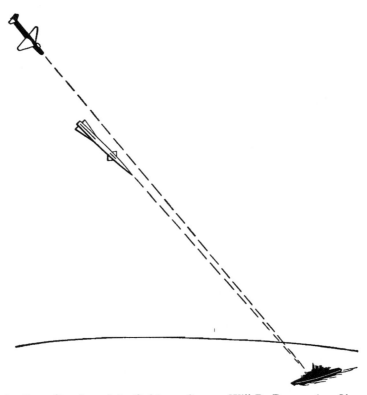

Fig. 1-3 Some Portion of the Guidance System Will Be Required to Observe the Target.

b. Since observation of the target will be involved, the range required of the guidance system will be limited by the range of the observation means employed.

c. It may be assumed that every effort will be made to make it difficult for the missile system to distinguish the target from its background, or that countermeasures will be taken to negate the effectiveness of the guidance system.

1-9 AIR-TO-AIR MISSILE GUIDANCE

The category of air-to-air guided missiles designates any guided missile launched from an aircraft the primary function of which is to destroy a target in the air. In this generalized classification, no distinction is drawn as to the type of aircraft carrying the missiles nor as to the type of aircraft target. The character of the missile and its guidance system is immaterial within the scope of this weapon classification.

Aircraft are employed as both defensive and offensive weapons. The defensive aircraft is used chiefly to intercept an airborne attack. The attack should be intercepted as early as possible after the threat becomes known so that the attack mission has less likelihood of being successfully completed. In order to make an interception, it is first necessary to know that an attack threatens, and it is desirable to know enough details about the attacking aircraft so that the interceptor aircraft may be directed to the engagement at a safe distance from the target being defended. The intercepting aircraft must be directed with sufficient accuracy so that the attacking aircraft may be sensed in some manner and engaged in battle. The accuracy of the interceptor direction may logically be expected to play an active part in placing the interceptor at the most favorable position to attack the enemy aircraft.

The attacking aircraft, depending upon its tactical mission, may be any of several different types. For a long-range bombing mission, intercontinental or otherwise, a large aircraft probably will be used, with a heavy payload encumbered by the requirement that the aircraft carry enough fuel for the return trip. The large bomber with its companion aircraft, represents such a vast investment of time and money that, even at the ultimate sacrifice of itself, it is committed, to the completion of the mission. In this case, the interceptor may well possess an advantage both as to speed and maneuverability over the bomber.

If the bombing or other type of attack is launched from short range, the attacking aircraft may be a fighter, equally ready to attack surface targets or engage in airborne combat with an interceptor. Also, a fighter duel may result if the bombing aircraft are protected by fighters. In the fighter-versus-fighter air battle, the advantages of speed and maneuverability may be in the favor of the attacker as readily as in favor of the interceptor. As speeds increase, two inherent effects are immediately apparent: the time available for the airplanes to locate and to engage each other in battle is reduced; aircraft become more difficult to observe from other aircraft.

The guided missile may be desired for use as a weapon in air-to-air combat by either the fighter or the bomber. For the fighter, use of the missile should not inhibit the fighter's ability to take defensive maneuvers during the time the missile is being guided to the target. Similarly, the bomber in employing defensive guided missiles must not be diverted from its main mission of attack because of the need to control its missiles. The bomber should be free to execute the tactics of its attack and be able, within its capabilities, to fly high or low, singly or in large numbers (Fig. 1-4), as the tactics of successful mission accomplishment dictate. In return, the defending fighter must be able to locate and destroy the bomber despite the tactics it employs. The guided missile, then, should not inhibit the individual mission, tactics, or probability of survival of the fighter or bomber using it and should be capable of successful operation despite the wide latitude of conditions imposed upon it.

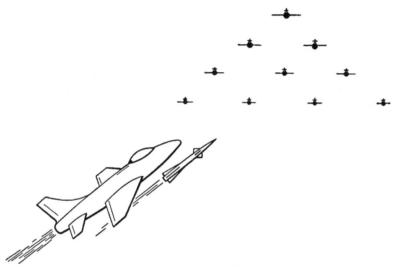

Fig. 1-4 The Missile Guidance System May Have to Isolate a Single Target to Effect a Kill.

From this superficial discussion, the following deductions, pertinent to air-to-air guidance systems, may be made:

a. For an interception to be made at a maximum range from the threatened target, early warning of the aircraft attack is essential.

b. The interceptor aircraft requires accurate direction and information regarding the attacking aircraft in order to locate them and be in the most favorable position for successful interception.

c. Some element of the guidance system must be able to sense the target in order to measure the position of the missile with respect to the target.

d. Since both the missile-carrying aircraft and its airborne target are capable of extremely high speed relative to each other, the operational time required to put the missile into useful service should be kept at a minimum.

e. The aircraft target is not necessarily inhibited in altitude, speed, or maneuverability; the missile must be capable of performance which will combat the target within its environmental limits.

f. Targets may exist simultaneously in large numbers. The missile guidance system may have to isolate a single target to effect a kill.

g. The guidance system should not inhibit the ability of the using aircraft to take evasive action for protection.

1-10 GUIDED MISSILES AGAINST UNDERWATER TARGETS

The submarine is a major offensive threat to the welfare of a seafaring nation at war. Its traditional function is to deny surface shipping access to the normal ocean trade routes and, by so doing, prevent the necessary transport of men, equipment, and materials. The submarine's traditional function has been augmented in that it may be used as a launching platform for surface-to-surface guided missiles. In view of the serious nature of the threat imposed by the submarine, all possible means of defense against it must be explored. The guided missile offers a possible means of defense. Two additional categories of missiles of a specialized type are therefore pertinent for consideration: (a) surface-to-subsurface and (b) air-to-subsurface. These are usually considered to be part of, or subordinate to, the categories of surface-to-surface and air-to-surface respectively.

The submarine as a target is unique only when it is operating beneath the surface of the water. When it is not submerged, the submarine is a mobile surface target and falls within normal classifications.

The primary defense of a submarine lies in its ability to avoid detection when submerged. The submarine, despite its relatively low velocity, is a mobile target, and it is necessary that some element of the guidance system be able to observe it with sufficient accuracy to permit guidance of the missile to it. The most commonly employed methods of locating a submerged submarine are by visual observation from the air, by sound transmitted through water, and by significant variations in the local magnetic field. Detection of a submerged submarine by sight is dependent upon many factors, such as the character of surface waves, contrast with ocean bottom, water depth, etc. Detection of a submarine by sound may be accomplished by passive listening for sounds emanating from the submarine or by a sonar device which emits a sound and "listens" for a discrete echo. Detection of a submarine by magnetometers may be accomplished by noting rapid variations of the local magnetic field. All of the methods mentioned have in common the required presence of a human observer who is trained to distinguish against a difficult background, a signal which represents the submerged submarine, from other objects having nearly similar signal characteristics. Further, by the very nature of the problem, the range of detection seems likely to be relatively small.

In antisubmarine warfare, it is not enough to wait until the submarine discloses its presence; the essence of the problem lies in locating and neutralizing the craft before it is in position to take offensive action. This requires the search for submarines over large areas of sea, on the periphery of convoys, and in coastal waters wherein the submarine might be employed for launching surface-to-surface missiles. Because of the vast areas involved, aircraft must be employed to supplement ships as vehicles for the conduct of the search.

If we assume, for the moment, that an aircraft in the process of searching has made positive contact with a submerged submarine, several alternatives emerge. The aircraft employed might be a long-range search

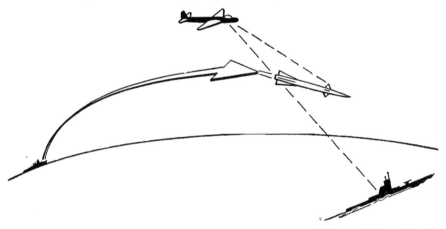

Fig. 1-5 The Missile May Be Launched from a Surface Ship and Guided by the Searching Aircraft.

airplane, a lighter-than-air craft, or, as in convoy protection, possibly a helicopter. Under some conditions, the searching aircraft may carry the missile, although this would not be practicable with a helicopter. Where the aircraft does carry the missile, the guided attack can be accomplished by the observing crew. Where the aircraft observing the submarine does not carry the missile, it is necessary to dispatch a missile to the scene of operations. Such a missile might be an air-to-subsurface missile carried by another aircraft and directed to the attack by the search aircraft, or it might be a surface-to-subsurface missile launched from a near-by surface ship and guided by the search aircraft, as in Fig. 1-5. If a submarine is contacted by a surface ship, since the range of contact is short the surface ship might best take direct action against the submarine without the necessity of recourse to guided missiles.

Examination of the subsurface guidance problem results in the deduction of several points pertinent to the guidance of both air-to-subsurface and surface-to-subsurface guided missiles:

a. Observation of the submarine and guidance of subsurface missiles will most frequently occur from aircraft.

b. It may be necessary to accomplish the guidance of the missile from an aircraft which does not launch it, but which assumes control of it at some phase during its flight.

c. If accurate knowledge of the location of the submarine exists because of continued contact and observation, the problem is essentially a specialized version of the surface target problem. However, in addition to considering the flight path, the motion and behavior of the missile at water entry and while underwater must be taken into account.

d. If the contact with the submarine is intermittent or the location of it is inaccurate, then some form of underwater terminal guidance is a probable requirement.

1-11 BASIS FOR MILITARY SERVICE REQUIREMENTS

The primary function of the Military Establishment of this nation is to defend the United States and its possessions against any aggressor. Allocations of responsibilities, for war or peace, have been made to describe the functions of each of the Military Services, operating either jointly or singly. The "Operations Research Section" of this series of volumes gives these functions in detail. However, brief observations may be made from them which tend to highlight some differences in missile guidance requirements of the various services.

The *Army* has primary interest in all operations on land and is responsible for the conduct of prompt and sustained land combat operations. It is required to defeat enemy land forces and to seize, occupy, and defend land areas. In order to accomplish this mission, the Army will require guidance systems for surface-to-surface missiles and for surface-to-air missiles to be used in defense of cities and other fixed locations, as well as for local defense of troops in the field. The Army is, by necessity, a mobile force and, in general, the weapons employed by it must be transportable. Choice of terrain is not always possible in mobile operations, so that the guidance systems of Army missiles should be as uninhibited as possible from effects of terrain.

The *Navy* is charged with obtaining and maintaining control of the seas, including the air over it, and has the primary interest in all operations at sea. To accomplish this mission, the Navy will employ surface-to-surface guided missiles to extend the range and increase the accuracy of its gunfire for engaging the enemy at sea, for bombardment of enemy-held seacoast cities, and for support of amphibious operations. The Navy will require guidance of surface-to-air guided missiles as a defense against air attacks on the Fleet or convoys and in defense of the United States against air attack through its coastal perimeter. Since the Navy must provide air support essential for its operations, it will augment the fighting power of its interceptor aircraft by the use of air-to-air guided missiles for defense of the Fleet and amphibious operations and for support of its combat aircraft over enemy-held territory. Guidance systems for air-to-surface missiles will be required for attacks against enemy shipping and for bombardment against naval targets ashore. In addition, since the Navy is responsible for antisubmarine warfare and the protection of shipping, it will require guidance for subsurface missiles. The Navy maintains the *United States Marine Corps*, which, in turn, is charged with the development, in coordination with all other armed services, of the techniques and equipment employed by landing forces in amphibious operations. The Marine Corps would thus be expected to have an active interest in mobile land-based missile guidance systems.

The *Air Force* is charged with the defense of the United States against airborne attacks and has primary interest in all operations in the air. One of its major responsibilities is to conduct strategic air warfare against an enemy nation. To accomplish the latter, the Air Force will have an interest in developing guidance systems for surface-to-surface missiles having intercontinental ranges as a substitute for and augmentation of piloted bomber attacks. To accomplish the former, the Air Force will require surface-to-air guided missiles as a defense against enemy air attack on the United States, augmenting its piloted interceptor defense. By reason of the tactical assignment, the surface equipment of Air Force guidance systems will tend to be permanent in location, as contrasted to the other services, since defense of fixed targets is the prime consideration in its surface-to-air category and because extremely long ranges are required of strategic surface-to-surface missiles. With permanent sites for surface-launched guided missiles, a choice of location can be made which will make terrain less of a guidance problem than for the Army requirements of the same category. The Air Force will increase the destructive power of its fighter aircraft by augmenting aircraft armament with air-to-air guided missiles. Such missiles will be utilized in fighter defense against enemy bomber attacks, in friendly bomber support, and in bomber defense. Air-to-surface missiles with appropriate guidance systems will be required by the Air Force to increase the accuracy of air strikes on selected surface targets. One of the collateral functions assigned to the Air Force is to conduct antisubmarine warfare and to protect shipping. The Air Force thus will also have a definite interest in the development of subsurface missile guidance systems.

1-12 GUIDANCE PHASES DURING MISSILE FLIGHT

There are three phases of missile flight which have, from a systems point of view, characteristics sufficiently different so as to require the use, in some missiles, of more than one guidance system during a single flight. In the interests of simplicity and reliability, a multiplicity of guidance systems is undesirable, and every consideration is employed to avoid this. Figure 1-6 shows a surface-to-air missile flight and illustrates the flight phases to be those of *launching*, *mid-course*, and *terminal* guidance.

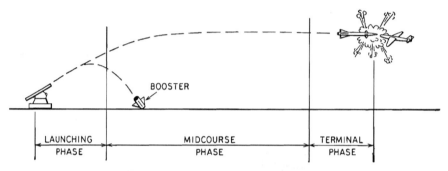

FIG. 1-6 Missile Guidance Phases.

Launching guidance. The launching phase is that portion of missile flight between initial firing and the time when the missile has reached a velocity at which it responds to normal control. As an example, a surface-launched missile, such as illustrated in Fig. 1-6, may be launched by use of a *booster*, which is an auxiliary propulsion system that separates from the missile after its impulse has been delivered. After the booster has separated from the missile, the missile continues in flight at some preselected velocity under its own power, or coasts, as the case may be.

During the period of flight when the booster is attached, the control characteristics of the combined missile and booster will vary radically from the characteristics of the missile alone at a higher velocity and after separation. Because these characteristics vary so radically, if a need exists for accurate guidance before the missile has separated from the booster and is flying at normal velocity, then a guidance system for the launching phase alone must be employed.

Midcourse guidance. In the case illustrated in Figure 1-6, let us assume that we have enough information from ground-based observation of the aircraft target to know where it is, but that the information is not sufficiently accurate to guide the missile to a collision with it. As part of the same assumption, the missile has an accurate but short-range guidance system contained within it. The missile, after launching, is guided from the ground-based information until the range to the target has decreased to the point where the missile-contained system can take over control. Midcourse guidance, then, is the guidance applied to a missile between the end of the launching phase and the start of the terminal phase of guidance.

Terminal guidance. Terminal guidance is the guidance applied to a missile between the end of the midcourse guidance and contact with or detonation in close proximity to the target.

1-13 MISSILE GUIDANCE FUNDAMENTALS

It has been pointed out that the two basic categories of targets are moving targets and stationary targets. From the discussion of type classifications of guided missiles as related to the targets which they are designed to hit, it will be noted that all guided missiles, launched to engage moving targets, have in common the requirement that some portion of the guidance system shall observe or sense the target. It has been indicated that the point of observation may vary—the target is conventionally observed at the launching or aiming point, but such observation may also be accomplished by a station outside the missile, approximately along the line of flight. Similarly, the target may be observed from the missile itself.

It is possible to observe a target, and from such observation determine its characteristics of behavior, in many ways. A target may be seen visually; it may be audible. A target, such as an aircraft, may emit infrared radiations from its engines so that it may be detected by an observer using some suitable device. In these cases the observer plays what may be called a *passive* role; he observes only the energy emitted from the target itself.

Since a target is not cooperative by choice, the observer is usually forced into a more active role. An airplane flying at night may be illuminated by a searchlight in order to be seen. This technique is obviously too limited for general use, since the airplane may take advantage of cloud-cover or fog, or may be difficult to distinguish against its background. There is available, however, energy over the entire electromagnetic spectrum, from X-rays to long radio waves, which may be transmitted by the observer playing an active role and observed by him as a reflection from the target. From a practical point of view, the immediate concern as to what part of the spectrum shall be employed is the characteristic behavior of the transmitted energy in the medium through which it is propagated. If the medium absorbs the energy, then the range of usefulness is limited; if the energy is radically distorted by anomalies, then the information obtained may be too unreliable for use; if the background of the target is such that it independently emits or returns energy in the band of frequencies being considered, the target is then indistinguishable from the background and no information of value on the target may be obtained.

Once we have examined the electromagnetic spectrum and determined the portions available for use (as well as the limitations and anomalies of propagation which exist within these portions), we may consider the methods of transmitting the energy and detecting its return from the target. Mere detection is not enough, since information on target motion is required; the detection must be accompanied by the ability to gather information on the motion of the target, with sufficient rapidity to guide the missile in flight.

In this discussion we have also indicated the possible use of another energy form, sound waves in the media of both air and water. Target detection and information gathering by sound can be employed for both passive and active usage. The importance of this type of target-information gathering in the guided missile field is relatively low as compared to electromagnetic energy because of the low propagation speed of sound.

When we consider the stationary target, an entirely different approach to the problem of guiding missiles results. When the target is at short range and amenable to close observation, the need for guided missiles is not acute, since conventional gunfire may be employed, in most instances, for destruction of the target. It is true that there are special targets of interest at short range where, because of gun trajectory and insufficient portable destructive power, the potential of guided missiles may be exploited. In general, however, the use of guided missiles against surface stationary targets has, as a first consideration, targets at long range, i.e., from beyond the reach of gunfire to intercontinental ranges of thousands of miles. For ranges of a few hundred miles, communication with, or navigation of, the missile by means of radio may conceivably be employed, so that propagation of electromagnetic waves is still of interest. As the range increases to the degree that this form of navigation becomes unusable, the logical method of locating the target is by means of some reference to its location on the earth, as by the earth's magnetic field, gravity, or celestial navigation. In very-long-range missiles, then, the guidance problem is primarily associated with terrestrial and celestial references that permit the missile to compute, independently, its own motion and the trajectory to carry it to the target at a known location with respect to the reference employed.

Although the fundamentals of the guidance intelligence problem evolve from propagated energy for some conditions and from earth's reference for others, both may be required in the course of a single missile flight.

A *servo system* is partially defined as a closed cycle automatic control system so designed that the output result of the system follows the input command to the system. If we review the definition of a missile guidance system (a group of components which measure the position of a guided missile with respect to its target and cause changes in the flight path as required), it is obvious, by definition, that a guided missile system is fundamentally a servo system in which the guidance intelligence is the input and the flight path of the missile the output. The two are related by computation, or other means, in common units for measurement and comparison. The same mathematical treatment and analysis employed for servo mechanisms should apply therefore for guidance systems, provided all the elements of the system are capable of being expressed in terms common to such treatment.

CHAPTER 2

PRIOR DEVELOPMENTS

There are four fields of interest which, together, encompass the major portion of the background for missile guidance system design. First is the field of the conventional weapon control systems—for guns, rockets, and bombs. These systems have similar tactical duties to perform and will compete with, as well as augment, guided missile systems. Second is the field of missile guidance systems which are now, or have been, in use. Third is the field of airborne navigation, with particular regard to automatic or semi-automatic systems. Fourth is the field of systems for the automatic control of aircraft. A review of these four fields of interest will be made, not with a view of cataloguing systems or system methodologies, but in an effort to point out applications to guidance systems, for further review or study by the reader.

2-1 CONVENTIONAL WEAPON SYSTEMS

The conventional weapons which guided missiles will compete with, replace, or augment are guns, rockets, and bombs. These weapons have been used for many years and, despite the introduction of guided missiles, have a high probability of continuing in use for a long time to come. For many reasons of economics and logistics, components of conventional weapons systems will also be employed as components of guided missile systems. Further, the vast problem of personnel training mitigates against too-rapid introduction of new techniques and devices.

In conventional weapon systems, intelligence with regard to the target is gathered by observation. This intelligence is evaluated, the weapon is aimed, and the projectile fired. From the time the bullet or rocket is fired, or the bomb is dropped, the trajectory is irrevocably dependent upon gravity, wind, and the ballistics of the projectile. The hit at the target is made at some time after the launching of the projectile. The elapsed time is called the *time of flight* of the projectile.

A missile guidance system is analogous to a gunfire control system wherein the missile, although in flight, is continuously re-aimed until the time of flight is reduced to zero; the general methods of gathering target intelligence differ but little between conventional weapon systems and missile guidance systems. Ordnance equipment, of which fire control systems are a part, is considered a product of heavy industry. Guided missiles, on the other hand, often are products of the aircraft industry. When a gulf exists between industries or technologies, as in this case, there is frequently a lack of awareness of the close similarity of problems.

2-2 ANTIAIRCRAFT GUNFIRE CONTROL

An antiaircraft gunfire control system usually consists of a gun director, a computer or computers, and a gun mount, as indicated in Fig. 2-1. The gun director may be one of many types, from a manually operated gun sight to an automatically operated radar. Regardless of type, it is the

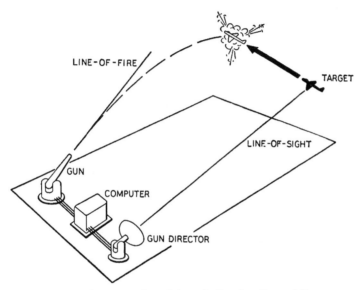

FIG. 2-1 Elements of Antiaircraft Gunfire Control System.

primary function of the gun director to observe, or track, the target continuously, and, by so doing, locate it in space with respect to some reference line, and to measure its motion. This information is transmitted to the computer, the primary function of which is to compute continuously the predicted future position of the target for a time of flight of the projectile later than the present position of the target, and to transmit the orders which position the gun along the line of fire.

Elements of this fire control system are also found in a surface-to-air missile guidance system. In order to guide a missile, the aircraft target must be tracked to gain intelligence as to its present position and motion. Precision tracking devices have been developed for gunfire control employing optics, infrared, radar, and sound. The fire control field has been the

24   PRIOR DEVELOPMENTS

major contributor to the art of precision measurement of position and motion of the high-speed aircraft target.

A vast background of experience in mechanizing computation exists in the field of gunfire control by reason of the complex problem which must be solved to predict the future position of the target and to develop the corresponding gun orders. Many types of computing devices have been employed. Mechanical, electromechanical, and electronic analog computers have been built and are in use. The use of electronic digital computers has been explored. Direct comparisons have been made between different methods of mechanizing computations in service use. Information as to type and component reliability and complexity has been built up by field experience.

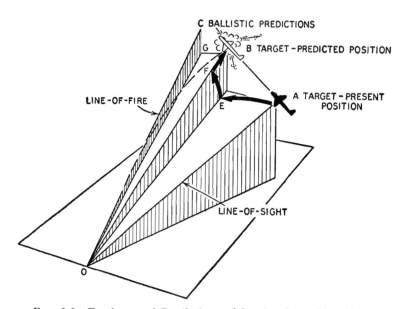

Fig. 2-2 Fundamental Predictions of Gunfire Control Problem.

Figure 2-2 illustrates some of the fundamentals of the antiaircraft gunfire control prediction problem. The target at A is being tracked by a gun director at O. It is assumed that the target has been tracked for a sufficient length of time to develop a knowledge of its motion. If the gun is fired when the target is at A, the time of flight of the shell from O to B should equal the time the target requires to go in a straight line from A to B, its predicted future position. A continuous prediction is usually generated from the angular rate of the change of bearing, which is shown as the total angle EOA when integrated over the time of flight; the angular change of elevation is shown similarly as EOF; and the change in direct (or slant) range FB. In addition to computing continuously the future target position, it is also necessary to predict the trajectory of the projectile. American guns are ordinarily rifled in such a manner that the projectile spins clockwise when viewed from behind. Complicated interactions between the gyroscopic effect of the spinning projectile and the air drag cause the shell to drift to the right; the force of gravity tends to pull it downward; wind motion will cause the shell to deviate from its still air trajectory; and changes in powder temperature and air density will cause variations in projectile velocity with corresponding trajectory changes. From these and similar factors the bearing angle BOG, usually called "ballistic deflection prediction," and a vertical angle COG, known as the "ballistic elevation prediction," are continuously computed. When the continuous ballistic predictions are added to the continuously predicted target position data, continuous gun orders are generated which point the gun along the line of fire, OC.

There are several mathematical formulations and corresponding methods of solution used in antiaircraft gunfire control systems, all of which involve the simultaneous solution of several interdependent integro-differential equations. The choice of solution in any one system is dependent upon practical considerations not related to the mathematics of the problem. For instance, Navy heavy calibre antiaircraft guns are sometimes used against surface targets. In this case it becomes desirable to obtain solutions of relative target and ship motions in the horizontal plane, in order that the computer may be used for the dual purpose of antiaircraft and surface fire.

In other types of gunfire control systems, the prediction of the future position of the target is accomplished by measurement of the rate of motion of the line-of-sight in the plane of target motion. Figure 2-3 shows the elements of the prediction problem, considering only a single plane through the path of the target and the tracking device. If it is assumed that the target moves in a straight line with a velocity V_T and that the average velocity of the projectile toward the predicted future position of the target is V_P, then

$$\sin AOB \text{ (lead angle)} = \frac{V_T \sin CAB}{V_P} \qquad (2\text{-}1)$$

As seen from the tracking device at point O, with the present range of R, the angular velocity ω of the line-of-sight is

$$\frac{V_T \sin CAB}{R} \qquad (2\text{-}2)$$

Combining Eq. (2-1) and (2-2) gives the

$$\text{lead angle } (AOB) = \sin^{-1}\frac{R\omega}{V_P} \qquad (2\text{-}3)$$

For small lead angles, in which the angle is approximately equal to its sine, Eq. (2-3) becomes

$$\text{lead angle} \cong \frac{R\omega}{V_P} \qquad (2\text{-}4)$$

or the functional relationships are

$$\text{lead angle} = f(R, \omega, V_P) \qquad (2\text{-}5)$$

It becomes obvious that simple prediction computers which approximate the solution can be mechanized from devices which measure these quantities. The rate gyroscope (which measures ω) has been developed as a

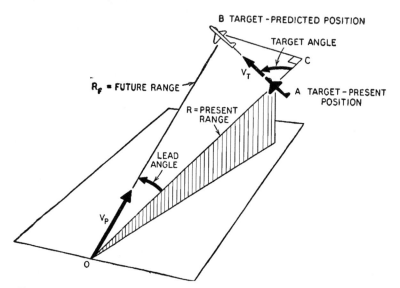

FIG. 2-3 Lead Angle Computation for Antiaircraft Gunfire Control.

versatile component for lead computing gun sights and fire control systems Its capabilities as an angular rate measuring device is in similar demand as an element of missile guidance systems.

The similarity of one type of missile guidance system with a gunfire control system is shown by comparing Fig. 2-4 with Fig. 2-2. The problem of tracking the target and predicting its future position B remains unchanged from that shown in Fig. 2-2. The missile is similarly tracked and its trajectory is generated and predicted. This corresponds, in essence, to the ballistic prediction of the gunfire control problem. A continuous solution of the two predictions can be established to provide an interception between the missile and target. Any deviation from the predicted trajectories of either the missile or target can be corrected by commands to the missile which cause changes in its flight path as required to result in a hit. Such a system is one type of command system.

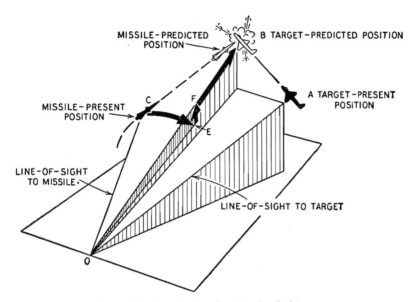

Fig. 2-4 Prediction for Missile Guidance.

2-3 SURFACE GUNFIRE CONTROL

A surface gunfire control system is usually comprised of the same general elements as the antiaircraft system—a director, a computer, and the gun. Indeed, many systems are designed explicitly for dual-purpose use of both surface and antiaircraft gunfire. The surface fire control problem requires a computer for prediction of motion only if relative motion exists between gun and target. Since a ship is a mobile platform, the Navy surface fire control systems always require a computer as part of the system. If no relative motion between target and gun exists, as is frequently the case in land surface gunfire, the only computation required is that of ballistic prediction.

Gun ballistics are divided into two general categories: interior ballistics, the study of the behavior of explosives and projectiles within the gun; and exterior ballistics, the study of projectiles in flight. Guided missiles have a background in interior ballistics by reason of the use of slow-burning explosives as missile propellants. Ballistic surface-to-surface missiles, such as the German V-2, are direct extensions of surface gunfire, and the study and prediction of trajectories of these missiles are an equally direct extension of the science of external ballistics.

2-4 SHIPBOARD STABILIZATION OF GUNFIRE CONTROL SYSTEMS

The Navy has a problem which is unique to that service, the necessity of stabilizing fire control systems against the motion of the ship. This problem also exists for guided missiles systems. A tracking device, such as a gun director or a radar, is, of course, fixed to the deck of the ship. Measurements of the present position of the target, commonly called "train" and "elevation" angles, are made, as shown in Fig. 2-5, in and

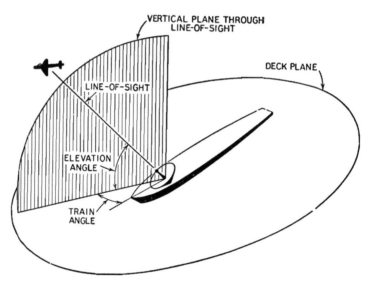

Fig. 2-5 Shipboard Measurements of Present Target Position.

from the plane of the deck of the ship. As the deck rolls and pitches, the angular measurement of train and elevation will change, even though the line-of-sight to the target is unchanged in space. In order to keep the line-of-sight on the target, the motion of the ship must be removed from the tracking device, and the line-of-sight orientation made stable as referred to space. This is usually accomplished by referring all measurements to a horizontal plane and by use of a stable vertical (a vertical-seeking gyroscope), and measuring the angles of level and cross-level, as shown in Fig. 2-6. By this device, all measurements of target position and rate may be referred to the horizontal plane (thereby satisfying needs of surface fire), and stabilized predictions may be computed. Stabilization will also be required for missile guidance systems, to remove ship's motion from the tracking system and to stabilize missile launchers.

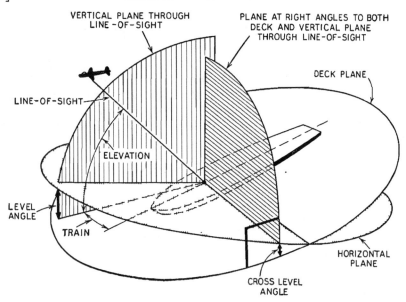

Fig. 2-6 Shipboard Measurements of Present Position Referred to a Horizontal Plane.

2-5 PARALLAX COMPUTATION

In locating the components of gunfire control systems, either in the field or aboard ship, it is usually necessary to place the gun director at some point well removed from the guns. Also, the director or tracking device usually will be at a different elevation, as indicated in Fig. 2-7. With

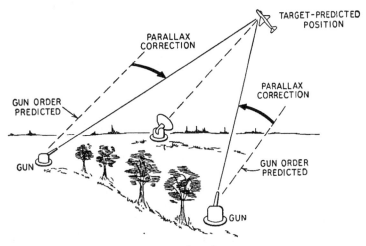

Fig. 2-7 Parallax Corrections.

the director tracking the target, the target position is observed, its motion measured, and its future position computed. Gun orders are transmitted in accordance with these predictions, as previously described. It is seen from Fig. 2-7 that the predicted gun order is incorrect by reason of the parallax which exists between the director and gun locations. The same computation may be required in any missile guidance system wherein the position of the missile at the end of the launching phase must be accurately known on the basis of ballistics predictions rather than observation.

2-6 AIRBORNE GUNFIRE CONTROL SYSTEMS

Air-to-air missile guidance systems are closely associated with airborne fire control systems. The reasons for this are obvious if consideration is given to the versatility of aircraft. An interceptor aircraft, for example, must be capable of fighting other aircraft with guns or missiles; of strafing, with guns or rockets; or of bombing. Because of the extreme penalty paid

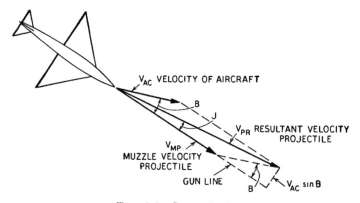

Fig. 2-8 Jump Angle.

for superfluous weight, every effort is made to use the same tracking device and weapon control system for multiple purposes. The ideal airborne weapon control system would be capable of use with guns, rockets, bombs, or missiles. The benefits of small size, weight, and versatility have brought the lead computing gyroscope into prominence for use in airborne fire control systems.

The airborne fire control problem involves one important element not present in surface fire control problems—high velocity of the weapon carrier. The muzzle velocity of a 20-mm projectile is approximately 2800 fps; the velocity of the aircraft may be as great as a third of this. The vector of motion of the projectile is the resultant of the vectors of motion of the projectile and the aircraft, as shown in Fig. 2-8. This situation arises to a limited degree even with fixed forward firing guns, particularly when the aircraft flies in a skid; and normally exists with guns which can be aimed and fired across the airstream, as is the case with bomber armament. The angle between the gun line and the resultant vector of motion of the projectile V_{PR} is usually termed "own ship's motion deflection angle," J, and by inspection

$$\sin J = \frac{V_{AC} \sin B}{V_{PR}} \tag{2-6}$$

Figure 2-9 shows the elements of the air-to-air gunfire control problem. In order to satisfy the problem (collision between target and projectile), where the *average* projectile velocity during the time of flight is assumed

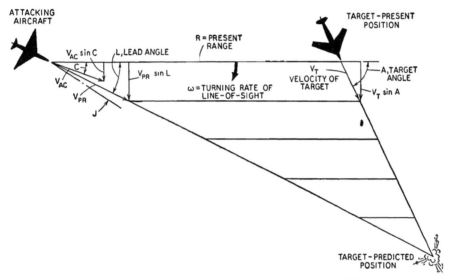

FIG. 2-9 Fundamentals of Air-to-Air Gunfire Control Problem.

equal to V_{PR}, the initial resultant projectile velocity, the velocity components of the projectile and target aircraft must fulfill the following equation:

$$V_{PR} \sin L = V_T \sin A \tag{2-7}$$

The angular rotation of the line-of-sight is

$$\omega = \frac{V_T \sin A - V_{AC} \sin C}{R} \tag{2-8}$$

Substituting Eq. (2-6) and (2-7) in (2-8) gives

$$\omega = \left[\sin L - \sin J \frac{\sin C}{\sin B} \right] \frac{V_{PR}}{R} \tag{2-9}$$

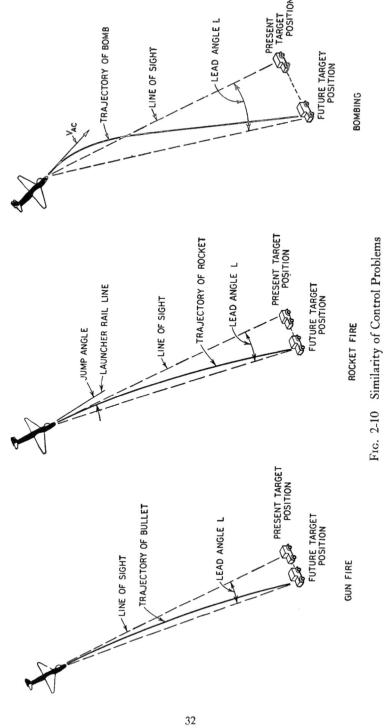

Fig. 2-10 Similarity of Control Problems

or, using the small angle approximation,

$$\omega \cong \left[L - J\frac{C}{B}\right]\frac{V_{PR}}{R} \qquad (2\text{-}10)$$

This illustrates that both the lead angle and the ship's motion deflection angle can be functionally related to the angular rate of turn of the line-of-sight, a fact which permits rate gyros and other angular rate measuring devices to be used as lead computing elements in airborne fire control systems.

The similarity between the development of the lead angle for gunfire, rocket fire, and bombs against a common moving surface target is illustrated in Fig. 2-10. A correction, usually called "jump," exists for rocket fire control, since a rocket fired from a moving launcher starts its acceleration period by turning into the relative wind ("weathercocking") by reason of the initial aerodynamic forces. The jump effect is modified by the accelerating jet action, so that the total jump is less than the angle between the launching line and the aircraft velocity vector. At the end of the accelerating, or burning period, the rocket has assumed an absolute velocity greater in magnitude that that of the aircraft, a direction at some angle with the direction of the launching rails prior to firing. The resultant angle is dependent upon the combined aerodynamic, propulsion, and gravity effects acting on the rocket.

The relative motion between the target and the intercepting aircraft may be extremely great, and it is necessary in firing air-to-air guided missiles that they be launched on a computed collision course with respect to the target in order that the guidance problem be minimized. The development of the correct lead angle at the moment of launching becomes similar in concept to the control of conventional weapons. It may be seen that in all cases the prediction of future target position changes only as a function of the time of flight; the ballistic prediction, however, is dependent upon the projectile employed. The concept of a single airborne fire control system for firing guns, rockets, bombs, and guided missiles with interchangeable (or plug-in) ballistic computers becomes theoretically possible of realization owing to this functional similarity.

2-7 MISSILE GUIDANCE SYSTEMS OF WORLD WAR II

Many guided missile research and development programs were initiated during World War II. The German developments, having been started at an earlier date, were further advanced than those of any other nation, and only the missiles employed by them could be said to have had an appreciable effect upon the conduct of the war. Work was initiated upon all categories of guided missiles, but only surface-to-surface and air-to-surface missiles were produced and used to any degree. Generally speaking, the German development of the missiles, as vehicles, proceeded at a more rapid pace and to a more satisfactory conclusion than that of the missile guidance systems. The Japanese ignored automatic control in their one effective missile and employed a human pilot as the guidance system. The reason for the advance of one technical field above the other is not too obvious; part of the answer undoubtedly lies in the complexity of the guidance system problems, the lack of electronic components and technology, and the urgency of the need for the weapons.

The most publicized of the German missiles were the surface-to-surface missiles, the V-1 (German FZG-76) and the V-2 (German A-4). However, the Germans and Japanese had under development and in use other guided missiles. Table 2-1 shows the more advanced of the many guided missile programs underway at the end of World War II. Work on the missiles listed here had progressed at least to the point of flight tests, although in some cases the guidance system had not been tested with the missile. The fact that this list is almost entirely of German missiles should not be interpreted to mean that the Allies were not working strenuously on guided missiles, but, in the main, the Allied effort was in the earlier development stages. The most advanced work in this country was in connection with guided bombs. Inspection of Table 2-1 shows that the powered guided missiles listed were to employ only four general types of guidance systems, excluding the human pilot of the Baka.

TABLE 2-1 WORLD WAR II GUIDED MISSILES

Missile Identity	Guidance System Type
Surface-to-Surface	
V-1 (German FZG-76)	Magnetic and ballistic
V-2 (German A-4)	Ballistic
Surface-to-Air	
Schmetterling (German Hs-117)	Radio command
Wasserfall (German)	Radio command
Enzian (German)	Radio command
Rheintochter I (German)	Radio command
Rheintochter III (German)	Radio command
Air-to-Air	
X-4 (German)	Wire command
Hs-298 (German)	Radio command
Hs-117-H (German)	Radio command
Air-to-Surface	
Hs-293 series (German)	Radio command
Baka (Japanese)	Human pilot
Weary Willy (United States)	Radio command
Assault Drone (United States)	Television radio command

2-8 V-1 GUIDANCE SYSTEM

The V-1 ("Buzz-Bomb") missile employed a simple and ingenious guidance system. During the launching and mid-course phases of flight it was controlled by a magnetic compass in azimuth and a barometric altimeter in altitude, as indicated in Fig. 2-11. The compass was manually set for the desired course of the missile in flight. The compass kept the spin axis of the directional gyro pointed along the line of the trajectory. The longitudinal axis of the missile in flight was aligned with the spin axis of the directional gyro. Since the gyroscope, once set, tended to remain fixed in space, any deviation of the flight axis of the missile caused a signal

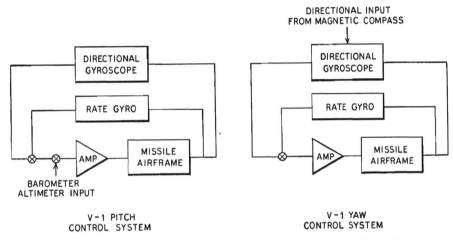

Fig. 2-11 Simplified Block Diagram of V-1 Pitch and Yaw Control Systems.

to be fed to the rudder correcting the alignment of the airframe. The yaw rate gyro acted as a limiting device to prevent imposition of maneuvers excessively severe on the airframe. The altitude control was equally simple, except that the altimeter did not position the directional gyro but added its signals directly into the elevator control system. All of the controls and amplifiers were pneumatic, rather than electrical. The energy required for operation of the controls during the flight was stored in two spherical, wire-wound, high-pressure (2000 psi) air containers. The system was simple, rugged, and reasonably reliable.

In addition to direction, the missile had to know the range to the target. This was determined by an air mileage measuring unit which consisted of a coarse pitch windmill driving a worm reduction gear, which in turn drove a counter. The counter carried electrical contacts which were manually set for the predetermined air mileage to the target. When the indicated target mileage was reached in flight, the following functions were performed: first, the warhead was armed; second, a radio transmitter was switched on; third, the missile controls were locked to cause the missile to dive. The accuracy of the terminal portion of the flight, then, depended upon the ballistics of the missile. The radio transmitter was used only on a relatively few missiles and was for the purpose of indicating to the operators the location of the missile at the start of its dive, and thus the accuracy of the flight. The information so obtained could be employed to correct the manual settings of direction and range of missiles fired subsequently.

2-9 V-2 GUIDANCE SYSTEM

The V-2 was a direct extension of long-range surface gunfire. Operationally, the problem of guiding this missile may be likened to pointing a gun with a long, flexible, curved barrel at a distant target. As with a gun for surface fire, the essentials of obtaining a hit were aiming the projectile in the correct direction in azimuth and pointing it at the correct

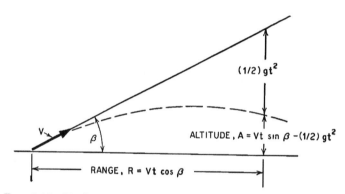

Fig. 2-12 Trajectory of a Projectile, Neglecting Air Resistance.

elevation angle so that the projectile would fall to the surface at the correct target range. Figure 2-12 indicates the trajectory of a projectile fired with a velocity, V, at an angle to the horizontal, β. The horizontal range, R, of the projectile at any time, t, after firing, neglecting air resistance, is

$$R = Vt \cos \beta \qquad (2\text{-}11)$$

Since the projectile, under the force of gravity g, falls a distance of $(\tfrac{1}{2})gt^2$ during any time t, the altitude A of the projectile indicated in Fig. 2-12 may be written as

$$A = Vt \sin \beta - (\tfrac{1}{2})gt^2 \qquad (2\text{-}12)$$

If we consider the horizontal range at the time when the projectile returns to the datum plane of firing, then the altitude $A = 0$, and Eq. (2-12) may be written as

$$V \sin \beta = (\tfrac{1}{2})gt \tag{2-13}$$

and the time of flight to return to the horizontal plane is

$$t = \frac{2V \sin \beta}{g} \tag{2-14}$$

If Eq. (2-14) is substituted in Eq. (2-11), the range when the projectile returns the horizontal plane is

$$R = \frac{V^2 \sin 2\beta}{g} \tag{2-15}$$

or Eq. (2-15) shows the range to be a function of

$$R = f(V^2, \beta) \tag{2-16}$$

The velocity of the projectile of a gun is fixed within narrow limits, since the powder charge for firing is fixed by the shell case or the powder bag. Variations from standards in temperature and gun barrel wear which can affect the muzzle velocity of the projectile are, in ordinary gunfire control practice, corrected in the ballistic computation, so that the only useful variable in the determination of gun range is the elevation angle, here equivalent to β.

In the case of a ballistic missile, the velocity is a controllable parameter, since the missile guidance system may be designed so as to shut off the propelling motor on command. This is the situation in the V-2. In essence, one more dimension of control was added to the ballistic missile that might improve its accuracy, as compared to the gun. The V-2 missile was controlled in azimuth, and, when the proper combination of elevation angle and velocity was reached, the motor was turned off. The trajectory of the missile, subsequent to motor shutoff, was dependent only upon gravity and aerodynamic forces (the latter only when the missile again returned to the more dense portion of the earth's atmosphere). No control was exerted after the motor was shut off.

The V-2 was controlled in heading during its burning period both by external vanes, which created aerodynamic moments, and by internal vanes, which were used to vary the direction of thrust of the rocket motor. The internal vanes, made of carbon and four in number, were located to the rear of the motor so that they projected into the exhaust gas stream. The four external vanes were located in the outer trailing edge of each large fin. Internal and external vanes for control in azimuth were interlocked; internal and external vanes in pitch were so connected as to permit separate control.

The specific types of control mechanisms that were employed varied considerably among rockets. In azimuth, the control was designed around a preset gyroscope which controlled the missile both in roll and in azimuth. In some missiles the manual settings of the gyro were augmented by radio command signals, which were transmitted from a tracking station near the launching site, to correct the azimuth trajectory. In elevation angle or pitch, the missile was controlled by a gyroscope that, after the vertical launching of the missile, had its axis driven by a constant-speed precession to effect a change of the missile pitch angle from the vertical to the computed pitch angle for the trajectory desired. Pickoffs on the gyroscopes furnished control voltages to electric amplifiers and electrohydraulic servo mechanisms which positioned the internal and external control vanes.

Early missiles used radio signals to control the reduction and cutoff of fuel supply, thus controlling missile velocity. The velocity of the missile was measured by the Doppler effect of retransmitted radio signals. The radio command velocity control was abandoned in favor of a gyroscope integrating accelerometer, which shut off the motor when a predetermined velocity and pitch angle were reached.

2-10 GERMAN RADIO COMMAND GUIDANCE SYSTEMS

It is notable, upon review of Table 2-1, that all of the guidance systems developed for powered missiles, other than of the surface-to-surface category, were "command" guidance systems. A command guidance system is one wherein the intelligence transmitted to the missile from an outside source causes the missile to traverse a directed path in space. This concept of a guidance system has the advantage of minimizing the equipment located in the missile, since all intelligence is generated elsewhere and the missile requires only a means of receiving the intelligence and an ability to act upon the commands so-ordered. The prefix of "radio" or "wire" in the guidance system type designation signifies the means of transmitting the intelligence to the missile.

In addition to the common use of command guidance for the many systems, the Germans planned to use similar operational techniques and the same components. Figure 2-13 illustrates the guidance system for the surface-to-air missile, Schmetterling (Hs 117). The complete system was called the Burgund system and was planned for use with subsonic surface-to-air missiles. The target tracker, seated in the director, kept the cross hairs of his optics centered on the target and, in so doing, caused the entire director to turn in azimuth and the optics to point in elevation. The missile tracker had a joystick control called the Knuppel. Theoretically, if the target was being tracked perfectly, the missile tracker would see it as a stationary object in his optics. By use of the joystick, the missile tracker would endeavor to keep the missile centered on the target. The missile was made more visible by the use of flares. As the joystick was moved (up or down, right or left) appropriate turn commands were transmitted from the Kehl radio transmitter on the ground and received by the Strassburg radio receiver in the missile. As the director moved in azimuth and elevation to follow the target, the loaded launcher was also caused to move, so that the missile was launched along the correct line to the target. Parallax and other required computations were made by the computers.

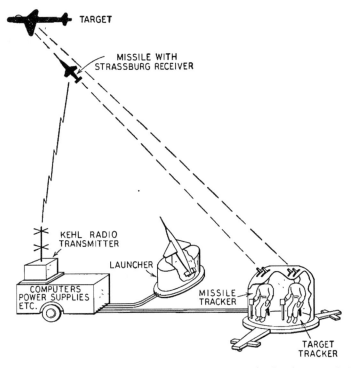

Fig. 2-13 Elements of the Burgund Guidance System for Surface-to-Air Missiles.

The radio command systems were planned to operate so as to keep the missiles continuously on the optical line-of-sight between the director and the target. This had the advantage of eliminating the computation required to predict the future position of the target and missile. However, the resulting trajectory is not economical of potential range and the maneuvers demanded of the missile tend to become excessive at the terminal portion of the flight. The joystick control (the Knuppel), the radio receiver (the Strassburg), and the transmitter (the Kehl) were components common to all of the radio command systems.

Figure 2-14 shows a simplified block diagram of the Burgund system. The operator observed visually the image of the missile with respect to the target, and upon detection of an error would put a command into the system by use of the joystick. The joystick unit contained a modulator consisting of two ceramic cylinders which were rotated at five cycles per second. The cylinders had a silver coating for electrical contact with brushes, the coating having been separated into two parts, insulated from each other. Each part encircled the cylinder at one end and tapered linearly to about five per cent near the other end. Continuous contacts were made at the end of the cylinders, and a movable brush rode the surface between the ends, positioned by the joystick. A closed circuit was completed alternately between the continuous contacts at the ends of the

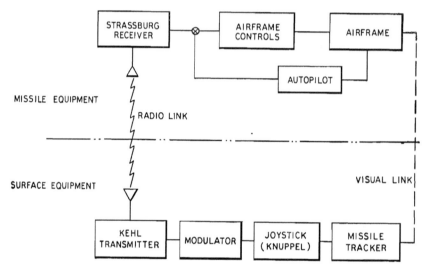

FIG. 2-14 Simplified Block Diagram of Burgund Missile Guidance System with Strassburg-Kehl Command Link.

cylinders and the movable brush. When the joystick, and consequently the movable brush, was centered, the alternate pulses were of equal duration; when the joystick was not in the center, the alternate pulses were of unequal duration. These pulses were fed into the modulator where they were converted to audio-frequency pulses. The audio-frequency pulses were, in turn, sent to the Kehl transmitter where they were used to modulate a single transmitted radio frequency. The transmitted radio frequency was selectable from any of a number of frequency channels; fourteen selectable frequencies were usually available.

When the signals were received in the missile, they were demodulated and fed as direct-current pulses to two polarized relays, one for pitch and one for yaw. The relays alternated between contacts and dwelt on opposing contacts for the duration of the original alternate pulses initiated by the joystick. The relays, in turn, caused solenoids to move the controlling air surfaces, spoilers, elevators, ailerons or rudder, as the case might be. These surfaces oscillated at a frequency corresponding to the rate of revolution of the cylinders in the joystick; the time of dwell in one direction varied in accordance to the joystick position. In addition to the command signals, a gyroscope, performing the function of an autopilot for stability, usually formed a part of the system.

The Strassburg-Kehl radio link was the only German radio command link to see service in a missile guidance system during World War II. There were several minor variations instituted from time to time in the production program, the only major addition being a channel for use as a detonation signal. The Kran-Brigg radio command link was developed late in the war as an alternate radio command link. This system was similar to the Strassburg-Kehl, except that different radio and audio command frequencies were used. Various modifications of the joystick were also proposed; certain of the missiles used different cyclic rates for the command pulses.

The Elsass command guidance system was proposed for use with the Wasserfall and Rheintochter missiles. This system was similar in operational concept to the Burgund command system, except that radar tracking of the target and missile was proposed as a substitute for optical tracking. The plan was to use the Strassburg-Kehl radio link with the Elsass system.

The susceptibility of the radio command link to electronic countermeasures led to the development of wire links which might be used effectively over short distances without fear of countermeasures. Wire command links were first devised for use with the X-4 air-to-air missile. Their use was also planned for a surface-to-surface antitank missile, called the X-7.

The X-4 missile was released and controlled by the pilot of the parent aircraft. The pilot aimed at the target, using an appropriate sighting device, and fired the missile. When the missile was fired, the gyroscopic autopilot was put into operation, the missile was armed for ready detonation, and flares on the wing tips of the missile were ignited. As in the Burgund system, the missile was continuously guided by command along the optical line of sight between the pilot and the target, by use of a joystick control. Two wire command links were developed, the Dortmund-Duisburg and the Duren-Detmold.

The Dortmund-Duisburg wire link provided for command transmission through two wires that connected the transmitting unit in the airplane to the receiving unit in the missile, employing pulses at two different audio frequencies. The Dortmund transmitting equipment, located in the missile-carrying aircraft, consisted of an oscillator operated by pulses from the joystick control unit, an audio power amplifier, suitable matching networks, and two spools, each containing 12 km of insulated wire. The oscillator transmitted two audio-frequency signals for pitch and yaw commands to the missile. These signals were modulated proportionally from the center frequency in accordance with the joystick commands, then amplified by the audio power amplifier for transmission by wire to the receiver in the missile. The Duisburg receiver was located in the fuselage of the X-4; two additional reels containing 18 km of wire were located on opposing wing tips. The audio signals were received through the wire and demodulated by the receiver to operate two polarized relays, one for pitch and one for yaw control.

The X-4 missile rotated about its longitudinal axis 60 rpm. Because of this rotation, there was a cancellation of aerodynamic misalignments resulting from production tolerances and a consequent simplification of the stabilizing problem. The X-4 was stabilized in line-of-flight by a single gyro which was employed to orient properly the yaw and pitch signals as the missile revolved.

The wire was made of insulated steel. The ejection of the wire was initiated by the detonation of a powder charge in the wire reels. It continued to pay out from both the airplane and the missile while the missile was in flight. To prevent the inductance of the wire on the reel from distorting the command signals, the insulation on a centimeter length of each layer of wire was removed so that all turns of the reel were shorted together. This wire proved to be a nuisance and hazard after it fell to earth.

The Duren-Detmold wire command link was a simple direct-current system which employed no vacuum tubes in its construction. In the Duren transmitter, the pitch commands changed the polarity of the transmitted signals, and the yaw commands changed the amplitude of the voltage by inserting a fixed resistance in the circuit.

In the Detmold receiver three relays were so connected that one was sensitive to the polarity of the direct-current signals; the second was sensitive to the amplitude of the signal; and the third operated to disconnect the first two in event the transmitting wire was broken. The missile was kept on course in obedience to the last command received. The reels of wire were similar to those used with the Dortmund-Duisburg equipment, except that the turns were not shorted, since it was essential that the resistance of the wire remain constant.

2-11 GUIDED BOMBS

Unpowered glide bombs with a variety of guidance system types were proposed as guided weapons in World War II. Table 2-2 lists some of the guided bomb projects. The first of the United States developments to see service (May 1944) was the GB-1, an Air Force general-purpose bomb which had attached to it a simple monoplane airframe assembly. The guidance system consisted simply of a preset autopilot, the operation of which was initiated immediately prior to launching. The results of the use of this bomb were encouraging but not spectacular.

TABLE 2-2 WORLD WAR II GUIDED BOMBS

Bomb Identity		Guidance System Type
FX-1400	(German)	Radio command
Bat	(U. S.)	Radar homing
Pelican	(U. S.)	Radar homing
Robin	(U. S.)	Television command
Azon	(U. S.)	Radio command
Razon	(U. S.)	Radio command
Tarzon	(U. S.)	Radio command
Felix	(U. S.)	Infrared homing
Roc	(U. S.)	Television command
GB-1	(U. S.)	Preset
GB-4	(U. S.)	Television command

The GB-4 also saw field service use. The GB-4 employed a television camera and radio transmitter in the bomb. An operator in the using aircraft monitored the picture seen by the camera in the bomb and, by use of a radio command link with the bomb, manually guided it to the surface target. The GB-4 guided bombs were first employed in August 1944 against the U-boat pens at Le Havre, France and later against discrete industrial targets in Germany.

Radio command systems were proposed for many of the bombs. Of these, the FX-1400 and the Azon saw military use. The FX-1400, of German design, employed the Strassburg-Kehl radio command link and used the standard operational tactics of visual guidance along the line-of-sight to the target, as previously described for powered German missiles. The Azon was, like the German systems, also visually guided (in azimuth only) along the line-of-sight of the operator to the target by use of radio command signals. The use of the Azon in Europe was limited, but it saw considerable service in the Burma Theater of Operations.

The concept of radar homing guidance was first introduced in the Bat, a glide bomb developed for the U. S. Navy by the National Defense Research Council. The Bat was a monowing glider containing a complete radar equipment which was capable of automatically tracking an isolated target. An operator in the parent aircraft would engage the target with the bomb's radar and the bomb would then be released. The information from the radar was employed to guide or "home" the bomb into collision with the target. The Bat was employed to a limited but satisfactory degree by the Navy against Japanese shipping in the Pacific. Other Navy developments of interest were the Pelican, which was essentially a forerunner of the Bat, using semiactive radar homing. The Robin employed a radio command link for guidance and, like the GB-4, obtained intelligence for guidance from a television camera located in the bomb.

One other method of obtaining intelligence for guiding bombs was proposed for the Felix, an Air Force guided bomb program. Felix made use of infrared radiation for observing the target. Steel mills, furnaces, and many other man-made activities are heat sources which transmit infrared radiation to a greater degree than the normal background of the earth's surface.

2-12 POSTWAR MISSILE GUIDANCE DEVELOPMENTS

It is evident, from the number and variety of publicity releases, that all major nations have instituted post-war guided missile programs of considerable magnitude. The information available in such releases is of general character, dealing with exterior parameters of the guided missiles and, as a rule, indicates only the type of guidance system employed. Detailed information on missile guidance systems is usually withheld from the public domain because of security reasons or, in some rare cases, because of corporate patent or design protection.

Post-war research in the upper atmosphere gained a new tool with the advent of high-altitude rockets. Captured V-2 rockets have been utilized to assist in scientific studies, and new rockets were designed as vehicles to further this work. Of these, the American Wac-Corporal and Viking are the better-known developments.

2-13 THE VIKING ROCKET *

The Viking rocket was conceived by Naval Research Laboratory scientists as a vehicle for exploring the upper atmosphere by means of direct measurements. Before the era of high-altitude rockets, direct access to altitudes above those obtainable by balloons had been denied to investigators of atmospheric phenomena. The higher layers had been studied, albeit by indirect means—reflection of radio waves transmitted from the ground, radiation from outer space which traverses the atmosphere, and others. With the advent of the German V-2 and the American Wac-Corporal it became possible to transport an instrument into the region of interest.

The V-2, which has been used extensively as an upper-air research vehicle, was designed as a military weapon and was adapted without redesign to scientific purposes. It had several shortcomings, particularly with regard to attitude stability. From the outset, Viking was designed with upper-air research requirements in view. The airframe was made

* Written by M. W. Rosen, Naval Research Laboratory.

as light as possible through a liberal use of aluminum and magnesium as structural materials. Hence it was possible to attain *mass ratios* up to 0.80 (fuels amounting to 80 per cent of the gross weight) and, as a result, to reach higher altitudes than the V-2, even though the Viking is only half the V-2's fully loaded weight and its power plant is no more efficient. In place of the heavy steel-walled warhead, designed for protecting the V-2's explosive charge against aerodynamic heating on the rocket's descent to the target, Viking substituted a thin-walled aluminum nose, adequate for the lower temperatures induced by the ascent and much better suited for cosmic ray measurements. Since the terminal portion of flight is not usable for most upper-air work, the airframe is broken into two large fragments before it reenters the atmosphere. The two fragments have poor aerodynamic shapes, are cushioned by the atmosphere, and land at relatively low velocities, thus permitting the recovery of instruments and records not otherwise possible.

Control of the orientation of the sensing instrument is important in most upper-air experiments, particularly where the phenomena being studied have directional properties, such as cosmic rays and solar radiation. The desired result can be achieved by stabilizing the individual instrument, but it is much more practical, especially when several instruments are involved, to stabilize the rocket. V-2's had no provisions for control of orientation after power cutoff and have been observed occasionally to tumble end-over-end in coasting flight in the upper atmosphere. An attempt was made in Viking to stabilize the airframe during coasting flight in pitch, yaw, and roll by means of an array of small jets under control of an autopilot which senses changes in orientation.

Continuous control of heading during powered flight is necessary to produce the desired near-vertical trajectory of Viking. This type of control in conjunction with power cutoff at a preset velocity was used to guide the V-2, even though it produced relatively large dispersion in impact points. In the Viking development, it was felt that a preset autopilot system would suffice, since the only requirement on impact was that it lie within the White Sands test range boundaries.

The powered flight control system of Viking is described with reference to Fig. 2-15. Of the three control channels—pitch, yaw, and roll—the pitch and yaw channels are identical. A single gyroscope, with its spin axis in the longitudinal direction, provides error signals in both pitch and yaw. From the gyro pickoff the error signal is fed to an amplifier where it is differentiated to produce a rate signal. The two signals, error and error rate, are added and amplified further in a push-pull stage which controls a hydraulic valve. The valve in turn controls a hydraulic servo which deflects the rocket motor away from the airframe's longitudinal axis to produce a pitch or yaw moment that rights the airframe. The rate term, of course, provides the necessary amount of damping. The motor is mounted in a gimbal so that it can be rotated about the pitch and yaw axes. Viking was the first large rocket to utilize a gimballed motor for steering, although Robert H. Goddard experimented with the idea as far back as 1936. The V-2, it will be recalled, was steered by four carbon vanes immersed in the jet exhaust and rotated individually.

Roll control in Viking is produced by a separate system of aerodynamic surfaces and small jets responding to gyroscopically detected errors.

It was pointed out previously that the requirements in Viking for guidance arise from the need for vertical flight and for producing impact within the range boundaries. It is important to know at every instant during powered flight whether or not the rocket will land within the range

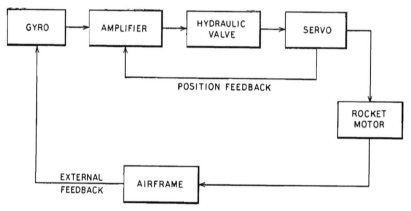

Fig. 2-15 Block Diagram of Viking Pitch (or Yaw) Control Channel.

so that, if an impact outside the limits is imminent, it can be prevented by cutting off the rocket motor (initiated by radio signal). For this purpose and specifically for Viking flights, the Naval Research Laboratory devised a *Rocket Impact-Point Predictor* based upon obtaining present position and velocity from optical trackers and predicting continuously the coordinates of impact. The elevation and azimuth angles from two optical trackers (at opposite ends of a seven-mile baseline) are fed to a computer which converts positions and velocities into rectangular coordinates. Time-to-go is computed as a function of vertical position, vertical velocity, and acceleration of gravity. The predicted impact point along either coordinate in an earth tangential plane is simply the present position plus the product of the coordinate velocity and time-to-go. The Coriolis deflection (See Par. 3-12) is computed for the east-west coordinate only. The coordinates of predicted impact are fed to a two-axis plotting board where they are traced continuously on a map of the range.

Using this information, the range safety officer may command cutoff of the rocket motor before a dangerous situation develops.

2-14 AIRBORNE NAVIGATION

The types of airborne navigation employed are usually classified as:

a. Contact navigation.
b. Celestial navigation.
c. Navigation by electronic aids.

This classification is essentially an equipment classification, without regard to the method of locating position on or above the surface of the earth. The designer of missile guidance systems is concerned with automatizing airborne navigation equipment as part of a complete system. A classification by navigational method, rather than by equipment, tends to simplify the problem, since different equipments which employ similar methods will tend to have essentially similar outputs to the system. A more fundamental classification of navigational methods is:

a. Navigation by observation and recognition.
b. Navigation by triangulation.
c. Navigation by use of earth or space references.

2-15 NAVIGATION BY OBSERVATION AND RECOGNITION

This method of navigation is, of course, the oldest and most commonly used. If one has been in a given place before, one can observe and recognize distinguishing characteristics and landmarks, and the location can be definitely established. When a pilot ventures into new areas, his memory is created from the accumulated memory of others—in the form of maps, charts, and photographs—so that he may observe and recognize his position.

When navigation of a guided missile is considered, the ability of the human pilot both to observe and to recognize must be replaced, at least within the missile proper, with less valuable equipment. The process of observation of an area beneath the missile can be accomplished in the visible light spectrum by the use of television; in the infrared spectrum by suitable infrared equipment; and in the radio frequency spectrum by suitable radar equipment. The area so observed can be displayed as a picture for purposes of recognition.

The process of recognition may be accomplished by a human, if the picture is transmitted to some operating point outside the missile, such as an airplane or ground station which would monitor and direct the missile. In this event, the guidance system would then be similar to the television command guidance systems developed for World War II glide

48 PRIOR DEVELOPMENTS

bombs. If, however, the range is so great as to prohibit the transmission of information to a human operator, then there must be created an automatic means of continually comparing the observed area with a mechanically stored memory (within the missile) of the area over which the missile should fly.

It must be pointed out that the three frequency spectrums mentioned for observation use will each "see" the same area as radically different pictures. Each would develop different characteristics of the terrain beneath the missile, so that recognition of distinguishing landmarks for navigational purposes must be developed in a memory form peculiar to the particular frequency employed for the observation. It is obvious that a system of this nature is of no value over areas, such as the sea, where no distinguishing landmarks exist.

2-16 NAVIGATION BY TRIANGULATION

Figure 2-16 illustrates an aircraft flying at P and able to measure its position with respect to known points on the chart, such as A, B, or C. The airplane can locate itself from one such point, if it can measure both the distance to the point and the bearing to it, with respect to some reference such as north. It can locate itself from two points if it knows the bearing to both of them, again, with respect to some common reference. The airplane can fix its position by measuring the distance to two of the known points. Similarly, the position of the airplane can be determined

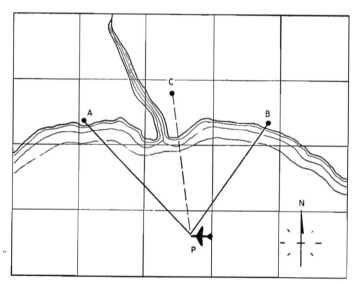

FIG. 2-16 Location by Triangulation.

at the ground stations, by any of these methods, and the position information communicated to the aircraft.

Navigation by the simultaneous measurement of both direction and distance may be accomplished by airborne radar. In order to identify and distinguish specific locations, devices known as *radar beacons* are frequently employed. A radar beacon, or transponder, consists of a receiver, which detects the radar signal, and a transmitter, which is triggered by the receiver and transmits, in return, signals to the radar. Beacon signals are usually coded for identification. Correspondingly, the aircraft may be tracked by ground-based radars and intelligence as to its present location may be communicated to the aircraft.

Navigation by the measurement of bearings to two or more ground stations is, of course, location by direction finding, a commonly used form of navigating aid for both ships and aircraft. A variation of ordinary direction finding techniques is known as *ground direction finding*, wherein the azimuth measurements to the position of the aircraft are made at two

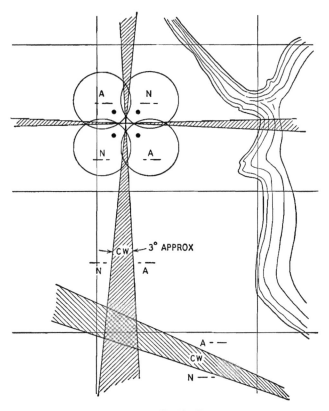

FIG. 2-17 Radio Ranges.

or more ground stations, the computation is accomplished on the ground, and the computed fix of the aircraft is communicated to it.

For aircraft navigation, radio range systems have been employed for many years. Such ranges generally do not indicate the distance between the observer and the signal transmitter, but only azimuth angle. The simplest form of radio range comprises two pairs of vertical antennas so located as to produce patterns as indicated in Fig. 2-17. A transmitter is switched from one pair to the other, producing an A, or dot-dash, on one pair and an N, or dash-dot, on the other. A continuous wave, or on-course, signal is heard over an angle of about three degrees where the two patterns overlap, thus superimposing the A and N signals. A pilot flying a known on-course leg of such a range has continuous indication only of his line of position as related to the transmitting location. He is able to fix his location by this means only where he flies over the station, as indicated by the cone of silence, or when he intercepts the leg of another range. Other

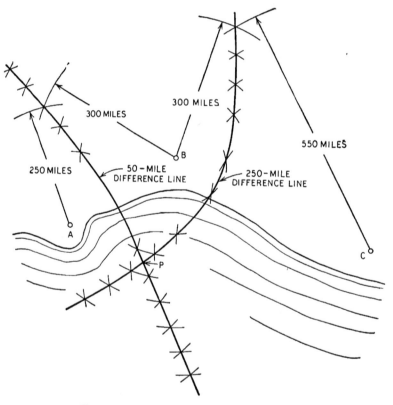

Fig. 2-18 Range Difference Hyperbolas.

aircraft navigating systems which employ azimuth data only are the German radio range *Sonne*, the *UHF radio range*, the *visual two-course range*, and the *omnidirectional beacon*.

Navigation by the measurement of distance to two or more ground locations can be done with considerable accuracy by electronic means, since accurate measurement of time, and therefore distance, is one of the outstanding contributions of this field. *Shoran* is a navigating system employing direct measurement of range to beacons at known locations in order to obtain a fix.

A variant of direct measure of range is employed by measuring the range difference between the response from beacon stations. In this case, three or more stations at known locations are required to obtain a fix. Figure 2-18 illustrates the development of the hyperbolic grid lines of a range difference navigation system. A, B, and C indicate three beacon stations which may be triggered by the interrogating aircraft. The beacons respond, and the receiver in the aircraft measures the difference in transit time of the signals from the three beacon stations, or the range of the aircraft to each of the three stations. If the range to B is 50 miles greater than the range to A, the airplane must be somewhere along the 50-mile difference line between A and B, as illustrated in Fig. 2-18. Correspondingly, if the range to C is 250 miles greater than the range to B, the airplane is located somewhere along the hyperbola, which is the 250-mile difference line. The location of the aircraft is obviously at a point, P, of intersection of the two hyperbolas. Since lines of constant range difference between two points are hyperbolas, systems which employ range or time difference as the primary measurements are called "hyperbolic" navigation systems or hyperbolic nets. Hyperbolic navigation systems now in use are *Loran* and *Gee*, which use pulsed radio energy; and *Decca*, which uses continuous-wave radio frequency transmission.

2-17 NAVIGATION BY EARTH OR SPACE REFERENCES

The primary method of all navigation is celestial navigation: the determination of position by the aid of celestial bodies—the sun, moon, planets, and stars. The practice of celestial navigation in its conventional form requires clear weather and visible celestial bodies; an accurate sextant with charts and tables; accurate knowledge of time; and a reasonably well-trained observer. The problem of developing an automatic celestial navigation system for missile guidance obviously poses a high order of difficulty. Other references of the earth exist which are used as aids to navigation, such as the earth's magnetic field and the earth's gravitational field. These and other terrestrial and celestial references will be considered in further detail.

2-18 AUTOMATIC CONTROL OF AIRCRAFT

The automatic control of moving vehicles was one of the possibilities visualized by the early radio enthusiasts. Automatic control of aircraft was early considered for military application. It is reported that the Germans, in 1914, conceived the idea of automatically guiding pilotless airplanes, loaded with explosives, into enemy installations. The idea was not exploited at the time; but the "Weary Willies" of World War II were a later version of the same idea.

The first successful automatic aircraft flight in this country was made at Dahlgren, Virginia in September 1924 when a radio-controlled pilotless seaplane took off from the water, was flown, and again landed. The equipment developed by C. B. Mirick of the Naval Research Laboratory employed a joystick control and was similar in many ways to the later German-developed command guidance systems.

The present uses of automatic control of aircraft are: for pilot relief and assistance; for aircraft gunfire and rocketfire control; for drones, as targets for antiaircraft gunnery practice; and for hazardous testing of experimental aircraft. Although the equipment and experience developed for all of these uses are of interest to the missile guidance system designer, information on commercially developed autopilots has the greater background and is more readily available.

2-19 AIRCRAFT AUTOPILOTS

Commercial and military aircraft have expanded rapidly in operating range, flight time, and control complexity. This expansion has been attended by a similar increase in the difficulty of performing piloting functions. Transoceanic and transcontinental flights with operating schedules of ten hours or more of flight time have become commonplace. In order to avoid pilot fatigue, it was necessary to develop automatic control equipment which relieved the pilot of the most tedious of his operations, permitting him to devote his time to major operational decisions.

Automatic pilots, as a rule, are so designed as to stabilize the aircraft in flight; to maintain aircraft at constant altitude and in constant direction of flight; and to permit interconnections for automatic approach and landing. The heart of the autopilot is, as with the control systems previously described, the gyroscope. The gyroscope can be made to maintain its spin axis in a true vertical position as indicated by the earth's gravitational force. The gyroscope will be discussed in greater detail subsequently.

Figure 2-19 shows a simplified diagram of three channels of an autopilot—the roll channel, pitch channel, and yaw channel. An examination of the roll channel reveals that any deviation of the airplane in roll from the horizontal position is detected by movement of the aircraft with respect to the vertical gyro. The difference between the gyro output and the aileron feedback signal is the servo actuating error signal.

The pitch channel operates in a similar manner, in that any deviation of the airframe in pitch with respect to the vertical gyro results in appropriate signals which move the airframe elevators. In turn, the airframe responds to the elevator motion and corrects its position with respect to the vertical gyro. It will be noted that the pitch channel can also be made to respond to a preset altimeter. Any deviation from the altitude set into the altimeter will cause the airframe to respond.

The yaw channel is similar to the channels just described except that the basic information is usually obtained from a gyro-stabilized magnetic

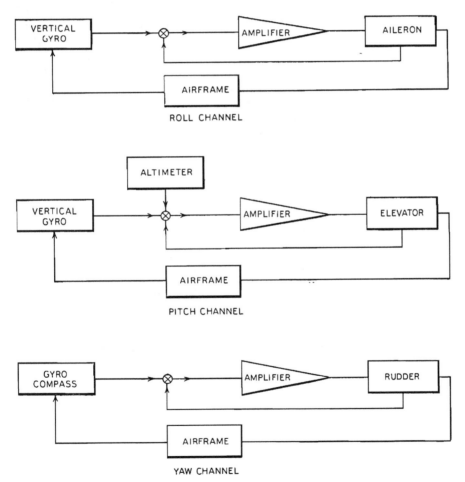

FIG. 2-19 Simplified Block Diagram of Autopilot Roll, Pitch and Yaw Channels.

compass. The deviation in azimuth from the manually inserted flight direction results in a correction of the airframe's direction by use of the aircraft rudder.

In conventional commercial aircraft, large turns must be coordinated both in azimuth and in roll. For this reason, large turns are normally inserted manually by the pilot, with both the yaw and roll channels responding to obtain a coordinated turn. Appropriate limits of rate of turn are generally established within the autopilot as demanded by safety according to the aircraft structural design. Appropriate interrelationships between the amount of change in yaw and the amount of roll for a given turn are usually maintained by aircraft autopilots.

If it is desired to make the landing operation dependent upon automatic approach and landing equipment, the same electrical signals that operate the cross pointer meters in systems such as the Instrument Landing System can be made to guide the aircraft automatically in its approach to an airport runway. It is apparent, even from this simplified description of aircraft autopilots, that the functions performed by such autopilots encompass, to a large degree, many of the functions which must be considered in stabilizing and controlling guided missiles. For example, the aircraft autopilot employed in the airborne fire control problem, involving high-speed and rapid-maneuvering fighter aircraft, has response characteristic requirements approaching those of a guided missile autopilot.

BIBLIOGRAPHY

1. K. L. Nielsen, J. F. Heyda, *The Mathematical Theory of Airborne Fire Control*, U. S. Government Printing Office, Washington, D. C.
2. A. R. Weyl, *Guided Missiles*, Temple Press, London.
3. F. Ross, Jr., *Guided Missiles, Rockets, and Torpedoes*, Lothrop, Lee & Shepard Co., New York.
4. K. W. Gatland, *Development of the Guided Missile*, Philosophical Library, New York.
5. J. A. Pierce, A. A. McKenzie, R. H. Woodward (Eds.), *Loran*, Vol. 4, Radiation Laboratory Series, McGraw-Hill Book Co., Inc., New York.
6. J. S. Hall, *Radar Aids to Navigation*, Vol. 2, Radiation Laboratory Series, McGraw-Hill Book Co., Inc., New York.

CHAPTER 3

TERRESTRIAL AND CELESTIAL REFERENCES

The earth is one of the smaller satellites of a medium-sized star and, considering the number and magnitude of other celestial bodies, would be completely insignificant were it not for the fact that we live on it. We are concerned herein with guiding a missile above the surface of the earth from one point on its surface to another point. This implies that we must know the location of the termination point of the flight with reference to the starting point. Since it is desirable to express these locations in a universally understandable form, this requires the creation of a universal reference frame over the surface of the earth. If the surface-to-surface missile is of extremely long range, so that it cannot be controlled from the launching point or other points along its path, it must contain within itself the ability to navigate from the launching to the terminal location. In order to accomplish this self-navigation during the flight, the missile must have some reference available in order to generate its location in terms of its eventual terminal point. In the case of the ballistic missile, the forces which act upon it after its propulsive acceleration has ceased must be known in order to predict its terminal point in the process of computing its proper aim.

In the process of navigating over the earth, a universal means of designating positions on the earth's surface has been adopted. Charts of many varieties have been made of the earth's surface configurations as the result of navigation and survey. The shape of the earth has been measured, in a general way, and its motions and relations to other parts of the solar system and celestial bodies have been computed. Terrestrial and celestial references for navigational use have been determined; these references are either fixed or variable in accordance with known laws of behavior. It is proposed herein to review briefly some of this knowledge, in an effort to indicate that part which is of value to missile guidance.

3-1 CHART PROJECTIONS [1]

In the establishment of a universal reference system to indicate position, the earth is assumed to be a sphere. If we define a *great circle* as a circle

---

[1] B. Dutton, *Navigation and Nautical Astronomy*, Chap. 1, United States Naval Institute, 1951, used as source material for chart projection discussions.

on the surface of the sphere marking the intersection of the sphere and a plane passing through its center, the *meridians* are great circles of the earth which pass through its poles. The *prime meridian* is the meridian used as the origin of measurement of longitude. The meridian of the original site of the Royal Observatory at Greenwich, England, is used by nearly all of the countries in the world as the prime meridian. *Longitude* is measured numerically in degrees east or west of the prime meridian.

The *latitude* of any place is its angular distance north or south of the equator and is also the angle at the earth's center subtended by the arc of the meridian contained between the equator and the place. Latitude is measured numerically in degrees north or south of the equator. Any position on the earth's surface is conventionally designated in terms of longitude and latitude.

The *distance* between any two positions on the surface of the earth is the length of the trajectory joining them, usually expressed in miles. In marine navigation, distance is customarily understood to be the rhumb line distance (a rhumb line being a line on the surface of the earth making the same angle with all meridians). The shortest distance between two points on the surface of the earth is the great circle distance between them. Navigators customarily express distance in nautical miles, measuring 6080.20 ft, which is practically the length of a minute of arc of a great circle on the surface of the earth.

The *direction* at any point along a trajectory is the inclination of the trajectory to the meridian of the point, measured clockwise from 000 deg at north through 360 deg. The *heading* of a vehicle is the direction in which it heads at any particular moment, similarly measured.

Let us consider some of the possible methods of guiding types of surface-to-surface missiles from one point on the surface of the earth to another such point. We have already mentioned, briefly, the following:

  a. Ballistic missile—guided to propulsion cutoff (V-2).
  b. Ballistic missile—guided after propulsion cutoff (Upper atmosphere research rocket, the Viking).
  c. Aerodynamic missile—guided from terrestrial or celestial references (V-1).
  d. Aerodynamic missile—guided by way stations, as by loran, radio range, etc.

The ballistic missile has been likened to a projectile fired from a gun, wherein the length of the gun barrel is the range of guidance. When the propulsion and guidance rockets cease operation, the projectile continues on its course subject only to the accelerations of the earth. Since gravity is the major acceleration acting upon the missile (other accelerations will will be considered later), the missile, after guidance ceases, will fly approximately in a plane which also passes through the center of the earth, so that its trajectory projected on the earth's surface will approximate a great circle. For the ballistic missile, then, the great circle distance between the launching and terminal points constitutes the range; the aiming angle is the proper initial heading along the great circle joining the two points.

The *aerodynamic missile*, so called because it depends on aerodynamic lift for flight, has much more versatile trajectory possibilities. The V-1 employed magnetic guidance; its trajectory, projected on the earth, was approximately a rhumb line since its heading was constant with respect to magnetic north. The V-1 then, employed the terrestrial reference of magnetism for its guidance. Another guidance method, mentioned previously, is that of navigation by observation and recognition of the terrain. In this case, the trajectory must be developed to take advantage of distinctive terrain that will simplify recognition. In any guidance system wherein the navigational method permits free choice of trajectory, such as celestial navigation, a great circle trajectory is the logical choice, since it is the shortest distance between two points on the surface of the earth and would be the most economical of fuel. For tactical reasons, such as to complicate the defense against missiles, it may be desirable to have the missiles arrive at the terminal point from different directions. In this event, the logical trajectory would be a great circle to some computed position, followed by a turn toward the terminal point.

Charts are used in navigation to represent the earth's spherical surface, or a part of it, on a convenient flat plane. Although there are many special instances that cannot be included in a generalization, the elements most desired in charts, from a missile guidance viewpoint, are:

a. The positions of origin and termination of the missile trajectory should be accurately determined.

b. For convenience, a great circle should be indicated by a straight line.

c. There should be a minimum of geometrical distortion of the surface areas.

d. Prominent physical features, such as land heights, etc., which could be required knowledge for the flight, should be recognizably displayed.

3-2 MERCATOR PROJECTION

The vast majority of charts used for marine navigation and many of those used for air navigation are made on the Mercator projection because position, distance, and direction can be measured easily; and because rhumb lines (of particular interest to the marine navigator) plot as straight lines. The construction of the Mercator projection is graphically illustrated in Fig. 3-1.

In Fig. 3-1a there is shown a portion of the earth's surface between two meridians projected to a plane surface. The two circles shown on the projected area are of equal size. In Fig. 3-1b, the parallels of latitude are expanded to plot the meridians parallel to each other. The circles are now distorted and become ellipses. This distortion of land areas, particularly in the higher latitudes, would make charts useless to a navigator, for he could not compare what he had on the chart with what he observed. Accordingly, to obtain the proper proportion, the meridians are expanded in the same ratio as the parallels. The original sector now appears on the

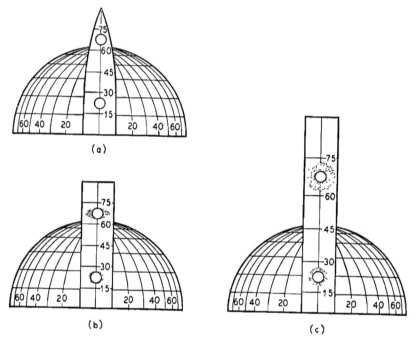

Fig. 3-1 Development of the Mercator Projection. (By permission from *Navigation and Nautical Astronomy* by Dutton. Copyright 1951, U. S. Naval Institute.)

completed chart as the rectangle of Fig. 3-1c. Note that, as the latitude increases, the parallels expand on an increasing scale, and accordingly the meridians expand in proportion. The circles resume their proper shapes, but are apparently larger than the original circles and are unequal. To compensate for this error, different scales must be used on Mercator charts for measuring distances in different latitudes.

The expansion of the latitude and longitude scales approximate the secant of the latitude for short distances. When great distances are involved, a more exact method must be used for accurate results. A convenient method is provided in *American Practical Navigator*, by Bowditch.

The length of a meridian on a Mercator chart, as expanded between the equator and any given latitude, expressed in units of one minute of arc at the equator, constitutes the number of *meridional parts* of that latitude. The expansion of the longitude is such as to make a given unit of it the same length, as shown on the chart, since the meridians are drawn parallel. Thus the number of meridional parts in one degree of longitude is everywhere 60. At the equator one degree of latitude is approximately the same length as one degree of longitude, but as the latitude increases, the ratio of latitude to longitude increases.

On the earth's surface one degree of latitude may be considered everywhere to be 60 nautical miles in length, whereas the length of one degree of longitude varies with the latitude. The latitude scale on a Mercator projection may therefore be used for measuring distance, at the proper latitudes.

The rhumb line was previously defined as a line making the same angle with all meridians, and it was also stated that one of the advantages of the Mercator projection to marine navigators was that the rhumb line appeared as a straight line. For great distances, however, if we neglect the special cases of the equator and the meridians, a rhumb line spirals toward the poles, as shown in Fig. 3-2. The resulting line is called a *loxodromic curve*.

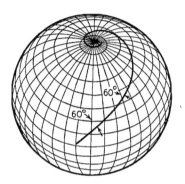

Fig. 3-2 A Loxodromic Curve. (By permission from *Navigation and Nautical Astronomy* by Dutton. Copyright 1951, U. S. Naval Institute.)

Although the Mercator projection as illustrated is the most universally available of all chart types, and will therefore frequently be employed, it does not satisfy the general requirements mentioned previously, since great circles do not appear as straight lines and there is considerable distortion at the higher latitudes.

3-3 TRANSVERSE MERCATOR PROJECTION

With reference to Fig. 3-1, when the development of the Mercator projection is continued around the equator for both hemispheres, the resultant complete projection is a cylinder, tangent to the sphere at the equator. The *transverse* Mercator projection is one which places the projected cylinder tangent to the earth at any great circle; in common usage this refers to an oblique great circle. The Mercator projection, described previously, is a special case of the transverse Mercator projection with the cylinder tangent at the equator. In a missile flight, planned along a great circle route between two points on the earth's surface, a transverse Mercator projection tangent at the trajectory would display the area adjacent to the trajectory with a minimum of distortion. The trajectory, which is the great circle of interest, would appear as a straight line and there would be a minimum of distortion in the areas adjacent to the trajectory. Such a projection does satisfy the general requirements of a chart for missile guidance use.

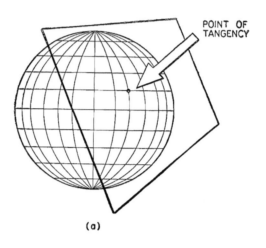

(a)

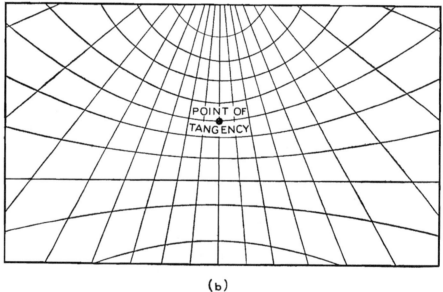

(b)

FIG. 3-3 A Gnomonic Projection and Chart. (By permission from *Navigation and Nautical Astronomy* by Dutton. Copyright 1951, U. S. Naval Institute.)

An *inverse* Mercator projection is another special case of the transverse Mercator projection, being that projection which results if the cylinder on which the earth's surface is projected is placed tangent to the earth at a meridian. This projection has found considerable favor in polar navigation use since it furnishes a familiar and simple means of measuring distances.

3-4 GNOMONIC PROJECTION

When the meridians and parallels of latitude are projected to a plane tangent to the earth at one point as shown in Fig. 3-3a, the result is called a *gnomonic projection*. Meridians appear as straight lines converging toward the pole, as illustrated in Fig. 3-3b, and parallels of latitude are projected as nonparallel curves. Distortion increases with increased distance from the point of tangency. Neither direction nor distance can be measured directly. The chief advantage of a gnomonic chart is that all great circles plot as straight lines. For this reason it is commonly called a *great circle* chart.

3-5 POLAR CHARTS

If the pole is chosen as the point of tangency for a gnomonic projection, the meridians appear as radial lines and the parallels of latitude appear as concentric circles. This projection is known as a *polar gnomonic* chart. A modification of the polar gnomonic chart is one on which the parallels of latitude increase uniformly in radius so that the latitude scale is constant. This projection is called the polar *azimuthal equidistant* chart.

Another projection used for polar charts is the *stereographic*, wherein the projecting plane is perpendicular to the axis of the earth and points on the earth are projected by straight lines from the opposite pole.

Gnomonic, azimuthal equidistant, and stereographic charts are so nearly alike in polar regions that it is difficult to distinguish the projection by appearance only. In practice all of these projections have found favor among navigators. Figure 3-4 shows a polar gnomonic chart with portions of several great circles illustrated.

3-6 LAMBERT CONFORMAL PROJECTION

The derivation of the *Lambert conformal* projection may be visualized by the following discussion. As shown in Fig. 3-5a, a cone is placed over a sphere representing the earth, with the axes of the cone and of the sphere in coincidences. The size of the cone is such that it cuts the surface of the sphere at the two parallels representing the parallels of latitude which have been selected as the standard parallels of the projection. The meridians of the sphere are projected onto the cone and so determine the meridians of the chart. The land masses on the sphere are then projected onto

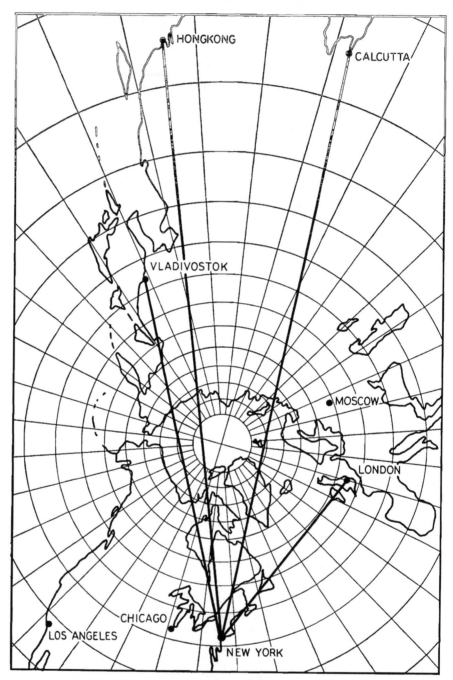

Fig. 3-4 Polar Gnomonic Chart with Some Great Circles Shown. (By permission from *Navigation and Nautical Astronomy* by Dutton. Copyright 1951, U. S. Naval Institute.)

the cone. In the Lambert conformal projection, the area lying between the standard parallels is compressed and the area lying outside the standard parallels is expanded.

The cone is then removed and developed as shown in Fig. 3-5b. Note that the standard parallels are arcs of concentric circles, with the apex of the cone as a center. The area between the standard parallels may be further divided by swinging additional arcs for other parallels of latitude. It will be noted that the meridians are straight lines converging at the apex of the cone.

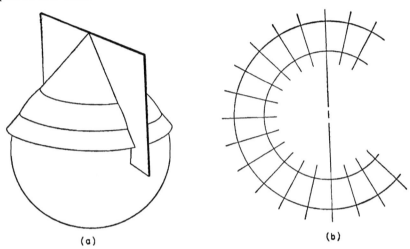

FIG. 3-5 A Lambert Conformal Projection and Chart. (By permission from *Navigation and Nautical Astronomy* by Dutton. Copyright 1951, U. S. Naval Institute.)

The advantages of the Lambert conformal projection are:

a. The distortion is comparatively minor. There is no distortion along the standard parallels.

b. The same distance scale may be used anywhere on the chart, with negligible error.

c. Meridians and parallels intersect at right angles, and the angles formed by any two lines on the surface of the earth are correctly represented on the chart.

d. A straight line on the chart closely approximates a great circle. The Lambert conformal projection thus also closely satisfies the requirements for missile guidance use.

3-7 POLYCONIC PROJECTION

If the projection is made on a series of cones tangent to the earth, the result is a *polyconic* projection as shown in Fig. 3-6. Meridians, except the central one, are represented as curved lines. Parallels of latitude are nonconcentric circles, but having their centers along the central meridians, usually beyond the limit of the map.

There is no distortion along the central meridian and, unless the spread in longitude is great, maximum distortion is small. Since shapes are more accurately shown on the polyconic than on any other projection commonly used, most maps (to the navigator a *map* in contradistinction to a chart is a representation which stresses political subdivision, physical features, etc.) are made on this projection. The polyconic projection is not suitable for navigational purposes because both direction and distance are difficult to measure accurately and both rhumb lines and great circles are curves.

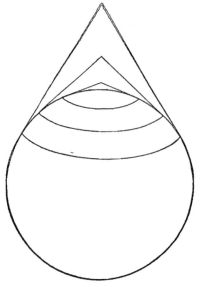

Fig. 3-6 The Polyconic Projection. (By permission from *Navigation and Nautical Astronomy* by Dutton. Copyright 1951, U. S. Naval Institute.)

3-8 MOTIONS OF THE EARTH

The principal motions of the earth are:

    a. Rotation about its polar axis once a day.

    b. Revolution about the sun once a year.

    c. Precession about the ecliptic axis once each 25,800 years.

    d. Space motion, or motion of the solar system through space with relation to other stars.

3-9 EFFECTS OF ROTATION OF THE EARTH

The physical effect of rotation of the earth has been to shape the earth as an oblate spheroid. The centrifugal force of the rotation causes a variation in the value of the gravitational force over the surface of the sphere. Motions of the wind and ocean currents moving above or on the surface of the earth are also affected by its rotation. Time, an essential element in navigation, is normally measured by the earth's rotation with respect to the sun and other celestial bodies.

3-10 SHAPE OF THE EARTH

The earth, because of its rotation, has the shape of an oblate spheroid, depressed at the poles and bulging at the equator. The amount of this departure from a truly spherical shape is sufficiently great to affect both the construction of charts and the absolute magnitude and direction of the vector of gravitational force. The amount of oblateness is difficult to measure; consequently authorities differ on the precise dimensions of the earth. Those determined by Clarke in 1866 have been generally used for the purpose of developing charts of North America, and are:

Equatorial diameter = 7926.5 statute miles = 6883.2 nautical miles
Polar diameter = 7899.6 statute miles = 6859.9 nautical miles
Mean diameter = 7917.5 statute miles = 6875.5 nautical miles
Difference = 26.9 statute miles = 23.3 nautical miles

The oblateness of the earth, then, as referred to the equatorial diameter, is 0.339 percent, approximately.

3-11 EFFECT OF ROTATION OF THE EARTH ON GRAVITY

The direction of the vector of gravitational force is the prime reference used by man. Buildings are constructed by use of the plumb line; vertical gyroscopes and gyrocompasses are directed by pendulous forces; measurements and chartings of land areas are made by use of the plumb bob and the level bubble.

Newton's third law of motion has been written to read that "every portion of matter in the universe attracts every other portion with a force directly proportional to the product of the masses and inversely as the square of the distance between them." Stating this in algebraic form, we have:

$$F = G \frac{m_1 m_2}{d^2} \tag{3-1}$$

where F is the force of attraction between two bodies of mass, m_1 and m_2, when separated by a distance d. The quantity G is called the Universal Gravitational Constant and is generally assigned the numerical value of 6.66×10^{-8} with the dimensions of $cm^3/gram\ sec^2$, when F is given in dynes, m_1 and m_2 in grams, and d in centimeters. The force of gravity per unit mass, g, on the surface of the earth is merely a special case of Newton's general law of gravitational attraction. If we assume the earth to be a homogeneous, stationary, isolated sphere (none of which is true), we may substitute $g = F$, the mass of the earth $M_e = m_1$, 1 gram at the earth's surface $= m_2$, and the radius $R = d$, and the equation becomes

$$g = G \frac{M_e}{R^2} \tag{3-2}$$

The mass of the earth, M_e, has been computed to be 6.15×10^{27} grams with an average density of approximately 5.5. This value for mean density indicates a high density for the core of the earth, since the density of surface rocks is in the order of 2.5 to 2.8.

The force of gravity at the surface of the earth is the resultant of the vectors of the force of attraction by the mass of the earth on a unit mass and the centrifugal force of the earth's rotation acting on the same mass, as shown in Fig. 3-7. The centrifugal force c may be written as

$$c = m\omega^2 r \qquad (3\text{-}3)$$

where m is the mass, ω is the angular velocity $\left(\omega = \dfrac{2\pi}{86,164.1 \text{ sec}} = 7.29211 \times 10^{-5} \text{ radian/sec}\right)$, and r the radius of gyration. By inspection of Fig. 3-7, it is obvious that the centrifugal force vector will be zero at the poles and a maximum at the equator.

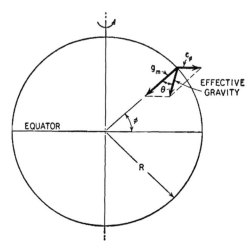

FIG. 3-7 The Effect on Gravity of Centrifugal Acceleration Due to Rotation of the Earth.

If we assume the earth to be a sphere with radius R, the gravitational attraction g_m is the same at all points on the surface. If c_e is the centrifugal force at the equator and m in Eq. (3-3) is a unit mass, we may write

$$c_e = \omega^2 R \qquad (3\text{-}4)$$

At any latitude ϕ, the centrifugal force at that latitude is

$$c_\phi = \omega^2 R \cos \phi = c_e \cos \phi \qquad (3\text{-}5)$$

The component of c_ϕ which directly opposes the gravitational attraction g_m is $c_\phi \cos \phi$, or $c_e \cos^2 \phi$, so that the total vertical gravitational force along the radius g_ϕ becomes

$$g_\phi = g_m - c_e \cos^2 \phi \qquad (3\text{-}6)$$

The value of the gravitational attraction may be expressed in terms of the resultant force at the equator, g_e, and the centrifugal force at the equator, c_e, as follows:

$$g_e = g_m - c_e \qquad (3\text{-}7)$$

Further, since the centrifugal force at the poles is zero, c_e may be expressed in terms of the resultant gravitational force at the pole, g_p, and at the equator, g_e, as

$$c_e = g_p - g_e \qquad (3\text{-}8)$$

If we substitute Eq. (3-7) and (3-8) in Eq. (3-6) and solve, we obtain

$$g_\phi = g_e \left[1 + \left(\frac{g_p - g_e}{g_e} \right) \sin^2 \phi \right] \qquad (3\text{-}9)[2]$$

The constant $\dfrac{g_p - g_e}{g_e}$ is known as the *gravitational flattening*. This equation does not consider the effect of the change of radius of the earth by reason of the oblateness at the poles. Berroth in 1916 published the following formula for determining the vertical component of gravity for various latitudes, including a correction for the oblateness of the earth:

$$g_\phi = 978.046(1 + 0.005296 \sin^2 \phi - 0.000007 \sin^2 2\phi) \qquad (3\text{-}10)$$

Table 3-1 shows the value of the force of gravity for various latitudes and is employed for determination of the latitude correction for gravity exploration and field work.

TABLE 3-1 VALUE OF $g\phi$ FOR VARIOUS LATITUDES

Latitude	cm/sec^2	ft/sec^2
0	978.046	32.08812
10	978.203	32.09327
20	978.652	32.10801
40	980.178	32.15807
50	981.078	32 18760
60	981.930	32.21555
70	982.623	32.23829
80	983.073	32.25305
90	983.223	32.25797

The angle θ between the true vertical, along the radius of the earth, and the direction of the effective gravitational force is of interest to missile guidance, since it represents a correction which must be applied to any pendulous vertical-indicating device in order that the true vertical may be indicated. The component of centrifugal force at latitude ϕ at right angles to the vertical is $c_\phi \sin \phi$ or $c_e \cos \phi \sin \phi$; hence

$$\theta = \tan^{-1} \frac{c_e \cos \phi \sin \phi}{g_\phi} \qquad (3\text{-}11)$$

[2] J. J. Jakosky, *Exploration Geophysics*, p. 253, Trija Publishing Co., 1950.

It can be seen by inspection that this correction is zero both at the poles and at the equator and will maximize at approximately 45 deg latitude. At 45 deg north latitude, a plumb line will be approximately 9 min from the vertical, downward toward the south.

Since the vertical component of gravity decreases inversely as the square of the distance between the center of the earth and a unit mass, and the centrifugal force increases as a function of the same distance, it is to be expected that a change in θ will result from a change in elevation. The change of θ with altitude is easily calculable, but it is extremely small. As an example, the difference in θ at latitude 45 deg, between sea level and 60,000 ft elevation, is in the order of 4.5 sec of arc. This deviation is an order of magnitude smaller than vertical-measuring devices can detect.

Gravitational anomalies exist which are caused by the presence of large bodies of abnormal density near the point of measurement. If the body is denser than the surrounding material, it will exert an unduly large force of attraction on a plumb bob or other pendulous mass and cause a deflection of the plumb line toward it. Although these anomalies do not usually exceed 10 sec of arc, except in mountainous regions, they are occasionally quite large. For example, between the north and south coasts of Puerto Rico, the anomalous deflection of the plumb line produced by local inhomogeneities may lead to an error in distance of 1 part in 50.

Charts, for navigational use, are developed from astronomical locations of pertinent places, land masses, coastal areas, and distinguishing landmarks. When an astronomical location of position is made, the measurements of the positions of the celestial bodies are related to the direction of the vector of effective gravitational force at that location. It does not matter whether a plumb line, or the ocean horizon, or a level bubble is employed; the reference so established is still based on the direction of effective gravity.

If, as an example, we have by astronomical measurements located a position as being 45 deg north latitude, then (since each minute of arc is a nautical mile) the great circle distance to the equator should be 2700 nautical miles. However, because of the rotation of the earth, the effective vertical at this latitude is in error by about 9 min, as previously noted, and the great circle distance, if the earth were a sphere, would measure 2691 nautical miles. Since the earth is not a sphere, the measured peripheral distance is still further altered by reason of its actual shape. As previously related, the effect of the oblateness of the earth is included in charts, but since the navigator is largely dependent upon celestial navigation, which in turn is dependent upon the reference of effective gravity, charts are based on astronomical observations and the distances are in error as compared to distances measured directly.

The effect of this on missile guidance problems is dependent upon the guidance method employed. If guidance is by celestial navigation, then astronomical positions are important, rather than the exact distance traversed. If guidance is accomplished by inertial means, wherein accelerations are integrated to obtain direction and distance traversed, then the actual distance between the launching point and the target is extremely important. If a ballistic missile is being considered, then the distance traversed and the effect of gravitational anomalies, both during its trajectory and at the terminus of the flight, are important.

3-12 THE CORIOLIS EFFECT

In our previous discussions of gravitational attraction and the effect of the centrifugal force of the earth's rotation, we tacitly assumed the existence of a fixed inertial frame of reference according to Newtonian mechanics. But there are also frames of reference in which such fundamental assumptions are not valid.

If we imagine a room in which the coordinate system has been established by the walls, floor, and ceiling, a particle falling within that room will have a specific trajectory or direction, within this coordinate system, to an observer within the room. If, however, we set this room and its coordinate system into a rapid rotation, and if the given applied forces remain unchanged, then the paths of the falling particles in the rotating coordinate system will no longer be the same.

An observer on the earth exists within a rotating frame of reference, both because of the daily rotation of the earth on its axis and the annual revolution of the earth about its sun. Coordinate frames on the earth, strictly speaking, are not inertial frames for these reasons. The effect of the revolution about the sun is so small that it may be neglected for our purposes. The effect of the rotation of the earth in creating a uniformly rotating frame of reference is appreciable in the consideration of long-range ballistic missiles. It was previously shown that the effective acceleration of a falling body was the resultant of the gravitational attraction and the centrifugal reaction. When the *apparent* acceleration of a freely falling body relative to the earth is considered, an additional acceleration is involved, called the *Coriolis acceleration*, after its discoverer.

The derivation of the Coriolis acceleration may be found in many theoretical physics texts.[3] It results in an eastward deviation of a falling body, and is, if x is the deviation to the *east*,

$$x = \tfrac{1}{3}\omega g t^3 \cos \phi \tag{3-12}$$

in which ω is the angular velocity of the rotating earth; g, the effective

---

[3] See, for example, Leigh Page, *Introduction to Theoretical Physics*, Chap. 1, D. Van Nostrand Co., Inc., N. Y., 1947.

gravity; t, the time of fall; and ϕ, the latitude. A physical recognition of this acceleration may be obtained by inspection of Fig. 3-8. A particle at P, above a section through the earth at the equator, is moving more rapidly toward the east than a point on the earth directly beneath it at A, since the particle is at a greater radius from the center of rotation. As the point A, on the earth directly beneath P, moves to A' during the time of fall, the particle falls to the eastward of A', since its initial eastward velocity was greater than that of the surface of the earth.

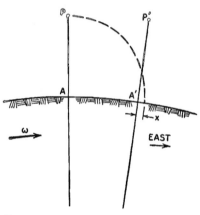

Fig. 3-8 The Coriolis Effect for a Falling Body.

If a body is projected vertically upward, it can be shown that it will fall to the *west* of its launching point by the amount

$$x = \tfrac{4}{3}\omega g t^3 \cos \phi \qquad (3\text{-}13)$$

Figure 3-9 again shows a section through the earth at the equator. As the body is projected vertically upward, the radius from the center of rotation increases. As the launching point A moves east, the projected body would have to increase its eastward velocity as its radius from the center increases in order to remain directly above it. Since its eastward velocity is limited to that of the surface of the earth at launching, it lags behind and falls to the earth *west* of A', which is the position of the launching point after the time of flight.

It should be noted that the Coriolis acceleration will not affect the direction of a stationary plumb line, which is always directed along the vector of effective gravity. The Coriolis effect involves freely falling bodies only. In the case of long-range ballistic missiles (which are freely falling bodies after the propulsive accelerations are removed), the times of flight will be correspondingly longer and an appreciable correction for the Coriolis acceleration must be made in the aiming computations in accordance with Eq. (3-13). For a missile that is guided to a position above the target and then is caused to fall ballistically (similar to the operation of the German V-1), Eq. (3-12) will apply. Since the height h through which a body falls may be closely expressed as being equal to $\tfrac{1}{2} g t^2$, Eq. (3-12) may be rewritten as a function of height of fall as

$$x = \tfrac{1}{3}\omega \sqrt{\frac{8h^3}{g}} \cos \phi \qquad (3\text{-}14)$$

The correction in this case will be rather small, since the height, for reasons of propulsion and aerodynamic control, will probably be within the troposphere. In the case of the V-1, the ballistic uncertainties of the diving missile were so great as to make such a correction meaningless.

We have discussed, thus far, only the effect of the Coriolis acceleration on freely falling particles. A particle moving horizontally in a straight line with respect to the earth, is moving in a curved path with respect to space and is therefore also subject to the Coriolis acceleration. This may, perhaps, be better visualized if we imagine an aircraft or guided missile flying a great circle course at constant speed above the surface of the earth. Its path is curved in space, by reason of the rotation of the earth. Any

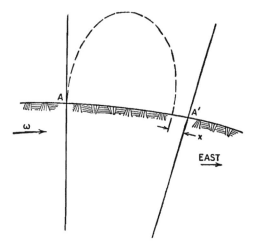

Fig. 3-9 The Coriolis Effect for a Body Projected Vertically Upward.

pendulous device, or level bubble, which is used to indicate the vertical in such a rapidly moving vehicle is thus affected by the Coriolis acceleration. The horizontal deviating acceleration y is

$$y = 2\omega v \sin \phi \qquad (3\text{-}15)$$

in which v is the horizontal velocity of the aircraft or missile and the other nomenclature is as before. It will be noted that the acceleration, as well as the consequent necessity for correction, increases directly as the velocity of the moving body and with increasing latitude. The correction, therefore, to a pendulous vertical-indicating device for high-speed guided missiles in great circle polar flight will be appreciable.

In the case of the ballistic missile, after the propulsive acceleration has been removed, its trajectory is determined by the accelerations acting upon it. The missile is fired at some angle to the horizontal and, if we consider its trajectory to be in a vacuum, has a constant horizontal component of velocity. The missile will be caused to deviate from great circle flight, by reason of the Coriolis acceleration, as a function of the horizontal component of its velocity and the latitude. Again, this deviation may be appreciable for high-speed missiles launched in the upper latitudes. The direction of the acceleration is always to the right in the Northern hemisphere and always to the left in the Southern, no matter what the direction of flight. The correction will, therefore, be in the opposite sense.

3-13 TIME

Time, as we use it, is an artificially developed reference, stemming from the daily rotation of the earth with respect to the sun. One rotation of the earth with respect to the sun depends upon the positions of the two bodies with respect to each other at the beginning and the end of the day. The speed of the earth in its orbit about the sun varies, and the length of the day, based on the rotation of the earth relative to the sun, varies. To overcome this objection and yet gain the advantages of solar time, an imaginary *mean sun* is used. The mean sun moves eastward in the celestial equator at a uniform rate equal to the average rate of the true sun in the ecliptic, thus removing the irregularities of apparent time. Time as measured by this means is called *civil* time. The difference between civil time and apparent time reaches a maximum value of nearly $16\frac{1}{2}$ min in November.

To avoid confusion, the earth is divided into time zones, each 15 deg wide in longitude, starting at the zero zone, extending $7\frac{1}{2}$ deg each side of the zero meridian at Greenwich. Conversion of longitude to time and vice versa is easily accomplished by these standards. Time at the zero meridian at Greenwich, England (*Greenwich Civil Time*), is of particular interest to navigators because the positions of the celestial bodies are tabulated in the almanacs for this time.

If we measure the rotation of the earth with respect to the stars, we have *sidereal* time. Sidereal time is useful to the navigator in locating fixed stars. The change in the celestial coordinates of most of the stars is too slight to be of apparent significance during any one lifetime. At any given sidereal time the stars are always in the same places in the sky, regardless of the time of day by civil time. Since the earth revolves about the sun, the sun appears to be changing its position with respect to the stars. When the earth rotates through 360 deg with respect to the sun, by reason of its multiple motions, it turns through more than 360 deg with respect to the stars. Hence, sidereal time units are shorter than solar time units. The solar day is about 4 min longer than the sidereal day.

In practice, correct time is determined by means of a small telescope mounted on an east-west axis so that the line of sight is north or south in the meridian. A hairline in the telescope is carefully lined up with the meridian and the exact instant a star crosses the meridian is determined. From this, the sidereal, and hence the solar, time can be computed. The correct time is broadcast by radio. In the United States, the correct time is determined by the Naval Observatory in Washington, D. C. and is broadcast either directly or indirectly from this source.

3-14 REVOLUTION, PRECESSION, AND SPACE MOTION OF THE EARTH

The earth, in addition to its daily rotation, revolves annually about the sun. In this trip, the earth follows an ellipse of small eccentricity, with the sun at one of the focal points. In January the earth is nearest the sun, the distance being about 91,300,000 miles; in July the distance is about 94,500,000 miles; the mean distance is about 92,900,000 miles. As the earth revolves about the sun its speed varies, being greater in January than in July, with an average speed of about 66,000 mph. The speed of the earth in its orbit is sufficient to cause the light from the stars to appear to shift forward, an effect known to the navigator as *aberration*. For those stars at right angles to the direction of the earth's travel the maximum effect is 20.5 sec of arc.

The rotation of the earth about the sun does create a Coriolis acceleration because it, too, represents a deviation from the earth's inertial frame. Since, however, the ratio of the revolution of the earth to the rotation is 1 to 365, the effect is so small as to be negligible.

The earth rotates about an axis which is not vertical to the plane of its revolution about the sun, usually referred to as the plane of the *ecliptic*. The moon, which is nearly in the plane of the ecliptic, exerts a gravitational force upon the earth. This tends to pull the axis of the earth vertical with respect to the ecliptic, but the gyroscopic motion of the earth causes the polar axis to precess. The earth's axis precesses in a direction opposite to the direction of rotation. The motion of precession of the earth refers to the conical motion of the earth's axis about the vertical to the plane of the ecliptic. The earth completes one precessional cycle in about 25,800 years, or the pole moves about 50.2 sec per year. The combined effects of other bodies cause slight variations in the rate of precession. In addition, the axis of the earth has periodic wandering motions of very small amplitude, an annual one believed to be associated with seasonal meteorological changes and one with a period of about 14 months, which may be the natural period of vibration of the earth. The movement is too small to be of any significance in ordinary navigation, for the poles do not wander more than 40 ft from their mean position.

The earth is one of the family of planets held together gravitationally by the sun. These planets, including the earth, move with the sun as it

74 TERRESTRIAL AND CELESTIAL REFERENCES

changes its position with respect to the stars. The average space relationship of the sun to the commonly known stars does not change sufficiently to be of interest in the navigation problem.

3-15 TERRESTRIAL MAGNETISM

The earth acts as a large spherical magnet with its field so distributed at the surface as to simulate a short bar magnet at the center of the earth. The earth is surrounded by a magnetic field having a strength of about 0.6 gauss, the moment of the hypothetical bar magnet has been estimated to be about 8×10^{25} cgs units. Figure 3-10 illustrates the familiar simu-

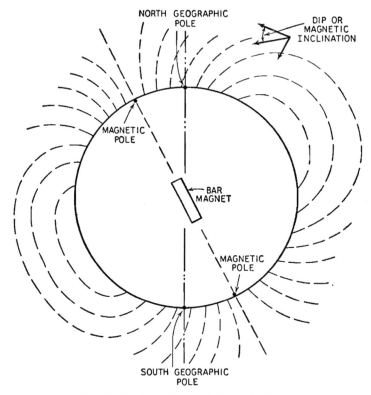

Fig. 3-10 The Earth's Magnetic Field.

lation of the earth as a magnet. If a bar magnet be freely suspended, it will position itself along a line of magnetic force. The horizontal vector will be the direction of the magnetic meridian at that point; the angle between the magnetic and true meridians is called *variation* or magnetic *declination*. The angle, in the plane of the magnetic meridian, that the magnet is inclined to the horizontal is called the *dip* or magnetic *inclination*. The common magnetic compass which is constrained to turn only in a horizontal plane indicates magnetic direction. However, since the dip varies from horizontal at the magnetic equator to 90 deg at the magnetic poles, the vertical component of the vector of the magnetic force is also an available reference and is sometimes referred to as *magnetic latitude*.

Magnetic charts of the world are available which show the dip, the intensity of the horizontal component, the intensity of the vertical component, the total magnetic force, the north-south component, the east-west component, and the variation. Large-scale charts of local areas are also available.

The earth's magnetic field is subject to changes in intensity and direction; in addition, there exist many severe anomalies. The changes are known as *secular*, *annual*, and *diurnal* variations. The secular variation has a period of about 1000 years; the annual rate of change of the secular variation is indicated on navigational charts, and although it varies widely in amplitude over the surface of the earth, the rate of change at any one location is relatively uniform. The annual variation, having approximately a one-year period, is of small amplitude with a maximum in an easterly direction in August and a westerly direction in February and is of no concern to navigators. The diurnal variation may have a range of 15 to 20 gammas in the total intensity of the magnetic field, but its effect upon the declination is unimportant, except in polar regions.

Unpredictable changes in the earth's magnetic field are termed *magnetic storms*. Magnetic storms have their origin in bursts of radiation from the sun. Such storms may occur with great suddenness and cause changes in the intensity of the earth's magnetic field of as much as 500 gammas within half an hour. The behavior of the magnetic field is not predictable during these storms.

Magnetic anomalies have been classified as continental, regional, and local in character. Continental anomalies are usually defined as variations of the earth's magnetic field associated with continental irregularities. Regional and local anomalies involve successively smaller areas, but the magnetic intensity may reach very high values. Such anomalies are caused by surface and subsurface material which imposes its own magnetic field over that of the earth. The change in intensity may be as great as 200,000 gammas.

3-16 ADDITIONAL TERRESTRIAL REFERENCES

Although the earth's gravitational and magnetic fields, together with time, form the principal references of the earth, both the pressure and motion of the air above the earth may also be employed. The use of air as an indication of altitude, by means of barometric altimeters, is so well known as to require no detailed discussion. A barometric altimeter was employed in the German V-1 to regulate the altitude of the missile in flight. The use of air motion for guidance seems unlikely until we consider the incendiary laden balloons released by the Japanese during World War II. In this operation the prevailing winds carried the balloons from Japan to the United States, serving both as the propelling and guiding means during the flight.

There are other references of the earth which are used in geophysical exploration that deserve no more than brief mention, since it is difficult to see how they may be used to obtain either directional or positional information. These are: surface electrical potential or resistivity, chemical variations of soil or atmosphere, thermal gradients of the air, soil, or oceans, and their radioactive characteristics. The motions of ocean currents will enter the guidance problem, as a secondary effect, since they are of interest in navigating a ship which may serve as a launching platform for surface-to-surface guided missiles.

3-17 CELESTIAL REFERENCES

The celestial bodies used for navigating purposes are members of our solar system—sun, moon, and some of the planets—and fixed stars of the first and second magnitude. The four planets most usually employed because of their apparent brilliance are Venus, Mars, Jupiter, and Saturn. The planetary motions are similar to earth motions; they rotate about their axes from west to east, they revolve around the sun in ellipses of small eccentricity from west to east with their orbits nearly in the plane of the ecliptic, and they move with the sun as it travels through space.

The moon has an equal period of rotation and revolution, so that the same side is always presented to the earth. The axis of rotation of the moon is tilted about 6.5 deg to its plane of revolution about the earth. This tilt, together with the moon's varying orbital speed, results in our seeing a little more than half the moon from the earth—a phenomenon called *libration*. The orbit of the moon is inclined a little more than 5 deg to the plane of the ecliptic. The apparent size of the moon to an observer on the earth is such that its diameter subtends an arc from about 29 to 33 min. The moon revolves about the earth in an ellipse of small eccentricity with a mean distance of about 253,000 miles. Actually, the earth and the moon revolve around each other, and it is the center of mass of the two that follows the path spoken of as the orbit of the earth. The center of the earth-moon system is about 2900 miles from the center of the earth, i.e., within the earth itself.

The sun is the most commonly used celestial reference for marine navigation. The sun contains about 99.9 percent of the total solar system mass and is the initial source of our light, heat, and useful energy. The surface temperature is about 10,000° F; each square foot of its surface transmits energy at the rate of about 8000 hp. The spectra of the transmitted energy extend from wavelengths shorter than visible light to wavelengths of radio frequencies. Like the earth the sun rotates from east to west, with its axis of rotation inclined about 7 deg to the ecliptic. The period of the sun's rotation varies with its latitude, being about 25 days at the equator and about 34 days at the poles. The diameter of the sun, when viewed from the earth, is of such apparent size as to subtend an arc of approximately 33 min.

The *American Nautical Almanac* tabulates stars of interest to the marine navigator. The major interest of the navigator lies in the apparent brightness of the stars and their availability for his immediate navigational needs. Stars were originally classified by Ptolemy according to brightness; the brightest stars (about 20 in number) were designated first magnitude; the dimmest that could be seen were designated sixth magnitude. By modern measurements, a first magnitude star gives about 100 times as much light as a sixth magnitude star. The fifth root of 100 is 2.512, and this is used as the standard magnitude ratio. Thus, a first magnitude star is 2.512 times as bright as a second magnitude star, and so on. Since a difference of 0.1 is the smallest change in magnitude that can be detected by the human eye, tabulated magnitudes are usually given to one decimal place. The magnitudes mentioned here are apparent magnitudes of brightness in the optical wavelength portion of the spectrum.

Astronomers compare stars on the basis of absolute magnitude, or the brightness of stars if they were all at a distance of 10 parsecs (a *parsec* being nearly 3.26 light years); and photographic magnitude, or the brightness as it appears on a photographic plate. In considering the problem of automatizing celestial navigation, it is obvious that in missile guidance the brightness of the stars in the particular spectrum of frequencies employed by the tracking device will be of considerable interest.

Stars differ in temperature and color. Several factors affect the color, but the chief one is temperature. The *blue stars* are the hottest, several being well over 20,000°K on the surface. The *red stars* are the coolest, some of them being less than 2000°K on the surface.

The stars vary considerably in size and density, but somewhat less in total mass. The stars vary in diameter from several hundred million miles to less than the diameter of the major planets of our solar system. Density varies from less than that of the air at the earth's surface, to tens of thousands of times as dense as water. Only a few of the stars, however, have less than one fifth or more than five times the mass of our sun.

Stars which are not of constant magnitude are called *variables*. In some stars, the variation in magnitude is predictable; in others, it is irregular. The change in some cases, particularly the long period of variables, may continue through several magnitudes. *Novae* are those stars which suddenly become many times brighter than previously and then gradually fade. Such stars are believed to have suffered a nuclear explosion.

The total number of stars is unknown. There are about 6000 stars of sixth apparent magnitude or brighter. Since only one half of the celestial sphere can be seen by an observer at one time, and since only the brighter ones can be seen near the horizon, probably the greatest number of stars that can be seen by the unaided eye at any one time does not exceed 2500. In the presence of interfering light, such as the moon, only a few hundred may be apparent.

Regardless of its size or magnitude, any star will appear as a point source of light which, because of the tremendous distance from the earth, cannot be resolved into a disc even with the most powerful telescope. The sun and the moon, as pointed out previously, subtend sizable arcs when viewed from the earth. When measurements on these two bodies are used for navigation, it is necessary to correct for their apparent size in order that the center of the body may be located. It would therefore seem that the use of a point source of light—a star—would be more desirable and less complex than the use of the sun or the moon for automatic celestial navigation.

3-18 THE NAVIGATIONAL TRIANGLE

Navigation by celestial references is accomplished by solution of the navigational triangle, shown in Fig. 3-11, as a geographical triangle on the earth and projected to an imaginary celestial sphere. The *celestial sphere* results from the assumption that all celestial bodies are located on a sphere of infinite radius, with the earth at the center. On the earth we have latitude, longitude, meridians, poles, etc. These references are extended to the celestial sphere, and the same terminology is employed to refer to locations on the celestial sphere. The term *navigational triangle* refers to either the geographical or the celestial triangle.

If we inspect the navigational triangle as portrayed on the earth, the vertices, labeled in standard navigational nomenclature, are: P_n, the pole of the earth (north in this example); AP, the position of the observer (which is the desired information); and GP, the geographical position on the earth having the celestial body in its zenith. Certain facts about this navigational triangle are immediately obvious. The sides of the triangle are all great circles. The side P_nAP is the co-latitude of the position of the observer. The side P_nGP is the co-latitude of the geographical position. The side $APGP$ is a great circle between the position of the observer and the geographical position of the celestial body. It was pointed out earlier that the arc subtended by great circles at the center of the earth may be translated directly into distance, since one minute of arc is nearly equal to one nautical mile. If the angle subtended at the center of the earth by *APGP* is known, then, of course, the side is known.

The angle at P_n is the difference in longitude between the observer and the geographical position of the celestial body. The angle at *AP* is the initial great-circle course angle from the observer to the *GP*. The angle at *GP* is the initial great-circle course angle from the *GP* to the observer.

If we inspect the triangle on the celestial sphere, the vertices are: P_n,

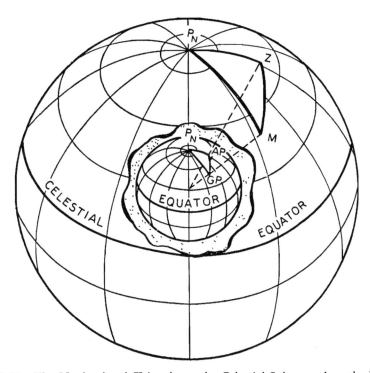

Fig. 3-11 The Navigational Triangle on the Celestial Sphere and on the Earth. (By permission from *Navigation and Nautical Astronomy* by Dutton. Copyright 1951, U. S. Naval Institute.)

the elevated pole; Z, the observer's zenith; and M, the celestial body. The side P_nZ is the co-latitude of the observer. The side ZM is known as the co-altitude of the star. The side P_nM is the co-declination of the celestial body. These terms will be defined shortly. The angles of the navigational triangle on the celestial sphere are t the meridian angle, Z the azimuth angle, and a third angle at the celestial body called the position angle (ZMP_n), not used in navigation.

The navigation problem is simply to determine enough about the navigational triangle from measurements on a celestial body so that *AP*, the observer's position, may be located in terms of the standard coordinates of the earth.

If a straight line is drawn from a celestial body *M* to the center of the earth, its interception point at the surface of the earth is the geographical position of that body (*GP*), as shown in Fig. 3-12. This line is perpendicular to a horizontal plane at the point of tangency. To an observer, standing at *AP*, the *altitude* of the body is its angular distance above the horizontal plane at *AP*, measured along the vertical circle, as indicated. The

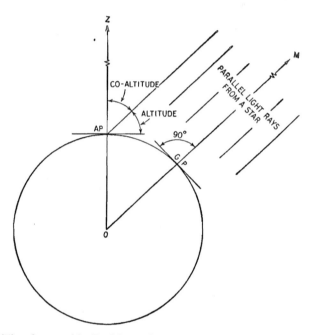

Fig. 3-12 The Geographic Position of a Celestial Body, Its Altitude and Co-Altitude.

complement of the altitude is the co-altitude, as shown. It will be noted by inspection that the angle *ZOM* is also the co-altitude of the celestial body, and that this quantity defines the great circle arc *APGP* of the navigational triangle. Hence, by measuring the altitude of a celestial body with respect to a horizontal plane, this side of the navigational triangle may be defined.

If we imagine the observer starting directly on the *GP* and moving away 200 nautical miles in any direction, he will move 200 min of arc across the surface of the earth. The altitude of the star would be 86° 40′ (90° minus 200′). As shown in Fig. 3-13 a circle of equal altitudes is created of 200-nautical mile radius. Equal altitude circles are all small circles until an altitude of zero is reached.

We have shown that, if the altitude of a celestial body is known, and this can be determined by measurement, the radius of the equal altitude circle is known and can be plotted, if we know the geographical position of the celestial body. If this circle can be plotted, we have a circular line of position, for we know that the observer must be on some point of this circle. For most altitudes it is not practical to plot the circle, because of the small scale and the distortion of charts. On a Mercator chart, the

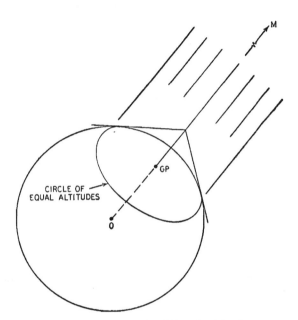

FIG. 3-13 A Circle of Equal Altitudes.

circle of equal altitude would not appear as a circle, because of the expansion at higher latitudes. But, if the body has an altitude of 87 deg or more, such circles can be plotted without appreciable error.

To determine the geographical position of the celestial body, tables are provided which list this information with respect to Greenwich time (as in the *American Nautical Almanac*). The longitude of the GP is equal to the Greenwich Hour Angle, *GHA* (which is a time measurement similar to longitude). The latitude is equal to the declination of the celestial body, which is defined as the angular distance from the celestial equator along the hour circle to the body. The coordinates of the position on the surface of the earth of the *GP*, then, may readily be determined from available tables, knowing the precise time at which the altitude of the celestial body was measured.

Figure 3-14 shows two circles of equal altitudes plotted. It is noted that an ambiguity exists in that the circles intersect at two points. To resolve the ambiguity, the azimuth of one of the celestial bodies can be observed and used to eliminate this possibility of error. A fix is possible from a single star if both the altitude and azimuth may be accurately measured. This is not done in marine or air-borne navigation because of the practical difficulty of measuring azimuth accurately.

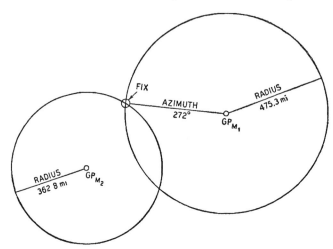

Fig. 3-14 Circles of Equal Altitudes Plotted to Determine Fix.

The farther the observer is removed from the GP, the greater becomes the radius of the circle of equal altitudes, and the less is the altitude of the celestial body. Although the radius of the circle of equal altitudes may increase, relative to the size of the chart employed, to where a segment of the circle may be represented as a straight line, the distance to the GP and the azimuth direction may be determined in the same manner and are still susceptible to being plotted.

3-19 MARINE AND AIR CELESTIAL NAVIGATION

Marine and air celestial navigation, as practiced, require the following:

a. An approximate knowledge of the location of the vehicle being navigated.
b. A sextant or other device to measure the altitude of the celestial bodies.
c. An accurate chronometer or precise knowledge of time referred to an appropriate standard.

d. Charts, tables, computation sheets, etc.

e. A reasonably experienced and competent observer.

The approximate position of the vehicle is usually obtained by dead reckoning, which is the process of integrating the position of the ship from estimates of its velocity, direction, wind and ocean currents, etc., over the period of time from the last established fix. Dead reckoning devices are sometimes employed which automatically accumulate such knowledge; to this mechanically obtained information is frequently added human estimation of unpredictable quantities.

The *sextant* is an instrument for measuring the angle between two objects by bringing into coincidence at the eye of the observer rays of light received directly from one object and by reflection from another, the measure being afforded by the inclination of the reflecting surfaces to each other. The marine sextant is used principally for measuring the altitudes of celestial bodies above the visible horizon. The air sextant is used principally to measure the altitude of celestial bodies as related to the horizontal by a bubble indicator. [4]

The positions of the celestial bodies employed in navigation are tabulated with respect to Greenwich, England, time. One minute of error in time is the equivalent of 15 minutes of error in longitude, so that the necessity for an accurate knowledge of time is apparent. At or near the equator a 4-sec error in time represents an error of a mile in the fix.

The charts, astronomical or navigation tables, and other such items required by the navigator are determined by his needs of the moment and the degree of precision required. There are many devices employed to minimize the computation and to render navigation a matter of rote. For example, Weems Star Altitude Curves provide a graphical method of obtaining a fix from three selected stars by plotting the altitudes directly and correlating them with the times of observation.

The navigator must have sufficient experience with the tools of navigation and sufficient competence in their handling to achieve a reasonably precise fix. The accuracy of marine and celestial navigation is usually partially determined by the competence of the navigator in making his measurements.

The usual method employed by the navigator in obtaining a fix is to measure the altitude of two or more stars. The approximate position, according to dead reckoning is known and plotted. On the basis of his approximate position the navigator determines, for each star, what the altitude and azimuth should be at the time the sight was taken. For each sight, the difference between his measured and calculated star altitudes is laid off on the chart along the corresponding azimuth line. For each

[4] See B. Dutton, *Navigation and Nautical Astronomy*, pp. 347-359, United States Naval Institute, 1951 for detail on sextants.

sight, the line of position is then perpendicular to the azimuth line at the distance from the dead reckoned position. The intersection of the lines of position, or more often the centroid of the enclosed space, indicates the fix.

Altitudes measured by a sextant are subject to certain errors which must be corrected before use of the measured data. These are:

a. *Index correction.* This is a correction for any error built into an individual sextant. Sextants are usually corrected to eliminate this error.

b. *Refraction* by the earth's atmosphere. The effect of atmospheric refraction is to cause a celestial body to appear higher in the sky. The degree of error is dependent somewhat upon local atmospheric conditions and principally upon the altitude of the celestial body.

c. *Dip* of the horizon resulting from the fact that the observer's eye is above the surface of the earth, causing a difference in the angle to the celestial and visible horizons. This does not apply to a bubble sextant.

d. *Semi-diameter of the sun or moon.* The upper or lower edge of these bodies are used in sextant observations; it is therefore necessary to correct the reading to indicate the center of the body.

e. *Parallax,* or the difference in the direction of a body of the solar system when viewed from the center of the earth and its surface.

f. *Coriolis,* the error caused by rotation of the earth when an observation is made using a bubble sextant in a fast-moving aircraft.

The total error in establishing a fix will vary with meteorological conditions as well as the ability of the navigator. With repeated readings, under reasonable meteorological conditions, marine navigators will plot a fix to an accuracy of about one to two miles; air navigation will normally be somewhat less accurate (about ten miles) because the precision of determining the horizontal using a bubble level in a moving aircraft is inherently less than sighting the actual horizon with a marine sextant. It must be remembered that an error of one minute of arc in establishing the horizontal plane from which star altitudes are measured results in an error of about one mile.

The human navigator has one great advantage that somewhat reduces the necessity for extreme precision in navigation—he usually may navigate by observation and recognition of the local area during the terminal portion of his voyage.

3-20 CELESTIAL NAVIGATION BY AUTOMATIC MEANS

Let us consider the general requirements for marine and air celestial navigation, listed previously, to determine comparable requirements for automatic celestial navigation for surface-to-surface missile guidance.

a. *Knowledge of approximate position.* The major advantage which may be derived from a continuous knowledge of the approximate position of the missile arises if there is a reasonable chance that the sight to the stars may be obscured during the missile flight. In this event, guidance by celestial navigation cannot exist, and a form of dead reckoning guidance may replace it during such intervals.

b. *A device to measure the altitudes of the stars.* The entire essence of automatic celestial navigation will lie in the ability to follow automatically the positions of the stars as referred to some usable reference plane.

c. An *accurate knowledge of time* will obviously be required.

d. The *charts and star tables* employed by the navigator form what might be called his memory as created by the prior observations, recordings, and mathematical abilities of others. For use in automatic celestial guidance, these same data must be translated into a memory form useful to the system employed.

e. The *human observer and computer* are, of course, eliminated in the automatic system. The computations must be made automatically, although the form such computations take may differ radically from the conventional.

If the necessity exists for a dead reckoning device to indicate continuously the approximate position of the missile, there also exists a fair amount of background for the design of such equipment, i.e., the indication and recording of aircraft motions have long been practiced. The integration of velocities, directions, and accelerations with respect to time to obtain position would only be required for guidance when the automatic celestial navigating equipment was not functioning; it would be expected that such periods would be of short duration and that the dead reckoning device would be corrected continually by the celestial navigator so that its information would be as accurate and up to date as possible.

The device employed to follow or track the stars automatically represents the key to employing automatic celestial navigation. The sensitivity of such a device would determine the magnitude of the stars which might be used in the navigation problem. It was previously noted that the stars might have different magnitudes if other than optical frequencies were employed. The accuracy of such a device would enter directly into the accuracy of the solution of the navigational problem and hence the accuracy of the ultimate hit on the target.

The knowledge of time may be obtained with sufficient accuracy any number of ways; by clock mechanisms, radio broadcast, crystal-controlled oscillators, etc.

There are many types and varieties of electronic, magnetic, and mechanical memories that might be employed. The problem here would seem to reside in determining which method or type was the lightest in weight and the most reliable for the amount and kind of data to be stored and the means employed to use it.

There are many ways, other than the conventional, that the navigational triangle may be solved, and the solution mechanized for missile guidance purposes. The actual mechanization and the computation required will depend largely upon the approach chosen by the designer. Certain general components would seem to be common to all approaches. The star-following mechanism will require stabilization with respect to space, so that motions of the missile will not cause the tracking device to lose the star. The horizon used for marine sextant navigation will not be available, and an equivalent reference, such as a stable vertical, will be required. A stored memory of star positions, limited to the stars to be employed, will be required as well as an accurate knowledge of time referred to the same standard as the stored memory.

If we assume that the foregoing are available, the problem of position determination may be solved in many ways. If a reference such as true north be known accurately, then the azimuth angle as well as altitude may be measured and position determined from a single star. If both azimuth and altitude are accurately known, then by tracking two or more stars, the vertical may be defined. If the problem lies in the northern hemisphere, Polaris, the north star, may readily be employed to determine both true north and the latitude of the missile. The major point, worthy of note, is that the designer of such a system is not restricted to conventional methods or solutions of the navigational problem, but is free to employ such simplifications as will result in equipment that is lightweight, rugged, and reliable.

The manner in which the total problem—of navigating from one point on the surface of the earth to another point—is solved is also susceptible to a variety of choices on the part of the designer. The system may conceivably be designed to measure the position of the missile and compute the correct heading to the position of the target. On the other hand, the trajectory may be predetermined and the error between it and the measured position used to correct the heading of the missile. Again, the choice will largely depend upon the equipment required to instrument the system design.

3-21 POLAR NAVIGATION

The polar regions, as far as we are here concerned, will be considered as those regions lying between 70 deg and 90 deg latitude, or within 20 deg of the geographic poles. These regions also include both magnetic poles. When the use of terrestrial references is considered for this area, it is found that many of the devices commonly employed in the middle latitudes become of little value to the polar navigator.

The greatest single problem in polar navigation is that of maintaining knowledge of direction.

The magnetic compass is not suitable for several reasons. Near the magnetic pole the horizontal vector of the magnetic field is too weak, and in the north polar regions this area of inadequate horizontal intensity includes the north pole as well. Magnetic variation is not accurately known over much of the polar regions. Some anomalies are known to exist and there are probably many others. Observations indicate that variation is not constant. Diurnal changes, which are unimportant in more moderate latitudes, may reach a magnitude of 7 deg in declination in polar regions. During severe magnetic storms, deviations on certain headings have been known to change as much as 45 deg, and such storms are by no means infrequent. Even if all these difficulties could be resolved, the rapid convergence of the isogonic lines prevents the magnetic compass from being a convenient instrument for maintaining direction.

The gyro compass loses its directive force at the geographic pole. With certain modifications, the gyro compass on a ship can be used as far as latitude 82 deg, the nearest approach so far of a surface ship to either pole.

Pendulous verticals, mounted in a stationary or slowly moving body, indicate the true vertical at the geographic poles, since the centrifugal force due to the earth's rotation is zero at these points. However, it will be noted that the Coriolis acceleration resulting from horizontal flight maximizes at the geographic poles. This must be considered in rapidly moving airborne vehicles in polar flight.

Dead reckoning is as accurate as the course and distance upon which it is based. Distance through the air can be determined nearly as accurately in the polar regions as elsewhere. Airspeed meters are usually calibrated for moderate temperatures and the corrections applied are approximations. The error tends to be greater at the polar regions because of the continued difference between the actual and standard temperatures.

Navigating by recognition and observation in polar regions tends to be uncertain because of the lack of distinguishing landmarks or man-made navigational aids. The perpetual cover of ice and snow is monotonous in character over large areas.

Celestial navigation and the determination of direction from celestial bodies constitute the most satisfactory form of navigation in the polar regions. Celestial navigation is not without its difficulties in these regions, however. During the long polar day, which may be several months in duration, the sun is continually above the horizon, which makes it difficult if not impossible to see the stars from the surface of the earth. Even when the sun is just below the horizon, because of reflected light, the stars still may not be visible to the unaided eye. Bright aurora often further delays the appearance of stars after sunset. Navigators try to avoid observations of bodies below 15 deg and will usually never employ bodies lower than 10 deg. The reason for avoiding observations on bodies of low altitude is because of the refraction of light by the atmosphere. Refraction varies with temperature and barometric pressure; it is therefore to be expected that in polar regions it will vary more widely than in lower latitudes. Refractions of several degrees have been observed in polar areas. The missile problem may be relieved somewhat, if the altitude of the missile is great enough. The missile will then be above most cloud cover, the refraction problem will be reduced, there is less reflection of light from the air at higher altitudes, and the stars will be more easily "seen."

BIBLIOGRAPHY

B. Dutton, *Navigation and Nautical Astronomy*, U. S. Naval Institute, Annapolis, Md., 1951.

L. Page, *Introduction to Theoretical Physics*, D. Van Nostrand Co., Inc., New York, 1952.

J. J. Jakosky, *Exploration Geophysics*, Trija Publishing Company, 1950.

CHAPTER 4

TRANSMISSION OF RADIO WAVES

It is the purpose of this chapter to discuss some of the fundamentals of, and the phenomena associated with, the transmission of energy in the form of radio waves that are of interest to the designer of missile guidance systems. The term "propagation," which has been used frequently heretofore, as applied to such radiated energy is generally accepted to include not only transmission phenomena, which are discussed here, but also the radiating and receiving properties of antennas—such as gain, directivity, and polarization. The radiating and receiving properties of antennas, as well as the imposition of intelligence on the radiated carrier, will be considered in Chapter 10 of this text.

The discussion in this chapter encompasses such factors as refraction, reflection, interference, diffraction, absorption, and scattering. The effects of both the transmission media and boundary media are considered. Since guided missiles are propelled by reaction motors such as jets and rockets, the interposition of flame in the transmission path of radio energy is of interest. Transmission phenomena are further complicated because some of the propagation factors are functions of the radio frequency or polarization, or both.

4-1 CLASSIFICATION OF RADIO FREQUENCIES

The spectrum of radio frequencies used for communication, radar, and other applications of radio transmission covers a range of frequencies from 15 kc to more than 30,000 mc. Within this overall spectrum, arbitrary names have been assigned to bands of frequencies. A classification of frequency groups and their nomenclature are given in Table 4-1.

Although, from a theoretical point of view, the entire spectrum of radio frequencies is available for use in missile guidance, the selection of a particular carrier frequency is based upon a number of considerations. The Federal Communications Commission allocates frequency bands for broadcasting, television, aeronautical and marine navigation, government and other public service use, and for miscellaneous and experimental purposes. These artificial allocations restrict the frequencies available for missile guidance to designated bands, but available frequencies do exist in all parts of the spectrum.

In the consideration of carrier frequencies, account must be taken of the variations in modes of transmitting radio waves of different frequencies. In the very low and low frequency ranges, the principal mode of propagation is along the surface of the earth, and reliable communication over distances up to several thousand miles may be carried on at these frequencies. However, because of energy absorption by the earth, large transmitting antennas and powerful transmitters are required for long-range communication. Since we are concerned with airborne missiles, and space and weight are at a premium, no further consideration will be given to very low and low frequency radio waves. Transmission in the

TABLE 4-1 CLASSIFICATION BY RADIO FREQUENCIES AND WAVELENGTHS

Classification	Frequency Range	Wavelength Range
Very low frequency	10-30 kc	30,000 to 10,000 meters
Low frequency	30-300 kc	10,000-1000 meters
Medium frequency	300-3000 kc	1000-100 meters
High frequency	3-30 mc	100-10 meters
Very high frequency	30-300 mc	10-1 meters
Ultra high frequency	300-3000 mc	100-10 cm
Super high frequency	3000-30,000 mc	10-1 cm

medium and high frequency ranges is mainly by waves that travel upward to the ionized layers of the atmosphere and are then refracted to the earth. In these frequency bands, communication may be carried on across great distances with relatively small transmitting antennas and low transmitter power outputs. However, the transmission is less reliable than at lower frequencies, being affected by such factors as the time of day, season of the year, and meteorological conditions. In the frequency ranges above 30 mc, transmission is essentially confined to straight-line paths between transmitter and receiver. The maximum transmission distance is then limited by the curvature of the earth. In precision-tracking radar applications, particularly those concerning airborne targets, the requirements for directivity and narrow beams have led to the use of ultra and super high frequencies. In missile-borne radars, the necessity for small component size and antenna directivity insures the continued interest of the missile guidance system designer in the super high frequency band.

For the guidance of surface-to-surface missiles we have previously pointed out the possibility of using loran or other hyperbolic navigational nets to obtain guidance intelligence. Since great transmission distances are a requirement of navigational nets, the radio frequencies employed are usually in the medium and high frequency bands. For the guidance of surface-to-air, air-to-air, and air-to-surface missiles, since the total range of guidance is likely to be relatively short, line-of-sight transmission is possible, and it is logical to expect that very high and ultra high radio frequencies may be employed. As pointed out in the preceding paragraph, super high frequencies will be of interest when radar is employed as a part of the guidance system.

4-2 THE ATMOSPHERE

The atmosphere is a gaseous layer enveloping the earth, consisting principally of dry gases—nitrogen and oxygen—and water vapor. It contains smaller amounts of the rare gases and some foreign matter. The atmosphere has been arbitrarily subdivided with increasing altitude into the *troposphere* (0 to 10 miles), the *stratosphere* (10 to 20 miles), the *chemosphere* (20 to 50 miles), the *ionosphere* (50 to 250 miles), and the *mesosphere* (from about 250 miles to space). The exact physical divisions are not too clearly defined in all instances, but gas molecules exist in all of the listed regions. The troposphere contains approximately three-quarters of the total weight of the atmosphere, and, since our major concern is transmitting intelligence to vehicles which depend on air for lift, it represents our chief area of interest in the atmosphere.

The temperature of the atmosphere varies considerably with altitude, dropping from ground temperatures through the troposphere to a low of about $-70°F$ at the lower limit of the stratosphere. The temperature is remarkably uniform throughout the stratosphere, with an estimated low about $-80°F$. The temperature rises and then falls with increasing altitude in the chemosphere reaching a low of about $-120°F$ at the beginning of the ionosphere, where it increases steadily because of the absorption of ultraviolet radiation from the sun.

The *ionosphere* is so called because of the ionization of the gases in this region of the atmosphere, resulting principally from ultraviolet solar radiation. Because of the variation of chemical composition of the air with altitude, and because the absorption of solar radiation differs between gases, there is a tendency for the ionization of the atmosphere to become stratified. Ionization does not decrease to zero between such strata, but has a value less than the maxima on either side. The altitude of the maximum electron density in a particular layer varies with the time of day and seasonally, as a result of variations of the composition and temperature of the atmosphere, and of solar radiation. The regions of ionization that are of interest to radio transmission and the typically approximate altitudes of their maxima are: the D layer, 35 to 40 miles; the E layer, 70 to 80 miles; the F_1 layer, 135 to 145 miles; and the F_2 layer, 190 to 230 miles.

The atmosphere is of interest in considering the transmission of radio waves, since they, like light waves, travel in straight lines through any isotropic, homogeneous medium, with a velocity $v = c/n$, where c is the velocity of light in a vacuum (essentially 3×10^8 meters per sec), and n

is the index of refraction of the medium. The index of refraction of air for radio waves is only slightly greater than unity, but it varies with the temperature, pressure, and water vapor content, and, since these change as a function of altitude, it is to be expected that the parameters of radio wave paths will be affected by the variations. Further, for medium, high, and a portion of the very high frequency bands, the ionized layers of the upper atmosphere can refract, reflect, and absorb energy from radio waves reaching them.

4-3 EFFECT OF THE IONOSPHERE ON RADIO WAVE TRANSMISSION

The ionized layers of the atmosphere have diurnal and seasonal characteristic variations. The E and the F_2 layers have a reasonably permanent existence. The F_1 layer appears in the early morning, persists throughout the day, and disappears again at night. The D layer exists in the daytime and has some influence on daytime broadcast signals at considerable distances. The E layer has a substantially constant virtual height throughout the day and from season to season. The F_2 layer varies greatly in virtual height during the day and from season to season. The characteristics of the ionized layers vary little with longitude; experimental data indicate that ionosphere characteristics, when considered as a function of local sun time, are much the same regardless of longitude. Latitude, however, is quite important, since the varying angle of incidence of solar radiation with latitude leads to greater ionization in equatorial regions than in polar regions.

The actual path that a radio wave follows in the ionosphere is controlled by the index of refraction. Variation in the index along the path causes the wave to follow a curved path such that the radius of curvature of the path $= n \frac{ds}{dn}$, where s is in the direction normal to the wave path and n is the index of refraction. The rate of curvature of the path is greatest when the index of refraction varies most rapidly, and the path becomes a straight line when the index of refraction is constant. The total angle through which a wave that has entered the ionosphere is deflected can be obtained, according to Snell's law, by the relation

$$\cos \alpha_0 = n \cos \alpha_n \tag{4-1}$$

Figure 4-1 illustrates the notation employed in Eq. (4-1). When α_n is zero the wave is at its highest point and is turning back toward the earth. The refractive index required to bend back to earth a wave entering the ionosphere with an angle α_0 is

$$n = \cos \alpha_0 \tag{4-2}$$

4-3] EFFECT OF THE IONOSPHERE ON RADIO WAVE TRANSMISSION

The index of refraction of an ionized medium in the presence of the earth's magnetic field is a function of many variables, among them being the dielectric constant of the medium, the number of electrons per cubic centimeter, the properties of the earth's magnetic field, and the frequency of the radio wave under consideration.

The electrons in the ionosphere exist in the presence of the earth's magnetic field. The effect of this field at the higher radio frequencies is to cause the electrons to vibrate in an elliptical path in response to electromagnetic excitation. There is a varying critical frequency associated with each of the electron layers, these critical frequencies having both diurnal and seasonal variations. Radio waves of frequency less than the critical frequency will be returned to earth irrespective of the angle of incidence at the ionosphere. When the frequency of the transmitted wave is greater than the critical frequency of the layer, then the only waves that will return to earth will be those which strike the ionosphere with an angle of incidence α_0 such that the $\cos \alpha_0 > n$, where n is the index of refraction at the point of maximum electron density for the frequency involved. Radio waves striking the ionosphere with an appreciably greater angle of incidence will pass on through the layer; waves with a lesser angle of incidence will be returned to earth.

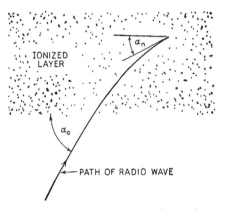

FIG. 4-1 Refraction in the Ionosphere.

Radio waves are sometimes returned to earth by the E layer at frequencies greater than the critical frequencies of the layer. These are termed *sporadic E layer reflections* and are thought to be the result of partial reflections from a sharp boundary of stratified ionization. These reflections apparently result from ion clouds that drift through space, causing reflections that come and go. Such clouds may range from one to several hundred miles in extent. There are other anomalies of the ionosphere which affect radio wave transmission of the medium and high frequency bands. Sky wave signals sometimes fade out suddenly. This phenomenon is the result of a burst of ionizing radiation from the sun that results in a rapid increase in absorption of the waves entering the ionized region. There are also prolonged periods of low-layer absorption, resulting from the same general cause, but with a longer duration and less severity than the sudden fade-outs. Ionosphere storms, usually accompanied by magnetic storms, are characterized by poor radio transmission above 500 kc and may last for one or more days. The effect of ionosphere storms are greater in or near the polar regions, with the most turbulent phase usually confined to within 20 deg of the magnetic poles

Frequencies in the range of 1.5 to 30 mc are most affected by refraction and other phenomena associated with the ionized layers of the atmosphere. Frequencies above 60 mc are almost never refracted or reflected to the earth by the ionosphere, and it is only under very special circumstances that frequencies in the range of 30 to 60 mc are so returned. Insofar as missile guidance is concerned, these frequencies are primarily associated with hyperbolic nets and other air navigation aids.

4-4 MULTIPATH TRANSMISSION

When the radio frequency employed is in the range of 1.5 to 30 mc and, therefore, is such that refraction and reflection from the ionosphere

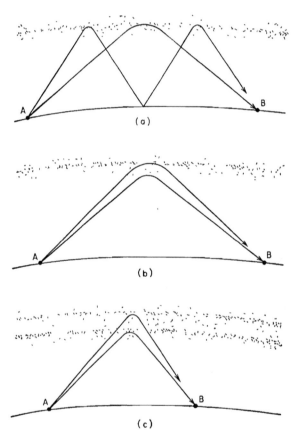

Fig. 4-2 Multiple Transmission Paths by Reason of Ionospheric Refraction.

occur, then there are normally two or more transmission paths by which energy may reach a distant receiving point in appreciable amplitude. Examples of such multiple transmission paths are illustrated in Fig. 4-2. In Fig. 4-2a, the multiple paths from the transmitter at A to the receiver B result from the fact that the energy may travel by routes involving different numbers of refractions from the ionosphere and reflections from the earth. In Fig. 4-2b, the multiple paths result from different depths of penetration into the same ionized layer. In Fig. 4-2c, the multiple paths result from the energy being refracted from two different layers of ionization. Other multiple paths are possible by reason of round-the-world transmission, with one signal path being the direct great circle route and a second path being the longer great circle route in the opposite direction. Indeed, the same signal may make multiple trips around the world and be received each time. It will be noted that since the individual path lengths vary in any case of multipath transmission, the same signal will arrive at the receiver at different times and by different paths.

4-5 EFFECT OF INDEX OF REFRACTION OF AIR ON TRANSMISSION

In free space a radio wave expands outward from its source, traveling radially and with a velocity equal to light in a vacuum. The ratio of the free-space velocity to the velocity in a medium is the index of refraction of the medium. The refractive index of the air for radio waves is essentially independent of frequency, except possibly for wavelengths of less than one centimeter, and is also independent of the polarization of the wave. The index of refraction of air for radio waves is primarily a function of the air's temperature, pressure, and moisture content. The index of refraction for radio waves may be obtained from the following empirical formula:

$$(n - 1) \times 10^6 = \frac{79p}{T} - \frac{11a}{T} - \frac{3.8 \times 10^5 a}{T^2} \qquad (4\text{-}3)[1]$$

where n = index of refraction of air

p = barometric pressure in millibars

T = temperature in degrees Kelvin

a = water vapor pressure in millibars

Since the atmosphere, within the troposphere, normally tends to have a gradual change in its physical characteristics with increasing altitude, the change in the index of refraction with altitude is therefore gradual. The earth is spherical, so that with increasing altitude the layers of constant index of refraction tend to follow the shape of the surface of the earth.

[1] *Summary Technical Report of the Committee on Propagation*, NDRC Radio Wave Propagation Experiments.

Figure 4-3 shows the curved path of the radio wave which results from the gradual change of refractive index with increasing altitude. If it is considered that the refractive index decreases linearly with height, it can be shown that

$$d\alpha = 0.358 \times 10^{-7} \frac{dh}{\alpha} \quad (4\text{-}4)^2$$

where α is the angle illustrated in Fig. 4-3, and $d\alpha$ is the change of that angle, with dh the change in height above the surface of the earth. The effect of the usual refraction by the atmosphere is negligible, except at small angles to the horizontal, but it causes a bending of the wave path at 2 deg or less to the horizontal, so that the effect is to create a radio horizon which differs from the visible horizon.

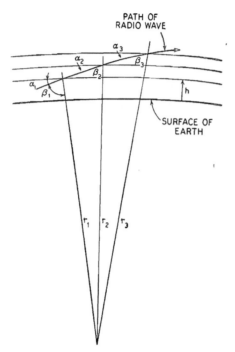

FIG. 4-3 Curvature of Wave Path by Reason of Change of Index of Refraction of Air with Altitude.

A convenient method of plotting lobe structures or wave paths has been developed in the *4/3 earth radius diagrams*. In these diagrams, the surface of the earth is drawn as a line having less curvature than the actual amount, so that the radio horizon line and wave paths may be plotted as straight lines. A convenient method of determining the approximate distance to the radio horizon for a given antenna height exists in the equation

$$d = \sqrt{2h} \qquad (4\text{-}5)$$

where d = the distance in statute miles to the radio horizon
h = the height of the antenna in feet

Since the radio horizon essentially limits direct wave path transmission, the approximate maximum direct transmission path distance from an antenna at height h to an airborne vehicle at a height h_1 may be determined by use of a modification of the same equation, as

$$d = \sqrt{2h} + \sqrt{2h_1} \qquad (4\text{-}6)$$

[2] H. R. Reed and C. M. Russell, *Ultra High Frequency Propagation*, p. 46, John Wiley & Sons, 1953.

Since anomalies exist in the character of the atmosphere, it is to be expected that such anomalies as affect the temperature, pressure, and moisture content will produce unusual refractions of radio waves. When a horizontal layer of warm air overlies a mass of cooler air, a *temperature inversion* is said to exist, since temperature normally decreases with height. If this horizontal layer of air results in a refractive index which decreases rapidly with height, a strong downward bending of the path of nearly horizontal radio waves will occur. This phenomenon is called "ducting." Ducts may occur close to the ground or at altitudes above it, being limited usually to heights under 10,000 ft. The effect on transmission depends upon the location of the transmitting and receiving antennas with respect to the duct. The path of the transmission may be such that it is refracted to the earth; it may be trapped within the duct; or it may pass through it with a considerable curvature of path within the duct. In radio communication, ducts may make possible transmission beyond the normal horizon to receivers not ordinarily geometrically capable of receiving the signal; with radars, targets may be observed at phenomenal distances beyond the normal radar horizon. Such transmission will, of course, be generally unpredictable.

4-6 POLARIZATION OF RADIO WAVES

The movement of energy in the form of expanding radiation fields constitutes a wave motion, whereby variations with time of the electric and magnetic fields in the region surrounding the propagating element are transmitted radially outward. With a sinusoidal current flow in the radiating element, the magnitude of each radiation field at any instant will vary sinusoidally with distance along the direction of propagation.

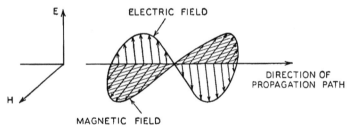

FIG. 4-4 Distribution of Electric and Magnetic Field Densities.

Figure 4-4 illustrates such a variation of the magnitudes of the fields at a given instant of time. The H lines represent the magnetic field; the E lines represent the electric field. The two fields are mutually perpendicular and both fields are so oriented as to be at right angles to the direction, or path, of propagation. The *plane of polarization* of a radio wave is determined by convention to be the direction of the electric field with respect to the earth's surface. The wave is *vertically polarized* if the electric field is vertical; it is *horizontally polarized* if the electric field is horizontal. Radio waves may also be *circularly* or *elliptically polarized*, in which instances the fields are caused to rotate correspondingly during propagation.

4-7 REFLECTION OF RADIO WAVES

Consider the simplest case of reflection of radio waves, when a plane wave strikes a plane surface. The incident wave is divided into two parts. One is the reflected wave, which is returned to the atmosphere, the other is the refracted wave which is absorbed by the reflecting medium. At the point of reflection, the ratio of any scalar quantity in the reflected wave to the same quantity in the incident wave is defined as the reflection coefficient of the reflecting medium. Thus defined, the *reflection coefficient*

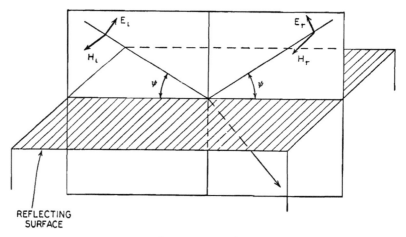

FIG. 4-5 Reflection of Vertically Polarized Wave.

can be different for the various components of the field. Figure 4-5 shows the reflecting plane to be the horizontal plane of a rectangular coordinate system and the vertical plane is the plane of incidence, with the grazing angle being ψ (angle of incidence = $90° - \psi$). The reflection coefficient **R**, considering the electric vectors, is equal to $\mathbf{E}_r/\mathbf{E}_i$.

For finite conductivity, the reflection coefficient may assume a variety of values. The general formulas have been derived from electromagnetic theory. For horizontal polarization

$$\mathbf{R}_h = \frac{\sin \psi - \sqrt{\varepsilon - \cos^2 \psi}}{\sin \psi + \sqrt{\varepsilon - \cos^2 \psi}} \tag{4-7}$$

For vertical polarization

$$\mathbf{R}_v = \frac{\varepsilon \sin \psi - \sqrt{\varepsilon - \cos^2 \psi}}{\varepsilon \sin \psi + \sqrt{\varepsilon - \cos^2 \psi}} \qquad (4\text{-}8)$$

where ε is the complex relative dielectric constant of the reflecting medium. These equations indicate that the magnitude of the reflected electric vector $\mathbf{E}_r$ is equal to $R\mathbf{E}_i$ and leads or lags it in phase, as the case may be, by a computable amount. Figures 4-6 and 4-7 show the relation of the reflection coefficient and the phase lag to the grazing angle for various surface media.

4-8 DUAL PATH TRANSMISSION

If we consider a transmitter to be located at A at a height h_1 above the surface of the earth, and a receiver located at B at height h_2, and that h_2 is above the radio horizon, then, as illustrated in Fig. 4-8, there occurs a dual path transmission of the radio waves between A and B. One path is, of course, the direct path between the transmitter and receiver; along the other path the energy is reflected from the surface of the earth to the receiver. The field at receiver B is the vector sum of the fields radiated along the direct and the reflected paths. The contribution from the reflected wave depends primarily on the manner in which the surface acts as a reflecting body. Upon reflection, the angle of incidence is equal to the angle of reflection, irrespective of the polarization of the wave. The strength of the field in the reflected wave, relative to the incident wave, depends upon the grazing angle ψ, the type of polarization, the reflecting coefficient of the surface, all of which have been previously discussed, and, in addition, a divergence factor. The *divergence factor* results from the fact that the earth is spherical, and the radiated paths diverge upon reflection from its surface to produce a decrease in strength of the reflected beam.

If, instead of a separate transmitter and receiver for communication, we consider that a radar transmitter and receiver are located at A and that B is an airborne target, then the energy to the target may be transmitted along both the direct and the reflected paths, and the energy reflected from the target will also return to the radar receiver by both paths. In considering the application of dual path transmission to radars, then, it is necessary to remember that dual path transmission normally will occur both in the energy transmitted to the target and the energy reflected from the target.

Figure 4-9 illustrates the interference phenomena which result from a uniformly radiating antenna, placed above a plane reflector. There exist regions of wave reinforcement, wherein the direct and reflected waves are in phase; similarly, there exist regions of cancellation, wherein the direct and reflected waves are in phase opposition. It should be noted that the regions of reinforcement represent a gain in field strength over propagation in free space. In this elementary diagram, it has been assumed, for simplicity, that the magnitude of the reflection coefficient is unity and the phase shift at reflection is zero degrees, with a constant index of refraction in the transmission medium. A is the position of the isotropic radiator; B is the location of a receiver or airborne target. As shown, B is located on one of the maxima, and the path length difference is two full wavelengths between the direct and reflected wave paths. B' illustrates a receiver or target in such location that there exists one and one-half wavelengths' difference between the two paths; the field, therefore, is zero at this point, under the assumed conditions. The solid lines are loci of the maxima in a vertical plane, the dashed lines are loci of minima in the same

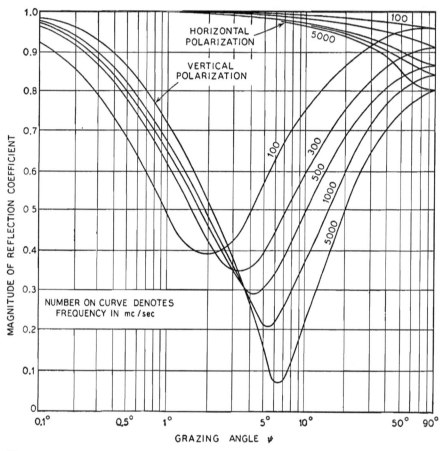

FIG. 4-6a Magnitude of the Reflection Coefficient as Related to Grazing Angle for Smooth Sea Water and for Various Frequencies. (By permission from *Ultra High Frequency Propagation*, by Reed and Russell. Copyright 1953, Wiley & Sons.)

plane. An aircraft, in horizontal flight toward or away from point A, would pass through successive regions of signal reinforcement and cancellation; in the case of a radar, the target would be first capable of detection and then fade away, through each successive period of reinforcement and cancellation. The loci of the maxima and minima, as illustrated, are hyperbolas. Signal reinforcement, or maxima, occur when the reflected waves have traveled an integral number of wavelengths farther than the direct wave. Signal cancellations, or minima, occur when the reflected waves have traveled an odd number of half wavelengths farther than the direct wave. The number of minima which exist is equal to the number of half wavelengths contained in the height of the radiating antenna above the reflecting surface.

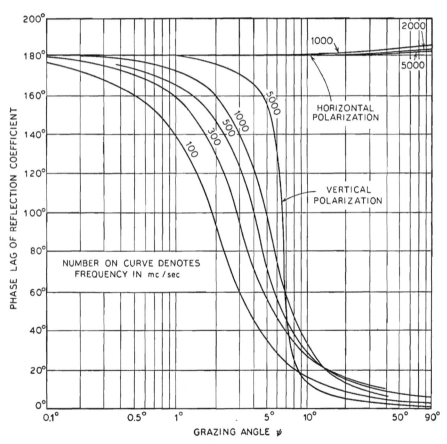

FIG. 4-6b Phase of the Reflection Coefficient as Related to Grazing Angle for Smooth Sea Water and for Various Frequencies. (By permission from *Ultra High Frequency Propagation*, by Reed and Russell. Copyright 1953, Wiley & Sons.)

There are many excellent texts, some of which are referenced, that discuss the interference phenomena in complete detail and illustrate methods of computing or estimating field strengths, including all of the many variables involved. Complete detailed coverage of a specialized field so thoroughly documented is not within the scope of this text. Sufficient detail, however, has been given to permit some general conclusions to be drawn that are pertinent to missile guidance.

Figure 4-10 illustrates typical theoretical interference patterns comparing vertical and horizontal polarizations in the ultra high frequency band, with sea water as the reflecting medium. The number of minima and maxima which occur are a function of the radio frequency and the height of the antenna above the reflecting surface. The magnitude of the maxima

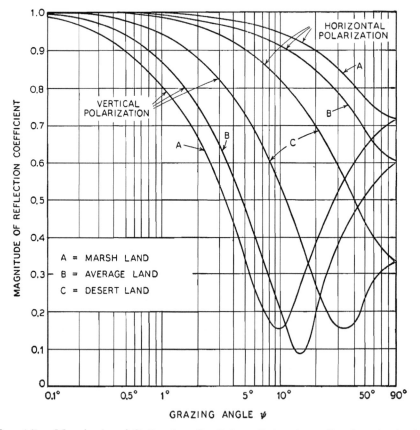

FIG. 4-7a Magnitude of Reflection Coefficient Related to Grazing Angle for Various Types of Smooth Land. Frequency—100 mc per sec. (By permission from *Ultra High Frequency Propagation*, by Reed and Russell. Copyright 1953, Wiley & Sons.)

and minima for each type of polarization is a function of the reflection coefficient and the grazing angle. When the parameters of a particular flight are held fixed, as in Fig. 4-10, then the magnitude and location of the maxima and minima are a function of the reflection coefficient, which is to say, the character of the terrain or reflecting surface. The higher the reflection coefficient, the greater will be the reinforcement, and, correspondingly, the greater the cancellation. It will be seen from Fig. 4-6 and 4-7 that the reflection coefficient will be greater for smooth sea water than for any other reflecting medium met in use. The interference phenomena, then, will be more severe over sea than over land. However, mountainous terrain may give rise to unpredictable interference problems not found over the relatively flat sea.

If we consider that Fig. 4-10 illustrates an aircraft flying directly toward

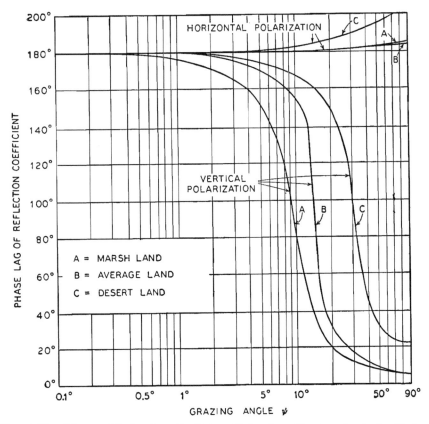

Fig. 4-7b Phase of Reflection Coefficient Related to Grazing Angle for Various Types of Smooth Land. Frequency—100 mc per sec. (By permission from *Ultra High Frequency Propagation*, by Reed and Russell. Copyright 1953, Wiley & Sons.)

the transmitting point A, then it will be observed that the more rapidly the aircraft flies, the higher will be the frequency at which it passes through the maxima and minima. This becomes of significance if the frequency approaches any employed in the transmission of intelligence to the guidance system.

4-9 FACTORS AFFECTING CHOICE OF POLARIZATION

In choosing the more desirable polarization for a specific use, the general considerations given will be concerned with the following items:

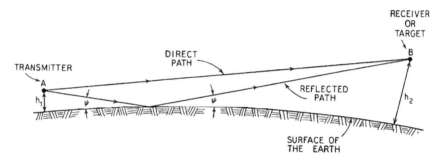

FIG. 4-8 Dual Path Transmission.

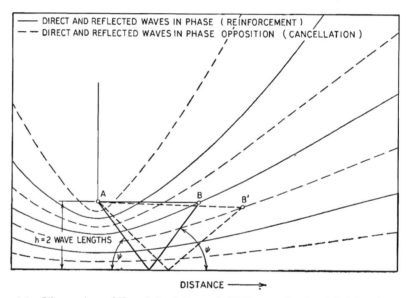

FIG. 4-9 Illustration of Equal Path Length Difference Loci, with Magnitude of Reflection Coefficient = 1.0, with 0° Phase Shift. (By permission from *Ultra High Frequency Propagation*, by Reed and Russell. Copyright 1953, Wiley & Sons.)

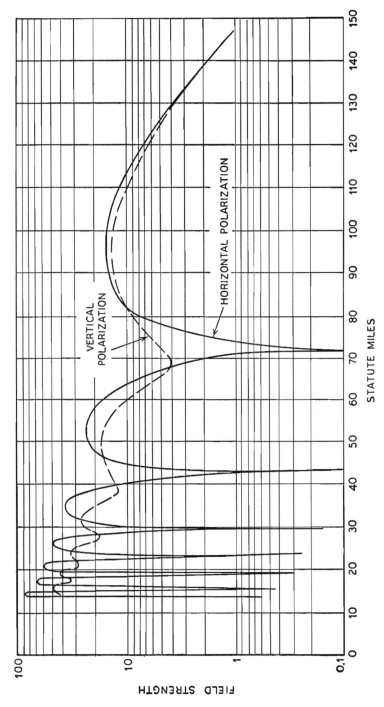

Fig. 4-10 Typical Interference Patterns with Surface-to-Air Transmission over Sea Water; the Aircraft Maintaining Constant Altitude of 10,000 ft. (By permission from *Ultra High Frequency Propagation*, by Reed and Russell. Copyright 1953, Wiley & Sons.)

a. The extent of reinforcement by reflection of the maxima.
b. The extent of signal cancellation in the minima.
c. The effects of surface roughness.
d. The effects of the foregoing on the manner in which the signal is treated by a specific system.

In communication between two stations at, or just above, the radio horizon, there seems to be little or no difference between vertical or horizontal polarization. The reflection coefficient is roughly the same for both polarizations when the grazing angle is approximately zero. The magnitude of the first maximum, in the practical situation, should be much the same with either polarization. When the receiving airborne vehicle is well above the radio horizon, horizontal polarization will produce greater reinforcement of signal strength than will vertical polarization for the maxima at the same grazing angles. At the same time, however, the minima produce much greater cancellation of signal strength with horizontal polarization. If maximum range be the greatest consideration and the specific use may accept loss of signal in the minima, then horizontal polarization is preferable. If, on the other hand, gapless coverage or continuity of information be desired, then vertical polarization is preferable.

Similarly, with radars, if maximum range is the prime consideration, as may be so with a search radar, then it would seem that horizontal polarization should be used. In a tracking radar, however, continuity of information is more important, and vertical polarization is preferable. This, of course, is a representation only of superficial considerations in making the choice of polarizations. There are other considerations of the interference problem associated with the particular manner in which intelligence is conveyed on the carrying radio wave, which must be treated in a more sophisticated selection.

4-10 DIFFRACTION OF RADIO WAVES

Radio waves normally travel outward from the antenna along radial lines, except when deviated by refraction or reflection. There is another condition under which radio waves deviate from their normal path, which is called "diffraction." When an obstructing object is interposed in the path of a radio wave, some of the energy of the wave is diffracted at the

Fig. 4-11 Diffraction Region Below Radio Horizon.

edge of the object and the path of the wave is bent around the edge. Since, by diffraction, some of the energy finds its way behind an object, this reduces the shadowing effect of objects which are opaque to radio waves. The earth's surface causes diffraction, as illustrated in Fig. 4-11. Buildings, mountains, structural parts of a ship, aircraft, or guided missiles will also cause diffraction. If the obstructing object is small, such as a guided missile, the region behind the object will suffer little or no shadowing effect. The effect on the field strength of a radio wave transmission by the earth's shadowing is indicated in Fig. 4-12.

4-11 TYPICAL FIELD STRENGTH CURVES

There are three types of graphical representations frequently employed to indicate the field strength or radio gain in a vertical plane through the antenna. These are:

a. Radio gain or field strength against height, at a constant distance from the antenna.
b. Radio gain or field strength against distance, at a constant height of the receiving antenna.
c. Contour lines representing constant radio gain or field strength.

Figure 4-12 illustrates the field strength plotted against distance between the transmitting and receiving antenna for a constant altitude of aircraft. It graphically depicts the reduction in signal strength that an aircraft will experience in the diffraction region, below the radio horizon, and the variations which occur in the interference region. The free-space field strength is also included, which may be used to illustrate the gain and the losses resulting from reflected signals following dual paths in the transmission to the receiver.

Although there are rigorous methods available for computing field strength in the interference and diffraction regions, such computations are usually based upon assumptions as to "standard" conditions of atmosphere and uniform reflecting coefficients. Limiting the parameters on the basis of reasonable assumptions is a necessity to avoid an unduly great amount of computation, but in nature there are many factors which cannot be considered in the computations, such as irregularities of the earth's surface, nonstandard atmospheric conditions, and other anomalies. The design engineer, to be sure of obtaining an adequate signal in shadow or fringe areas, must resort to the application of a safety factor in his design. Considerations are usually limited by space and weight requirements, particularly in guided missile design. The designer must weigh the requirements as dictated by a study of all relevant factors against that which is economically and physically possible.

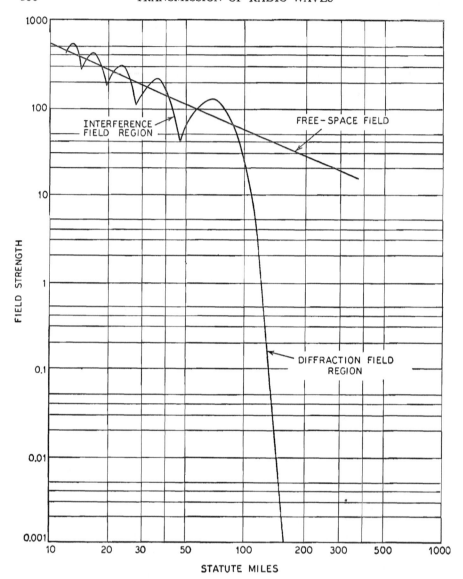

Fig. 4-12 Range versus Field Strength Curve at 5000-ft Elevation. (By permission from *Ultra High Frequency Propagation*, by Reed and Russell. Copyright 1953, Wiley & Sons.)

4-12 ABSORPTION OF RADIO WAVES

When some or all of the energy contained in a radio wave is irreversibly converted to some other form, such as heat, *absorption* is said to occur. Oxygen and water vapor molecules, precipitation in all its forms, and foreign matter such as dust, all absorb energy from radio waves in the atmosphere. The amount of absorption is independent of the polarization of the radio wave and is a function of its frequency. Molecular absorption is negligible at frequencies below 5000 mc, so that this phenomena is of interest only to the user of radio waves in the super high frequency band.

If we consider molecular absorption only, the ingredients in the atmosphere which absorb microwave energy are:

  a. Oxygen, which has a magnetic interaction with the transmitted radio waves because the O_2 molecule is normally in a paramagnetic state.
  b. Water vapor, by reason of the electric polarity of the H_2O molecule.

In both instances, there are certain frequency regions where the absorption is abnormally large because of molecular resonance. For the oxygen molecule, this region occurs at radio wavelengths in the vicinity of 0.5 cm and 0.25 cm. For the water vapor molecule, the resonance center is at 1.35 cm, but because of the character of the water vapor molecule there also exist many sharp resonances at frequencies above the super high frequency band.

To have appreciable absorption, it is necessary that the incident radio wave frequency not differ too much from the molecular resonant frequency. The nitrogen and oxygen molecules, which constitute the important elements of dry air, are both devoid of a permanent electric moment active in the infrared or microwave frequency regions. The oxygen molecule, however, is paramagnetic, or, in other words, has a permanent magnetic moment and can absorb radio waves in the microwave region. Absorption is usually thought of as arising only from electric dipoles, but it can arise from magnetic polarity also. Superficially, it might appear that the effect of molecular absorption would be negligible, but the attenuation which results is appreciable because of the great path lengths of radio wave transmission in the atmosphere. Figure 4-13 shows the theoretical attenuation due to oxygen absorption, for frequencies of interest.

Since the atmosphere is never dry, consideration must be given to the absorption of radio waves by uncondensed water vapor molecules. At radio wavelengths much less than one millimeter, the absorption by water vapor is so high as to make such wavelengths useless for transmission except over short distances. This statement does not apply, obviously if the wavelength is reduced indefinitely. The atmosphere opens up to transmission only when the frequency becomes high compared with the rotational frequencies of the water molecule, which occurs in the infrared rather than the super high radio frequency region. In considering the effect of water vapor absorption in the use of microwaves, allowance must be made for the variation of the fractional water vapor constant of the atmosphere as a function of altitude or of temperature and pressure. It is of interest to note that the absorption of radio waves by the water vapor

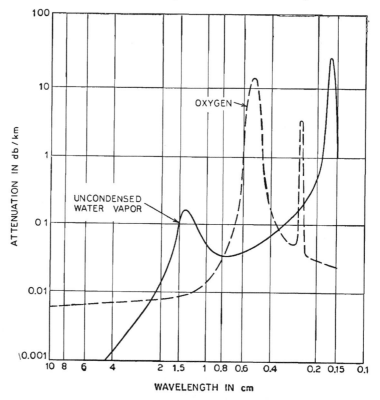

FIG. 4-13 Theoretical Values of Atmospheric Attenuation by Oxygen and Uncondensed Water Vapor at Sea Level for Temperature of 20°C in an Atmosphere Containing One Per Cent Water Molecules. (By permission from *Propagation of Short Radio Waves*, by Kerr. Copyright 1951, McGraw-Hill Book Co., Inc.)

molecules is the result of the electric polarity rather than the paramagnetic moment, as was the case with the oxygen molecule. Figure 4-13 also shows the theoretical attenuation which results because of water vapor absorption for frequencies of interest to the problem of missile guidance.

4-13 SCATTERING OF RADIO WAVES

Scattering of a radio wave is said to occur when it strikes a surface too rough to support specular (or mirrorlike) reflection. The energy reflected by a rough terrain or by high water waves may be scattered in various directions. Since, in the ultra high and super high frequency bands, directive antennas are frequently employed to channel the radio energy in narrow beams, the scattered energy may be lost from the beam. Scattering may occur when a wave passes through a nonhomogeneous medium. Anomalies of the index of refraction of the earth's atmosphere produce some scattering. Scattering also occurs when a radio wave strikes raindrops, fog, hail or snow in the earth's atmosphere. Condensed water and other forms of precipitation are capable of both scattering the incident radiation and absorbing energy from the radio waves. The amount of energy which is lost by scattering is a function of the radio frequency and the size, shape, distribution, and index of refraction of the particles in the atmosphere.

4-14 ATTENUATION BY CONDENSED WATER AND OTHER FORMS OF PRECIPITATION

Radio waves in the super high frequency band are attenuated by precipitation through two mechanisms:

a. Energy is absorbed and converted irreversibly to heat.
b. Energy is scattered out of the beam of a directive antenna.

The effect of the two mechanisms which result in attenuation is partially dependent upon the size of the liquid drop in the case of rainfall. For very small drops, as in fog, the attenuation is caused principally by absorption, and is almost directly proportional to the total volume of the water drops, per unit volume of the atmosphere. For large drop sizes, scattering of the radio waves plays an increasingly greater part in the attenuation. Experience indicates that precipitation is never uniform over an extended region. The attenuation resulting from rainfall can be computed only if the drop size distribution is known or assumed. As a result of nonuniformity of precipitation as it occurs in nature and the difficulty of measuring drop size distribution, exact calculations of attenuation for any practical path are not feasible.

Precipitation is usually measured in inches per hour or millimeters per hour, as the most practical index of rainfall intensity. By assuming relationships, based on generalized empirical data, between the intensity of rainfall per hour, the amount of water per unit volume, and the drop sizes, theoretical curves have been computed for the attenuation of radio waves due to fog or rain. Figure 4-14 indicates such theoretical values. It should be noted that attenuation by rainfall and fog, at wavelengths of 10 cm and greater, is unimportant. The importance of attenuation by rainfall and fog increases rapidly with decreasing wavelengths for radio waves in the region of 3 cm and less. The attenuation from even moderate rainfall exceeds that from uncondensed water vapor or oxygen for radio wavelengths of 1.25 cm and less.

Attenuation by the mechanics of absorption by solid particles, such as hail or snow, is much less than from liquid drops of equal water content. Scattering of the radio waves by such solid particles does occur, but except for wavelengths in the millimeter region, the attenuation from dry hailstones is small compared with that from rainfall of equivalent precipitation

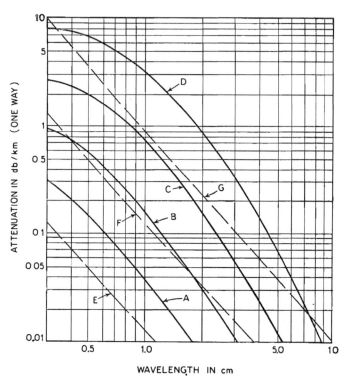

FIG. 4-14 Theoretical Values of Attenuation by Rain and Fog. Solid Curves Show Attenuation by Rain of the Following Intensities:

A	Drizzle	0.25 mm/hr
B	Light Rain	1.0 mm/hr
C	Moderate Rain	4.0 mm/hr
D	Heavy Rain	16 mm/hr

Dashed Curves Show Attenuation by Fog or Cloud of the Following Intensities:

E	Visibility	2000 ft	0.032 g/m³
F	Visibility	400 ft	0.32 g/m³
G	Visibility	100 ft	2.3 g/m³

(By permission from *Propagation of Short Radio Waves*, by Kerr. Copyright 1951, McGraw-Hill Book Co., Inc.)

rate. Attenuation caused by snow or ice crystals can almost always be neglected.

4-15 FACTORS AFFECTING CHOICE OF FREQUENCY

The choice of frequency for a specific application is, in general, concerned with range and equipment requirements and applications. When communication at long ranges is the prime requirement, as for air navigational aids, frequencies in the medium and high bands are employed. It will be recalled that long-range transmission at these frequencies is possible with relatively small antennas and low power transmitters because of the refraction from the ionosphere and the reflection from the earth.

When a line-of-sight transmission path is possible, more reliable communication can be obtained with frequencies in the very high and ultra high bands. The selection of precise frequencies within these bands is partly determined by the available frequencies, as determined by Federal Communications Commissions allocations, the requirements dictated by the equipment, and the method of imposing intelligence on the radio wave carrier.

In considering the super high frequency band, the factors of atmospheric and precipitation attenuation, in the light of the specific application, will play a large part in the choice of frequency. For missile-borne equipment, size and weight are partially governing factors and must be considered in selection of the frequency. Chapter 10 will discuss this at greater length.

4-16 RADOMES

Radar scanning antennas present a difficult aerodynamic problem, since they do not easily lend themselves to incorporation in a streamlined fuselage or wing. Such antennas must be provided with streamlined housings, capable of sustaining large aerodynamic loads, without interfering with the performance of either the radar or the airborne vehicle. The shape of the housing depends largely upon the location of the radar in or on the aircraft, which in turn depends largely upon the function of the radar. Search radars may be located under the wing or fuselage; tail warning radars are located in the fuselage tail; tracking radars for fire control are usually located in the nose of fighter aircraft.

Radars in guided missiles are normally located in the nose of the missile. It is obvious that, as speeds of airborne vehicles increase, the necessity for streamlining all surfaces, including the radar housing, must also increase. These housings for radars are called "radomes."

Figure 4-15a illustrates a normal incidence radome, one in which the waves from the center of the radar beam are at normal incidence to the dielectric material of the radome, despite the motion of the antenna in following a target. It may be seen from Fig. 4-15a that some oblique incident waves exist at the perimeter of the beam, but that any distortion of the beam which may occur as a result of this is uniform throughout the motion of the antenna, as long as the dielectric material and its thickness are uniform.

As the shape of the radome becomes more streamlined, as shown in Fig. 4-15b, the problem of maintaining integrity of the beam beyond the

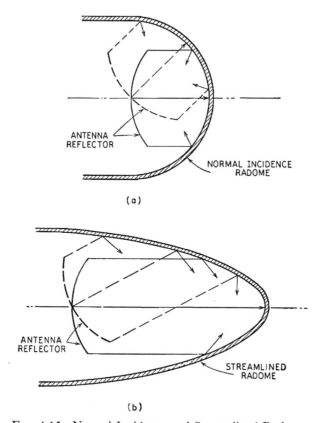

Fig. 4-15 Normal Incidence and Streamlined Radomes.

radome becomes more difficult. The angle of incidence of the path of the radio waves at the radome changes rapidly as the aspect of the antenna is changed. If the radome is constructed of a sheet of dielectric material of uniform thickness, the amounts of reflection and attenuation will change with a change of the antenna aspect. If the radio wave propagated at the antenna has plane polarization, since the oblique incidence with respect to the plane of polarization may also change with antenna motion, the resultant wave transmitted beyond the radome will suffer nonuniform phase changes with antenna motion. The result will be a change in direction of the beam, as well as a distortion of the beam shape, for the energy transmitted to, or received from, the medium beyond the radome. Further, the rate of change of the beam direction may not be uniform per unit of antenna motion. These effects are pointed out to stress the necessity for careful and considered radome design.

The problems of radome design do not reside only in having the proper electrical characteristics. The radome must be structurally capable of supporting the aerodynamic loads imposed upon it without undue physical or electrical distortion. For this reason, it is not usually possible to build radomes of extremely thin sheets of materials. The materials used for radome construction must have compatible structural and dielectric properties. It is not necessary that the radome be of the same material throughout. There are many combinations of materials possible, such as the sandwich type of radome wherein tough outer skins are combined with low-loss or low-density core materials. Sandwich panels of this type have been made using fiber glass cloth bonded with plastics for the inner and outer skins, and with an inner core of fiber glass honeycomb or isocyanate foam.

Radome materials should be impervious to moisture, at least insofar as the outer skin is concerned, since they must be used in all weather conditions. Further, materials employed in radome construction must not be hygroscopic, or water-absorbing, inasmuch as the presence of moisture in a material will radically affect its electrical characteristics.

Since an aircraft must fly through rain, hail, and snow, the outer skin of a nose radome must be capable of resisting the abrasive action of precipitation when the airborne vehicle is traveling at high speeds. If the airspeed is sufficiently high, it is to be expected that air friction may give rise to high temperatures on the surface of nose radomes. It is therefore necessary that materials with the ability to withstand the temperatures encountered, without undue change in electrical or structural properties, be employed.

4-17 TRANSMISSION THROUGH A SHEET OF DIELECTRIC MATERIAL

Normal Incidence. When the path of a radio wave impinges at normal incidence on a plane sheet of dielectric material, part of the energy is reflected, and the remainder enters the material. If no absorption of the energy occurs within the material, it is called "lossless" material. Conversely, when absorption does occur within the material, it is termed "lossy" material. Consider a radio wave which has entered the material and reaches the far surface. At this boundary, part of the energy is reflected and the remainder enters the atmosphere beyond the dielectric sheet. In general, for a lossless dielectric, the energy reflected from the far surface is about equal in magnitude, but opposite in phase, to the energy reflected from the near surface.

Some of the energy which is reflected from the far surface reemerges at the near surface and is directly superimposed on the energy originally reflected; part of it may undergo continued multiple reflections and contribute to both the resultant reflected energy and the resultant energy transmitted beyond the dielectric sheet. When the thickness of the dielectric material equals one quarter wavelength of the radio wave in that dielectric material, the wave reflected from the far surface will have traveled a half wavelength more than the wave reflected from the near surface and will therefore be in phase with it. For a quarter wavelength thickness and other thicknesses of odd numbers of quarter wavelengths the reflection should be maximum.

Considering a sheet of dielectric material whose thickness is an integral number of half wavelengths of the radio wave in that particular material, the wave reflected from the far surface will be out of phase when combined with the wave reflected from the near surface. Cancellation should ensue, and the resultant energy reflection should be a minimum.

From electromagnetic theory, the maximum value of the power-reflection coefficient for lossless sheets of dielectric material is developed as

$$|R|_{max}^2 = \left[\frac{\frac{\epsilon}{\epsilon_0} - 1}{\frac{\epsilon}{\epsilon_0} + 1}\right]^2 \qquad (4\text{-}9)[3]$$

where ϵ = permittivity of material
ϵ_0 = permittivity of free space
$\frac{\epsilon}{\epsilon_0}$ = specific dielectric constant $\left(\text{note, index of refraction, } n = \sqrt{\frac{\epsilon}{\epsilon_0}}\right)$.

Since actual dielectrics are always somewhat lossy, we may discuss how this modifies the reflection coefficient. The same general considerations are relevant, but it is necessary to consider the attenuation of any wave that is propagated in the lossy material. The power transmitted through the sheet is less because the wave traverses the sheet of dielectric once or more. The waves reflected from the far surface, which combine with the primary reflected wave from the near surface, will have made at least two traverses of the dielectric sheet and are attenuated in each passage. The resultant reflected energy from the far surface will, therefore, be smaller than in the lossless material and will never be great enough to cancel the primary wave completely. A lossy medium is usually char-

[3] Cady, Karelitz, and Turner, *Radar Scanners and Radomes*, Vol. 26, Radiation Laboratory Series, McGraw-Hill Book Co., Inc., 1948. See Chapter 10, p. 261, by H. Leaderman.

acterized by a dielectric constant that is a complex quantity. It may be written:

$$\varepsilon = \epsilon(1 - j \tan \delta) \qquad (4\text{-}10)^3$$

in which the quantity tan δ is called the "loss tangent" of the material and is a determining factor in both the refraction and absorption coefficients. When tan δ is very small, the magnitude of the reflection approaches that for a lossless sheet of dielectric material.

Other Than Normal Incidence. Figure 4-16 illustrates the paths of radio waves resulting from an incident wave impinging on a sheet of dielectric material at other than normal incidence. The internal and external reflections and transmissions to the region beyond the sheet are shown. At each surface boundary, part of the energy will be reflected and part will be transmitted past the boundary. Those waves emerging on the far side of the dielectric sheet combine to give a resultant transmitted wave; those waves which are reflected and reemerge from the near side of the material combine with the primary reflected wave to give a resultant reflected wave.

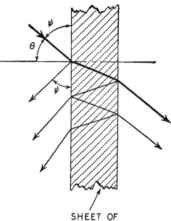

FIG. 4-16 Multiple Reflections and Refractions; Wave Path at Oblique Incidence to Sheet of Dielectric Material.

It can be shown that the expression for the reflection coefficient for normal incidence can be used for other than normal incidence, provided that, in place of the ratios of the indices of refraction or specific dielectric constants, there be substituted instead equivalent or fictitious values that depend on the angle of incidence. The polarization of the radio waves now becomes a factor. For parallel polarized waves (electric vector in the plane of incidence, similar to vertical polarization in the problem of surface reflection of the earth), the effective dielectric constant to be used, represented by ϵ_θ, is given by

$$\frac{\epsilon_\theta}{\epsilon_0} = \frac{(\epsilon/\epsilon_0)^2}{1 + \frac{(\epsilon/\epsilon_0) - 1}{\cos^2 \theta}} \qquad (4\text{-}11)^4$$

The ratio $\epsilon_\theta/\epsilon_0$ is to be used for a wave incident at angle θ in place of the ratio of the actual specific dielectric constant of the medium ϵ/ϵ_0. Similarly, the value of the effective dielectric constant for perpendicularly polarized

---

[4] *Op. cit.* See Chapter 11, p. 287, by H. Leaderman, W. Ellis, and L. A. Turner.

radiation (electric vector perpendicular to the plane of incidence) is

$$\frac{\epsilon_\theta}{\epsilon_0} = 1 + \frac{(\epsilon/\epsilon_0) - 1}{\cos^2 \theta} \tag{4-12}[5]$$

Figure 4-17 shows the reflection coefficients, plotted against the angle of incidence, for a single interface between air and the dielectric medium for a value of $\epsilon/\epsilon_0 = 4$. It is apparent that, for all angles of incidence, parallel polarized radiation is reflected to a lesser degree than is perpendicularly polarized radiation.

It is obvious, then, that when a plane polarized wave passes through a panel of dielectric material at oblique incidence, the amount of reflection is different for parallel and perpendicular polarization; and it follows that

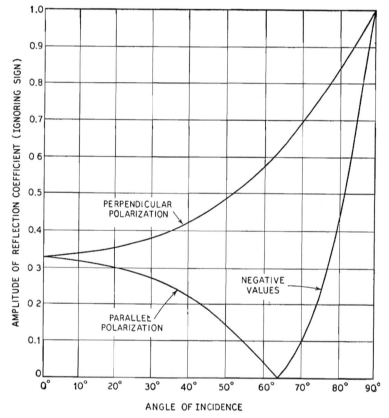

FIG. 4-17 Amplitude of Reflection Coefficient for a Single Interface between Air and the Dielectric Medium at Oblique Incidence for $\epsilon/\epsilon_0 = 4$. (By permission from *Radar Scanners and Radomes* by Cady, Karelitz, and Turner. Copyright 1948, McGraw-Hill Book Co., Inc.)

[5] *Ibid.*, p. 288.

with a lossy material having a complex value for its dielectric coefficient, the wave will suffer a retardation in phase that is different for parallel and perpendicular polarizations. If the sheet of dielectric material lies at an angle between the parallel and perpendicular polarizations, the wave can be thought of as consisting of two polarized components. These components will undergo a relative shift of phase in passing through the sheet of material and the emerging resultant wave will be elliptically polarized. The result is always an attenuation of the radio energy.

For a more complete treatment of the problems of electrical design of radomes, and structural considerations of them, the reader is referred to "Theory of Lossy High-Incidence Radomes," *Report No. NADC-EL-5116* and "Electrical Design of Lossy High-Incidence Radomes," *Report No. ADC EL-123-50*, both written by Samuel Wolin of the U. S. Naval Air Development Center, Johnsville, Pa.

4-18 EFFECT OF FLAMES ON RADIO WAVE TRANSMISSION*

For some types of missile guidance systems, the launching position of a guided missile is also the site of a radio or radar transmitter which propagates radio energy carrying intelligence to the missile. In the geometry of such a system, the guided missile flies away from the radio transmitter, presenting a rear aspect to it. When the propulsion motor is a jet or rocket, and propulsion is continued during the guidance phase, the emitted flame may be interposed between the transmitter at the launching point and the receiver antenna in the missile. When the signals pass through the flames, reflection, absorption, and random amplitude modulation of the transmitted signals may occur. Even though the direct signal may reach the antenna without passing through the exhaust trail, signals reflected from the flame may reach the antenna, and such signals will vary in amplitude and phase. The variations may be caused either by changes in the orientation of the missile with respect to the propagation path or by changes in the character of the flame. Consequently, the electrical properties of flames and the interaction between the flames and radio waves are of interest to the designer of missile guidance systems.

During the past seventy years, numerous investigators have been interested in the electrical properties of conducting gases and flames and some works on this subject have been published. Much of the interest in recent years has been directed toward a study of the interaction between flames and electromagnetic waves at super high frequencies. The early workers using microwave frequencies investigated the properties of cool ionized gases; more recently the desire for knowledge of the propagation

* Paragraphs 4-18 to 4-22 inclusive have been written by William W. Balwanz of the Naval Research Laboratory.

of electromagnetic waves through reaction type exhausts and other high temperature flames has stimulated interest in this phase of the problem. The sensitivity of experimental results to small variations in the flame parameters, the strict requirements placed upon measuring equipment by flame discontinuities, and the relatively large influence of the physical environment upon the exploratory fields are factors of difficulty in the investigations of this field. However, considerable progress in understanding the phenomena encountered has been made.

4-19 CONDUCTIVITY OF A GASEOUS MEDIUM WITH A FREE CHARGE

One of the earliest developments of an expression for the conductivity of a gaseous medium with free charge is quite simple, yet it gives results with sufficient accuracy for many present needs. The charged particle is accelerated by the force of the electric field of the radio wave and is retarded by a frictional force, proportional to the velocity of the charged particle, caused by collision with other particles. The equation of motion (in cgs electrostatic units) is thus given by

$$m \frac{dv}{dt} + gv = qE_m e^{j\omega t} \qquad (4\text{-}13)$$

where m = mass of the charged particle (grams)
 v = velocity of the charged particle (cm per sec)
 g = average frictional constant
 E_m = magnitude of the applied electric field (statvolts per cm)
 ω = angular frequency of the electric field (radians)
 q = electric unit charge (esu)

A solution of this equation is given by

$$v = \frac{g - j\omega m}{\omega^2 m^2 + g^2} qE_m e^{j\omega t} \qquad (4\text{-}14)$$

and the current i is

$$i = Nqv = Nq^2 \frac{g - j\omega m}{\omega^2 m^2 + g^2} E_m e^{j\omega t} \qquad (4\text{-}15)$$

where N is the number of electrons per cubic centimeter. Charged particles other than electrons follow this same relationship but contribute negligibly to the current, by reason of their greater mass. Consequently, the conductivity σ of such a medium is given by

$$\sigma = \frac{i}{E_m e^{j\omega t}} = Nq^2 \frac{g - j\omega m}{\omega^2 m^2 + g^2} \qquad (4\text{-}16)$$

From Eq. (4-13), g is seen to have the dimension of mass divided by time and may be assumed to have the form

$$g = \frac{m}{\tau} \tag{4-17}$$

where τ is the mean free time between electron collisions. This assumption has been justified experimentally by investigators in the field to within the desired accuracy, within limited areas, but is not generally correct. One criticism of this treatment is that it assumes the mean free time τ independent of electron velocities. Margenau[6] has developed an expression for the conductivity based on the assumption that the mean free path between collisions is independent of particle velocities. Although this assumption is more logical than one of independent mean free time, it is not generally correct for all possible parameter variations. This is particularly so at elevated temperatures. Here neither the mean free path nor the mean free time between electron collisions is independent of the electron velocities.[7] In certain limiting regions these two assumptions yield identical results[8] and in other regions do not differ greatly, insofar as numerical results are concerned. The Margenau treatment requires a knowledge of flame temperatures which are not conveniently measured. Consequently, a mean free time is assumed, since it provides a workable method of attack.

Substitution of the value of g from Eq. (4-17), into the conductivity expression, gives

$$\sigma = \sigma_r - j\sigma_i = \frac{Nq^2\tau}{m}\left(\frac{1 - j\omega\tau}{1 + \omega^2\tau^2}\right) \tag{4-18}$$

or

$$\sigma_r = \frac{Nq^2\tau}{m(1 + \omega^2\tau^2)} \tag{4-19}$$

and

$$\sigma_i = \omega\tau\sigma_r \tag{4-20}$$

4-20 ABSORPTION IN A GASEOUS MEDIUM WITH A FREE CHARGE

With this value of conductivity, an expression for the absorption of electromagnetic waves in an unbounded homogeneous isotropic gaseous medium is obtained from Maxwell's equations. One convenient development of such an expression assumes that there exists a uniform charge distribution throughout the medium of the flame, an assumption which is known to be incorrect for flame gases of the type considered. The actual

---

[6] H. Margenau, "Conduction and Dispersion of Ionized Gases at High Frequencies," *Phys. Rev.* **69**, 508 (1946).

[7] R. B. Brode, "The Quantitative Study of the Collisions of Electrons with Atoms," *Rev. Mod. Phys.* **5**, 257 (1933).

[8] J. H. Cahn, "Electron Velocity Distribution in High Frequency Alternating Fields, Including Electronic Interaction," *Phys. Rev.* **75**, 838 (1949).

distribution is an unknown, which unknown must be determined in the investigation of specific flames. However, the assumption becomes more rational if we consider uniform distribution in regions small compared to flame dimensions, but large compared to the focal area for the electromagnetic waves. On this basis, the absorption loss for signals propagated through such media may be expressed, in rationalized mks units, as

$$\text{Absorption loss, in db/meter} = -8.68\omega\mu^{\frac{1}{2}}k \qquad (4\text{-}21)$$

where k, the index of absorption, is determined from

$$k^2 = \frac{1}{2}\left[-\left(\epsilon - \frac{4\pi\sigma_i}{\omega}\right) + \sqrt{\left(\epsilon - \frac{4\pi\sigma_i}{\omega}\right)^2 + \left(\frac{4\pi\sigma_r}{\omega}\right)^2}\right] \qquad (4\text{-}22)$$

and the relative phase shift for the same signal may be expressed as

$$\text{Relative phase shift, in radians per sec} = \omega\mu^{\frac{1}{2}}n \qquad (4\text{-}23)$$

where n, the index of refraction, is determined from

$$n^2 = \frac{1}{2}\left[+\left(\epsilon - \frac{4\pi\sigma_i}{\omega}\right) + \sqrt{\left(\epsilon - \frac{4\pi\sigma_i}{\omega}\right)^2 + \left(\frac{4\pi\sigma_r}{\omega}\right)^2}\right] \qquad (4\text{-}24)$$

and where μ = the permeability of the medium
ϵ = the dielectric constant of the medium

and all other notation as previously indicated. The contributions of the regions of uniform distribution must then be combined to give the total absorption loss.

4-21 REFLECTION AT A BOUNDARY BETWEEN AIR AND A GASEOUS MEDIUM WITH A FREE CHARGE

If the simplifying assumption of normal incidence is made, with the further assumption of a flat infinite boundary between the air and the flame, the reflection coefficient can be determined in terms of the variables used above. If the permeability of the flame is taken to be the same as for air, the magnitude of the reflection coefficient is

$$R = \frac{(1-\eta)^2 + \kappa^2}{(1+\eta)^2 + \kappa^2} \qquad (4\text{-}25)$$

where $\eta = \dfrac{n}{\sqrt{\epsilon_{\text{air}}}}$

$\kappa = \dfrac{k}{\sqrt{\epsilon_{\text{air}}}}$

4-22 EXPERIMENTAL AND THEORETICAL STUDIES

Experiments on a particular rocket motor flame[9] have shown that in the vicinity of the motor throat the flame temperature and pressure vary

[9] F. P. Bundy, R. H. Johnson and H. M. Strong, "Final Report on Optical Studies at Malta Test Station," *Project Hermes Report No. R50A0506* (General Electric), June 1950.

from 2000° to 2700°K and from 0.5 to 2.8 atm (absolute) respectively. If the electrons are assumed to be in equilibrium with the other flame gases, the mean free time between electron collisions (τ) is calculated to be of the order of 10^{-12} to 10^{-11} sec. Measurements with electromagnetic wave flame probes indicate these values to be of the proper order of magnitude.

The absorption path length through a flame is difficult to evaluate. The apparent flame dimensions vary by as much as 4 to 1, depending upon the method of determination. To the eye, the flames appear larger in the dark than in the light. Photographically great dimensional variations are observed, depending upon the exposure and type of film used. It cannot be assumed that electron boundaries agree with visible flame boundaries. Such methods give no indication of the electron distribution within the flame, and when nonuniformities exist, the distribution is more important than the total path length.

Thermodynamic methods are available[10] for calculating the electron concentration in high temperature gases as a function of temperature, pressure, and the types and concentration of particles present in the flame. However, characteristics of the gases in the various parts of the flame are difficult to evaluate. The calculations may also be complicated by combustion processes which occur in exhaust flames. Further, electrons released by collision processes occurring in the flame shock nodes (resulting from the high velocity of mass transport) appear to be greater than indicated by temperature measurements using emission and absorption methods. In spite of these difficulties, thermodynamic methods appear to be feasible, provided the variables can be evaluated. Calculated electron concentration for carefully controlled experiments range up to 10^{13} electrons per cu cm. Experiments measuring the absorption loss of electromagnetic waves transmitted through the flames indicate the same order of electron concentration.

Calculations based on these theories show some variation in the loss of electromagnetic signal propagated through rocket motor flames as a function of the electromagnetic frequency. However, the signal loss may either increase or decrease with frequency, depending upon flame parameters, which in turn are determined by rocket motor and fuel characteristics. In any event the loss does not appear to vary more than one (or possibly two) orders of magnitude for electromagnetic waves in the super high frequency region. Theoretical considerations indicate that the absorption loss in the exhaust flames should vary according to the fuels used, the contaminants present in the fuels, motor combustion efficiency, and other related parameters. High-speed pictures (4000 frames per sec) of rocket motor flames[11] have shown high frequency variation of luminosity along different stream lines. As may be expected from such data, high

---

[10] N. M. Saha and N. K. Saha, *A Treatise on Modern Physics*, Vol. I, Indian Press, 1934.
[11] Bundy, Johnson, and Strong, *op. cit.*

frequency variations in absorption loss have been observed, the magnitude of such variations being 50 percent of the absorption loss.

BIBLIOGRAPHY

1. "The Propagation of Radio Waves Through The Standard Atmosphere," *Summary Technical Report of the Committee on Propagation*, NDRC Volume 3, Edited by Stephen S. Attwood.
2. H. R. Reed and C. M. Russell, *Ultra High Frequency Propagation*, John Wiley & Sons, Inc., New York, 1953.
3. D. E. Kerr, *Propagation of Short Radio Waves*, Vol. 13, Radiation Laboratory Series, McGraw-Hill Book Co., Inc., New York, 1947.
4. W. M. Cady, M. B. Karelitz, and L. A. Turner (Eds.), *Radar Scanners and Radomes*, Vol. 26, Radiation Laboratory Series, McGraw-Hill Book Co., Inc., New York, 1947.
5. F. E. Terman, *Radio Engineers Handbook*, McGraw-Hill Book Co., Inc., New York, 1943.
6. A. Sheingold, *Fundamentals of Radio Communication*, D. Van Nostrand Co., Inc., New York, 1951.

Symbols Used in Chapter 5

A = area (cm²) (subscripts refer to specific areas)
c = velocity of light
c_1 = constant = 3.732×10^{-12} watt cm²
c_2 = constant = 1.436 cm deg
C = heat capacity of detector (joules per deg)
d = diameter (cm)
dJ_λ/dT = derivative J_λ with respect to T
dP/dT = derivative P with respect to T
D = distance (cm)
e = d-c voltage (volts)
E = total emissive power (watts cm⁻² per hemisphere)
f = focal length of mirror (cm)
F = flux density (watts cm⁻²) (subscripts refer to specific examples)
h = Planck's constant
i_g = galvanometer current (amp)
I = intensity of radiation (watts cm⁻² per steradian)
J_λ = the emissive power of a unit area in the wavelength interval $d\lambda$ (watts cm⁻² per cm per 2π steradians)
$J_{\lambda max}$ = spectral emissive power of the source for $\lambda = \lambda_{max}$ (watts cm⁻² per cm per 2π steradians)
k = Boltzmann gas constant
K_1 = constant
M = meter deflections (subscripts refer to specific examples)
n = number of atoms
P = power (watts) (subscripts refer to specific examples)

ΔP = net exchange of power (watts)
r_g = galvanometer resistance (ohms)
r_t = internal resistance (ohms)
S_λ = relative spectral sensitivity of the detector
t = transmission
t_h = transmission of haze
t_w = window transmission
t_λ = spectral transmission of the atmosphere
T = absolute temperature (°K) (subscripts refer to specific examples)
ΔT = differential temperature (°K)
w = amount of precipitable water vapor
V = visual range (nautical miles)
x = thickness of column of atmosphere
X = length of optical path

α = the attenuation coefficient due to scattering by haze
β_λ = absorption coefficient
ϵ = emissivity of surface
ϵ_λ = spectral emissivity
λ = wavelength (cm)
λ_{max} = wavelength in microns at maximum spectral emissive power
$\Delta\lambda$ = wavelength interval (cm)
Λ = rate of energy loss from thermocouple (watts per deg)
μ = micron = 10^{-4} cm
σ = the Stefan-Boltzmann constant (5.7×10^{-12} watt cm⁻² deg⁻⁴)
τ = time constant (sec)

CHAPTER 5

EMISSION, TRANSMISSION, AND DETECTION OF THE INFRARED

This chapter deals with radiation emitted by objects by virtue of their temperature. This "thermal" radiation is distributed over the ultraviolet, the visible, and the infrared regions of the spectrum, the fraction appearing in each part of the spectrum being dependent on the temperature. The ultraviolet, comprising wavelengths less than 0.4 micron, is relatively weak except from objects at very high temperatures and is therefore of minor importance to missile guidance. The visible spectrum and the visibility of objects through the atmosphere constitute an involved subject about which much information has been collected.[1] The discussion will, in the main, relate to the emission and detection of thermal radiation in the infrared region between the long wavelength limit of the visible spectrum at about 0.7 micron and 15 microns, where atmospheric absorption by carbon dioxide and water vapor becomes exceedingly strong. This is a region of considerable interest because a large part of the radiation emitted by objects at ordinary temperatures lies within it. The thermal radiation spectrum does not end at 15 microns, but extends essentially to infinity and can be detected and measured at wavelengths of one or a few centimeters, where the atmosphere is again transparent, by means of microwave radiometers.[2] The concepts and methods which apply to the infrared spectrum are equally applicable at shorter wavelengths in the visible or the ultraviolet.

5-1 TOTAL RADIATION

All objects radiate energy by virtue of their temperature. In this section the fundamental laws governing the emission of radiation and some of their corollaries are presented. For the purpose in mind it is convenient to begin with the relationships governing the total radiation of all wavelengths emitted by an object and the measurement of this radiation with a radiometer equally sensitive at all wavelengths. Later we shall proceed

---

[1] W. E. Knowles Middleton, *Vision through the Atmosphere*, University of Toronto Press, 1952.
[2] R. H. Dicke, "The Measurement of Thermal Radiation at Microwave Frequencies," *Rev. Sci. Instr.* **17**, 268 (1946).

to the more elaborate problems of the measurement in selected wavelength bands with a radiometer which is selectively sensitive, through an atmosphere which is selectively transmitting.

Total Emissive Power. The total emissive power of a surface of unit area is the amount of energy of all wavelengths radiated per second into a solid angle of 2π steradians, or a hemisphere. It is given by the Stefan-Boltzmann Law,

$$E = \epsilon \sigma T^4 \qquad (5\text{-}1)$$

where E = total emissive power (watts cm^{-2} per hemisphere)
  σ = the Stefan-Boltzmann constant (5.7×10^{-12} watt cm^{-2} deg^{-4})
  T = absolute temperature (°K)
  ϵ = the total emissivity of the surface

The *emissivity* ϵ is unity for a black body, or perfect radiator. A *black body* may be defined as an object that absorbs all of the radiation falling on it, neither reflecting nor transmitting any of the radiation. Black bodies rarely occur naturally, although most materials except metals and a few transparent substances may be considered to be black for the long portion of the infrared wavelength range. Close approximations to black bodies can be realized through the use of any enclosure of uniform interior wall temperature and with a very small opening in one wall. Examples of black bodies are: a cylindrical electric furnace of uniform temperature with an aperture much smaller than the furnace diameter in one end; the Mendenhall wedge,[3] a strip of platinum a few thousandths of a centimeter thick and perhaps a centimeter wide bent into a sharp wedge and heated electrically; or, on a larger scale and at a lower temperature, the narrow mouth of a large cave of uniform internal temperature.

It will be noted that nothing has been said about the "blackness" of the interior surfaces of the furnace, the wedge, or the cave. "Blackness" does not matter for the reason that radiation entering the openings of the specified structures is, in part, reflected but also, in part, absorbed on each encounter with a wall, so that after the many reflections and partial absorptions which occur, there is only an infinitesimal fraction of the entering radiation eventually reflected out of the opening. A simple demonstration of this phenomenon of light trapping can be made in the following way: Five or ten razor blades of the thin variety are stacked one on the other. The edge of the stack made up of the cutting edges of the blades is, then, a stack of very thin wedges, the polished faces of the cutting edges of adjacent blades making up the individual wedge faces. If the observer looks directly into this edge of the stack of blades it will be seen to be extremely

---

[3] For this and other types of black body see *Temperature, Its Measurement and Control in Science and Industry*, Reinhold Publishing Corporation, New York, 1941, Ch. 12, pp. 1164-1187, especially.

black, even though the individual blade edges are shiny reflectors. That is, light entering the wedges is almost completely absorbed and virtually none returns to the observer. Since the absorption is nearly perfect, such an array is also a close approximation to a perfect black body emitter.

It follows from the Stefan-Boltzmann Law (Eq. (5-1)) that the total emissivity of an object is the ratio of its emissive power at temperature T to the emissive power of a black body at the same temperature. Although the method of measuring ϵ is implicit in the equations and procedures to be described below, many intricacies of method beyond the scope of this chapter are documented.[3]

Intensity of Radiation. Equation (5-1) describes the total emissive power of unit area of a surface into a solid angle of 2π steradians. The *intensity of radiation* I of a surface is the emissive power per steradian normal to the surface and is given by

$$I = \frac{E}{\pi} = \frac{\epsilon \sigma T^4}{\pi} \qquad (5\text{-}2)$$

This quantity is sometimes called the *steradiancy*. This relationship applies for surfaces which obey the *Lambert cosine law* that the emissive power at any angle with the normal is proportional to the cosine of that angle. It is not strictly obeyed by many actual materials, particularly polished metals,[3] but deviations are small for rough surfaces and the law may be assumed without serious error in many cases.[4a] Note that the relationship between the intensity and the emissive power is

$$I = E/\pi \qquad (5\text{-}3)$$

and not $E/2\pi$. This is the result of a well-known photometric theorem[4] which is often overlooked.

The Flux Density. Equations (5-1) and (5-2) relate to radiative properties of a unit surface. The *flux density* F of radiation from a surface of area A at a distance D is the radiant energy per second passing through a unit area lying perpendicular to the line-of-sight to the emitting surface,

$$F = \frac{\epsilon \sigma T^4 A}{\pi D^2} \qquad (5\text{-}4)$$

D must be about ten times the lateral dimensions of the radiating object for this simple equation to apply. That is, the object must be far enough away to be treated as a point source of radiation. Otherwise, as for example in computing the flux density at a point 10 cm from an object 10 cm square, the cosine law must be applied and an integration carried out over the entire solid angle subtended by the object at the point in question.

[4] F. K. Richtmyer and E. H. Kennard, *Introduction to Modern Physics*, p. 141, McGraw-Hill Book Company, Inc., New York, 1947.

[4a] See Max Jakob, *Heat Transfer*, Vol. 1, p. 42, John Wiley and Sons, Inc., 1949, for the variation of emissivity with angle for smooth dielectrics.

130 EMISSION, TRANSMISSION, AND DETECTION OF THE INFRARED

Details of treatment required can be found in standard texts,[5] but this condition can usually be avoided in practice. The value of the area A to be used in computing the flux density from a distant object is the projected cross-sectional area, as illustrated in Fig. 5-1.

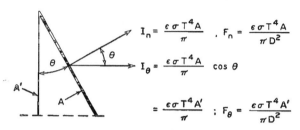

FIG. 5-1 Illustration of the Relationship between the Normal Intensity I_n and the Intensity at an Angle θ, I_θ, for a Diffusing Surface.

Use of the Equations. For the time being, attention will be restricted to thermal detectors, i.e., to sensitive elements which depend on a slight change in temperature for their response when exposed to a radiation field. Thermocouples and bolometers fall in this category; photoconductive cells do not, but it will develop that equivalent considerations apply. However, only thermal detectors can be made black over the entire spectrum, and it is appropriate to restrict attention to them.

It is clear that, if a thermal detector is exposed to a flux of radiation from some other object, its temperature rise and, therefore, its response will depend not alone on the value of the flux density computed by Eq.

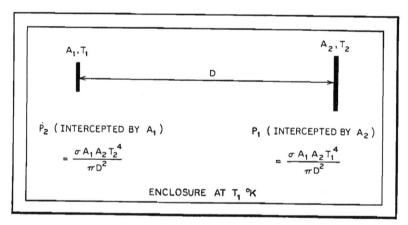

FIG. 5-2 Exchange of Radiation between Two Surfaces of Different Temperature.

[5] J. W. T. Walsh, Photometry, 2nd Rev. Ed., pp. 140*ff*, Constable and Company Ltd., London, 1953.

(5-4) but, rather, on the net exchange of radiant energy between object and detector. In Fig. 5-2, let the shorter line represent a detector, say, a thermocouple, of area $A_1(\text{cm}^2)$ and at room temperature $T_1(°K)$, separated by a distance D from a warmer black body object of area A_2 and temperature T_2. By Eq. (5-4), the flux density of radiation produced at the detector by the object A_2 is

$$F_2 = \frac{A_2 \sigma T_2^4}{\pi D^2} \tag{5-5}$$

The radiant power P_2 intercepted by the detector A_1 is, therefore,

$$P_2 = A_1 F_2 = \frac{A_1 A_2 \sigma T_2^4}{\pi D^2} \tag{5-6}$$

Similarly, the radiant power supplied to the surface A_2 by A_1 is

$$P_1 = \frac{A_1 A_2 \sigma T_1^4}{\pi D^2} \tag{5-7}$$

The net exchange of power is

$$\Delta P = P_2 - P_1 = \frac{A_1 A_2 \sigma}{\pi D^2} (T_2^4 - T_1^4) \tag{5-8}$$

The response of the thermocouple is proportional to ΔP and will be positive if $T_2 > T_1$, negative if $T_2 < T_1$, and zero if $T_2 = T_1$.

Emissivity of Object Less Than Unity. Let the detector A_1 be a black receiver and the emitter A_2 be a gray body of emissivity ϵ_2. By "gray body" is meant that ϵ_2 has the same value at all wavelengths and is less than unity in value. In this case, Eq. (5-5) becomes

$$F_2 = \frac{\epsilon_2 A_2 \sigma T_2^4}{\pi D^2}$$

and it would appear at first glance that Eq. (5-8) becomes

$$\Delta P = \frac{\sigma A_1 A_2}{\pi D^2} (\epsilon T_2^4 - T_1^4)$$

That it cannot be correct is immediately apparent upon putting $T_2 = T_1$, in which event a negative meter reading would be predicted, and the system would constitute a means for the transfer of energy between two reservoirs at equal temperature without performance of work.

The problem is cleared up simply by consideration of the fact that P_1 and P_2 are the powers absorbed by A_1 and A_2, respectively. Since we are assuming that the detector A_1 is a perfect black body, the power which it absorbs is, as before,

$$P_1 = A_1 F_2 = \frac{A_1 A_2 \sigma \epsilon_2 T_2^4}{\pi D^2}. \tag{5-9}$$

however, the power which the object A_2 absorbs is

$$P_2 = A_2\epsilon_2 F_1 = \frac{A_2\epsilon_2 A_1 \sigma T_1^4}{\pi D^2} \tag{5-10}$$

inasmuch as the emissivity is numerically equal to the absorption coefficient. Hence the net exchange of power in this case is

$$\Delta P = P_2 - P_1 = \frac{A_1 A_2 \sigma \epsilon_2}{\pi D^2}(T_2^4 - T_1^4) \tag{5-11}$$

It can be shown by similar treatment that, if the receiver is a gray body of emissivity ϵ_1, the product $\epsilon_2\epsilon_1$ is a multiplier of the term $(T_2^4 - T_1^4)$.

Equation (5-11) was derived for the special, simple case of uniform surroundings, achievable only in an enclosed laboratory space, and it will be immediately obvious that it cannot be applied haphazardly in many actual situations. For example, if a block of ice at 273°K were placed alongside the detector A_1 at room temperature T_1°K but shielded so that the detector could not view it directly, the detector could nevertheless *receive radiation* from it by reflection from A_2, and a negative meter reading could result, even when $T_2 > T_1$. It is necessary to apply Eq. (5-11) twice in this case, once for the A_2, A_1 exchange and then for the A_1 ice exchange. The meter reading is the algebraic sum of the two ΔP's.

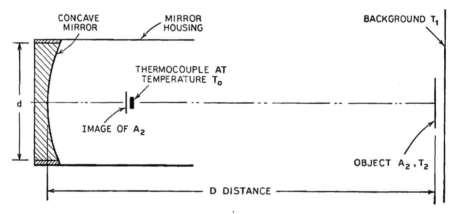

Fig. 5-3 Simple Radiometer.

Radiometry. A *radiometer* is any device for measuring the flux density of radiation or total radiant power falling on it, such as the detector A_1 in the foregoing examples. Radiometers usually comprise a sensitive detector, such as a thermocouple; an optical system, such as a paraboloidal mirror aluminized on its front surface, to form an image of an object or a selected area on the thermocouple; and some means of measuring the thermocouple voltage, such as a galvanometer or an ultra-sensitive voltmeter. Figure 5-3 is a diagram of a simple radiometer. In order to

5-1] TOTAL RADIATION

illustrate the application of the foregoing equations to its use, the assumptions will be retained that D is large with respect to the size of the object A_2 and that the atmosphere is completely transparent. In Fig. 5-3, the object at temperature T_2 is shown against a background at temperature T_1, and the temperature T_0 is assigned to the detector. The results illustrate that the temperature of the detector is immaterial in detecting the radiation from the object relative to its background.

By Eq. (5-4), the flux density of radiation produced at the mirror by A_2 is

$$F_2 = \frac{\sigma T_2^4}{\pi D^2} \cdot (\text{Area})$$

The total radiant power intercepted by the mirror is found by multiplying the flux density of radiation by the area of the mirror, $\pi d^2/4$:

$$P_2 = \frac{\pi d^2}{4} \frac{\sigma T_2^4}{\pi D^2} \cdot (\text{Area})$$

The value of the area to be used depends on the size of the image in relation to the size of the thermocouple.

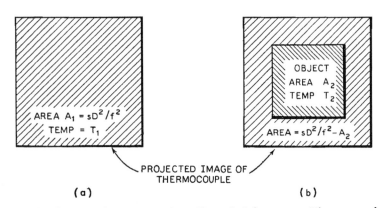

Fig. 5-4 (a) Image of Background or Extended Source on Thermocouple, and (b) Image of Small Object Against Background.

Case (a): Image larger than thermocouple. This is the case illustrated in Fig. 5-4a. Obviously, only that part of the image which lies on the thermocouple is of use, and this corresponds to an area on the object equal to the projected area of the thermocouple: sD^2/f^2, where s is the area of the thermocouple, and f is the focal length of mirror. The power intercepted by the thermocouple is

$$P_2 = \frac{\pi d^2}{4} \frac{\sigma T_2^4}{\pi D^2} \frac{sD^2}{f^2} = \frac{d^2 \sigma T_2^4 s}{4f^2} \qquad (5\text{-}12)$$

It will be noted that the power received does not depend on the distance D.

If the radiometer is swung to view the background at temperature T_1, a similar relation applies, and the net signal due to the presence of the object A_2 is

$$\Delta P = \frac{d^2 s \sigma}{4 f^2} (T_2^4 - T_1^4) \tag{5-13}$$

If T_2 and T_1 are nearly equal, the differential may be used, and the differential power (or the change in power) is

$$\frac{dP}{dT} = \frac{d^2 s \sigma}{f^2} T^3$$

These relations show that, for the case in question, the signal is independent of the distance and varies inversely with the square of the F number of the optical system (f/d), i.e., inversely with the square of the focal length and directly with the square of the mirror diameter. It also varies with the area of the thermocouple and the field of view (s/f^2). For a given ΔT, the signal varies with T^3.

The order of magnitude of quantities involved in radiation pyrometry, where usually extended objects are viewed, can be shown by a computation for a specific case by choosing

$$d = 30 \text{ cm}$$
$$f = 30 \text{ cm}$$
$$s = 1 \text{ mm} \times 1 \text{ mm} = 10^{-2} \text{ cm}^2$$
$$T = 300°K$$
$$\Delta T = 1°K$$

Then $\Delta P = 1.5 \times 10^{-6}$ watt. A typical thermocouple may have a sensitivity of about 1 volt per watt, leading to a voltage signal of about 1.5 microvolts in a thermocouple of about 5-ohm resistance. Amplifiers now exist in which the noise level is about 5×10^{-9} volt, which, in the case illustrated, would correspond to a radiation temperature difference of about 3×10^{-3} deg to produce a signal equal to noise. The limits of detection will be discussed briefly in a later section. It should be remarked at this point that the foregoing results apply to the measurement of an extended source under ideal conditions, including a long time interval in which to make the measurement. The measurement at high speed of the radiation from remote objects cannot be carried to such limits.

Case (b): Image smaller than the thermocouple. In this case, the radiant intensity of the object is measured by aiming the radiometer first at the extended background, when the foregoing relations apply, and then at the object, when the object and the background surrounding it will be imaged on the thermocouple, as shown in Fig. 5-4b.

The radiant power falling on the thermocouple in Fig. 5-4b is

$$P_2' = \frac{\pi d^2 \sigma}{4\pi D^2}\left[A_2 T_2^4 + \left(\frac{sD^2}{f^2} - A_2\right)T_1^4\right]$$

and, in Fig. 5-4a, it is

$$P_1' = \frac{d^2 s \sigma T_1^4}{4f^2}$$

as in Eq. (5-12). The net power, which constitutes the signal, is

$$\Delta P' = \frac{d^2 A_2 \sigma}{4 D^2}(T_2^4 - T_1^4) \qquad (5\text{-}14)$$

The radiant signal depends on the square of the mirror diameter and the actual area of the target, and it falls off as the inverse square of the distance. For thermocouples of equal sensitivity in volts per watt, the response is independent of thermocouple size, provided it be large enough to receive the entire image of the object. It should not be construed, however, that thermocouple size is unimportant; the noise signal and other considerations dictate that the thermocouple should be just large enough to receive the entire image of the object.

Although the preceding results were worked out for a single sensitive element, they apply for a two-element compensated system as well, in which one thermocouple views (a) in Fig. 5-4 at the same time that the other views (b), thereby giving the net power difference directly.

Calibration of a Radiometer. A total radiation detector can be calibrated conveniently by applying the conditions of Case (a) and Eq. (5-13) in a laboratory experiment. Two thin-walled rectangular one-gallon cans painted on the outside with a granular pigment paint and filled with water at known temperatures T_1 and T_2 often provide adequate sources. The emissivity of such a painted surface is usually 0.90 to 0.95 for total radiation at temperatures up to 100°C or higher. If greater precision is required, a more perfect emitter can be constructed by building into one side of a can a re-entrant cone of 20 or 30 deg angle with its vertex inside the can and surrounded by water at uniform temperature. It is a difficult matter to construct a black body which can be known to be absolutely black, both with respect to its blackness and its uniformity of temperature.

Of course, any convenient source can be calibrated by means of a calibrated thermocouple used in the manner illustrated in Fig. 5-2 or, by comparison, with a National Bureau of Standards secondary source of radiation.

Measurement of Emissivity. The normal emissivity of any surface is determined under the conditions of Case (a) and Eq. (5-13) by measuring first the signal from the surface at temperature T_2 when the thermocouple (or an intermediate reference surface) is at temperature T_1, and then measuring the signal from a perfectly emitting surface, also at temperature T_2. The emissivity is then simply the ratio of the meter deflections M_1 and M_2 in the two cases; i.e.,

$$\frac{M_1}{M_2} = \frac{\epsilon(T_2^4 - T_1^4)}{(T_2^4 - T_1^4)} \qquad (5\text{-}15)$$

The normal emissivities of a number of materials at ordinary temperatures are given in Table 5-1. It may be emphasized that the emissivity of an opaque material is a surface property. Any alteration of the surface will change it; for example, roughening a metallic surface. The emissivity can only be considered to be a physical property of the material when it is measured for an opaque, polished specimen. Composite materials such as paint films, anodized aluminum, or shiny mirrors coated with thin lacquer will possess emissivities which depend on thickness of film, nature of the organic vehicle, and so on. Excluding polished metals and restricting attention to ordinary earth temperature, say, 273°K to 500°K, many objects are essentially black. The earth, foilage, water and ice, bricks

TABLE 5-1 NORMAL TOTAL EMISSIVITY OF SELECTED MATERIALS AT ORDINARY TEMPERATURES

MATERIAL	TEMPERATURE (°C)	EMISSIVITY
Paint Films		
Granular pigment, any color[6]	100	0.90–0.94
Aluminum paint[6]	100	0.25
Special aluminum paint[7]	100–370	0.18
Metals		
Cold-rolled steel, clean, gray[6]	150	0.60
Same, scrubbed with steel wool[6]	150	0.46
Same, pickled in HCl[6]	150	0.35
Same, buffed to bright finish[6]	150	0.11
Aluminum foil[8]	100	0.04
Aluminum sheet, smooth[6]	150	0.08
Same, roughened with emery[6]	—	0.70
Stainless steel[8]	100	0.09
Brass, burnished[8]	100	0.05
Brass, oxidized to blue interference color[8]	100	0.07
Carbon, rough plate[9]	100	0.77
Carbon, rough plate[9]	500	0.72

[6] J. A. Sanderson, "The Emissivity of Navy Aluminum Paints and of Granular Pigment Paints," *NRL Report H-2024* (March 1943).

[7] J. A. Sanderson, "The Emissivity at 700°F of Heat Resisting Aluminum Paints," *NRL Report H-2122* (July 1943).

[8] Memorandum Report from A. H. Pfund to J. A. Sanderson (1943).

[9] B. T. Barnes, W. E. Forsythe, and E. Q. Adams, "The Total Emissivity of Various Materials at 100-500°C," *J. Opt. Soc. Am.* **37**, 804 (1947).

and stones, granular paint films of whatever color, cloth, glass, wood, and the human skin are essentially black so far as their emission of radiation at ordinary temperatures is concerned.

Polished metals and metal flake paints such as aluminum paint are generally of low emissivity. The remarkable difference in emissivity of granular pigment and aluminum flake paints is due to different roles of the pigments. In each case, the principal emitter is the organic vehicle which absorbs strongly because of the natural frequencies of vibration of the chemical bonds, C—H, C=C, CH_2, CH_3, etc., which lie mainly in the spectral interval 3 to 15 microns. In the case of a granular pigment paint, multiple scattering of incident radiation in all directions has the effect of increasing the optical path of an incident ray within the film of organic vehicle and thus of increasing the fraction of radiation absorbed by the film. The monochromatic absorption coefficient is equal to the monochromatic emission coefficient; therefore, the addition of a granular pigment in a layer of organic paint vehicle increases the total infrared emissivity. Even the addition of ground rock salt, which is transparent in the infrared and which, by itself, is of low emissivity in the infrared, will increase the emissivity of a film of organic vehicle through the scattering action described.

Metallic flake pigments exercise a different effect through the remarkable phenomenon called "leafing" which describes the action of the flakes in adjusting themselves to lie mainly parallel to the surface as fallen leaves lie on the ground, so that the scattering of incident radiation by the pigment is chiefly back in the direction from which it came through a thin overlying layer of vehicle. Thus, the optical path of incident radiation into and back out of the paint film is through a minimum thickness of vehicle; the absorption of radiation by the vehicle and, therefore, the emissivity are low.

It must be emphasized that the foregoing remarks, which relate to the total emissivity over all wavelengths, apply only within the wavelength region where the materials are opaque and therefore only to temperatures which give rise to negligible intensities of radiation outside of those wavelength bands. Thus glass, which is opaque in ordinary thickness at wavelengths longer than about 3 microns, is essentially a black-body emitter of radiations at temperatures below about 400°K, for at those temperatures the intensity of radiation at wavelengths shorter than 3 microns is negligible. But a glass bead heated to incandescence will emit more strongly at infrared wavelengths where it is opaque than at visible wavelengths where it is semitransparent. The experimentalist therefore must, at all times, take into account the physical properties of the material and the spectral distribution of radiant intensity as function of temperature in reaching his conclusions.

5-2 THE SPECTRAL DISTRIBUTION OF RADIATION

The foregoing paragraphs have dealt with the total emissive power, integrated over all wavelengths from zero to infinity, of a black body of any temperature T or of a gray body of emissivity ϵ which was constant for all wavelengths. This paragraph deals with the law describing the emissive power as a function of both wavelength and temperature and with corollaries of that law and simplified forms of it which are useful in special cases.

The Planck Distribution Law. The spectral emissive power of a black body is given by the radiation law of Max Planck.[4] It describes the emission of thermal radiation within an interval $\Delta\lambda$ at wavelength λ from unit area of a black body, into a hemisphere as follows:

$$J_\lambda = \frac{c_1}{\lambda^5} \frac{1}{e^{c_2/\lambda T} - 1} \qquad (5\text{-}16)$$

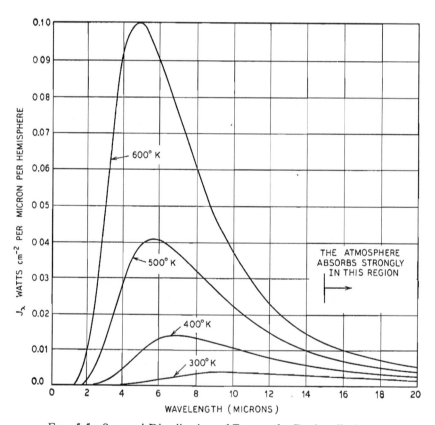

FIG. 5-5 Spectral Distribution of Energy for Perfect Emitters.

where J_λ = the emissive power of unit area in the wavelength interval $\Delta\lambda$
$c_1 = 3.732 \times 10^{-12}$ watt cm^2
$c_2 = 1.436$ cm deg
λ = wavelength in centimeters
T = absolute temperature (°K)

The spectral intensity is, as in earlier sections, J_λ/π. J_λ cannot have a finite value except as it applies to a finite $d\lambda$, for an infinitely narrow spectral band can contain no energy. In computing values of J_λ, λ is expressed in centimeters, and the results will be in the units: watts cm^{-2} per cm per hemisphere. The results may be plotted in any form convenient to the worker, and usually the micron ($\mu = 10^{-4}$ cm) is chosen both for λ and $d\lambda$, although frequently other units for $d\lambda$ may be more convenient as, watts cm^{-2} per 100 angstrom units.

For example, to compute J_λ at $2.892\mu = 2.892 \times 10^{-4}$ cm, for $T = 1000°K$, substitution in Eq. (5-16), using centimeters, produces the result

$$J_\lambda = 1.30 \times 10^4 \text{ watts cm}^{-2} \text{ per cm}$$
$$J_\lambda = 1.30 \text{ watts cm}^{-2} \text{ per micron}$$
$$J_\lambda = 0.013 \text{ watt cm}^{-2} \text{ per 100 A}$$

and so on.

Eq. (5-16) is awkward to use, and for that reason considerable effort has been given to the computation of tables of its values for a wide range of values of λT.[10,11,12] In addition, radiation slide rules sufficiently accurate for many purposes are available. (General Electric Company, Schenectady, N. Y., and A. G. Thornton, Ltd., Manchester, England.

Figure 5-5 shows four distribution curves for temperatures 300°K, 400°K, 500°K, and 600°K. It will be noted that the total area under a curve, which is proportional to the total emissive power, increases rapidly with increasing temperature. The total emissive power is the integral of J_λ over all wavelengths from zero to infinity, and its value is[13]

$$\int_0^\infty J_\lambda \, d\lambda = \int_0^\infty \frac{c_1}{\lambda^5} \frac{1}{e^{c_2/\lambda T} - 1} \, d\lambda = \frac{2\pi^5 k^4 T^4}{15 c^2 h^3} = \sigma T^4 \qquad (5\text{-}17)$$

[10] Frederick E. Fowle, *Smithsonian Physical Tables*, 8th Rev. Ed., Tables 310, 311, 312, Smithsonian Institution, Washington, D. C., 1934. Tables of J_λ for selected temperatures 23°K to 25000°K. Table for computing J_λ for any value of λT.

[11] A. N. Lowan and G. Blanch, "Tables of Planck's Radiation and Photon Functions," *J. Opt. Soc. Am.* **70**, 70-81 (1940). Tables of $J_\lambda/J_{\lambda\text{max}}$, $\frac{J_0 - \lambda}{J_0 - \infty}$, and similar tables for number of photons emitted for $\lambda T = 0.050$, to $\lambda T = 2.00$; equations for $J_{\lambda\text{max}}$, etc.

[12] L. L. Holladay, "Proportion of Energy Radiated by Incandescent Solids in Various Spectral Regions," *J. Opt. Soc. Am.* **17**, 329 (1928). Relative intensity $J_\lambda/J_{\lambda\text{max}}$ and proportion in region from ultraviolet to λT for values of λT 400 micron degrees to infinity.

[13] The method of integration is given, for example, in A. E. Ruark and H. C. Urey, *Atoms, Molecules and Quanta*, p. 59, McGraw-Hill Book Company, Inc., New York, 1930.

where k = the Boltzmann gas constant
c = the velocity of light
h = Planck's constant
σ = the Stefan-Boltzmann constant

The use of this equation has already been discussed. With reference to Fig. 5-5, and by anticipating the discussion of atmospheric transmission, it can be concluded that use of the Stefan-Boltzmann equation when treating with radiation which must pass through a real atmosphere inevitably leads to error because a considerable fraction of the energy is radiated at wavelengths longer than 14μ where the atmosphere absorbs strongly. For example, reference to the Tables of Lowan and Blanch[11] shows that for $T = 600°K$ and $\lambda = 14\mu = 14 \times 10^{-4}$ cm, i.e., $\lambda T = 0.84$ cm deg,

$$\int_0^{14\mu} J_\lambda\, d\lambda \Big/ \int_0^\infty J_\lambda\, d\lambda = 0.87$$

so that 13 percent of the total emissive power lies beyond 14μ. The fraction of the total appearing at longer wavelengths increases at lower temperatures, and, for the 300°K curve, 48 percent of the total area is included between 14μ and infinity.

The rise of each distribution curve is steeper on the short than on the long wavelength side of the maximum, and the fraction of the radiation between $\lambda = 0$ and $\lambda = \lambda_{max}$ is one-fourth of the total[14]; i.e.,

$$\int_0^{\lambda_{max}} J_\lambda\, d\lambda = \frac{1}{4} \int_0^\infty J_\lambda\, d\lambda = \frac{1}{4} \sigma T^4 \qquad (5\text{-}18)$$

The wavelength of maximum spectral intensity falls progressively at shorter wavelengths as the temperature rises, and the value of the intensity at the maximum increases sharply with temperature. The first of these phenomena is described by the *Wien displacement law*, which is obtained by setting the derivative of Eq. (5-16) with respect to wavelength equal to zero and solving.[15] The result is

$$\lambda_{max} T = \text{constant} = 2892 \text{ micron deg} \qquad (5\text{-}19)$$

where λ_{max} = wavelength in microns of maximum spectral emissive power

The value of J_λ at the maximum depends on the fifth power of the temperature, which can be shown by solving Eq. (5-16) for J_λ at $\lambda = \lambda_{max}$. The result[11] is

$$J_{\lambda_{max}} = 21.201 c_1 \left(\frac{T}{c_2}\right)^5 \qquad (5\text{-}20)$$

[14] Frank Benford, "Laws and Corollaries of the Black Body," *J. Opt. Soc. Am.* **29**, 92-96 (1939).
[15] See, for example, F. K. Richtmyer, *Introduction to Modern Physics*, p. 242, McGraw-Hill Book Company, Inc., New York, 1928.

5-2] THE SPECTRAL DISTRIBUTION OF RADIATION

The Rate of Change of J_λ with Temperature. It is often useful to know the rate of change of the spectral emissive power with temperature. For example, a practical problem of measuring or controlling the temperature of a surface at fairly high temperatures, say, 500°K, could involve a choice between systems which are equally sensitive for equal energies but which are sensitive in different spectral regions. Figure 5-5 shows that J_λ (500°K) has equal values at 3.5μ and 10.5μ. All other things being equal, in which of these spectral regions will the greatest change in J_λ occur for a small change in temperature?

Differentiating Eq. (5-16) with respect to T, we obtain

$$\frac{dJ_\lambda}{dT} = \frac{c_1 c_2}{\lambda^6 T^2} \frac{e^{c_2/\lambda T}}{(e^{c_2/\lambda T} - 1)^2} \tag{5-21}$$

This equation is tedious to compute, but a simplification of the work can be made by taking its ratio to J_λ, thereby obtaining multiplying factors which can be applied to the readily available tables of J_λ. The ratio of Eq. (5-21) to Eq. (5-16) is

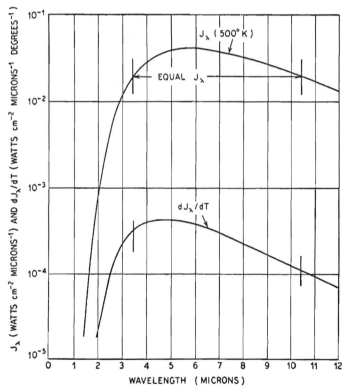

FIG. 5-6 J_λ and dJ_λ/dT for $T = 500°$K.

$$\frac{dJ_\lambda/dT}{J_\lambda} = \frac{c_2}{\lambda T^2} \frac{e^{c_2/\lambda T}}{(e^{c_2/\lambda T} - 1)} \tag{5-22}$$

If $e^{c_2/\lambda T}$ is large, the ratio $e^{c_2/\lambda T}/(e^{c_2/\lambda T} - 1)$ will be nearly unity. Specifically, an error of one percent or less will result from placing the ratio equal to unity if $\lambda T < 0.31$ cm deg, and an error of 10 percent or less will result if $\lambda T < 0.62$ cm deg. Thus, for a 500°K source, the approximation is valid within one percent for $\lambda < 6.2\mu$, and within 10 percent for λ between 12.4μ and 6.2μ. Or, for a 300°K source, the approximation is valid within one percent for all wavelengths less than 10μ.

Figure 5-6 shows J_λ for $T = 500°K$ and dJ_λ/dT plotted on a logarithmic scale. This figure shows that, in the case cited, the choice of a radiometer sensitive at 3.5μ would be the choice to make, for a change in temperature of 1°C would produce three times the change in J_λ at 3.5μ as at 10.5μ. Consideration of atmospheric attenuation, to be discussed in a later paragraph, would show that the 3.5μ region would be favorable to radiometry

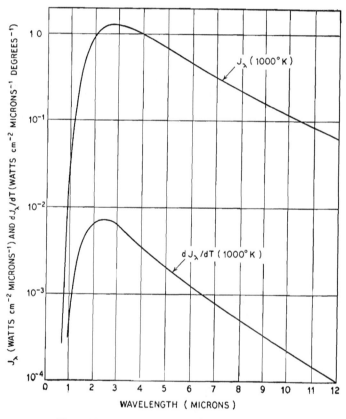

FIG. 5-7 J_λ and dJ_λ/dT for $T = 1000°K$.

at a distance; and, all other things being equal, the experimenter would, in this case, do well to choose a system sensitive at 3.5μ, for by so doing he would largely eliminate the problem of discrimination against the background at ordinary temperature for which the spectral emissive power at 3.5μ is weak.

Figure 5-7 shows J_λ and dJ_λ/dT for $T = 1000°K$, and inspection shows that, in this case also, a detector sensitive at shorter wavelengths should be chosen to provide maximum response for a given small change in temperature. This is because both the response of the detector, depending on J_λ, and the sensitivity to a small change in temperature of the source will be large at short wavelengths, in the region of the maximum of J_λ.

The Spectral Emissivity. The foregoing discussion of the spectral distribution related to black-body radiators. The spectral emissive power of objects which do not emit as black bodies is obtained by multiplying the appropriate distribution equation by the spectral emissivity, ϵ_λ. This quantity has been measured for relatively few materials, notably tungsten and other lamp filament materials, and at the relatively high temperatures which produce visible radiations. The values of total emissivity (Table 5-1) constitute a guide to the spectral emissivities when considered in conjunction with the spectral distribution of radiation for the temperatures quoted, for all of which the main emission is in the infrared. A further guide, and one which is adequate for many purposes, is the absorption spectrum of the material. In spectral regions where the material is transparent or of high reflectivity, the emissivity is low. If, however, the material is opaque and the opacity is due to absorption rather than to high reflectivity, the emissivity will be high.

5-3 SIMPLIFIED FORMS OF THE DISTRIBUTION LAW

Planck's distribution law, Eq. (5-16), applies for all values of λT. It is analytically difficult, and therefore approximate forms of it are often used for small and large values of λT.

The Wien Law. If λT is less than 0.3 cm deg, the denominator $e^{c_2/\lambda T} - 1$ takes the large value 119, and therefore an error of less than one percent results from writing the equation

$$J_\lambda = \frac{c_1}{\lambda^5} \frac{1}{e^{c_2/\lambda T}} \quad (5\text{-}23)$$

This is the Wien distribution equation which preceded the Planck law, historically. It applies in the visible spectrum ($\lambda < 0.7\mu$) for temperatures up to 4000°K and therefore is a convenient equation to use in optical pyrometry.

The Rayleigh-Jeans Equation. If λT is large, $c_2/\lambda T$ is small, and the denominator of Eq. (5-16) can be expanded and the equation written as

$$J_\lambda = \frac{c_1}{\lambda^5} \frac{1}{1 + (c_2/\lambda T - 1)} = \frac{c_1}{c_2} \frac{T}{\lambda^4} \qquad (5\text{-}24)$$

This is the Rayleigh-Jeans equation. It is valid within one percent for $\lambda T > 77$ cm deg. Thus, for a 1000°K source, it is valid for $\lambda > 0.077$ cm = 770μ, or for a 300°K source it is valid for $\lambda > 2.6$ mm.

The integral of Eq. (5-24) between wavelengths λ_1 and λ_2 is the total emissive power:

$$E = \int_{\lambda_1}^{\lambda_2} J_\lambda \, d\lambda = -\left. \frac{c_1 T}{3 c_2 \lambda^3} \right|_{\lambda_1}^{\lambda_2} \qquad (5\text{-}25)$$

where $\lambda_2 > \lambda_1$, and $\lambda_1 T > 77$ cm deg.

Equations (5-24) and (5-25) apply to problems in microwave radiometry. A reference to their use has been cited.[2]

5-4 DETECTORS OF THERMAL RADIATION

Two types of radiation detectors will be discussed: (a) thermal detectors, including thermocouples and bolometers which depend for their response on a small change in their temperature produced by absorbed incident radiation; and (b) photoconductive detectors which depend for their response on a change in electrical conductivity induced by absorbed incident quanta.

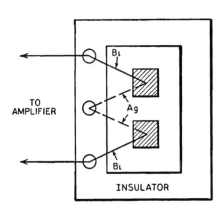

FIG. 5-8 A Simple Type of Thermocouple.

Thermocouples. A radiation thermocouple[16] consists of two extremely fine wires of two different materials having a large difference in thermoelectric power, spot-welded or otherwise joined together to form a thermoelectric junction. To this junction is attached a small receiver of thin metal foil, say, 1 mm square, to intercept the incoming radiation. The receiver is blackened by one of several methods to make it a good absorber.

The free ends of the thermoelectric wires are attached to relatively massive metallic posts set in an insulating supporting frame and then to a galvanometer or suitable low voltage amplifier.

[16] See, for details, F. A. Firestone, "Radiation Thermopile Design," *Rev. Sci. Inst.* **1**, 630 (1930).
John Strong, *Procedures in Experimental Physics*, Ch. VII (Prentice-Hall, Inc., New York, 1946).
D. F. Hornig and B. J. O'Keefe, "Design of Fast Thermopiles and the Ultimate Sensitivity of Thermal Detection," *Rev. Sci. Inst.* **18**, 474 (1947).

Figure 5-8 represents a form of construction which could be used in constructing a "compensated" thermocouple in which there are two junctions connected in opposition. An assembly such as that illustrated is enclosed in a glass or metal case fitted with a transparent window to admit the radiation. The radiation is focused by an optical system on one of the receivers while the other views only the adjacent background; therefore, no thermoelectric voltage appears unless one of them receives or loses more radiation than the other in accordance with equations already developed.

Whereas the response of a thermocouple exposed to a given field of radiation will be larger the greater the receiving area, simply because more radiation will be intercepted, the sensitivity, or the response in volts per watt of radiation received, varies inversely with the square root of the receiver area. If a receiver of large area is required for any purpose, an advantage is gained, within limits, by constructing a *thermopile* of several thermocouples, each with a small receiver, connected in series.

A number of thermoelectric materials are useful, the most common pairs being bismuth-silver, copper-constantan, and Hutchins alloys (97% Bi, 3% Sb; 95% Bi, 5% Sn). Special semiconducting materials are sometimes used.

The result of a slight warming of the receiving area of a thermocouple is the development of a small internal d-c voltage e. If the internal resistance of the thermocouple is r_t, and if it is connected to a galvanometer of resistance r_g, the galvanometer current, i_g, will be

$$i_g = \frac{e}{r_t + r_g} \tag{5-26}$$

It therefore is essential that the thermocouple resistance and the matching galvanometer or amplifier resistance be low. In practice, thermocouples are constructed with resistances of 5 to 10 ohms. Efforts to construct high-resistance thermocouples of semiconductors having large thermoelectric powers and which could be coupled direct to vacuum tubes have not met with success. Thermocouples made of semiconductors, mentioned earlier, employ a unique construction which results in low resistance, as by making the two "wires" relatively large with needle-shaped or chisel-shaped ends which are joined to a gold-foil receiver.

The warming ΔT of the thermocouple receiver by an absorbed flux of radiation depends on several factors. The smaller the heat capacity and the lower the rate of loss of absorbed energy, the larger is ΔT. In a steady-state condition

$$\Delta T = \frac{\Delta P}{\Lambda} \tag{5-27}$$

where ΔP = the net steady-state inflow of radiant power in watts
Λ = the rate of energy loss from the thermocouple in watts per degree

The *time constant* τ, or the time in seconds required for the detector to reach $\frac{e-1}{e} = 0.63$ of the ultimate steady-state response, is

$$\tau = \frac{C}{\Lambda} \tag{5-28}$$

where C is the heat capacity of the detector in joules per degree. Thus

$$\Delta T = \frac{\tau \Delta P}{C} \tag{5-29}$$

and large response is associated with long time constant and low heat capacity.

The loss of heat from the thermocouple is by conduction through the wires, by convection cooling, and by radiation. Thermal conduction can be reduced by minimizing the size of the wires and by making them long, but this also increases the electrical resistance, and a compromise must always be made. Radiation losses are minimized by blackening only one side of the metal foil receiver, leaving the opposite side a bright reflector. Convection losses can be eliminated by evacuating the thermocouple case

TABLE 5-2 CHARACTERISTICS OF MODERN THERMOCOUPLES

Name	Receiver Size (mm)	Resistance (ohms)	Time Constant (sec)	Sensitivity (volts/watt)
Epply:				
Unevacuated spectrum type	1.1 × 16	12	2	0.3
Unevacuated circular type	0.7 cm²	3	2	0.03
Farrand:				
Hornig type evacuated	0.75 × 0.75	6–10	0.03–0.04	7–10
Hilger-Watts:				
Schwartz type (semi-conductors)				
Unevacuated	1.0 × 10	150	0.03	2.3
Unevacuated	0.2 × 2	150	0.005	3.5
Evacuated	0.2 × 2	160	0.03	85.0
Reeder:				
Evacuated	0.2 × 2	—	—	6.0
Evacuated	0.6 × 4	10–15	0.07	4.0
Evacuated	1.0 × 10	4	0.10	2.0

with resulting increase in sensitivity of 10 to 40 times, but with corresponding increase in time constant.

These elementary considerations which barely touch on the problem of thermocouple design show clearly that, in any problem of radiometry, a design compromise has to be reached through consideration of the several factors of flux of radiation available, field of view required, and time allowable for the measurement.

Table 5-2 gives the characteristics of a few thermopiles, including certain ones deliberately made insensitive for special purposes where large fluxes of radiation are involved.

Bolometers. The bolometer was invented by S. P. Langley[17] at the Allegheny Observatory in 1881. He conceived the idea of using a thin blackened strip of platinum foil as a resistance in one arm of a Wheatstone bridge so that the small change in resistance resulting from the warming of the strip by incoming radiation could be measured. The unbalance of the bridge was measured with a high-sensitivity galvanometer, and, needless to say, the problem of maintaining constancy of ambient temperature to avoid drift was severe.

The roles of heat capacity and of conduction of heat away from the bolometer are the same as in the case of the thermocouple, and extremely thin metal strips are used. In modern practice the strips are formed by the evaporation of metals in vacuum[18, 19] or by rolling a *Wollaston wire* (platinum encased in a silver sheath) into a thin ribbon and subsequently dissolving the silver[20].

By either of these methods, bolometer strips only a few hundred angstrom units in thickness can be produced. An advantage of the rolled strip is that the temperature coefficient of resistance of the massive metal obtains, whereas evaporated films are of lower temperature coefficient of resistance than the massive metal.

The dimensions of a metal bolometer strip may be 1×10 mm or a few tenths of a millimeter wide by 1 or 2 mm long, and the resistance is usually a few ohms. The difficulties of d-c drift have largely been overcome through the development of electronic circuits which amplify the voltage pulses resulting from modulation of the incoming radiation or by scanning the bolometer across the object to be measured. The bolometers must be coupled to their amplifiers through special well-shielded low input-im-

[17] S. P. Langley, *Proc. Am. Acad. Arts and Sciences* **16**, 342 (1881).

[18] C. B. Aiken, W. H. Carter and F. S. Phillips, "The Production of Film Type Bolometers with Rapid Response," *Rev. Sci. Inst.* **17**, 377 (1946).

[19] B. H. Billings, W. L. Hyde and E. E. Barr, "An Investigation of the Properties of Evaporated Metal Bolometers," *J. Opt. Soc. Am.* **37**, 123 (1947), and "Construction and Characteristics of Evaporated Nickel Bolometers," *Rev. Sci. Inst.* **18**, 429 (1947).

[20] William G. Langton, "A Fast Sensitive Metal Bolometer," *J. Opt. Soc. Am.* **36**, 355A (1946).

pedance transformers which are now available. The sensitivity of metal strip bolometers is about 1 volt per watt. The limiting sensitivity will be discussed briefly later in the chapter.

Thermistor Bolometers. The thermistor bolometer, developed by the Bell Telephone Laboratories,[21] is a thin flake made by sintering certain mixtures of semiconducting oxides of relatively large, negative temperature coefficient of resistance. Two types of material are used: one, a mixture of oxides of nickel and manganese, having a resistivity of 2500 ohm cm at 25° C; and the other, a mixture of oxides of nickel, manganese, and cobalt, having a resistivity of 250 ohm cm at 25° C. The bolometer flakes are usually about 10μ thick and they may vary in lateral dimensions from 0.2 × 0.2 mm to 5 × 5 mm with resistance of 1 to 5 megohms, which permits them to be connected directly to vacuum tubes.

The flakes are usually cemented to a quartz or glass plate to provide a thermal sink to hasten the dissipation of absorbed energy and thereby decrease the time constant, as well as to provide strength, although they can be used completely suspended in air.

Table 5-3 presents selected average values of backed-thermistor characteristics as given by Wormser,[22] who has also described many other characteristics of these detectors in detail.

TABLE 5-3 CHARACTERISTICS OF THERMISTOR BOLOMETERS (AFTER WORMSER)

Length (mm)	Width (mm)	Area (mm²)	Resistance at 27°C (megohms)	Bias Voltage	Sensitivity (volts/watt)	Time Constant (millisec)	Equivalent Noise Input (watts)
Quartz-backed, 62.5-cps bandwidth							
5.55	2.54	14.1	0.48	242	4.10	4.56	1.0×10^{-8}
6.35	0.76	4.84	1.54	207	110.5	3.5	1.2×10^{-8}
1.0	1.0	1.00	2.07	184	284.0	4.8	5.2×10^{-9}
1.0	0.5	0.5	4.65	216	1070.0	4.5	2×10^{-9}
0.5	0.5	0.25	2.1	170	1105.0	1.9	1.4×10^{-9}
Glass-backed, 37.5-cps bandwidth							
5.55	2.25	12.5	0.60	145	35.5	5.8	1.6×10^{-8}
6.34	0.5	3.17	2.96	282	189	6.4	6.5×10^{-9}
0.82	1.42	1.16	0.11	31	85.5	6.2	3×10^{-9}
2.5	0.2	0.5	3.0	130	585	5.9	2.2×10^{-9}
1.0	0.2	0.2	1.25	54	750	6.3	1.2×10^{-9}

[21] W. H. Brattain and J. A. Becker, "Thermistor Bolometers," *J. Opt. Soc. Am.* **36**, 354A (1946).

[22] Eric M. Wormser, "Properties of Thermistor Infrared Detectors," *J. Opt. Soc. Am.* **43**, 15 (1953).

The Pneumatic, or Golay, Detector. The pneumatic detector,[23] commonly known as the Golay cell, is one of the most remarkable of sensitive elements, although it has proved more useful in laboratory than in field applications, mainly because it must be protected from shock and vibration.

Figure 5-9 illustrates the principle of the pneumatic detector in a simple way, but in a form which can be constructed and used as a demonstration device for large signals. A brass tube about 1 cm in diameter and 1 cm long is closed at one end by a polished plate of rocksalt or other material

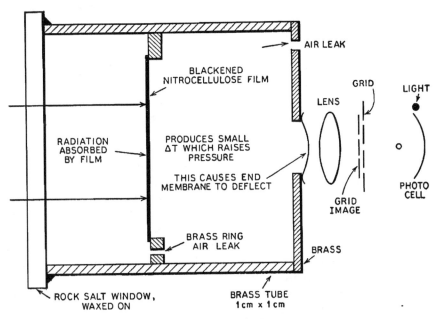

FIG. 5-9 Pneumatic Detector.

transparent to long wavelength radiation. Somewhere in the cell, near the middle, is placed a brass ring which supports a thin nitrocellulose film, blackened to make it an absorber of radiation. The film may be blackened by a layer of a metallic black that is evaporated on, as in blackening thermocouples or bolometers (see below); or, as in the actual case in the construction of pneumatic detectors, a semitransparent film of metal, say, aluminum, is evaporated on in such a thickness that its resistance is 189 ohms per square. (The term "per square" relates to a square of any dimension.) At infrared wavelengths, such a film absorbs 50 percent of

---

[23] M. E. J. Golay, "Theoretical Considerations in Heat and Infrared Detection, with Particular Reference to the Pneumatic Detector," *Rev. Sci. Inst.* **18**, 347 (1947); "A Pneumatic Infra-Red Detector," *Ibid.*, **18**, 357 (1947); "A New Receiver of Radiant Energy," Hammond Vinton Hayes. *Rev. Sci. Inst.* **7**, 202 (1936).

the incident radiation, reflects 25 percent, transmits 25 percent, and is reasonably neutral over a wide band of wavelengths. Its transmission varies between 15 percent and 30 percent over the interval 2μ to 15μ.

The back of the cell is closed by a brass plate with a small aperture, about 5 mm in diameter, covered with an extremely thin nitrocellulose film. The back plate also contains a small air leak to the outside.

The action of the cell is as follows: An incoming pulse of radiant energy $\Delta P \times \Delta T$ (joules) is absorbed by the blackened film within the cell, and the absorbed energy is dissipated in warming the air within the cell, thereby producing a small increase in pressure. The increase in pressure causes the terminal membrane to deflect, and it is by measurement of this mechanical deflection that the intensity of the incident radiation is determined.

An air leak from the cell to the outside allows equilibrium to be restored, returning the terminal membrane to its rest position and allowing a second pulse of radiation to be measured. The time constant and, therefore, the sensitivity depend on this air leak: if it is large, the system will restore itself quickly and pulses of energy in rapid repetition can be measured. If it is small, a longer time interval between pulses of energy must be allowed, but the magnitude of each pulse, to provide a given deflection of the terminal membrane, will be correspondingly smaller.

The air leak in a demonstration model ought to be quite small. A satisfactory method of making it is to drill a No. 50 hole, fill the hole with soft wax, and perforate the wax as required with a thin needle.

The deflection of the terminal membrane can be observed in three ways. If a demonstration model such as that illustrated is held so that window light or a room light is reflected from the flat membrane, the eye will readily detect the deflection of the membrane when the cell receives a strong signal, as by passing a cigarette rapidly before it.

In an early application of the cell,[24] the deflection of the membrane was observed by placing an optical flat in close juxtaposition to it and observing the appearance of Newton's interference fringes under mercury green line illumination when the membrane was distended. A movement of the membrane of one wavelength of green light, or 5000 angstrom units, was observable.

In the most refined form of the cell as it is currently manufactured,* the terminal membrane is coated with a reflecting film of evaporated antimony to make it a mirror surface. A grid of parallel bars, like a picket fence, is placed in a position to the right of the membrane in Fig. 5-9 and illuminated by a small tungsten light. A lens between the grid and the

[24] Harold A. Zahl and Marcel J. E. Golay, "Pneumatic Heat Detector," *Rev. Sci. Inst.* **17**, 511 (1946).

* Eppley Laboratories, Newport, Rhode Island.

membrane forms an image of the grid back on itself after reflection of the light by the membrane. The image is so adjusted that images of the bars fall on top of the spaces between bars when the membrane is flat, and no light reaches the photocell shown in Fig. 5-9. If, however, the membrane is distended ever so slightly, the image is deflected and transparent spaces of the grid are imaged back on themselves so that light passes back through the grid to the photocell, the response of which is measured by conventional means.

This method of measuring a small displacement was first used by Hardy[25] in a unique system for amplifying galvanometer deflections. As applied to the Golay cell, it is capable in theory and by extrapolation of experimental results of measuring a displacement of the membrane of about one angstrom unit, although the physical meaning of so small a displacement is vague, to say the least.

The pneumatic detector is a fascinating study because of the several basic processes from the interaction of radiation and matter to sheer mechanical effects involved and because it represents a remarkable innovation in thermal detectors. The ultimate sensitivity of the device proves to be about the same as those of the thermocouple and the bolometer, which depend on quite different physical phenomena. A unique property of the detector is that sensitivity does not fall off with increasing area and, therefore, it can be made large enough for use at very long wavelengths in the millimeter region.

Limits of Detection. The smallest flux of radiant energy that can be detected depends not only on the sensitivity of the detecting device but also on the noise level inherent in the device. The latter may arise from vacuum tube noise in the amplifier, or from thermal noise in the detector, or, ultimately, from random fluctuations in the emission of radiation by a souce at constant temperature. In general, the longer the time allowed for a measurement (which is to say, the longer the time constant of the detector and the narrower the bandpass of the associated amplifier), the smaller is the quantity of radiant energy detectable. Experience has shown that estimates of the minimum detectable energy of a system ought to be made with considerable conservatism, for only occasionally do completed systems perform as estimated beforehand.

A guide to ultimate sensitivity is the *Havens limit*, which was formulated by R. J. Havens[26] on the basis of extensive study of materials useful in thermocouple and bolometer construction and of the performance of infrared detectors. It applies for detectors at room temperature used in

---

[25] James Daniel Hardy, "A Theoretical and Experimental Study of the Resonance Radiometer," *Rev. Sci. Inst.* **1**, 429 (1930).

[26] R. J. Havens, "Theoretical Comparison of Heat Detectors," *J. Opt. Sci. Am.* **36**, 355A (1946).

systems which take full advantage of the time constant of the detector. The Havens limit is written

$$\Delta P_{min} = 3 \times 10^{-12} \frac{A^{1/2}}{\tau} \qquad (5\text{-}30)$$

where ΔP_{min} = minimum detectable change in radiant power (watts)
A = area of the detector in square millimeters
τ = time constant in seconds

It is of interest that all practical detectors—whether they be low-resistance metal-strip bolometers, high-resistance thermistor bolometers, thermocouples, or pneumatic cells—possess approximately equal ultimate limits of detection of radiation which are well above the Havens limit, except for an occasional detector where all factors of construction seem to have been favorable in a way not generally reproducible in quantity. Jones[27] has collected response data on many detectors and has commented that ". . . no bolometer or thermocouple known to the writer which operates at room temperature has better performance than is indicated by the Havens estimate, although several detectors have approached it within a factor of two. . . ." Thus, an excellent thermocouple, evacuated, and of area 1 mm^2 and time constant about 1 sec may permit the detection, in practice, of about 5×10^{-11} watt, whereas the Havens limit would predict 3×10^{-12} watt; either metal or thermistor bolometers of shorter time constant, say, 5 millisec, and area about 1 mm^2 may permit the detection of 5×10^{-9} watt to 10^{-8} watt.

It is to be emphasized that there is no "best" thermal detector. Each of the types mentioned has features which point to its use in some problems and exclude its use in other problems. The radiation thermocouple is perhaps the most reliable and easily handled of them all and it remains in widespread use in problems where relatively long measuring times can be used.

Blackening of Thermal Detectors. Since absorbed radiation of any wavelength will produce a temperature rise, blackened thermal detectors are useful throughout the spectrum. However, some care must be exercised to assure that a bolometer or thermocouple is truly black at all wavelengths. Visual inspection is a poor guide.

Perhaps the earliest and most obvious method of blackening receivers was to coat them with candle soot or camphor soot, a method which did not require touching the delicate devices. However, soot, although an excellent absorber of visible and ultraviolet radiation, may be quite transparent in the infrared. When measurements could only be made with high sensitivity galvanometers whose time constants were several seconds,

---

[27] R. Clark Jones, "Factors of Merit for Radiation Detectors," *J. Opt. Soc. Am.* **39**, 344 (1949).

the time constant of the sensitive element itself was of little consequence, and blackness could be assured by applying fairly thick layers of carbon black or bone black in an organic vehicle such as shellac which itself absorbs strongly in the long infrared.

The introduction by Pfund[28] of the method of depositing black metallic powders, as of zinc or gold, by evaporation of the metal at a pressure of a few millimeters, permitted blackening of receivers without touching them. In thick layers, such metallic blacks are extremely effective throughout the spectrum. However, efforts to reduce time constant in order to achieve electronic amplification of modulated thermocouple or bolometer voltages led to the use of quite thin layers of gold black which may be completely absorbing at short wavelengths and highly transparent at long wave-

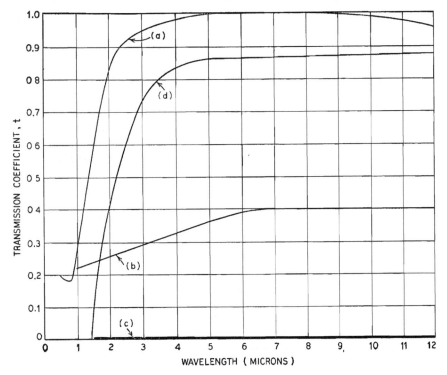

FIG. 5-10 Transmission of Metallic Powder Film:
(a) Gold, Surface Density 56×10^{-6}, gm/cm^2, Evaporated;
(b) Gold, Same Thickness, Evaporated;
(c) Heavy Film of Efficient Gold or Zinc Black;
(d) Tellurium Black.

[28] A. H. Pfund, "Bismuth Black and Its Applications," *Rev. Sci. Inst.* **1**, 397 (1930); "The Optical Properties of Metallic and Crystalline Powders," *J. Opt. Soc. Am.* **23**, 375 (1933).

lengths. The problem has been extensively investigated by Harris et al.[29], who found that gold black, to be uniformly absorbing, should be evaporated at a pressure of about 1 mm Hg in nitrogen which is free of oxygen.

Several transmission curves of metallic blacks, taken from various sources, are shown in Fig. 5-10. It is evident from inspection of these curves that a metallic black under some conditions may be a poor absorber in the infrared. The curve for tellurium powder, a semiconductor, is introduced to emphasize the danger of judging blackness by appearance. This curve was obtained for a thick, evaporated powder film which was remarkably black by visual inspection and yet quite transparent in the infrared.

Thermistor materials are themselves absorbers in the infrared, but the thin flakes used are semitransparent and are usually blackened with a thin film of black lacquer. Even after this treatment, they remain selectively sensitive in the infrared. The absorption coefficient may vary between 1.0 and about 0.90 in the 5-to-15-micron region.

The metallic absorbing film of the pneumatic detector does not possess uniform absorption coefficient throughout the spectrum.

Therefore, if absolute measurements are to be made, the chosen detector should be checked for uniformity of spectral response against a thermocouple of the older, thickly blackened type in order to assure that its absorption coefficient is reasonably constant throughout the spectrum.

Photoconductive Cells. In recent years rapid advances in the theory of photoconductivity and in the technology of constructing practical radiation detectors based on this phenomenon have greatly improved the facility with which measurements can be made in the region 1 to 5 microns. The materials of greatest current usefulness are lead sulfide and lead telluride; the development of lead selenide is progressing rapidly. Simpson and Sutherland[30] and Smith[31] have given recent comprehensive reviews of the subject, and these papers are recommended for the study of details and for the many references cited.

The photoconducting layers are prepared chemically or by evaporation in vacuum in thicknesses of 0.1 to 1 micron. Infrared sensitization is accomplished by introducing oxygen into the layer. Lead sulfide cells are commercially available in the form of layers which operate fully exposed to air, as well as in the more conventional form of layers deposited on the inside wall of an evacuated glass cell. Lead telluride and lead selenide cells are usually in the form of a *Dewar flask* which can be filled with liquid nitrogen, the sensitive layer being on the wall of the nitrogen

---

[29] Louis Harris, Rosemarie McGinnies, and Benjamin M. Siegel, "The Preparation and Optical Properties of Gold Blacks," *J. Opt. Soc. Am.* **38**, 582 (1948).

[30] O. Simpson and G. B. B. M. Sutherland, "Photoconductive Cells for Detection of Infrared Radiation," *Science* **115**, 1-4 (1952).

[31] R. A. Smith, "Infrared Photoconductors," *Phil. Mag. Supplement* **2**, 321-369 (1953).

reservoir to allow effective cooling. A window of sapphire or other transparent material such as magnesium oxide may be placed in the outer wall of the cell to admit longer wavelength radiation. The sensitivity of these cells is poor unless they are cooled. Lead sulfide operates satisfactorily at room temperature, but both the sensitivity and the long wavelength limit of sensitivity are increased by cooling the cell either with dry ice or liquid nitrogen. However, cooling the cell increases the time constant. The time constants of all of these materials are, nevertheless, much smaller than those of thermal detectors. These are listed by Simpson and Sutherland as follows: Pbs, 4 to 10×10^{-5} sec at 20°C; 2 to 7×10^{-4} sec at -190°C; PbTe, 1 to 5×10^{-4} sec at -190°C; PbSe, 3 to 10×10^{-5} sec at -190°C.

Each of the materials is sensitive throughout the visible spectrum as well as in the infrared. PbS cells are useful to about 3 microns uncooled and to about 3.75 microns when cooled to 90°K. Lead telluride is useful to 5.5 microns. Lead selenide, although still an experimental material, is sensitive to wavelengths as long as 8 microns when cooled to 90°K, and to about 6 microns at 290°K.[31]

Minimum Detectable Signal. The limiting sensitivity of photoconductors has been discussed on theoretical grounds by Jones[27], Felgett[32], and Moss[33]. Typical results have been summarized by Smith[31] for monochromatic radiation in the region of maximum spectral response for each of the cells, and for amplifier bandwidth of 1 cps, i.e., for approximately 1 sec measuring time. For lead sulfide, a minimum detectable energy of about 10^{-12} watt is possible. For lead telluride, 10^{-12} to 10^{-13} watt may be detectable. The minimum detectable energy for lead selenide cells appears to be about equal to that of good thermal detectors at the present time.

Choice of a Photoconductive Cell. It does not follow that the cell which is sensitive over the widest wavelength range is the best to be chosen for a given application, or even that the most sensitive cell is the best choice. The engineering implications of cooling a cell, for example, add considerably to the complexity of its use. Availability must also be considered in all applications except pure research, where a single good cell, if it can be obtained, may open up to the spectroscopist a wide avenue of investigation in which, for the first time, the full optical capabilities of his spectrometers may be realized.

Figure 5-11 shows three typical spectral response curves for photoconductive cells. That for PbS at 293°K is for an Eastman Kodak cell;[34]

[31] R. A. Smith, "Infrared Photoconductors," *Phil. Mag. Supplement* **2**, 321-369 (1953).

[32] P. B. Felgett, "On the Ultimate Sensitivity and Practical Performance of Radiation Detectors," *J. Opt. Soc. Am.* **39**, 970 (1949).

[33] T. S. Moss, "The Ultimate Limits of Sensitivity of Lead Sulfide and Telluride Photo-Conductive Detectors," *J. Opt. Soc. Am.* **40**, 603 (1950).

[34] *Information Bulletin on Ektron Detectors*, Eastman Kodak Co., 1953.

that for PbS at 90°K is for a British Thompson Houston Company cell;[33] and that for PbTe is for a British experimental cell.[33] It should be emphasized that the curves of Fig. 5-11 have no relationship to the absolute sensitivities of the several cells, for the curves are relative, with peak sensitivity arbitrarily set at unity. They will be used in examples to be given later which illustrate the computation of cell response to radiation from objects at various temperatures.

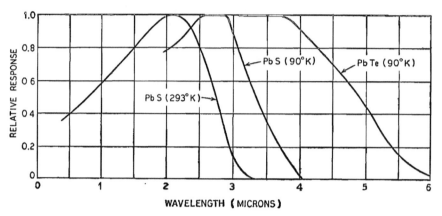

Fig. 5-11 Relative Spectral Response Curves of PbS and PbTe Photoconductive Cells.

5-5 ATMOSPHERIC TRANSMISSION

Investigations of the transmission of the atmosphere followed relatively rapidly the discovery of the infrared spectrum by Sir William Herschel in 1800. His son, Sir John Herschel, published results in 1840 showing broad bands of absorption by the atmosphere in the infrared, and J. W. Draper, using phosphors as detectors, also observed atmospheric absorption in the solar spectrum in 1842. A brief review of the discovery of the infrared spectrum and subsequent developments has been given by Langley,[35] who made the first great strides in understanding it more than 70 years ago by mapping the absorption bands to 5 microns.

The Attenuating Processes. The attenuation of radiation in the optical spectrum by the earth's atmosphere is due to three processes: (a) absorption by molecular constituents of the atmosphere; (b) scattering by haze particles and fog or cloud particles; and (c) scattering by air molecules.

Atmospheric Absorption by Gases. Absorption by O_2 and N_2 molecules and ozone, O_3, when it is present, occurs in the ultraviolet at wavelengths shorter than 0.3μ. Throughout the region, 0.3μ to 0.7μ, scattering by air

[35] S. P. Langley, *Annals of the Astrophysical Observatory*, Vol. 1, Smithsonian Institution, Washington, D. C., 1900.

molecules and haze is the main attenuating process, although weak water vapor and oxygen absorption bands appear in the red end of the visible spectrum. In the infrared, water vapor and carbon dioxide are the principal absorbers. Ozone absorption appears only in the spectrum of the sun when the radiation has traversed the layer of ozone at high altitude, in the neighborhood of 15 to 20 miles, in the earth's atmosphere.

The infrared absorption bands of a molecule occur at discrete wavelengths corresponding to resonant frequencies of the molecule. As in the case of two weights joined by a spring, the resonant frequencies of a molecule depend on the masses of the atoms and the binding force between them. It happens that these frequencies lie in the infrared, mainly between about 2μ and 15μ, and the infrared absorption spectrum of a molecule is of great usefulness in analysis of its structure. It is not sufficient that a molecule possess a natural frequency of vibration in order that it absorb radiation. The vibration must produce an oscillation of electric charge in the molecule, or a change in dipole moment, in order for the vibration to produce absorption. Thus, molecules such as O_2 and N_2 do not show absorption bands in the infrared because the complete symmetry of their vibrations can produce no change in the dipole moment. A diatomic molecule like HCl, for example, produces strong infrared absorption at its natural frequency and at overtones of it. The reason is that the hydrogen, being of much lower mass, makes relatively large excursions while the chlorine atom makes relatively small excursions, and change in the dipole moment accompanies the mechanical vibration of the molecule. In like manner, the triatomic molecules, H_2O, CO_2, and O_3, vibrate in a way to produce a change in dipole moment and accompanying infrared absorption. In general, a polyatomic molecule can execute $(3n - 6)$ vibrations, where n is the number of atoms, except for linear molecules, where the number of vibrations is $(3n - 5)$. It will be apparent that not all of these vibrations produce infrared absorption. For example, it is known that CO_2 is a linear molecule which is arranged O—C—O. Obviously, the vibration in which the carbon remains motionless while the two oxygen atoms vibrate in phase, both moving toward and away from the carbon together, would be inactive in the infrared. In contrast, if one oxygen moves toward the carbon while the other is moving away from it, or if a bending vibration occurs, the oxygens moving in one direction perpendicular to the axis of the molecule while the carbon moves in the opposite direction, infrared absorption would occur.

Distinction from Absorption by Liquids. The foregoing remarks apply to absorption by gases, including water vapor. Since water often exists both as vapor and as liquid, it should be pointed out that the infrared absorption by liquid water is quite different than the absorption by water vapor. A centimeter thickness of liquid water is completely opaque at wavelengths longer than about 2μ in the infrared and, indeed, the absorption of liquid water can be investigated at longer wavelengths only by the use of capillary layers squeezed between plates of some insoluble transparent material. However, water vapor equivalent to a column of liquid 1 cm² in cross section and several centimeters long remains relatively transparent in the windows between absorption bands in the infrared. The length of the column of liquid water which would be produced if all the water vapor in a column 1 cm² in cross section were condensed to the liquid form is known as the "precipitable water vapor." For example, a 2000-yard path of atmosphere at 80°F, relative humidity 100 percent, contains 4.7 cm of precipitable water.

Liquid water in the form of large fog particles attenuates radiation mainly by scattering of radiation out of the beam. Particles which are extremely large with respect to the wavelength, such as raindrops or snowflakes, absorb as well as scatter the incident radiation, but because of the extreme opacity of water in the infrared, each particle takes out of the beam all of the radiation that falls on it, either by scattering it out or by absorbing it. Therefore, the cross-sectional area of the particles and the

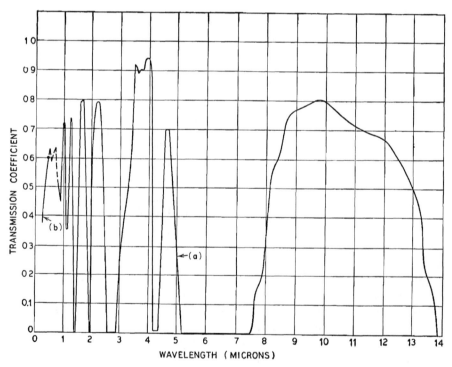

Fig. 5-12a Transmission Spectra of the Atmosphere.

number of them per cubic centimeter determine their attenuation coefficient, and absorption and scattering need not be treated separately in this case.

Scattering will be discussed in greater detail later in this chapter.

Map of the Atmospheric Absorption Bands. Figure 5-12 was constructed using data from a number of sources to show the positions of the major bands between 0.3μ in the ultraviolet and 14μ in the infrared and to illustrate the effect of amount of water vapor on the several bands. The curve (a) shown in Figure 5-12a was adapted from a recent and renowned work by Gebbie and others.[36] It shows the transmission spectrum of a 2000-yard path containing a total of 17 mm of precipitable water and atmospheric haze of such a concentration that the transmission of red light of wavelength 0.61μ was 60 percent, as shown by a large dot at that wavelength. Curve (b) in Figure 5-12a is a visible and near ultraviolet curve constructed from

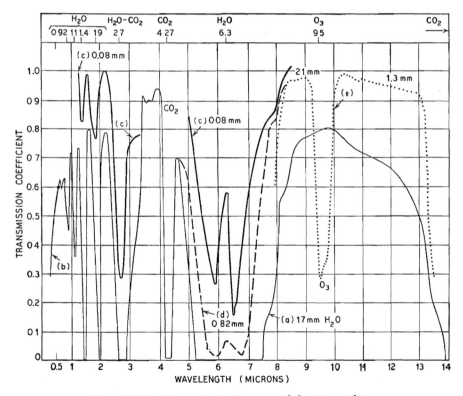

Fig. 5-12b Transmission Spectra of the Atmosphere.

[36] H. A. Gebbie, W. R. Harding, C. Hilsum, A. W. Pryce, and V. Roberts, "Atmospheric Transmission in the 1 to 14μ Region," *Proc. Roy. Soc.* A, **206** (1951).

data of Curcio and others[37] to match the 0.60μ point of Gebbie. The dotted portion connecting curves (a) and (b) is without significance except to indicate the presence of a weak water vapor band at 0.76μ. Curve (c) in Fig. 5-12b in two sections was taken from the classical work of Fowle.[38] It refers to 0.08 mm precipitable water and no haze. Curve (d), from the same source, illustrates the effect of increasing water vapor in the great 6μ band. It was not reproduced throughout the spectrum to avoid crowding.

Curve (e), in Figure 5-12b, was constructed from data of Adel and Lampland.[39] It represents the transmission of the entire atmosphere, with the sun as source, and it illustrates the great ozone absorption band at 9.5μ as well as the relatively weak absorption of small amounts of water in the 10μ window.

Beginning at the ultraviolet end of Fig. 5-12a and following curves (b) and (a) through, we can see that the transmission coefficient increases steadily toward longer wavelengths in the visible spectrum and that this increase continues in the infrared in the "windows" between the absorption bands until the window between 3μ and 4μ is reached. Water vapor absorption is considered to be weak in the near infrared windows, and increasing transparency with wavelength illustrates decreasing attenuation by haze at longer wavelengths in this region. The state of haze for which these curves apply may be defined through the transmission coefficient for visible light of wavelength 0.55μ. The transmission coefficient of 0.59 shown corresponds to a visible detection range of a large dark object against the horizon of about 8 nautical miles. Although such a day is quite hazy, it definitely is not foggy. Fog particles are large with respect to the wavelength throughout the spectral range shown, and the attenuation which they produce is approximately the same at all wavelengths. No increase in the transparency of fog occurs in the infrared.

Attenuation by Scattering. The reader is referred to Middleton[1] and Kuiper[40] for detailed discussion of scattering theory. It has been noted that Fig. 5-12b shows lower attenuation by aerial haze with increasing wavelength. Figure 5-13, plotted from selected data of Table 1 in Gebbie,[36] shows the effect in greater detail. Each curve describes the transmission of a 2000-yard path in several window regions for a given state of haze specified by the transmission of red light of wavelength 0.61μ and for equal

---

[37] J. A. Curcio, L. F. Drummeter, Jr., C. C. Petty, H. S. Stewart, and C. P. Butler, "An Experimental Study of Atmospheric Transmission," *J. Opt. Soc. Am.* **43**, Fig. 6, 100 (1953).

[38] F. E. Fowle, "Water Vapor Transparency to Low-Temperature Radiation," *Smithsonian Misc. Collections*, p. 23, Vol. 68, No. 8, Publication 2484, Smithsonian Institution, Washington, D. C., 1917.

[39] Arthur Adel and C. O. Lampland, "Atmospheric Absorption of Infrared Solar Radiation at the Lowell Observatory," *Astrophysical Jour.* **91**, 481 (1940).

[40] Gerard P. Kuiper, ed., *The Atmospheres of the Earth and Planets*, Ch. III, Rev. Ed., University of Chicago Press, Chicago, 1952.

water vapor, 17 mm, in all cases. The visible range for which each curve applies has been noted, but this was done by extrapolating each curve to obtain a value of transmission coefficient at 0.55μ, and computing the visibility from that value. The visible ranges noted do not, therefore, represent observations of Gebbie *et al.*; they may be inexact and they are recorded only to assist in visualizing the haziness of the several atmospheres.

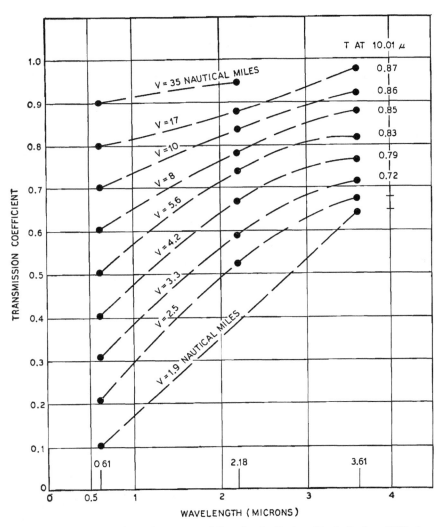

Fig. 5-13 Transmission of 2000 yd of Haze in the Red and in the Infrared Windows at 2.18μ and 3.61μ. The State of Haziness Is Specified by the Transmission at 0.61μ and Also by Visual Detection Ranges V Noted on the Curves.

The connecting lines between the several plotted points serve mainly to identify corresponding points, but probably do represent reasonably well the march of haze attenuation over the spectral range covered by them. It will be noted that the transmission coefficients for 10.01μ, from the same source of data, are slightly lower than those for the 3.61μ window. This does not indicate a lower transmission of haze in the 10μ window than in the 3.6μ window, but, rather, a stronger water vapor absorption at 10μ than at 3.6μ

Fog and Clouds. The particles of water which make up fog and clouds are distributed between 5μ to 100μ in diameter, and there are always many particles which are large with respect to the wavelength throughout the useful infrared spectrum. The attenuation coefficient of fog is, on this account, approximately constant throughout the visible and infrared regions of the spectrum to 15μ.[41] At extremely long wavelengths, fog would transmit radiation, but the absorption of water vapor becomes stronger with increasing wavelength and absorbs strongly even at 200μ to 300μ. In the microwave region water vapor becomes relatively transparent, and fog particles produce no serious attenuation because of their small size with respect to the wavelength.

Computation of Atmospheric Attenuation. The attenuation by haze obeys Beer's exponential law

$$I_\lambda = I_{0\lambda} e^{-\alpha_\lambda X} \quad (5\text{-}31)$$

where $I_{0\lambda}$ = incident intensity of radiation at wavelength λ
I_λ = intensity transmitted at wavelength λ
α_λ = the attenuation coefficient due to scattering by the haze
X = length of the optical path

The transmission t is obviously I/I_0. The distance X may be in any convenient unit. If X is expressed in kilometers, for example, then α has the dimension km^{-1}. α depends on the size and the size distribution of the particles, on their index of refraction, and on the number of particles per cubic centimeter. These quantities are never known in practice, and the value of α or of I/I_0 at some chosen wavelength (as 0.61μ in Fig. 5-13) is ordinarily used to describe the haze. In many cases the visual range V, in nautical miles, is used to describe the haze through the relation

$$V = 3.92/\alpha \quad (5\text{-}32)$$

Thus, if the distance at which a large dark object can just be distinguished against the horizon is observed to be 10 miles, then $\alpha = 0.39$ mile^{-1}, for visible light. The transmission curve (b) of Fig. 5-12a shows that t_λ and therefore α_λ vary considerably between the blue and red ends of the spec-

[41] J. A. Sanderson, "Transmission of Infra-Red Light by Fog," *J. Opt. Soc. Am.* **30**, 405 (1940).

trum. Furthermore, it is known that α_λ may vary markedly from day to day even when the visual range remains essentially constant.[37] This means only that the particle sizes of hazes differ considerably from place to place, and even from day to day and that one cannot specify a haze completely either by a visibility measurement or a transmission measurement at a single wavelength.

However, the measurement of the complete spectral attenuation curve of a haze is difficult and infrequently attempted. Perforce, one must estimate or measure α or α_λ at a chosen wavelength and then proceed to apply the data of Fig. 5-13 to the estimation of α_λ over a wider band of the spectrum.

In dealing with thick fog, the value of α determined in the visible may be applied throughout the spectrum.

Computation of water vapor transmission presents its own complication, for although the amount of water vapor can be estimated from a measurement of relative humidity, water vapor absorption does not follow in every instance Beer's law. Equation (5-31) only applies if α_λ remains nearly constant over the spectral interval under consideration. If it changes rapidly with wavelength, then the computations must be made in detail at such close intervals in wavelength that the labor becomes prodigious, even when adequate values of α_λ are available.

The absorption bands of molecules contain a feature not disclosed in Fig. 5-12 and not mentioned in the earlier discussion, namely, closely spaced absorption lines produced by rotational frequencies of the molecule. These rotational lines appear only when the bands are examined with a spectrometer of extremely high resolving power, and the bands illustrated in Fig. 5-12 are therefore only the envelopes of the combined rotation-vibration bands. α_λ changes rapidly in the rotation lines.

The large mass of calculations required if individual α's are used is reduced by employing a relation which describes the integrated absorption over a wide spectral interval. Such a relation and one of great usefulness has recently been proposed and tested against many experimental data by Elder and Strong.[42] They divided the spectrum into eight window regions as shown in Table 5-4.

These regions extend from center to center of the successive absorption bands shown in Fig. 5-12. Strong and Elder took note of the fact that, as the amount of precipitable water vapor w in the path increases, the additional absorption produced by an additional small amount of water dw becomes less, and they tried an empirical equation

$$dI = -I_0 K_1 \, dw/w \qquad (5-33)$$

---

[42] Tait Elder and John Strong, "The Infrared Transmission of Atmospheric Windows," *Jour. Franklin Inst.* **255**, 189 (1953).

164 EMISSION, TRANSMISSION, AND DETECTION OF THE INFRARED

to take this into account. Integration leads to

$$t = I/I_0 = -K_1 \log w + t_0 \tag{5-34}$$

where K_1 and t_0 are constants for a particular region. The values of K_1 and t_0 are given in Table 5-4, and with them Eq. (5-34) can be quickly

TABLE 5-4 WINDOW REGIONS IN THE INFRARED
(AFTER ELDER AND STRONG)

	Window Wavelengths (μ)	K_1	t_0
I	0.72–0.92	15.1	106.3
II	0.92–1.1	16.5	106.3
III	1.1–1.4	17.1	96.3
IV	1.4–1.9	13.1	81.0
V	1.9–2.7	13.1	72.5
VI	2.7–4.3	12.5	72.3
VII	4.3–5.9	21.2	51.2
VIII	5.9–14	—	—

evaluated and plotted on semilog paper, as in Fig. 5-14, to form working curves for reading off the window transmission in any of the regions. It is to be noted that K_1 and t_0 were derived from experimental data from many sources for amounts of water up to 200 mm; therefore Eq. (5-34) is an experimental or empirical equation with a strong basis for validity. Although the simple form of the equation invites extrapolation to larger

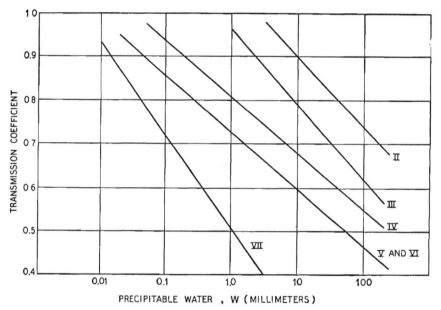

FIG. 5-14 Plot of $t = -k \log w + t_0$, for Several Window Regions.

amounts of water, it cannot be said with certainty that extrapolation is justified.

Region VIII was not treated. Also, Eq. (5-34) does not account for the transmission of haze; it applies only for haze-free atmospheres. But the transmission of haze can be estimated separately and applied as a multiplying factor. If we choose region V, 1.9μ to 2.7μ, for example, Fig. 5-14 shows that the transmission of 10 mm of haze free water vapor is $t_w = 0.60$. Suppose the optical path to be 2000 yards and the day quite hazy, $V = 2.5$ nautical miles. From Fig. 5-13 it is learned that the haze transmission t_h varies from 0.47 at 1.9μ to 0.59 at 2.7μ, and that the average of these is 0.53, which is also approximately the value 0.54 of t_h at the center of the window of region V. Therefore it can be guessed that the haze transmission at the center of the window is valid and can be applied, and the overall transmission of the window is, approximately

$$t = t_w \times t_h = 0.3$$

Since transmission by haze decreases exponentially whereas the window transmission does not, state of haze rather than water vapor may play the larger role in determining the transmission of long paths. In the foregoing example, which applied to fairly thick haze, if the distance is increased to 10 miles containing 100 mm of water vapor, from Fig. 5-14 it is found that t_w decreases only to 0.47, while the haze transmission would decrease to $(0.54)^{10}$, or 0.002.

Yates[43] has prepared a set of tables and curves from which the total transmission of the atmosphere can be obtained for path lengths 100 to 20,000 yards, for water vapor concentrations ranging from 4.6 mm to 18 mm per 1000 yards of path, and for states of haze ranging from 100 percent to 50 percent transmission by a 2000-yard path at wavelength 0.61μ. By total transmission is meant the integrated transmission over the spectral interval 0.7μ to 12μ for radiation from a source of specified temperature, which defines the spectral distribution of energy. The tables and curves present data for sources at temperatures 373°K to 6000°K. The wavelength interval 0.7μ to 12μ is subdivided into 12 smaller intervals which do not coincide with those of Strong and Elder but which serve the same purpose of permitting the treatment of selected narrow bands of the spectrum at will. The greatest usefulness of the results is, however, in obtaining integrated total transmission. Yates employed the data of Gebbie[36] to establish the attenuation by haze and of Howard[44] for water vapor for amounts of water 0.02 to 2.0 mm. Elder and Strong have

---

[43] Harold Yates, "Total Transmission of the Atmosphere in the Near-Infrared," *Naval Research Laboratory Report 3558* (September 1951).

[44] J. N. Howard, "The Absorption of Near-Infrared Black Body Radiation by Atmospheric Carbon Dioxide and Water Vapor," Ohio State University Research Foundation, *Project 407, Report No. 1* (March 1950).

pointed out that the results of Yates agree well with Eq. (5-34) in the region of low water content but sometimes deviate from it for large amounts of water.

5-6 INTEGRATED RESPONSE OF A DETECTOR

Computation of Response. In earlier sections illustrating the application of the black-body laws, atmospheric transmission was not considered, and the detectors were considered to be nonselective with wavelength. It is possible now to illustrate the method of estimating the response of a selective receiver to radiation which has penetrated a layer of the atmos-

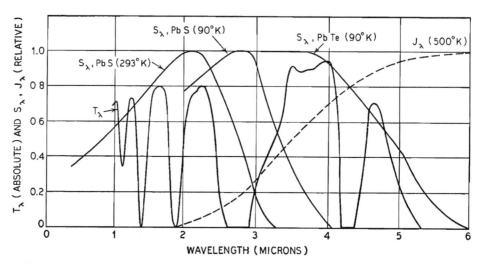

FIG. 5-15 J_λ for 500°K Source, S_λ for PbS and PbTe, and t_λ for 2000 yd of Atmosphere Containing 17 mm of Precipitable Water.

phere. Figure 5-15 repeats the relative spectral response curves of Fig. 5-11 and the transmission curve of 17 mm of water vapor from Fig. 5-12, and it shows in addition the relative spectral intensity of a part of the 500°K black-body curve to the maximum of this curve at 6μ. To estimate the response of a photoconductive cell it is necessary to evaluate the integral

$$E = \int_0^\infty J_\lambda S_\lambda t_\lambda \, d\lambda \qquad (5\text{-}35)$$

where J_λ = the spectral distribution of the source
S_λ = relative spectral response of the detector
t_λ = spectral transmission of the atmosphere

The evaluation is made by multiplying ordinates of the several curves wavelength by wavelength throughout the spectrum and plotting the products obtained against wavelength as in Fig. 5-16. This figure shows clearly the advantage of extension of PbS sensitivity to longer wavelength by cooling, and the greater advantages of using cooled PbTe cells through utilization at longer wavelengths both of higher values of J_λ for the source selected and of t_λ in the 3.6μ window of the atmosphere.

With the thought in mind that the results plotted in Fig. 5-16 are relative through the use of relative instead of absolute values of S_λ, it is of interest to compare the total energy available in three cases. Integration of the curves with a planimeter showed the following ratios of response to 500°K radiation.

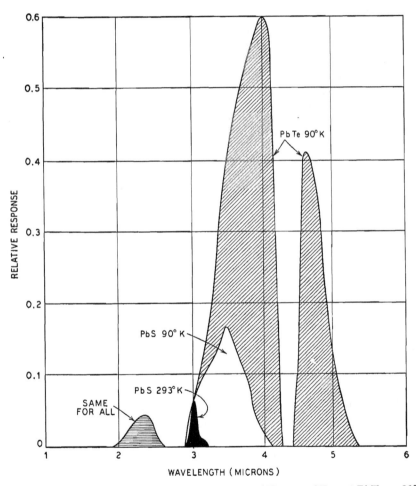

FIG. 5-16 The Products J_λ, S_λ, t_λ for PbS at 293°K and 90°K, and PbTe at 90°K for 500°K Source and 17 mm Precipitable Water.

PbS(90°K)/PbS(293°K) 4.5
PbTe(90°K)/PbS(90°K)   . . . 5.2
PbTe(90°K)/PbS(293°K)   24.0

Thus, if the several cells were of equal absolute sensitivity at the respective wavelengths of maximum response, the actual meter deflection produced by cold PbTe would be about 24 times that produced by PbS at room temperature. If, however, the absolute sensitivity of PbTe were $\frac{1}{24}$ that of PbS, there would be no advantage in its use to measure the total radiation of a 500°K source, and, in fact, the avoidance of cooling would greatly favor PbS.

Contrast Against Background. In the discussion of thermal detectors it was emphasized that the exchange of thermal radiation between detector and object is the quantity measured. This is not true in the case of photoconductive detectors, which do not depend for their response on being warmed by the incoming radiation. Thus, if the increase in response above dark current is measured when the cell is exposed to a source of radiation, the response is proportional to the value of Eq. (5-35). In many practical cases an object is compared with the surrounding area or background which may be nearly at the same temperature, as, for example, if an area of the full moon (about 400°K) were being compared with adjoining areas, or if a photoconductive cell were being used in a control circuit for regulating furnace temperature. In such cases, the net response is proportional to

$$\Delta E = \int_0^\infty J_\lambda S_\lambda t_\lambda \, d\lambda - \int_0^\infty J_{b\lambda} S_{b\lambda} t_\lambda \, d\lambda \qquad (5\text{-}36)$$

where the subscript b denotes the background. This is a similar expression to Eq. (5-8), (5-11), and (5-17) where, however, both S_λ and t_λ were considered to be unity and $\int_0^\infty J_\lambda \, d\lambda = \sigma T^4$.

Other conditions relating to computation of flux density, spectral radiant intensity, and the use of optical systems apply as in earlier examples. If the optical system itself is selectively transmitting, as, for example, when lenses or filters are used, appropriate t_λ's must be introduced in Eq. (5-36).

Effect of Atmospheric Radiation. The example illustrated in Fig. 5-16 took into account only the transmission of the atmosphere. In regions where the atmosphere absorbs strongly, it also emits strongly. If an exponential law were followed in absorption, which it has been pointed out is not the case over reasonably wide wavelength intervals for water vapor, the spectral emissive power of a column of the atmosphere x centimeters thick would be

$$J_\lambda = \int_0^t \epsilon_\lambda e^{-\beta_\lambda x}\, dx = \frac{\epsilon_\lambda}{\beta_\lambda}(1 - e^{-\beta_\lambda t}) \tag{5-37}$$

where ϵ_λ = emissivity per cubic centimeter as function of wavelength
β_λ = absorption coefficient

By Kirchhoff's Law, if thermal equilibrium obtains, $\epsilon_\lambda/\beta_\lambda$ is simply the Planck function for a black body at the temperature of the radiating gas. As $\beta_\lambda t$ increases, the term in parentheses approaches unity, and therefore, a relatively thin layer of atmosphere may radiate like a black body in a region of high β. For example, in Fig. 5-12b the integrated transmission coefficient for 0.82 mm of water in the region between 5μ and 6μ is approximately 0.09. The emissive power of this thin layer of water vapor would be 0.91. Figure 5-5 shows that a black body at 300°K radiates appreciably in the 5μ to 6μ region where PbTe, for example, retains sensitivity. Therefore, a steady signal current from the first several hundred feet of atmosphere would be indicated by a PbTe cell exposed to a moist atmosphere, and fluctuations in this signal due to fluctuating atmospheric temperature would constitute an undesirable noise signal.

5-7 OPTICAL MATERIALS

Reflectors. Paraboloidal glass mirrors are ordinarily used in infrared spectrometers, radiometers, and other infrared devices, to collect radiation and bring it into focus on the detecting element. There are a number of advantages to the use of a mirror. All wavelengths are brought to the same focus so that the image is free of chromatic aberration. Glass can be worked with relative ease to produce near perfect surfaces, whereas refracting materials available for use in infrared lenses are difficult to work, are in general less durable than glass, and are not available in sufficient variety of dispersive qualities to permit achromatization of lenses, as is possible with lenses for the ultraviolet and visible regions. Spherical mirrors give rise to spherical aberration, and paraboloidal mirrors, which overcome this defect for incoming parallel rays, produce marked coma in the image when used slightly off-axis. Spherical aberration and coma can be corrected in spherical mirrors by means of Schmidt[45] or Maksutov[46] or Bouwers[47] correcting plates of a refracting material placed in the path of the incoming radiation. These systems increase the width of field of view over which sharp images can be obtained and permit large light gathering power, aperture numbers less than $f/1$ being achievable. These

---

[45] B. Schmidt, "Mitt. Hamb. Sternwarte," *Bergedorf* **7**, 36 (1932); also Eric M. Wormser, "On the Design of Wide Angle Schmidt Optical Systems," *J. Opt. Soc. Am.* **40**, 412 (1950).

[46] D. D. Maksutov, "New Catadioptric Meniscus Systems," *J. Opt. Soc. Am.* **34**, 270 (1944).

[47] A. Bouwers, *Achievements in Optics*, Elseview Publishing Company, Inc., New York, Amsterdam, 1946.

systems are well known in astronomy where small *f*-number and wide field of view are often valuable, and where the excellent optical working properties of glass permit careful figuring. In the infrared, the difficulty of working the materials available for the correcting plates is more severe.

A mirror is made highly reflecting through a wide band of the spectrum by depositing a film of metal such as gold or aluminum on its front surface by evaporation of the metal in vacuum. Aluminum is commonly used because it is highly reflecting throughout the ultraviolet, visible, and infrared. It also can be washed with a detergent in water. However, gold is often used in cases where its low reflectivity in the visible is an advantage. Evaporated metal surfaces are sometimes protected from abrasion with a thin layer of silicon monoxide. Rhodium, electroplated on a substrate of some evaporated metal, is useful when the greatest resistance to the elements is required.

The reflectivity of gold rises from about 47 percent at 0.5μ to 95 percent at 0.8μ and to about 98 percent at 10μ. The reflectivity of aluminum is about 90 percent in the visible spectrum and 95 percent or higher in the 10μ region. The reflectivity of electroplated rhodium rises from 70 percent in the visible to 95 percent in the 10μ region.

Materials Transparent to Long Wavelengths. Transparent "window" materials are required for sensitive elements and often for closing the open end of a radiometer telescope tube (Fig. 5-3). Solids which transmit infrared radiation in the 1μ to 15μ region are, in general, crystalline materials for which the natural frequencies of the crystalline lattice vibrations are in the remote infrared. The best-known materials are alkali halides, which transmit readily from the ultraviolet through the visible and infrared to the approximate wavelength shown for each: sodium chloride, useful to 15μ; potassium chloride, useful to 20μ; potassium bromide, useful to 30μ. These materials can be brought to excellent polish by skilled craftsmen. They are highly soluble in water and must therefore be protected from humid air. A thin lacquer or varnish coat will not insure that water will not gain entry through a pinhole and ultimately destroy the figure of the entire surface. It is possible, however, to cement a thin sheet of transparent material such as a rubber hydrochloride (Pliofilm) over the entire face of the crystal, using thin rubber cement, and thereby achieve reasonable permanence against water damage. This procedure produces marked changes in the optical transmission because of absorption bands in all sheets of organic materials, and it results in an optical surface inferior to that of a well-polished crystal.

In laboratory instruments, such as thermocouples for infrared spectrometers, sodium chloride and potassium bromide are the best and most generally used materials, without any protective coating.

Silver chloride in the form of rolled sheets as developed by Kremers[48] receives wide use in many applications where the highest optical quality is less desirable than insolubility in water. The transmission coefficient is about 0.80 throughout the infrared to wavelength 18μ, the loss of light being principally due to the high reflectivity of the material which in turn is due to the high index of refraction, approximately 2.

Silver chloride is photosensitive to blue light and the ultraviolet, and therefore cannot be exposed to daylight or strong incandescent lights. It can be coated with a film of some red material such as evaporated selenium or stibnite which excludes the blue light but which, through even higher index of refraction, reduces the transmission somewhat. High transmission can be restored and even brought higher than 0.80 by applying an anti-reflection coating of a $\frac{1}{4}$ wavelength film of polystyrene or other transparent material[49]—but, again, with the introduction into the transmission spectrum of absorption bands of the coating material.

A material known as KRS5 was developed in Germany during World War II. It is a eutectic mixture of thallium iodide and thallium bromide

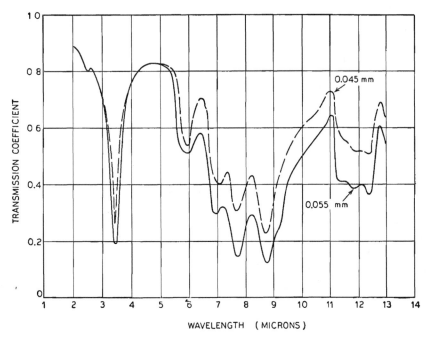

FIG. 5-17 Transmission Spectra of Pliofilm.

[48] H. C. Kremers, "Optical Silver Chloride," *J. Opt. Soc. Am.* **37**, 337 (1947).
[49] Mark Hyman and Bruce H. Billings, "High Transmission Windows for Radiation of 3 to 14 microns Wavelength," *J. Opt. Soc. Am.* **37**, 113 (1947).

which is red in color but relatively transparent between 1μ and 40μ. The transmission coefficient is 0.70 throughout most of the infrared spectrum, the light loss again being due to high reflectivity. KRS5 is difficult to work optically, but it can be brought to an excellent finish by skilled craftsmen.

Organic Materials. All organic films show strong band absorption at the natural frequencies of vibration of the chemical bonds of their complex

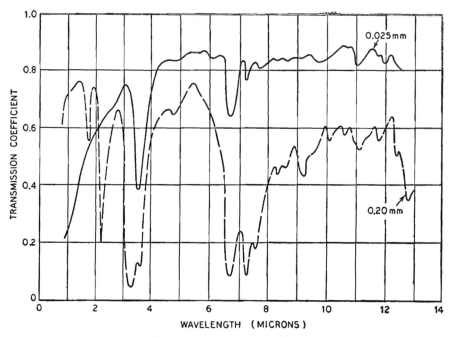

FIG. 5-18 Transmission Spectra of Polyethylene.

molecules. In general, only thin layers of the order of a thousandth of an inch are useful. The transmission spectra of two thicknesses of Pliofilm (a rubber hydrochloride) are shown in Fig. 5-17 and of two thicknesses of polyethylene in Fig. 5-18. The very dissimilarity of certain absorption bands in the polyethylene curves indicates a difference in the molecular structure of the two samples measured and illustrates the usefulness of infrared absorption spectroscopy in discovering such differences. Tetrafluorethene (Teflon), a polymer of the structure $-\underset{\underset{F}{|}}{\overset{\overset{F}{|}}{C}}-\underset{\underset{F}{|}}{\overset{\overset{F}{|}}{C}}-$ in which fluorene atoms replace the more familiar hydrogen atoms is relatively transparent in the near infrared in thicknesses as great as 4 mm. The transmission curves of three thicknesses of this material are shown in Fig. 5-19. Low transmission in the visible portion of these samples was due to the circumstance that they were translucent, like opal glass, rather than clear. Visible light was scattered, but not absorbed by the materials. At longer wavelengths near 1μ, scattering became inconsequential, and the materials transmitted freely.

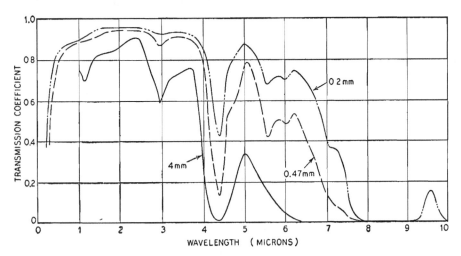

FIG. 5-19 Transmission Spectra of Teflon.

Materials Useful in the Near Infrared. A number of durable materials are available for use in the near infrared. Figure 5-20 shows transmission curves for miscellaneous thicknesses of quartz, artificial sapphire, magnesium oxide, lithium fluoride, and fluorite. The curves are of interest in indicating the long wavelength cutoff of these materials.

Progress has been made in the development of arsenic trisulfide glass. Frerichs[50] has described samples of such glass which transmit 50 percent to 75 percent of the incident radiation in the region 1μ to 12μ. This glass is becoming commercially available.* It is probable that continued advances in glass technology will greatly increase the choice of materials for use throughout the infrared.

Filters. Powder filters often are used to eliminate the visible spectrum and the very short infrared while transmitting longer wavelengths. The curve for tellurium powder in Fig. 5-10 illustrates the performance of such a filter. The filtering effect depends on the scattering of short wave-

[50] Rudolf Frerichs, "New Optical Glasses with Good Transparency in the Infrared," *J. Opt. Soc. Am.* **43**, 1153 (1953).

* American Optical Company.

lengths out of the beam by particles in the filter which are larger than the wavelength. When wavelength and particle size become approximately equal, transmission sets in and rises rapidly to a constant value. The scattering powder must, in general, be made of a material which is transparent in the infrared; it has been noted that a metallic black may become transparent in the infrared. Powder filters of magnesium oxide can be made by burning magnesium ribbon and condensing a suitable layer of the smoke on rock salt or some other transparent material.[51] Silver

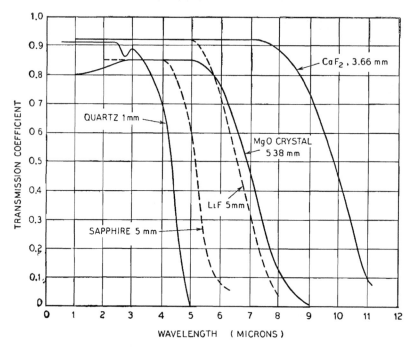

FIG. 5-20 Transmission Spectra of Crystalline Materials.

chloride can be treated to form a black powder film of silver sulfide on its surface, producing a filter which is opaque to visible light but transparent at wavelengths 1μ to 3μ or longer.[48] In general, powder filters are transparent throughout the long wavelength region of the spectrum except at wavelengths where the parent material is opaque or strongly reflecting. Thus, powdered quartz absorbs strongly at 9μ where polished quartz exhibits strong metallic reflection. Filters which are useful in a restricted region of the spectrum are so-called heat transmitting glasses and dyed

[51] R. L. Henry, "The Transmission of Powder Films in the Infra-Red," *J. Opt. Soc. Am.* **38**, 775 (1948).

plastic films, such as Cellophane or Nylon. Filters of the latter type have been described by Blout et al.[52]

Either glass or dyed plastic filters may begin to transmit at wavelengths 0.7 to 0.85μ, depending on the thickness of the glass or the concentration of dye in the film. The transmission coefficients of either type are about 0.80 in the region 1.5μ to 2μ. The rise in transmission is much steeper for the plastic filters than for glass, i.e., they have a sharper cutoff at the short wavelength side. Glass filters become opaque in the neighborhood of 3μ, depending on the thickness. Plastic filters exhibit strong infrared absorption at 3.5μ and other wavelengths where the characteristic vibration bands of the chemical bands in the plastic occur.

BIBLIOGRAPHY

1. W. E. Knowles Middleton, *Vision Through the Atmosphere*, University of Toronto Press, 1952.
2. *Temperature, Its Measurement and Control in Science and Industry*, Reinhold Publishing Corporation, New York, 1941.
3. F. K. Richtmyer and E. H. Kennard, *Introduction to Modern Physics*, McGraw-Hill Book Co., Inc., New York, 1947.
4. J. W. T. Walsh, *Photometry*, 2nd Ed. Rev., Constable and Company Ltd., London, 1953.
5. A. E. Ruark and H. C. Urey, *Atoms, Molecules and Quanta*, McGraw-Hill Book Co., Inc., New York, 1930.
6. F. K. Richtmyer, *Introduction to Modern Physics*, McGraw-Hill Book Co., Inc., New York, 1928.
7. J. Strong, *Procedures In Experimental Physics*, Prentice-Hall, Inc., New York, 1946.
8. S. P. Langley, *Annals of the Astrophysical Observatory*, Smithsonian Institution, Washington, D. C., 1900.
9. Gerard P. Kuiper, ed., *The Atmospheres of the Earth and Planets*, University of Chicago Press, Chicago, revised ed. 1952.
10. A. Bouwers, *Achievements in Optics*, Elsevier Publishing Company, Inc., Houston, Amsterdam, 1946.

[52] E. R. Blout, W. F. Amon, R. G. Shepherd, Jr., A. Thomas, C. D. West, and E. H. Laud, "Near Infra-Red Transmitting Filters," *J. Opt. Soc. Am.* **36**, 460 (1946).

CHAPTER 6

MATHEMATICAL GROUNDWORK

Symbols Used in Chapter 6

a = gain margin
$\varepsilon(t)$ = error voltage in a feedback system
$\varepsilon(s)$ = Laplace transform of $\varepsilon(t)$
ε^2 = sum of the squares of the deviations δ_i
$\text{erf}(t)$ = the error function
$f'(t)$ = first derivative of $f(t)$ with respect to t
$f^{(-1)}(t)$ = indefinite integral of $f(t)$ with respect to t
$G(s)$ = transfer function of a network
$G(j\omega)$ = frequency-response function of a network
h = constant finite difference
$h(t)$ = impulse response of a network
$i(t)$ = current as a function of time
$I(s)$ = Laplace transform of $i(t)$
Im = imaginary part of
$KG(s)$ = general servo open-loop transfer function
$\mathcal{L}$ = direct Laplace transform
$\mathcal{L}^{-1}$ = inverse Laplace transform
$n_i(t), n_o(t)$ = input and output noise functions
$n!$ = n factorial = $n(n-1)(n-2) \cdots 2 \cdot 1$
p = probability of success
q = probability of failure = $1 - p$
r = fractional factor
Re = real part of

$s = \sigma + j\omega$ = complex variable used in $\mathcal{L}$ transformation
$u(t)$ = unit step function
$\bar{x}$ = mean value
$\beta = \beta(s)$ = feedback-path transfer function
γ = phase margin
δ_i = deviations used in least-squares method
$\Delta, \Delta^2, \ldots$ = first, second, ... ordinary differences
$\underset{x_0,x_1}{\triangle}$ = first divided difference
ζ = damping factor
$\theta_i(t)$ = input voltage of a network
$\theta_i(s)$ = Laplace transform of $\theta_i(t)$
$\theta_i(j\omega)$ = Fourier transform of $\theta_i(t)$
$\theta_o(t)$ = output voltage of a network
$\theta_o(s)$ = Laplace transform of $\theta_o(t)$
$\theta_o(j\omega)$ = Fourier transform of $\theta_o(t)$
$\mu = \mu(s)$ = open-loop transfer function
ρ = correlation coefficient
σ = standard deviation
σ^2 = variance
τ = time-delay parameter
ϕ = phase angle of $KG(s)$
$\phi_{11}(\tau)$ = autocorrelation function
$\phi_{12}(\tau)$ = crosscorrelation function
$\Phi_{11}(\omega)$ = power-density spectrum
$\omega = 2\pi f$ = general angular frequency variable
ω_n = undamped natural resonant angular frequency

Subsequent chapters of this book require a mathematical background somewhat specialized in character. It is the purpose of this chapter to present sufficient groundwork in the specialized mathematics to enable the reader, on the basis of elementary algebra and calculus, to proceed through the book without encountering insurmountable mathematical stumbling blocks. The first portion of the chapter is devoted to a development of the mathematical concepts and tools required for the study of the behavior of linear networks and servo systems discussed at length in Chap. 7 and subsequent chapters. The auto- and crosscorrelation functions, of particular interest in radar design, are discussed briefly for further use in connection with Chap. 10. Considerable attention is given to operational techniques which will be of value in Chap. 12 and in other volumes of this series. One section is devoted to a description of some of the more powerful methods of curve fitting. Finally, the last portion of the chapter is devoted to a summary of some of the elementary concepts of probability theory.

6-1 LINEAR NETWORKS

In the study of servo systems the dynamic behavior of the mechanical elements and the electronic circuits is of fundamental importance in determining operational performance. A complete system in the research and drawing board stages is made up of a number of block elements, each of which must be described by some mathematical characterization in order that an overall system analysis can be performed. Since a large number of these elements are mechanical or nonelectrical in nature, it would be convenient if a common method could be employed to characterize mathematically both electrical and nonelectrical elements. In recent years the electrical-analogy approach to the study of nonelectrical systems has become increasingly important. Electrical analogs can be established for mechanical, hydraulic, thermal and other physical elements.[1] It is found that the use of electrical analogs simplifies greatly the understanding of many nonelectrical systems and enables the use of a common mathematical method of solution in handling all of the elements of a servo system. It is the purpose here to develop those common mathematical processes required for defining the action of the separate elements, both electrical and nonelectrical, in the system as well as the mathematics required to understand the operation of the system as a whole.

Only systems which are linear in the mathematical sense will be considered. The word *linear* here is meant to imply that the individual block elements which make up the whole system behave linearly over their operating range so that they may be represented by systems of linear equa-

---

[1] For an excellent discussion of electrical analogs see: Thaler, George J., and Brown, Robert G., *Servomechanism Analysis*, Chap. 3, McGraw-Hill Book Co., Inc., New York, 1953.

tions. The elements of primary concern in this chapter will be two-terminal linear networks. A *linear network* is an electrical network in which the currents and voltages can be related by a set of linear integro-differential equations with constant coefficients; these coefficients are functions of the parameters of the network. Thus the basic elements or parameters of the network are time-invariant. In a linear network the *principle of superposition* applies, which principle can be expressed as follows: if several inputs are applied to a linear network, the resultant output is the sum of the outputs produced by the individual inputs.

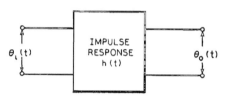

FIG. 6-1 General Two Terminal-Pair Network.

Since a large part of the theory of servo systems concerns itself with the treatment of linear networks, a definition of the terms used to describe network behavior will be given as a background for the mathematics to follow. Consider any general network as shown in Fig. 6-1. The classical manner of describing a network is by means of an ordinary linear integro-differential (i-d) equation relating the output and the input. In the case of servo systems this i-d equation might take a form such as

$$a_n \frac{d^n \theta_o(t)}{dt^n} + a_{n-1} \frac{d^{n-1} \theta_o(t)}{dt^{n-1}} + \cdots + a_0 \theta_o(t) + \int \theta_o(t)\, dt = F[\mathcal{E}(t)] \quad (6\text{-}1)$$

where the a_n's are the time-invariant parameters of the system. When a set of boundary conditions is associated with equations of the form (6-1), complete information regarding the action of the network is provided; however, such i-d equations are frequently tedious to solve and they do not lend themselves readily to design work.

Another manner of describing a network is by means of the response of the network to an impulse.

> The *impulse response* of a network is the response of the network to a unit impulse.

In Par. 6-9 it will be shown why the impulse response $h(t)$ is frequently referred to as a *weighting function*. The impulse response is a function of time, which completely describes the behavior of the network. There are two transformations associated with $h(t)$ which are generally employed to describe a network:

1. The *transfer function* is the Laplace transform of the impulse response. It is also the ratio of the Laplace transform of the network output to the Laplace transform of the network input, with all initial conditions set equal to zero.

2. The *frequency-response function* is the Fourier transform of the impulse response. It is also the ratio of the Fourier transform of the network output to the Fourier transform of the network input.

The Laplace transform is considered in Par. 6-2 and the Fourier transform in Par. 6-8.

For a set of initial conditions equal to zero, both the transfer function and the frequency-response function provide a complete description of the behavior of a network.

> The expression *transfer characteristic* will be used to refer to either the transfer function or the frequency-response function when the initial conditions are all equal to zero.

If the initial conditions are not actually zero, then the transfer function permits the solution of a given problem to be obtained more easily than does the frequency-response function. Considerably more detail on the relationship between these two functions will be found in Par. 6-11.

The following paragraphs will be devoted to a discussion of the basic mathematical tools required to understand the meaning and application of the preceding definitions in regard to network behavior and servo system operation.

6-2 THE LAPLACE TRANSFORMATION

There exist a number of different methods for solving linear integro-differential equations. Of all these methods by far the most useful are those employing the *transformation calculus*. The most powerful of all is the *Laplace-transform method*. The Laplace-transform method is also the simplest method for handling a set of nonzero boundary conditions. The method reduces the problem of solving a complicated i-d equation of the form (6-1) to the far simpler and more easily handled problem of solving an algebraic equation.

The *direct Laplace transform* is defined by

$$\mathcal{L}[f(t)] = \int_0^\infty f(t)e^{-st}\, dt = F(s) \tag{6-2}$$

in which s is a complex variable usually written as $s = \sigma + j\omega$. An interpretation of the significance of the transformation (6-2) is beyond the scope and purpose of this work; suffice it to say that it changes a function of the real time variable into a new function of a complex frequency variable for the specific purpose of simplifying the mathematics required in solving i-d equations. Definition (6-2) can be used to determine by straightforward integration the transforms $F(s)$ corresponding to the time functions $f(t)$. In the solution of i-d equations it is also required to recover the original time function corresponding to a given transform $F(s)$. This is called the *inverse Laplace transform* and is defined as the operation

$$\mathcal{L}^{-1}[F(s)] = f(t), \quad 0 \leqslant t \tag{6-3}$$

The explicit expression for $f(t)$ in terms of $F(s)$ requires a greater knowledge of the theory of functions of a complex variable than is needed here; the reader is referred to advanced texts[2] if more detail is desired.

6-3 DEVELOPMENT OF FUNCTION-TRANSFORM PAIRS

In solving problems by the $\mathcal{L}$-transform method, use is continuously made of the functional correspondence between $f(t)$ and $F(s)$. To save time in the actual use of this transformation, tables of *function-transform pairs* are prepared in advance which display the most frequently used transforms. Table 6-1 presents some of the most commonly used function-transform pairs. In order to illustrate the method employed to develop such a table, several of the most important functions will be discussed here.

Unit Step Function $u(t)$. Here $f(t)$ is the unit step function $u(t)$ defined by

$$u(t) = \begin{cases} 0, & t < 0 \\ 1, & t \geqslant 0 \end{cases} \tag{6-4}$$

The use of Eq. (6-2) gives

$$\mathcal{L}[u(t)] = \int_0^\infty (1)e^{-st}\,dt = \left. -\frac{1}{s}e^{-st} \right|_0^\infty = \frac{1}{s} \tag{6-5}$$

Unit Ramp Function. Here $f(t)$ is a function which increases linearly with the time:

$$f(t) = \begin{cases} 0, & t < 0 \\ t, & t \geqslant 0 \end{cases} \tag{6-6}$$

Using Eq. (6-2) gives

$$\mathcal{L}[f(t)] = \int_0^\infty te^{-st}\,dt = \left. -\frac{te^{-st}}{s} \right|_0^\infty + \frac{1}{s}\int_0^\infty e^{-st}\,dt$$

$$= 0 + \frac{1}{s} \cdot \left. \frac{-1}{s}e^{-st} \right|_0^\infty = \frac{1}{s^2} \tag{6-7}$$

This type of input corresponds to a unit step function input in velocity.

The Damped Exponential. This is an example of a transcendental function:

$$f(t) = e^{-\alpha t}, \quad 0 \leqslant t \tag{6-8}$$

where α is a real number. Using Eq. (6-2) gives

$$\mathcal{L}[e^{-\alpha t}] = \int_0^\infty e^{-\alpha t}e^{-st}\,dt = \int_0^\infty e^{-(s+\alpha)t}\,dt = \frac{1}{s+\alpha} \tag{6-9}$$

[2] Churchill, Ruel V., *Modern Operational Mathematics in Engineering*, McGraw-Hill Book Co., 1944.

Table 6-1 Function—Transform Pairs

No.	$F(s)$	$f(t)$ $0 \leq t$
1	$\dfrac{1}{s}$	1, or unit step function $u(t)$ at $t = 0$
2	$\dfrac{1}{s^2}$	t
3	$\dfrac{1}{s+\alpha}$	$e^{-\alpha t}$
4	$\dfrac{\omega_0}{s^2+\omega_0^2}$	$\sin \omega_0 t$
5	$\dfrac{s}{s^2+\omega_0^2}$	$\cos \omega_0 t$
6	1	unit impulse at $t = 0$
7	$\dfrac{s+\omega_0}{s^2+\beta^2}$	$\dfrac{1}{\beta}(\omega_0^2+\beta^2)^{\frac{1}{2}} \sin(\beta t + \psi)$ $\psi = \tan^{-1} \beta/\omega_0$
8	$\dfrac{1}{s(s^2+\beta^2)}$	$\dfrac{1}{\beta^2}(1 - \cos \beta t)$
9	$\dfrac{1}{(s+\alpha)^2+\beta^2}$	$\dfrac{1}{\beta} e^{-\alpha t} \sin \beta t$
10	$\dfrac{s+\omega_0}{(s+\alpha)^2+\beta^2}$	$\dfrac{1}{\beta}[(\omega_0-\alpha)^2+\beta^2]^{\frac{1}{2}} e^{-\alpha t} \sin(\beta t + \psi)$ $\psi = \tan^{-1} \beta/(\omega_0-\alpha)$
11	$\dfrac{s+\alpha}{(s+\alpha)^2+\beta^2}$	$e^{-\alpha t} \cos \beta t$
12	$\dfrac{1}{s[(s+\alpha)^2+\beta^2]}$	$\dfrac{1}{\beta_0^2} + \dfrac{1}{\beta\beta_0} e^{-\alpha t} \sin(\beta t - \psi)$ $\psi = \tan^{-1} \beta/-\alpha$ $\beta_0^2 = \alpha^2 + \beta^2$
13	$\dfrac{s+\omega_0}{s[(s+\alpha)^2+\beta^2]}$	$\dfrac{\omega_0}{\beta_0^2} + \dfrac{1}{\beta\beta_0}[(\omega_0-\alpha)^2+\beta^2]^{\frac{1}{2}} e^{-\alpha t} \sin(\beta t + \psi)$ $\psi = \tan^{-1} \beta/(\omega_0-\alpha) - \tan^{-1} \beta/-\alpha$ $\beta_0^2 = \alpha^2 + \beta^2$
14	$\dfrac{1}{(s+\alpha)^n}$	$\dfrac{1}{(n-1)!} t^{n-1} e^{-\alpha t}$

This is a good example of how the $\mathcal{L}$ transform simplifies a function. The transcendental exponential function transforms into a relatively simple algebraic function. Another such example follows.

Sinusoidal Input. If the input is of the form

$$f(t) = \sin \omega_0 t, \quad 0 \leqslant t \tag{6-10}$$

where ω_0 is a positive real number, then the $\mathcal{L}$ transform is

$$\begin{aligned}
\mathcal{L}[\sin \omega_0 t] &= \int_0^\infty \sin \omega_0 t \, e^{-st} \, dt \\
&= \frac{1}{2j} \int_0^\infty (e^{j\omega_0 t} - e^{-j\omega_0 t}) e^{-st} \, dt \\
&= \frac{1}{2j} \left(\frac{1}{s - j\omega_0} - \frac{1}{s + j\omega_0} \right) \\
&= \frac{\omega_0}{s^2 + \omega_0^2}
\end{aligned} \tag{6-11}$$

Evaluations of the type illustrated lead to the construction of tables of the form of Table 6-1.

6-4 BASIC THEOREMS OF THE LAPLACE TRANSFORMATION

In addition to function transforms which frequently simplify the functions of real variables involved, the Laplace transformation is even more useful in the simplification of certain operations. The following notation will be employed to make these *operation-transforms* easy to tabulate:

$$f'(t) = \frac{df(t)}{dt}$$

and

$$f^{(-1)}(t) = \int f(t) \, dt = \int_0^t f(t) \, dt + f^{(-1)}(0+)$$

where $f^{(-1)}(0+)$ is interpreted to be the value of the indefinite integral of $f(t)$ as t approaches zero from the positive side.

The simplest operation theorem is in respect to the linearity of the direct and inverse transforms.

THEOREM 1—LINEARITY:

$$\left. \begin{aligned}
\mathcal{L}[af_1(t) \pm bf_2(t)] &= aF_1(s) \pm bF_2(s) \\
\mathcal{L}^{-1}[aF_1(s) \pm bF_2(s)] &= af_1(t) \pm bf_2(t), \quad 0 \leqslant t
\end{aligned} \right\} \tag{6-12}$$

This theorem follows at once from the linear property of the definition (6-2) and from a definition of the inverse transform[3] not stated here.

[3] Churchill, *op. cit.*, pp. 157-178.

THEOREM 2—REAL DIFFERENTIATION. *If the function $f(t)$ and its first derivative $f'(t)$ are $\mathcal{L}$ transformable, and if $\mathcal{L}[f(t)] = F(s)$, then*

$$\mathcal{L}[f'(t)] = sF(s) - f(0+) \qquad (6\text{-}13)$$

THEOREM 3—REAL INTEGRATION. *If the function $f(t)$ is $\mathcal{L}$ transformable, and if $\mathcal{L}[f(t)] = F(s)$, then*

$$\mathcal{L}[f^{(-1)}(t)] = \frac{1}{s}[F(s) + f^{(-1)}(0+)] \qquad (6\text{-}14)$$

These two very important theorems are relatively easily proved by employing Eq. (6-2) and then integrating by parts. Detailed proofs are given in Gardner and Barnes.[4] Two other important theorems will be stated without proof:

THEOREM 4—REAL TRANSLATION. *If the function $f(t)$ is $\mathcal{L}$ transformable, and if $\mathcal{L}[f(t)] = F(s)$, then*

$$\mathcal{L}[f(t-b)] = e^{-bs}F(s) \qquad (6\text{-}15)$$

for $f(t-b) = 0$ in $0 < t < b$ where b is a positive real number.

THEOREM 5—COMPLEX TRANSLATION. *If the function $f(t)$ is $\mathcal{L}$ transformable, and if $\mathcal{L}[f(t)] = F(s)$, then*

$$\mathcal{L}[e^{-bt}f(t)] = F(s+b) \qquad (6\text{-}16)$$

where b is a complex number with non-negative real part.

Two additional theorems are given which are particularly useful in servo theory:

THEOREM 6—FINAL VALUE. *If the function $f(t)$ and its first derivative are $\mathcal{L}$ transformable, and if $\mathcal{L}[f(t)] = F(s)$, then*

$$\lim_{s \to 0} sF(s) = \lim_{t \to \infty} f(t) \qquad (6\text{-}17)$$

provided $sF(s)$ is analytic on the axis of imaginaries and in the right half-plane.

This provision means that the denominator of $sF(s)$ cannot contain factors of the form $(s - s_0)$ where the real part of $s_0 \geq 0$. This will be explained in greater detail in Par. 6-13.

THEOREM 7—INITIAL VALUE. *If the function $f(t)$ and its first derivative are $\mathcal{L}$ transformable, and if $\mathcal{L}[f(t)] = F(s)$, then*

$$\lim_{s \to \infty} sF(s) = \lim_{t \to 0} f(t) \qquad (6\text{-}18)$$

provided the $\lim_{s \to \infty} sF(s)$ exists.

---

[4] Gardner, Murray F. and Barnes, John L., *Transients in Linear Systems.* Vol. I, pp. 126-130, John Wiley & Sons, Inc., New York, 1947.

The limit as $t \to 0$ means that the limit is approached from the right passing through positive values of t. Detailed proofs of Eq. (6-17) and (6-18) will be found in Gardner and Barnes.[5]

Table 6-2 is a table of operation-transform pairs analogous to Table 6-1 containing the theorems that have been given plus a few others for reference.

TABLE 6-2 OPERATION—TRANSFORM PAIRS

No.	$f(t)$ $0 \leq t$	$F(s)$
1	$af_1(t) \pm bf_2(t)$	$aF_1(s) \pm bF_2(s)$
2	$f'(t) = \dfrac{df(t)}{dt}$	$sF(s) - f(0+)$
3	$f^{(-1)}(t) = \int f(t)\, dt$	$\dfrac{1}{s}[F(s) + f^{(-1)}(0+)]$
4	$f(t-b)$ for $f(t-b) = 0$, $0 < t < b$ b is a positive real number	$e^{-bs} F(s)$
5	$e^{-bt} f(t)$ b is complex with non-negative real part	$F(s+b)$
6	Convolution Theorem: $\int_0^t f_1(t-\tau) f_2(\tau)\, d\tau$	$F_1(s)F_2(s)$
7	$f^{(n)}(t) = \dfrac{d^n f(t)}{dt^n}$	$s^n F(s) - s^{n-1}f(0+) - s^{n-2}f'(0+)$ $- \cdots - f^{(n-1)}(0+)$
8	Final Value Theorem: $\lim\limits_{s \to 0} sF(s) = \lim\limits_{t \to \infty} f(t)$ provided $sF(s)$ is analytic on the axis of imaginaries and in the right half plane	
9	Initial Value Theorem: $\lim\limits_{s \to \infty} sF(s) = \lim\limits_{t \to 0} f(t)$	

6-5 THE SOLUTION OF A SIMPLE I-D EQUATION

As an example of the power of the $\mathcal{L}$-transform method for solving linear i-d equations consider the very simple RC circuit of Fig. 6-2. Here

---

[5] *Loc. cit.*, pp. 265-269.

E is a constant voltage and both R and C are constant. If it is assumed that there is no initial charge on the capacitor with the switch open, then how does $i(t)$ behave after the switch is closed? It will be assumed that the reader has a working knowledge of Kirchhoff's Laws, the use of which yields the equation of equilibrium

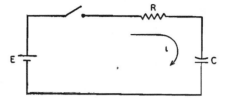

FIG. 6-2 Simple RC Circuit.

$$Ri(t) + \frac{1}{C}\int i(t)\,dt = E \quad (6\text{-}19)$$

Taking the $\mathcal{L}$ transform of both sides yields

$$\mathcal{L}[Ri(t)] + \mathcal{L}\left[\frac{1}{C}\int i(t)\,dt\right] = \mathcal{L}[E]$$

which, upon using Tables 6-1 and 6-2, produces

$$RI(s) + \frac{1}{sC}[I(s) + i^{(-1)}(0+)] = \frac{E}{s} \quad (6\text{-}20)$$

where

$$\mathcal{L}[i(t)] = I(s)$$

The initial condition that the charge on C was zero means that $i^{(-1)}(0+) = 0$ and therefore solving for $I(s)$ in Eq. (6-20) just as though this were an ordinary algebraic equation yields

$$I(s) = \frac{E}{s\left(R + \dfrac{1}{sC}\right)} = \frac{E/R}{s + \dfrac{1}{RC}} \quad (6\text{-}21)$$

If $T = RC$, then Eq. (6-21) can be written as

$$I(s) = \frac{E}{R}\frac{1}{s + 1/T} \quad (6\text{-}22)$$

Taking the inverse transform and using No. 3 of Table 6-1, we obtain

$$\mathcal{L}^{-1}[I(s)] = i(t) = \frac{E}{R}\mathcal{L}^{-1}\left[\frac{1}{s + 1/T}\right] \quad (6\text{-}23)$$

$$\therefore i(t) = \frac{E}{R}e^{-t/T}$$

This illustrates the standard procedure for solving differential equations by the $\mathcal{L}$-transform method. However, frequently the result is not so simple as in Eq. (6-22) and a short digression into the use of partial fraction expansions will be helpful before taking up more complicated examples.

6-6 THE $\mathcal{L}^{-1}$ TRANSFORM OF RATIONAL FRACTIONS

The solution of differential equations by use of the $\mathcal{L}$ transform follows in general the procedure used in example 1 of Par. 6-6. However, the final function whose inverse transform yields the solution is usually considerably more complicated than that of Eq. (6-22). In general, this end product is a rational algebraic fraction of the form

$$F(s) = \frac{A(s)}{B(s)} = \frac{a_m s^m + a_{m-1} s^{m-1} + \cdots + a_1 s + a_0}{s^n + b_{n-1} s^{n-1} + \cdots + b_1 s + b_0} \qquad (6\text{-}24)$$

where the a's and b's are real constants and m and n are positive integers. Only in rare cases can the inverse transform of a function written in the form of Eq. (6-24) be found in the tables. The procedure, in general, for $n \geqslant m$ is to factor $B(s)$ and then to express $F(s)$ as the sum of partial fractions. There are two important cases to be considered: (1) the roots of $B(s)$ are all real or zero and all different (i.e., no multiple roots), and (2) there are multiple roots.

Case 1: No multiple roots. Let the n roots of $B(s)$ be $s_1, s_2, \cdots, s_n$ where any one may be zero but no two are equal. Then $F(s)$ may be written as

$$F(s) = \frac{A(s)}{(s - s_1)(s - s_2) \cdots (s - s_{n-1})(s - s_n)} \qquad (6\text{-}25)$$

This may be expressed as the sum of n partial fractions of the form

$$F(s) = \frac{K_1}{s - s_1} + \frac{K_2}{s - s_2} + \cdots + \frac{K_n}{s - s_n} \qquad (6\text{-}26)$$

where the undetermined coefficients can be determined as follows. To find K_1, for example, multiply both sides of Eq. (6-26) by the factor $(s - s_1)$ and then let $s - s_1 = 0$. This procedure can be expressed formally for the general coefficient K_p as

$$K_p = \left[(s - s_p) \frac{A(s)}{B(s)} \right]_{s = s_p} \qquad (6\text{-}27)$$

After this procedure is completed for all the K's the inverse transform may easily be accomplished for each fraction; for example,

$$\mathcal{L}^{-1} \left[\frac{K_p}{s - s_p} \right] = K_p e^{s_p t}, \quad 0 \leqslant t \qquad (6\text{-}28)$$

where use has been made of No. 3, Table 6-1.

Example 1. Find the $\mathcal{L}^{-1}$ transform of $F(s) = \dfrac{K(s + \omega_0)}{s(s + \omega_1)(s + \omega_2)}$ where the ω's are real positive constants and different.

By Eq. (6-26) this can be expressed as

$$F(s) = \frac{K_1}{s} + \frac{K_2}{s + \omega_1} + \frac{K_3}{s + \omega_2}$$

where the evaluation of the coefficients by Eq. (6-27) is

$$K_1 = \left[\frac{K(s + \omega_0)}{(s + \omega_1)(s + \omega_2)}\right]_{s=0} = \frac{K\omega_0}{\omega_1\omega_2}$$

$$K_2 = \left[\frac{K(s + \omega_0)}{s(s + \omega_2)}\right]_{s=-\omega_1} = \frac{K(-\omega_1 + \omega_0)}{-\omega_1(-\omega_1 + \omega_2)} \quad (6\text{-}29)$$

$$K_3 = \left[\frac{K(s + \omega_0)}{s(s + \omega_1)}\right]_{s=-\omega_2} = \frac{K(-\omega_2 + \omega_0)}{-\omega_2(-\omega_2 + \omega_1)}$$

Since all the K's are constants, the $\mathcal{L}^{-1}$ transform of $F(s)$ by Eq. (6-28) is

$$\mathcal{L}^{-1}\left[\frac{K(s + \omega_0)}{s(s + \omega_1)(s + \omega_2)}\right] = \frac{K\omega_0}{\omega_1\omega_2} - \frac{K(\omega_0 - \omega_1)}{\omega_1(\omega_2 - \omega_1)} e^{-\omega_1 t} - \frac{K(\omega_0 - \omega_2)}{\omega_2(\omega_1 - \omega_2)} e^{-\omega_2 t} \quad (6\text{-}30)$$

It can be seen that in this simple case where all the roots of $B(s)$ are real and different the coefficients, Eq. (6-29), can be written by inspection.

Case 2: At least one multiple root. Let the n roots of $B(s)$ be $s_1, s_2, s_3, \cdots, s_{n-q}$ where the root s_1 occurs q times. Then $F(s)$ may be written as

$$F(s) = \frac{A(s)}{(s - s_1)^q(s - s_2) \cdots (s - s_{n-q-1})(s - s_{n-q})} \quad (6\text{-}31)$$

This may be expanded as the sum of n partial fractions as follows:

$$F(s) = \frac{K_{11}}{(s - s_1)^q} + \frac{K_{12}}{(s - s_1)^{q-1}} + \cdots + \frac{K_{1q}}{(s - s_1)}$$

$$+ \frac{K_2}{(s - s_2)} + \frac{K_3}{(s - s_3)} + \cdots + \frac{K_{n-q}}{(s - s_{n-q})} \quad (6\text{-}32)$$

The coefficients $K_2, K_3, \cdots, K_{n-q}$ may be evaluated according to the method of Case 1. However, the first q coefficients $K_{11}, \cdots, K_{1q}$ require a new method. To find K_{1l}, for example, multiply both sides of Eq. (6-32) by the factor $(s - s_1)^q$ and then differentiate both sides of the resulting equation $(l - 1)$ times. If the factor $(s - s_1)$ is set equal to zero, then K_{1l} results. This procedure can be expressed formally for the $(1l)^{\text{th}}$ coefficient as

$$K_{1l} = \frac{1}{(l - 1)!}\left[\frac{d^{l-1}}{ds^{l-1}}\frac{(s - s_1)^q A(s)}{B(s)}\right]_{s=s_1} \quad (6\text{-}33)$$

It can be appreciated that this method could become very tedious if q is large. If there are other repeated roots in $B(s)$, the procedure must be repeated for each. The following illustrative example may be helpful.

188   MATHEMATICAL GROUNDWORK

Example 1. Find the $\mathcal{L}^{-1}$ transform of $F(s) = \dfrac{K(s + \omega_0)}{s^2(s + \omega_1)^3}$ where the ω's are real positive constants.

According to Eq. (6-32) we may write $F(s)$ in the form

$$F(s) = \frac{K_{11}}{s^2} + \frac{K_{12}}{s} + \frac{K_{21}}{(s + \omega_1)^3} + \frac{K_{22}}{(s + \omega_1)^2} + \frac{K_{23}}{(s + \omega_1)}$$

and the evaluation of the coefficients by Eq. (6-33) is

$$K_{11} = \left[\frac{K(s + \omega_0)}{(s + \omega_1)^3}\right]_{s=0} = \frac{K\omega_0}{\omega_1^3}$$

$$K_{12} = \left[\frac{d}{ds}\frac{K(s + \omega_0)}{(s + \omega_1)^3}\right]_{s=0} = \left[\frac{K(s + \omega_1) - 3K(s + \omega_0)}{(s + \omega_1)^4}\right]_{s=0} = \frac{K(\omega_1 - 3\omega_0)}{\omega_1^4}$$

$$K_{21} = \left[\frac{K(s + \omega_0)}{s^2}\right]_{s=-\omega_1} = \frac{K(\omega_0 - \omega_1)}{\omega_1^2}$$

$$K_{22} = \left[\frac{d}{ds}\frac{K(s + \omega_0)}{s^2}\right]_{s=-\omega_1} = \left[\frac{-K(s + 2\omega_0)}{s^3}\right]_{s=-\omega_1} = \frac{K(2\omega_0 - \omega_1)}{\omega_1^3}$$

$$K_{23} = \frac{1}{2!}\left[\frac{d^2}{ds^2}\frac{K(s + \omega_0)}{s^2}\right]_{s=-\omega_1} = \frac{1}{2}\left[\frac{d}{ds}\frac{-K(s + 2\omega_0)}{s^3}\right]_{s=-\omega_1} = \frac{K(3\omega_0 - \omega_1)}{\omega_1^4}$$

In the case of K_{23}, use is made of the previous work in obtaining K_{22}. With the use of Table 6-1 the inverse transform is

$$\mathcal{L}^{-1}\left[\frac{K(s + \omega_0)}{s^2(s + \omega_1)^3}\right] = K_{11}t + K_{12} + \left(\frac{K_{21}t^2}{2} + K_{22}t + K_{23}\right)e^{-\omega_1 t} \quad (6\text{-}34)$$

for $0 \leqslant t$ where the K's are given above.

6-7 THE SOLUTION OF SOME IMPORTANT I-D EQUATIONS

The material in Par. 6-6 enables the solution of some of the more important i-d equations found in servo theory. The behavior of the circuit

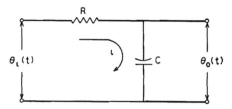

Fig. 6-3   Simple Low-Pass RC Circuit.

in Fig. 6-3 is frequently required for unit step and unit ramp functions as inputs. The i-d equations for the input and output of the network in Fig. 6-3 are

6-7]   THE SOLUTION OF SOME IMPORTANT I-D EQUATIONS   189

$$\left. \begin{array}{l} \theta_i(t) = Ri(t) + \dfrac{1}{C} \int i(t)\, dt \\[2mm] \theta_o(t) = \dfrac{1}{C} \int i(t)\, dt \end{array} \right\} \quad (6\text{-}35)$$

where $\theta_i(t)$ and $\theta_o(t)$ represent voltages.

If we assume the boundary condition of no initial charge on C, then $i^{(-1)}(0+) = 0$ and the $\mathcal{L}$ transforms of Eq. (6-35) are

$$\left. \begin{array}{l} \theta_i(s) = RI(s) + \dfrac{1}{sC} I(s) \\[2mm] \theta_o(s) = \dfrac{1}{sC} I(s) \end{array} \right\} \quad (6\text{-}36)$$

where $\theta_i(s) = \mathcal{L}[\theta_i(t)]$ and $\theta_o(s) = \mathcal{L}[\theta_o(t)]$.*

From the definition 1 in Par. 6-1 the *transfer function*† $G(s)$ is

$$G(s) = \frac{\theta_o(s)}{\theta_i(s)} = \frac{\theta_o}{\theta_i}(s) = \frac{1}{Ts + 1} \quad (6\text{-}37)$$

where $T = RC$ as before. In the equation

$$\theta_o(s) = G(s)\theta_i(s) \quad (6\text{-}38)$$

the $\theta_o(s)$ is referred to as the *response transform* and $\theta_i(s)$ is frequently called the *excitation function* which includes the driving transform and initial conditions. The *driving transform* is the $\mathcal{L}$ transform of the *driving function*, $\theta_i(t)$.

Unit Step Driving Function. Here according to Eq. (6-5) the excitation function is $\theta_i(s) = 1/s$ and hence the response transform is

---

* The $\mathcal{L}$ transform of a function is, as observed in Par. 6-2, an entirely different function in the s-domain; hence strictly $\mathcal{L}[\theta(t)] = \Theta(s)$, i.e., a new symbol is used. Usually lower-case letters are used to represent functions in the time domain, whereas the corresponding upper-case letters represent the $\mathcal{L}$ transforms. However, it has become prevalent in engineering practice to use the same symbol to represent both the time domain function and its $\mathcal{L}$ transform; hence, $\mathcal{L}[\theta(t)] = \theta(s)$. As long as the argument is present there need be no confusion, since $\theta(t)$ stands for a given time function and $\theta(s)$ represents its $\mathcal{L}$ transform—$\theta(s)$ *does not* mean that s has replaced t in $\theta(t)$ as in the conventional algebraic sense. In cases where the argument is not explicitly given, the correct interpretation will depend upon the context. For example, d/dt implies $\theta \equiv \theta(t)$, $\theta_o = \mu\theta_i$ implies $\theta_o \equiv \theta_o(s)$, and $\theta_i \equiv \theta_i(s)$ since μ is a transfer function and is a function of s; $\mu \equiv \mu(s)$.

† The symbol $\dfrac{\theta_o}{\theta_i}(s)$ is used to represent the transfer function, and the symbol $\dfrac{\theta_o}{\theta_i}(j\omega)$ to represent the frequency-response function of a network or system. The transfer characteristic, which is either the transfer function or the frequency response function, is a *characteristic of the network or system* and *is not dependent* upon any *particular input*—hence the use of the symbolic representation. On the other hand, the output response $\theta_o(s) = \dfrac{\theta_o}{\theta_i}(s)\theta_i(s)$ *does* depend upon the input and its associated initial conditions.

$$\theta_o(s) = \frac{1}{s(Ts+1)} \quad (6\text{-}39)$$

Using the partial fraction expansion method of Par. 6-6 yields

$$\theta_o(s) = \frac{K_1}{s} + \frac{K_2}{Ts+1} = \frac{1}{s} + \frac{-T}{Ts+1}$$

$$\therefore \theta_o(s) = \frac{1}{s} - \frac{1}{s+1/T} \quad (6\text{-}40)$$

Taking the $\mathcal{L}^{-1}$ transform recovers $\theta_o(t)$ as

$$\theta_o(t) = 1 - e^{-t/T} \quad (6\text{-}41)$$

It is easily seen that the behavior of $\theta_o(t)$ is described by Fig. 6-4, where $\theta_o(t)$ starts off at zero for $t = 0$ and approaches unity as $t \to \infty$. For a step input the i-d equation has a solution which comprises both transient and steady state solutions.

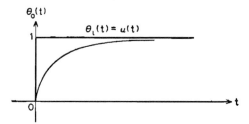

FIG. 6-4 Response of Low-Pass RC Circuit to Unit Step Input.

Unit Ramp Driving Function. Here according to Eq. (6-7) the input transform is $\theta_i(s) = 1/s^2$ and hence

$$\theta_o(s) = \frac{1}{s^2(Ts+1)} \quad (6\text{-}42)$$

which, by Case 2 of Par. 6-6, yields

$$\theta_o(s) = \frac{K_{11}}{s^2} + \frac{K_{12}}{s} + \frac{K_2}{Ts+1}$$

$$= \frac{1}{s^2} - \frac{T}{s} + \frac{T^2}{Ts+1} \quad (6\text{-}43)$$

$$\therefore \theta_o(s) = \frac{1}{s^2} - \frac{T}{s} + \frac{T}{s+1/T}$$

Taking the $\mathcal{L}^{-1}$ transform recovers $\theta_o(t)$ as

$$\theta_o(t) = t - T(1 - e^{-t/T}) \quad (6\text{-}44)$$

A plot of $\theta_o(t)$ in Fig. 6-5 shows that even after the transient term dies out the output never quite reaches the input but is less by an amount T.

The type of analysis illustrated in the two foregoing cases is typical of circuit theory in general. Next an illustration will be given of the differential equations encountered in the study of closed loop servo systems. A typical differential equation relating the error ε and the input θ_i for a position control or proportional-error servo system is

$$\frac{d^2\varepsilon(t)}{dt^2} + 2\zeta\omega_n\frac{d\varepsilon(t)}{dt} + \omega_n^2\varepsilon(t) = \frac{d^2\theta_i(t)}{dt^2} + 2\zeta\omega_n\frac{d\theta_i(t)}{dt} \quad (6\text{-}45)$$

where the constant ζ is called the damping factor and ω_n the undamped natural resonant angular frequency. Taking the $\mathcal{L}$ transform gives

$$s^2\varepsilon(s) - s\varepsilon(0+) - \varepsilon'(0+) + 2\zeta\omega_n[s\varepsilon(s) - \varepsilon(0+)] + \omega_n^2\varepsilon(s)$$
$$= s^2\theta_i(s) - s\theta_i(0+) - \theta_i'(0+) + 2\zeta\omega_n[s\theta_i(s) - \theta_i(0+)] \quad (6\text{-}46)$$

where $\mathcal{L}[\varepsilon(t)] = \varepsilon(s)$. From Eq. (6-46) it is obvious that before a solution can be obtained it is necessary to specify the input and a set of boundary

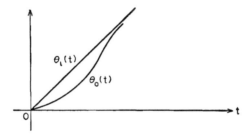

Fig. 6-5 Response of Low-Pass RC Circuit to Unit Ramp Input.

conditions. A very common input in testing servo response is the step velocity or ramp displacement input with the initial conditions:

$$\left.\begin{array}{l}\theta_i(t) = \omega_i t, \quad 0 \leqslant t \\ \theta_i(t) = \varepsilon = 0, \quad t = 0+ \\ \theta_i'(t) = \varepsilon' = \omega_i, \quad t = 0+\end{array}\right\} \quad (6\text{-}47)$$

By use of these conditions Eq. (6-46) becomes

$$s^2\varepsilon(s) - \omega_i + 2\zeta\omega_n s\varepsilon(s) + \omega_n^2\varepsilon(s) = s^2\theta_i(s) - \omega_i + 2\zeta\omega_n s\theta_i(s) \quad (6\text{-}48)$$

Since $\theta_i(t) = \omega_i t$ and hence $\theta_i(s) = \omega_i/s^2$, this becomes

$$\varepsilon(s) = \frac{\omega_i(s + 2\zeta\omega_n)}{s(s^2 + 2\zeta\omega_n s + \omega_n^2)} \quad (6\text{-}49)$$

Let the roots in the quadratic factor of the denominator be denoted by

$$\left.\begin{array}{l}\alpha_1 = -\zeta\omega_n + \omega_n\sqrt{\zeta^2 - 1} \\ \alpha_2 = -\zeta\omega_n - \omega_n\sqrt{\zeta^2 - 1}\end{array}\right\} \quad (6\text{-}50)$$

so that $\mathcal{E}(s)$ becomes

$$\mathcal{E}(s) = \frac{\omega_s(s + 2\zeta\omega_n)}{s(s - \alpha_1)(s - \alpha_2)} \tag{6-51}$$

Expansion by partial fractions is now possible; however, it is seen from Eq. (6-50) that the result depends upon the value of ζ. If $\zeta > 1$, then α_1 and α_2 are real and different and a solution of Eq. (6-51) is possible by the method of Case 1, Par. 6-6. The system is said to be *overdamped*. If $\zeta = 1$, called *critical damping*, then $\alpha_1 = \alpha_2$, and Case 2, Par. 6-6, applies. If $\zeta < 1$ the system is *underdamped* and α_1 and α_2 are complex conjugates. Since this condition was not considered in Par. 6-6 it will be developed here. Let the roots be denoted by

$$\left.\begin{array}{l}\alpha_1 = -\alpha + j\beta \\ \alpha_2 = -\alpha - j\beta\end{array}\right\} \tag{6-52}$$

so that the response transform can be written as

$$\begin{aligned}\mathcal{E}(s) &= \frac{\omega_s(s + 2\zeta\omega_n)}{s(s + \alpha - j\beta)(s + \alpha + j\beta)} \\ &= \frac{\omega_s(s + 2\zeta\omega_n)}{s[(s + \alpha)^2 + \beta^2]}\end{aligned} \tag{6-53}$$

According to No. 13, Table 6-1, the inverse transform is

$$\mathcal{E}(t) = \frac{2\zeta\omega_s\omega_n}{\beta_0^2} + \frac{\omega_s}{\beta\beta_0}[(2\zeta\omega_n - \alpha)^2 + \beta^2]^{\frac{1}{2}} e^{-\alpha t} \sin(\beta t + \psi) \tag{6-54}$$

where

$$\beta_0 = [\alpha^2 + \beta^2]^{\frac{1}{2}}, \quad \psi = \tan^{-1}\frac{\beta}{2\zeta\omega_n - \alpha} - \tan^{-1}\frac{\beta}{-\alpha}$$

The solution is seen to consist of a constant steady-state term and an exponentially decaying sinusoidal transient. Although Eq. (6-53) could have been solved by use of partial fractions, it is always simpler to use the function-transform pairs whenever the proper ones can be found. The complete solution of the servo problem posed in Eq. (6-45) is then available from Eq. (6-49), depending upon the value of ζ for the step velocity input assumption. The preceding example illustrates the use of the $\mathcal{L}$-transform method for boundary conditions which are not all zero. It is seen that the method handles such problems without difficulty and will thus yield simultaneously both that part of the transient resulting from the boundary conditions and the part due to the excitation function alone. The Laplace transform offers a tremendous advantage over all other methods for treating arbitrary initial conditions.

6-8 THE FOURIER TRANSFORM

In the study of both circuit analysis and servo problems it is frequently unnecessary to obtain the transient response due to nonzero initial conditions. In such cases it is possible to use the *Fourier-transform* method which leads to the *frequency-response functions* defined in Par. 6-1 and discussed in more detail in Par. 6-9. The Fourier transforms are defined by

$$f(t) = \frac{1}{2\pi} \int_{-\infty}^{\infty} F(j\omega) e^{j\omega t} \, d\omega \qquad (6\text{-}55)$$

$$F(j\omega) = \int_{-\infty}^{\infty} f(t) e^{-j\omega t} \, dt \qquad (6\text{-}56)$$

Some writers call Eq. (6-56) the *direct* Fourier transform and Eq. (6-55) the *inverse* Fourier transform; however, usually both are called simply Fourier transforms. It should be noted that the factor $1/2\pi$ could have as well been associated with Eq. (6-56) instead of Eq. (6-55) or a factor $1/\sqrt{2\pi}$ could be placed before each integral. In order that $f(t)$ possess a Fourier transform it is necessary that

$$\int_{-\infty}^{\infty} |f(t)| \, dt < \infty$$

Hence there are many functions which do not have a Fourier transform. In this respect the Laplace transform is considerably more general than the Fourier transform. There exist tables of Fourier-transform pairs very similar to the function-transform pairs for the Laplace transform. Perhaps the most extensive such table is that of Campbell and Foster in *Bell System Monograph B584*.[6]

6-9 THE FREQUENCY-RESPONSE FUNCTION

The impulse response $h(t)$ of a network was defined in Par. 6-1 to be the response of the network to a unit impulse at time $t = 0$. For time-invariant networks the output response to a unit impulse applied at time $t = t_1$ is given by $h(t - t_1)$. Since only linear networks are being considered, for which the superposition principle holds, the output response for any arbitrary input, $\theta_i(t)$, may be determined as follows. Consider $\theta_i(t)$ to be made up of samples of height $\theta_i(t)$ and width dt. These samples can be considered impulses of area $\theta_i(t) \, dt$ at times t. The output of a network at any time t_0 due to this impulse is $\theta_i(t) \, dt \, h(t_0 - t)$. The resultant output to all such inputs making up $\theta_i(t)$ will hence be

$$\theta_o(t_0) = \int_{-\infty}^{t_0} \theta_i(t) h(t_0 - t) \, dt \qquad (6\text{-}57)$$

since only inputs prior to t_0 will contribute. By changing the variable of integration from t to $\tau = t_0 - t$ and then replacing t_0 by t, Eq. (6-57) becomes

[6] Campbell, George A. and Foster, Ronald M., "Fourier Integrals for Practical Application," *Bell Tel. System Tech. Pub., Monograph B584*.

$$\theta_o(t) = \int_0^\infty \theta_i(t-\tau)h(\tau)\,d\tau \qquad (6\text{-}58)$$

Since $h(\tau) = 0$ for $\tau < 0$ this may be written

$$\theta_o(t) = \int_{-\infty}^\infty \theta_i(t-\tau)h(\tau)\,d\tau \qquad (6\text{-}59)$$

A study of Eq. (6-59) shows why the impulse response is frequently called the *weighting function*, for $h(\tau)$ actually weights the input at time t according to its age τ. Now if the input is sinusoidal in form expressed by $\theta_i(t) = Ae^{j\omega t}$, then the output is given according to Eq. (6-59) by

$$\theta_o(t) = A\int_{-\infty}^\infty e^{j\omega(t-\tau)}h(\tau)\,d\tau$$
$$= Ae^{j\omega t}\int_{-\infty}^\infty h(\tau)e^{-j\omega \tau}\,d\tau \qquad (6\text{-}60)$$

If the integral is designated by

$$G(j\omega) = \int_{-\infty}^\infty h(\tau)e^{-j\omega \tau}\,d\tau \qquad (6\text{-}61)$$

then it is seen from

$$\theta_o(t) = Ae^{j\omega t}G(j\omega) \qquad (6\text{-}62)$$

that for sinusoidal inputs the output of a linear network is also sinusoidal, modified in amplitude and phase by $G(j\omega)$. The function $G(j\omega)$ is called the *frequency-response function*. It is seen from Eq. (6-61) that the frequency-response function is the Fourier transform of the impulse response. The input $\theta_i(t)$ is related to its Fourier transform $\theta_i(j\omega)$ by

$$\theta_i(t) = \frac{1}{2\pi}\int_{-\infty}^\infty \theta_i(j\omega)e^{j\omega t}\,d\omega \qquad (6\text{-}63)$$

Using Eq. (6-61) and (6-63) in Eq. (6-59) yields the following:

$$\theta_o(t) = \int_{-\infty}^\infty d\tau \frac{1}{2\pi}\int_{-\infty}^\infty d\omega\, \theta_i(j\omega)e^{j\omega(t-\tau)}h(\tau)$$
$$= \frac{1}{2\pi}\int_{-\infty}^\infty d\omega\, \theta_i(j\omega)e^{j\omega t}\int_{-\infty}^\infty h(\tau)e^{-j\omega \tau}\,d\tau \qquad (6\text{-}64)$$
$$= \frac{1}{2\pi}\int_{-\infty}^\infty d\omega\, \theta_i(j\omega)G(j\omega)e^{j\omega t}$$

From Eq. (6-64), the integrand must contain the Fourier transform of $\theta_o(t)$ and hence

$$\theta_o(j\omega) = G(j\omega)\theta_i(j\omega) \qquad (6\text{-}65)$$

This is the mathematical expression of the definition of the frequency-response function as the ratio between the Fourier transforms of the output and input.

6-10 SIMPLIFICATION BY REPLACING d/dt BY $j\omega$ FOR STEADY-STATE OPERATION

For steady-state operation with sinusoidal inputs it is always possible to obtain the Fourier-transform operational form of the differential equation representing a system by replacing the operator $\dfrac{d}{dt}$ by $j\omega$ and the operator $\int dt$ by $\dfrac{1}{j\omega}$. This can readily be demonstrated if the applied sinusoidal voltage is written in exponential form. For example, if the input is

$$\theta_i(t) = A \cos \omega t \tag{6-66}$$

this can be represented by the real part of $Ae^{j\omega t}$, so that

$$\theta_i(t) = Ae^{j\omega t} \tag{6-67}$$

remembering that in the end result the real part only is to be retained. Then,

$$\frac{d\theta_i(t)}{dt} = A \frac{d \cos \omega t}{dt} = -A\omega \sin \omega t \tag{6-68}$$

from Eq. (6-66), and from Eq. (6-67)

$$\frac{d\theta_i(t)}{dt} = Aj\omega e^{j\omega t} \tag{6-69}$$

Taking the real part of Eq. (6-69) yields

$$\begin{aligned}
\operatorname{Re}\left[Aj\omega e^{j\omega t}\right] &= \operatorname{Re}\left[Aj\omega(\cos \omega t + j \sin \omega t)\right] \\
&= \operatorname{Re}\left[-A\omega \sin \omega t + jA\omega \cos \omega t\right] \\
&= -A\omega \sin \omega t
\end{aligned} \tag{6-70}$$

which result is the same as Eq. (6-68). Hence

$$\frac{d\theta_i(t)}{dt} = j\omega \theta_i(t) = Aj\omega e^{j\omega t} \tag{6-71}$$

It can be shown in a similar manner that

$$\int \theta_i(t)\, dt \equiv \int dt \cdot \theta_i(t) \equiv \frac{1}{j\omega} \theta_i(t) \tag{6-72}$$

Proof will be left to the reader.

In steady-state network analysis it is not necessary to write down the differential equation; analysis by the impedance method is simpler. The impedance of a pure inductance L is simply $j\omega L$ and that of a capacitance is $1/j\omega C$; thus the elementary circuit of Fig. 6-6 may be analyzed by relating the complex current and voltage by

$$\left(R + j\omega L + \frac{1}{j\omega C}\right) i = E e^{j\omega t} \\ \frac{1}{j\omega C} i = \theta_o(t)$$ (6-73)

Thus

$$\theta_o(t) = \frac{E e^{j\omega t}}{(1 - \omega^2 LC) + j\omega RC}$$ (6-74)

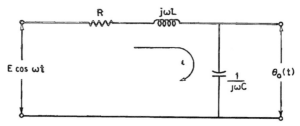

FIG. 6-6 Simple RLC Circuit with Sinusoidal Input.

where the real part of the result is to be used. Here we see the fact demonstrated that the output will be of the same frequency as the input but altered in amplitude and phase. From Eq. (6-73) and (6-74) where

$$\theta_i(t) = E e^{j\omega t}$$ (6-75)

the frequency-response function is

$$\frac{\theta_o(t)}{\theta_i(t)} = G(j\omega) = \frac{1}{(1 - \omega^2 LC) + j\omega RC}$$ (6-76)

In this special case, where sinusoidal inputs only are used, the ratio of the output-to-input time functions provides the frequency-response function which can be used to relate the Fourier transform of the output to the Fourier transform of any general input, if such a transform exists.

6-11 THE TRANSFER CHARACTERISTIC OF A SYSTEM

The *transfer characteristic* is the system function relating the transforms of the output and input. If the Laplace transform method of analysis is employed to obtain the system function, all initial conditions are made zero, and the resultant transfer function is written in terms of the complex variable s. If s is now replaced by $j\omega$ the result is the frequency-response function, which can be used to plot the amplitude and phase response to sinusoidal inputs.

If the given functional relationship between the output and the input is the frequency-response function, then the transfer function can be obtained from this by replacing $j\omega$ by s. The resultant transfer function can be used to obtain the transient response for any input, provided the initial conditions are actually zero. If, in fact, the initial conditions are not zero, then the transient solution can be obtained from the frequency-response function as follows: replace $j\omega$ by d/dt in the frequency-response function; solve the resulting differential equation by the Laplace-transform method, putting in the actual initial conditions.

6-12 CORRELATION FUNCTIONS

Two functions which are receiving an increasing amount of attention in the fields of information theory and communication theory are the *autocorrelation function* defined by

$$\phi_{11}(\tau) = \lim_{T \to \infty} \frac{1}{2T} \int_{-T}^{T} f(t)f(t - \tau)\, dt \qquad (6\text{-}77)$$

and the *crosscorrelation function* defined by

$$\phi_{12}(\tau) = \lim_{T \to \infty} \frac{1}{2T} \int_{-T}^{T} f_1(t)f_2(t - \tau)\, dt \qquad (6\text{-}78)$$

where τ is a time delay parameter. In these definitions the functions $f(t)$ are considered to be continuous and

$$\lim_{T \to \infty} \frac{1}{2T} \int_{-T}^{T} f^2(t)\, dt < \infty \qquad (6\text{-}79)$$

It is readily observed that $\phi_{11}(\tau)$ is an even function, so that

$$\phi_{11}(\tau) = \phi_{11}(-\tau) \qquad (6\text{-}80)$$

whereas for the crosscorrelation function

$$\phi_{12}(\tau) = \phi_{21}(-\tau) \qquad (6\text{-}81)$$

The autocorrelation function discards phase information in regard to $f(t)$, whereas the crosscorrelation function retains phase information, provided at least one of the functions, $f_1(t)$ or $f_2(t)$, is periodic.

There is an important relationship between the autocorrelation function and the power spectrum of $f(t)$ given by the Fourier-transform pair:

$$\phi_{11}(\tau) = \frac{1}{2\pi} \int_{-\infty}^{\infty} \Phi_{11}(\omega) e^{j\omega\tau}\, d\omega \qquad (6\text{-}82)$$

$$\Phi_{11}(\omega) = \int_{-\infty}^{\infty} \phi_{11}(\tau) e^{-j\omega\tau}\, d\tau \qquad (6\text{-}83)$$

where $\Phi_{11}(\omega)$ represents the power density spectrum of $f(t)$. Since $\phi_{11}(\tau)$ and $\Phi_{11}(\omega)$ are even functions, these relations can be simplified to

$$\phi_{11}(\tau) = \frac{1}{\pi} \int_{0}^{\infty} \Phi_{11}(\omega) \cos \omega\tau\, d\omega \qquad (6\text{-}84)$$

$$\Phi_{11}(\omega) = 2\int_{0}^{\infty} \phi_{11}(\tau) \cos \omega\tau\, d\tau \qquad (6\text{-}85)$$

The autocorrelation function as defined by Eq. (6-77) is a time domain concept representing the following steps: (1) the given function is delayed by a time τ, (2) the given function is multiplied by the delayed function, and (3) the average is taken over a period which is allowed to become infinite. An example follows for a periodic function.

Example 1. Find $\phi_{11}(\tau)$ for $f(t) = A \sin(\omega_0 t + \psi)$. Here from Eq. (6-77) and (6-80) the autocorrelation function is

$$\phi_{11}(\tau) = \lim_{T \to \infty} \frac{1}{2T} \int_{-T}^{T} A \sin(\omega_0 t + \psi) A \sin[\omega_0(t - \tau) + \psi] \, dt \quad (6\text{-}86)$$

Trigonometric manipulation yields

$$\phi_{11}(\tau) = \lim_{T \to \infty} \frac{A^2}{4T} \int_{-T}^{T} [\cos \omega_0 \tau - \cos(2\omega_0 t - \omega_0 \tau + 2\psi)] \, dt$$

$$= \frac{A^2 \cos \omega_0 \tau}{2} - \lim_{T \to \infty} \frac{A^2}{8\omega_0 T} \left[\sin(2\omega_0 t - \omega_0 \tau + 2\psi) \right]_{-T}^{T}$$

$$= \frac{A^2 \cos \omega_0 \tau}{2} - \lim_{T \to \infty} \frac{A^2}{8\omega_0 T} [\sin(2\omega_0 T - \omega_0 \tau + 2\psi)$$
$$+ \sin(2\omega_0 T + \omega_0 \tau - 2\psi)]$$

$$= \frac{A^2 \cos \omega_0 \tau}{2} - 0$$

$$\therefore \phi_{11}(\tau) = \frac{A^2}{2} \cos \omega_0 \tau \quad (6\text{-}87)$$

It is seen that the phase angle ψ is disregarded and the autocorrelation function is also sinusoidal and an even function.

The crosscorrelation function has an interesting application in network analysis. It can be shown[7] by the use of the convolution integral that the impulse response of any network or system is given by the crosscorrelation function between the output and input for an input of wide-band random noise.

If the input noise is $n_i(t)$ and output $n_o(t)$, then

$$\phi_{12}(\tau) = \lim_{T \to \infty} \frac{1}{2T} \int_{-T}^{T} n_o(t) n_i(t - \tau) \, dt = h(\tau) \quad (6\text{-}88)$$

This, of course, can be transformed into the system transfer function. This method has the advantage that the results will not be appreciably affected by extraneous noise; however, it requires: (1) wide-band input noise, (2) multiplication circuits capable of handling wide-band noise, and (3) sufficiently long integration time to give good smoothing. These requirements could be rather severe in some cases since the input noise bandwidth must be wider than the effective bandwidth of the system under test.

[7] Goldman, Stanford, *Information Theory*, pp. 278-279, Prentice-Hall, Inc., New York, 1953.

6-13 POLES, ZEROS, AND ANALYTIC FUNCTIONS

In Par. 6-6 it was stated that the end product of the $\mathcal{L}$-transform solution was generally a function of the form

$$F(s) = \frac{A(s)}{B(s)} \qquad (6\text{-}89)$$

where $A(s)$ and $B(s)$ are polynomials in s with real coefficients. By obtaining the roots of $A(s) = 0$ and $B(s) = 0$ the numerator and denominator can be factored and Eq. (6-89) can be expressed as

$$F(s) = \frac{(s - z_1)(s - z_2) \cdots (s - z_m)}{(s - p_1)(s - p_2) \cdots (s - p_n)} \qquad (6\text{-}90)$$

The values $z_1, z_2, \cdots, z_m$ are called the *zeros* of the function $F(s)$ and $p_1, p_2, \cdots, p_n$ are called the *poles* of the function $F(s)$. As illustrated in Eq. (6-90) there are only *first-order* zeros and poles; however, if $F(s)$ can be written as

$$F(s) = (s - z_1)^b G(s) \qquad (6\text{-}91)$$

where b is a positive integer, then $F(s)$ has a *zero of order b* at the point z_1. Further, if $F(s)$ can be written as

$$F(s) = \frac{G(s)}{(s - p_1)^b} \qquad (6\text{-}92)$$

where b is a positive integer, then $F(s)$ has a *pole of order b* at the point p_1. For example, in Par. 6-7 it was found that the transform of the output of a simple RC integrator for a unit ramp input was

$$\theta_o(s) = \frac{1}{s^2(Ts + 1)} \qquad (6\text{-}93)$$

Here $\theta_o(s)$ has no zeros but has a second-order pole at 0 and a first order pole at $-1/T$.

A function, $F(s)$, is said to be *analytic* at the point s_1 if the function has a unique derivative at the point s_1. The necessary condition for a function to possess a unique derivative, i.e., for the derivative at the point to be independent of how that point is approached, is that the function satisfy the *Cauchy-Riemann equations*. These equations are

$$\frac{\partial u}{\partial \sigma} = \frac{\partial v}{\partial \omega} \quad \text{and} \quad \frac{\partial v}{\partial \sigma} = -\frac{\partial u}{\partial \omega} \qquad (6\text{-}94)$$

where the u and v are defined by

$$\left. \begin{array}{c} F(s) = u(\sigma, \omega) + jv(\sigma, \omega) \\ u = \text{Re}\,[F(s)] \quad \text{and} \quad v = \text{Im}\,[F(s)] \end{array} \right\} \qquad (6\text{-}95)$$

If these partial derivatives exist and are continuous in a region containing s_1, then the truth of the Cauchy-Riemann equations is also a sufficient

MATHEMATICAL GROUNDWORK

condition for analyticity. From these definitions it is readily seen that s itself is analytic everywhere in the complex plane. A function is analytic in a region, R, of the complex plane if the function is analytic at every point in that region.

6-14 STABILITY IN FEEDBACK SYSTEMS

Determination of the stability of a feedback system is of the utmost importance in the design and development of servomechanisms. In any control system it is absolutely essential that the transient response of the system be such that transient disturbances decay rapidly and do not ever build up or cause self-sustained oscillation. A system will be considered *stable* if a small transient disturbance in the input results in a response which ultimately dies out. A system will be called *unstable* if such an input disturbance results in a response of self-sustained oscillations or a response which increases indefinitely until it is limited by the nonlinearity of the system.

There are a number of methods for determining whether or not a system is stable. The first methods to be presented here are based upon the integro-differential equation representing the system and they determine absolute stability. These methods do not indicate just *how* stable a system is; i.e., they do not give any quantitative information on the *margin of stability*. Hence they are not so important as a later method to be presented, called *Nyquist's Criterion*, which gives a considerable insight into the whole stability problem.

Characteristic Equation Method. If a system is represented by an i-d equation of the form

$$a_0 \frac{d^n \theta_o(t)}{dt^n} + a_1 \frac{d^{n-1} \theta_o(t)}{dt^{n-1}} + \cdots + a_{n-1} \frac{d\theta_o(t)}{dt} + a_n \theta_o(t)$$

$$+ a_{n+1} \int \theta_o(t)\, dt + \cdots + a_{n+m} \overbrace{\int \cdots \int}^{m \text{ times}} \theta_o(t)\, dt_1 \cdots dt_m = \theta_i(t) \quad (6\text{-}96)$$

then the *characteristic equation* for the system is given by

$$a_0 s^{n+m} + a_1 s^{n+m-1} + \cdots + a_{n-1} s^{m+1} + a_n s^m + a_{n+1} s^{m-1} + \cdots + a_{n+m} = 0 \quad (6\text{-}97)$$

To obtain the characteristic equation in this case the driving function is first set equal to zero, thus bringing the i-d equation into reduced form. Next, the operator d/dt is replaced by s and $\int dt$ by $1/s$. Finally, the resulting equation is multiplied through by the highest power of s in the denominators, thus leaving one constant term.

It can readily be seen that the characteristic equation is also easily obtained from the transfer function. A simple single-loop servo system containing a feedback element is shown in Fig. 6-7. The transfer function for this sytem is determined symbolically as follows:

$$(\theta_i + \beta\theta_o)\mu = \theta_o$$
$$\theta_o(1 - \mu\beta) = \mu\theta_i$$
$$\therefore \frac{\theta_o}{\theta_i} = \frac{\mu}{1 - \mu\beta} \qquad (6\text{-}98)$$

In terms of the elements of Fig. 6-7 this is

$$\frac{\theta_o}{\theta_i}(s) = \frac{K_1 G_1(s)}{1 - K_1 G_1(s) K_2 G_2(s)} \qquad (6\text{-}99)$$

According to the definition above the characteristic equation for this servo system is

$$1 - K_1 G_1(s) K_2 G_2(s) = 0 \qquad (6\text{-}100)$$

where K_1 and K_2 are constants independent of s.

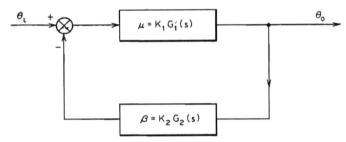

Fig. 6-7 Simple Single-Loop Servo System with Feedback Element.

THEOREM 8. *In order that a system be stable, all of the zeros of the characteristic equation must lie in the left half of the complex plane.*

This means that the real part of all of the zeros must be negative. From the exponential form of the solution of linear differential equations, it is seen that the transients decay more rapidly as the magnitude of the real parts of the zeros increases. This offers some qualitative idea as to how stable a system may be.

The characteristic-equation method just outlined can become very laborious if the equation is higher than fourth degree, since the zeros must be obtained, necessitating the solution of the polynomial. The next method is an attempt to avoid such computation.

Routh's Criterion. In order to eliminate the need for actually evaluating the zeros of the characteristic equation, Routh's criterion can be employed to determine the presence of zeros in the right half-plane. Consider a system having the following characteristic equation

$$a_0 s^n + a_1 s^{n-1} + \cdots + a_{n-1} s + a_n = 0 \qquad (6\text{-}101)$$

where all coefficients are present. If any coefficient is missing the system is unstable. The following triangular array is calculated from the original coefficients

$$\begin{array}{cccccc} a_0 & a_2 & a_4 & a_6 & a_8 & \ldots \\ a_1 & a_3 & a_5 & a_7 & a_9 & \ldots \\ b_1 & b_3 & b_5 & b_7 & \ldots \\ c_1 & c_3 & c_5 & \ldots \\ d_1 & d_3 & \ldots \\ e_1 & \ldots \end{array} \qquad (6\text{-}102)$$

where the calculations are made as follows:

$$b_1 = \frac{-\begin{vmatrix} a_0 & a_2 \\ a_1 & a_3 \end{vmatrix}}{a_1} = \frac{a_1 a_2 - a_0 a_3}{a_1} \qquad (6\text{-}103)$$

$$b_3 = \frac{-\begin{vmatrix} a_0 & a_4 \\ a_1 & a_5 \end{vmatrix}}{a_1} = \frac{a_1 a_4 - a_0 a_5}{a_1} \qquad (6\text{-}104)$$

$$b_5 = \frac{-\begin{vmatrix} a_0 & a_6 \\ a_1 & a_7 \end{vmatrix}}{a_1} = \frac{a_1 a_6 - a_0 a_7}{a_1} \qquad (6\text{-}105)$$

$$c_1 = \frac{-\begin{vmatrix} a_1 & a_3 \\ b_1 & b_3 \end{vmatrix}}{b_1} = \frac{b_1 a_3 - a_1 b_3}{b_1} \qquad (6\text{-}106)$$

$$c_3 = \frac{-\begin{vmatrix} a_1 & a_5 \\ b_1 & b_5 \end{vmatrix}}{b_1} = \frac{b_1 a_5 - a_1 b_5}{b_1} \qquad (6\text{-}107)$$

$$d_1 = \frac{-\begin{vmatrix} b_1 & b_3 \\ c_1 & c_3 \end{vmatrix}}{c_1} = \frac{c_1 b_3 - b_1 c_3}{c_1} \qquad (6\text{-}108)$$

and so on. This process is continued until all zeros are obtained for additional coefficients. Array (6-102) is then inspected.

THEOREM 9. *The system represented by Eq. (6-101) is stable if, and only if, all of the terms in the left-hand column of the array (6-102) have the same algebraic sign.*

If all the terms in the left-hand column do have the same sign, then the characteristic equation has no zeros with positive real parts. If changes in sign do exist, then the system is unstable and the number of changes in sign is equal to the number of zeros with positive real parts.

Example 1

$$s^6 + 3s^5 + 5s^4 + s^3 + 2s^2 + 6s + 1 = 0$$

Routh Array:

1	5	2	1
3	1	6	
$\frac{14}{3}$	0	1	
1	$\frac{75}{14}$		
-25	1		
$\frac{1889}{350}$			
1			

From this array it is seen that the system is unstable and since there are two changes in sign there are two zeros of the characteristic equation with positive real parts.

The Nyquist Stability Criterion. System stability was discussed in Theorem 8 in connection with the zeros of the characteristic equation of the system given by (6-100). The characteristic-equation method becomes especially laborious in practice when the equation is of fifth degree and higher. A much more useful criterion was developed by H. Nyquist;[8] this has now become known as the *Nyquist stability criterion.* Although this criterion as such will not be used in Chapter 7 in discussing system stability, the method will be briefly expounded here for the following reasons: (a) the attentuation-frequency diagram method of Chapter 7 is based on the Nyquist criterion, (b) the method of Nyquist is widely employed by servo engineers, and (c) it will afford some measure of comparison between the two methods most commonly used in stability studies.

The Nyquist stability criterion is based upon the closed loop transfer characteristic which provides the characteristic equation (Eq. 6-100). For a single-loop system with $\beta = -1$ the characteristic equation can be written as $1 + KG(s) = 0$. The Nyquist criterion makes use of the complex plane plot of $KG(j\omega)$, hereafter referred to as the *KG locus.* It might be noted that $KG(j\omega)$ also represents the open loop response for the simple servo system under consideration.

The first step in applying the Nyquist criterion is to plot the *KG* locus or *Nyquist diagram* on the complex plane. Whereas in pole-zero analysis the imaginary axis of the *s*-plane is the boundary line between the regions of stability and instability, in *KG*-locus analysis the behavior of the locus in the vicinity of the $-1 + j0$ point determines system stability. The following theorems are offered without proof.

THEOREM 10. *A system is stable, provided the KG locus does not pass through or enclose the $-1 + j0$ point.*

[8] Nyquist, H., "Regeneration Theory," *Bell Tel. System Tech. Pub., Monograph B642*, 1932.

THEOREM 11. *A system will go into sustained oscillation if the KG locus passes through the $-1 + j0$ point.*

THEOREM 12. *Destructive oscillation exists whenever the KG locus encloses the $-1 + j0$ point; such oscillation will continue to increase until some nonlinearity provides limiting, or until system failure provides a system breakdown.*

These three conditions are illustrated in Fig. 6-8 for the simple open loop frequency-response function

$$KG(j\omega) = \frac{K_c}{(j\omega + \omega_0)(j\omega + \omega_1)(j\omega + \omega_2)} \qquad (6\text{-}109)$$

Note that the *KG* locus is shown as a complex plane plot in which the real part is plotted along the horizontal axis and the imaginary part along the

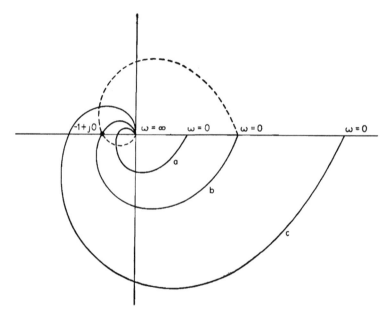

FIG. 6-8 Examples of Stable and Unstable KG(s) Loci.

vertical axis. In practice the locus is usually plotted in polar coordinates for convenience. For low gain, Theorem 10 applies since the *KG* locus (a) of Fig. 6-8 does not encompass the $-1 + j0$ point. Curve (b) shows a case in which the gain is sufficiently high to cause instability. The *KG* locus passes through the $-1 + j0$ point, thus illustrating Theorem 11. As the gain is further increased, the *KG* locus encloses the $-1 + j0$ point as shown in curve (c) and Theorem 12 applies. The Nyquist criterion is thus seen to be very simple for single loop servo systems with $\beta = -1$.

When multiple loop systems are considered, the Nyquist criterion is extended by means of Cauchy's integral theorem to handle the stability problem. That this problem is more difficult to handle results from the fact that poles may exist in the right half s-plane for $KG(s)$, i.e., in the open loop response, whereas the closed loop system could still be stable. The first step in applying the *generalized* Nyquist criterion is, as before, to plot the $KG(s)$ locus for $s = j\omega$. Here, however, the $KG(s)$ will not in general be a simple function, but will represent the composite function

$$KG(s) = K_1G_1(s)K_2G_2(s) \cdots \qquad (6\text{-}110)$$

A vector is next drawn from the $-1 + j0$ point to any arbitrary point on the KG locus. Let this vector traverse the KG locus and observe the net change in phase $-2\pi N$ as ω varies from $-\infty$ to $+\infty$. The net number of counterclockwise revolutions about the $-1 + j0$ point is given by N. Let P be the number of poles of $KG(s)$ in the right half plane.

THEOREM 13.[9] *A system is stable if, and only if, the number of counterclockwise revolutions N of a vector from the $-1 + j0$ point to the KG locus is equal to P, the number of poles of KG(s) with positive real parts.*

A logical corollary to Theorem 13 is the case of $P = 0$ which leads to the simpler criteria of Theorems 10, 11, 12.

The three plots in Fig. 6-8 are all closed plots in that the complete plot of KG for $-\infty \leqslant \omega \leqslant \infty$ forms a continuous curve which is closed on itself. For servo systems, in general, this is not true because of the presence of poles at the origin. Such cases give rise to open plots in which the KG locus becomes infinite at $\omega = 0$. It is of importance to know how to close the plot since this will determine the stability of the system.

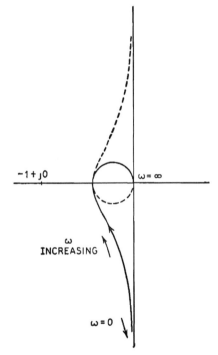

FIG. 6-9 Example of an Open KG(s) Locus.

---

[9] A good discussion of the Theorem can be found in: Chestnut, H. and Mayer, C. W., *Servomechanisms and Regulating System Design*, Vol. I, pp. 138-146, John Wiley & Sons, Inc., N. Y., 1951.

One example of an open-plot *KG* locus is shown in Fig. 6-9. Here $KG \to \infty$ as $\omega \to 0$ and the question to be settled is just how the plot is joined from $\omega = 0-$ to $\omega = 0+$. In order to resolve the pole at $\omega = 0$ consider the *s*-plane plot of Fig. 6-10. Let the path of a point begin at $s = -j\infty$ and proceed along the negative imaginary axis until ω gets very small. Then the path detours the origin on a small semicircle in the positive half plane as shown until it reaches a very small positive value of ω after which it proceeds along the positive imaginary axis until $s = +j\infty$.

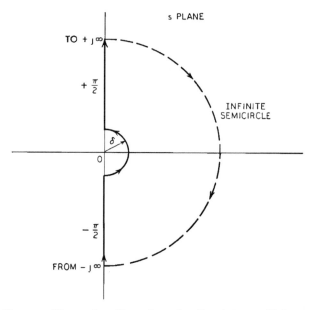

Fig. 6-10 Contour Illustrating Procedure for Resolving a Pole at the Origin.

The usual procedure for handling this situation in function theory is to let the small semicircular path about the pole at the origin be denoted by

$$s = \delta e^{j\phi} \quad (6\text{-}111)$$

where $\delta \to 0$ and $-\frac{\pi}{2} < \phi < \frac{\pi}{2}$. If the *KG* locus of Fig. 6-9 is given by

$$KG(s) = \frac{K}{s(s + \omega_0)(s + \omega_1)} \quad (6\text{-}112)$$

then as $s \to 0$ this becomes

$$KG \to \frac{K}{\omega_0 \omega_1 s} = \frac{K e^{-j\phi}}{\omega_0 \omega_1 \delta} \quad (6\text{-}113)$$

using Eq. (6-111). Now as $\delta \to 0$ the magnitude of the *KG* locus becomes infinite and as ϕ goes from $-\pi/2$ to $\pi/2$ the phase angle of the *KG* locus goes from $+\pi/2$ to $-\pi/2$. This means that the points $\omega = 0-$ and $\omega = 0+$ are joined by means of the infinite semicircle as shown in Fig. 6-10. It can be shown in an analogous manner that for a $KG(s)$ function containing s^n in the denominator, the KG locus makes n clockwise semicircles of infinite radius about the origin as ω passes through zero.

Applications. In order to illustrate the use of the Nyquist stability criterion and in particular the application of Theorem 13, a couple of illustrative examples will be given. These will be representative of system transfer functions which might be found in practice.

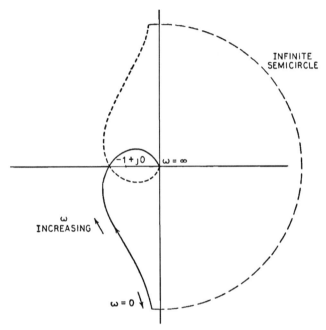

FIG. 6-11 Unstable Position Control Servo System with an Open-Loop $KG(s) = \dfrac{K}{s(s + \omega_0)(s + \omega_1)}$.

Example 1. Basic Type I Position Control Servo System:

$$KG(s) = \frac{K}{s(s + \omega_0)(s + \omega_1)} \qquad (6\text{-}114)$$

The stability of a system whose open loop transfer function is given by Eq. (6-114) depends upon the values of gain K and of ω_0 and ω_1. Figure 6-11 illustrates a choice of parameters which make the system unstable. The system can be made stable by lowering the system gain or by employing suitable compensation. The latter method is illustrated in Fig. 6-12 and is represented by

$$KG(s) = \frac{K(s + \omega_2)}{s(s + \omega_0)(s + \omega_1)} \qquad (6\text{-}115)$$

It should be noted that these $KG(s)$ plots are not drawn to scale but merely indicate the general shape of the KG loci.

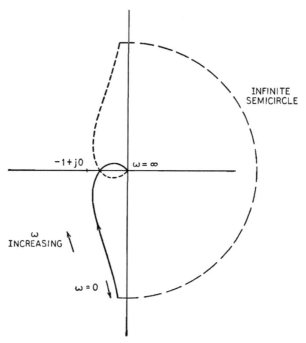

FIG. 6-12 Stable Position Control Servo System with an Open-Loop $KG(s) = \dfrac{K(s + \omega_2)}{s(s + \omega_0)(s + \omega_1)}$.

Example 2. Basic Type II Velocity Control Servo System:

$$KG(s) = \frac{K(s + \omega_0)}{s^2(s + \omega_1)(s + \omega_2)} \qquad (6\text{-}116)$$

This transfer function represents a servo system frequently referred to as a "zero-velocity error" system; i.e., no error exists for a constant velocity input.

Figure 6-13 shows a choice of parameters yielding an unstable system. Here there are no poles in the right half plane, or $P = 0$, whereas a vector from the $-1 + j0$ point to the KG locus makes two clockwise revolutions as ω varies from $-\infty$ to $+\infty$, i.e., $N = -2$. Since $N \neq P$, the system is unstable. By reducing the gain, the system can be made stable as shown in Fig. 6-14. Here $N = 0$; hence $N = P$ and the system is stable.

Relative Stability. In discussing the Nyquist criterion up to this point, only *absolute* stability has been considered. The $KG(s)$ locus,* however, affords considerable insight into the *degree* of stability or just how much stability *margin* there is, i.e., how critical the gain setting is. Consider the arbitrary KG locus of Fig. 6-15. It can be seen that the factor a and the phase angle γ are intimately connected with stability. The system as

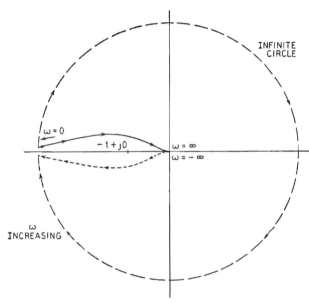

FIG. 6-13 Unstable Velocity Control Servo System with an Open-Loop $KG(s) = \dfrac{K_1(s + \omega_0)}{s^2(s + \omega_1)(s + \omega_2)}$.

illustrated is stable; however, increasing the gain of the $KG(s)$ response so that $a \leqslant 0$ would create instability and likewise decreasing the phase angle γ until it becomes zero or negative would create instability. The phase angle γ is called the *phase margin* and is related to the phase angle ϕ of $KG(s)$ by

$$\gamma = 180° + \phi \tag{6-117}$$

where the angles are taken in degrees with the direction as indicated in Fig. 6-15. The *phase angle ϕ* is *positive* when measured counterclockwise from zero; the *phase margin* is *positive* when measured counterclockwise

---

* The KG locus also provides information concerning the transient response of the system, but this will not be considered here.

from 180°. The gain factor *a* is called the *gain margin* and is *positive* whenever the $KG(s)$ locus crosses the negative real axis to the right of the $-1 + j0$ point. Application of the Nyquist criterion readily yields the following theorem:

THEOREM 14: *A system is stable if and only if it has both positive phase margin and positive gain margin.*

Furthermore, it is obvious that the degree of stability of a system depends upon the relative magnitudes of phase and gain margin. The setting of safety margins has been done by the servo engineers and is discussed in Chap. 7.

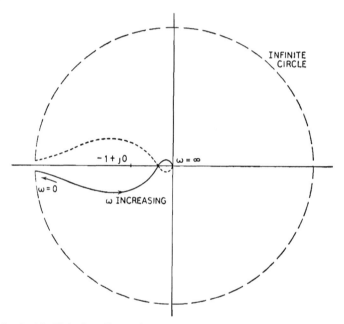

FIG. 6-14 Stable Velocity Control Servo System with an Open-Loop $KG(s) = \dfrac{K_2(s + \omega_0)}{s^2(s + \omega_1)(s + \omega_2)}$.

Attenuation-phase Diagrams. The discussion in the preceding paragraphs points the way to a different manner of plotting the $KG(s)$ response with the viewpoint of stability determination. This method is referred to as the *attenuation-and-phase-frequency-diagram* or *log-decibel plot* method. Here, the absolute magnitude $|KG(s)|$ is plotted in decibels vs. frequency on a logarithmic scale and the phase angle ϕ of $KG(s)$ or the phase margin γ is plotted also vs. frequency on a logarithmic scale. On such a plot the 0-db line corresponds to the unit circle of Fig. 6-15 and the frequency at which $|KG(s)|$ crosses this line is called *gain crossover*. An application of the Nyquist criterion results in the realization that, in order for a system to be stable, it must possess a *positive phase margin* at *gain crossover*. On a log-db plot, the *gain margin* is the number of db by which the magnitude curve would have to be *increased* to make gain crossover occur at $\phi = -180°$ or at zero phase margin. These concepts will be amplified and illustrated in Chap. 7. They were brought up here to show how they are obtained as a result of the Nyquist criterion.

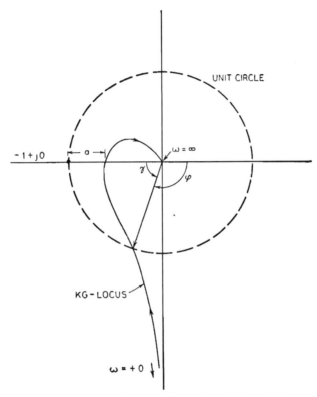

Fig. 6-15 Arbitrary KG(s) Locus Illustrating Gain and Phase Margin.

6-15 TWO METHODS OF CURVE FITTING

There exist a large number of problems in which the information required as part of the solution is in the form of raw data. In some cases the raw data can be used directly, whereas in many others it is convenient and frequently necessary to represent the data by an analytical expression or function. For example, part of the data from a guided missile test might be presented in the form of a set of discrete points locating the flight in space vs. time of flight. It would be extremely helpful to be able to obtain an analytic expression for the trajectory of the missile; for such a function could be used in determining servo operation, maximum turning radius of the missile, dynamic flight characteristics, etc. Two of the most powerful methods for fitting a curve to raw data will be outlined. The first of these is the *method of least squares* and the second is the method of *finite differences*.

The Method of Least Squares. The viewpoint of the user of the method of least squares is somewhat as follows. There is a considerable amount of acceptable experimental data on hand, no particular units of which are favored over any others, i.e., each unit of data is subject to the same probable error of observation. It is desired to fit a relatively simple curve to these data, say, a straight line or a parabola. Now only two points are required to fit a straight line, and only three points to fit a parabola, and there is no basis upon which to select any particular two or three points; in fact, it would be better if all the data could be used. The *method of least squares* is indicated. The method uses all of the acceptable data and hence it will not, in general, yield a curve passing through any of the points, but the resultant curve will be a "best fit" in the sense that it will come as close as possible to each point (using the *least-square error criterion*). The least-square error criterion, now widely adopted in many fields, consists in minimizing the sum of the squares of the deviations of the data points from the curve being fit.

Although the method of least squares can be used to fit many types of curves, it is used most for fitting polynomials, which are the simplest to handle. Furthermore polynomials are usually the best suited for subsequent operations. To illustrate the method, let it be required to fit the n data points $(x_1, y_1), (x_2, y_2), \cdots, (x_n, y_n)$ to a straight line

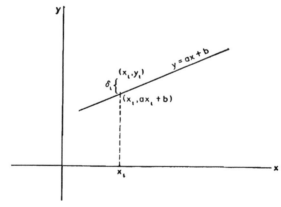

FIG. 6-16 Deviation of Data from Line for Least-Square Method.

6-15] TWO METHODS OF CURVE FITTING

$$y = ax + b \qquad (6\text{-}118)$$

Now, in general, the point (x_i, y_i) will not satisfy (6-118). If the deviation of the point from the line is denoted by δ_i as shown in Fig. 6-16, then

$$\delta_i = y_i - (ax_i + b) \qquad (6\text{-}119)$$

It should be noted it is implied here that there is more scatter in the y data coordinates than in x. Should there be more scatter in x, then the deviations could be measured parallel to the x-axis. The least-square error criterion requires the minimum value of

$$\mathcal{E}^2 = \sum_{i=1}^{n} \delta_i^2 = \sum_{i=1}^{n} \left\{ y_i - (ax_i + b) \right\}^2 \qquad (6\text{-}120)$$

The minimization of $\mathcal{E}^2$ is the problem of minimizing a function of the parameters a and b, which requires the simultaneous solution of

$$\frac{\partial \mathcal{E}^2}{\partial a} = 0 \quad \text{and} \quad \frac{\partial \mathcal{E}^2}{\partial b} = 0 \qquad (6\text{-}121)$$

From Eq. (6-120) these two simultaneous equations are

$$a \sum_{i=1}^{n} x_i^2 + b \sum_{i=1}^{n} x_i = \sum_{i=1}^{n} x_i y_i \qquad (6\text{-}122)$$

$$a \sum_{i=1}^{n} x_i + bn = \sum_{i=1}^{n} y_i \qquad (6\text{-}123)$$

These are linear equations and are easily solved for a and b.

Example 1. Fit a straight line to the following experimental data:

t	0.5	0.8	1.0	1.25	1.65	2.0	2.5	2.9	3.25	3.5
$f(t)$	3.6	4.0	4.4	5.1	5.5	6.5	7.0	8.0	8.3	9.0

Calculation of Eq. (6-122) yields for the line $f(t) = at + b$

$$a \sum_{i=1}^{10} t_i^2 + b \sum_{i=1}^{10} t_i = \sum_{i=1}^{10} t_i f(t_i)$$

where

$$\sum_{i=1}^{10} t_i^2 = 47.65, \quad \sum_{i=1}^{10} t_i = 19.35, \quad \sum_{i=1}^{10} t_i f(t_i) = 137.02;$$

$$\therefore 47.65a + 19.35b = 137.02$$

Also, from Eq. (6-123),

$$a \sum_{i=1}^{10} t_i + bn = \sum_{i=1}^{10} f(t_i)$$

where

$$\sum_{i=1}^{10} f(t_i) = 61.40$$

$$\therefore 19.35a + 10b = 61.40$$

The set of simultaneous equations to be solved is

$$\left.\begin{array}{r} 47.65a + 19.35b = 137.02 \\ 19.35a + 10b = 61.40 \end{array}\right\}$$

These yield

$$a = 1.78; \quad b = 2.69$$

and the best fit in the least-square sense is

$$f(t) = 1.78t + 2.69$$

Figure 6-17 shows the raw data and the best straight-line fit. In fitting the raw data given by a simple straight line one of the following assumptions is made: (1) the data points probably differ from the straight line by experimental error only, or (2) a straight line is desired for some specific purpose. If it is felt or known that the excursions from the straight line *are significant*, then a higher degree polynomial is required or perhaps in this particular case a sinusoidal variation could be superimposed upon the line already obtained.

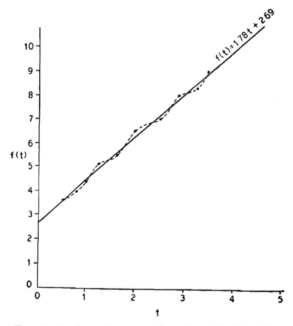

FIG. 6-17 Raw Data and Best Straight-Line Fit.

To develop the method of least squares for a general polynomial, let it be required to fit the m points $(x_1, y_1), (x_2, y_2), \cdots, (x_m, y_m)$ by the nth degree polynomial

$$y = a_n x^n + a_{n-1} x^{n-1} + \cdots + a_1 x + a_0 \tag{6-124}$$

where $m > n$. Following a procedure analogous to that for fitting the simple straight line, it is required to minimize

$$\mathcal{E}^2 = \sum_{i=1}^{m} \delta_i^2 = \sum_{i=1}^{m} (a_n x_i^n + a_{n-1} x_i^{n-1} + \cdots + a_1 x_i + a_0 - y_i)^2 \tag{6-125}$$

As before, to minimize $\mathcal{E}^2$, the first partial derivatives must all simultaneously vanish, or

$$\frac{\partial \mathcal{E}^2}{\partial a_n} = \frac{\partial \mathcal{E}^2}{\partial a_{n-1}} = \cdots = \frac{\partial \mathcal{E}^2}{\partial a_1} = \frac{\partial \mathcal{E}^2}{\partial a_0} = 0 \tag{6-126}$$

The n linear equations which result are

$$a_{n-1} \sum_{i=1}^{m} x_i^{2n-1} + a_{n-2} \sum_{i=1}^{m} x_i^{2n-2} + \cdots + a_0 \sum_{i=1}^{m} x_i^{n} = \sum_{i=1}^{m} x_i^{n} y_i$$

$$a_n \sum_{i=1}^{m} x_i^{2n-1} + a_{n-2} \sum_{i=1}^{m} x_i^{2n-3} + \cdots + a_0 \sum_{i=1}^{m} x_i^{n-1} = \sum_{i=1}^{m} x_i^{n-1} y_i$$

$$\cdots \cdots \cdots \cdots \cdots \cdots \cdots \cdots \cdots \cdots \cdots \tag{6-127}$$

$$a_n \sum_{i=1}^{m} x_i^{n} + a_{n-1} \sum_{i=1}^{m} x_i^{n-1} + \cdots + a_1 \sum_{i=1}^{m} x_i = \sum_{i=1}^{m} y_i$$

These are known as the *normal equations*. It can be seen that the numerical complexity of obtaining the coefficients increases directly with the degree of the polynomial assumed.

Example 2. Fit a parabola to the following data obtained from a missile flight (see Fig. 6-18):

t	2.0	3.0	4.0	5.0	6.0	7.0	7.9	8.6	9.3
$f(t)$	5.5	7.3	8.8	9.5	9.4	8.5	7.0	5.0	3.0

Let the parabola be

$$f(t) = at^2 + bt + c$$

then

$$\mathcal{E}^2 = \sum_{i=1}^{9} \delta_i^2 = \sum_{i=1}^{9} \left\{ at_i^2 + bt_i + c - f(t_i) \right\}^2$$

The normal equations are

$$a\Sigma t_i^4 + b\Sigma t_i^3 + c\Sigma t_i^2 = \Sigma t_i^2 f(t_i)$$
$$a\Sigma t_i^3 + b\Sigma t_i^2 + c\Sigma t_i = \Sigma t_i f(t_i)$$
$$a\Sigma t_i^2 + b\Sigma t_i + c\Sigma 1 = \Sigma f(t_i)$$

where $\sum \equiv \sum_{i=1}^{9}$ in all cases. With the help of a desk calculator the required summations are found to be

$$\Sigma t_i^4 = 21{,}520.61 \qquad \Sigma t_i^2 f(t_i) = 2287.04$$
$$\Sigma t_i^3 = 2716.45 \qquad \Sigma t_i f(t_i) = 357.70$$
$$\Sigma t_i^2 = 361.86 \qquad \Sigma f(t_i) = 64$$
$$\Sigma t_i = 52.80 \qquad \Sigma 1 = 9$$

The normal equations become

$$\left. \begin{array}{r} 21{,}520.61a + 2716.45b + 361.86c = 2287.04 \\ 2716.45a + 361.86b + 52.80c = 357.70 \\ 361.86a + 52.80b + 9c = 64 \end{array} \right\}$$

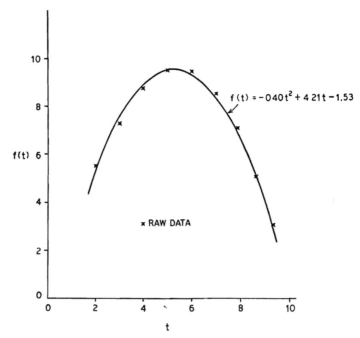

Fig. 6-18 Raw Data and Parabola Fitted by Least Squares.

The solution of this set of simultaneous equations yields
$$a = -0.40, \quad b = 4.21, \quad c = -1.53$$
The parabola of best fit by least squares is thus
$$f(t) = -0.40t^2 + 4.21t - 1.53$$
Figure 6-18 shows that the fit is indeed excellent.

To fit curves other than polynomials by the method of least squares, it is best to follow the fundamental concept of the method from the start: (1) Form the deviation for the ith data point, (2) square this deviation; (3) sum these squares over all data points; (4) take the first partial derivative of this sum with respect to each of the unknown parameters; (5) set all of these partial derivatives equal to zero; and (6) attempt to solve the resulting simultaneous equations for the unknowns. If the resulting equations are not easily soluble, a trick is frequently required. For example, to fit the curve
$$y = ke^{ax}$$
take the logarithm of each side; the result is
$$\ln y = \ln k + ax$$
which is of the form
$$Y = K + ax$$
and is readily fitted by the method.

A similar device works for curves of the form $y = ax^n$.

Curve Fitting by Finite Differences. Fitting a curve by the use of finite differences requires a considerably different viewpoint than that of the method of least squares. In the first place, only a polynomial curve can be fitted by finite difference techniques. Second, the curve passes through each of the points selected to be fit. This means that some predetermined idea must exist as to just which points are the most significant. Finally, the degree of the polynomial does not need to be specified in advance, assuming there are a sufficient number of data points. Therefore in some respects the method of finite differences is more general and in others more restrictive than the method of least squares.

The first requirement for using the method of ordinary finite differences is to have discrete data points with a constant interval between successive values of the independent variable. Experimental data are generally taken at regular intervals, so that this requirement is usually easy to meet. The method of divided differences to be mentioned later waives this requirement. The selected points are next used to construct a *difference table* as now shown.

x	y	Δ	Δ^2	Δ^3	Δ^4
x_0	y_0				
		Δy_0			
x_1	y_1		$\Delta^2 y_0$		
		Δy_1		$\Delta^3 y_0$	
x_2	y_2		$\Delta^2 y_1$		$\Delta^4 y_0$
		Δy_2		$\Delta^3 y_1$	
x_3	y_3		$\Delta^2 y_2$		
		Δy_3			
x_4	y_4				

Here $x_1 - x_0 = x_2 - x_1 = \cdots = x_4 - x_3 = h$, a constant finite difference and $y = f(x)$. The table is constructed as follows:

$$\Delta f_0 = f_1 - f_0,$$
$$\Delta f_1 = f_2 - f_1, \text{ etc.;}$$
$$\Delta^2 f_0 = \Delta f_1 - \Delta f_0,$$
$$\Delta^2 f_1 = \Delta f_2 - \Delta f_1, \text{ etc.;}$$

where $f(x_0) = y_0 \equiv f_0$, etc.

In the construction of such a table, care must be taken that the higher differences represent true differences and do not merely reflect data inaccuracy. For example, if $\Delta f_0 = 0.05$ and $\Delta f_1 = 0.07$, and it is known that the probable error of measurement in the f's is ± 0.02, then Δf's = ± 0.04 and $\Delta^2 f$'s = ± 0.08 cannot be considered significant.

Example 1. Construct a difference table for $y = 3x^2 - 2x + 1$ for $h = 0.2$ and $x_0 = 0$.

x	y	Δ	Δ^2	Δ^3
0	1			
		−0.28		
0.2	0.72		0.24	
		−0.04		0
0.4	0.68		0.24	
		0.20		0
0.6	0.88		0.24	
		0.44		
0.8	1.32			

This example illustrates the fact that the nth differences of an nth degree polynomial are constant and all higher order differences vanish. In practice, if m^{th} differences are constant to within 2^m times the experimental accuracy of the data, the tables must be terminated at the mth differences.

6-15] TWO METHODS OF CURVE FITTING

Although there are a large number of formulas in the theory of finite differences which could be used for curve fitting, the most important is perhaps the *forward Gregory-Newton interpolation formula*:

$$y(x_0 + rh) = y_0 + r\Delta y_0 + \frac{r(r-1)}{2!}\Delta^2 y_0 + \frac{r(r-1)(r-2)}{3!}\Delta^3 y_0 + \cdots \qquad (6\text{-}128)$$

In order to use Eq. (6-128) to fit a polynomial it is necessary to set

$$x \equiv x_0 + rh \qquad (6\text{-}129)$$

which provides $y(x)$ in terms of the entries in the difference table. Then the fractional factor $r = (x - x_0)/h$.

Example 2. Fit a polynomial to the following data which have a probable error of ± 0.02 for each measured value.

t	0	0.2	0.4	0.6	0.8	1.0
$f(t)$	1	0.70	0.69	0.88	1.30	2.01

t	$f(t)$	$\Delta f(t)$	$\Delta^2 f(t)$	$\Delta^3 f(t)$
0	1			
		−0.30		
0.2	0.70		0.29	
		−0.01		−0.09
0.4	0.69		0.20	
		0.19		0.03
0.6	0.88		0.23	
		0.42		0.06
0.8	1.30		0.29	
		0.71		
1.0	2.01			

Here the accuracy in $f(t)$ is ± 0.02, the 2nd differences *are not* constant to within $2^2(\pm 0.02) = \pm 0.08$, whereas the 3rd differences *are* constant to within $2^3(\pm 0.02) = \pm 0.16$ and thus the table must be terminated here. The polynomial would fit the data better if $\Delta^2 f(t)$ and $\Delta^3 f(t)$ would be used which are the averages of the values in the table; this is $\overline{\Delta^2 f(t)} = 0.25$ and $\overline{\Delta^3 f(t)} = 0$. Using Eq. (6-128) for $t_0 = 0$ and $t = 0.2r$, we obtain

$$f(t) = 1 + 5t(-0.30) + \frac{(5t)(5t-1)}{2}(0.25)$$
$$= 3.12t^2 - 2.12t + 1$$

Fig. 6-19 shows a plot of $f(t)$ passing through the first point and near the next three points. If the exact values of Δ^2 and Δ^3 had been used instead of the averaged values, the curve would have passed through all of the first four points.

The Gregory-Newton formula of Eq. (6-128) can also be used to determine the polynomial fitting the derivative of a tabular function. This can be accomplished in two ways: (1) find the function first and then differentiate or (2) use the derivative formulas directly. The derivative formulas are obtained by differentiating Eq. (6-128) with respect to r, yielding for the first

$$h \frac{dy(x_0 + rh)}{dr} = \Delta y_0 + \frac{2r - 1}{2!} \Delta^2 y_0 + \frac{3r^2 - 6r + 2}{3!} \Delta^3 y_0 + \cdots \quad (6\text{-}130)$$

Since x_0 and h are constants, if $x \equiv x_0 + rh$, then Eq. (6-130) can be considered to yield $y'(x) \equiv \dfrac{dy(x)}{dx}$ from

$$y'(x) = \Delta y_0 + \frac{2r - 1}{2!} \Delta^2 y_0 + \frac{3r^2 - 6r + 2}{3!} \Delta^3 y_0 + \cdots \quad (6\text{-}131)$$

where

$$r = \frac{x - x_0}{h}$$

In case the data to be fitted were not taken at equispaced intervals, the method of using ordinary finite differences as just developed does not apply.

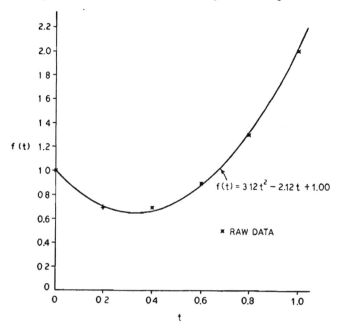

FIG. 6-19 Raw Data and Parabola Fitted by Finite Differences.

For this purpose the concept of *divided differences* has been established. A table of divided differences is formed in a manner analogous to the table of ordinary finite differences as shown below.

x	y	$\triangle$	$\triangle^2$
x_0	y_0		
		$\underset{x_0,x_1}{\triangle} y_0 \equiv \dfrac{y_1 - y_0}{x_1 - x_0}$	
x_1	y_1		$\underset{x_0,x_1,x_2}{\triangle^2} y_0 \equiv \dfrac{\underset{x_1,x_2}{\triangle} y_1 - \underset{x_0,x_1}{\triangle} y_0}{x_2 - x_0}$
		$\underset{x_1,x_2}{\triangle} y_1 \equiv \dfrac{y_2 - y_1}{x_2 - x_1}$	
x_2	y_2		$\underset{x_1,x_2,x_3}{\triangle^2} y_1 \equiv \dfrac{\underset{x_2,x_3}{\triangle} y_2 - \underset{x_1,x_2}{\triangle} y_1}{x_3 - x_1}$
		$\underset{x_2,x_3}{\triangle} y_2 \equiv \dfrac{y_3 - y_2}{x_3 - x_2}$	
x_3	y_3		

Here the symbol $\underset{x_0,x_1}{\triangle}$ is used to indicate a divided difference, and the subscripts (x_0, x_1) on the symbol refer to the values of x involved in forming the difference. For curve fitting, *Newton's divided difference formula* is

$$y = f(x) = y_0 + (x - x_0) \underset{x_0,x_1}{\triangle} y_0 + (x - x_0)(x - x_1) \underset{x_0,x_1,x_2}{\triangle^2} y_0 + \cdots \tag{6-132}$$

This formula is used in exactly the same manner as the ordinary finite difference formula of Eq. (6-128).

Example 3. Construct a divided difference table and fit a polynomial to the following data:

t	0	0.1	1.0	1.3	2.0
$f(t)$	5	5.281	7	7.717	11

t	$f(t)$	$\triangle$	$\triangle^2$	$\triangle^3$
0	5			
		2.810		
0.1	5.281		−0.900	
		1.910		1.000
1.0	7		0.400	
		2.390		1.000
1.3	7.717		2.300	
		4.690		
2.0	11			

Using Eq. (6-132) yields

$$f(t) = 5 + (t - 0)(2.810) + (t - 0)(t - 0.1)(-0.900)$$
$$+ (t - 0)(t - 0.1)(t - 1.0)(1.000)$$
$$= 5 + 2.810t - 0.900t^2 + 0.090t + t^3 - 1.100t^2 + 0.100t$$
$$\therefore f(t) = t^3 - 2t^2 + 3t + 5$$

6-16 BRIEF DISCUSSION OF PROBABILITY THEORY

The theory of probability plays an important role in the study of guided missile behavior. Questions frequently asked are: What is the probability of kill? What is the deviation or dispersion of missiles about the control beam? How does launching error affect the probability of capture? etc. These questions can be intelligently discussed only by a person who has at least an introductory understanding of the fundamental concepts of probability theory. It is the purpose of this paragraph to present only the meager necessities.[10] (A treatment of probability theory, as it pertains to Operations Research, is to be found in the section of this title in another volume of this series.)

Basic Concepts of Probability. Discrete variables will be considered first, two very important ideas from statistics being presented as a brief background. Consider the variable x which assumes the discrete values $x_1, x_2, \cdots, x_N$: the *mean value* of x is given by

$$\bar{x} = \frac{1}{N} \sum_{i=1}^{N} x_i \qquad (6\text{-}133)$$

It is obvious that, in general, the discrete values x_i are dispersed about the mean, $\bar{x}$. The most significant *measure of dispersion* is called the *standard deviation*. It is defined by

$$\sigma_x = \left[\frac{1}{N} \sum_{i=1}^{N} (x_i - \bar{x})^2 \right]^{\frac{1}{2}} \qquad (6\text{-}134)$$

The square of the standard deviation is called the *variance*. It is recognized that the variance is the second moment about the mean which, in mechanics, is known as the moment of inertia.

The classical definition of *a priori probability* can be expressed as follows:

> If there are n possible, mutually exclusive, and equally likely ways of obtaining successes and failures of an event, and if m of these ways give successes, then the mathematical probability of the event succeeding is given by $p = m/n$.

---

[10] For further details, see Kenney, *Mathematics of Statistics*, Part I (1947) and Kenney and Keeping, *Mathematics of Statistics*, Part II (1951), D. Van Nostrand Co., Inc., N. Y.

By *mutually exclusive* events is meant that if any particular event occurs on a specific occasion it is not possible for any other event to occur on the same occasion. Events are considered *equally likely* if no single one of them can be expected to occur in preference to the others. As defined, then, the probability p is a number between 0 and 1. If $p = 0$, the event is impossible, and if $p = 1$, the event is certain. The events of a set are said to be *independent* if the occurrence of any one of them *does not* affect the occurrences of the others.

Several of the most important fundamental theorems will be given without proof. The proofs are relatively simple and require merely the application of a little logical thought to the foregoing definitions.

THEOREM 15. ADDITION LAW. *If the probabilities of the mutually exclusive events $x_1, x_2, \cdots, x_n$ are $p_1, p_2, \cdots, p_n$ respectively, then the probability that any one of these events should happen when all are in question is the sum of the probabilities,* $\sum_{i=1}^{n} p_i$.

THEOREM 16. LAW OF COMPOUND PROBABILITY. *If the events $x_1, x_2, \cdots, x_n$ are independent with probabilities $p_1, p_2, \cdots, p_n$ respectively, then the probability that all of the events should happen simultaneously when all are in question is the product of the probabilities,* $\prod_{i=1}^{n} p_i$.

THEOREM 17. REPEATED TRIALS. *If p is the probability of the success of an event in a single trial, and $q = 1 - p$ is the probability of failure, then the probability P that the event will succeed exactly m times in n trials is given by the $(m+1)^{st}$ term in the binomial expansion $(q+p)^n$; or*

$$P = \frac{n!}{m!(n-m)!} p^m q^{n-m}.$$

The following examples illustrate the application of these three theorems.

Example 1. In a single throw of a die, the probability of getting either a 1 or a 7 is, by Theorem 15,

$$\tfrac{1}{6} + \tfrac{1}{6} = \tfrac{1}{3}$$

Example 2. In a single throw of a pair of dice, what is the probability of throwing a 7?

A 7 can be obtained in the following six ways: $(1+6), (2+5), (3+4), (4+3), (5+2), (6+1)$, all of which are mutually exclusive and equally probable. Now, by Theorem 16, the probability of any one of the six ways is $(\tfrac{1}{6})(\tfrac{1}{6}) = \tfrac{1}{36}$ since the two numbers coming up on the dice for any throw are independent. Thus, by Theorem 15, the required probability is

$$P = \sum_{i=1}^{6} p_i = 6(\tfrac{1}{36}) = \tfrac{1}{6}$$

Compare this to the probability of getting "snake-eyes" (two 1's), which is $\tfrac{1}{36}$.

Example 3. There are 4 black marbles and 7 white marbles in a bag. Two marbles are drawn at random. What is the probability that one marble drawn is black, and one is white?

The solution requires the application of both Theorems 15 and 16. There are two mutually exclusive possibilities: (1) the black marble is drawn first and (2) the white marble is drawn first. For Case 1, out of a total of the the 11 marbles, the probability of drawing a black one is $\tfrac{4}{11}$ and now, out of the remaining 10 marbles, the probability of drawing a white one is $\tfrac{7}{10}$. Hence the compound probability, for Case 1, is $\tfrac{4}{11} \cdot \tfrac{7}{10} = \tfrac{28}{110}$. For Case 2, the probability of first drawing a white marble is $\tfrac{7}{11}$ and then next of drawing a black one is $\tfrac{4}{10}$, or a compound probability of $\tfrac{7}{11} \cdot \tfrac{4}{10} = \tfrac{28}{110}$. The answer is the sum of these

$$\tfrac{28}{110} + \tfrac{28}{110} = \tfrac{28}{55} \doteq \tfrac{1}{2}$$

Example 4. In 8 tosses of a penny, find the probability of exactly 3 heads.

Apply Theorem 17. Here $n = 8$, $m = 3$, $p = q = \tfrac{1}{2}$.

$$P = \frac{8!}{3!5!}\left(\tfrac{1}{2}\right)^3 \left(\tfrac{1}{2}\right)^5 = \frac{8 \cdot 7 \cdot 6}{6}\left(\tfrac{1}{2}\right)^8$$

$$\therefore P = \tfrac{7}{32}$$

Example 5. Experimental data indicate that, in every dozen firings of a certain guided missile, only 7 effect a kill. If 3 missiles are fired in sequence at a single target, what is the probability of kill?

Here, kill will be effected if any one of the 3 missiles destroys the target; the constant, and independent, probability for any one kill being $\tfrac{7}{12}$. There are three mutually exclusive possibilities:

(1) First missile succeeds; $p_1 = \tfrac{7}{12}$
(2) First fails, second succeeds; $p_2 = \tfrac{5}{12} \cdot \tfrac{7}{12} = \tfrac{35}{144}$
(3) First and second fail, third succeeds; $p_3 = \tfrac{5}{12} \cdot \tfrac{5}{12} \cdot \tfrac{7}{12} = \tfrac{175}{1728}$

$$P = p_1 + p_2 + p_3 = \tfrac{7}{12} + \tfrac{35}{144} + \tfrac{175}{1728}$$

$$\therefore P = \tfrac{1603}{1728} \doteq 0.93$$

If a set of N discrete variables exists such that f_1 are of type x_1, f_2 of x_2, $\cdots$, f_n of x_n, then the definitions of mean value and variance can be extended to be

$$\bar{x} = \frac{\sum_{i=1}^{n} f_i x_i}{\sum_{i=1}^{n} f_i} = \frac{1}{N} \sum_{i=1}^{n} f_i x_i \qquad (6\text{-}135)$$

$$\sigma_x^2 = \frac{1}{N} \sum_{i=1}^{n} f_i (x_i - \bar{x})^2 \qquad (6\text{-}136)$$

These can be expressed in terms of probability for $p_i = f_i/N$;

$$\bar{x} = \sum_{i=1}^{n} p_i x_i \qquad (6\text{-}137)$$

$$\sigma_x^2 = \sum_{i=1}^{n} p_i (x_i - \bar{x})^2 \qquad (6\text{-}138)$$

At this point a brief introduction to the concept of *random variables* is required. In many scientific fields the only method available which affords an explanation of a particular phenomenon is a repetition of experimental observations. Suppose a sequence of observations or experiments is made, and that the results vary in such an irregular way that it is impossible to give an exact prediction for any individual observation. It can then be said that the phenomenon in question is represented by a sequence of *random experiments*. It should be noted that, even though the individual results behave in an irregular manner, the sequence of random experiments taken as a whole show a decided *statistical regularity*, which is the basis of the mathematical theory of statistics and probability.

The definition of *empirical probability* will be developed as follows: Suppose a random experiment is repeated a large number of times, say, n times, and an event A is observed to take place exactly m times; then the ratio m/n will be called the *frequency* of the event A. If this ratio is observed as n is increased, it is found in general that it shows a decided tendency to become constant. The *probability of the event A* is that number P such that, as n becomes increasingly large, it is almost certain that $P = m/n$. This definition is not inconsistent with the previous one for a priori probability.

Given a random experiment which may be repeated many times, each result being represented by n numbers $\xi_1, \xi_2, \cdots, \xi_n$, the vector ξ is called an n-dimensional *random variable*. The random variables considered in this chapter will all be one-dimensional, i.e., $n = 1$. The random variable ξ has an unique *probability distribution* defined by

$$F(x) = P(\xi \leq x) \qquad (6\text{-}139)$$

The function $F(x)$ is also referred to as the *probability function* or the *dis-*

tribution function. The probability that the random variable ξ belongs to the interval $a < \xi \leq b$ is $F(b) - F(a)$. If $f(x)$ represents the derivative of $F(x)$ with respect to x, than $f(x)$ is called the *probability density* or *frequency function* of ξ. Then

$$f(x)\, dx = P(x < \xi < x + dx) \qquad (6\text{-}140)$$

Functions of random variables, such as $g(\xi)$, are also random variables whose probability distributions are determined by the distribution of ξ. The mean value of the random variable $g(\xi)$ is

$$\overline{g(\xi)} = \int_{-\infty}^{\infty} g(x) f(x)\, dx \qquad (6\text{-}141)$$

where $f(x)$ is the probability density of ξ. The following important theorems regarding mean values are stated without proof:

THEOREM 18. ADDITION. *The mean value of the sum of random variables is equal to the sum of their mean values.*

THEOREM 19. MULTIPLICATION. *The mean value of the product of independent random variables is equal to the product of their mean values.*

The variance or square of the standard deviation of the random variable ξ is

$$\sigma^2 = \int_{-\infty}^{\infty} (x - m)^2 f(x)\, dx \qquad (6\text{-}142)$$

where m is the mean value of ξ.

Distribution Functions. One of the most important distribution functions is the *normal distribution function*

$$F(x) = \frac{1}{\sigma \sqrt{2\pi}} \int_{-\infty}^{x} e^{\frac{-(x-m)^2}{2\sigma^2}}\, dx \qquad (6\text{-}143)$$

where m stands for the mean value and σ for the standard deviation. The *normal frequency function* corresponding to Eq. (6-143) is given by

$$f(x) = \frac{1}{\sigma \sqrt{2\pi}} e^{\frac{-(x-m)^2}{2\sigma^2}} \qquad (6\text{-}144)$$

The standardized variable $t = \dfrac{x - m}{\sigma}$ is frequently employed to reduce these functions to

$$F(x) = \frac{1}{\sqrt{2\pi}} \int_{-\infty}^{x} e^{-t^2/2}\, dt \qquad (6\text{-}145)$$

$$f(t)\, dt = \frac{1}{\sqrt{2\pi}} e^{-t^2/2}\, dt \qquad (6\text{-}146)$$

Figures 6-20 and 6-21 show plots of $F(x)$ and $f(t)$ respectively. The normal distribution is frequently referred to as the *Gaussian distribution* and Eq. (6-144) is called *Gauss' error curve*. A large number of problems in missile guidance involve the analysis of random errors which follow a

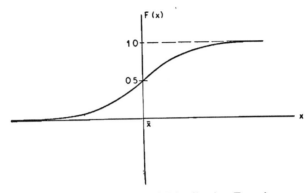

FIG. 6-20   The Normal Distribution Function.

Gaussian distribution. Extensive tables of Eq. (6-145) and (6-146) exist. Also tabulated is the *error function* or *probability integral* defined as

$$\text{erf}(t) = \frac{2}{\sqrt{\pi}} \int_0^t e^{-y^2} dy = 2F(t\sqrt{2}) - 1 \qquad (6\text{-}147)$$

The maximum height of the normal frequency function of Eq. (6-144) is at $x = m$, at which point $f(m) = \dfrac{1}{\sigma\sqrt{2\pi}}$. A change in the value of m

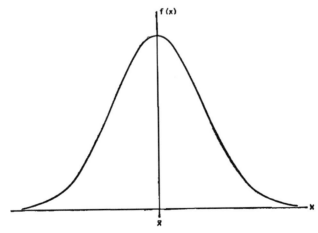

FIG. 6-21   The Normal Frequency Function.

amounts merely to a linear translation of the curve along the x-axis. However, a change in σ actually changes the shape of the curve. Increasing σ reduces the maximum value of $f(x)$ and spreads out the curve. Figure 6-22 shows $f(x)$ for $m = 0$ and several values of σ. The total area under the curves $f(x)$ is always equal to 1. The curve has inflexion points at $x = m - \sigma$ and $x = m + \sigma$.

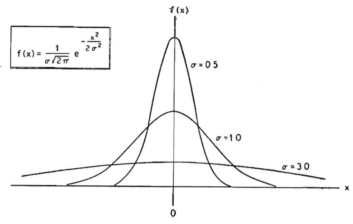

FIG. 6-22 The Normal Frequency Function for $m = 0$ and $\sigma = 0.5$, 1.0, and 3.0.

The normal frequency function can be used to determine the probability that any experiment represented by it has a value lying in any specified interval. For example, the probability that ξ lies in the interval (a, b) is

$$P(a < \xi < b) = \int_a^b f(x)\, dx \qquad (6\text{-}148)$$

From Eq. (6-148) it can be calculated that 50 percent of the data would be observed in the interval $m \pm 0.6745\sigma$, 68 percent in $m \pm \sigma$, 95 percent in $m \pm 2\sigma$, and 99.97 percent in $m \pm 3\sigma$.

The normal frequency function can be extended to handle the two-variable case. The definition is

$$f(x, y) = \frac{1}{2\pi\sigma_x\sigma_y\sqrt{1-\rho^2}} \qquad (6\text{-}149)$$
$$\exp\left[-\frac{1}{2(1-\rho^2)}\left\{\frac{(x-m_x)^2}{\sigma_x^2} - 2\rho\left(\frac{x-m_x}{\sigma_x}\right)\left(\frac{y-m_y}{\sigma_y}\right) + \frac{(y-m_y)^2}{\sigma_y^2}\right\}\right]$$

where ρ is called the *correlation coefficient* defined by

$$\rho = \frac{\overline{(x-m_x)(y-m_y)}}{\sigma_x\sigma_y} \qquad (6\text{-}150)$$

The correlation coefficient is a measure of the dependency or correlation between x and y; in a normal distribution $\rho = 0$ implies that x and y are independent.

Another important distribution is the *Rayleigh distribution* whose frequency function is

$$f(x) = \frac{1}{m} e^{-x/m} \tag{6-151}$$

defined for $x \geq 0$ only. The Rayleigh distribution is used extensively in radar analysis since both target noise and receiver noise after square-law rectification follow this distribution closely.

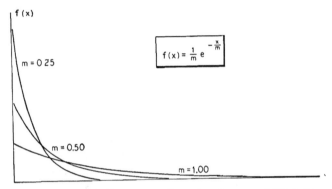

Fig. 6-23 The Rayleigh Frequency Function for $m = 0.25$, 0.50, and 1.00.

Fig. 6-23 shows a plot of the Rayleigh frequency function for several values of m. The mean value is

$$\text{Mean value} = \frac{1}{m} \int_0^\infty x e^{-x/m}\, dx = m \tag{6-152}$$

and the variance is

$$\sigma^2 = \frac{1}{m} \int_0^\infty (x - m)^2 e^{-x/m}\, dx = m^2 \tag{6-153}$$

It is seen that the Rayleigh distribution is characterized by a single parameter m which represents both the mean value and the standard deviation. An excellent discussion of additional distribution functions will be found in Cramer.[11]

[11] Cramer, Harold, *Mathematical Methods of Statistics*, Princeton University Press, 1946.

CHAPTER 7

SERVO SYSTEM THEORY

Symbols Used in Chapter 7

a_1, a_2 = resistances
A_1, A_2 = magnitudes of voltage ratios
b_1, b_2 = reactances
B_1, B_2 = phase of voltage ratios
C = capacitance, farads
db = decibels, $A_{db} = 20 \log_{10} A$
E = actuating error signal
  $= \theta_i + \beta\theta_o$
E_o = output voltage
E_i = input voltage
ε = error quantity = $\theta_i - \theta_o$
f = frequency, cps
$F = \omega/\omega_0$, normalized real frequency variable
$G(s)$ = function of complex frequency, s
H = target altitude, in ft
⊕ = circular junction indicating summing action
⊖ = circular junction indicating differencing action (error detector)
K = parameter, gain factor
  = ω_0/ω_1 for Type I systems
$\mathcal{L}$ = Laplace transform
$\mathcal{L}^{-1}$ = inverse Laplace transform
N = numerical factor, ω_3/ω_1
N = network transfer function
R = resistance, ohms
R = range to target, yd

R_h = horizontal range to target
R_0 = slant range to target at crossover
R_{h0} = horizontal range to target at crossover
$\mathcal{R}$ = response, percentage of input
$\dot{R}$ = range velocity, yd/sec
$\ddot{R}$ = range acceleration, yd/sec²
$\dddot{R}$ = rate of change of range acceleration, yd/sec³
$\ddddot{R}$ = second rate of change of range acceleration, yd/sec⁴
$|\dot{R}_{max}|$ = absolute magnitude of maximum value of $\dot{R}$
$|\ddot{R}_{max}|$ = absolute magnitude of maximum value of $\ddot{R}$
$|\dddot{R}_{max}|$ = absolute magnitude of maximum value of $\dddot{R}$
$\ddot{R}_i$ = range input acceleration component
$\dddot{R}_i$ = range input rate of change of acceleration component
$s = \sigma + j\omega$, the complex frequency operator
t = time, sec
$\tan^{-1}$ = the angle whose tangent is
⟶ = unidirectional flow, in direction of arrow
V = target horizontal speed, knots
Z_g = generator or source impedance
Z_l = load impedance

SYMBOLS USED IN CHAPTER 7

Z_1 = series arm impedance
Z_2 = shunt arm impedance
Z_{12} = input open-circuit driving-point impedance
Z_{34} = output open-circuit driving-point impedance
α_1 = negative of quadratic root
α_2 = negative of quadratic root
β = feedback circuit transmission factor
ζ = dimensionless damping ratio (see Eq. 7-34)
θ = target bearing angle, in deg ($\theta = 0$ at crossover)
θ_i = input quantity (desired value)
θ_o = output quantity (controlled variable)
$\theta_i(s)$ = generalized input function
$\dot{\theta} = \dfrac{d\theta}{dt}$, velocity
$\ddot{\theta} = \dfrac{d^2\theta}{dt^2}$, acceleration
$\dddot{\theta} = \dfrac{d^3\theta}{dt^3}$, time rate of change of acceleration
$\ddddot{\theta} = \dfrac{d^4\theta}{dt^4}$, time rate of change of $\dddot{\theta}$
$\dot{\theta}_{max}$ = maximum value of $\dot{\theta}$
$\ddot{\theta}_{max}$ = maximum value of $\ddot{\theta}$
$\dddot{\theta}_{max}$ = maximum value of $\dddot{\theta}$
μ = gain of forward circuit
$\sigma = 0$, for steady-state analysis
τ = delay time
ϕ = target elevation angle, in deg
ϕ_0 = target elevation angle, at crossover
$\omega = 2\pi f$, angular frequency in radians per sec
ω_0 = -1 slope intercept at zero db line, frequency in radians/sec
ω_1 = -1 slope, -2 slope break-frequency
ω_2 = geometric mean of ω_0 and ω_1 ($= \sqrt{\omega_0 \omega_1}$), -2 slope intercept with zero db line
ω_3 = high frequency intersection of -2 slope and -1 slope
ω_4 = second -1 slope intersection with unity gain line
ω_5 = geometric mean of ω_3 and ω_4
ω_n = system undamped natural angular frequency
$u = j\dfrac{\omega}{\omega_0}$, nondimensionalized complex operator

Even a book limited to the *principles* of missile guidance provides ample evidence of the manifold nature of the problems embraced within the field. After all of the multifarious considerations of target detection, missile launching and propulsion, and transmission of guidance intelligence to the missile have been resolved, the actual guidance problem remains. The design and construction of missile control systems to obtain accurate performance under dynamic conditions constitute the "hard core" problem of guided missiles. Although it is like stating the obvious, one is led to say that missiles could not perform without guidance. The key to the design of control systems is servo system theory. The purpose of the present chapter is to give enough basic background material in the general field of analysis of *linear* servo systems to establish the fundamental concepts upon which a discussion of missile guidance design procedures may be made. Throughout the chapter, the system point of view will be emphasized.

That is, even though one's concern is in regard to a single component within the servo loops, the larger "system" point of view should be maintained. The guided missile tactical problem will be explored for guides to servo system performance requirements. Design methods based upon both the frequency response and the transient response analysis will be discussed.

7-1 SERVO SYSTEM DESIGN PROBLEM

A servo system may be defined as a combination of elements for the control of a source of power in which the output of the system, or some function of the output, is fed back for comparison with the external input intelligence and the difference between these quantities is used in controlling the power. Perhaps the most compactly phrased definition possible is: *A servo system is defined as an error-closing closed-cycle system.* Servo systems found in guided missiles vary widely in the amount of power controlled, from a very small fraction of a horsepower to the extremely large power of the main propulsion motor producing thousands of horsepower during limited intervals. There is no theoretical limit to the amount of power that can be controlled. The servo system may contain electrical, mechanical, hydraulic, pneumatic, or optical units in almost any combination. Because a relatively wide separation of the control point and the controlled device is involved, an electrical system combined with a mechanical or hydraulic system is most frequently used. The guided missile may be thought of as a large servo system comprising many small servo systems. In these systems, various forms of electromagnetic radiation are used with many variations in the means of modulating or transmitting the required basic control intelligence.

Nature of Initial Specifications. The designer is faced with demands that are basically contradictory. There is often a limitation on the servo system size, weight, and complexity, as well as on the amount of power that may be consumed in producing controlled power output during a given interval of time. At the same time, high performance specifications of rapid response in following input commands and in reducing errors due to load variations are demanded. In addition, the language in which the requirements are given necessitates translation into terms that are more directly related to the system design parameters. In all too many cases, the designer has assumed that the problem starts from the specifications given to him, that they are not to be questioned, and that he must design a system which in every way meets the requirements as initially stated. The portion of the system for which he is directly responsible may, indeed, meet the specifications perfectly, but partial responsibility for faulty overall system operation may come back to the individual component designer, albeit perhaps unjustly. The obvious suggestion is that one must concern himself as much as practicable with the entire system so that the importance of all the factors affecting the design of a particular portion is not underestimated.

Fundamental Design Concepts. The two approaches to servo system design of most importance are (1) the differential equation of motion method and (2) the transfer-function method. The classical approach to servo system design is that of establishing an integrodifferential equation relating the input quantity, the output quantity, the error or difference between the input and the output, and coefficients that are functions of the system parameters. In writing such an equation, the assumption is usually made that the system is linear. All subsequent studies are then influenced by the necessary approximations that are inherent in such a procedure. Effort is then applied to obtain the solution of the system equation for various standard test inputs, such as an input step in position, to determine system performance. The basic aims of engineering studies are to arrive at an optimum design. The procedure described lacks sufficient clues as to suitable remedies should the initial design prove inadequate. Transient analysis does predict the time required for the system to return to steady-state conditions after an input or output disturbance, the magnitude of the excursions of the output and consequently the maximum deviations from the input, and the frequency of an oscillation, if any is present. The important deficiency of the method lies in the difficulty of determining, in complex systems, the effect of the inertia, time-lags, friction, stiffness, or compliance of any component of the system so that modifications to meet particular requirements can be made.

A more satisfactory design procedure is the transfer-function method which is based upon ordinary transmission-network theory. The proposed servo system design may be studied unit by unit. That is, the transfer of energy through a unit as specified by the ratio of output to input (in the presence of the preceding and following units to allow for possible loading or interaction effects) is determined. The role of the unit becomes clearly evident in expressions for overall system performance. The foregoing is not to say that a final check on system transient performance is not important, but rather that the transfer-function method shows superiority in the initial design phase.

Tactical Problem Dynamics. A specific missile is developed because a tactical problem exists, and it is believed that the missile, as planned, will solve the problem. The importance of translating the tactical problem into relationships from which the servo system parameters may be given particular values is apparent. In the previous paragraphs the utility of servo specifications stated in terms of the frequency domain factors of transfer-function analysis was mentioned. Expansion of the sinusoidal steady-state error expressions into series form and use of higher derivatives of the input motion are aids to design. Guided missile servo systems are

SERVO SYSTEM THEORY

subjected to transients, e.g., at the end of the boost phase The effect of such factors is found by a transient response analysis. The ever-present necessity of excluding noise from the system by employing a minimum bandwidth is in direct opposition to the requirements for high dynamic performance. The best compromise becomes the best design.

7-2 CLOSED LOOP RELATIONSHIPS

Basic relations that apply to all servo systems may be derived from a consideration of the block diagrams of Fig. 7-1 which show the equivalent circuits for simple, closed loop control systems. The symbols used are:

θ_i = input quantity (desired value)
θ_o = output quantity (controlled variable)
ε = error quantity = $\theta_i - \theta_o$
E = actuating error signal = $\theta_i + \beta\theta_o$
μ = gain of forward circuit
β = feedback circuit transmission factor
$\rightarrow$ = unidirectional flow, in direction of arrow
⊕ = junction indicating summing action
⊖ = junction indicating differencing action (error detector)
K = constant
$G(s)$ = function of complex frequency
$s = \sigma + j\omega$
$\sigma = 0$ for steady-state analysis
$\omega = 2\pi f$, frequency in radians per second
f = frequency in cycles per second

For the simple servo system of Fig. 7-1a, two measures of the system performance are the error ε as a function of the input θ_i, and the expression specifying the overall transfer characteristic, θ_o/θ_i, of the closed loop system. For negative feedback systems, i.e., for systems with $\beta = -1$,

$$\varepsilon = \theta_i - \theta_o \tag{7-1}$$

and

$$\frac{\varepsilon}{\theta_o} = \frac{1}{\mu} \tag{7-2}$$

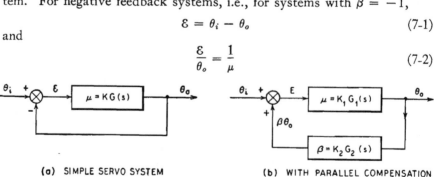

(a) SIMPLE SERVO SYSTEM   (b) WITH PARALLEL COMPENSATION

FIG. 7-1 Block Diagrams of Single Loop Servo Systems.

7-2] CLOSED LOOP RELATIONSHIPS

Under conditions of small error, we may replace θ_o by θ_i to obtain the approximate relationship

$$\frac{\varepsilon}{\theta_i} \cong \frac{1}{\mu} \tag{7-3}$$

In using Eq. (7-3) the computed error must be compared with the input to verify that θ_o is closely approximated by θ_i. The usual interest in error computation is for inputs that are a function of time.

The transfer characteristic is the other relationship of interest and is obtained from Eq. (7-1) and (7-2) used simultaneously. Thus, the overall closed loop transfer characteristic is

$$\frac{\theta_o}{\theta_i} = \frac{\mu}{1+\mu} \tag{7-4}$$

The transfer characteristic may be used to determine system response for sinusoidal and other time function inputs.

Systems with elements in the feedback path ($\beta \neq -1$), see Fig. 7-1b, have no point within the system where the system error ε appears. Instead, there is a system actuating-error signal

$$E = \theta_i + \beta\theta_o \tag{7-5}$$

The forward path relationship is

$$\frac{E}{\theta_o} = \frac{1}{\mu} \tag{7-6}$$

Simultaneous solution of Eq. (7-5) and (7-6) yields the actuating-error input-quantity ratio

$$\frac{E}{\theta_i} = \frac{1}{1-\mu\beta} \tag{7-7}$$

and the transfer characteristic

$$\frac{\theta_o}{\theta_i} = \frac{\mu}{1-\mu\beta} \tag{7-8}$$

Equation (7-3) relates the error ε to the input by the approximate expression $1/\mu$. By setting $\beta = -1$ in Eq. (7-7), we have the exact expression for the simple servo system error-input ratio

$$\frac{\varepsilon}{\theta_i} = \frac{1}{1+\mu} \tag{7-9}$$

which may be expressed as a series obtained by direct division of $(\mu + 1)$ into unity. Thus,

$$\frac{\varepsilon}{\theta_i} \cong \frac{1}{\mu} - \frac{1}{\mu^2} + \frac{1}{\mu^3} - \frac{1}{\mu^4} + \cdots \tag{7-10}$$

Equation (7-10) is convergent, provided $\mu > 1$, and has utility in derivation of steady-state error expressions.

A servo system is employed, in general, when a high degree of correspondence is required between the input and the output. A measure of this ability is the error input ratio given by Eq. (7-3), (7-9), and (7-10) for the simple servo system ($\beta = -1$), and Eq. (7-7) for the servo system with elements in the feedback path. The performance of a servo system under dynamic conditions may be investigated for inputs of sinusoidal, step function, and ramp function form by proper use of the transfer characteristic. For the simple servo system and the system with parallel compensation shown in Fig. 7-1, the transfer characteristics are given by Eq. (7-4) and (7-8), respectively. In addition to small error and excellence of performance under dynamic conditions, an early concern regarding a new design is its stability. A system is termed *absolutely stable* if any free oscillations in the system do not continue indefinitely. Once it has been determined that a system is stable in the *absolute* sense, the next question is its *relative* stability, i.e., the nature of the system transient response. The magnitude of overshoots and the damping, and the magnitude of any resonant rise in the frequency response, are aids in answering this question of relative stability.

Absolute stability may be determined by any of several methods. It is clear that an individual element of a system, e.g., the μ part of Fig. 7-1, cannot oscillate because there is no path for energy feedback within the element. When the feedback or β path is provided, oscillation is possible if the phase shift from the input through the μ and the β path totals 360 deg to cause the system to become regenerative. The involvement of all the elements of the entire loop is recognized. In the transfer characteristic expression given by Eq. (7-8), the elements of the complete loop appear in the denominator in the quantity $(1-\mu\beta)$. If a linear system is not absolutely stable, then the transfer characteristic should approach infinity at some frequency. The only way in which this is possible is for the denominator of the transfer characteristic to equal zero. It is helpful to inspect directly the $(1-\mu\beta)$ term for the system to determine that all terms of the polynomial are present and that they are of the same sign, but this inspection is not definitive in the case of small positive roots. One of the universally applicable methods of determining absolute stability, known as Routh's[1] criterion (see Chapter 6), will be applied in later examples.

7-3 BASIC TYPE I SERVO SYSTEM

As mentioned at the beginning of the chapter, the transfer-function approach has proved of great utility during the design phase of a servo system development. To emphasize this approach, the basic equations specifying system response and error characteristics are derived from

---

[1] See Routh, E. J., *Advanced Part of the Dynamics of a System of Rigid Bodies*, Vol. II, 6th Edition, Macmillan and Company, London, 1930.

consideration of the open loop log-magnitude vs. log-frequency plot of Fig. 7-2. By *open loop characteristic* is meant the response for no feedback —i.e., the β path (see Fig. 7-1) is opened. Under these conditions, any input θ_i is modified only by the forward loop to become $\mu\theta_i$ at the output. The actual characteristic is a smooth curve asymptotic to the straight line segments with a maximum deviation of -3 db at the break from the -1 slope to the -2 slope. The frequency at which the break occurs is called a *corner frequency*, ω_1. Extension of the initial (low frequency) -1 slope to its intersection with the unity gain (0-db) line at ω_0 defines a parameter of the system that is related to error due to velocity of the input.

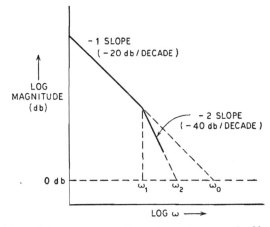

Fig. 7-2 Type I Servo System Open Loop Asymptotic Characteristic.

Extension of the -2 slope to the 0-db line to ω_2 defines the *geometric mean frequency* between ω_0 and ω_1 ($\omega_2 = \sqrt{\omega_0 \omega_1}$) which is another important parameter in that this frequency is often taken as a measure of bandwidth effective in reducing system error. The entire characteristic may be described as having a -1 ("single-integrator") slope through ω_0 together with a low-pass filter section having a corner frequency at ω_1. This is expressed in the complex frequency domain by

$$\mu = \left(\frac{\omega_0}{s}\right)\left(\frac{\omega_1}{s + \omega_1}\right) \qquad (7\text{-}11)$$

where $s \equiv \sigma + j\omega$, σ is the real part of s, and $j\omega$ is the imaginary part. Note that the magnitude of ω_0 is a direct function of the gain employed in the μ path. One can visualize the effect of an increase in gain as a downward shifting of the 0-db reference line of Fig. 7-2. The value of ω_1 is not affected by a change in gain since it is established as a constant by physical components in the system. We may rewrite Eq. (7-11) to introduce a gain factor and obtain

$$\mu = \underbrace{\left(\frac{\omega_0}{\omega_1}\right)}_{\text{gain factor}} \cdot \underbrace{\left(\frac{\omega_1}{s}\right)\left(\frac{\omega_1}{s+\omega_1}\right)}_{\text{frequency terms}} \qquad (7\text{-}12)$$

which is in the form $\mu = KG_1(s)$ shown on Fig. 7-1a. The advantage of separating μ into a parameter independent of frequency and grouping all other terms into a complex frequency factor is principally that of facilitating gain level checks from unit to unit in a complicated system.

The closed loop transfer-function for the μ characteristic of Eq. (7-12) is found, for $\beta = -1$, by substitution into Eq. (7-4). Letting the gain factor $\omega_0/\omega_1 = K$, we find

$$\frac{\theta_o}{\theta_i} = \frac{K \frac{\omega_1}{s} \frac{\omega_1}{s+\omega_1}}{1 + K \frac{\omega_1}{s} \frac{\omega_1}{s+\omega_1}} \qquad (7\text{-}13)$$

$$= \left[\frac{s^2}{K\omega_1^2} + \frac{s}{K\omega_1} + 1\right]^{-1} \qquad (7\text{-}14)$$

In factor form we may write the closed loop response as

$$\frac{\theta_o}{\theta_i} = \frac{\frac{\omega_1}{2}(1 - \sqrt{1-4K})}{s + \frac{\omega_1}{2}(1 - \sqrt{1-4K})} \cdot \frac{\frac{\omega_1}{2}(1 + \sqrt{1-4K})}{s + \frac{\omega_1}{2}(1 + \sqrt{1-4K})} \qquad (7\text{-}15)$$

The ability to glance at an equation like Eq. (7-14) and "rough out" the corresponding amplitude and phase diagram without factoring or manipulation is easily acquired. As an aid certain rules may be written as follows:

1. Slope of low frequency asymptote is set by lowest degree term present. In Eq. (7-14), we have a constant term with an indication of an initial zero-slope asymptotic segment.

2. Slope of high frequency asymptote is set by highest degree term present. In Eq. (7-14), the s^{-2} term indicates a -2 slope at high frequencies.

3. Asymptotic segments (or their extensions) intersect the 0-db line at a value found by considering either extreme term singly and finding ω for $\theta_o/\theta_i = 1$. In Eq. (7-14), the constant term is unity so that the zero slope line is through unity, or 0 db. The second order term gives, on substituting $j\omega$ for s and remembering that we are concerned only with magnitude, $1 = K\omega_1^2/\omega^2$, so that the -2 slope (extended) intersects the 0-db line at $\omega = \sqrt{K}\omega_1$.

4. The phase is 90° times the slope of the amplitude characteristic with negative slopes corresponding to phase lags. In Eq. (7-14) the phase is

zero at zero frequency, approaches $-180°$ at high frequencies, and is the average value of $-90°$ at the geometric mean frequency $\omega = \sqrt{\omega_0 \omega_1} = \omega_1 \sqrt{K}$. In Eq. (7-14), we note that the low frequency transmission is asymptotic to the zero-slope 0-db line at zero frequency. The phase starts from zero at zero frequency. The high frequency asymptote has a slope of -2 intersecting the low frequency asymptote at $\omega = \sqrt{K}\omega_1$. The phase at high frequencies approaches $180°$ lag.

Amplitude and Phase Characteristics. The amplitude and phase characteristics may be derived using relationships written for θ_o/θ_i in the form

$$\theta_o/\theta_i = a + jb \tag{7-16}$$

which are

$$|\theta_o/\theta_i| = |\sqrt{a^2 + b^2}| \tag{7-17}$$

$$\underline{/\theta_o/\theta_i} = \tan^{-1}\frac{b}{a} \tag{7-18}$$

and

$$|\theta_o/\theta_i|_{db} = 20 \log_{10} |\theta_o/\theta_i| \tag{7-19}$$

For steady-state conditions $s = j\omega$, and the transfer function of Eq. (7-14) becomes the frequency response function

$$\frac{\theta_o}{\theta_i} = \left[\frac{(j\omega)^2}{K\omega_1^2} + \frac{j\omega}{K\omega_1} + 1\right]^{-1} \tag{7-20}$$

Change of the frequency variable ω to a normalized frequency ratio $\omega/\omega_1 = F$ results in

$$\frac{\theta_o}{\theta_i} = \left[\left(1 - \frac{F^2}{K}\right) + j\frac{F}{K}\right]^{-1} \tag{7-21}$$

which has an amplitude, expressed in decibels,

$$|\theta_o/\theta_i|_{db} = -10 \log_{10}\left[F^4\left(\frac{1}{K^2}\right) + F^2\left(\frac{1}{K^2} - \frac{2}{K}\right) + 1\right] \tag{7-22}$$

and a phase

$$\underline{/\theta_o/\theta_i} = -\tan^{-1}\left[\frac{F}{K - F^2}\right] \tag{7-23}$$

Figure 7-3 shows the closed loop response for three values of gain. Another aid to a quick estimate of the response curve shape is the fact that, in the system under consideration, the amplitude curve is always tangent to the -1 slope open loop asymptote at the geometric mean frequency. This means that a gain of 10, for instance, results in a resonant rise of $\sqrt{10}$, or an output of approximately 3.1 times the input at a frequency of $\omega = \sqrt{10}\omega_1$. In general, the desired response is one with a minimum resonant rise commensurate with usable bandwidth. A value of $K = 1$ is often taken as a design objective. By setting the coefficient of the F^2 term

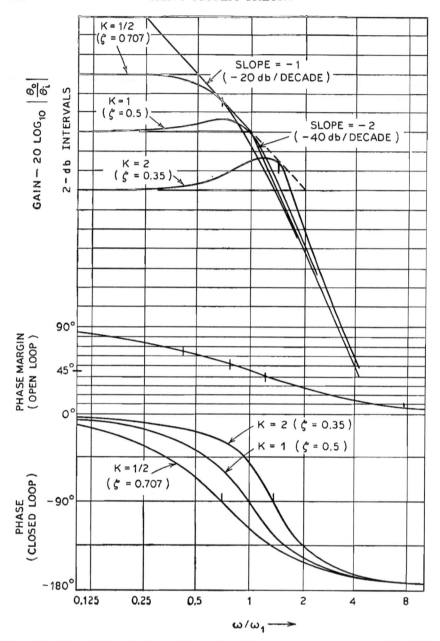

Fig. 7-3 Type I Servo System Closed Loop Response as a Function of Gain for Sinusoidal Input.

in Eq. (7-22) to zero, the requirement on gain for no resonant rise is found to be $K \leq \frac{1}{2}$.

Gain Margin and Phase Margin. Gain and phase margins are quantities determined from the open loop characteristic. The gain margin, expressed in decibels, is the number of decibels below unity gain at the frequency for which the phase magnitude equals 180°. For the system shown in Fig. 7-3 the gain margin is infinite since the greatest slope is a -2 slope with which 180° phase occurs at infinite frequency. The phase magnitude at the frequency corresponding to unity gain is subtracted from 180° to obtain the phase margin. For the system of Fig. 7-3, the phase margins are approximately 66° for $K = \frac{1}{2}$, 52° for $K = 1$, and 39° for $K = 2$.

Transient Response for Position Step Input. As stated in the introduction to the chapter, the frequency response function approach to design is of great utility, but a servo system design should be verified by checking the transient response. In the Laplace transform procedure to be used, we first take the Laplace transform of the input expressed as a function of time, $\theta_i(t)$, to obtain a generalized input function, $\theta_i(s)$, as follows:

$$\mathcal{L}[\theta_i(t)] = \theta_i(s) \tag{7-24}$$

The system output is then expressed in the s-domain as

$$\theta_o(s) = \frac{\theta_o}{\theta_i}(s) \cdot \theta_i(s) \tag{7-25}$$

The system output expressed in the time domain is then obtained by taking the inverse Laplace transform as follows:

$$\mathcal{L}^{-1}[\theta_o(s)] = \theta_o(t) \tag{7-26}$$

For an input step in position from initial condition zero we have the unit function

$$\theta_i(t) = u(t) \tag{7-27}$$

Applying the procedure outlined above, we have, as explained in Chapter 6, Eq. (6-5),

$$\theta_i(s) = \mathcal{L}[\theta_i(t)] = \mathcal{L}[u(t)] = \frac{1}{s} \tag{7-28}$$

For the Type I servo system indicated by Fig. 7-2, θ_o/θ_i is given by Eq. (7-14). For an input step in position, with initial conditions zero,

$$\theta_o(s) = \frac{K\omega_1^2}{s(s^2 + s\omega_1 + K\omega_1^2)} \tag{7-29}$$

To facilitate finding the inverse Laplace transform by consulting the usual tables, we first obtain an alternate form for Eq. (7-29) by the use of partial fraction theory. Accordingly,

$$\theta_o(s) = \frac{1}{s} + \frac{\alpha_2}{(\alpha_1 - \alpha_2)(s + \alpha_1)} - \frac{\alpha_1}{(\alpha_1 - \alpha_2)(s + \alpha_2)} \tag{7-30}$$

where the factors of the quadratic are indicated as $(s + \alpha_1)$ and $(s + \alpha_2)$. From Laplace transform tables, we find the time domain equivalent of Eq. (7-30) to be

$$\theta_o(t) = 1 + \frac{\alpha_2}{\alpha_1 - \alpha_2} e^{-\alpha_1 t} - \frac{\alpha_1}{\alpha_1 - \alpha_2} e^{-\alpha_2 t} \tag{7-31}$$

For Eq. (7-29)

$$\alpha_1 = \frac{\omega_1}{2}(1 + \sqrt{1 - 4K}) \tag{7-32}$$

$$\alpha_2 = \frac{\omega_1}{2}(1 - \sqrt{1 - 4K}) \tag{7-33}$$

Critical damping corresponds to $K = \frac{1}{4}$, i.e., $\omega_0 = \omega_1/4$. The commonly used dimensionless damping ratio ζ is defined as the ratio of the actual system damping to that required for the system to be critically damped. Since, in general, $\omega_0 = K\omega_1$, the system discussed here is characterized by $\zeta = K\omega_1 \div \omega_1/4 = 1/(2\sqrt{K})$.

In the more frequently used differential equation of motion derivation, the system response is written in the form

$$\frac{d^2\theta_o(t)}{dt^2} + 2\zeta\omega_n \frac{d\theta_o(t)}{dt} + \omega_n^2 \theta_o(t) = \omega_n^2 \theta_i(t) \tag{7-34}$$

or in alternate forms derived by using the relation $\theta_i - \theta_o = \varepsilon$. The parameter ω_n is the system undamped natural angular frequency where $\omega_n = \sqrt{\omega_0 \omega_1} = \sqrt{K}\omega_1$. The parameter ζ is the dimensionless damping ratio, $\zeta = \omega_1/2\omega_2 = 1/(2\sqrt{K})$. For overdamped response $K < \frac{1}{4}$ and Eq. (7-31) becomes

$$\theta_o(t) = 1 - \frac{\sqrt{1 - 4K}}{2(1 - 4K)} e^{-\frac{\omega_1 t}{2}} \left\{ (1 + \sqrt{1 - 4K})e^{\sqrt{1 - 4K}\frac{\omega_1 t}{2}} \right.$$
$$\left. - (1 - \sqrt{1 - 4K})e^{-\sqrt{1 - 4K}\frac{\omega_1 t}{2}} \right\} \tag{7-35}$$

System output specified by Eq. (7-35) consists of a constant term minus two terms with exponential decay. For values of $K > \frac{1}{4}(\zeta < 1)$, the complex quantities that appear in Eq. (7-35) require rearrangement for evaluation. The expression for the underdamped case consists of a constant term minus a damped sinusoid as follows:

$$\theta_o(t) = 1 - \frac{2\sqrt{K}}{\sqrt{4K - 1}} e^{-\frac{\omega_1 t}{2}} \sin\left(\sqrt{4K - 1}\frac{\omega_1 t}{2} + \tan^{-1}\sqrt{4K - 1}\right) \tag{7-36}$$

Figure 7-4 shows the response for the same three values of gain used in the sinusoidal study. The time axis is normalized with respect to system natural frequency. A value of $K = 1$ is often taken as a satisfactory compromise in the desire for speed of response[2] without unduly large overshoots or long decay time. There is no overshoot for $K \leq \frac{1}{4}$ as compared with no resonant rise for $K \leq \frac{1}{2}$. The system response shows zero steady-state error for position step-function inputs. A single-section, resistance-capacitance, low-pass filter response to a step-function input is a simple exponential rise with the shape of the curve of output versus time everywhere concave downward. The initial slope projects to unity at one time

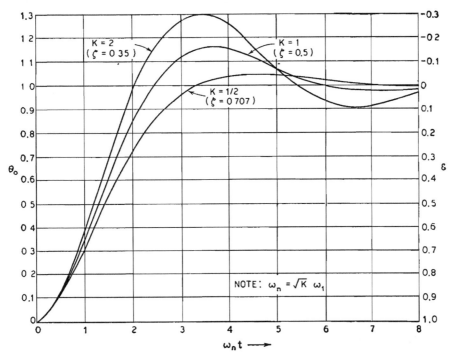

Fig. 7-4 Type I Servo System Closed Loop Response as a Function of Gain for Position Step Function Input.

constant at which time the response has risen to $1/e$, or approximately 63.2 percent of the final value. For the second-order system considered here, a better description of the transient response may be made using the quantities shown in Figure 7-5. The point of inflection of the curve is found at t_I and a tangent is drawn. The intersection with the zero line defines a delay time, τ_D. The intersection with the final value line estab-

---

[2] Speed of response in the physical sense as distinguished from the mathematical sense is to be understood. See Thaler, G. J., and Brown, R. G., *Servomechanism Analysis*, 1st Ed., p. 90, McGraw-Hill Book Co., Inc., New York, 1953.

lishes the response time τ_R for rise to $\mathcal{R}\%$ of the input. The performance may now be characterized as displaying a delay of τ_D and a response time of τ_R to $\mathcal{R}\%$ of the input. The foregoing is more satisfactory than a loose extension of the single-order system concepts with its definition of a system time constant by selection of the 63 percent response time.

Steady-state Error Expression. Bandwidth requirements not to exceed initially specified maximum errors may be related to any input function

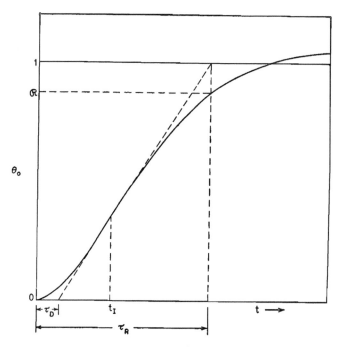

FIG. 7-5 Quantities Used in Description of Second-Order System Transient Response.

by way of an approximate steady-state error expression derived (for $\beta = -1$ systems) using Eq. (7-3) which is, repeated,

$$\frac{\varepsilon}{\theta_i} \cong \frac{1}{\mu} \qquad (7\text{-}3)$$

By substitution of Eq. (7-12), the expression used for Type I system μ, into Eq. (7-3) gives

$$\frac{\varepsilon}{\theta_i} = \frac{1}{K\dfrac{\omega_1}{s}\dfrac{\omega_1}{s+\omega_1}} \qquad (7\text{-}37)$$

$$\varepsilon(s) = \frac{s\theta_i}{K\omega_1} + \frac{s^2\theta_i}{K\omega_1^2} \qquad (7\text{-}38)$$

If we apply to Eq. (7-38) the operation-transform pair No. 9 in Table 6-2 of Chap. 6 and assume all initial conditions to be zero, then we obtain

$$\varepsilon(t) = \frac{\dot{\theta}_i}{K\omega_1} + \frac{\ddot{\theta}_i}{K\omega_1^2} \qquad (7\text{-}39)$$

By the use of the relationship given in Eq. (7-39), the system error may be plotted as a function of time. The original quantity is a plot of input position θ_i as a function of time. In many cases it is sufficient to use successive graphical differentiations to obtain $\dot{\theta}_i$ and $\ddot{\theta}_i$. For a specific input as a function of time, a selection between systems may be made by comparison of the error-time plots.

If the error expression is derived by the more exact method of Eq. (7-10), then Eq. (7-39) becomes

$$\varepsilon(t) = \frac{\dot{\theta}_i}{K\omega_1} + \frac{\ddot{\theta}_i}{K\omega_1^2}\left(1 - \frac{1}{K}\right) - \frac{\dddot{\theta}_i}{K^2\omega_1^3}\left(2 - \frac{1}{K}\right) \\ + \frac{\ddddot{\theta}_i}{K^3\omega_1^4}\left(3 - \frac{1}{K} - K\right) - \cdots \qquad (7\text{-}40)$$

For large gain ($K > 1$), Eq. (7-40) is closely approximated by Eq. (7-39). For gain less than unity ($K < 1$), we actually have attenuation, and Eq. (7-40) may not be used since it does not converge.

The foregoing emphasizes the system difficulties that arise when the bandwidth of the intelligence to be transmitted exceeds the servo bandwidth. In actual practice, the spectrum of the intelligence to be transmitted is always greater than the servo bandwidth in that high frequency components of relatively low amplitude are not passed. This discrepancy gives rise to the servo system error which, for adequate design, is held to low values. The utility of the error expressions discussed here is seen to lie principally in checking system design during the initial phases. If inadequate bandwidth is being employed, it becomes evident immediately. When the errors computed by this method are large, one may not attach too much significance to the exact value computed but, instead, merely conclude that the error is large and that a redesign is in order.

For the $-1, -2$ system under discussion, the error expressions for the three values of gain used are, employing Eq. (7-39),

$$\text{For } K = \tfrac{1}{2}, \quad \varepsilon = \frac{\dot{\theta}_i}{\omega_1/2} + \frac{\ddot{\theta}_i}{\omega_1^2/2} \qquad (7\text{-}41)$$

$$\text{For } K = 1, \quad \varepsilon = \frac{\dot{\theta}_i}{\omega_1} + \frac{\ddot{\theta}_i}{\omega_1^2} \qquad (7\text{-}42)$$

$$\text{For } K = 2, \quad \varepsilon = \frac{\dot{\theta}_i}{2\omega_1} + \frac{\ddot{\theta}_i}{2\omega_1^2} \qquad (7\text{-}43)$$

246 SERVO SYSTEM THEORY

To use the error expressions, values are needed for the derivatives of the input expressed as a function of time.

Pass-course as Tactical Problem. To develop an appreciation for the significance of the effect of gain with respect to system error, consider the following specific tactical situation. A beam-rider guided missile is to be employed against high-speed aircraft attacking a target other than the defending guided missile installation. Assume that the target passes and that it travels at constant speed on a straight line at a constant altitude. From this single situation the demands upon the radar train, elevation, and range servo systems and upon the missile pitch and yaw channel servo systems may be derived. Since the geometry of the radar servo problem is less complicated than that for the beam-rider missile, the

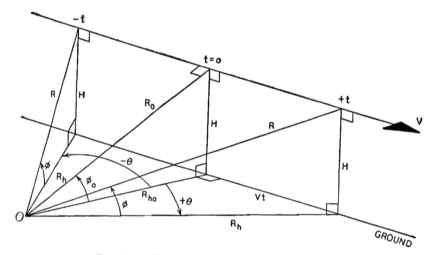

FIG. 7-6 The Pass-course Tracking Problem.

radar problem will be studied here. The problem is depicted graphically in Fig. 7-6 in which

V = target horizontal speed in knots
H = target altitude in ft
R = range to target in yd
R_h = horizontal range to target
R_0 = slant range to target at crossover
R_{h0} = horizontal range to target at crossover
ϕ = target elevation angle in deg
ϕ_0 = target elevation angle at crossover
θ = target bearing angle in deg
  ($\theta = 0$ at crossover)

t = time in sec ($t = 0$ at crossover)
O = observation point

The train angle in radians is given by the relationship

$$\tan \theta = K_1 \frac{Vt}{R_{h0}} = K_1 \frac{Vt}{R_0 \cos \phi_0} \tag{7-44}$$

where K_1 adjusts for units. The value of K_1 is

$$K_1 = \frac{6080.20}{3600 \cdot 3} \frac{\text{yd hr}}{\text{naut. mi sec}} = 0.5630 \tag{7-45}$$

The additional multiplying factor

$$K_2 = \frac{180}{\pi} \frac{\text{deg}}{\text{radian}} \cong 57.296 \tag{7-46}$$

is needed to convert radians to degrees.

By successive differentiations, we obtain

$$\dot{\theta} = \left[\frac{K_1 V}{R_0 \cos \phi_0}\right] \cos^2 \theta \tag{7-47}$$

$$\ddot{\theta} = -\left[\frac{K_1 V}{R_0 \cos \phi_0}\right]^2 \cos^2 \theta \sin 2\theta \tag{7-48}$$

$$\dddot{\theta} = 2\left[\frac{K_1 V}{R_0 \cos \phi_0}\right]^3 \cos^4 \theta (4 \sin^2 \theta - 1) \tag{7-49}$$

The maximum values of $\dot{\theta}$, $\ddot{\theta}$, and $\dddot{\theta}$ are found by setting the next higher derivative to zero and using value of θ found. They are, with units of radians for the second members of the continued equalities and units of degrees for the final members,

$$|\dot{\theta}_{\max}| = \frac{K_1 V}{R_0 \cos \phi_0} = 32.26 \frac{V}{R_0 \cos \phi_0} \tag{7-50}$$

$$|\ddot{\theta}_{\max}| = \frac{3\sqrt{3}}{8}\left[\frac{K_1 V}{R_0 \cos \phi_0}\right]^2 = 11.80 \left[\frac{V}{R_0 \cos \phi_0}\right]^2 \tag{7-51}$$

$$|\dddot{\theta}_{\max}| = 2\left[\frac{K_1 V}{R_0 \cos \phi_0}\right]^3 = 20.44 \left[\frac{V}{R_0 \cos \phi_0}\right]^3 \tag{7-52}$$

Since few servo systems have such low gain that a significant position error is involved, instead of plotting θ, $\dot{\theta}$, $\ddot{\theta}$, and $\dddot{\theta}$ as a function of time, the derivatives are plotted versus θ in Fig. 7-7. Each derivative is normalized with respect to its peak value and plotted as a percentage. To facilitate relating θ to time, Eq. (7-44) was used to plot the curve labeled t for which a separate scale at the right applies. Figure 7-8 gives the magnitudes of the maximum values of the derivatives as a function of a factor involving target velocity, slant range to the target at crossover, and the target elevation angle at crossover. The values obtained from Fig. 7-8 times the system error series coefficients provides a scale factor adjustment by which the relative importance of a given derivative is found.

As an intentionally somewhat unrealistic example using the pass-course as an input, assume the following:

$$V = 500 \text{ knots}$$
$$R_0 = 1000 \text{ yd}$$
$$H = 1500 \text{ ft}$$

The maximum rates are determined at

$$\frac{V}{R_0 \cos \phi_0} = \frac{500}{1000 \cdot 0.866} = 0.577$$

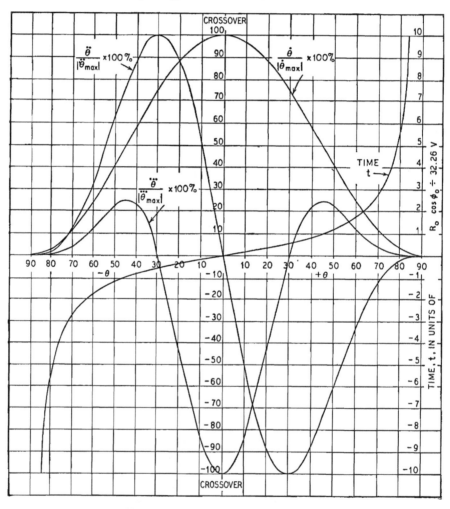

Fig. 7-7 Pass-course Train Rates.

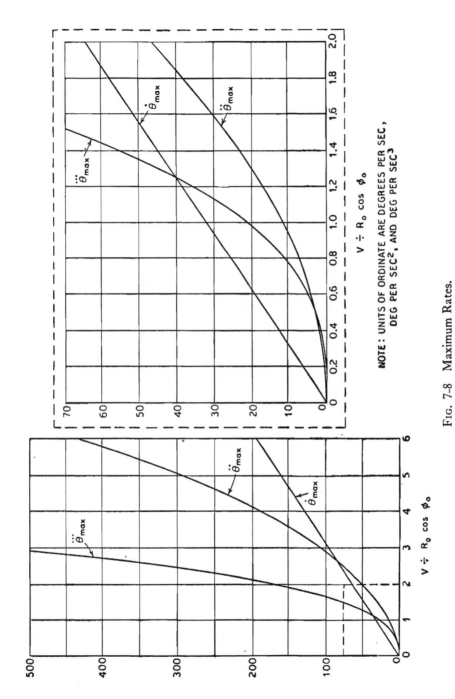

Fig. 7-8 Maximum Rates.

and from Fig. 7-8 are read as $\dot{\theta}_{max} = 18.6$ deg per sec and $\ddot{\theta}_{max} = 4$ deg per sec². We assume a given value of $\omega_1 = 10$ in the error expression, Eq. (7-42), for the $-1, -2$ servo system under study. Accordingly,

$$\varepsilon = \frac{\dot{\theta}_i}{10} + \frac{\ddot{\theta}_i}{100} \qquad (7\text{-}53)$$

is to be evaluated as a function of θ, first, and then converted to a function of time. The product of $18.6 \cdot 0.1 = 1.86$ is large as compared with $4 \cdot 0.01 = 0.04$. Hence, the system error curve should have almost ex-

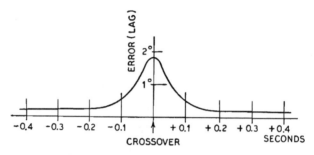

FIG. 7-9 Train Tracking Error.

actly the shape of the input velocity component. When converted to a time base, ε takes the form shown in Fig. 7-9. To follow the entire process, take $\theta = +30°$ as an example. Read $\dot{\theta}/|\dot{\theta}_{max}| = 75\%$ and compute $\dot{\theta} = 0.75 \cdot 18.6 = 13.94$. Read $\ddot{\theta}/|\ddot{\theta}_{max}| = -100\%$ and compute $\ddot{\theta} = -1 \cdot 4 = -4$. The value of ε at $\theta = 30°$ is then found to be $0.1 \cdot 13.94 - 0.01 \cdot 4 = 1.353°$. Reading the time curve, $\theta = 30°$ corresponds to $0.58 \cdot (R_0 \cos \phi_0 \div 32.26V) = 0.58(1000 \cdot 0.866 \div 32.26 \cdot 500) = 0.031$ sec after crossover. For the particular conditions that have been imposed in this example, a radar with a beamwidth in the neighborhood of 3° to 4° would be required. The maximum lag of about 1.8° occurs at crossover. The system is too simple and needs improvement in the basic transfer characteristic.

7-4 IMPROVED TYPE I SERVO SYSTEM

In the majority of cases, the open loop response of the so-called Type I system does not actually start with an initial slope of -1, for such a specification implies infinite gain at zero frequency. This d-c gain is, in general, very large so that the approximation involved in assuming it to be infinite is not great. Extension of the single-integrator slope back from the ω_0 intersection with the 0-db line to the d-c gain level results in an intersection at the ignored initial low frequency corner. The frequency at which the asymptotic slope changes from -1 to -2 is recognized as the second low-pass filter corner. The frequency of this corner is established by system parameters difficult to modify. In the presence of requirements for better dynamic performance the designer would like to use more gain but, as concluded from the study in Par. 7-3, the optimum design places the 0-db level through the $-1, -2$ corner frequency. Higher gain could be employed if the -2 slope is brought back to a -1 slope. To investigate this possibility, we will consider under the heading "improved Type I system" a system described by the slope of its open-loop asymptotic segments as a $-1, -2, -1$ system. Figure 7-10 shows the improved Type I system

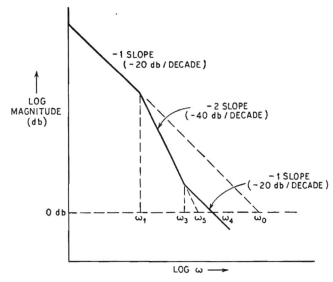

FIG. 7-10 Improved Type I System Open Loop Asymptotic Characteristic.

with the "reciprocal low-pass" corner located at a frequency ω_3. The actual open loop characteristic is a smooth curve passing through the asymptotic segment that has a -2 slope at a frequency equal to the geometric mean of ω_1 and ω_3, i.e., $\omega = \sqrt{\omega_1 \omega_3}$. The maximum deviation from the asymptotes occurs at the break frequencies and is somewhat less than 3 db, depending upon the proximity of ω_1 and ω_3. The μ characteristic is given by

$$\mu = \left(\frac{\omega_0}{s}\right)\left(\frac{\omega_1}{s + \omega_1}\right)\left(\frac{s + \omega_3}{\omega_3}\right) \tag{7-54}$$

Since ω_5 in Fig. 7-10 is the geometric mean of two pairs of omegas, i.e., $\omega_0 \omega_1 = \omega_5^2 = \omega_3 \omega_4$, we may define the bandwidth effective in reducing system error, ω_4, in terms of other parameters by $\omega_4 = \omega_0 \omega_1 \div \omega_3$. Let $N = \omega_3/\omega_1$ and $K = \omega_0/\omega_1$, and we may write

$$\mu = K\left(\frac{\omega_1}{s}\right)\left(\frac{\omega_1}{s + \omega_1}\right)\left(\frac{s + N\omega_1}{N\omega_1}\right) \tag{7-55}$$

which is of the form

$$\mu = KG_1(s) \tag{7-56}$$

For a negative feedback system ($\beta = -1$),

$$\frac{\theta_o}{\theta_i}(s) = \frac{K\dfrac{\omega_1}{s}\dfrac{\omega_1}{s + \omega_1}\dfrac{s + N\omega_1}{N\omega_1}}{1 + K\dfrac{\omega_1}{s}\dfrac{\omega_1}{s + \omega_1}\dfrac{s + N\omega_1}{N\omega_1}} \tag{7-57}$$

$$= \frac{s + N\omega_1}{N\omega_1} \cdot \frac{\alpha_1}{s + \alpha_1} \cdot \frac{\alpha_2}{s + \alpha_2} \tag{7-58}$$

where

$$\alpha_1 = \frac{\omega_1}{2}\left(\frac{N + K}{N} + \sqrt{\left(\frac{N + K}{N}\right)^2 - 4K}\right) \tag{7-59}$$

$$\alpha_2 = \frac{\omega_1}{2}\left(\frac{N + K}{N} - \sqrt{\left(\frac{N + K}{N}\right)^2 - 4K}\right) \tag{7-60}$$

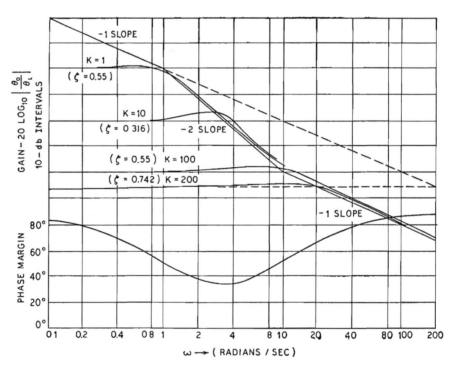

FIG. 7-11 Improved Type I System Sinusoidal Response.

Amplitude and Phase Characteristics. In Fig. 7-11, the closed loop gain for the improved Type I system is shown for a particular value of $N = \omega_3/\omega_1 = 10$ and for four values of gain, K. Note that the damping ratio is the same for both $K = 1$ and for $K = 100$. Phase margin is shown on the same frequency base. Figure 7-11 shows that, for even a full decade of -2 slope, the minimum phase margin is approximately 35° which is associated with a closed loop resonant rise of approximately 3 db. A gain level between $K = 100$ and $K = 200$ appears nearly ideal. The improved Type I system is seen to permit an increase in gain by a factor in excess of 100 over that usable in the basic Type I system. In actual practice, high frequency parasitic cutoffs would modify the second -1 slope to higher values. A measure of system bandwidth effective in reducing system error is the frequency of unity open loop gain which, for $K = 100$, is approximately $\omega = 10\omega_1$.

Response for Position Step Input. To confirm as satisfactory the selection of gain level chosen on the basis of the frequency response, investigate the response to an input step in position. Proceeding as indicated by Eq. (7-25), using Eq. (7-28) and Eq. (7-58), we have

$$\theta_o(s) = \frac{\alpha_1\alpha_2(s + N\omega_1)}{N\omega_1 s(s + \alpha_1)(s + \alpha_2)} \tag{7-63}$$

where α_1 and α_2 are defined by Eq. (7-59) and (7-60). With the use of partial fraction theory, the alternate form found is

$$\theta_o(s) = \frac{1}{s} - \frac{\alpha_1 - N\omega_1}{N\omega_1} \frac{\alpha_2}{\alpha_1 - \alpha_2} \frac{1}{s + \alpha_1} + \frac{\alpha_2 - N\omega_1}{N\omega_1} \frac{\alpha_1}{\alpha_1 - \alpha_2} \frac{1}{s + \alpha_2} \tag{7-64}$$

In view of Eq. (7-59) and (7-60) critical damping occurs for the conditions that make the radical equal to zero. The damping ratio ζ may accordingly be written as

$$\zeta = \frac{N + K}{2N\sqrt{K}} \tag{7-65}$$

for the $-1, -2, -1$ system under discussion. Equation (7-64) is in a form permitting a direct use of Laplace transform tables to obtain for the overdamped case, i.e., $N + K > 2N\sqrt{K}$

$$\theta_o(t) = 1 + \frac{N - K - \sqrt{(N + K)^2 - 4KN^2}}{2\sqrt{(N + K)^2 - 4KN^2}}$$
$$\exp\left[-\left(\frac{N + K}{N} + \sqrt{\left(\frac{N + K}{N}\right)^2 - 4K}\right)\frac{\omega_1 t}{2}\right]$$
$$- \frac{N - K + \sqrt{(N + K)^2 - 4KN^2}}{2\sqrt{(N + K)^2 - 4KN^2}}$$
$$\exp\left[-\left(\frac{N + K}{N} - \sqrt{\left(\frac{N + K}{N}\right)^2 - 4K}\right)\frac{\omega_1 t}{2}\right] \tag{7-66}$$

A more convenient form for the underdamped case, $2N\sqrt{K} > N + K$, is

$$\theta_o(t) = 1 + \sqrt{\frac{4KN^2 - (N+K)^2 + (N-K)^2}{4KN^2 - (N+K)^2}} \exp\left[-\frac{N+K}{N}\frac{\omega_1 t}{2}\right]$$
$$\cdot \sin\left(\sqrt{4K - \left(\frac{N+K}{N}\right)^2}\frac{\omega_1 t}{2} + \tan^{-1}\frac{\sqrt{4KN^2 - (N+K)^2}}{-(N-K)}\right) \quad (7\text{-}67)$$

Figure 7-12 shows the system response for a position step input as a function of gain for the special case of $N = 10$. The gain levels used are given by $K = 1$, $K = 10$, $K = 100$, and $K = 200$. These values correspond to those of Fig. 7-11. Note that the time axis of Fig. 7-12 is nondimen-

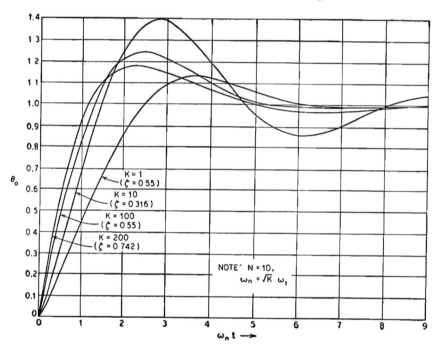

FIG. 7-12 Transient Response of Improved Type I System for Position Step Input.

sionalized with respect to the system natural undamped resonant frequency $\omega_n = \sqrt{K}\,\omega_1$, to permit a fair comparison of equal-bandwidth systems. Choice of gain level on the basis of minimum resonant rise consistent with wide bandwidth is again found to give satisfactory transient response with respect to the conflicting requirements both of rapid response and of minimum overshoot.

Error Characteristics. Using the approximate relationship given in Eq. (7-3) and the μ characteristic specified by Eq. (7-55) and (7-56), we obtain for system error

$$\frac{\varepsilon}{\theta_i} \cong \frac{1}{K\left(\frac{\omega_1}{s}\right)\left(\frac{\omega_1}{s+\omega_1}\right)\left(\frac{s+N\omega_1}{N\omega_1}\right)}$$

$$\varepsilon(s) = \frac{s\theta_i}{K\omega_1} + \frac{s^2\theta_i}{K\omega_1^2}\left(1-\frac{1}{N}\right) - \frac{s^3\theta_i}{K\omega_1^3}\frac{1}{N}\left(1-\frac{1}{N}\right)\cdots \quad (7\text{-}68)$$

$$\varepsilon(t) = \frac{\dot\theta_i}{K\omega_1} + \frac{\ddot\theta_i}{K\omega_1^2}\left(1-\frac{1}{N}\right) - \frac{\dddot\theta_i}{K\omega_1^3}\frac{1}{N}\left(1-\frac{1}{N}\right)\cdots \quad (7\text{-}69)$$

For the values of $N = 10$ and $K = 100$,

$$\varepsilon(t) = \frac{\dot\theta_i}{100\omega_1} + \frac{\ddot\theta_i}{111\omega_1^2} - \frac{\dddot\theta_i}{1111\omega_1^3}\cdots \quad (7\text{-}70)$$

Comparison of Eq. (7-70) with Eq. (7-53) shows the improvement obtained by the introduction of the second -1 slope. To complete the comparison,

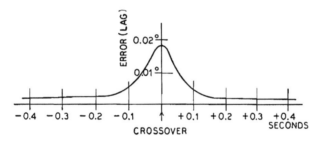

FIG. 7-13 Train Tracking Error of Improved System.

the same pass-course example previously employed was used to plot the system error shown in Fig. 7-13. The maximum error of the basic system is seen to be about 100 times that of the improved Type I system (the factor representing the difference in gain).

7-5 BASIC TYPE II SERVO SYSTEM *

A servo system in which the open loop asymptotic characteristic has an initial slope of a double integrator, i.e., a slope of -2 on a log-magnitude vs. log-frequency plot, may be called a *Type II system*. The open loop asymptotic characteristic is depicted in Fig. 7-14 in which the initial -2 slope is followed by a -1 slope at high frequencies. The system is characterized in the complex frequency domain as follows:

$$\mu = \left(\frac{\omega_5}{s}\right)^2\left(\frac{\omega_3+s}{\omega_3}\right) \quad (7\text{-}71)$$

* See Fig. 19-20 and associated text for a discussion of another Type II system.

Since ω_5 is the geometric mean of ω_3 and ω_4, we may substitute and write

$$\mu = \underbrace{\left(\frac{\omega_4}{\omega_3}\right)}_{\text{Gain Factor}} \cdot \underbrace{\left(\frac{\omega_3}{s}\right)^2 \left(\frac{\omega_3 + s}{\omega_3}\right)}_{\text{Frequency Terms}} \qquad (7\text{-}72)$$

We now have the forward loop gain μ expressed in the form $KG_1(s)$ shown on Fig. 7-1a. For $\beta = -1$, use Eq. (7-4) to obtain the closed loop

$$\frac{\theta_o}{\theta_i} = \frac{K\dfrac{\omega_3(\omega_3 + s)}{s^2}}{1 + K\dfrac{\omega_3(\omega_3 + s)}{s^2}} \qquad (7\text{-}73)$$

$$= \frac{s + \omega_3}{\omega_3} \cdot \frac{K\omega_3^2}{s^2 + sK\omega_3 + K\omega_3^2} \qquad (7\text{-}74)$$

$$= \frac{s + \omega_3}{\omega_3} \cdot \frac{\alpha_1}{s + \alpha_1} \cdot \frac{\alpha_2}{s + \alpha_2} \qquad (7\text{-}75)$$

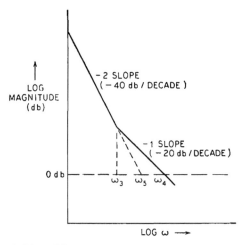

FIG. 7-14 Basic Type II System Open Loop Asymptotic Characteristic.

In Eq. (7-73) through (7-75), $K = \omega_4/\omega_3$ and the α_1 and α_2 of the factors of the quadratic are

$$\alpha_1 = \frac{\omega_3}{2}(K + \sqrt{K^2 - 4K}) \qquad (7\text{-}76)$$

$$\alpha_2 = \frac{\omega_3}{2}(K - \sqrt{K^2 - 4K}) \qquad (7\text{-}77)$$

Note that the product of α_1 and α_2 in the numerator of Eq. (7-75) is the $K\omega_3^2$ in the numerator of Eq. (7-74).

Amplitude and Phase Characteristics. The basic Type II system gain

7-5] BASIC TYPE II SERVO SYSTEM

is plotted together with phase margin in Fig. 7-15 as calculated from

$$|\theta_o/\theta_i|_{db} = 10\log_{10}\left[\frac{K^2(F^2+1)}{F^4 + F^2K(K-2) + K^2}\right] \quad (7\text{-}78)$$

$$\underline{/\theta_o/\theta_i}_{\text{(closed loop)}} = -\tan^{-1}\left[\frac{F^3}{F^2(K-1)+K}\right] \quad (7\text{-}79)$$

$$\text{Phase margin} = 180° + \underline{/\theta_o/\theta_i}\Big|_{\substack{\text{(open loop)} \\ |\theta_o/\theta_i|=1}}$$

$$= 180° - \tan^{-1}\left(\frac{2F}{F^2-1}\right) \quad (7\text{-}80)$$

where $K = \omega_4/\omega_3$ and $F = \omega/\omega_3$. Three values of gain specified by $K = 1$, $K = 2$, and $K = 10$ were used with gain in the neighborhood of $K = 2$ giving wide bandwidth without excessive resonant rise.

Response for Position Step Input. The system response for a step function input is found from

$$\theta_o(s) = \frac{K\omega_3^2}{s(s^2 + sK\omega_3 + K\omega_3^2)} \cdot \frac{s + \omega_3}{\omega_3} \quad (7\text{-}81)$$

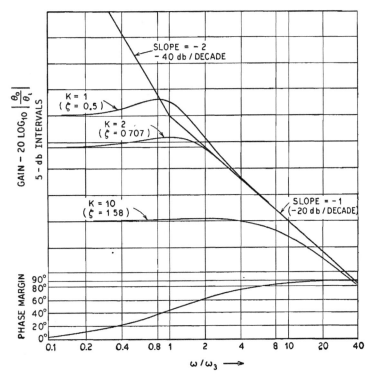

FIG. 7-15 Type II Servo System Sinusoidal Performance.

Partial fraction expansion yields

$$\theta_o(s) = \frac{1}{s} + \frac{K\omega_3(\omega_3 - \alpha_1)}{\alpha_1(\alpha_1 - \alpha_2)} \cdot \frac{1}{s + \alpha_1} - \frac{K\omega_3(\omega_3 - \alpha_2)}{\alpha_2(\alpha_1 - \alpha_2)} \cdot \frac{1}{s + \alpha_2} \quad (7\text{-}82)$$

where $(s + \alpha_1)$ and $(s + \alpha_2)$ are the factors of the quadratic with α_1 and α_2 the same expressions specified in Eq. (7-76) and (7-77). Critical damping occurs for $\sqrt{K^2 - 4K} = 0$, i.e., $K = 4$. The dimensionless damping ratio ζ is thus

$$\zeta = \frac{\sqrt{K}}{2} = \frac{1}{2}\sqrt{\frac{\omega_4}{\omega_3}} \quad (7\text{-}83)$$

Taking the inverse Laplace transform of Eq. (7-82) gives, for overdamped cases ($K > 4$), the time domain expression

$$\theta_o(t) = 1 - \frac{K + \sqrt{K^2 - 4K}}{2\sqrt{K^2 - 4K}} \exp\left[-(K + \sqrt{K^2 - 4K})\frac{\omega_3 t}{2}\right]$$
$$+ \frac{K - \sqrt{K^2 - 4K}}{2\sqrt{K^2 - 4K}} \exp\left[-(K - \sqrt{K^2 - 4K})\frac{\omega_3 t}{2}\right] \quad (7\text{-}84)$$

which, for underdamped cases ($K < 4$) becomes

$$\theta_o(t) = 1 + \frac{2}{\sqrt{4-K}} \exp\left[-\frac{K\omega_3 t}{2}\right] \cdot \sin\left(\sqrt{4K - K^2}\frac{\omega_3 t}{2} - \tan^{-1}\sqrt{\frac{4-K}{K}}\right) \quad (7\text{-}85)$$

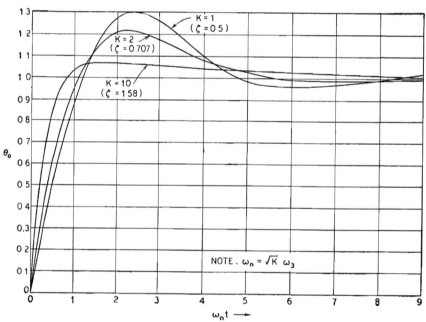

FIG. 7-16 Transient Response of Type II System for Position Step Input.

The response of the $-2, -1$ system to a step input is shown in Fig. 7-16 for the three values of gain specified by $K = 1$, $K = 2$, and $K = 10$. Speed of response without excessive overshoot is realized for gain in the neighborhood of $K = 2$. To afford the same basis for comparison previously used, the time base has been normalized with respect to the system natural undamped resonant frequency $\omega_n = \sqrt{K}\,\omega_3$. The more rapid response and smaller overshoot associated with the overdamped case $K = 10$ are not chosen because of the wide noise bandwidth ($\omega = K\omega_3$). In the system under discussion, the dividing line between overshoot and no overshoot is *not* that of critical damping.[3] The pitfalls of generalization are again emphasized.

System Error Expression. The Type II system error expression is found using the approximation of Eq. (7-2) and the open loop expression of Eq. (7-72), to be

$$\frac{\varepsilon}{\theta_i} \cong \frac{1}{K\left(\dfrac{\omega_3}{s}\right)^2 \left(\dfrac{\omega_3 + s}{\omega_3}\right)}$$

$$\varepsilon(s) = \frac{s^2 \theta_i}{K\omega_3^2} - \frac{s^3 \theta_i}{K\omega_3^3} \cdots \tag{7-86}$$

$$\varepsilon(t) = \frac{\ddot{\theta}_i}{K\omega_3^2} - \frac{\dddot{\theta}_i}{K\omega_3^3} \cdots \tag{7-87}$$

Type II systems are the type used in radar range units. Accordingly, a range input as a function of time would be a suitable tactical problem to use in determining the significance of Eq. (7-87).

Pass-course as Range Servo Problem. In Par. 7-3, the tactical problem of a beam-rider missile launched against a high-speed bomber passing at constant speed and at constant altitude was related to the determination of the guidance radar train servo bandwidth. The same problem may be used to determine bandwidth and gain requirements for the radar automatic range servo system. The same procedure is employed with position versus time, using Fig. 7-6, given by

$$R = [R_0^2 + (K_1 V t)^2]^{\frac{1}{2}} \tag{7-88}$$

where adjustment for difference in units (range in yards, speed in knots, time in seconds) is accomplished by the constant previously given as

$$K_1 = \frac{6080.20}{3 \cdot 3600} \frac{\text{yd hr}}{\text{naut. mi sec}} = 0.5630 \tag{7-45}$$

The higher derivative quantities may be obtained by simple slope determination of a curve for range position versus time or by taking successive derivatives with respect to time of Eq. (7-88). The analytic procedure

---

[3] See Den Hartog, J. P., *Mechanical Vibrations*, 3rd Ed., p. 51, McGraw-Hill Book Co., Inc., 1947, regarding free vibrations with viscous damping.

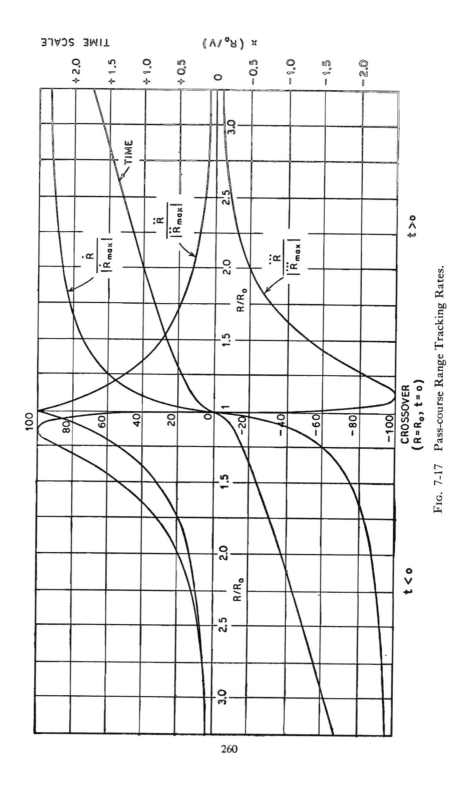

FIG. 7-17 Pass-course Range Tracking Rates.

gives

$$\dot{R} = \frac{K_1^2 V^2 t}{[R_0^2 + (K_1 V t)^2]^{\frac{1}{2}}} \qquad (7\text{-}89)$$

$$\ddot{R} = \frac{K_1^2 V^2 R_0^2}{[R_0^2 + (K_1 V t)^2]^{\frac{3}{2}}} \qquad (7\text{-}90)$$

$$\dddot{R} = -\frac{3 K_1^4 V^4 R_0^2 t}{[R_0^2 + (K_1 V t)^2]^{\frac{5}{2}}} \qquad (7\text{-}91)$$

$$\ddddot{R} = \frac{3 K_1^4 V^4 R_0^2 (4 K_1^2 V^2 t^2 - R_0^2)}{[R_0^2 + (K_1 V t)^2]^{\frac{7}{2}}} \qquad (7\text{-}92)$$

The maximum values of a given derivative are found by setting the next higher derivative equal to zero. Equation (7-90) shows $|\dot{R}_{max}|$ to be at $t \to \infty$, Eq. (7-91) shows $|\ddot{R}_{max}|$ to be at $t = 0$, and Eq. (7-92) shows $|\dddot{R}_{max}|$ to occur at $t = R_0/2K_1 V$. To provide the greatest utility to plots of the various derivatives, the ordinates are normalized to the absolute value of the maximum magnitude. Figure 7-17 shows, as a function of R/R_0,

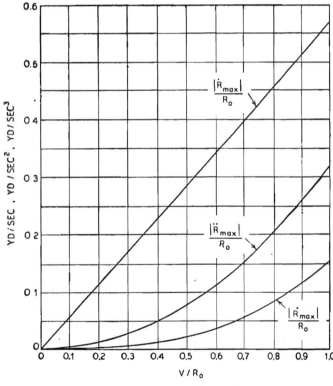

Fig. 7-18 Maximum Range Rates.

$$\frac{\dot{R}}{|\dot{R}_{max}|} = \left[1 - \left(\frac{R_0}{R}\right)^2\right]^{\frac{1}{2}} \qquad (7\text{-}93)$$

$$\frac{\ddot{R}}{|\ddot{R}_{max}|} = \left(\frac{R_0}{R}\right)^3 \qquad (7\text{-}94)$$

$$\frac{\dddot{R}}{|\dddot{R}_{max}|} = -\frac{5^{\frac{5}{2}}}{16}\left(\frac{R_0}{R}\right)^4\left[1 - \left(\frac{R_0}{R}\right)^2\right]^{\frac{1}{2}} \qquad (7\text{-}95)$$

The values of the maximum rates, shown in Fig. 7-18 as a function of $K_1 V/R_0$, are

$$\frac{|\dot{R}_{max}|}{R_0} = \left[\frac{K_1 V}{R_0}\right] = 0.563\left(\frac{V}{R_0}\right) \qquad (7\text{-}96)$$

$$\frac{|\ddot{R}_{max}|}{R_0} = \left[\frac{K_1 V}{R_0}\right]^2 = 0.317\left(\frac{V}{R_0}\right)^2 \qquad (7\text{-}97)$$

$$\frac{|\dddot{R}_{max}|}{R_0} = \frac{48}{5^{\frac{5}{2}}}\left[\frac{K_1 V}{R_0}\right]^3 = 0.153\left(\frac{V}{R_0}\right)^3 \qquad (7\text{-}98)$$

In using the pass-course range rate values as a servo input, it is contemplated that all calculation be made as a function of range so that percentage error may be found if desired and, at the very last, conversion to a time base. The time curve on Fig. 7-17 aids in this operation and is a plot of Eq. (7-88) rearranged to read

$$t = \left(\frac{R_0}{K_1 V}\right)\left[\left(\frac{R}{R_0}\right)^2 - 1\right]^{\frac{1}{2}} \qquad (7\text{-}99)$$

Range Error Due to Target Motion. Setting the gain in the Type II system at the slightly higher than optimum value represented by $K = 2$ ($\zeta = 0.707$), the general error expression of Eq. (7-87) becomes, for range,

$$\varepsilon(t) = \frac{\ddot{R}_t}{2\omega_3^2} - \frac{\dddot{R}_t}{2\omega_3^3} \qquad (7\text{-}100)$$

If the allowable range error due to target motion is specified as ±5 yd, we may substitute $\varepsilon(t) = 5$ in Eq. (7-100) and solve for the required value of ω_3. Thus,

$$10\omega_3^3 - \ddot{R}_t\omega_3 + \dddot{R}_t = 0 \qquad (7\text{-}101)$$

If the same tactical problem as described in Par. 7-3 is assumed, where $V = 500$ knots and $R_0 = 1000$ yd, we find from Fig. 7-18 at $V/R_0 = \frac{1}{2}$ the values $|\ddot{R}_{max}| = 79$ yd/sec^2 and $|\dddot{R}_{max}| = 19$ yd/sec^3. If the system error due to target motion is assumed to be principally from the acceleration component, take values at crossover for computation. From Fig. 7-17, at crossover we find $\ddot{R}/|\ddot{R}_{max}| = 100\%$ and $\dddot{R}/|\dddot{R}_{max}| = 0$. Equation (7-101) then becomes $10\omega_3^3 - 79\omega_3 = 0$ or $\omega_3 = 2.81$ radians per sec. If, instead, we choose the instant corresponding to maximum rate of change of acceleration for calculation purposes, we have $\ddot{R}/|\ddot{R}_{max}| = 72\%$ and Eq. (7-101) becomes $10\omega_3^3 - 57\omega_3 - 19 = 0$ or $\omega_3 = 2.54$ radians per sec. Range tracking errors computed as a function of R/R_0 may be converted to a time plot with the aid of the TIME curve of Fig. 7-17. The result for the example in which a 500-knot bomber passes within a radar range of 1000 yd is shown for the Type II system with $\omega_3 = 2.81$ in Fig. 7-19. Since for the value of ω_3 used the acceleration error is approximately 11.7 times as significant as the rate of change of acceleration, the curve

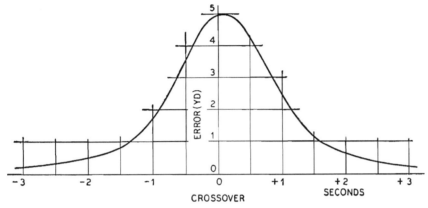

FIG. 7-19 Range Tracking Error.

in Fig. 7-19 is similar in shape to that of the acceleration component. The performance depicted is for a system with a bandwidth effective in reducing system error of approximately twice ω_3 or slightly in excess of 5 radians per sec. The system natural frequency is $\omega_n = \sqrt{K}\,\omega_3$ or almost exactly 4 radians per sec.

7-6 TRANSFER-FUNCTION DESIGN TECHNIQUE

The most readily applied procedure of the various methods or techniques for analyzing and designing servo systems is that known as transfer-function analysis. In the earlier sections of this chapter, the assumed starting point has been a transfer characteristic equation with no specific statements regarding its derivation. The transfer function of any component, part of a servo loop, or entire servo system is a mathematical expression stating the complex ratio of the output of the device to its input. The transfer function may be obtained either from the Laplace transformation or from circuit theory. In Chapter 6 the justification for interchange of the frequency response variable $j\omega$ and the Laplace transformation variable s is explained from complex-variable theory and the discussion of the Nyquist stability criterion. The derivations here are limited to the frequency response or circuit theory approach since it is believed that the earlier communications theory and feedback amplifier theory are more familiar to the greater number.

Adjustment of a servo system transfer characteristic, either for the purpose of stabilizing or to obtain performance required by specifications, is often accomplished by introduction into the loop, either in the forward or μ path, or into the feedback or β path, of electrical networks known as equalizers or filters. Because of the low frequencies involved in servo system work, these usually, but not always, consist of resistance-capacitance networks. In order to develop simultaneously the transfer-function concept and information of importance in the general field of guided missile servo system development, a selected group of RC (resistance-capacitance) networks and of servo components is studied.

The L-section Network. Before the analysis of a specific network configuration is undertaken, the general procedure used in the determination of the steady-state response of a network should be outlined. It should be noted that the effect produced by the insertion of a network into an electrical circuit is not only a function of the character of the network itself, but also of the terminating impedances, i.e., the nature of the input and output circuits. The immediate interest here is in the individual

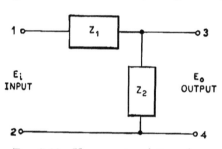

FIG. 7-20 Unsymmetrical *L*-section.

effects of the network itself. That is, the analysis is based upon the assumption that the input circuit impedance, referred to as the *generator impedance* Z_g, is negligibly small and that the output circuit impedance, referred to as the *load impedance* Z_L, is effectively infinite. The unsymmetrical *L*-section of Fig. 7-20 is considered here as the basic configuration.

The quantities Z_1 and Z_2 may contain resistance and reactance as indicated in complex form by

$$Z_1 = a_1 + jb_1 \tag{7-102}$$

and

$$Z_2 = a_2 + jb_2 \tag{7-103}$$

where a_1 and a_2 have values of zero or positive real numbers, and b_1 and b_2 have any real number values including zero with the limitation, for restriction of our consideration to resistance-capacitance or resistance-inductance networks only, that b_1 and b_2 cannot have unlike signs. For resistance-inductance networks, b_1 and b_2 may be zero or positive. The symbol j indicates the imaginary number, $\sqrt{-1}$.

Before obtaining the steady-state response equation, another term called the *open-circuit driving-point impedance* must be introduced. As used here, the impedance between terminals 1 and 2 of Fig. 7-20 measured with terminals 3 and 4 open-circuited is designated the *input open-circuit driving-point impedance*, Z_{12}. Similarly, the impedance between terminals 3 and 4 with terminals 1 and 2 open-circuited is designated the *output open-circuit driving-point impedance*, Z_{34}. The steady-state transfer characteristic, E_o/E_i, may now be given the general form

$$\frac{E_o}{E_i} = \frac{Z_{34}}{Z_{12}} = \frac{Z_2}{Z_1 + Z_2} = a + jb \qquad (7\text{-}104)$$

The magnitude of E_o/E_i is, in the case of passive networks, an attenuation term

$$\left|\frac{E_o}{E_i}\right| = \sqrt{a^2 + b^2} \qquad (7\text{-}105)$$

whereas the phase of the output voltage relative to the input voltage is the *phase shift angle*

$$\underline{/E_o/E_i} = \tan^{-1}\frac{b}{a} \qquad (7\text{-}106)$$

Since the quantity a is never negative, the sign of b determines whether the output voltage leads or lags the input. For a positive value of b/a, a leading phase shift occurs; for a negative value of b/a, a lagging phase shift is involved. In all single-section RC or RL networks the phase shift never exceeds 90 deg.

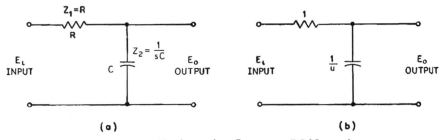

FIG. 7-21 Single-section, Low-pass RC Network.

Single-section, Low-pass Filter. The procedure outlined may be applied to the single-section, low-pass RC network of Fig. 7-21. A careful study of such basic networks leads to a generally applicable method of analysis by which all RC networks, and by extensions all systems, may be analyzed. In this case, the series-branch impedance Z_1 becomes R and the shunt-branch impedance Z_2 becomes $1/sC$ where s is defined as $j\omega$ under steady-state conditions and C is the capacitance. Changes of variable as defined by the sequence of equalities

$$u = sCR = \frac{s}{1/CR} = \frac{s}{\omega_0} = j\frac{\omega}{\omega_0} = jF \qquad (7\text{-}107)$$

are found an aid in various phases of the analysis of more complicated systems and will be employed. Figure 7-21b shows the form adopted to facilitate analysis in which, without loss of generality, the resistance is normalized to unity. The transfer function becomes

$$\frac{E_o}{E_i} = \frac{\frac{1}{u}}{1 + \frac{1}{u}} = \frac{1}{u+1} \qquad (7\text{-}108)$$

or the alternative

$$\frac{E_o}{E_i} = \frac{\omega_0}{s + \omega_0} \qquad (7\text{-}109)$$

where

$$\omega_0 = \frac{1}{RC} \qquad (7\text{-}110)$$

The magnitude of the transfer function is given by

$$|E_o/E_i| = \left[1 + \left(\frac{\omega}{\omega_0}\right)^2\right]^{-\frac{1}{2}} \qquad (7\text{-}111)$$

and the phase by

$$\underline{/E_o/E_i} = -\tan^{-1}\left(\frac{\omega}{\omega_0}\right) \qquad (7\text{-}112)$$

The plotting of both attenuation and phase on a logarithmic frequency scale has special merit in network studies and, in general, in servo system studies. If attenuation be expressed in terms of decibels, as determined by the formula*

$$|E_o/E_i|_{db} = 20 \log_{10} |E_o/E_i| \qquad (7\text{-}113)$$

the transfer characteristic exhibits approximately straight-line low and high frequency portions called asymptotic segments when plotted on a logarithmic frequency scale as indicated by Fig. 7-22 (since decibels are a logarithmic quantity, the scales are actually log-log). The asymptotic segments extended to intersection define a frequency having a particularly important relationship to the parameters of the network being analyzed. Substitution of Eq. (7-111) into (7-113) gives a decibel expression for the attenuation of the network:

$$|E_o/E_i|_{db} = -10 \log_{10}\left[1 + \left(\frac{\omega}{\omega_0}\right)^2\right] \qquad (7\text{-}114)$$

* Values of decibels determined on a voltage ratio basis may not be used in power level calculations unless the input and output impedances are equal in value and pure resistance.

from which it is possible to determine the asymptotes by retaining the portion within the bracket having importance at extremely low and at extremely high frequencies. For low frequencies the equation of the asymptote,

$$|E_o/E_i|_{db} = 0 \tag{7-115}$$

is a zero-slope line at zero-gain level. For very high frequencies the equation of the asymptote,

$$|E_o/E_i|_{db} = -20 \log_{10}\left(\frac{\omega}{\omega_0}\right) \tag{7-116}$$

is the equation of a line crossing the zero decibel gain line at a frequency specified by $\omega/\omega_0 = 1$, i.e., $\omega = \omega_0 = 1/RC$. To distinguish from the variable ω, a subscript zero has been used. The intersection of the asymptotes thus defines an angular frequency ω_0 which may be used as a reference angular frequency. The significant nature of the value of ω_0 is emphasized by the fact that the reciprocal of ω_0, namely, RC, is the circuit time constant of transient analysis. Before discussing the slope of the high frequency asymptotic segment, it is desirable to introduce the term *decade*. In conformity with a rising usage, the term *decade* serves to mean a frequency interval of ten to one, i.e., an interval of one cycle of graduations in a plot on common log paper. From a value of zero decibels for $\omega = \omega_0$, Eq. (7-116) gives a value of -20 db for $\omega = 10\omega_0$. Accordingly, the slope of the high frequency asymptotic segment is -20 db/decade (-1 on a log-log plot).

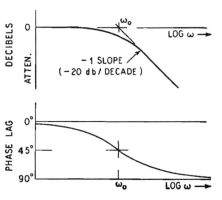

FIG. 7-22 Transfer-function Magnitude and Phase for RC Low-pass Network.

The actual transfer-function magnitude is a smooth curve deviating from the asymptotes by the greatest amount, -3 db, at the reference frequency. For a given number of decades either side of the reference frequency, the attenuation characteristic deviates from the asymptotes by the same amount. Accordingly, only a limited number of deviation values are needed in order to graph the characteristic. A study of the equation for phase shift, Eq. (7-112), reveals the fact that the phase characteristic has odd-function symmetry about the reference frequency. The values given in Table 7-1 are worth committing to memory if much work in this field is done.

268 SERVO SYSTEM THEORY

TABLE 7-1 MAGNITUDE AND PHASE OF THE TRANSFER FUNCTION
$\left(\dfrac{\omega_0}{s+\omega_0}\right)$

$\dfrac{\omega}{\omega_0}$	$\|E_o/E_i\|_{db} = -10\log_{10}\left[1+\left(\dfrac{\omega}{\omega_0}\right)^2\right]$	$\angle E_o/E_i = -\tan^{-1}\left(\dfrac{\omega}{\omega_0}\right)$
$\tfrac{1}{16}$	$-.02$	-3.6
$\tfrac{1}{8}$	$-.07$	-7.1
$\tfrac{1}{4}$	$-.26$	-14.0
$\tfrac{1}{2}$	$-.97$	-26.6
1	-3.0	-45
2	$-.97 - 6.02$	$+26.6 - 90$
4	$-.26 - 12.04$	$+14.0 - 90$
8	$-.07 - 18.06$	$+7.1 - 90$
16	$-02 - 24.08$	$+3.6 - 90$

Single-section, High-pass Filter. The transfer function for the single-section, RC high-pass network shown in Fig. 7-23 is obtained in the same

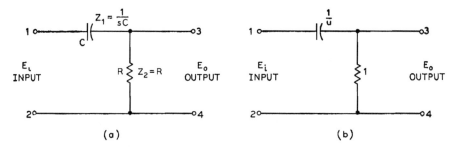

FIG. 7-23 Single-section, RC High-pass Network.

manner used in deriving the low-pass network transfer function. Thus,

$$\frac{E_o}{E_i} = \frac{1}{1+\dfrac{1}{u}} = u\left(\frac{1}{u+1}\right) \qquad (7\text{-}117)$$

or, in the alternate form, where $\omega_0 = 1/RC$,

$$\frac{E_o}{E_i} = \left(\frac{s}{\omega_0}\right)\left(\frac{\omega_0}{s+\omega_0}\right) \qquad (7\text{-}118)$$

In Eq. (7-117) and (7-118), the same function found in the low-pass study appears together with a new term which has the magnitude and phase

$$u = \frac{s}{\omega_0} = j\frac{\omega}{\omega_0} = \left(\frac{\omega}{\omega_0}\right)\angle{+90°} \qquad (7\text{-}119)$$

In decibel form,

$$|u| = 20 \log_{10}\left(\frac{\omega}{\omega_0}\right) \qquad (7\text{-}120)$$

Equation (7-120) is that of a straight line (on log-log or decibel log-frequency plots) which has a slope of $+1$ or $+20$ decibels/decade crossing the unity gain or zero decibel line at $\omega/\omega_0 = 1$, i.e., $\omega = \omega_0$.

Both of the two terms of Eq. (7-117) and (7-118) are known as complex functions of the real variable ω, since $u = sCR$ and $s = j\omega$. By use of the subscripts 1 and 2 to refer to the first and the second function respectively, the functions may be indicated in the equivalent rectangular and polar forms:

$$(E_o/E_i)_1 = a_1 + jb_1 = A_1 \underline{/B_1} \qquad (7\text{-}121)$$

and

$$(E_o/E_i)_2 = a_2 + jb_2 = A_2 \underline{/B_2} \qquad (7\text{-}122)$$

The product of two such functions is given by[4]

$$(E_o/E_i)_1 \cdot (E_o/E_i)_2 = (A_1 \underline{/B_1})(A_2 \underline{/B_2}) = A_1 \cdot A_2 \underline{/B_1 + B_2} \qquad (7\text{-}123)$$

Finally, since the magnitude expressed in decibels is desired,

$$|E_o/E_i|_{db} = (A_1 \cdot A_2)_{db} = A_{1db} + A_{2db} \qquad (7\text{-}124)$$

and

$$\underline{/E_o/E_i} = B_1 + B_2 \qquad (7\text{-}125)$$

We are now able to combine the results given for the function (s/ω_0) and those for $\left(\dfrac{\omega_0}{s + \omega_0}\right)$ to exhibit the steady-state transfer function of the high-pass network by its two aspects, magnitude and phase, as follows:

$$|E_o/E_i|_{db} = -10 \log_{10}\left[1 + \left(\frac{\omega_0}{\omega}\right)^2\right] \qquad (7\text{-}126)$$

$$\underline{/E_o/E_i} = \tan^{-1}\left(\frac{\omega_0}{\omega}\right) \qquad (7\text{-}127)$$

Figure 7-24 shows the important concept of graphical synthesis of the overall transfer function from the "building block" graphs of the two fundamental transfer-function forms, s/ω_0 and $\dfrac{\omega_0}{s + \omega_0}$. The forms appear as indicated and are called a *differentiator function* and a *low-pass function*. They also appear in reciprocal form in which case they are referred to as an *integrator function* and a *reciprocal low-pass function*. In the latter instance, the sign of the magnitude expressed in decibels and the sign of the phase are changed from those of the functions involved in Fig. 7-24.

---

[4] For a detailed discussion see a text on circuit theory; e.g., *Electric Circuits*, M.I.T. Staff, John Wiley & Sons, Inc., 1943.

270 SERVO SYSTEM THEORY

Extension of Asymptotic Segment Concept. In more involved examples, quadratic forms appear in transfer-function expressions which, upon factoring, yield conjugate-complex roots* (instead of the negative-real quantities discussed to this point). These cannot be given a general characterization but require individual analysis since the response is a function of the damping ζ (a parameter that differs from case to case). It is possible,

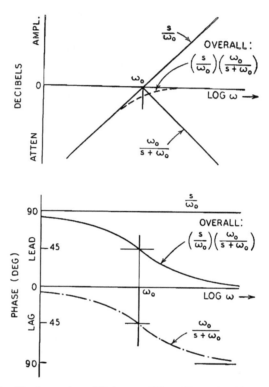

FIG. 7-24 Single-section, High-pass Filter Transfer Characteristics.

however, to draw asymptotic segments for such transfer functions. When the quadratic appears as

$$\frac{E_o}{E_i} = \left[\frac{s^2 + 2\zeta\omega_0 s + \omega_0^2}{\omega_0^2}\right]^{-1} \tag{7-128}$$

the asymptotes are zero slope through a gain level of unity or zero db, a plus infinity (straight up) slope starting from unity gain and $\omega = \omega_0$, a minus infinity slope ending at unity gain and $\omega = \omega_0$, and finally a -2

---

* See Chap. 6, Par. 6-7, for a discussion of the mathematical background involved here.

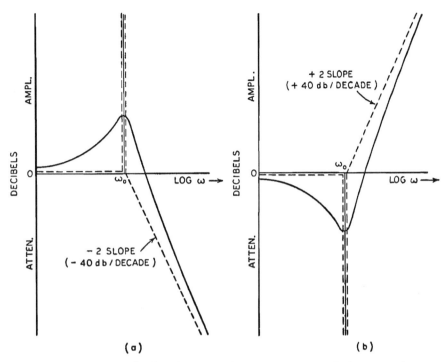

Fig. 7-25 Transfer-function Magnitude and Asymptotic Segments for
(a) $\dfrac{E_o}{E_i} = \left[\dfrac{s^2 + 2\zeta\omega_0 s + \omega_0^2}{\omega_0^2}\right]^{-1}$ and
(b) Its Reciprocal.

(-40 db/decade) slope from unity gain and $\omega = \omega_0$. The foregoing is clarified by Fig. 7-25 in which the reciprocal function is also shown.

Application of Transfer-function Procedure to a Network. The details of the application of the method are best shown by analyzing a more complicated configuration, namely, the circuit of Fig. 7-26. The procedure may be separated into six steps:

1. Write equation for transfer function.
2. Note the factors of which the transfer function is composed.
3. Draw individual asymptotic segments and combined overall asymptotic attenuation characteristic.
4. Draw individual phase and combined overall phase curves.
5. Compute values, using specific circuit values.
6. Prepare accurate graphs, using values assembled in 5.

These steps are applied to the circuit of Fig. 7-26 as follows:

272   SERVO SYSTEM THEORY

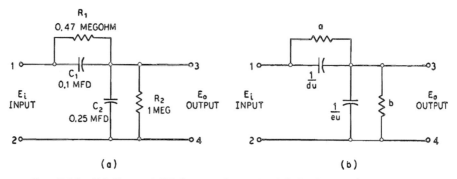

Fig. 7-26 *RC* Shunted, High-pass Network with Resistance Termination.

1. *Write equation for transfer function:*

$$\frac{E_o}{E_i} = \frac{b\dfrac{1}{ue}}{b + \dfrac{1}{ue}} \bigg/ \left(\frac{a\dfrac{1}{ud}}{a + \dfrac{1}{ud}} + \frac{b\dfrac{1}{ue}}{b + \dfrac{1}{ue}} \right)$$

$$= \left[\frac{b}{a+b}\right] \left[\frac{u + \dfrac{1}{ad}}{\dfrac{1}{ad}}\right] \left[\frac{\dfrac{a+b}{ab} \cdot \dfrac{1}{d+e}}{u + \dfrac{a+b}{ab} \cdot \dfrac{1}{d+e}}\right] \quad (7\text{-}129)$$

$$= \left[\frac{b}{a+b}\right] \left[\frac{s + \dfrac{\omega_0}{ad}}{\dfrac{\omega_0}{ad}}\right] \left[\frac{\dfrac{a+b}{ab} \cdot \dfrac{\omega_0}{d+e}}{s + \dfrac{a+b}{ab} \cdot \dfrac{\omega_0}{d+e}}\right] \quad (7\text{-}130)$$

2. *Note the functions involved:*

(1) $\dfrac{b}{a+b}$, a constant attenuation, no phase shift.

(2) $\dfrac{s + \dfrac{\omega_0}{ad}}{\dfrac{\omega_0}{ad}}$, a reciprocal low-pass filter characteristic with an angular reference frequency $\omega_{02} = \omega_0/ad$.

(3) $\dfrac{\dfrac{a+b}{ab} \cdot \dfrac{\omega_0}{d+e}}{s + \dfrac{a+b}{ab} \cdot \dfrac{\omega_0}{d+e}}$, a low-pass filter characteristic with an angular reference frequency $\omega_{01} = \dfrac{a+b}{ab} \cdot \dfrac{\omega_0}{d+e}$.

3. *Draw individual asymptotic segments and overall attenuation characteristic:*
See Fig. 7-27.

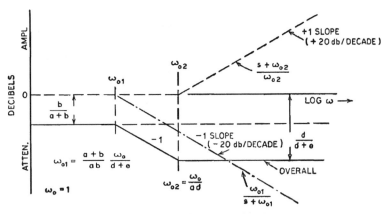

Fig. 7-27 Asymptotic Characteristics.

4. *Draw individual phase shifts and combined overall phase curves:*
See Fig. 7-28.

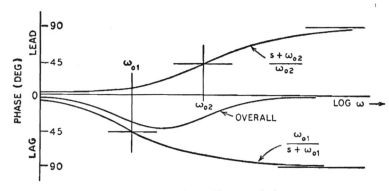

Fig. 7-28 Phase Characteristics.

5. *Compute values using specific circuit values:*

$$\frac{b}{a+b} = \frac{1}{0.47+1} = 0.68; \quad \underline{-3.35 \text{ db}}$$

$$\frac{\omega_0}{ad} = \frac{1}{0.47 \cdot 0.1} = \underline{21.28} = \omega_{02}$$

$$\frac{a+b}{ab} \cdot \frac{\omega_0}{d+e} = \frac{0.47+1}{0.47 \cdot 1} \cdot \frac{1}{0.1+0.25} = \underline{8.94} = \omega_{01}$$

274 SERVO SYSTEM THEORY

6. *Prepare accurate graphs:*

Each characteristic may be plotted on graph paper easily by use of the values integral numbers of octaves each side of ω_{01} and ω_{02} (see Table 7-1) and then combined, using dividers to perform the summations.

RC Networks Important in Servo System Design. In servo system design, the stabilization answer when found is in the form of a transfer function demanded of a missing unit often supplied by an equalization network. Resistance-capacitance networks are widely used in this con-

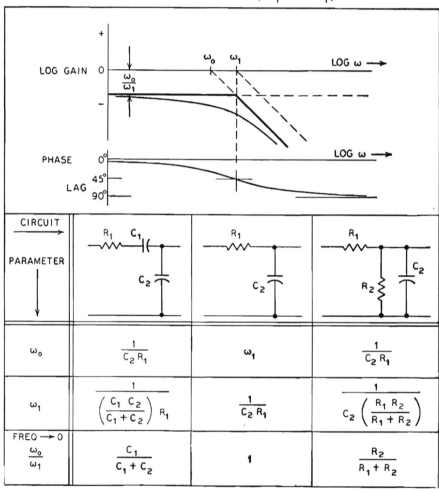

FIG. 7-29 *RC* Low-pass Networks.

7-6] TRANSFER-FUNCTION DESIGN TECHNIQUE

TRANSFER CHARACTERISTIC: $\left(\dfrac{\omega_0}{\omega_1}\right)\left(\dfrac{\omega_1}{s+\omega_1}\right)\left(\dfrac{s+\omega_2}{\omega_2}\right)$

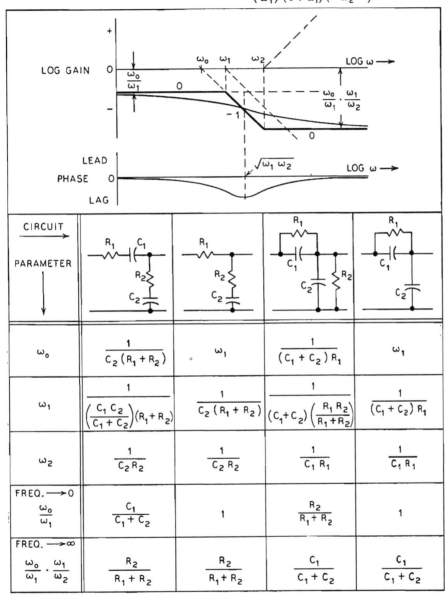

FIG. 7-30 *RC* Phase-lag Networks.

nection and in shaping the open loop characteristic to meet previously established specifications. The procedure explained in this section has been applied to various L-section, RC networks and they are grouped according to transfer functions. Single-section, low-pass RC networks with the transfer function

$$\frac{E_o}{E_i} = \left(\frac{\omega_0}{\omega_1}\right)\left(\frac{\omega_1}{s + \omega_1}\right) \qquad (7\text{-}131)$$

are grouped in Fig. 7-29. Single-section, phase-lag RC networks with the transfer function

$$\frac{E_o}{E_i} = \left(\frac{\omega_0}{\omega_1}\right)\left(\frac{\omega_1}{s + \omega_1}\right)\left(\frac{s + \omega_2}{\omega_2}\right) \qquad (7\text{-}132)$$

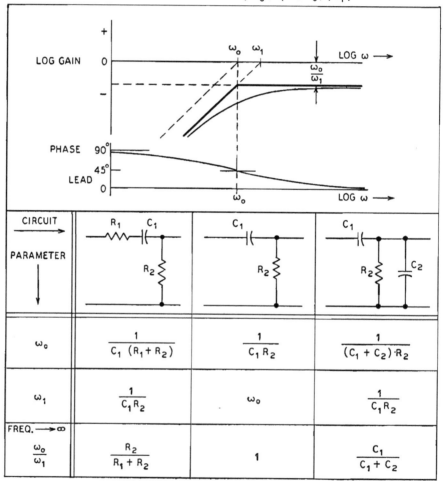

Fig. 7-31 RC High-pass Networks.

7-6] TRANSFER-FUNCTION DESIGN TECHNIQUE

TRANSFER CHARACTERISTIC: $\left(\dfrac{s+\omega_0}{\omega_0}\right)\left(\dfrac{\omega_0}{\omega_1}\right)\left(\dfrac{\omega_1}{s+\omega_1}\right)\left(\dfrac{\omega_1}{\omega_2}\right)$

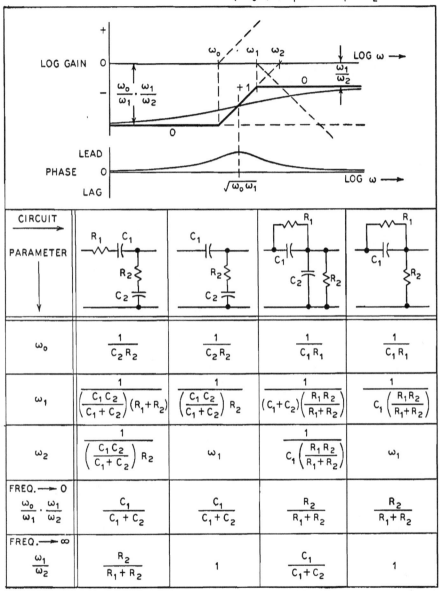

FIG. 7-32 *RC* Phase-lead Networks.

TRANSFER CHARACTERISTIC: $\left(\dfrac{s+\omega_0}{\omega_0}\right)\left(\dfrac{\omega_0}{\omega_1}\right)\left(\dfrac{\omega_1}{s+\omega_1}\right)\left(\dfrac{s+\omega_2}{\omega_2}\right)\left(\dfrac{\omega_2}{\omega_3}\right)\left(\dfrac{\omega_3}{s+\omega_3}\right)$

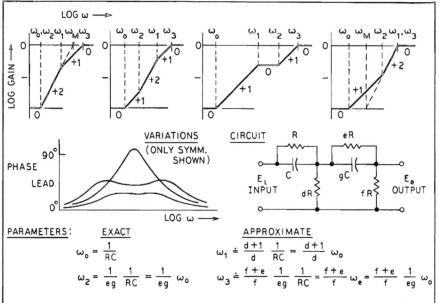

PARAMETERS:

EXACT:
$$\omega_0 = \dfrac{1}{RC}$$
$$\omega_2 = \dfrac{1}{eg}\dfrac{1}{RC} = \dfrac{1}{eg}\omega_0$$

APPROXIMATE:
$$\omega_1 \doteq \dfrac{d+1}{d}\dfrac{1}{RC} = \dfrac{d+1}{d}\omega_0$$
$$\omega_3 \doteq \dfrac{f+e}{f}\dfrac{1}{eg}\dfrac{1}{RC} = \dfrac{f+e}{f}\omega_e = \dfrac{f+e}{f}\dfrac{1}{eg}\omega_0$$

DESIGN PROCEDURE: (NO APPROXIMATIONS, NO COMPONENT VALUE RESTRICTIONS)

(1) SPECIFY $\omega_0, \omega_1, \omega_2, \omega_3$.

(2) SELECT R AND C USING THE RELATIONSHIP $\omega_0 = 1/RC$. VALUES OF R AT LEAST 10 TIMES THE EQUIVALENT SOURCE IMPEDANCE ARE DESIRABLE IF PRACTICAL. SMALL VALUES OF C DESIRABLE BECAUSE OF COMPONENT SIZE.

(3) FOR $\omega_2 > \omega_1$ DESIGNS, SELECT g ON THE BASIS
$$0 < g < [(\omega_3 - \omega_0)(\omega_1 - \omega_0)/(\omega_3 - \omega_2)(\omega_2 - \omega_1)].$$

(4) FOR $\omega_1 > \omega_2$ DESIGNS, SELECT g ON THE BASIS
$$0 < g < [(\omega_3 - \omega_1)^2/4(\omega_3 - \omega_2)(\omega_1 - \omega_2)].$$

(5) COMPUTE e USING THE EQUATION $e = (1/g)(\omega_0/\omega_2)$.

(6) INSERT VALUES OF $\omega_0, \omega_1, \omega_2, \omega_3$, AND g INTO QUADRATIC
$$f^2\left(\dfrac{\omega_1}{\omega_0} - \dfrac{\omega_2}{\omega_0} + \dfrac{\omega_3}{\omega_0} - \dfrac{\omega_1\omega_3}{\omega_0\omega_2}\right) + f\dfrac{1}{g}\left(\dfrac{\omega_1}{\omega_2} + \dfrac{\omega_3}{\omega_2} - 2\right) - \dfrac{g+1}{g^2}\left(\dfrac{\omega_0}{\omega_2}\right) = 0$$
AND SOLVE FOR f.

(7) INSERT VALUES OF $\omega_0, \omega_1, \omega_2, \omega_3, g$, AND f INTO THE EQUATION
$$d = \left[\left(\dfrac{\omega_3}{\omega_0} - \dfrac{\omega_2}{\omega_0} + \dfrac{\omega_1}{\omega_0} - 1\right) - \dfrac{g+1}{g}\dfrac{1}{f}\right]^{-1}$$
TO FIND d AND COMPLETE THE DESIGN.

REF: NAVAL RESEARCH LAB. RPT. NO. 4100 OR NATIONAL ELECTRONICS CONFERENCE PROC. VOL. 9, 1953, "RESISTANCE - CAPACITANCE SHUNTED HIGH-PASS NETWORK SYNTHESIS" C.F. WHITE.

FIG. 7-33 *RC* Two-section Shunted, High-pass Network.

are shown in Fig. 7-30. In Fig. 7-31, single-section, high-pass RC networks with the transfer function

$$\frac{E_o}{E_i} = \left(\frac{s}{\omega_0}\right)\left(\frac{\omega_0}{s+\omega_0}\right)\left(\frac{\omega_0}{\omega_1}\right) \tag{7-133}$$

are shown. Single-section, phase-lead RC networks with the transfer function

$$\frac{E_o}{E_i} = \left(\frac{s+\omega_0}{\omega_0}\right)\left(\frac{\omega_0}{\omega_1}\right)\left(\frac{\omega_1}{s+\omega_1}\right)\left(\frac{\omega_1}{\omega_2}\right) \tag{7-134}$$

are grouped in Fig. 7-32. The two-section, shunted, high-pass RC network characteristics and design are the subjects of Fig. 7-33, where the network transfer function

$$\frac{E_o}{E_i} = \left(\frac{s+\omega_0}{\omega_0}\right)\left(\frac{\omega_0}{\omega_1}\right)\left(\frac{\omega_1}{s+\omega_1}\right)\left(\frac{s+\omega_2}{\omega_2}\right)\left(\frac{\omega_2}{\omega_3}\right)\left(\frac{\omega_3}{s+\omega_3}\right) \tag{7-135}$$

provides a wide variety of attenuation and phase variations, depending upon the values of the parameters ω_0, ω_1, ω_2, and ω_3. The network permits the following four variations in the transfer function shown in Eq. (7-135):

1. $\omega_0 = \omega_2 < \omega_1 < \omega_3$
2. $\omega_0 < \omega_2 < \omega_1 < \omega_3$
3. $\omega_0 < \omega_1 < \omega_2 < \omega_3$
4. $\omega_0 < \omega_2 < \omega_1 = \omega_3$

Multiple-section low-pass and high-pass networks and special combinations have been analyzed and the characteristics published in many places.[5]

Transfer Function of Servo Motor. In electromechanical servo systems an electric motor provides the motive power. To provide an entirely different type of example of the application of the transfer-function approach to servo system design, consider the typical, small, two-phase servo motor. The first characteristic of importance is the relationship between motor

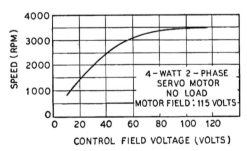

Fig. 7-34 Typical Servo Motor Speed-Voltage Characteristic.

[5] White, C. F., "Resistance-Capacitance Low- and High-pass Filters," *Naval Research Laboratory Report R-2587*, 1945; Tschudi, E. W., "Transfer Functions for R-C and R-L Equalizer Networks," *Electronics*, p. 116, May 1949.

speed and control voltage. Figure 7-34 shows a typical characteristic. The usual basis for the initial design of a servo system is linear theory. That is, all parts of the system must perform in a linear fashion with variation of signal amplitude. Application of such a requirement to the motor of Fig. 7-34 limits the allowable control voltage to a value considerably below the 75-volt control field rating of the motor. Above such a limit, the speed saturation effect is to produce a distorted sine wave motion of the motor shaft for an applied sine wave voltage. If lower voltages are used, the approximate linear characteristic of Fig. 7-34 may be expressed as follows:

$$\dot{\theta} = KE_m = KE_m \sin \omega t \qquad (7\text{-}136)$$

Equation (7-136) states that the motor speed, or angular velocity $\dot{\theta}$, is equal to a constant, K, times E_m the applied voltage. In making an experimental test of motor performance, voltage is made sinusoidal. The actual shaft position is indicated in Eq. (7-137) as the integral of $\dot{\theta}$ and is again of sinusoidal form with a 90-deg phase shift from the applied signal.

$$\theta = \int \dot{\theta}\, dt = \int KE_m \sin \omega t\, dt$$
$$= \frac{-KE_m}{\omega} \cos \omega t = \frac{KE_m}{\omega} \sin\left(\omega t - \frac{\pi}{2}\right) \qquad (7\text{-}137)$$

The amplitude of shaft motion, θ, varies inversely with ω, the angular frequency of the applied signal. The corresponding log-magnitude

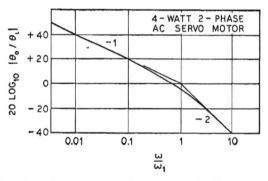

FIG. 7-35 Servo Motor Transfer-function Magnitude Based on Linear Theory.

log-frequency characteristic is a straight line with a -1 slope. In the low frequency region, the motor response to a constant-amplitude, variable-frequency sine wave input voltage drops at a rate of 20 db per decade of frequency increase. This is consistent with the concept of a motor acting as a perfect integrator with respect to time of the applied voltage. These conditions are valid only for low frequencies. At higher frequencies the response drops at a rate initially equal to twice the low-frequency slope, or −40 db per decade. The frequency at which the slope changes from −1 to −2, the "corner frequency," is the frequency at which the response is 3 db down from the response for perfect integrator response, and from data usually available on motor performance, it is possible to predict the

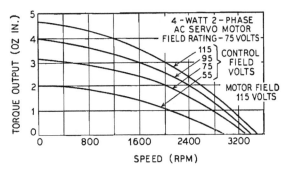

Fig. 7-36 Torque-Speed Characteristics for a Typical Small Servo Motor.

"corner frequency." Figure 7-35 shows the motor characteristic expressed mathematically by the transfer function.

$$\frac{\theta_o}{\theta_i} = \left(\frac{\omega_1}{s}\right)\left(\frac{\omega_1}{s + \omega_1}\right) \qquad (7\text{-}138)$$

A family of motor torque-speed characteristics for the same motor are shown in Fig. 7-36. From the intercepts along the zero speed axis the motor torque-voltage gradient characteristic is determined, while the intercepts along the zero torque axis provide data for speed-voltage gradient calculations. A set of sample calculations of corner frequency is given in Fig. 7-37. With the use of the data of Fig. 7-36, a total of four

TORQUE−VOLTAGE GRADIENT	SPEED−VOLTAGE GRADIENT
$\mu = \dfrac{\text{TORQUE}}{\text{VOLTAGE}}$	$g = \dfrac{\text{ANGULAR VELOCITY}}{\text{VOLTAGE}}$
$= \dfrac{4 \text{ OZ IN.}}{95 \text{ VOLT}} \cdot \dfrac{1}{16 \cdot 12} = 2.2 \cdot 10^{-4} \dfrac{\text{LB FT}}{\text{VOLT}}$	$= \dfrac{3400 \text{ RPM}}{95 \text{ VOLT}} \cdot \dfrac{2\pi}{60} = 3.75 \dfrac{\text{RADIANS}}{\text{SEC VOLTS}}$
EQUIVALENT VISCOUS RESISTANCE	CORNER FREQUENCY
$R = \dfrac{\text{TORQUE}-\text{VOLTAGE GRADIENT}}{\text{SPEED}-\text{VOLTAGE GRADIENT}} = \dfrac{\mu}{g}$	$\omega_1 = \dfrac{\text{EQUIVALENT VISCOUS RESISTANCE}}{\text{MOMENT OF INERTIA}} = \dfrac{R}{I}$
$= \dfrac{2.2 \cdot 10^{-4}}{3.75} = 58.5 \cdot 10^{-6} \text{ LB FT SEC}$	$= \dfrac{58.5 \cdot 10^{-6}}{1.04 \cdot 10^{-6}} = 56.3 \dfrac{\text{RADIANS}}{\text{SEC}}$

Fig. 7-37 Sample Calculations of Servo Motor Corner Frequency.

evaluations of corner frequency may be made. The solid line curve in Fig. 7-38 shows the variation of the corner frequency with change in the amplitude of the voltage applied to the control field of the motor. By way of eliminating the possibility of arriving at conclusions valid only for a particular motor, a similar study made on a larger motor gave the results shown by the dashed line in Fig. 7-38. As previously mentioned, the initial approach to design of a servo system is on the basis of *linear* operation. The curves of Fig. 7-38, however, show a nonlinear performance. That is, the motor corner frequency is not a fixed quantity char-

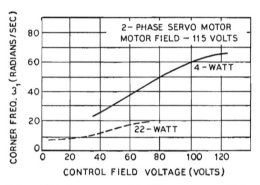

Fig. 7-38 Servo Motor Performance with Nonconstant Value of Corner Frequency as a Function of Control Voltage Showing Nonlinear Characteristics.

acteristic of a given motor but is a function of the amplitude of the applied signal. Use of high loop gain to establish servo characteristics by the β-path transfer function mitigates the servo motor nonlinearity effects.

7-7 IMPROVEMENT OF SYSTEM PERFORMANCE

Many excellent references are available on the subject of methods for improvement of servo system performance. The discussion here is based upon the use of the transfer-function concept previously developed. The methods available to the designer for improving system performance may be placed into four categories, namely, (1) the use of series (cascade) networks for stabilization, (2) the use of feedback (parallel) stabilization, (3) the adjustment of system gain, and (4) the adjustment of existing component frequency bandwidths (component time-constants). These four means are interrelated and in large systems are all employed. Although the attenuation-versus-frequency concept is used in the preliminary design phase, it is understood that the transient performance is investigated before the design is completed. In using series networks various combinations of phase-lag and of phase-lead networks may be utilized. In parallel stabilization arrangements, frequency-sensitive networks are

7-7]   IMPROVEMENT OF SYSTEM PERFORMANCE   283

used effectively in stabilization of the complete system by controlling the characteristics of a local loop.

Series Network Approach. To illustrate the use of series networks, consider the system depicted in Fig. 7-39. The motor transfer function indicated is that given in Eq. (7-138). The amplifier is shown with a gain of

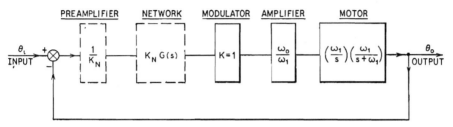

Fig. 7-39   Stabilization by Use of Series Network.

ω_0/ω_1. In dashed lines are indicated a preamplifier with a gain of $1/K_N$ and a network labeled with a transfer function, $K_N G(s)$, to be determined. The preamplifier exactly cancels the loss introduced by the network at $\omega \to 0$. Figure 7-40 shows the uncompensated servo system, a-b-c, to be a Type I with the gain level at such a high level that highly oscillatory

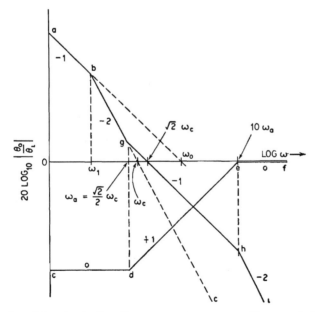

Fig. 7-40   Log-Magnitude Log-Frequency Asymptotic Characteristics for Servo System of Fig. 7-39.

response to a step-function input would occur as determined in Par. 7-3. The remedy is the improvement suggested in Par. 7-4 and may be obtained by use of a single-section, RC shunted high-pass network shown as the fourth phase-lead network of Fig. 7-32 and as c-d-e-f in Fig. 7-40. A gain of 10 is easily obtained in a single-stage preamplifier. Placement of the lower network corner at $\omega_a = \dfrac{\sqrt{2}}{2}\omega_c$ provides one octave of -1 asymptotic slope before gain crossover and performance comparable to that for $K = 200$ in Fig. 7-11 and 7-12. The compensated characteristic is a-b-g-h-i in Fig. 7-40.

Phase lag networks may be successfully employed in similar situations.[6]

Feedback Path Network Approach. To illustrate the use of networks in the feedback path for stabilization purposes, consider the system depicted in Fig. 7-41 in which the desired transfer characteristic for the portion of the complete system shown between section $A\text{-}A'$ and $B\text{-}B'$ is

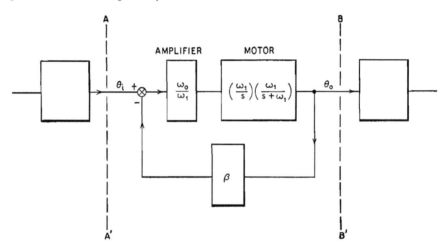

FIG. 7-41 Servo System Incorporating Elements in Feedback Path.

that of a perfect integrator over as wide a frequency range as practical. The availability of the amplification required will be assumed. A possible design procedure is to set the closed loop transfer function equal to the desired characteristic and solve for the unknown feedback transfer function. Accordingly,

$$\frac{\theta_o}{\theta_i} = \frac{\dfrac{\omega_0}{\omega_1}\dfrac{\omega_1}{s}\dfrac{\omega_1}{s+\omega_1}}{1 - \dfrac{\omega_0}{\omega_1}\dfrac{\omega_1}{s}\dfrac{\omega_1}{s+\omega_1}N} = \frac{\omega_3}{s} \qquad (7\text{-}139)$$

[6] Chestnut, H. and Mayer, R. W., *Servomechanisms and Regulating System Design*, Volume I, p. 249, John Wiley & Sons, Inc., New York.

where N indicates the transfer function of the network to be found and the desired integrator characteristic is shown as ω_3/s. Solving for N, we have

$$N = \frac{s}{\omega_3 / \left(\frac{\omega_3}{\omega_0} - 1\right)} \cdot \frac{s + \left(1 - \frac{\omega_0}{\omega_3}\right)\omega_1}{\left(1 - \frac{\omega_0}{\omega_3}\right)\omega_1} \qquad (7\text{-}140)$$

For the purposes of the illustration shown in Fig. 7-42, assume $\omega_3 = 2\omega_0$. The design objective is shown by the heavy line through $\omega_3 = 2\omega_0$. The required network characteristic is

$$N = \frac{s}{2\omega_0} \cdot \frac{s + \frac{\omega_1}{2}}{\frac{\omega_1}{2}} \qquad (7\text{-}141)$$

If we assume the original amplifier gain to be $\omega_0/\omega_1 = 10$, we may show the open loop asymptotic characteristic by the dotted lines in Fig. 7-42. Equation (7-141) then becomes

$$N = \frac{s}{2\omega_0} \cdot \frac{s + \frac{\omega_0}{20}}{\frac{\omega_0}{20}} \qquad (7\text{-}142)$$

The first term of Eq. (7-142) can be realized by the use of a tachometer generator. The second term cannot be obtained physically except as a

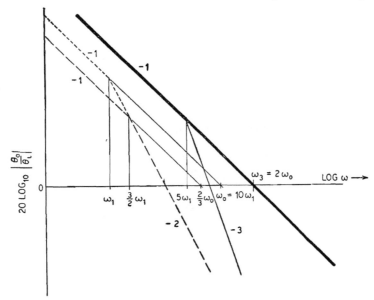

Fig. 7-42 Asymptotic Characteristics for Fig. 7-41.

part of a complete transfer function for a network like the shunted high-pass RC phase-lead network of Fig. 7-32. The transfer function

$$\frac{\text{output}}{\text{input}} = \frac{\theta_o}{\theta_i} = \frac{\theta_3}{\theta_2} = \frac{s + \omega_4}{\omega_4} \cdot \frac{\omega_4}{\omega_5} \cdot \frac{\omega_5}{s + \omega_5} \quad (7\text{-}143)$$

contains an undesired attenuation factor ω_4/ω_5 and an undesired low-pass transfer function with corner at ω_5. To make ω_5 desirably high relative to ω_4, assume the availability of a gain of 100 in the β path by setting $\omega_5 = 100\omega_4$. Let ω_4 of Eq. (7-143) equal $\omega_0/20$ of Eq. (7-142). The closed loop characteristic becomes

$$\frac{\theta_o}{\theta_i} = \frac{10\frac{\omega_1}{s} \cdot \frac{\omega_1}{s+\omega_1}}{1 - 10\frac{\omega_1}{s} \cdot \frac{\omega_1}{s+\omega_1} \cdot \frac{s}{20\omega_1} \cdot \frac{s + \frac{\omega_1}{2}}{\frac{\omega_1}{2}} \cdot \frac{50\omega_1}{s + 50\omega_1}}$$

$$= \frac{2\omega_0}{s} \cdot \frac{25\omega_1^2}{s^2 + s\omega_1 + 25\omega_1^2} \cdot \frac{s + 50\omega_1}{50\omega_1} \quad (7\text{-}144)$$

Equation (7-144) follows the heavy solid line until $\omega = \sqrt{25\omega_1^2} = 5\omega_1$ at which frequency the asymptotic slope becomes -3.

If we assume that no gain is available in the feedback path, i.e., the tachometer generator gain is limited by the specification $\omega_3 = 2\omega_0$, the best that can be done is

$$\frac{\theta_o}{\theta_i} = \frac{10\frac{\omega_1}{s} \cdot \frac{\omega_1}{s+\omega_1}}{1 + 10\frac{\omega_1}{s} \cdot \frac{\omega_1}{s+\omega_1} \cdot \frac{s}{20\omega_1}}$$

$$= \frac{\frac{2}{3}\omega_0}{s} \cdot \frac{\frac{3}{2}\omega_1}{s + \frac{3}{2}\omega_1} \quad (7\text{-}145)$$

The dashed line on Fig. 7-42 which shows the corner frequency break between the -1 and -2 slopes occurring at $3/2\omega_1$ is the conpensated response using tachometer-only feedback.

Thus, the initial design objective is seen impossible of exact accomplishment. However, while one degree of approximation is obtainable by the use of tachometer feedback, a much closer approximation is obtained by the use of gain in the feedback path together with a shunted high-pass network excited from a tachometer generator.

Active Filters. In complicated servo systems, there is a common requirement for data smoothing at some point in the system, e.g., at an indicator in systems in which an operator closes the loop. Such smoothing usually takes the form of RC low-pass networks of one or more sections.

Since the low-pass filters introduce time delays or phase lags directly in the servo loop, they affect system stability.

Figure 7-43 shows a method by which it is possible to introduce the filter as needed for smoothing and then operate on the smoothed data by a reciprocal filter to cancel (from a system stability point of view) the effects of the smoothing filter phase lag. The reciprocal filter is formed by utilization of a network identical with the smoothing filter placed in the feedback path of a high-gain feedback amplifier. Such an arrangement is known as an *active filter*.

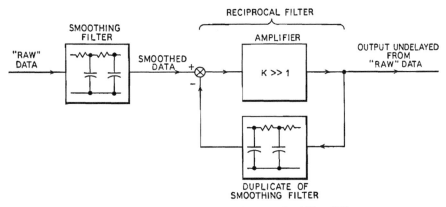

FIG. 7-43 Filtering without System Stability Effects.

Reference Frequencies. In discussions regarding design criteria, several reference frequencies are employed that, under certain conditions in simple systems, are nearly coincident. To avoid confusion, a list of those most frequently employed follows:

1. *Noise Bandwidth.* The frequency at which the open-loop gain equals unity defines the bandwidth effective in reducing system tracking error, also frequently referred to as the noise bandwidth since below this frequency there is system gain and above there is attenuation. This frequency is used in determining phase margin. In some instances the asymptotic gain characteristic may, without great error, be used in this connection in place of the actual gain characteristic.

2. *Undamped Natural Frequency.* The transient responses for step function inputs depicted in Par. 7-3, 7-4, and 7-5 have been normalized with respect to the system undamped natural frequency, ω_n. In the example illustrated in Fig. 7-3, $\omega_n = \sqrt{K\omega_1}$.

3. *Damped Natural Frequency.* The damped natural frequency $\omega_d = \sqrt{1-\zeta^2}\,\omega_n$ is the reciprocal of the period between any two successive maxima

in a transient step-function response, independent of the amplitude of vibration or of the time.

4. *Resonant Frequency.* The resonant frequency or the "frequency of maximum forced amplitude" is the frequency corresponding to the maximum closed loop response. In many cases this frequency differs only slightly from the frequency ω_n where the phase is 90 deg.

5. *System Bandwidth.* Little used except in some "rules of thumb" correlating frequency and transient response. A bandwidth defined as in communications work, i.e., the frequency corresponding to the half-power point (closed-loop gain = -3 db).

Depending upon the relative importance of the noise problem in the servo system under development, attention to the noise bandwidth as compared with the natural frequency for the system should be given.

Application of Stability Criterion. To relate the procedure followed in a design study of an actual servo system, the transfer function was found to be, in a preliminary phase,

$$\frac{\theta_o}{\theta_i}(s) = \frac{24(s + 1.5)}{s^5 + 4.5s^4 + 28.5s^3 + 36s^2 + 96s + 36} \quad (7\text{-}146)$$

Before any further work is justified, a test for system stability is in order. Using Routh's criterion in the manner explained in Chap. 6, we write the coefficients of the denominator in the two-line array shown below and compute the succeeding numbers of the array as required:

1	28.5	96
4.5	36	36
20.5	88	
16.7	36	
43.8		

Since all numbers of the first column are of the same sign, positive, the system is concluded to be stable in the absolute sense. At this point in

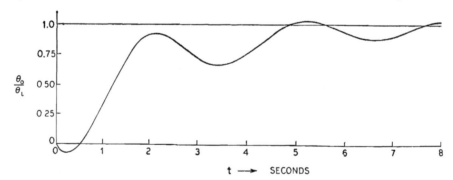

FIG. 7-44 Transient Response of System for Which Error Series Coefficients Are Greater Than Unity.

the development, a look at the error expression series for sinusoidal input is suggested. This expression was found by dividing the s-domain expression for $(1 + \mu)$ into unity with the result in the t-domain that

$$\varepsilon(t) = 2\dot{\theta}_i - 1.67\ddot{\theta}_i + \cdots \tag{7-147}$$

Since the coefficients of the error expression are not numbers less than unity, it is clearly apparent that the bandwidth of the servo system is entirely too restricted when compared to the bandwidth of the intelligence to be transmitted through the servo. There is actually no point to further analysis of the system as constituted. However, since all systems in this particular field previously analyzed were poor by comparison, the next procedure of subjecting the system to an input transient step of position was taken with the attendant necessity of quintic root finding. The result, shown in Fig. 7-44, indicates stability on a long-time basis and a rather oscillatory response with poor rise time. This example is given to show the role of each step in the design procedure and the possibility of stopping at any point to redesign when such is indicated.

7-8 INTERPLAY OF FREQUENCY RESPONSE AND TRANSIENT RESPONSE THEORY IN SYSTEM DESIGN

Throughout the chapter, effort has been directed toward fostering the system point of view. The importance of taking the larger system point of view rather than being content with accepting a component development without personally making every practicable effort to check the suitability as a part of the system cannot be overstressed. The interplay of design approaches based upon the frequency response or transfer-function method and the historically older system integrodifferential equation and transient response method has been discussed.

In using design procedures based upon the transfer-function approach the first step is to determine the job to be done by the servo system. In guided missile developments, the missile job is specified as an input varying in a prescribed manner with time. The specification may be a nonanalytical description (perhaps graphical) or the usually more satisfactory analytic specification. An example of the latter is the constant-velocity, straight-line pass-course employed in Par. 7-3, 7-4, and 7-5. Analysis of flight paths is the subject of an entire chapter, Chap. 12. The variation of input with time, while specified by the geometry of the problem, in some cases may not be obtained readily in the form of an analytic expression as a function of time. By taking small increments of distances or time, an approximate graphical or analytic solution leading to a table of values of position as a function of time may be obtained. The details of the mathematics by which the various derivative quantities may be obtained from such a table are given in Chap. 6.

To use the frequency-response methods, it is desirable to translate the input-time-function into an equivalent frequency-domain function to aid in selecting a servo transfer characteristic of only just-adequate bandwidth to transmit the frequency spectrum of the input information with error just inside the maximum allowed by the specified problem. The good engineering job is the one that limits the servo bandwidth to a minimum without exceeding the allowable system error. Expressions for servo system error due to restricted bandwidth were developed in Par. 7-3, 7-4, and 7-5 for the so-called Type I and Type II systems to illustrate the method so that the same procedure could be followed in a particular system study. The closed-form error expressions are, in general, of little utility as compared with the error series expressions. In the series form, the requirements for convergence are specified in the frequency domain, i.e., the expression converges for all input frequencies for which the open loop transfer characteristic has gain greater than unity. The precision of the calculated error when a limited number of terms is used may be determined by inspection of the last term evaluated since the error in the approximation will always be less than the magnitude of the last term used.

In translating the error expression into the time domain there is involved the concept of translation of the convergence requirement into an equivalent time domain specification. This may be a requirement that a computing time equivalent to several time constants (reciprocal of the unity open loop gain frequency) must be allowed. That is to say, the input must not vary too rapidly.

Finally, in system designs based upon frequency response theory, the designer investigates various likely characteristics to determine the best basic type. Having chosen a given type, the proper gain setting is selected to obtain a closed loop response with suitably limited resonant rise (or, if one prefers, the desirable gain and phase margins). Next, the bandwidth necessary to limit system error just to meet requirements is determined. The system transient response for the type of disturbances that the system may be subjected to is investigated as a final check upon the design.

System design based upon transient response theory starts with the assumption that no flight path requirements will place demands upon the system in excess of those resulting from some transient disturbance, e.g., the initial misalignment with the called-for flight path position at the instant of initial guidance (at the end of the missile boost phase). Specifications are written based upon the maximum misalignment possible and still reliably effect capture. The minimum range demanded in the tactical application is established. The system is then designed, using any methods preferred, to provide just fast enough performance to bring the missile to within the lethal distance of the target at the required minimum range.

Such functions as a position step input are among a limited number of readily applied time domain test signals. Special functions, e.g., a flight path, are difficult to employ in a transient analysis. The final check on a system design dictated by transient response considerations is a verification that flight path dynamics do, indeed, impose no excessive demands upon the system.

As presented, the relative emphasis upon frequency response or upon transient response theory is somewhat arbitrary with the individual. The ease of application of transfer-function design procedures remains as the greatest aid in design regardless of the assumed relative importance of the frequency or of the transient response approaches.

BIBLIOGRAPHY

1. H. L. Hazen, *Theory of Servomechanisms*, J. Franklin Inst., 1934.
2. M. F. Gardner and J. L. Barnes, *Transients in Linear Systems*, McGraw-Hill Book Co., Inc., New York, 1951.
3. J. P. Den Hartog, *Mechanical Vibrations*, McGraw-Hill Book Co., Inc., New York, 1947.
4. H. Lauer, R. Lesnich, and L. E. Matson, *Servomechanism Fundamentals*, McGraw-Hill Book Co., Inc., New York, 1947.
5. H. M. James, N. B. Nichols, and R. S. Phillips, *Theory of Servomechanisms*, McGraw-Hill Book Company, Inc., New York, 1947.
6. H. W. Bode, *Network Analysis and Feedback Amplifier Design*, D. Van Nostrand Co , Inc., New York, 1945.
7. L. A. MacColl, *Fundamental Theory of Servomechanisms*, D. Van Nostrand Co., Inc., New York, 1945.
8. R. E. Graham, "Linear Servo Theory," *Bell System Tech. J.*, 1946.
9. G. J. Thaler, and R. G. Brown, *Servomechanism Analysis*, McGraw-Hill Book Co., Inc., New York, 1953. See Bibliography.

CHAPTER 8

TACTICAL CONSIDERATIONS

The need for and the concept of new weapons are formulated and developed by operations research within the Department of Defense. When the necessity for a new weapon is shown to exist by postulating either the specific tactics for defense or the means to mount a critical offense, operational requirements for the weapon are developed. An operational requirement is a document which spells out the tactical need for a weapon and, as a rule, assigns the specific area of cognizance within the structure of the military establishment. The operational requirements are then translated into performance specifications for the new weapon by the cognizant group bearing the responsibility for the development and use of the weapon. The matériel and research groups of the military service issue the performance specifications to contractors, with the intent of purchasing the new weapon to meet the operational needs. In the case of a proposed guided missile system, the performance specifications may define the explicit type of guidance system to be employed. Usually the contract requires that the contractor shall make a thorough preliminary study which determines, among many other parameters, the type of guidance system that shall be used. When this study has been completed and the recommendations resulting therefrom approved, the contractor proceeds with the necessary research and development work limited to the general area of the approved recommendations.

It is the purpose of this chapter to develop the effect of tactical considerations on the choice and evolution of the design of the guidance system or systems which form a part of the overall guided missile system. The tactical problem is the basis for the operational requirement, and tactical considerations are, therefore, the overriding considerations in all phases of the design of a missile guidance system.

From the examination of the target and the damage probability required of the missile there can be evolved the armament specifications. These in turn will define the accuracy requirements for the missile guidance system. From considerations of the tactical problem the possible methods of transmitting intelligence to the missile are determined. In some cases, the method of transmitting intelligence to the missile, or the manner by which the missile acquires the guidance intelligence, may limit the trajectory or flight path of the missile. The dynamics of the trajectory, in turn, establish the characteristics of the control loops and servomechanisms that are employed.

The tactical situation may impose the requirement for separate guidance systems during the launching and terminal phases of the missile flight. The system concept must be kept paramount because all of these many considerations are interdependent and a decision in one particular design area on one specific component may radically affect other portions of the guidance system design.

Because the subject is complex, the easiest way to gain an appreciation of the interrelationships of the design elements of a missile guidance system is to postulate an example in each of the missile categories and discuss the tactics which concern the choice of the missile guidance method. The numerical values employed in the hypothetical cases are chosen for convenience only.

8-1 TARGET DAMAGE DEFINITIONS

The purpose of a guided missile system is to destroy the target. The degree of destruction or damage of a specific target is subject to many possible definitions. A target may be totally destroyed; it may suffer partial damage. In the case of defense against an attacking aircraft, the aircraft may be (a) destroyed instantly; (b) so damaged that it is forced to return to base without completing its mission; or (c) so damaged that, although it completes its mission, it fails to return to its base. In the case

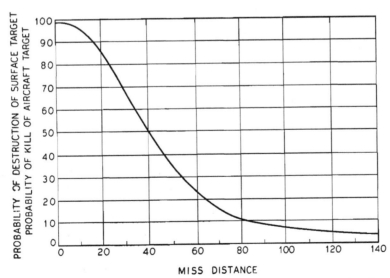

FIG. 8-1 Generalized Curve of Kill or Destruction Probability as Related to Miss Distance.

of a surface target, a specific target such as a tank or a ship may be totally destroyed or may be partially destroyed. An industrial area may be destroyed by rendering it uninhabitable, or a percentage of damage may be assessed.

An evaluation of the kill potential of a guided missile against a particular target under various tactical situations is desirable in order to effect comparison between weapons. In the consideration of a guidance system, if the damage parameters of the warhead are known, the accuracy required of the guidance system for placing the missile in the vicinity of the target may be estimated.

Surface Targets. Small targets or isolated single targets may be considered "killed" when wholly incapacitated from further action or totally destroyed. In this category might be placed tanks, ships, surface vehicles of all types, gun emplacements, single buildings, and small troop concentrations. It is possible to plot a curve, such as Fig. 8-1, wherein the probability of total destruction can thus be related to miss distance for a specific warhead.

Large surface targets such as cities, industrial areas, etc., may be assigned a percentage of probable damage in assessing the capabilities of warheads.

Aircraft Targets. An aircraft is vulnerable in many ways to the explosion of a warhead: the fragments of the warhead and missile, the blast effect of the explosion, or the incendiary quality of the target's fuel. There is even the possibility of detonation of the target's own bombs. In considering the kill of an attacking aircraft, the important criterion is the destruction of the aircraft before the aircraft completes its mission.

Standard recognition is given:

a. The K kill, wherein the aircraft falls out of control immediately, without any reasonable doubt.
b. The B kill, wherein the aircraft fails to return to its base as a result of damage.

The K kill, in addition to the destruction of the target, denotes frustration of the target's mission if the kill is made prior to the range of release of the weapon employed by the target in its attack. The B kill denotes failure to survive and is primarily useful in attrition studies. Figure 8-1 may, for discussion purposes, also be used to illustrate the relationship between miss distance and K kill probability for an hypothecated warhead employed against an aircraft target.

Probability Relationships. In view of its complexity and cost, a guided missile system (and hence the associated guidance system) can scarcely be justified unless it has a probability of kill or destruction that is superior to the conventional weapons it replaces. The probable effectiveness of a single missile, P, may be defined as the ratio of kills to the number of missiles which are launched. Since statistical analysis is based upon a population of data, the number of missiles launched to determine this probability must be large.

Some of the missiles which are launched fail to reach the target area. The two general reasons for this are: (a) failure of an element of the missile system which aborts the flight; (b) defeat of the missile by enemy action. If a sufficiently large number of missiles were launched, the probable reliability of the missile system, P_r, could be determined statistically as the ratio of the number of missiles which reached the target area without failure of equipment to the total number of missiles launched. Similarly, if sufficient data existed, the probability of the missile surviving enemy action, P_s, could be defined as the ratio of reliable missiles which survived to detonate at the target area to the total number of reliable missiles launched.

When the missile reaches the target area and the warhead detonates, there is a probability, P_d, that the missile will "kill" the target, if some explicit definition of the term "kill" is made. The probable effectiveness of a single missile may be defined as

$$P = P_r \cdot P_s \cdot P_d \tag{8-1}$$

The probability of damage P_d may be arbitrarily defined as the product of the conditional probability P_k that the target will be "killed" if the missile passes through a significant area normal to the trajectory and P_e, which represents the guidance error probability distribution of the trajectories. By definition, the distribution of the detonation points along the trajectory is included in P_k. An expression may be written for the probability of damage in integral form as

$$P_d = \int_A P_k \cdot P_e \, dA \tag{8-2}$$

in which A is the area surrounding the target in a plane normal to the trajectory that contains significant values of P_k and P_e.

The opportunity of obtaining population quantities of statistical data on reliability, survival, and damage does not, as a rule, exist, except under the condition of actual warfare. The data are then employed for the purpose of analysis, whereas in designing a guidance system the information is required for intelligent synthesis. In establishing the kill probability for a nonexistent warhead, in lieu of experimental data, mathematical models may be constructed which facilitate an approximation of missile effectiveness. It should be remembered that this area of operations research is based only on assumptions drawn from experience; they may be called intelligent assumptions, albeit major in scope and effect. Similarly, in design of missile guidance systems, a normal or Gaussian distribution of errors and a lack of bias errors are both assumed. This process permits the establishment of criteria for design, but it should be kept in mind that the design effectiveness of the system is based on assumptions which are subject to reassessment as the work progresses and statistical data become available.

8-2 TERMINOLOGY OF ERRORS[1]

It is the universal desire to speak about the errors of a weapon system by means of a few numbers which may be used on a common basis for comparison with other weapon systems. Any description of errors by means of a few quantitative values rather than a complete tabulation of every item of data involves definite assumptions about the distribution of errors. Experience with radar tracking equipment and gunfire control systems has indicated that the following simple assumptions are reasonable and avoid the confusion which results from attempts to give a more complex description of system errors:

a. The distribution of errors follows a simple normal distribution, or Gaussian, law.
b. When errors in more than one dimension are involved, as for example, traverse and elevation, the distributions are independent of each other.

On the basis of these assumptions, the following simple figures can be properly used to condense error data used in assessing the performance of missile guidance equipments:

a. *Mean Error* (also called *MPI*, arithmetic mean, algebraic average and bias).
b. *Standard Error* (also called root-mean-square error, standard deviation and standard dispersion).

It will be noted that the first figure indicates the mean value of the error and the second figure indicates the spread of errors about that mean value. For example, in sighting-in a rifle by a number of shots, the average error of the total grouping represents the mean error and is corrected by boresighting the rifle; the spread of shots about the mean may be attributed to errors resulting from the ballistics of the piece and imperfect aiming. The dispersion is sometimes measured in various other units, such as mean absolute error, circular probable error, (c.p.e.) median error, variance, etc. On the basis of these fundamental assumptions, any of the various measures of dispersion can be converted by a simple factor to any of the others. Thus, the unit of measure of error is not important, but it

---

[1] Adapted in part from "Usage of Statistical Formulas and Proposed Standard Terminology in Fire Control Applications," J. J. Fleming, Operational Research Branch, NRL.

must be stated clearly. The mean absolute error (definition follows) is the easiest to calculate; therefore, the other measures of dispersion are generally obtained from it by the use of correction factors.

In statistical terminology, a *population* of data is an infinite collection of data, while a *sample* is the finite number of data items encountered in experiments. The equations employed herein will be expressed in terms of sample quantities, even though the equations refer, in the strict sense, only to population quantities. The sample taken in laboratory tests of missile guidance and control equipment is generally large enough to justify the assumption that it obeys the laws of the population for all practical purposes.

Single Variable, Normal Distribution. Assuming that our test data include a sufficiently large number n of error items of a single variable x (such as errors in the elevation plane only of a tracking radar), then $\bar{x}$, the mean error, is equal to $\frac{\Sigma x_i}{n}$. The deviation of any single error item, x_i, from the mean error is equal to $x_i - \bar{x}$. The standard deviation, σ_x, is defined as

$$\sigma_x = \sqrt{\frac{\Sigma(x_i - \bar{x})^2}{n}} = \sqrt{\frac{\Sigma(x_i^2) - n\bar{x}^2}{n}} \qquad (8\text{-}3)$$

The *mean absolute error*, (m.a.e., also called the average error, mean dispersion, etc., is the arithmetic mean of all errors without regard to sign and may be expressed as

$$\text{m.a.e.} = \frac{\Sigma |x_i - \bar{x}|}{n} \qquad (8\text{-}4)$$

The *probable error* is defined by the fact that 50 percent of the errors have absolute magnitudes greater than the probable error, p.e., or expressed algebraically,

$$\text{p.e.} = \int_{\bar{x}-\text{p.e.}}^{\bar{x}+\text{p.e.}} p(x)\, dx \qquad (8\text{-}5)$$

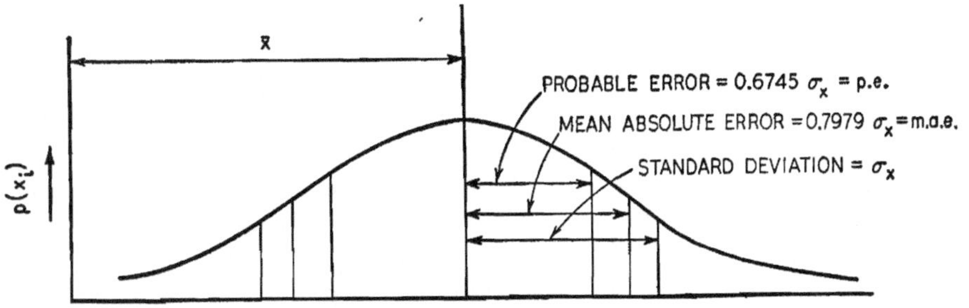

FIG. 8-2 Illustrating Normal Distribution and Relation of Probable Error, Mean Absolute Error, and Standard Error.

Figure 8-2 illustrates a normal distribution curve for a probability $p(x)$ of x lying between x and dx and shows the notation employed. This function is normalized to unity, i.e., the total area under the curve represents 100 percent probability. This curve may be expressed in terms of the standard deviation as

$$p(x) = \frac{1}{\sigma_x \sqrt{2\pi}} e^{-\frac{(x-\bar{x})^2}{2\sigma_x^2}} \tag{8-6}$$

Table 8-1 tabulates the probability that a single error item will fall within the value of $\bar{x} \pm k\sigma_x$. Let us examine what this means in a pertinent example. If we assume that test data indicate that a radar range unit has a standard deviation of 50 ft under given conditions, the probability that a single representative measurement will be within 50 ft of the target in range is, from Table 8-1, 68.3 percent. It must be remembered, however, that this applies only in the case of a *single* variable with normal distribution.

TABLE 8-1 PROBABILITY THAT AN x_i WILL LIE INSIDE $\bar{x} \pm k\sigma_x$

k	$\leq k\sigma$ (%)	$\leq k$(m.a.e.) (%)	$\leq k$(p.e.) (%)
1	68.3	57.5	50.0
2	95.5	88.9	82.3
3	99.7	98.3	95.7
4	99.98	99.9	99.3

Two Variables, Normal Distribution. Using the same general notation as in the case of a single variable, with y as the second variable, with x and y assumed to be statistically independent, we may write

$$p(x, y) = p(x)p(y) = \frac{1}{2\pi\sigma_x\sigma_y} e^{-\left[\frac{(x-\bar{x})^2}{2\sigma_x^2} + \frac{(y-\bar{y})^2}{2\sigma_y^2}\right]} \tag{8-7}$$

If the exponent of Eq. (8-7) is set equal to a constant $\frac{1}{2}c^2$, then the relation between x and y becomes

$$\frac{(x-\bar{x})^2}{\sigma_x^2} + \frac{(y-\bar{y})^2}{\sigma_y^2} = c^2 \tag{8-8}$$

This equation defines an equi-probability ellipse with $p(x, y)$ constant along the perimeter. Table 8-2 shows the value of c for equi-probability ellipses having a value of P percent probability.

Under most conditions of tracking moving targets the value of the standard deviation in one coordinate approaches or is nearly equal to the value of the standard deviation in the second coordinate. Similarly, when the miss distance at an aircraft target is considered, the standard error up and down tends to be in the same order of magnitude as the right-left error. Because of this, the errors are most frequently considered on the

TABLE 8-2 VALUES OF c FOR P PERCENT PROBABILITY ELLIPSES

P (%)	c
25.0	0.7585
39.3	1.000
50.0	1.177
54.6	1.253
75.0	1.665
90.0	2.146
95.0	2.448
99.0	3.035

basis of circular distribution, which case is defined when $\sigma_x = \sigma_y = \sigma$. Substitution for the circular case in Eq. (8-7) obtains

$$P(x, y) = \frac{1}{2\pi\sigma^2} e^{-\left[\frac{(x-\bar{x})^2+(y-\bar{y})^2}{2\sigma^2}\right]} \tag{8-9}$$

Contours for constant values of $p(x, y)$ are circles and obtained by

$$(x - \bar{x})^2 + (y - \bar{y})^2 = c^2\sigma^2 \tag{8-10}$$

with the radius of the circles being equal to $c\sigma$.

Equation (8-9) may be expressed in polar coordinates, where r is the magnitude of the radial error and θ is the angular direction of the error, as

$$p(r, \theta) = \frac{1}{2\pi\sigma^2} e^{-\frac{r^2}{2\sigma^2}} \tag{8-11}$$

In addition to the standard deviation σ, the following measures of dispersion are sometimes employed:

a. Mean radial error = m.r.e. = $\Sigma r_i/n$.
b. Circular probable error = c.p.e. Fifty percent of the radial errors is contained within a circle having a radius equal to the circular probable error.

The majority of test data on radars and similar tracking elements discloses a distribution which is nearly circular, but not rigorously so. An equivalent circular distribution may be substituted for the slightly elliptical distribution if the value of σ employed is obtained from

$$\sigma = \sqrt{\sigma_x \sigma_y} \tag{8-12}$$

The various circular measures of dispersion may be converted from one measure to another by the following conversion factors:

$$\sigma = 0.7979 \text{ m.r.e.} = 0.8493 \text{ c.p.e.} \tag{8-13}$$

Table 8-3 gives the radii of the p percent probability circles in each of the three circular measures of dispersion commonly employed. It will be noted that when two variables with normal distribution are considered the standard deviation (or r.m.s. error, standard dispersion, etc.) is the radius of a circle enclosing 39.3 percent of the single error items. In other words, if a guided missile system is determined by test to have a standard deviation of 50 ft against an aircraft target, the probability that a single representative missile will pass within 50 ft of the target is approximately 40 percent.

TABLE 8-3 RADIUS OF PROBABILITY CIRCLES FOR VALUES OF PERCENT PROBABILITY

Probability (%)	Radius of Probability Circle
25	0.7585σ = 0.6052 m.r.e. = 0.6442 c.p.e.
39.3	(σ) = 0.7979 m.r.e. = 0.8493 c.p.e.
50	1.177σ = 0.9394 m.r.e. = (c.p.e.)
54.6	1.253σ = (m.r.e.) = 1.065 c.p.e.
75	1.665σ = 1.329 m.r.e. = 1.414 c.p.e.
90	2.146σ = 1.712 m.r.e. = 1.823 c.p.e.
95	2.448σ = 1.953 m.r.e. = 2.079 c.p.e.
99	3.035σ = 2.421 m.r.e. = 2.578 c.p.e.

As a further example of the use of Table 8-3, if a guidance system is required to have an accuracy such that 90 percent of the missiles must pass within a circle of 50-ft radius around the target, the standard error of the system, which is employed for test and design purposes, must be no greater than 50/2.146, or approximately 23.3 ft.

The two-variable, normal distribution case is the one most frequently encountered in considering errors in the design of missile guidance systems. In the consideration of surface targets, the target may be looked upon as a point or an area on a two-dimensional surface. In the case of an aircraft target, if the missile is fused independently of the guidance system, then again the error, or miss distance, is considered in a two-dimensional plane normal to the trajectory of the missile.

Three Variables, Normal Distribution. Using the same general notation as in the previous cases, with z as the third variable, and with the distributions of x, y, and z assumed to be statistically independent, we may write

$$p(x, y, z) = p(x)p(y)p(z) = \frac{1}{\sigma_x \sigma_y \sigma_z (\sqrt{2\pi})^3} e^{-\left[\frac{(x-\bar{x})^2}{2\sigma_x^2} + \frac{(y-\bar{y})^2}{2\sigma_y^2} + \frac{(z-\bar{z})^2}{2\sigma_z^2}\right]} \quad (8\text{-}14)$$

If the exponent of Eq. (8-14) is set equal to a constant, then the relation between x, y, and z may be written

$$\frac{(x-\bar{x})^2}{\sigma_x^2} + \frac{(y-\bar{y})^2}{\sigma_y^2} + \frac{(z-\bar{z})^2}{\sigma_z^2} = c^2 \quad (8\text{-}15)$$

which defines an equi-probability ellipsoid with $p(x, y, z)$ constant along the surface. In the symmetrical case wherein the standard deviations of all three variables are equal, i.e., $\sigma_x = \sigma_y = \sigma_z = \sigma$, a spherical distribution is defined by substitution in Eq. (8-14) to obtain

$$p(x, y, z) = \frac{1}{(\sqrt{2\pi})^3 \sigma^3} e^{-\left[\frac{(x-\bar{x})^2 + (y-\bar{y})^2 + (z-\bar{z})^2}{2\sigma^2}\right]} \quad (8\text{-}16)$$

In addition to the standard error σ, the following measures of dispersion may be employed in the symmetrical three-variable case:

   a. Spherical probable error   = 1.5382σ.
   b. Mean spherical radial error = 1.5958σ.

Table 8-4 gives the radii of the p percent probability spheres in each of the three spherical measures of dispersion commonly employed. The three-variable case applies to guidance systems wherein the detonation order is part of the guidance, so that the three-dimensional miss must be considered in determination of system effectiveness. It will be noted that the standard deviation, in the case of three symmetrical variables, includes only 19.9 percent of the probable item locations.

TABLE 8-4 RADIUS OF PROBABILITY SPHERES
FOR VALUES OF PERCENT PROBABILITY

Probability (%)	Radius of Probability Spheres
19.9	1.000 σ = .6501 s.p.e. = 6267 m.s.r.e.
25	1.101 σ = .7159 s.p.e. = 6900 m.s.r.e.
50	1.538 σ = 1.000 s.p.e. = 9639 m.s.r.e.
75	2.027 σ = 1.318 s.p.e. = 1.270 m.s.r.e.
90	2.500 σ = 1.625 s.p.e. = 1.567 m.s.r.e.
95	2.795 σ = 1.817 s.p.e. = 1.752 m.s.r.e.
99	3.368 σ = 2.190 s.p.e. = 2.111 m.s.r.e.

8-3 SURFACE-TO-SURFACE MISSILE GUIDANCE

Case One. In order to discuss the impact of the tactical situation on the choice and development of the guidance system for a surface-to-surface guided missile, let us postulate an operational requirement and performance specification for the development of a guided missile of intercontinental range carrying an atomic warhead for use against targets of strategic importance. The following facts, pertinent to the missile guidance system, have been abstracted from the hypothetical performance specifications:

Target: The target shall be considered to be industrial buildings constructed of masonry, concrete, and steel.
Maximum Range: The maximum range of the missile, propulsion and guidance system shall be 3000 nautical miles.
Missile Parameters: The missile shall have a cruising speed of $M = 3.5$ at 60,000 ft altitude. It shall be capable of a 2-g. maneuver at this altitude.
Guidance System: The guidance system shall be capable of guiding the missile

along a preselected trajectory at constant altitude. The guidance system shall be capable of inserting evasive maneuvers in the flight path without harmful effect to the system accuracy. The missile shall have a standard miss distance (error) no greater than 10 miles at maximum range.

Reliability: The reliability of the system shall be at least 80 percent.

Effectiveness of Missile: A single missile shall be capable of inflicting a damage probability of at least 50 percent at the maximum range.

Accuracy Requirements. The item of prime importance to the designer of the guidance system is that the missile shall have a standard miss distance no greater than 10 miles at maximum range. Let us examine how this statement came into being. As discussed in Par. 8-1 the probability that a representative missile will inflict specific damage upon a target is the result of considering a series of probabilities. The missile flight may be aborted by reason of a failure of a component of the missile, the guidance system, the launching equipment, or by reason of human errors in setting up the problem. The flight may also fail by reason of effective defensive measures on the part of the enemy. The probability that the warhead will inflict the required destruction on the target must be considered. Most important to the guidance system designer is the fact that the error in delivering the missile to the target represents another probability in the overall effectiveness of the system. The probable effectiveness of a single missile is the product of all the single probabilities.

The operational research accomplished has placed an assumed value on the probable reliability P_r of the entire missile system of 80 percent, as indicated in the specifications. This figure in itself is composed of a series of probabilities, one of which is assessed against the guidance system.

The probability P_s that the missile will survive enemy defensive action in the form of interceptors, surface-to-air guided missiles, antiaircraft guns and rockets has also been determined as part of the operational research study. We shall assume that this missile type has a probability of survival of 85 percent.

The probability that any single representative missile will reach the target is the product of the probability of survival and the probability that the missile is reliable. In the case specified the probability that a specific single representative missile will reach the target area is 0.80 × 0.85, or 68 percent. If we consider only a single missile, it should arrive at the target area with a miss distance of such value that the combined probabilities of reliability, survival, and kill should be 50 percent, as defined by the specifications. In the process of the operations research an integration of damage probability and probable guidance errors has been performed as discussed in paragraph 8-1 to determine that a standard error of 10 miles at maximum range will produce the required destruction, with the specified missile system effectiveness. As the development and testing of the missile proceed, the values of the pertinent probabilities may be reassessed many times. Inability to meet one contributing probability may force another to bear a greater share of meeting the overall effectiveness figure, or conversely, an improvement in one may permit a relaxation in another.

Reliability. Reliability is defined as that quality of a guided missile or its components which permits unfailing performance in all of the natural environments of operation. It is also the probability that the missile or its components will not fail. The entire guided missile system may be considered as several separate systems wherein the distributions of the probabilities of success or failure of the several systems are independent of each other, yet the probabilities of each contribute to the overall success or failure of the mission of the missile.

Although we have not yet begun to postulate the possible missile guidance system or systems which might be required, let us inspect for a moment the items which conceivably may enter into the reliability probability requirements.

(a) We know that the guidance problem must be set up by humans to determine the location of the target as related to guidance system employed.

(b) The missile must be launched, and consequently a launching device and possibly a launching system of guidance may be necessary.

(c) The missile structure may fail, so that it has a probability of success or failure associated with it.

(d) The guidance system represents another system independent of the others in its probable success or failure.

If we assign an equal reliability to each of these four independent items, then the reliability required of each will be the fourth root of 0.8 or, in this case, 94.5 percent reliability. When we consider the total number of components in a missile guidance system that must give unfailing performance, it becomes obvious that every precaution must be taken to insure reliability of all components of the system.

Trajectory. We can logically deduce much about the probable trajectory from the tactical requirements for the guided missile. The maximum range is sufficiently great that the shortest and therefore most economical trajectory will possess an advantage. The shortest trajectory in this case will be a great circle course from the launching point to the target. If we consider that the launching area will be within the United States or its possessions, such as Alaska, then it is probable that a great circle course to potential targets will involve flights over or near the polar regions. (See Chap. 3, Fig. 3-4.) The length of the trajectory is sufficiently great so that the type of guidance used must be either from stations along the path of the missile or such that the missile employs terrestrial or celestial references for its guidance intelligence. It is logical to expect that the trajectory will be a straight flight (essentially) with the possible exception of evasive maneuvers near the target. In this case the critical trajectory response requirements will be concerned principally with the maneuvers; as indicated by the specifications these have been arbitrarily maximized at 2 gravities. The relationship between trajectory dynamics and the guidance system will be discussed in greater detail in later chapters.

Launching. We have discussed the trajectory during the major portion of the postulated missile flight, but before the flight is fully underway, the missile must be launched and put on the desired trajectory with the knowledge that its guidance equipment is functioning and that it will reach and maintain the specified altitude. There are several areas of interest to the guidance system designer: the environmental conditions imposed by the launching on the guidance system; the question of whether the guidance system should be made operative either before or after launching; and the necessity for a separate guidance system during the launching phase.

These considerations can be resolved only by a detailed examination of the tactics of the use of the missile and a knowledge of the midcourse guidance system that will be used. It is obvious that a missile of this range requirement will be large in size and that the facilities needed for handling are not easily movable, in the sense of being portable. This means that the launching installation will be of permanent nature. Further, since every opportunity must be taken to advance the launching site toward the possible targets in order to obtain full benefit from the requirement for maximum range, the launching installation will be located, in some instances, far from populated areas. The equipment required, therefore, should be kept at a minimum for reasons of transport. If the missile is launched by means of a booster arrangement, the boosters, when they are dropped off in flight, must not present a hazard to any surrounding population.

Target. The first question that must concern the guidance system designer in connection with the missile arriving at the target is the accuracy of the guidance system. If, after study and test, it can be shown that the guidance system proposed meets the accuracy requirements, then the operational knowledge of the target need only include its location in terms of the reference used. If, on the other hand, the projected accuracy of the guidance system is such that the performance specifications cannot be adequately met by midcourse guidance alone, then the designer must consider the feasibility of incorporating a terminal guidance system which will depend upon some unique quality of the target in order to receive information during the terminal portion of the flight. The terminal guidance system, for example, might home on an adjacent radio station or on heat from a blast furnace. The employment, however, of more than one type of guidance system in separate phases of missile guidance should be avoided, if possible, in the interests of simplicity, reliability, and economy.

Airframe Performance and Structure. The guidance system designer must have full knowledge of the characteristic behavior of the airframe in response to an order from the guidance system. If the entire guidance system is considered as a servo system, the airframe forms a major component in the guidance loop; as such it must be stable and the characteristics of its behavior known.

The guidance designer is vitally interested in the weight allowance assigned the guidance equipment and the dimensions and location of the space allocated for it. It is necessary that there be a continuing interchange of information between the guidance and missile designers as the development of the missile system progresses, since it is to the interest of the missile designer to minimize the weight and space reserved for the guidance equipment. The designer of the guidance equipment is always prepared to demand additional weight and space allocations as the exigencies of his design become more apparent. The location of some elements of the guidance system may be quite critical, as in the case of gyros that measure or integrate spatial motions. If such elements are so located in the structure that they are subject to unusual vibratory modes, their effectiveness is materially diminished.

Environment. All equipment purchased by the government must meet standard environmental specifications for equipment of that particular type. In addition, the contractor must develop environmental specifications, tests, and even test equipment, based on the intimate knowledge of environmental demands of the specific guided missile system and its use. The dictates of military service use necessitate that the equipment be capable of operating both in tropical heat and in arctic cold. The missile must be so designed as to operate under any meteorological extreme that the service may conceivably indicate. In addition, the design of the system will impose its own environmental requirements. If the missile is boosted at launching, the airframe must withstand the shock of the booster ignition and takeoff. If accelerations are developed by maneuvers in flight, the structure must withstand them. The temperatures in flight must be taken into account. The handling and shipping of the missiles in transit must be considered, and the design of all components as well as the shipping containers must be capable of withstanding the shocks and vibration imposed. Not only is it necessary that the guidance equipment be constructed to withstand the environment imposed upon it, but the rigorousness of the design must be demonstrated by test while the equipment is in operation. Further details on general design practice are to be found in the "Structures and Design Practice" section of this series of volumes.

Choice of Midcourse Guidance. The 3000-nautical mile range of the missile in our example limits the choice of midcourse guidance to intelligence obtained from either terrestrial or celestial references, or to guidance by means of a radio navigation system. The various possibilities within these guidance system types will be studied by the contractor in considerable detail, so that the ultimate recommendation for research and development may proceed on a rational basis on one system type after all of the arguments for each system have been fully explored.

We will review the problem, which normally involves a study of considerable depth, in superficial detail. If the use of radio navigation, such as loran or radio ranges, is considered, guidance stations along the possible flight paths must be established. Several factors tend to mitigate against this type of system: the guiding stations in the forward area must be constructed, maintained, and defended; the logical locations for some of the stations may be uninhabitable and unsupportable areas; radio interference is great in the polar regions which may specifically prevent the use of radio frequencies for guidance; and when the guidance stations are "on the air" they may serve to warn the enemy of the impending attack.

If, on the basis of these reasons, we rule out the use of guidance by radio navigation, then there remain the alternatives of celestial and terrestrial references as possible sources of guidance intelligence. We can discount the use of terrestrial magnetic references because of the probability of polar flights; the prevalence of magnetic storms and the magnetic anomalies of the polar area prevent serious consideration of this kind of guidance. We have for consideration, then, only celestial navigation and inertial guidance.

Each of these two remaining methods of obtaining guidance intelligence has some factors which mitigate against its use and other factors which favor its choice. Consider first the case against celestial navigation—it is necessary that the stars be visible at all times during the flight. It is obvious that there is always a possibility that the weather will be overcast when it is desired to launch the missile. On the favorable side, there is no apparent reason why the accuracy of a celestial navigation device should decrease with increasing range from the launching location, since the accuracy of celestial navigation is inherently independent of the distance the vehicle travels. Consider the case against inertial guidance—an inertial system is essentially a dead reckoning device; the motions of the aircraft are integrated with time to obtain the present position and heading of the aircraft. It is obvious that, as the time of flight increases, the errors of position determination will also increase. On the other hand, an inertial system is independent of the weather.

The two systems, however, tend to complement each other. We shall now conclude that the most satisfactory midcourse guidance system for a missile with the specified tactical demands is a celestial navigation system in combination with a dead reckoning system. The resultant system is herein superficially estimated to have the accuracy of the celestial navigation equipment, plus the ability to be launched from beneath cloud cover in any weather or time of day. If at any time the sight to the stars or sun be obscured while the missile is in flight, the dead reckoning system will serve to carry on until the prime intelligence is again available. The conclusions derived here are entirely superficial; in the real case, a detailed study would be made by the contractor and the results of such a study, by virtue of many additional parameters, might differ radically from these conclusions.

Launching Guidance. The task of launching guidance may now be consigned to the inertial guidance system. The inertial system may be employed to integrate the motions of the vehicle during launching and to determine its position in space until the celestial navigation system acquires bodies that will be used for navigation.

Terminal Guidance. The necessity for terminal guidance is dependent upon the accuracy with which the midcourse guidance brings the missile to the target area. In Case One, it was specified that the standard miss distance should be no greater than 10 nautical miles at the maximum range. Since the accuracy of the chosen navigation system is essentially independent of range, piloted aircraft tests may be made to obtain statistical data which will indicate whether or not the system has the required accuracy. If the data indicate that the system accuracy meets the specifications, then no terminal guidance will be required. The contractor will be expected to indicate to the using service the probable accuracy of the midcourse system and the feasibility of including a provision for terminal guidance. In this particular case, since the accuracy demanded is well below the accuracy obtained in the practice of shipboard celestial navigation, it will be assumed that the requirements may be met with automatic celestial navigation equipment, providing no insoluble problems arise during the research and development work.

The requirement for evasive action during the terminal portion of the flight may be obtained by programmed maneuvers around the desired trajectory. The inertial system may again be used to advantage in integrating the course made good by the missile during such a phase of hypothetical flight.

Solution. The solution of the problem of determining the guidance system to be recommended for Case One, from the tactical aspects of the assumed case, results in the recommendation that the development proceed on an automatic celestial navigation system in combination with an inertial dead reckoning system, and that the inertial system be employed for launching guidance and programmed maneuvers during the evasive phase of the flight.

8-4 SURFACE-TO-AIR MISSILE GUIDANCE

Case Two. In order to consider the effect of the tactical situation on the choice of a guidance system for a surface-to-air missile, let us assume that an operational requirement and performance specification have been issued for the purchase of a surface-to-air guided missile system to defend a warship or task force against the attack of bombing aircraft. The following facts are assumed to have been abstracted from the hypothetical performance specifications:

Target: The target is assumed to be a 300-knot aircraft, capable of maneuvering at 3 g. The target may fly at any altitude from 10,000 to 40,000 ft in pursuit of its mission.

Maximum Range: The maximum effective range of the missile, propulsion and guidance system shall be at least 40,000 yd.

Missile Parameters: The missile shall have a sustained velocity of $M = 2.0$ at 30,000-ft altitude. It shall be capable of maneuvers as required to combat the target aircraft.

Guidance System: The guidance system shall be capable of guiding the missile to an interception with the target with such accuracy that 80 percent of the missiles pass within 200 ft of the target at 40,000-yd range.

Reliability: The reliability of the missile guidance system shall be at least 90 percent.

Effectiveness of Missile: A single representative missile shall have a kill probability of at least 50 percent at the maximum range.

Launching: The missile launching equipment shall be so constructed as to permit the launching of two missiles in salvo. The launcher shall be automatically loaded and shall not require more than 10 sec between salvos.

Ship: The ship used as the vehicle shall be a cruiser having a maximum roll amplitude of 15 deg with a period of 20 sec and a maximum pitch amplitude of 5 deg with a period of 15 sec.

Tactical Situation. The tactical situation may best be developed by listing the sequence of events which lead to the interception of the target aircraft by the postulated surface-to-air missile. It is assumed that the cruiser carrying the missile and guidance equipment is part of a group of ships consisting of carriers and appropriate escort vessels. The following events would normally be expected to occur in sequence:

a. DETECTION. The attacking aircraft is detected in some manner. The detection may be made from an aircraft or surface ship and by either visual or radar contact.

b. IDENTIFICATION. The traget must be identified as friend or foe. If the target is friendly, procedures must be taken to protect it from action on the part of elements of the task group; if the target is identified as an enemy, an alert must be given.

c. EVALUATION. Information as to position and altitude, direction of motion, and probable type of attack is needed in order to direct the specific means of interception that may best be employed at least risk to the elements of the group.

d. ASSIGNMENT. After the target has been evaluated, the responsibility is assigned to those elements, or that element, of the task force which may best accomplish the interception.

We shall assume that the target has been assigned to the guided missile cruiser for interception. The proper authorities aboard the cruiser have received, and will continue to receive, the latest information on the target from other elements of the task group, but it is desired that direct knowledge of the target be obtained aboard the cruiser. Since the target is at considerable range, the radar operators on the cruiser will attempt to acquire the target by searching the area of reported contact. When the search radar operators have taken the target under observation, information about the target is relayed to the operators of the guided missile system. The target, when within range of the guided missile system, must be acquired by the operators of this system, thus relieving all other elements of responsibility for the interception of this particular target. The process of detection and assignment is thus repeated aboard the ship, but on the basis of greater and more specific knowledge than the original detection. If the ship were operating as an autonomous unit, then it must be able to accomplish all of the operations without assistance.

Since the specified maximum missile range is 40,000 yd, or 20 nautical miles, we shall assume, by reason of the magnitude of the range, that a radar for tracking the target must be employed as part of the guided missile system. To determine the maximum range requirements of this radar, let us examine the time that may expire between acquisition of the target by the search radar and acquisition of the target by the tracking radar. If it be assumed that the missile tracking radar was alerted and already warmed up and in operation, the missile operators must turn the radar in the direction indicated by search information; acquire the target; and, when the target is in range, fire the missile. The total time required will depend upon the speed of rotation of the radar mount, the angle the mount must be turned through, the missile firing processes, the alertness of the crew, and other similar factors. Let as assume that, in the worst case, the target may be acquired by the tracking radar and the missile readied for firing within 30 sec.

The velocity of the missile is specified to be $M = 2.0$, or twice the speed of sound, so that the time required for the missile to fly 40,000 yd is approximately 55 sec. The total time between indication of the target to the operators of the missile system tracking radar and the interception by the missile may be as much as 85 sec. The target, if it is flying directly toward the ship with a velocity of 300 knots (500 ft per sec), will move something over 6000 yd in range toward the ship during this time. The range capability of the missile system tracking radar should be for this type of target at least 46,000 yd in order to obtain an interception at the maximum missile range.

There is a probability associated with the range of acquisition of a specific aircraft target with a particular radar. Repeated tests on the radar equipment, using the same target and indication means in a simulated tactical situation, will result in a distribution of maximum acquisition range data such as is shown in Fig. 8-3, wherein the units of range are, for the moment, assumed to be in thousands of yards.

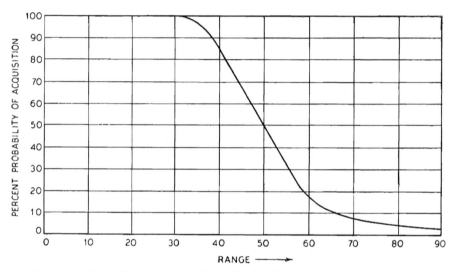

FIG. 8-3 Generalized Relationship of Probability of Acquisition to Range.

If a radar having the acquisition characteristics shown in Fig. 8-3 be planned for use as part of the missile system, then we observe that the effectiveness of the system at maximum interception range has been reduced, since the probability of acquisition at this range (46,000 yd) is only 62 percent. When multiplied by the previous design figure for system effectiveness of 50 percent, the probability of an interception of this target by a representative missile deteriorates to 31 percent. This presents a problem—the missile effectiveness of 50 percent is not realizable until the probability of acquisition is 100 percent, which occurs at an acquisition range of 31,000 yd. The interception occurs, under this circumstance, at approximately 25,000 yd.

There are several alternatives: the radar can be redesigned to meet the specifications so that it will have a probability of acquisition of unity at

46,000 yd; or the specifications may be waived in the matter of missile effectiveness, so that the 50 percent value at 25,000 yd is considered acceptable; or the effectiveness of the remainder of the system may be arbitrarily increased to compensate for the probability of acquisition. The decision as to the proper alternative will, in part, be dependent upon the launching range of the weapons which are carried by the target aircraft. If the target were assumed to carry a bomb with a release point only 8000 yd horizontal range from the ship under attack, then a waiver might be obtained. On the other hand, if the maximum missile range specification had, as a basis, a guided missile attack from the bomber, then the radar must be redesigned or the design parameters of the missile changed, or both. The search radar which indicates target position to the missile system tracking radar must have its capabilities examined in a similar manner to be sure that it is not a limiting factor in the system effectiveness.

At the maximum range demanded of the missile system tracking radar, the target, flying at the minimum specified altitude of 10,000 ft, is at an elevation angle of approximately 3.5 deg, as measured from the radar. A precision tracking radar such as would be employed here inherently has a narrow, highly directive beam. Interference due to surface reflection should not exist in the tactical problem from which these specifications evolve.

Choice of Guidance Method. On the basis of the tactical situation outlined and the general conclusions on surface-to-air missile guidance of Chap. 1, there are several alternatives presented in the choice of guidance method for this problem. Since it has already been determined that the target will be observed by use of a tracking radar, the decision remains as to the best means by which the missile position and motion may be sensed in order that it may be guided to an interception.

The following alternatives will be considered:

a. The missile may be tracked by the same radar that is tracking the target. If the trajectory of the missile is along the beam of the radar, the missile may be tracked by using a beacon in the missile and a separate receiver in the radar. From this observation of the missile's position and its motion, commands may be transmitted to maintain it along the beam of the radar. This is one type of command guidance system. But the specifications call for the launching of two missiles in salvo fire; the tracking of three moving bodies simultaneously by the same radar, while not theoretically impossible, becomes in practice extremely complicated and difficult of accomplishment.

b. The missile may be tracked by a radar other than the one tracking the target, and the interception with the target can be commanded by a suitable radio link. This is also a type of command guidance system.

This method has the advantage of permitting freedom in the choice of trajectory for the missile; but again, since there are two missiles in salvo to be considered, two additional radars would be required. Since the weight of equipment which may be located topside aboard a ship must be kept at a minimum, this guidance method does not seem feasible for shipboard use.

c. The missile may contain within itself a means of determining the target's position and motion, i.e., a homing guidance system. The maximum range to the target at the instant of launching is about 44,500 yd. A radar homing system with this range capability would be both too large and too expensive to be employed in a missile of this type. A possible variety of homing which might be considered is one in which the target is illuminated by the ground radar, with a radar receiver only within the missile. This method of guidance is called "semiactive homing." Again, however, the maximum range is the deciding criterion. It will be assumed in this instance that the range requirements are too great and that the semiactive system cannot be employed.

d. The missile may contain within itself a means of seeking the center of the radar beam which is tracking the target. This method of guidance is called *beam riding*. In this method, the tracking radar transmitter supplies the necessary information to permit a receiver in the missile to sense both the magnitude and the direction of error of any departure of the missile from the center of the radar beam. The center of the beam of the tracking radar is automatically maintained on the target; the missile follows it to eventual interception. The problem of two missiles in salvo is solved by firing one slightly before the other. Since the missiles are small, the probability of one missile physically shielding intelligence from the other is low. Moreover, diffraction of the radio energy around the second missile permits the information to reach the first missile without harmful interference. The traffic capabilities of this guidance method are therefore considered to be excellent.

Of the alternative guidance methods suggested, the beam-riding method has obvious advantages in this particular tactical situation. The contractor for this hypothetical missile would make a study in greater detail than the superficial considerations given here, and because of other possible factors, might come to a different conclusion. Before proceeding with research or design on a specific guidance method or system, a thorough study of all of the interrelated parameters would be made, reaching conclusions and recommendations for the guidance system development.

Accuracy Requirements. The specifications read: ". . . 80 percent of the missiles (shall) pass within 200 ft of the target at 40,000-yd range." These accuracy requirements result from an operations research study of the probable reliability of the equipment; the probability that the missile

8-4] SURFACE-TO-AIR MISSILE GUIDANCE

will survive enemy action; and the interrelated probabilities of error and kill probability as related to the miss distance and warhead lethality. The study has concluded that the design criterion of effectiveness is that a representative missile shall have a 50 percent chance of destroying the target aircraft. This criterion is commonly called the *single-shot kill probability*.

It has been specified that the reliability of the missile system shall be at least 90 percent. The specification does not make it arbitrarily possible that a system can be built with such reliability; but it represents a goal that must be met if the operations planning is to have realistic value. If it cannot be met, then the specifications on other parts of the system, such as guidance accuracy, must be made more stringent.

The ability of the enemy bomber to destroy this missile is judged to be nonexistent. The speed of the missile, its small size and consequent relative immunity to detection and observation, together with the fact that two missiles are to be fired in salvo, have led to the conclusion that the missile will not be destroyed by the armament carried by the bomber or made ineffective by means of electronic countermeasures. The probability of survival from enemy action is thus assumed to be 100 percent.

Of the missiles fired, then, it may be assumed that 90 percent arrive at the target area. The specifications speak of the accuracy requirements in terms of 80 percent of the missiles launched. It is obvious that the specifications have been evolved from the 90 percent probability circle in considering the guidance errors of those missiles which reach the target (i.e., $0.90 \times 0.90 = 81$ percent, which has been rounded off to the 80 percent figure of the specifications).

The miss distance may be converted to the r.m.s. figure by using the ratio of the radius of the 39.3 percent probability circle to the radius of the 90 percent probability circle (refer to Table 8-3). The r.m.s. miss distance then becomes $(200 \times 1.00)/2.146$, or approximately 94 ft. This figure may be used as a guide in establishing the criterion for the missile guidance system error. As the design progresses, a reassessment of this and the other factors involved in the determination of the effectiveness of the missile system will be required to maintain the effectiveness at the specified standard.

In the case of the beam-riding missile, there are two separate probable errors which must be related: (a) the errors of the target tracking radar, and (b) the errors of the missile and receiver combination in following the radar beam. In lieu of specific knowledge of the abilities of the two interrelated systems, it can be assumed that the total guidance error will be divided equally between them in order to establish design criteria for each. Although there exists a tenuous relationship between the errors of the guiding radar and those of the guidance system riding the beam, it can be assumed that the distribution of errors of the two is independent, and that each system error is the square root of the sum of the squares of the two independent errors. On this basis, the standard error for each of the independent systems becomes $\sqrt{94^2/2}$, or approximately 67 ft.

The errors of tracking radars are normally stated in angular values, since the measurements of a tracking radar are in polar coordinates. The design standard error for the radar is almost invariably expressed in mils (the term being derived from milliradians). The Navy definition of a *mil* is the angle subtended by an arc equal to one one-thousandth of the arc's radius, and hence is equal to one one-thousandth of a radian (approximately 3′26″). The Army's definition of a mil is 1/6400 of a circle. In either case, to facilitate computation for small angles, a mil is assumed to be that angle whose tangent is best defined by 1 yd measured laterally at 1000 yd range. At 40,000 yd, the maximum range at interception, the standard error for design use is $67/(3 \times 40,000)$, or 0.55 mil for the tracking radar. This value will be assumed to be feasible.

Tracking Radar. The tracking radar employed in the system may be one which is already available for shipboard use, or a new design may be required. In the event that an existing radar is to be employed, a study of its capabilities must be made to assure that its use will not compromise the required system performance. If an available radar fulfills the design requirements as to range and accuracy capabilities, then a study of the modifications required to impose the beam-riding intelligence on the existing radar transmitting equipment must be made.

If a new radar design is required, then, in addition to the design criteria already discussed, the dynamic capabilities of the radar tracking servomechanisms must be developed by a review of both the target motion and the roll and pitch of the ship. It is necessary that the radar line-of-sight be made stable with respect to space despite the motion of the ship. The development of equipment to accomplish this has been accomplished many times in the field of naval firecontrol with acceptable accuracy.

Reliability. The specifications state that the reliability of the missile guidance system shall be at least 90 percent. If we arbitrarily divide the complete system into three more or less independent systems—the missile with its controls and launcher, the beam-riding receiver, and the tracking radar—and assign equal reliability to each, then the reliability of each becomes the third root of 90 percent, or approximately 97 percent. The necessity for conservative design becomes apparent.

Trajectory. In the case of a beam rider, the guidance method determines the trajectory, since the missile will always seek the center of the tracking radar beam. The response that will be demanded from the missile depends upon: (a) the dynamics of the trajectory for specific tactical situations, (b) the maneuvers of the target, and (c) the initial entry of the missile into the beam. Study of these factors will be required to determine the design criteria for the bandwidth and response of the missile guidance system.

Launching. There are three aspects of launching which require detailed study on the part of the contractor: (a) the physical design of the launching and handling equipment to permit salvo fire of two missiles and the loading of an additional two missiles, ready to fire, within 10 sec after the previous firing; (b) the dispersion of the missiles prior to capture by the guiding beam; and (c) the necessity for a booster, and, if a booster is required, its effect upon launching guidance requirements.

Target. The equivalent radar area of the target is a determining factor in the establishment of the power requirements of the tracking radar. The dynamic capabilities of the target are determining factors in the design of the servomechanisms for the tracking radar in order that it may follow the maneuvers of the target without contributing serious dynamic lags to the system.

Airframe Performance and Structure. The missile guidance system designer must know the frequency response characteristics of the airframe which forms such an important part in the guidance loop. He is vitally interested in the physical aspects of space and weight availability and must be intimately involved in the airframe design and space allocation in order that proper location of motion-sensitive elements may be made.

Environment. The contractor must examine, both in theory and by test, the shocks, vibrations, and all other physical environments that the missile will be subject to in handling, shipping, storage, and use. As a result of such a survey, environmental specifications, test and, if necessary, test equipment must be developed to prove that the equipment will be reliable despite the adverse conditions to which it may be subjected. These tests should be designed scientifically in order to measure reliability as a finite probability that failure will not take place in the expected environment. Equipment must be tested to failure in sufficient quantities to assure statistical validity. (See "Structures and Design Practice" of this series.)

Terminal Guidance. The necessity for terminal guidance depends upon the accuracy of the midcourse guidance system—in this case, the beam-rider system. In the foregoing brief survey of the error requirements, it was indicated that the standard error requirement for the tracking radar (0.55 mil) was assumed to be feasible of attainment. The ability of the missile to meet its requirements (67 ft r.m.s. from the beam center), will have to be determined by test. It will be assumed that in Case Two the contractor proceeds on the basis that no terminal guidance is required.

Launching Guidance. The necessity for launching guidance will depend upon the inherent ability of the missile to be launched into and to be captured by the guiding and tracking radar beam. Exact knowledge as to the probable ballistic stability of the missiles in the launching phase will require considerable test and analysis. The contractor will be required to study this phase of missile flight in great detail and will evolve a design criterion for launching accuracy. The need for launching guidance will be determined as a result of both theoretical studies and tests of missile flights.

Solution. The solution for Case Two, from the tactical aspects of the case, results in the recommendation that a beam-rider guidance system be employed, without terminal guidance, and that the necessity for launching guidance be determined as a result of further study and tests as the design of the missile and launching equipment proceeds.

8-5 AIR-TO-SURFACE MISSILE GUIDANCE

Case Three. It will be assumed that a need has been demonstrated for a guided missile launched from the air against ground targets such as bridges, troop concentrations, fortified enclosures, and similar targets. The following information, of interest to the guidance system designer, has been excerpted from the hypothetical performance specifications:

Target: Possible targets shall be highway and railway bridges, troop concentrations, vehicles in convoy, gun emplacements, etc.

Maximum Range: The maximum range of the missile shall be at least 10,000 yd.

Missile Parameters: The missile shall be propelled to a velocity of $M = 0.9$ and shall coast to maximum range with a velocity at maximum range of $M = 0.6$. The missile shall be stable and capable of control despite the variation in velocity.

Guidance System: The guidance system shall be capable of guiding the missile to an accuracy such that the r.m.s. miss at the target shall not be greater than 50 ft from the center of the target. Maneuvers of the parent aircraft shall be possible for evasive action during guidance.

Reliability: The reliability of the guided missile system shall be at least 90 percent.

Miscellaneous: The missiles shall be arranged for launching from a single-seater radar-equipped aircraft. The missiles shall be wing-mounted: two missiles shall be carried on the aircraft. The missiles shall be fired singly. The speed of the aircraft at firing and during the guidance period will be approximately 300 knots. Altitude at launch shall be from sea level to 5000 ft.

Target. The specifications indicate that the target may be any of a number of unrelated objects. There is no single distinguishing feature, common to all target types, that permits the use of other than visual detection and observation of the targets. It may be assumed immediately that the pilot of the aircraft will accomplish the tracking of the target during the guidance period and that he, therefore, will become a part of the guidance system. The use of this system is possible only when visibility permits.

Tactical Situation. It may be assumed that the pilot of the missile-carrying plane is briefed prior to his mission and has a knowledge of: the location of the target so that it may be identified; the character of the surrounding terrain; the preferable direction of approach; the character and location of antiaircraft guns defending the target; and the probability of sufficient visibility at the target to permit the successful conclusion of his mission. If the mission is aborted by reason of poor visibility at the target area, it is probable that alternate targets of opportunity will be suggested. The maximum range of visibility required is the same as the maximum specified for missiles, 10,000 yd.

Choice of Guidance Method. It has already been determined that, because of the varying character of the target, the observation of the target will be visual. There remains to be determined, then, the manner by which the position of the missile will be measured so that it may be guided in flight to the target. The following alternatives will be considered:

a. The missile may be observed visually and maintained on the line-of-sight between the pilot and the target. This is the method used by the Germans for the command of the Hs 293 and other missiles. However, we are here concerned with a single-seater aircraft, and the complete attention of the pilot will be required to keep the target under accurate observation and fly the aircraft, without imposing the additional problem of tracking the missile.

b. The missile may contain within it a means of sensing the target position, i.e., homing on the target. However, it has already been postulated that, by reason of the variety of targets, there is no single distinguishing factor common to all. Many of the targets indicated are indistinguishable from their background by other than optical means, so that the use of a homing system of any type does not lend itself as a guidance method to this problem.

c. The missile may contain within it a means of seeking the center of a radar beam which is pointed at the target. The target types do not lend themselves to the use of an automatic tracking radar, as previously mentioned. However, it would be possible to servo the radar antenna, and thus the center of the radar beam, to the optical tracking device employed by the pilot in observing and tracking the target. This method of guidance is called *optical beam riding*.

d. The missile may contain a beacon which is automatically tracked by the aircraft radar. In this event the position of both the target and missile may be related to each other and appropriate commands transmitted to the missile to accomplish a hit.

Of the alternative methods of guidance considered, the optical beam rider and the command system using the radar to track the missile are, from a superficial inspection, the most desirable. The choice between these two methods may be made on the basis of the requirement that the aircraft must not be inhibited in its ability to take evasive maneuvers to increase its survival probability. If the beam-rider system is used, a maneuver on the part of the aircraft while the missile is riding the beam must be restrained by the necessity that the radar beam center point at the target and that the beam not be translated beyond the ability of the missile to follow. The dynamics of the situation severely restrict the maneuvers of the parent aircraft during the missile flight. So far as the command system is concerned, the radar automatically tracks the missile. Maneuvers of the aircraft with respect to the line-of-sight to the missile are limited only by the limits of antenna motion. In this case, either the pilot may track the target during the maneuver or the maneuver may be programmed by programming the optical line-of-sight to the target. A computer is required to relate the tracking lines to the target and missile and to compute the commands to the missile that will result in a hit.

The contractor for this hypothetical missile would be expected to make a study in much greater detail than the superficial examination made herein; it is entirely possible that the eventual conclusions of a more detailed study would result in the recommendation for research and development on another guidance method.

Accuracy Requirements. The accuracy requirements for the missile guidance system have been specified to be ". . . the r.m.s. miss at the target shall not be greater than 50 ft from the center of the target." Since this specification is already stated in terms usable for design, a review of the manner by which the specification was evolved will not be repeated.

The method of guidance selected for this case involves two tracking systems, independently operated. In addition, the missile is commanded by a separate radio link, wherein the command intelligence is generated in a computer. We may, for design purposes, allocate the errors among three independent systems: the optical tracking of the target by the pilot; the automatic radar tracking of the missile; and the computer, command and missile following system. If we assume, in lieu of accurate test information, that the total specified system error is divided equally among the three subsidiary systems, then design criteria for the independent subsidiary systems may be established. On the basis that the errors of the three subsidiary systems are independent of each other, the total system error is the square root of the sum of the squares of the errors of the subordinate systems; thus the r.m.s. error allocated to each of the three systems for design purposes becomes: $\sqrt{50^2/3}$, or 29 ft approximately.

Let us assume that the missile has been fired at its maximum specified range, 10,000 yd. The velocity of the missile varies from that of the speed of the aircraft at the instant of launching, to a maximum of $M = 0.9$ at the end of the propulsion period, and reduces to $M = 0.6$ at maximum range. The average velocity will be assumed to be $M = 0.75$, or 825 ft per sec. The time of flight for the missile to travel 10,000 yd is approximately 36 sec. During this time of flight it is assumed that the aircraft has continued to approach the target despite its evasive action. The aircraft velocity is specified to be 300 knots, or 500 ft per sec, and therefore travels 6000 yd during this time. If we assume, arbitrarily, that the aircraft has traveled only 5000 yd toward the target by virtue of evasive action, then the range to the target from the aircraft at the instant of missile impact is 10,000 − 5000, or 5000 yd. The errors of polar coordinate tracking systems are usually measured and reported in test data in mils. The r.m.s. or standard error of the optical tracking system and the radar tracking system thus becomes 29/(3 × 5000), or approximately 2 mils for each.

The feasibility of the subsidiary systems' meeting the design criteria may be determined, in part, on the basis of past experience. The assignment of such criteria permits investigation by tests in relatively small areas where study might indicate that the ability to meet the accuracy requirements was a critical factor in adopting this particular guidance method. It will be assumed, in this case, that study has indicated that the tracking systems can meet the accuracy requirements without difficulty, but that research and tests are required to demonstrate the accuracy of the computer-command link-missile combination. The contractor will study the systems and components of the systems in an attempt to assess the contributions to error of each under assumed dynamic tactical conditions, and he will conduct such tests and research as are required to indicate the feasibility of the complete system. This study will indicate the necessity of reassessing the errors of the various parts of the system, keeping the total system error (50 ft r.m.s.) as a constant which must be met in the ultimate design.

Trajectory. With a command system of this type, wherein two independent tracking elements simultaneously observe the target and the missile, the trajectory is uninhibited, within limits, by the guidance method. If there exists any advantage of fuel enonomy, survival probability, or increased damage effectiveness by one type of trajectory as opposed to others, then this guidance method permits a freedom of choice.

Terminal Guidance. The character and variety of the possible targets in this case rule out detailed consideration of a terminal guidance system.

Launching Guidance. In order for the aircraft's radar to track the missile, it is necessary that the radar be positioned in such a manner that the missile intercepts the beam and is acquired by the radar. The problem is much simpler in this instance than in that of the beam rider, Case Two, since the radar is not engaged in tracking the target but is free to move in manner and direction to optimize the probability of acquiring the missile. Further, the location of a beacon in the missile should eliminate any possibility of ambiguity in the acquisition. From this superficial survey of the launching problem, it does not seem that a special launching guidance system will be required. A requirement for inherent ballistic accuracy of the unguided missile during the pre-acquisition stage will exist; the parameters of this may be developed by study.

Solution. From the tactical aspects of Case Three, there will result a recommendation that a command system be employed, that a radio link be used to convey the intelligence to the missile, that a computer be used to relate the missile and target positions and thus obtain the proper commands to the missile to result in a target hit, that the target be tracked optically, and that the missile be tracked by the airborne radar.

8-6 AIR-TO-AIR MISSILE GUIDANCE

Case Four. It will be assumed that, as the result of an operations research study, a need has been shown for the development of an air-to-air guided missile to be used by interceptor aircraft against bombers. The following information, of interest to the contractor for the missile guidance system, has been digested from the hypothetical performance specifications issued by one of the military services:

Target: The target shall be assumed to be a 300-knot bomber attacking the continental United States. The attack may develop over either land or water. The bomber may fly at altitudes from 10,000 to 40,000 ft. The bomber is capable of sustained maneuvers of 2 g. The bomber defensive armament is assumed to be 20-mm guns.

Maximum Range: The maximum usable range of the missile shall be 10,000 yd.

Missile Parameters: The missile shall have an average velocity of $M = 3.0$.

Guidance System: The guidance system shall be capable of guiding the missile with such accuracy that the r.m.s. error at the target shall not be greater than 50 ft from the target center, despite the maneuvers of the target and during day or night operation.

Interceptor Aircraft: The missiles shall be designed for launching from an aircraft flying at a speed of 360 knots. Six missiles shall be wing-mounted and shall be capable of being fired either singly or in salvos of two.

Reliability: The reliability of the guided missile system shall be at least 85 percent.

Missile Effectiveness: The effectiveness of the guided missile system shall be such that a single representative missile shall have a K kill probability of at least 50 percent.

Tactical Situation. The tactical situation may be hypothecated from the performance specifications and the discussion on this category of missiles in Chapter 1. A clear picture of the impact of the tactical situation on the ultimate choice of missile guidance system may best be obtained by a review of the steps which are logically required in effecting an interception with the attacking bomber. The following events would normally be expected to occur:

a. EARLY WARNING AND IDENTIFICATION. The target bomber or bombers must be detected and identified by some form of early warning system capable of alerting the interceptors in sufficient time to vector them into position for the interception. The interceptors could be either already in the air on patrol or could be located on the ground in sufficient readiness to take off in the defense of the area of operations. The need for an early warning system is required, whatever type of weapons is employed by the interceptors.

b. VECTORING. The flight path of the target is observed by the early warning system and the interceptors are commanded along a course that will bring the interceptor into position to observe the target directly. Since it was specified that this system must operate during the day or night, it must therefore be assumed that both the early warning system and the interceptor will employ radar for detection of the target aircraft. The interceptor must be vectored into such position that the target will be detected by the interceptor's radar.

c. INTERCEPTOR SEARCH. To avoid penetration of the area being defended, it is logical to assume that the early warning radar equipment will be optimized for maximum range. By reason of the dynamics of the tactical situation, combined with long-range operation, it is necessary that the interceptor be equipped to search a limited sector in order to acquire the target. The accuracy of the vectoring information given the interceptor pilot determines the volume of space he must be prepared to search in order to find the target.

d. RADAR TRACKING. Having searched the sector and acquired and identified the target, the interceptor, in order to use its weapon, must be able to observe the target's position and motion. In a night weapon system, it may be assumed that the pilot will not observe the target visibly, but will employ his radar in a tracking mode of operation in order to sense the target.

e. WEAPON USE. When the pilot has detected and acquired the target and is tracking it, he must not only place himself in the most favorable position to destroy it with the weapon he is using, but accomplish the destruction in such a manner that he has a high probability of survival.

Choice of Guidance Method. The decision has already been made to observe the target by means of the interceptor's radar. It remains to be determined how the position of the missile shall be related to the target in order to achieve a destructive hit. The following alternatives will be considered:

a. The position of the missile may also be observed by the interceptor's radar and commands computed and transmitted for guiding the missile. However, the specifications state that the system shall be capable of firing two missiles in salvo. All types of command systems may therefore be dismissed from further consideration because of the complexity involved.

b. The missile may be designed to follow the interceptor radar beam to the target, i.e., by beam riding. This method has the advantage of large traffic capacity, but, as previously discussed, tends to limit the maneuverability of the guiding aircraft.

c. The missile may contain within itself a means of homing on the target. Three varieties of the homing method may be considered: (1) The missile may transmit energy and home on the reflection of this energy from the target; (2) the missile may home on the energy of the interceptor's radar reflected from the target; (3) the missile may home on energy originating at the target, such as the heat of the motors, the energy from the bomber's radar, etc. The first method (known as "active" homing) requires that the missile shall transmit energy of sufficient power that the maximum range requirement may be met. Since the missile is expended, this portion of the system is lost with the missile. This method also requires that the missile have the necessary space for this stored power and the additional equipment to make it usable. Since any weight or space that can be eliminated is undesirable, active homing will be decided against on this basis. The second variety of homing mentioned requires that the interceptor's radar shall illuminate the target during the flight of the missile. This is called "semiactive" homing. Since the semiactive type of homing does not require a transmitter in the missile, it should result in a smaller and lighter missile as compared with an active system. The third type of homing is known as "passive" homing and presumes that the target will emit energy of a specific character of such amplitude that the missile will have sufficient range to meet the requirements. This suggests a knowledge of the target that might not be available; further, the characteristics of one target type as compared to another might radically limit the application of this system.

It will be assumed, then, that, since a homing method of guidance inherently permits salvo fire and does not unduly inhibit the maneuvers of the interceptor, a homing system will be used for this case. Of the three varieties of homing methods, the semiactive type will be chosen on the basis of the preceding superficial examination. It is again pointed out that a contractor will make a detailed study covering many additional parameters, and that the conclusions reached as a result of such study may vary quite radically from the conclusions herein derived.

Accuracy Requirements. In this case it is required that the missile home on the target with such accuracy that the r.m.s. error (or standard deviation) will not be greater than 50 ft. We can assume that the homing radar receiver observes the target as a point source of energy at long range, and that errors of the system are generated (a) by sources of noise inherent to the radar tracking the target and (b) by systematic errors introduced as a result of the dynamics of missile and target motion. As the missile approaches the target, the target has a finite size and is no longer a point source of returned energy. The energy may appear to be radiated from different parts of the target as its aspect changes. This may be considered an additional source of error, inherent to the target rather than the radar receiver which observes it. An investigation of the radar receiver is required to compile data which may indicate the probable accuracy against this particular target type. A study of the dynamics of homing against a maneuvering target will indicate the system design criteria in this regard; such studies are usually accomplished by use of analog simulators. The data of the two studies may then be combined to determine the probable guidance accuracy of the homing system.

Interceptor Radar. In the guidance method proposed for this case, the accuracy of the interceptor radar does not enter into the accuracy of the guidance system, after the missiles have been fired. Before launching, the interceptor's radar is required to observe the target and relate the homing system of the missile to the target in such a manner that the radar receiver in the missile will engage the correct target. This may be accomplished in several ways: as one example, the antenna of the missile receiver may be positioned by the tracking radar so that it is pointed in the correct direction to assure acquisition of the target. The missile receiver antenna is thus said to be "slaved" to the tracking radar. After the missile is launched, the interceptor radar need track the target with only enough accuracy to assure that a sufficient signal returns to the missile radar receiver to permit the homing to be accomplished.

The radar of the interceptor also serves the function of a search radar in the initial phase of the weapon system operation. The effectiveness of the radar in the search mode of operation must form part of the overall effectiveness of the missile system, for if it does not have a high probability of acquiring the target at sufficient range for the missile to be employed, the effectiveness of the system is correspondingly lowered. The probability that the interceptor will detect and acquire the target aircraft is a function of many parameters, such as the accuracy of vectoring the interceptor to the target, the effective target area presented by the aspect of the bomber with respect to the interceptor, the relative velocity of the two aircraft, and other similar representations of the dynamic tactical situation. In the interests of simplicity, let us assume that Fig. 8-3, with the ordinate of range in units of feet, illustrates the detection and acquisition ability of an available interceptor radar for the target being considered. To illustrate graphically the effect of the tactical situation, let us investigate the range requirements of the radar under two discrete situations: (a) a tail approach to the bomber and (b) a head-on approach to the bomber.

a. TAIL APPROACH. The maximum range specified for the missile is 10,000 yd, with a missile velocity of $M = 3.0$, or approximately 3300 ft per sec. In traveling the specified 10,000 yd, the missile consumes approximately 9 sec of time. During this time of flight, the bomber, traveling at 300 knots, or 500 ft per sec, has gone a distance of 1500 yd. The maximum range between the two aircraft at the instant of launching should then be 10,000 − 1500 yd, or 8500 yd. Let us assume that the computing and firing processes will consume 50 sec between detection of the target and the firing of the missile. During this period of time, the 360-knot interceptor is overtaking the 300-knot bomber at the rate of 100 ft per sec. The range at detection should be approximately 10,200 yd, by the process of simple arithmetic. If we consult Fig. 8-3, remembering that the units of range are in feet, it will be observed that at this range there is a 100 percent probability of detecting the target.

b. HEAD-ON APPROACH. Since the missile and target are now approaching each other, the range at missile launching between the target and the interceptor, to take full advantage of the maximum missile range, becomes 10,000 + 1500, or 11,500 yd. During the 50 sec consumed by the computing and firing processes, the interceptor and target are approaching each other at a relative velocity of 1100 ft per sec, so that, in the 50 sec allotted, they travel approximately 18,000 yd toward each other. The total range required of the radar for a head-on approach now becomes 29,500 yd. Referring again to Fig. 8-3, we note that the probability of detection of this target with this radar is only 2 percent. It is obvious that the effectiveness required of the missile system cannot be obtained by using this hypothetical radar with a head-on approach to the target.

The important lesson to be learned from this example is that the parameters of the interceptor and the radar are very much a part of the missile system, despite the fact that the missile and guidance system *per se* are frequently looked upon as independent components. The tactical application must consider all factors in reaching conclusions and recommendations for the development of weapon systems of this character. In this specific case, the decision with regard to the use of the radar as part of the system would be predicated upon a study of the effect of a vectoring doctrine which can place the interceptor in position for a rear hemisphere attack, as compared to a forward hemisphere attack.

Trajectory. Since the missile guidance system is independent of the parent aircraft after firing, the trajectory of the missile may be chosen for any critical advantage, such as ease of computation, minimum maneuver requirements, economy of fuel, etc. In general, a homing system will employ a computed intercept course.

Launching. One requirement for a homing system is that it must engage the target by its own guidance system. This may be accomplished prior to launching, or the system may be required to search for and lock on the target after the missile has been fired. Which method is to be used is partly dependent upon the ability of the pilot to handle the additional operations of monitoring the missile radars prior to launching, partly upon the effectiveness that can be built into an automatic acquisition system in the missile, and partly upon the choice of radar type. In any event, the decision can be made only as a result of study and investigation of the specific system the contractor will employ; the decision will involve launching and firing processes and not a separate launching guidance system.

Solution. From the tactical review of Case Four, the contractor will recommend the use of a semiactive homing guidance system, using the interceptor radar as the illuminating source. Additional study and research work will be recommended in order to outline specific design criteria for the interceptor radar.

CHAPTER 9

MEASUREMENTS OF MISSILE MOTION

It is the purpose of this chapter to discuss the measurement of the components of the vector of missile motion and the devices that may be so employed in missile guidance systems. A rigid body, such as a missile, moving freely through space is said to have six degrees of freedom: three translations and three rotations. In order to express its position completely, six numbers or coordinates are required. The principal missile motions of interest to the guidance problem are: (1) translation along the longitudinal axis (velocity); (2) rotation about the longitudinal axis (roll); (3) rotation about the lateral horizontal axis (pitch); and (4) rotation about the vertical axis (yaw).

The devices employed to measure motion separate naturally into two categories: those which establish a datum from which position may be measured, and those which measure the rate and change of rate of motion. Devices in the first category do not, as a rule, enter into the dynamics of the guidance system response. The major concerns in the design of these devices are accuracy and the endurance of accuracy in relation to the time of missile flight. Devices which measure rates and accelerations of the missile are usually intimate components of the guidance and control loops, and the response characteristics of these components must be determined for use in system design.

9-1 DATUM DETERMINATION

A datum employed in a guidance system may be established in relation to the reference frame of the earth, to a space reference, or to an arbitrary reference frame established by the coordinates of the missile or its guidance system. The particular datum employed is dependent upon the use of the missile and the demands of the guidance system.

The earth's magnetic field is commonly used to establish a datum line (or plane) in airborne vehicles by the employment of gyromagnetic and gyrostabilized compasses. The local effective vertical is commonly indicated in airborne vehicles by the use of a pendulous mass or a vertical-seeking gyroscope. A space reference may be established by the use of a free gyroscope. The missile flight may be maintained at a constant altitude by the use of barometric or radio altimeters.

The accuracy of establishing the datum and the sensitivity of the measurement of it may enter directly into the accuracy of the guidance system. As an example, in the case of a celestial navigation system using a vertical reference for measuring altitude of a star, it will be recalled that an uncertainty of one minute in establishing the datum may result in an error of one mile in determining the position of the missile. When a free gyro is used to establish a space reference, the ability of the gyro to retain its position with respect to space also enters directly into the accuracy of position determination. The outputs of these devices, in compatible form, are inputs to the guidance and control systems of the missile. By definition, these outputs are fixed quantities once the datum has been established. The response characteristics of datum-establishing devices are of little interest in the design of the guidance system as long as: (a) no errors of datum measurement are created by motions of the missile; (b) the output of the datum-establishing device contains no unwanted frequency (natural resonance or other) within the usable bandpass of the guidance system; and (c) the time required to establish the datum initially is satisfactory for the guidance system requirements.

9-2 THE GYROSCOPE

The gyroscope in its many forms is probably the most commonly used device in the field of flight motion measurement and indication. The two qualities of a gyroscope which account for its usefulness are: the axis of a free gyroscope will remain fixed with respect to space, provided no external forces act upon it; and a gyroscope can be made to deliver a torque (or a signal) which is proportional to the angular velocity about a per-

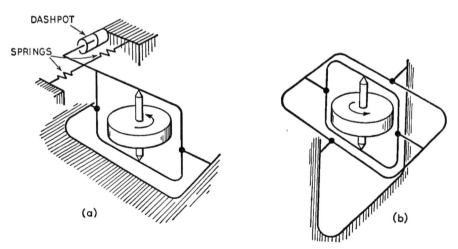

Fig. 9-1 Gyroscope Gimbal Systems.

pendicular axis. Both qualities stem from the principle of conservation of angular momentum, which may be stated as follows: *in any system of particles, the total angular momentum of the system relative to any point fixed in space remains constant, provided no external forces act on the system.*

Gyroscopes are frequently spoken of as having *one* or *two* degrees of freedom, or as being *free* gyroscopes. This terminology is confusing because it results from the conventional use of the number of degrees of freedom of the vector of angular momentum rather than from the actual degrees of rotational freedom. Figure 9-1a shows diagrammatically the mounting of what is commonly called a *single-degree-of-freedom,* or "rate," *gyroscope.* Although there are obviously two rotational axes involved, in its use it is a single-degree-of-freedom system. Figure 9-1b illustrates

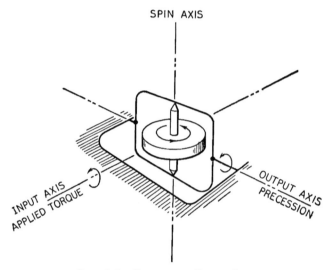

FIG. 9-2 Gyroscopic Precession.

the gimballing arrangement for what is sometimes called a *two-degree-of-freedom gyroscope*. As can be seen, a gyro wheel so mounted has three degrees of rotational freedom, *except when all three axes are in the same plane*. When the measurements of motion are made only from two coordinate axes, or when the outer axes lie in the same plane, this arrangement is frequently called a two-degree-of-freedom gyroscope. A *free gyroscope* is defined as one wherein the wheel has three degrees of rotational freedom and is unconstrained with respect to rotation. Although the wheel illustrated in Fig. 9-1b fulfills this definition as long as the axes are not aligned, a wheel so mounted as to be capable of rotation about five intersecting axes has three degrees of rotational freedom, whatever the direction of the axes.

Precession. The phenomenon of gyroscopic precession is explained readily by Newton's law of motion for rotation, which may be stated: *The time rate of change of angular momentum about any given axis is equal to the torque applied about the given axis.* When a torque is applied about the input axis of the gyroscope illustrated in Fig. 9-2 and the speed of the wheel is held constant, the angular momentum of the rotor may be changed only by rotating the projection of the spin axis with respect to the input axis, i.e., the rate of rotation of the spin axis about the output axis is proportional to the applied torque. This may be stated in equation form as

$$T = I\omega_r\Omega \tag{9-1}$$

where T = torque
 I = inertia of the gyroscope rotor about the spin axis
 ω_r = rotor speed
 Ω = angular velocity about the output axis

The rule for determination of the direction of precession about the output axis is: *Precession is always in such direction as to align the direction of rotation of the rotor with the direction of rotation of the applied torque.* This is illustrated in Fig. 9-2 which indicates the direction of precession about the output axis as a result of the applied torque. The output axis (or axis of precession) is always at right angles to the input axis.

Gyroscopic precession differs from angular acceleration about a fixed axis in that it is theoretically possible for the fixed axis acceleration to continue indefinitely, whereas the precessional response to torque has a well-defined limit. The limit is reached when the spin axis is turned sufficiently to align itself with the torque axis. No further precessional response to torque input is possible when this condition has been reached, because all the angular momentum of the system is already about the input axis.

The Free Gyroscope. The function of a free gyroscope in a missile guidance system is to establish a datum from which missile motion or position may be measured. If a free gyroscope, perfect in balance and without frictional torques, were to have its spin axis directed at any point in space, it would continue to remain fixed with respect to space despite any motion of the missile or rotation of the earth beneath the missile. If it be assumed that the axis is pointed at a star, then a measurement of the direction of the axis with respect to the local vertical or horizontal will define the position of the missile in exactly the same manner that it is determined in celestial navigation by using the same star. It is apparent that any datum convenient for computation may be employed.

In practice, there is obvious difficulty in constructing a free gyroscope with such perfect balance and small frictional torques that it will remain fixed in space with sufficient accuracy during the time of flight of a missile of intercontinental range. As the missile moves in flight, and as the earth rotates beneath the missile during the flight, the position of the rotor changes with respect to the gimballing system which retains it. Any friction of the gimbal bearings creates a torque which will precess the rotor from its fixed space position; any unbalance of the system when subjected to the accelerations of the missile motion may introduce other precessing torques. It is necessary that the position of the rotor be continuously measured; this requires that "pick-offs" or measuring devices of some type be used to determine the angles between gimbals (or other convenient internal reference). Pick-offs for gyroscopic use may be selected from many different types—capacitative, inductive, resistive, even light beams may be employed; the essential qualities of the pick-off are that it shall be light in weight to minimize unbalance and shall not introduce torques to the detriment of the gyroscope operation.

The free gyroscope is frequently used as a datum for roll and pitch of missiles for flights of relatively short duration. The datum may be established before the missile is launched; in this case it is necessary that the shocks and accelerations of the missile launching do not precess the gyroscope from its established position. The tolerance on the error resulting from precession determines the permissible unbalance and frictional torques of the gyroscope and its measuring system. Obviously, the longer the time of flight of the missile, the better must be the ability of the gyroscope to maintain its fixed space position.

9-3 THE VERTICAL GYROSCOPE

The vertical gyroscope is a gyroscope which is positioned by a gravity-sensitive element such as a pendulum or bubble level. The gyroscope is used to integrate the short time variations of the gravity-sensitive element position. There have been many ingenious arrangements developed to erect, and to maintain erect, vertical gyroscopes. In principle, all of the arrangements employ a means of measuring the direction of the effective gravity and, in the event of an error between this direction and the vertical as indicated by the gyroscope, of applying a torque to the rotor to precess it in the direction to correct the error. Owing to the nature of gyroscopic precession, the axis about which the torque is applied is at right angles to the direction of precession required to correct the measured error.

Figure 9-3 shows the principle employed, although the methods indicated are used for illustration only. Figure 9-3a shows a vertical gyroscope with an error in the plane of the input axis of the rotor. The effective vertical is indicated by the arrow; an angle of θ exists between the spin axis and the direction of the effective vertical in the plane of the input axis. There is suspended from the rotor gimbal a cylinder containing an appropriate conducting fluid and electrical contacts. The device (usually called an erection mechanism) is counterbalanced as required. Figure 9-3b shows a sectional view through the rotor gimbal, illustrating that the conducting liquid has completed a circuit between contact point A and the common contact C because of the tilt of the rotor. The completion of the circuit through the conducting fluid energizes the torque motor indicated in Fig. 9-3a. The torque motor, as its name implies, exerts a torque along the input axis in the direction indicated by the arrow, causing the rotor to precess as indicated by the arrow on the output axis. When the rotor is vertical, as in Fig. 9-3c, the circuit is broken and the precession ceases. If the rotor had been tilted in the opposite direction, the circuit would have been made through contact B and the direction of the torque applied would

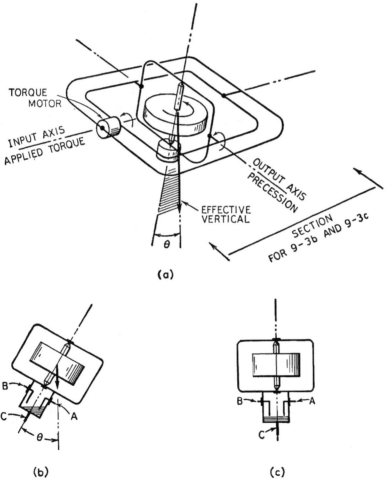

Fig. 9-3 Principles of Vertical Gyroscope Operation.

be reversed. Similar contacts and a torque motor would also be used in the plane of what is called the output axis in Fig. 9-3.

There are practical difficulties in constructing a precise vertical gyroscope. Regardless of the arrangement employed, the only means of knowing the direction of the vertical is by the direction of gravity as indicated by some form of pendulous mass. When an error exists, such as the angle θ in Fig. 9-3a, the component of the gravitational force which tends to restore the vertical-indicating mass is a function of the sine of the angular error. As the error approaches zero, so does the restoring force; the sensitivity of the erection mechanism is low as the gyroscope approaches the vertical. Because the sensitivity is low about the zero position and the gyroscope serves to integrate the oscillations about the zero, if there is a continuous error introduced into the system from one direction only, there tends to be a lag of erection in that direction, with a consequent average error. In many vertical gyroscopes it is desirable to correct by torque input any calculable precession that is continuously applied from one direction. Some erection mechanisms may introduce a dead spot near the vertical. The system described in Fig. 9-3 will cease any erection action when contacts A and B are both out of the conducting fluid. The angular uncertainty around the vertical is the measure of the precision of the device.

The rotation of the earth causes an apparent precession of the rotor, while the steady-state motion of the missile over the surface of the earth creates another apparent precession. The mass which is used to measure the direction of the gravitational force actually measures the resultant of all accelerations acting upon it. The Coriolis acceleration also will cause a deviation of the mass from the direction of the effective vertical. These factors must be considered in the design of a vertical gyroscope for long-range missile flight; for other than long range, the importance of some of them is reduced in accordance with accuracy demands.

Effect of Earth's Rotation. If we imagine a free gyroscope, perfect in lack of friction and unbalance, with its spin axis vertical on the equator, as the earth rotates the upper end of the spin axis will precess toward the west. The rotor turns about a horizontal axis in the plane of the meridian. The gyroscope is, of course, retaining its position with respect to space while the earth rotates beneath it. Figure 9-4a indicates a gyroscope of the same perfect character with its spin axis vertical at A located at other than the equator. As the earth rotates to A' and then to A'', the gyroscope, as viewed from the reference frame of the earth, apparently precesses, as shown in Fig. 9-4b. The apparent precession caused by the earth's rotation may be countered by applying the proper torque, and thus developing a counter rate of precession, as given by

9-3] THE VERTICAL GYROSCOPE 333

$$\Omega = \omega_e \cos \phi \qquad (9\text{-}2)^1$$

where Ω = the rate of precession
ω_e = angular velocity of the earth
ϕ = latitude

The correcting precession is about an axis in the plane of the meridian.

Effects of Missile Motions. If we again visualize the perfect free gyroscope with its spin axis vertical in the plane of the equator and further imagine it in a missile flying westward in the same plane with a constant velocity exactly equal to the surface velocity of the earth, then there would

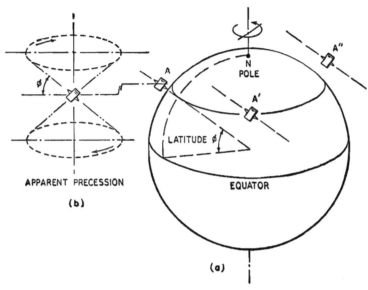

FIG. 9-4 Effect of Rotation of the Earth, Showing Apparent Gyroscopic Precession.

be no apparent precession as a result of the earth's rotation. If the missile were to fly eastward at the same speed, the apparent rate of westward precession of the upper end of the spin axis would be double that created by the earth's rotation. The E-W component of the motion of the missile, then, creates an apparent precession around a N-S horizontal axis in the plane of the meridian. The precession caused by the E-W component of the motion of the missile, in combination with the precession caused by the earth's rotation, may be countered in a vertical gyroscope by applying the proper torque and thus developing an opposing rate of precession,

[1] Martin Davidson, *The Gyroscope and Its Applications*, p. 68, Hutchinson's Scientific and Technical Publications.

as given by
$$\Omega = \omega_e \cos \phi + \omega_m \sin \lambda \qquad (9\text{-}3)^2$$

where Ω = the rate of precession
 ω_e = the angular velocity of the earth
 ω_m = the angular velocity of the missile about a diameter of the earth
 ϕ = the latitude
 λ = the missile course

The sense of the sign of the precession to correct for the motion of the missile is positive for angles of missile course from 0° to 180° and negative from 180° to 360°.

If the direction of the missile flight were due north, then the upper end of the gyroscope's spin axis will move toward the south as a result of the motion of the missile. This apparent precession is about a horizontal E-W axis. The N-S component of the missile motion, then, creates an apparent precession around an E-W horizontal axis. The apparent precession caused by the N-S component of the missile motion may be countered by applying the proper torque and thus developing a correcting rate of precession as given by

$$\Omega = \omega_m \cos \lambda \qquad (9\text{-}4)^3$$

The correcting rate of precession is around a horizontal E-W axis.

The foregoing description of the effect of the flight of the missile on the vertical gyroscope was premised upon steady-state conditions, i.e., no accelerations. The missile in flight is subjected to accelerations by reason of corrections to the trajectory, the trajectory itself, and external forces such as gusts of wind. When accelerations exist, the effective vertical is the resultant of the various accelerative forces. The pendulous mass which indicates the vertical to the gyro becomes liable to error when accelerations other than gravity exist. The accelerations imposed upon the pendulous mass may be either linear due to translation of the airframe or angular due to rotation.

If the acceleration (other than gravity) in any direction is prolonged, then the vertical gyroscope assumes an erroneous position, if no corrective action is taken. There are several possible corrective actions. For example, the existence of an acceleration can be determined by an accelerometer and the erection mechanism of the vertical gyro prevented from applying torques until the acceleration ceases. During the period of time when the acceleration persists, the vertical gyroscope is "free" and maintains its position with respect to space.

[2] Davidson, *loc. cit.*
[3] Davidson, *loc. cit.*

Effect of Coriolis Acceleration. In Par. 3-12, it was shown that, in a missile flying at constant altitude on a great circle course, any pendulous mass is subject to the Coriolis acceleration. The horizontal deviating acceleration y, as given in Eq. (3-15), is

$$y = 2\omega_e v \sin \phi$$

in which v is the horizontal velocity of the missile and the remaining notation is the same as before. The direction of the acceleration is always to the right in the Northern hemisphere and always to the left in the Southern, no matter what the direction of flight of the missile. By inspection, it will be noted that the acceleration is directly proportional to the horizontal velocity of the missile and to the sine of the latitude.

The Coriolis acceleration causes the pendulous mass to indicate other than the normal effective vertical; since the erecting mechanism is in error, the output of the vertical gyroscope will contain a similar error. The correction for the the effect of the Coriolis acceleration is made by compensating for it in the output of the gyroscope.

Response Characteristics. The requirements of the guidance system establish the criteria for the response characteristics of the erecting system of a vertical gyroscope to a step function input. Rapid response is not compatible with accuracy, i.e., the longer the integration time employed, the more accurate will be the integrated position. In a vertical gyroscope for use in a long-range missile, the time permitted for erection can be considerably longer than in a short-range missile where the erection time may be an appreciable part of the time of flight of the missile. Correspondingly, the accuracy requirements for the short-range missile gyroscope will be less stringent. The response characteristics in many vertical gyroscopes are made nonlinear. If the error exceeds some fixed amount, a large constant torque is applied to bring the gyroscope to the near vertical, after which the precession rate will depend upon the response characteristics of the erection system. The greatest step function input usually occurs as a result of launching. The gyroscope may be either caged (gimbals locked) or free during the launching phase of the flight, and when it first functions as a vertical gyroscope there may be considerable error as a result of launching accelerations.

9-4 AIRBORNE MAGNETIC COMPASSES

Because of the motions common to airborne flight and the character of the earth's magnetic field, it is necessary to provide some form of stabilization for an airborne magnetic compass. It will be recalled from Chap. 3 that in the upper latitudes the vertical component of the magnetic force is greater than the horizontal component which is used to indicate direction. Conventional airborne vehicles make coordinated turns, i.e., the aircraft banks when a turn is made. If a magnetic compass is not maintained in the horizontal plane during a banked turn, the direction indicated by the compass is the resultant of both the horizontal and vertical components of the magnetic field as related to the angle of roll of the aircraft or missile. In many instances, the magnetic compass may indicate the wrong direction of turn.

There are two types of airborne magnetic compasses in general use, the gyromagnetic compass and the gyrostabilized compass. The gyromagnetic compass consists of a gyroscope which is positioned by a magnetic compass. The gyrostabilized magnetic compass consists of a magnetic compass which is maintained in a horizontal plane by the outputs of a vertical gyroscope.

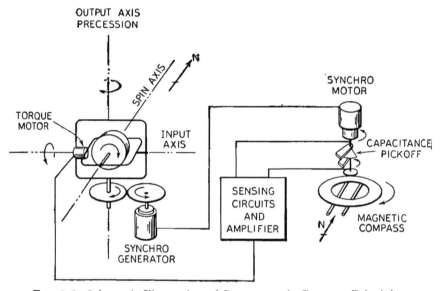

FIG. 9-5 Schematic Illustration of Gyromagnetic Compass Principles.

Figure 9-5 shows the principles of a gyromagnetic compass. There are many specific design methods employed in the manufacture of these devices; the method shown in Fig. 9-5 is for the purpose of illustration only. The function of the gyroscope in the gyromagnetic compass is to integrate the oscillations of the magnetic compass and so maintain a steady directional indication. The device illustrated consists of a magnetic compass with suitable pick-offs to sense the direction and measure the amplitude of its motion, a gyroscope, and a follow-up system to close the loop and indicate error between the gyroscope and compass positions.

Let us assume that the compass turns in the direction as indicated by the arrow. The lower plate of the capacitance pick-off, which is suitably connected to the compass, turns in relation to the upper plates, which are on the shaft of the synchronous motor of the follow-up system. The capacitance pick-off is here indicated to be a multiplate variable capacitor. The direction and amplitude of the error as indicated by the capacitor are sensed and measured, and a suitable current is impressed on the torque motor of the gyroscope. The torque causes the gyroscope to precess around its output axis and, in doing so, turns the rotor of the synchronous generator. The synchronous motor follows the motion of its generator, returning the upper plate of the capacitor to the neutral position and removing the initial error signal.

The gyrostabilized magnetic compass is one in which the magnetic compass element is stabilized by a vertical gyroscope so that it measures only the horizontal component of the earth's magnetic field. In the "flux gate" compass, which is a type of gyrostabilized magnetic compass, the directional reference is obtained from an earth induction compass. The magnetic sensitive element consists of triangularly mounted cores with primary and secondary windings. The primary windings are excited by an alternating current which saturates the cores. Induction takes place between the primary and secondary windings; the secondary windings are Y-connected and balanced so that the only voltages in the outputs of these windings are those caused by the earth's magnetic field. The output voltage of each of the secondary windings is determined by the angle at which its core is positioned with respect to the earth's magnetic field. Because of the physical arrangement of the cores, only one possible combination of voltages will exist for any given compass heading.

9-5 THE SINGLE-DEGREE-OF-FREEDOM MECHANICAL SYSTEM

A single-degree-of-freedom mechanical system is one in which its geometric position at any instant of time can be expressed by one number only. The classic example of a single-degree-of-freedom system is a mass suspended from a spring so that it is restrained in motion to move only in the direction of the axis of the spring. Figure 9-6 shows a single-degree-of-freedom system in which the mass m is suspended by a spring having a spring constant k. Between the mass and the rigid member from which it is suspended is a dashpot. The dashpot, which symbolizes the viscous friction of the system, transmits no force to the mass as long as it is at rest, but with any movement of the mass the dashpot develops a damping force proportional to the velocity in the opposite direction. The damping force may be written $c\, dx/dt$, wherein c is the *damping constant* or the *coefficient of viscous friction*.

Let an alternating force $P \sin \omega t$ act upon the mass. From Newton's second law of motion may be derived the differential equation for a single-degree-of-freedom system with the distance x, between any instantaneous position of the mass and its equilibrium position, as a function of time for the applied input. The differential equation of motion may be written as

$$m\frac{d^2x}{dt^2} + c\frac{dx}{dt} + kx = P \sin \omega t \tag{9-5}$$

Let the dashpot be removed from the linear single-degree-of-freedom system shown in Fig. 9-6. If the mass be pulled downward and released, the system continues to move about its position of equilibrium. This alternating motion represents the undamped natural frequency of the system, f_n, which may be written as

$$f_n = \frac{1}{T} = \frac{1}{2\pi}\sqrt{\frac{k}{m}} = \frac{\omega_n}{2\pi} \tag{9-6}$$

where T = the period of the natural frequency

$\omega_n = \sqrt{k/m}$ = the natural rotational frequency

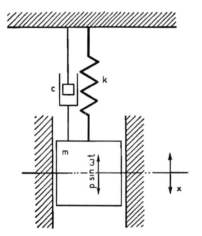

Fig. 9-6 Linear Single-Degree-of-Freedom System.

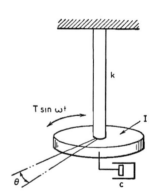

Fig. 9-7 Torsional Single-Degree-of-Freedom System.

Let the dashpot be again installed in the system and consider what occurs if the parameter of damping is varied. If the damping constant be very large, when the mass is pulled away from its position of equilibrium it will slowly creep back to that position. If, on the other hand, the damping be small, the mass will oscillate around the position of equilibrium with continually reducing amplitude. The damping which permits the most rapid asymptotic return to the position of equilibrium, without overshoot, is, under the stated system conditions, the critical damping constant, c_c. The critical damping constant may be expressed as

$$c_c = 2\sqrt{mk} = 2m\omega_n \qquad (9\text{-}7)$$

Figure 9-7 shows a rotational single-degree-of-freedom system in which k is the spring constant of the shaft in torsion, c is the damping coefficient, and I the moment of inertia of the disk to which is applied an alternating torque, $T \sin \omega t$. The differential equation of motion for the rotational single-degree-of-freedom system may be written in terms of a single dimension θ as

$$I\frac{d^2\theta}{dt^2} + c\frac{d\theta}{dt} + k\theta = T \sin \omega t \qquad (9\text{-}8)$$

In correspondence to the linear system, it may be shown that the natural circular frequency ω_n of the rotational single-degree-of-freedom system may be expressed as

$$\omega_n = \sqrt{k/I} \qquad (9\text{-}9)$$

and that the critical damping constant c_c is

$$c_c = 2\sqrt{Ik} = 2I\omega_n \qquad (9\text{-}10)$$

9-6 LINEAR ACCELEROMETERS

Accelerometers are widely used to measure both oscillatory and transient motions in guided missiles. They are used both as elements of missile guidance systems and as measuring devices to determine the shocks and vibrations of the guidance equipment environment. The fidelity with which these instruments respond both to oscillatory motion and to transient inputs is of considerable interest.

A linear accelerometer is represented in Fig. 9-8. The frame of the accelerometer is attached to the missile, and the motion of the mass m with respect to the frame is utilized to measure the component of the motion in the direction of the axis of the accelerometer. The linear accelerometer is a single-degree-of-freedom mechanical system. The motion of the missile, and therefore of the frame, with respect to space is indicated as the input x_i; the motion of the mass with respect to space is indicated as z; the motion of the mass *with respect to the frame* is the output x_o; therefore, $x_o = z - x_i$.

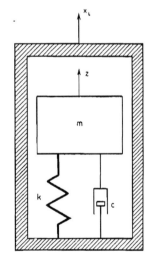

FIG. 9-8 Linear Accelerometer as Single-Degree-of-Freedom System.

From Fig. 9-8 it may be seen that the differential equation of motion

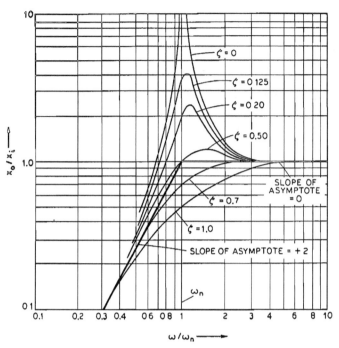

FIG. 9-9a Relationship between x_o/x_i and Frequency for Linear Accelerometer (Sketched).

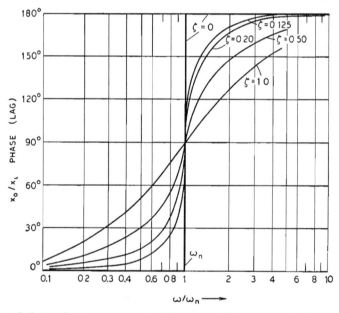

FIG. 9-9b Relationship between x_o/x_i Phase and Frequency for Linear Accelerometer (Sketched).

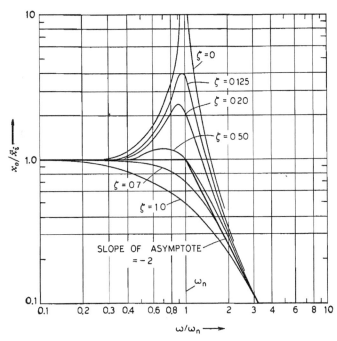

FIG. 9-9c Relationship between x_o/x_i and Frequency for Linear Accelerometer (Sketched).

for the mass m is

$$m\frac{d^2z}{dt^2} + c\left(\frac{dz}{dt} - \frac{dx_i}{dt}\right) + k(z - x_i) = 0 \qquad (9\text{-}11)$$

By substitution of the relationship between x_o, x_i, and z to eliminate z and by rearranging, Eq. (9-11) becomes

$$\frac{d^2x_o}{dt^2} + \frac{c}{m}\frac{dx_o}{dt} + \frac{k}{m}x_o = -\frac{d^2x_i}{dt^2} \qquad (9\text{-}12)$$

Let c be the damping constant of the system under consideration. The ratio between the damping constant c and the critical damping constant c_c is called the damping ratio ζ and is

$$\zeta = \frac{c}{2\sqrt{mk}} \qquad (9\text{-}13)$$

Since ω_n, the undamped natural rotational frequency, is from Eq. (9-6)

$$\omega_n = \sqrt{k/m} \qquad (9\text{-}14)$$

Eq. (9-12) becomes, after substitution,

$$\frac{d^2x_o}{dt^2} + 2\zeta\omega_n\frac{dx_o}{dt} + \omega_n^2 x_o = -\frac{d^2x_i}{dt^2} \qquad (9\text{-}15)$$

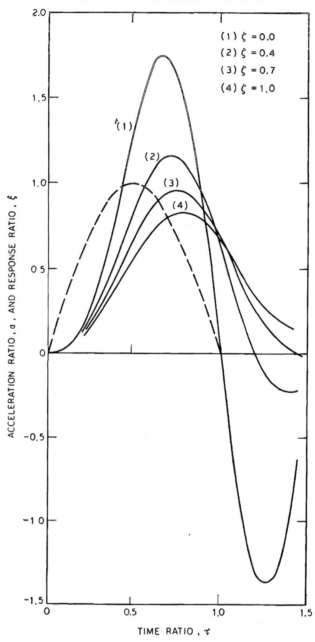

Fig. 9-10a Response to a Half Sine Wave Pulse of Acceleration of an Accelerometer Whose Natural Period Is 1.014 of the Duration of the Pulse.

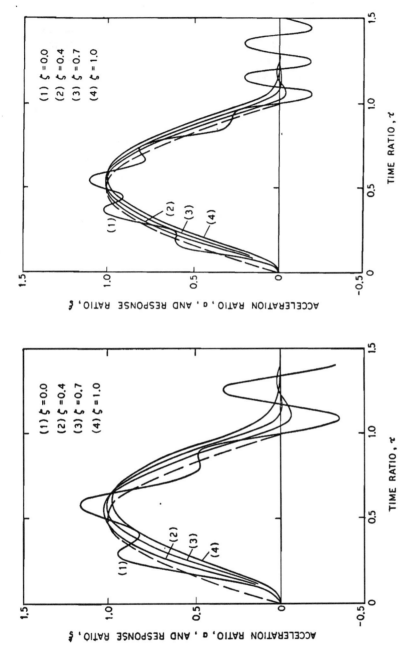

Fig. 9-10b Response to a Half Sine Wave Pulse of Acceleration of an Accelerometer Whose Natural Period Is 0.338 of the Duration of the Pulse.

Fig. 9-10c Response to a Half Sine Wave Pulse of Acceleration of an Accelerometer Whose Natural Period Is 0.203 of the Duration of the Pulse.

344   MEASUREMENTS OF MISSILE MOTION

The motion of the missile $x_i = x_i(t)$ is the input to the accelerometer; the motion of the mass with respect to the frame $x_o = x_o(t)$ is the output of the instrument. By stating Eq. (9-15) in operational form, the transfer characteristic of the system becomes

$$\frac{\text{Output}}{\text{Input}} = \frac{x_o}{x_i}(s) = -\frac{s^2}{s^2 + 2\zeta\omega_n s + \omega_n^2} \qquad (9\text{-}16)$$

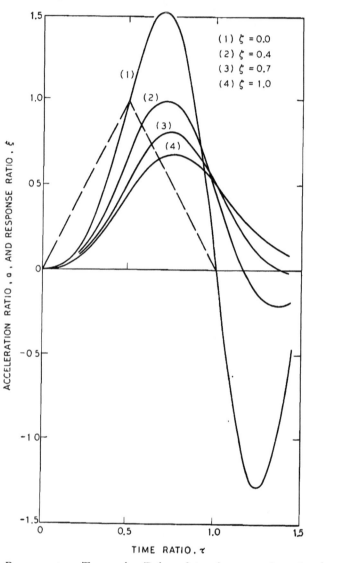

Fig. 9-11a Response to a Triangular Pulse of Acceleration of an Accelerometer Whose Natural Period Is 1.014 of the Duration of the Pulse.

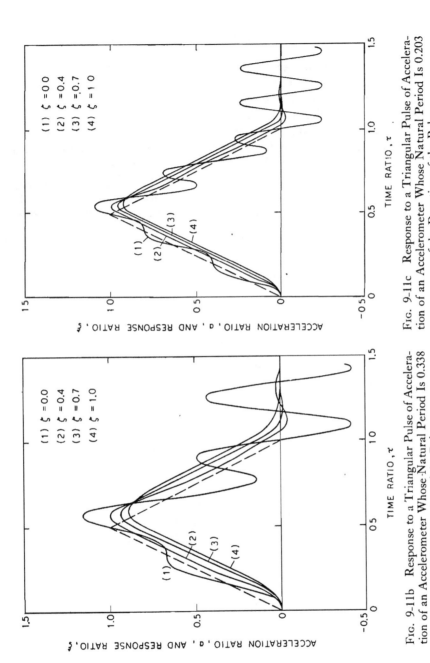

FIG. 9-11b Response to a Triangular Pulse of Acceleration of an Accelerometer Whose Natural Period Is 0.338 of the Duration of the Pulse.

FIG. 9-11c Response to a Triangular Pulse of Acceleration of an Accelerometer Whose Natural Period Is 0.203 of the Duration of the Pulse.

For steady-state conditions, $s = j\omega$, wherein ω is the steady-state frequency being employed.

In a particular system, let the spring constant k and the mass be held constant. Figure 9-9 shows in sketch form the generalized frequency response of a linear accelerometer for several damping ratios. It will be observed that below the natural frequency the output response of a linear accelerometer to a steady-state oscillation falls off with decreasing frequency and the curves become asymptotic to a $+2$ slope on the log-log plot. For frequencies above the natural resonant frequency of the accelerometer the curves become asymptotic to a 0 slope. The corresponding phase of the output with respect to the input signal is shown in Fig. 9-9b.

It is important to remember that the pick-offs employed in an acceler-

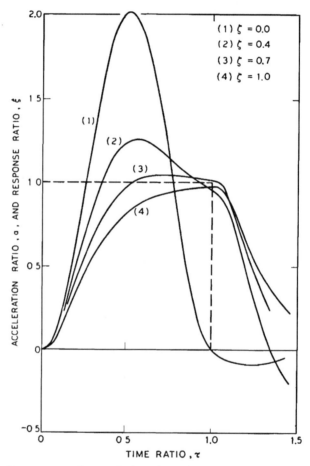

Fig. 9-12a Response to a Square Pulse of Acceleration of an Accelerometer Whose Natural Period Is 1.014 of the Duration of the Pulse.

ometer measure the positional *differences* between the frame of the accelerometer and the mass employed in it. Because of this, as indicated in Fig. 9-9a, the accelerometer is a poor device to measure steady-state oscillations at frequencies which are low with respect to the natural frequency of the accelerometer. In such instances the mass follows the input motion faithfully and the output signals indicating the difference between the frame and mass motions may fall below system noise.

The motion of the output may be related to an input acceleration as

$$\frac{x_o}{x_i}(s) = -\frac{1}{s^2 + 2\zeta\omega_n s + \omega_n^2} \qquad (9\text{-}16a)$$

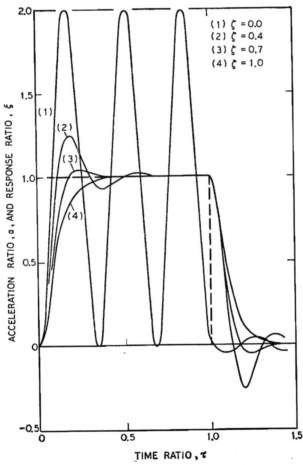

FIG. 9-12b Response to a Square Pulse of Acceleration of an Accelerometer Whose Natural Period Is 0.334 of the Duration of the Pulse.

The corresponding frequency response of the output related to input motions is shown in Fig. 9-9c for several damping ratios.

The response of accelerometers to three different types of transient inputs has been computed by Levy and Kroll.[4] The three types of transient inputs were: (a) half sine wave pulse, (b) triangular pulse, and (c)

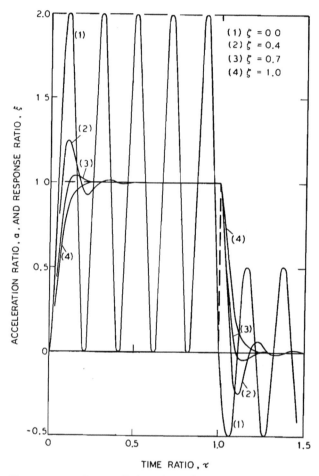

FIG. 9-12c Response to a Square Pulse of Acceleration of an Accelerometer Whose Natural Period Is 0.203 of the Duration of the Pulse.

---

[4] "Response of Accelerometers to Transient Accelerations," by Samuel Levy and Wilhelmina D. Kroll, *Journal of Research of the National Bureau of Standards*, Vol. 45, No. 4, October 1950. *Research Paper 2138*. Figures 9-10, 9-11, and 9-12 are from this paper.

square pulse. Figures 9-10, 9-11, and 9-12 show the results of this numerical integration. For each type of transient input, three relationships between the natural period of the accelerometers and the duration of the pulse were explored: (1) the natural period about equal to the duration of the pulse, (2) the natural period about equal to one-third the duration of the pulse, and (3) the natural period about equal to one-fifth the duration of the pulse. Four values of damping ratio were employed in developing the curves for each of the cases, $\zeta = 0, 0.4, 0.7,$ and 1.0. To give the analysis a wider range of usefulness, the ordinates of the curves are in the following dimensionless form:

$$\left.\begin{array}{c} a = \left(\dfrac{d^2x_i}{dt^2}\right) \bigg/ \left(\dfrac{d^2x_i}{dt^2}\right)_{\max} \\ \xi = -kx/m\left(\dfrac{d^2x_i}{dt^2}\right)_{\max} \\ \tau = t/T_p \end{array}\right\} \quad (9\text{-}17)$$

in which T_p = duration of the acceleration pulse to be measured
τ = ratio of time to pulse duration
a = dimensionless acceleration
ξ = dimensionless response

and all other notation is as before.

It is evident from an inspection of the figures that for none of the accelerometers considered does the time history of the dimensionless response ξ coincide with the time history of the dimensionless acceleration a. In many cases the coincidence can be markedly improved by considering the response curves to be shifted a small distance to the left. On the basis of the few cases illustrated, an optimum value of damping is indicated to be between 0.4 and 0.7 of the critical value. It is also indicated that, to obtain an accuracy better than 5 percent of the peak acceleration in measuring acceleration pulses having the general characteristics of the triangular or sinusoidal pulses, an accelerometer must have a natural period of less than one third the duration of the acceleration pulse.

9-7 ANGULAR ACCELEROMETERS

The angular accelerometer is essentially a rotational single-degree-of-freedom mechanical system such as was illustrated in Fig. 9-7. It is employed to measure oscillations and transients in rotation about its input axis. As in the case of the linear accelerometer it may readily by demonstrated that the differential equation, when θ_i is the angular input and θ_o the angular output, is

$$\frac{d^2\theta_o}{dt^2} + \frac{c}{I}\frac{d\theta_o}{dt} + \frac{k\theta_o}{I} = \frac{-d^2\theta_i}{dt^2} \quad (9\text{-}18)$$

the damping ratio ζ is

$$\zeta = \frac{c}{2\sqrt{Ik}} \qquad (9\text{-}19)$$

Substituting Eq. (9-9) and (9-19) into Eq. (9-18) and rearranging gives

$$\frac{d^2\theta_o}{dt^2} + 2\zeta\omega_n \frac{d\theta}{dt} + \omega_n^2\theta = -\frac{d^2\theta_i}{dt^2} \qquad (9\text{-}20)$$

By stating Eq. (9-20) in operational form, the transfer characteristic of the system becomes

$$\frac{\text{Output}}{\text{Input}} = \frac{\theta_o}{\theta_i}(s) = -\frac{s^2}{s^2 + 2\zeta\omega_{ns} + \omega_n^2} \qquad (9\text{-}21)$$

which is identical to the linear case.

9-8 RATE GYROSCOPES

Rate gyroscopes, because of their small size and versatility, are probably the most commonly used instrument for measuring motion and accomplishing computation involving rates in the gunfire and missile control fields. It is therefore important to know their frequency response characteristics and the bandwidth limits over which their output is proportional to the rate of change of the input signal. The frequency response characteristic and the sensitivity are the important elements in the proper selection of rate gyroscopes for the purposes intended.

The function of the rate gyroscope is to give an output signal proportional to the velocity of the rotation of the device about its input axis.

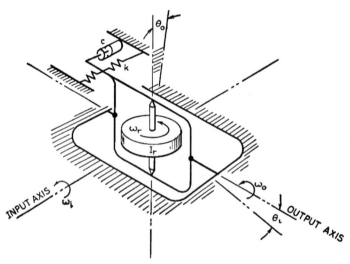

Fig. 9-13 Simplified Diagram of Rate Gyroscope Operation.

As long as the motion of the output axis is limited by the design of the instrument, the rate gyroscope is essentially a single-degree-of-freedom mechanical system. Figure 9-13 is a simplified diagram of a rate gyroscope. The differential equation describing the performance of the rate gyroscope, omitting considerations of secondary axis inputs, is

$$I_g \frac{d^2\theta_o}{dt^2} + c\frac{d\theta_o}{dt} + k\theta_o = H\omega_i \cos\theta_o - I_g \frac{d\omega_{oA}}{dt} + M_c + M_i + M_u \quad (9\text{-}22)$$

where θ_o = gimbal angular displacement about output axis with respect to the gyro case
θ_i = input angular displacement about input axis
I_g = moment of inertia of the gimbal assembly about the output (gimbal) axis
c = viscous damping constant
k = spring constant
ω_i = angular velocity about the input axis
ω_{oA} = angular velocity about output axis
H = angular momentum of rotor
M_c = correction torque applied to output shaft as from unbalanced weights
M_i = torque on output shaft caused by indicating system
M_u = torque on output shaft caused by uncertainties, nonviscous and coulomb friction, etc.

The following simplifications and assumptions may be made:

a. Let $\cos\theta_o = 1$. The maximum motion of the output axis of a high performance rate gyroscope is on the order of 2 deg, in order to minimize cross coupling errors: in this case, the $\cos\theta_o = 0.9994$.
b. $M_c = M_i = M_u = 0$. In a well-designed rate gyroscope these torques will presumably be small enough that they may be neglected, at least for the purpose of this analysis.
c. The motion ω_{oA} is unimportant and may be neglected.

By introducing the simplifications and assumptions, Eq. (9-22) now becomes

$$\frac{d^2\theta_o}{dt^2} + \frac{c}{I_g}\frac{d\theta_o}{dt} + \frac{k}{I_g}\theta_o = \frac{H}{I_g}\omega_i \quad (9\text{-}23)$$

The undamped resonant frequency of the rate gyroscope may be readily shown to be

$$\omega_n = \sqrt{k/I_g} \quad (9\text{-}24)$$

The damping ratio ζ is

$$\zeta = \frac{c}{2\sqrt{kI_g}} \quad (9\text{-}25)$$

Substituting Eq. (9-24) and (9-25) into Eq. (9-23), we have

$$\frac{d^2\theta_o}{dt^2} + 2\zeta\omega_n \frac{d\theta_o}{dt} + \omega_n^2 \theta_o = \frac{H}{I_g}\frac{d\theta_i}{dt} \qquad (9\text{-}26)$$

The transfer characteristic of the rate gyroscope, on the basis of the assumptions and simplifications, is

$$\frac{\theta_o}{\theta_i}(s) = \frac{sH/I_g}{s^2 + 2\zeta\omega_n s + \omega_n^2} \qquad (9\text{-}27)$$

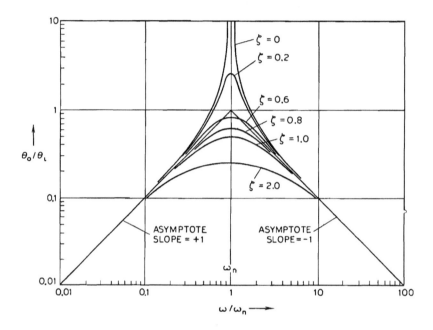

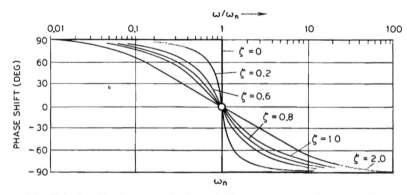

FIG. 9-14 Relationship between θ_o/θ_i and Frequency and between Phase and Frequency for a Rate Gyroscope.

Figure 9-14a shows the relation between the gain θ_o/θ_i, and the frequency, normalized to the undamped natural resonant frequency of the gyroscope system for steady-state conditions. It will be observed that the slopes of asymptotes of the system transfer characteristics on a log-log plot are $+1$ below the natural resonant frequency and -1 for frequencies above it. The corresponding phase of the output with respect to the input is shown in Fig. 9-14b.

9-9 USE OF MOTION-MEASURING DEVICES

The two general applications of motion-measuring devices such as described in this chapter are: (1) as components of autopilots which stabilize missile flight and (2) as instruments for the measurement of missile motions, shocks, and vibrations in the various phases of missile flight.

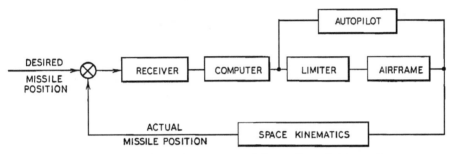

FIG. 9-15 Simplified Block Diagram of Generalized Guidance System.

The function of the guided missile autopilot is to translate the input command accelerations from the guidance system into output missile accelerations by means of control surface deflections. Figure 9-15 illustrates a simplified block diagram of a generalized missile guidance system, including the autopilot. If an error exists between the actual position of the missile and the desired position of the missile as established by the guidance system, the receiver in the missile receives an input command for a correcting acceleration. (Although the term "command" is used, the received signal could be the result of an error in beam riding, or homing, etc.) The output of the receiver is applied to a computer which translates the error information to the correct missile command. In turn, this information is transmitted to a limiting device, the character of which is dependent upon the aerodynamics of the missile. The purpose of the limiting device is twofold: (1) to prevent the applications of accelerations to the missile beyond its structural ability, and (2) to prevent the missile from assuming angles of attack (the angle between the longitudinal axis of the missile and the vector of flight motion) that will cause the missile to become unstable. The limiting device is usually also a measuring device; there are many types of instruments which may be used.

A brief explanation will make clear why limiting is usually necessary. At low altitude, a given command will cause the missile to turn with a given acceleration. The magnitude of acceleration that the missile can stand is determined by its structural qualities, i.e., its ability to stay in one piece despite the aerodynamic loading. The error signal input from the guidance system may be considerable, particularly as a result of large transients at launching. If the full error signal were applied, the acceleration demanded at low altitude might destroy the missile. As the altitude increases, however, the equivalent response of the missile to a control surface deflection is greatly reduced because of the less dense air. If the

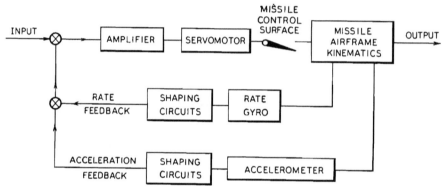

Fig. 9-16 Simplified Block Diagram of Autopilot.

missile responds to too great an acceleration demand at higher altitudes, the angle of attack increases to the point where the missile may become unstable and control is lost completely. The response to input commands at high altitudes, then, must be limited by the stability criteria of the missile.

The problem may be solved in many ways. The angle of attack may be measured by pitot tubes or by vanes on the missile and appropriate devices employed to limit the signal to the autopilot. The density of the air mass through which the missile is moving and the velocity of the missile may both be measured and the information employed to act as a gain monitoring device on the input to the autopilot. These devices also fall into the category of instruments which measure missile motion, but there are so many possible types that a detailed review of them is not possible in this text.

Figure 9-16 illustrates a simplified block diagram of a generalized autopilot system for a missile. This diagram is included to indicate the use of rate gyroscopes and accelerometers in the feedback paths of the autopilot system. The use and the method of use of these devices will depend upon the transfer characteristics of the missile airframe.

Accelerometers are employed in missiles undergoing aerodynamic tests to measure the accelerations, oscillations, and similar vibratory phenomena of the missiles in flight. The result of such measurements is used in establishing the environmental tests which must be imposed upon the guidance and other missile-borne equipment. The vibratory modes of the missile are of particular importance in selecting the proper location of motion-measuring gyroscopes. A thorough examination of the motions of the missile structure under aerodynamic loading in conditions of flight must be made to be sure that no effects are created by compliance (aerolastic bending) of the airframe structure that can lead to instability of the guidance system. In a homing missile, for example, if there is compliance in the structure between the homing head and a gyroscope which measures the missile motion, a positive feedback may result and so create an unstable control system.

BIBLIOGRAPHY

1. J. P. Den Hartog, *Mechanical Vibrations*, McGraw-Hill Book Co., Inc., New York, 1947.
2. E. S. Ferry, *Applied Gyrodynamics*, John Wiley & Sons, Inc., New York, 1932.
3. M. Davidson, Ed., *The Gyroscope and Its Applications*, Hutchinson's Scientific and Technical Publications, London.
4. S. Levy and W. D. Kroll, "Response of Accelerometers to Transient Accelerations," *Journal of Research of the National Bureau of Standards*, Vol. 45, No. 4, October 1950, Research Paper 2138.

CHAPTER 10

DETECTION AND INFORMATION GATHERING

Symbols Used in Chapter 10

a = signal amplitude	Δt = an increment of time
A = area	T = absolute temperature
B = bandwidth, cps	T_p = pulse repetition period
c = velocity of propagation of electromagnetic waves	v = linear velocity
	V = electric potential difference
C = capacitance, farads	w = noise power per cycle of bandwidth
d = linear distance	
E, e_1 = electric potential difference	X = linear distance
f = frequency, cps	y = probable error
Δf = an increment of f	Y = a particular value of ω
$f(t)$ = function of time	Z = impedance
F = noise figure	
g = modulation gain	
g_m = grid-to-plate transconductance	α = complex transmission factor
	β = feedback transfer characteristic
G = gain	Γ = antenna pattern propagation factor
$G(t)$ = function of time	
h = height above surface	δ = an increment of time
i = current	Δ = pulse width
$j = \sqrt{-1}$	ϵ = 2.71828
K = a constant	θ = geometric angle
L = inductance henrys	λ = wavelength
m = modulation index	μ = transfer characteristic
n = order of harmonic	ξ = electric field magnitude
N = noise power, watts	Σ = probable error
p = precision factor	τ = propagation time
P = probable distance	ϕ = electrical phase angle
$\mathcal{Q}$ = loran position line	ψ = geometric angle
S = power, watts	ω = angular frequency, radians per sec
t = time	

An important portion of the guided missile system is that dealing with the interchange of intelligence between the launching or guiding station, the missile, and the target. Since the missile must travel through some distance to locate within a killing distance of its target, some sort of information must be propagated through this space to enable the missile to fulfill its mission. Alternatively the missile must use some field already existing in space, such as the earth's magnetic field, to arrive at its potentially killing position. The mechanics of this latter alternative are described elsewhere in this book. It is with those systems which propagate and use radio frequency electromagnetic energy with which we shall be principally concerned in this chapter.

Many excellent works have been written concerning the intimate details of parts of guidance systems. There are, for example, hundreds of references on the subject of multivibrators. Such electronic devices are frequently used in guidance systems. Any detailed treatment in this chapter of topics fully discussed in available design literature would be unnecessarily repetitious. Rather, the task of this chapter is to reacquaint the reader with already known basic facts, but in a way that will display more clearly their utility in missile guidance.

10-1 TYPICAL COMMUNICATIONS SYSTEMS

Intelligence is transmitted via radio through space as a traveler or modulation upon what radio engineers call a "carrier." The interesting nature of the carrier is its ability to transmit information. In some guidance systems, such as radar homing, for example, the existence of the carrier is sufficient for the successful guidance of a missile to a target. There may be in such a system, however, a "hidden" modulation of the carrier to overcome some physical limitations of the detecting device such as its inability to determine the angle of arrival of the carrier with sufficient accuracy. For instance, conical scanning or lobing may be employed to modulate the carrier in a radio detection system in order to improve the accuracy of determining the angle of arrival.

The carrier wave, depending on the type and its frequency, can be modulated either in amplitude or frequency by a number of mechanisms. As a result of the modulation process, whether amplitude or frequency modulation is employed, modulation sidebands are produced which actually contain the important intelligence. The aim of the guidance designer is to treat the carrier and its sidebands in such a way as to retain all essential information but to reject as much other information (noise) as possible.

10-2 MODES OF INTELLIGENCE TRANSMISSION

All of the common modes of intelligence transmission utilizing a carrier and sidebands can be basically expressed as variations of either carrier amplitude or carrier frequency.* Although no attempt will be made to

---

* Pulse-time and pulse-width modulation can, for instance, be expressed as forms of frequency modulation.

exhaust the possibilities in this discussion, three fundamental systems of amplitude modulation and two of frequency modulation are in common use and there are several combinations of both used. Where the systems operate in combination they may be used separately to transmit or receive two or more channels of information or they may be used in an interrelated fashion where one modulation becomes a carrier for a new modulation. The latter system is usually referred to as a "subcarrier" system.

10-3 AMPLITUDE MODULATION—CARRIER AND TWO SIDEBANDS

The classic example of modulation system is one wherein a carrier sine wave is amplitude-modulated by a signal sine wave. This combination produces, at the detector of a receiver having sufficient bandwidth, three discrete frequencies: one at the carrier frequency, and an upper and a lower sideband which are displaced from the carrier by the signal frequency and which contain all of the information the original modulating signal contained. The carrier has no value except that it is generally necessary in the detection process, for, in the usual detector, the carrier and at least one sideband must combine in a nonlinear device to cause the carrier wave to be demodulated. In the usual envelope detector for amplitude modulation, the carrier, once used, is discarded in a filter and the information contained in the sidebands is retained. Since the carrier is not necessary except at the terminal end of the communication circuit, it is frequently discarded at the transmitter. This leads to the consideration of another mode of transmission.

10-4 AMPLITUDE MODULATION—SUPPRESSED CARRIER, TWO SIDEBANDS

The designer could, in the foregoing example, choose not to utilize the carrier; thus the power required for its generation would be reduced. He must, however, resupply the carrier at the detector end of the circuit to allow the detection process to take place. In order to regain the intelligence contained in the sidebands he must supply to the detector a local carrier which is an accurate reproduction of the original suppressed carrier in waveform, frequency, and phase. If he does not, he distorts the demodulated information. A good example of this system is a selsyn circuit containing a generator and a motor. If the rotor of the generator selsyn is mechanically rotated in an oscillatory manner, a double sideband suppressed carrier signal is sent to the motor on the stator leads. An accurate reproduction of the carrier in waveform, phase, and frequency must be sent to the rotor terminals of the motor if the motor's rotor shaft is to reproduce the input oscillation accurately. This is usually accomplished by connecting the rotor terminals of both the motor and the generator to

10-5 AMPLITUDE MODULATION—SINGLE SIDEBAND, SUPPRESSED CARRIER

In actuality, each sideband of either of the previous systems contains all of the information it is possible to transmit. It is therefore proper to consider conservation of even greater power and bandwidth by the transmission of only one sideband. If this is done, the bandwidth required to

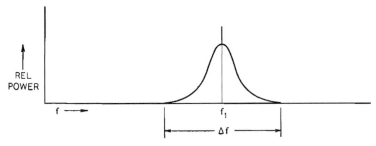

Fig. 10-1 Spectrum of Signal To Be Modulated on Carrier.

transmit the spectrum of information is reduced by a factor somewhat greater than two.

This important fact is displayed in Fig. 10-1 and 10-2. Suppose a signal centered at a frequency of f_1 and having a width of Δf is modulated upon a carrier having a frequency, f_2. Figure 10-1 shows the spectrum of the signal and Fig. 10-2 the spectrum of the modulated carrier. It is clear

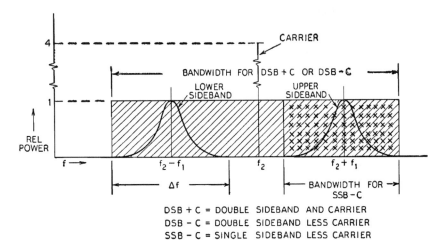

Fig. 10-2 Spectrum of Modulated Carrier.

that the band width required for the faithful transmission of single-sideband, suppressed-carrier information is somewhat less than half of that required for either double-sideband, with-carrier or double-sideband, without-carrier information. Here the guidance designer has an opportunity to separate his information from noise. As it will be seen later, noise from various sources is present with the signal. This noise power, N, can be expressed as a product of the noise power per cycle per second of bandwidth, w, times the bandwidth, B, in cycles per second thus:

$$N = wB \qquad (10\text{-}1)$$

The noise power varies directly with the bandwidth. In the case of single-sideband, suppressed-carrier and double-sideband, suppressed-carrier, all of the available power capacity of the system can be used to generate or transmit sidebands. For single-sideband, suppressed-carrier, the signal power is S. For double-sideband, suppressed-carrier, the signal power in each sideband is $S/2$.

For a 100-percent-modulated, double-sideband, with-carrier system of the same power capacity, the signal power in each sideband is $S/6$, the power in the carrier being $S/1.5$. A résumé of the competitive situation between these systems regarding bandwidth and ultimate signal-to-noise ratios is given in Table 10-1. The single-sideband, suppressed-carrier

TABLE 10-1 COMPARISON OF AMPLITUDE-MODULATED COMMUNICATION SYSTEMS

System	Sideband Power	Carrier Power	Transmission Bandwidth	Power S/N Ratio
Double-sideband, with carrier	$S/3$	$S/1.5$	$\geq 2B$	$\leq 1/6$
Double-sideband, suppressed-carrier	S	0	$\geq 2B$	≤ 1
Single-sideband, suppressed-carrier	S	0	B	1

system has obvious advantages in regard to utilization of bandwidth and system power capability. The state of the art, however, sometimes limits the design from a practical standpoint.

10-6 FREQUENCY MODULATION

Although the applications of amplitude modulation are more or less obvious in the missile guidance field, particularly in pulsed radar or loran, the applications of frequency modulation may be more obscure. Some of the uses of frequency modulation are in the detection of moving targets by the use of the Doppler principle as applied to radar, and in the telemetering systems used to analyze missile performance in the test phases. Again, the literature is rather complete in its theoretical approach to frequency modulation. However, some basic review may be in order.

Frequency modulation as a radio term refers to the modulation of the frequency of a carrier wave. Although it is usual to discuss frequency modulation and phase modulation together, they are distinctly individual, but related. This general type of modulation is referred to by various authors as frequency modulation, phase modulation, angle modulation, time modulation, or by other similar names.

In the case of amplitude modulation it was shown, indirectly, that the spectrum of the modulated wave was dependent upon the frequency of the modulating signal. For frequency or phase modulation this is no longer entirely the case. The spectrum width can be shown to be proportional to the modulating signal frequency spectrum *and amplitude*. These latter two quantities are further related by a quantity called the "modulation index."

$$\text{Modulation index} = \frac{\text{Carrier frequency deviation}}{\text{Modulating frequency}} \quad (10\text{-}2)$$

The frequency of the carrier wave is modulated at a rate proportional to the modulating signal frequency; the maximum excursions of frequency of the carrier being proportional to the modulating signal amplitude. The usable spectrum width B_u of the modulated wave is given as [1]

$$B_u = k_0 \Delta f_0 + k_1 f_1 \quad (10\text{-}3)$$

where Δf_0 = increment of unmodulated carrier frequency
f_1 = modulating signal frequency
k_0 and k_1 are constants

Equation (10-2) substituted into Eq. (10-3) gives

$$\begin{aligned} B_u &= k_0 m f_1 + k_1 f_1 \\ &= f_1 (k_0 m + k_1) \end{aligned} \quad (10\text{-}4)$$

where m = modulation index.

The values of k_0 and k_1 depend upon how many terms of a series expansion are used to resolve the large actual bandwidth into a usable finite bandwidth, the criterion being the tolerable distortion. For instance, in high-quality FM broadcasting where the tolerable distortion is, say, one percent, the necessary bandwidth is given in terms of Eq. (10-3) as

$$B_u = 2\Delta f_0 + 8 f_1 \quad (10\text{-}5)$$

Starr has shown that signal-to-noise ratio, $(S/N)_{\text{FM}}$, of an FM system is related to that of a single-sideband system in the following manner:

---

[1] Starr, *Radio and Radar Technique*, Pitman Press, 1953.

$$(S/N)_{\text{FM}} = \tfrac{3}{8}(B_{\text{FM}}/B)^2 (S/N)_{\text{SSB}} \qquad (10\text{-}6)$$

where B_{FM} = the bandwidth of the FM signal
B = bandwidth of the single-sideband signal

It can be seen from this relationship that, for $B_{\text{FM}}/B \geq \sqrt{8/3}$, the wideband FM system is potentially more noise-free than the best AM system, namely, single-sideband.

A similar equation is derived by Starr for phase modulation, PM.

$$(S/N)_{\text{PM}} = \tfrac{1}{8}(B_{\text{PM}}/B)^2 (S/N)_{\text{SSB}} \qquad (10\text{-}7)$$

The use of PM is obviously not so fruitful in improving signal-to-noise ratio as the use of FM.

The use of FM in the guidance and control systems of missiles can take a number of forms, most of which will reduce to two basic ones: (a) a system can be intentionally frequency modulated or (b) some use can be made of a natural frequency modulation. An example of form (a) is the standard FM altimeter (for which see Par. 10-18) which could have obvious use in the control of the altitude of a missile. An example of form (b) is the Doppler principle sometimes used in radar systems to detect only targets which move. Further examples of FM systems will be developed later.

10-7 SUBCARRIERS

An extension of the earlier discussion of either amplitude-modulated or frequency-modulated systems is the use of one modulating signal as

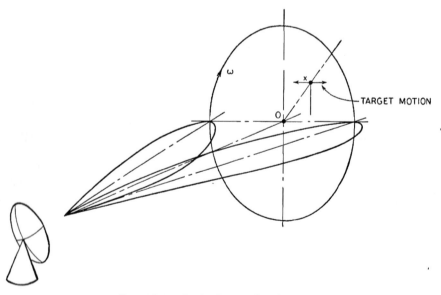

Fig. 10-3 Conical Scanning Radar.

the carrier wave for another signal. An example of such a system is that of a fire control radar. In such a radar equipment a radio frequency carrier at, say, 3000 mcs per sec is amplitude-modulated by a series of short pulses. This modulated carrier is emitted by an antenna system and reflected from a target. However, the phase* of the reflected pulses after detection at the radar will have been modulated by the range to the target. Stated another way, the pulse wave has become the carrier for the range phase-modulating signal.

The center line of the antenna beam of a scanning-type fire control radar is made to describe a cone in space by rotation of the antenna feed system at some angular velocity, ω. Reference to Fig. 10-3 may be of

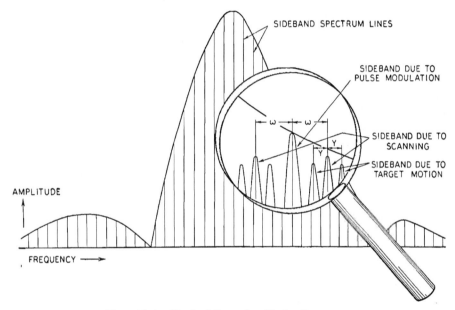

Fig. 10-4 Conical Scanning Radar Spectrum.

some help in visualizing this action. If a target is located at point O in the center of the circle described by the center line of the beam, the received radar signal will consist of a radio frequency carrier whose amplitude is pulse-modulated.

If the target has moved to a position X not in the center of the circle of Fig. 10-3, the received signal at the radar will consist of a radio frequency carrier amplitude-modulated by the reflected pulses which in turn are amplitude-modulated by the angular scan frequency, ω. The amount of amplitude modulation is proportional to the distance, OX, from beam center, and the phase of ω is proportional to the angular direction of OX

---

* Phase is defined as relative time position with respect to a reference.

referred to some reference line. If the target could be made to vary its position about point X in a sinusoidal fashion, at an angular frequency Y, the scanning wave of frequency ω would become the carrier for a modulating signal proportional to the amplitude of the sinusoid about point X. The phase modulation of the carrier ω indicates the direction of target motion.

The spectrum of the signal received by the radar set under these conditions is shown in Fig. 10-4. The radar set, then, is a system utilizing numerous subcarriers. The gathering of information about target motion has been the purpose of the construction of the set. It is important that the radar designer process the various subcarriers through the set in such a manner as to preserve the important target motion information.

10-8 THE NATURE OF GUIDANCE INTELLIGENCE

The very existence of a target implies that information is available either directly or indirectly about its location in some field such as electromagnetic or sound. The missile must obtain this information directly or indirectly through some intermediary such as its launching station. The guidance designer, to generate a successful system, must have a quantitative knowledge of the available information and of the tactical situation. Someone must set down a clear statement of the objective of the missile system and define the limits of operation.

Given the objective, the designer can investigate the modes of variation of the information available from the target and the information required by the missile for various means of guidance. Also, the objective being given, some guidance systems will not be suitable. For instance, the designer would not want to attack a target near the land masses of mountainous islands with a system using inertial navigation, because of the error in the determination of the direction of the center of the earth. A more inclusive discussion of selection of guidance method appears in Chap. 8 of this book. Once the general form of the guidance system has been determined, it is possible to investigate some basic facts which, in the processing of the information, are important to the outcome. It is at this stage of development that information bandwidths are determined.

10-9 SPECTRUM OF THE PRIMARY CARRIER

The radio frequency spectra of interest here are the medium frequency (300 kc to 3000 kc), the high frequency (3000 kc to 30,000 kc), the very high frequency (30 mc to 300 mc), the ultra high frequency (300 mc to 3000 mc), and the super high frequency (3000 mc to 30,000 mc). The transmission characteristics of space for these spectra are discussed in Chap. 4. For missile guidance purposes the use of medium, high and very high frequency spectra is principally confined to loran and other forms of hyperbolic navigation systems. Radar systems for guidance use mostly the ultra and super high frequency spectra. The selection of a frequency depends on factors such as size, weight, and component availability. It is well to avoid absorption bands of water vapor and molecular oxygen, as shown in Chap. 4. It is probable that, in many cases, compatibility with other system components may entirely determine the frequency selection.

10-10 LORAN [2]

Loran is a radio navigation system which makes use of pulse techniques. It provides a means for determining position as well as a means for establishing a course toward a given point or along a particular path. Position determination is accomplished by locating the point in question as the intersection of two imaginary lines on the earth's surface. Each line is determined by measuring the difference in distances to each of two transmitting stations. On a plane surface, the locus of a point moving so that the difference in distances to two selected points is constant defines a hyperbola. Thus loran is referred to as a hyperbolic navigation system. Since the earth is an oblate spheroid, these lines are not exactly hyperbolic, but the distortion thus introduced is allowed for in preparing loran charts covering large areas.

10-11 BASIC CONCEPTS IN LORAN

The speed of propagation of radio waves in air is about 0.162 nautical mile per microsec, or one nautical mile in about 6 microsec. A pulse of radio frequency energy emitted by a transmitter travels outward in all directions at this speed. Thus, if this pulse is received simultaneously at two points, these points necessarily lie on a circle at whose center is the transmitter. If two stations transmit pulses coincidentally and these pulses are received simultaneously at a given point, that point is equidistant from the two stations. If there is a time difference between the arrival of the two signals, the receiving point is closer to one than to the other by a matter of 0.162 nautical mile for each microsecond of time difference. Figure 10-5 illustrates the fact that time differences are measures of distance differences, and that the lines of constant difference define a family of hyperbolas. In loran navigation the time difference between signals from two pairs of stations whose lines of position cross is measured, thereby establishing a fix. Actually, the two transmitters of a loran pair are not keyed simultaneously, but alternately.

One station, called the "master," transmits the first pulse, which is received at the second, or "slave" station, and is used as a reference for synchronizing the slave transmissions. Since the timing circuits are free

---

[2] Pierce, McKenzie, and Woodward, *Loran*, McGraw-Hill Book Co., Inc., New York, 1950.

running under crystal control, either an operator or automatic equipment is required initially to establish and maintain exact synchronization.

In Fig. 10-6, if the distances from the master and slave stations are d_m and d_s respectively, the baseline distance or separation of the two stations is such that the transmission time between stations is τ, and if the slave pulse is emitted a time δ after reception of the master pulse, then the time difference observed is given by

$$\Delta t = \tau + \delta + d_s/c - d_m/c \qquad (10\text{-}8)$$

where c is the propagation velocity. If the observer is located on the baseline at zero distance from the master,

$$\Delta t = \tau + \delta + \tau - 0 \qquad (10\text{-}9)$$

Similarly if he is located at the slave station,

$$\Delta t = \tau + \delta + 0 - \tau \qquad (10\text{-}10)$$

The maximum possible variation of Δt is thus $+\tau$ to $-\tau$ and the absolute values of Δt lie between the limits $\tau + \delta \pm \tau$. In order to insure that the first signal received at any point will be the master, it is only necessary that δ be made greater than zero.

The method of measuring time differences in the loran system dictates that the delay between reception of the master pulse at the slave station and the transmission of the slave pulse be greater than δ by an increment

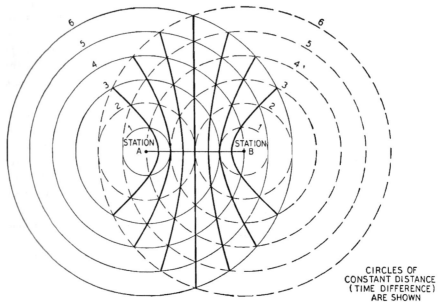

Fig. 10-5 Plane Hyperbola Generation.

$T_p/2$, where T_p is the pulse repetition period. Since loran repetition rates are approximately 25 or approximately $33\frac{1}{3}$ pulses per sec, $T_p/2$ is about 20,000 or 15,000 microsec. This additional delay causes the reception of the slave pulse to follow reception of the master pulse by more than half the repetition period.

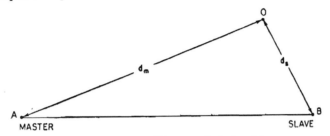

FIG. 10-6 Loran Distance Relationships.

In the terminal equipment the quantity $T_p/2$ is ignored. The quantity obtained is the so called "indicated" rather than the true time difference. Loran charts are labeled in the former values and true time differences are not used in practice. Since the equipment ignores the $T_p/2$ delay, Eq. (10-8), (10-9), and (10-10) and the deductions made from them are valid if we define Δt as indicated rather than true time difference.

10-12 IDENTIFICATION OF LORAN PAIRS

In order to conserve space in the radio frequency spectrum and to permit faster operation of the measuring equipment each chain of adjacent

TABLE 10-2 PULSE REPETITION RATES

Channel Designation	Approximate Pulses/sec	Repetition Period μ sec
L0	25	40,000
L1	$25\frac{1}{16}$	39,900
L2	$25\frac{2}{16}$	39,800
L3	$25\frac{3}{16}$	39,700
L4	$25\frac{4}{16}$	39,600
L5	$25\frac{5}{16}$	39,500
L6	$25\frac{6}{16}$	39,400
L7	$25\frac{7}{16}$	39,300
H0	$33\frac{3}{8}$	30,000
H1	$33\frac{4}{8}$	29,900
H2	$33\frac{5}{8}$	29,800
H3	$33\frac{6}{8}$	29,700
H4	$33\frac{7}{8}$	29,600
H5	$33\frac{8}{8}$	29,500
H6	34	29,400
H7	$34\frac{1}{8}$	29,300

loran pairs is assigned a single radio frequency channel, and the various pairs in the chain are distinguished by slight differences in repetition rate. Standard 2.0-mc-per-sec loran stations operate at either 1.75, 1.85, 1.90, or 1.95 mc per sec. Two basic repetition rates are used, 25 pulses per sec or $33\frac{1}{3}$ pulses per sec. Each basic rate is further divided into seven specific rates, each differing from the adjacent rate by approximately $\frac{1}{16}$ or $\frac{1}{8}$ of a pulse per sec. Table 10-2 shows the system of repetition rates and their designations. Each pair of stations is designated by a code which indicates channel number, basic rate, and specific rate in that order. A pair designated 413 would operate on Channel 4 (1.95 mc per sec) at the basic rate of 25 pulses per sec, but at a specific rate of about $25\frac{2}{16}$ pulses per sec. If the receiving equipment is within range of several pairs of stations, there may be a multiplicity of pulses received, but only one pair will be closely synchronized with the receiving circuits and hence have a low rate of drift.

10-13 SERVICE AREAS FOR LORAN

Since signals from both stations of a pair are necessary to determine a line of position, the receiving equipment must be within the effective zones of both transmitters. If it is assumed that the service areas of the two stations are identical circles, the navigator must be within that area common to the two circles. If the baseline is short, this area is nearly circular, whereas if the baseline approaches the effective range of a transmitter it is

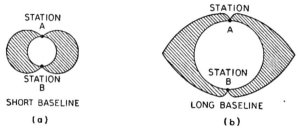

FIG. 10-7 Service Area of a Loran Pair. (By permission from *Loran*, by Pierce, McKenzie, and Woodward. Copyright 1948, McGraw-Hill Book Co., Inc.)

flattened considerably, as shown in Fig. 10-7. The precision with which a line of position can be determined in regions far from the baseline is higher for long baselines than for short ones. It is necessary, however, to determine two position lines to establish a fix, and this implies concern with the service areas common to two loran pairs. It becomes necessary in practice to use baselines much shorter than propagation difficulties alone would permit. Figure 10-8 shows the effect of baseline length on service area in a loran triplet (two pairs having one station common to each pair). If the two baselines are not colinear, the service area is larger and the precision greater on the side where the included angle is smaller. A particularly favorable situation is obtained when the angle between the baseline is 60 to 90 deg, as shown on Fig. 10-9a, and the baseline length is comparable to the diameter of the area to be served. In some cases it is possible to locate four stations so as to obtain excellent coverage and accuracy over a large area surrounding the intersection of the baselines. An idealized arrangement of a loran quadrilateral is shown in Fig. 10-9b.

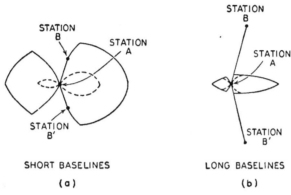

FIG. 10-8 Service Area of a Triplet. (By permission from *Loran*, by Pierce, McKenzie, and Woodward. Copyright 1948, McGraw-Hill Book Co., Inc.)

10-14 PROPAGATION EFFECTS ON LORAN

As pointed out in Chap. 4, ionization of the gases in our atmosphere affects the propagation of electromagnetic waves by absorption, reflection, refraction, and diffraction. The part of the earth's gaseous blanket which is known to affect the transmission of radio frequency energy is called the

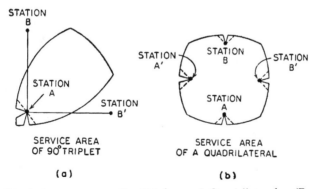

FIG. 10-9 Ideal Arrangements for Triplet and Quadrilateral. (By permission from *Loran*, by Pierce, McKenzie, and Woodward. Copyright 1948, McGraw-Hill Book Co., Inc.)

ionosphere, and various more or less well-defined regions of appreciable ionization are known as the D, E, F, and $F2$ layers in order of increasing height. Standard loran signals are propagated mainly by ground waves during daylight hours, at least as far as transmission to appreciable distances is concerned. Under these conditions the matching of two signals can be done very precisely, to within 1 microsec if signal-to-noise ratio is fairly high. During the hours of darkness the D and $F1$ layers disappear, leaving only the E and $F2$ layers to affect propagation of skywaves. The effect of these ionized layers is to cause one or more skywave pulses to be received in the loran equipment. Under severe conditions when multiple-hop transmission exists, six or more signals may be received from a transmitter.

When a ground wave is present it will arrive first, and provided ground waves from both stations of a pair are received, these are used. The ground wave is usually not subject to appreciable fading or splitting, although its shape and amplitude may vary rapidly unless it is considerably stronger than the noise. Within perhaps 500 miles of the station the ground wave is generally used, and the $E1$ (one reflection from the E layer) wave is ignored. Between the ground wave limit and about 1500 miles the $E1$ signal arrives first, followed by either the $E2$ (two reflections from the E layer) or the $F1$. Although at times the $E1$ signal is very steady, in general the pulse received is the result of integration of the various signals arriving by slightly differing paths. Consequently the differing phase relationships result in a pulse whose amplitude varies with time and which is subject to wide variations in shape, even splitting into more than one pulse. $E2$ and F signals are so variable in amplitude and shape that they are unusable for matching. In the region where both ground wave and $E1$ signals are received their separation will be some 75 to 100 microsec. Toward the limit of skywave reception the first signal may be either $E1$ or $E2$. When both are present their separation will also be 75 to 100 microsec. The nighttime E layer is remarkably stable, varying only slightly from hour to hour, from latitude to latitude, and varying only moderately from winter to summer. Because a skywave travels farther than a ground wave in reaching a given point and because it is somewhat slowed in its passage through the ionized layer, the E layer signal takes longer to arrive than does a ground wave signal. This delay is about 160 microsec for points separated 200 miles and falls approximately exponentially to a constant value of about 65 microsec at 1000 miles and beyond. If skywave signals are used in a loran observation, corrections are required unless the observer is near the center line between the pair or else at a great distance from each station. Skywave corrections are printed on loran charts. The possible variation in delay of the skywave at short distances is so great that when the observer is within 250 miles of either station skywave measurements are of no value.

10-15 LORAN SYSTEM ACCURACY

Computed Time Differences. It is considered that the propagation velocity of radio waves is constant at the speed of light. All loran observations seem to confirm that this is the case, at least over sea water. No experimental evidence is at hand either to confirm or refute this assumption as far as overland transmission is concerned. Loran is not intended for use over land areas, but should this become necessary more knowledge of the behavior of propagation velocity would become an immediate necessity. It is assumed that the coding delay introduced at slave stations is exactly the assigned value. The actual delay introduced may be affected by distortion introduced into the local transmitter signal when it is attenuated for matching with the remote signal from the master station. The positions of loran sites are often computed from celestial observations, since frequently the sites cannot be tied in optically with accurately known geodetic reference points. The pitfalls in position determination by celestial means have been mentioned in Chap. 3. Fortunately loran itself may be used as a means of establishing more accurately the true positions of stations by measuring, in a series of statistically designed tests, the time differences at several geodetic reference points.

Measured Time Differences. Inability to match pulses exactly, combined with unknown differences in propagation time of the two signals, leads to errors in time difference measurement. If we call the probable error in this measurement Σ, the observer establishes the fact that he is locating

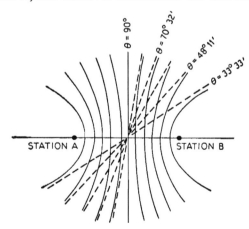

FIG. 10-10 Family of Plane Hyperbolas. (By permission from *Loran*, by Pierce, McKenzie, and Woodward. Copyright 1948, McGraw-Hill Book Co., Inc.)

himself with respect to a region on the loran chart bounded by the lines $\mathscr{D} + \Sigma$ and $\mathscr{D} - \Sigma$, and he is just as likely to be within these lines as outside them. The width of this strip is not solely dependent upon the error Σ, as reference to Fig. 10-10 will show. The asymptotes of the hyperbolas are radii emanating from the midpoint of the baseline between the two stations. A time difference measurement can be converted to an indication of the angle between the baseline and the radius to the observer, if the distance to the midpoint is large. A cursory inspection shows that this angle changes rapidly with measured time difference when much nearer one station than the other. Therefore, to determine how wide the strip determined by the lines $\mathscr{D} + \Sigma$ and $\mathscr{D} - \Sigma$ really is, the difference, 2Σ, must be multiplied by the factor of geometrical precision, p. The value p is given by

$$p = \frac{d_1}{d_2} \csc \theta \tag{10-11}$$

where d_1 and d_2 are distance to midpoint and length of baseline respectively, and θ is the angle between the baseline and the radius from midpoint to the observer. This expression is reasonably accurate only if $(d_1/d_2) \gg 1$. The exact value of p is given by

$$p = \tfrac{1}{2} \csc \tfrac{1}{2}\psi \tag{10-12}$$

in which ψ is the angle subtended by the baseline between stations as seen by the observer. The probable error in the observer's line of position for a probable error in time difference measurement is

$$y = Kp\Sigma \tag{10-13}$$

If K is chosen to make the unit of y one nautical mile per microsec,

$$Kp = 0.081 \csc \tfrac{1}{2}\psi \tag{10-14}$$

The minimum possible value of p is unity, and this occurs if the observer is on the baseline, making $\psi = 180$ deg.

The equipment must ascertain two position lines to determine a fix, but actually it ascertains two strips which intersect. The area common to the two strips is a parallelogram to a very close approximation. (See

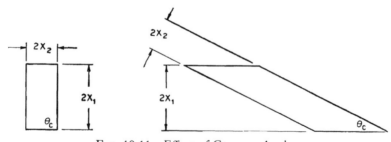

Fig. 10-11 Effect of Crossing Angle.

Fig. 10-11.) The area is $4X_1X_2 \csc \theta_c$, where X_1 and X_2 are the widths and θ_c is the angle of intersection. The minimum area is obtained if θ_c is 90 deg. The probability of the observer's being within the parallelogram is only $\frac{1}{4}$, since his probability of being within either strip composing it is $\frac{1}{2}$. The probable distance between the actual location and the point represented by the intersection of the lines of position on the chart, if the errors in time measurement on the two pairs of stations is the same, is approximately[3]

$$P = 1.15 K\Sigma \csc \theta_c (p_1^2 + p_2^2)^{\frac{1}{2}} \qquad (10\text{-}15)$$

If ground wave signals are being used, an error of perhaps 1 microsec in matching may be expected. This leads to a probable error of[4]

$$P = 0.186 \csc \theta_c (p_1^2 + p_2^2)^{\frac{1}{2}} \text{ nautical miles} \qquad (10\text{-}16)$$

Matching skywave signals leads to greater errors, and the probable error in measuring time difference between stations of a pair runs about 2 microsec at the range limit and 6 microsec at 300 miles from either station. A fix determined from skywave measurements will have a probable error of approximately

$$P_s = 1.15 \csc \theta_c (p_{s1}^2 + p_{s2}^2)^{\frac{1}{2}} \text{ nautical miles} \qquad (10\text{-}17)$$

where $p_{s1} = \dfrac{400}{d_1 \csc \theta_1}$ and $p_{s2} = \dfrac{400}{d_2 \csc \theta_2}$, d and θ having been already defined.

10-16 POSSIBLE LORAN MISSILE APPLICATION

It is evident that, at least in theory, loran navigation could be applied as a guidance method for long-range missiles. In order to use loran for missile navigation, two general requirements must be met. First, it must be possible to place loran stations so that the area around the destination of the missile is adequately covered. This implies signals well above noise, a low value for the geometrical precision factor, and crossing angles of high value. Even if these conditions are met, with present loran equipment the probable accuracies are so poor that the system could be used only for placing a missile within a rather large area. At this point it could be "dumped" into the area or some short-range system such as radar or infrared homing could be used to select and guide the missile toward a specific objective.

The second general requirement is that it be possible to make automatic the operation of loran measuring devices and produce information suitable for use in generating steering orders. This appears to be within the realm of practicability considering the present state of the art. It would involve

[3] Pierce, McKenzie, and Woodward, *loc. cit.*
[4] Pierce, McKenzie, and Woodward, *loc. cit.*

servo control of delay circuits which would cause slave pulses to coincide automatically with their respective master pulses, thereby generating some mechanical or electrical quantities which are analogs of time differences. Once available, these quantities might be used as inputs to a computer in the missile or relayed to some guidance station for computation, the steering information being sent to the missile by a command guidance radio link.

Regardless of where the computation is accomplished, loran may be used in two fundamental ways. It can be used as a system complete within itself, independent of all other navigation devices, or it can be used in conjunction with other instruments. In the latter category, loran might furnish accurate position checks either continuously or periodically, and steering information would be generated by a computer which utilized this information plus compass heading of the missile and required heading to the target. Used wholly by itself, the most simply visualized system would cause the missile to follow one of the two hyperbolas which passes through the target until it reached the other hyperbola. In general, this is uneconomical of fuel, since the missile is caused to follow a hyperbola rather than a great circle or a rhumbline. It is, however, relatively easy to implement, since a voltage proportional to the difference between the hyperbola the missile is tracking and the one it should be tracking is easily obtained and modified with derivatives to make it suitable for right-left guidance.

A method of producing a shorter path would be to let the missile cross both families of hyperbolas as required to reach the destination. If, for example, the time difference line at the target was 3500 and at the initiation point it was 2600 microsec for one pair, and the corresponding readings for the second pair were 1900 and 1600, the missile might be controlled so as to successively pass through the coordinates (3500, 1900), (3400, 1867) .... (2700, 1633), and (2600, 1600). The rate at which the two sets of lines were crossed is the same as the ratios of final to initial time differences, in this case 3:1. Control of the missile might be accomplished as follows: the first pair of stations could be automatically tracked, the servo output voltage being proportional to the difference between the initial and the measured time difference. The second pair would also be tracked, and its output voltage compared with the first servo output in the ratio of 1:3. The comparator output voltage would operate the missile steering system. Thus any discrepancy between the desired 1:3 ratio of output voltages would cause the missile's course to be altered to reduce the discrepancy.

10-17 RADAR

Radar is a word coined in the early days of the art from the longer name "Radio Detection and Ranging." The word carries the implication of a transmitted radio signal and a received echo. In its use in missile guidance the term "radar" no longer has this meaning entirely. Rather the radar techniques developed during World War II have been applied in whole or in part and have become *radar guidance* techniques whether they use a transmitted signal and a received echo or only the transmitted signal or only the received echo.

A modern pulsed radar system has been shown in a previous example to be a complex collection of carriers and subcarriers, including both amplitude and frequency modulations. Perhaps a more enlightening way

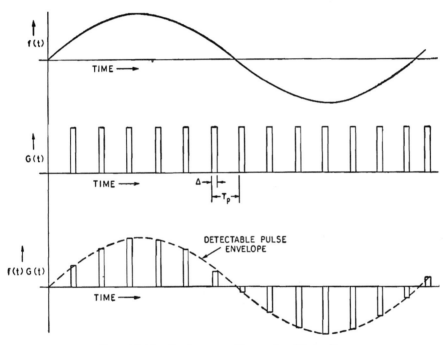

FIG. 10-12 Radar as an Example of Sampling.

to show some of the relationships in a fire or missile control radar is to consider it as a problem in sampling.[5] A continuous signal, such as target position, must be transmitted through space in short bursts or pulses which are used to reconstruct the target position with sufficient accuracy for the guidance intelligence requirements.

Refer to Fig. 10-12. A continuous symmetrical signal, $f(t)$, is to be transmitted by the discontinuous signal, $G(t)$, which is to serve as a carrier.

Expressed as a Fourier series,

$$f(t) = \sum_{n=0}^{n=\infty} a_n \cos(\omega_n t + \phi_n) \qquad (10\text{-}18)$$

[5] Starr, *loc. cit.*

and

$$G(t) = \frac{\Delta}{T_p} + \frac{2\Delta}{T_p} \sum_{K=1}^{K=\infty} \frac{\sin K\pi \frac{\Delta}{T_p}}{K\pi \frac{\Delta}{T_p}} \cos 2K\pi \frac{\Delta}{T_p} \quad (10\text{-}19)$$

where a_n = amplitude of the nth signal harmonic
n = order of the signal harmonic
ω_n = signal frequency in radians per second
ϕ_n = relative phase of the nth harmonic
Δ = pulse width
T_p = pulse repetition period
t = time

The modulation product of these signals is

$$f(t)G(t) = \frac{\Delta}{T_p} \sum_{n=0}^{\infty} a_n \cos(\omega_n t + \phi_n)$$

$$+ \frac{2\Delta}{T_p} \sum_{n=0}^{\infty} \sum_{K=1}^{\infty} a_n \frac{\sin K\pi \frac{\Delta}{T_p}}{K\pi \frac{\Delta}{T_p}} \cos 2K\pi \frac{\Delta}{T_p} \cos(\omega_n t + \phi_n) \quad (10\text{-}20)$$

Equation 10-20, through the use of trigonometric identities, can then be expressed as

$$f(t)G(t) = \frac{\Delta}{T_p} \sum_{n=0}^{\infty} a_n \cos(\omega_n t + \phi_n)$$

$$+ \frac{\Delta}{T_p} \sum_{n=0}^{\infty} \sum_{K=1}^{\infty} a_n \frac{\sin K\pi \frac{\Delta}{T_p}}{K\pi \frac{\Delta}{T_p}} \left\{ \cos[(K\omega_r + \omega_n)t + \phi_n] \right.$$

$$\left. + \cos[(K\omega_r - \omega_n)t - \phi_n] \right\} \quad (10\text{-}21)$$

where ω_r = repetition frequency in radians per second.

The second term of Eq. (10-21) can be removed by a low-pass filter which removes all frequencies greater than the maximum signal frequency if the restriction $\omega_r \geq 2\omega_n$ is observed. The restriction is caused by the nature of the last part of the second term, in that components of frequency $(\omega_r - \omega_n)$ would begin to appear in the pass band of the low-pass filter if the restriction were not observed. The action of the low-pass filter leaves

$$f(t)G(t) = \frac{\Delta}{T_p} \sum_{n=0}^{n \leq \frac{\omega_r}{2\omega}} a_n \cos(\omega_n t + \phi_n) \quad (10\text{-}22)$$

which is approximately* Δ/T_p times the original continuous signal. Δ/T_p is usually much less than unity. It can be made to approach unity if $\Delta \approx T_p$ through the use of a 100 percent pulse stretcher. Such a pulse stretcher is examined in detail in Par. 10-29. The signal wave can thus be reconstructed at the far end of a radar circuit with essentially no distortion.

10-18 FM RADAR SYSTEMS

This general class of radar systems includes those utilizing frequency modulation as a means of generating or measuring intelligence. The mod-

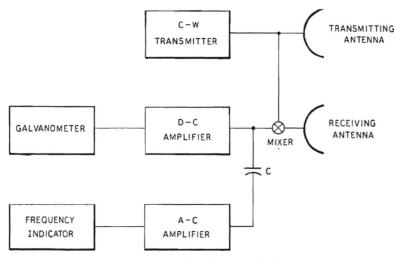

FIG. 10-13 C-w Doppler Radar.

ulation may be impressed at the transmitter in the electronic circuitry or at the target by means of the Doppler principle. Four systems will be discussed, namely:

1. Continuous-wave Doppler.
2. Range-measuring Doppler.
3. Pulsed Doppler.
4. Transmitted FM (Radio Altimeter).

C-w Doppler. A simple c-w radar system is shown in Fig. 10-13. If the target is stationary, its presence may be detected by rectifying the energy returned from the target and displaying it upon a d-c galvanometer. No other property of the target may be deduced except its presence and possibly its direction. If, however, the target is moving, its radial velocity

---

* Approximation and upper limit of Eq. (10-22) are caused by the restriction $\omega_r \geq 2\omega_n$.

also may be detected by comparing the echo frequency against the transmitted frequency. The echo radio frequency will differ from the transmitted frequency because of the Doppler shift. The Doppler shift is completely analogous to that occurring in sound propagation. The amount of the shift is doubled because of the two-way transmission (to the target and return). The comparison between the transmitted and received frequencies results in a difference or beat frequency sometimes called the Doppler frequency, f_D, where

$$f_D = 89.4 \frac{v}{\lambda} \qquad (10\text{-}23)[6]$$

when v = target radial velocity in miles per hour
λ = transmitted wavelength in centimeters.

To make use of this principle we discard the d-c value of the echo and retain only the a-c component proportional to target radial velocity. Since this is easily done by means of a blocking capacitor, we have available a technique whereby only targets which move are detected; all fixed targets or *clutter* (random echoes) are rejected by the capacitor. At first impression, the range to the target would seem to be available by integration of the range rate. However, this is not true because no reference point is inherent in the system from which a constant of integration can be obtained to make the integral a definite one. The indicated system cannot measure range. This technique is fine in theory, but its satisfactory operation is in proportion to the freedom of the transmitter from frequency and amplitude modulation noise. The maximum tolerable transmitter noise depends upon the expected range of Doppler frequencies and how the apparatus is mechanized. The required short-time transmitter frequency stability may be as great as one part in 10^{10}. The bandwidth of the receiver may be made very small compared to that of a pulsed radar. This, of course, limits the information rate. However, in guidance systems the information rate required depends upon the ability of the system to use information, i.e., the system bandwidth requirements. The system bandwidth requirements are usually only a few cycles per second, or less, as will be shown in later chapters. The receiver bandwidth, then, need not be greater than a few hundred cycles at most. For a given maximum range, the ratio of the required peak power of a pulsed radar to the required power of a c-w Doppler radar is a linear function of the bandwidth ratios.

For comparable maximum range performance, the peak power of a pulsed radar is likely to be in the order of hundreds of kilowatts and that of a c-w Doppler radar in tens of watts. The average powers of these two radar systems, however, will be equal if they are designed to have the same

---

[6] Ridenour, L., *Radar System Engineering*, McGraw-Hill Book Co., 1947.

maximum range capability. A Doppler system, unless gated, is capable of unambiguous tracking under the special condition that only one moving target exist within the antenna beam. This condition is no different than that encountered in a pulsed radar, in that some special feature of the target, usually its range, allows it to be selected from all others for tracking. In a Doppler system only two means of selection are available, namely, Doppler signal frequency and Doppler signal amplitude. The basis of selection is usually Doppler frequency and the mechanism is commonly a highly selective tunable filter such as is contained in commercial wave analyzers. Narrowing the filter bandwidth gives a greater amount of definition just as reducing the range gate duration in a pulse radar improves definition.

The successful use of this system (and actually *all* c-w systems) requires that the transmitter leakage into the receiver be controlled so that only the amplitude required for optimum mixer operation be admitted. This requirement makes it difficult to use a common receiving and transmitting antenna. In an experimental system it is possible, by the use of separate receiving and transmitting antennas and a leakage canceling network consisting of an attenuator and a phase shifter, to obtain a receiver sensitivity limited only by receiver input circuit noise.

Range-measuring Doppler. In order to measure the range to a target a reference must be included to provide a point from which to measure range. The reference point must be emitted by the transmitter in the form of either frequency or amplitude modulation. In pulsed radar the transmitter pulse forms the reference from which range (time) is measured. The range to the target causes the phase of the various sidebands of the pulse to be shifted to produce (ideally) at the receiver a replica of the transmitted pulse whose time displacement is proportional to range. Here we wish to reverse the process, i.e., determine range by measuring the relative phase shift of the sidebands. Intuitively, one can see that to determine the range by measuring sideband phase shift only two sidebands are required. Such a signal is easily produced by many methods. An elementary radar could be constructed about such a pair of frequencies. (See Fig. 10-14.) The range to the target modulates the phase of the sidebands so that the relative phase is proportional to the range. Such a system, to be unambiguous, would have to have a sideband frequency separation great enough, so that, at maximum range, the path lengths would differ by one cycle at the chosen radio frequencies. The radar would respond to fixed as well as moving targets. If, however, it is desired only to measure range to targets having a radial velocity, it is necessary to use the Doppler frequency as a means of excluding fixed targets.

The use of two sidebands is equivalent to transmitting two separate frequencies. Target radial motion causes a Doppler sideband to be modulated upon each of the transmitted frequencies. Each Doppler sideband is displaced from its transmitted carrier by an amount determined by Eq. (10-23). It can be shown[7] that the relative phase of the Doppler sidebands is a linear function of range to the target. This simple radar could measure range and rate of change of range.

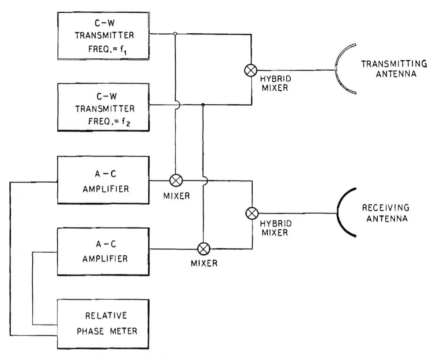

FIG. 10-14 Range-measuring Doppler Radar.

Pulsed Doppler. The range-measuring Doppler radar just discussed is in reality a very crude pulsed Doppler radar whose sidebands form a sort of pulse whose length is very great. In the period between pulses the amplitude of the pulse does not go to zero. Although the range rate information could be very accurate, the range position data obtained from the radar would be very inaccurate because of the difficulty of accurately measuring phase when one cycle of the signal to be measured corresponds to the maximum range of the radar. If phase can be measured accurately in increments of one degree and the maximum range of the radar is to be 10 nautical miles, the smallest detectable change of range would be 10/360 nautical miles, or 56 yd. Using the same criteria, we see that a pulsed radar could, in theory, measure in increments of about 3 yd. (Of course,

[7] Ridenour, *loc. cit.* p. 140.

neither of these incremental ranges can be measured in practice, but the order of difficulty for each type is the same.) One means of obtaining the range-measuring ability of a pulsed radar and the clutter-rejection ability of a Doppler radar is to build a set with the combined features. This technique has been called "pulsed Doppler." Such a system is diagrammed on Fig. 10-15. In such a radar the pulse delay is used as a measure of range and time of signal occurrence may be used for target selection (gating) as in a conventional pulsed radar. However, only those echoes affected by Doppler shift are allowed to actuate the indicators and

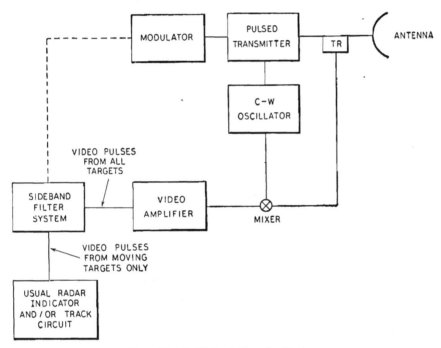

FIG. 10-15 Pulsed Doppler Radar.

tracking circuits. The separation of the pulses which have Doppler shift from those which do not is accomplished by utilizing a very complex filter network. In general, the filter network can be mechanized in one of several ways which are equivalent in theory but different in practice.

One method makes use of the frequency displacement of pulse sidebands caused by Doppler shift. The other method operates in the time domain and makes use of the fact that the phase angle between successive echo pulses for a moving target is different from that between successive transmitter pulses. This second form of filtering is the one most commonly utilized in systems for obtaining moving target indication, or "MTI."

The analysis and synthesis of these filter networks are very complex and beyond the scope of this book.

FM Altimeter. As mentioned previously, in order to measure range it is necessary to mark the transmitted signal with some form of reference modulation. The reference may be impressed as frequency modulation. If the transmitter frequency is varied, one may measure range by comparing the received against the transmitted frequency. Figure 10-16 is a block diagram of the system. Here, it is necessary to apply the restriction that the target have no radial velocity. If this is the case, the frequency comparison yields a frequency proportional to the range to the target. If radial velocity is present, the received frequency differs from that trans-

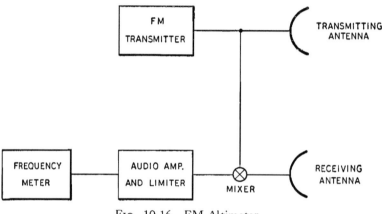

Fig. 10-16   FM Altimeter.

mitted by an amount proportional to range plus range rate. The system has been applied to the determination of altitude from an aircraft whose vertical velocity is essentially zero.

10-19 PULSED RADAR SYSTEM PARAMETERS

It will be the purpose of the following paragraphs to portray the design of system parameters as influenced by the information the system must pass. Again, many references are available on the subject of intimate design details of most parts of a radar system. It will not be necessary to review these here. Rather, the design philosophy will be stressed from the standpoint of communication theory. Important areas of discussion could center about the antenna, transmission lines, r-f transmitters, pulse modulators, receivers, range detecting circuits, angle (bearing and elevation) detecting circuits, and power supplies. The elements of servo system design as applied to radar are discussed in detail in other chapters.

The initial phases of the discussion will apply, more generally, to both search and tracking radars. The latter portions will have greater application to the dynamic conditions prevalent in tracking radars.

10-20 RADAR ANTENNAS

The design of radar antennas is a complex art bordering on a science. The permutations and combinations of variables in the design problems and the many solutions given in the literature make this field very large indeed. It will be necessary to offer here only a selected treatment.

Antennas useful in the guidance and control of missiles by means of radar techniques generally fall into the category of quasi-optical antennas rather than into the category of multielement array antennas. Such a quasi-optical antenna system usually consists of a feed mechanism which excites either a paraboloid or a lens. The paraboloid or lens is trusted (sometimes mistakenly) to exercise the majority of the control of the pattern of the emitted beam. This pattern is called the "secondary pattern." The feed system itself radiates toward the secondary radiator in a controlled pattern called the "primary pattern."

The state of the art in the development of large antennas (physically large compared to the wavelength transmitted) has progressed into the design stages and it is possible to state, more or less categorically, some known design facts.

(a) *The gain and secondary pattern of a large antenna vary in a known fashion with the area in square wavelengths and with the degree of illumination of the secondary radiator by the primary feed.*

If the transmitting antenna[8] were to radiate energy isotropically—i.e., uniformly in all directions—the power flow through unit area at a distance, d, from the antenna could be found by dividing S, the total radiated power, by $4\pi d^2$. A directive antenna, however, will concentrate the energy in certain directions. The power flow observed at some distant point will differ by some factor G from that which would be produced by an antenna radiating isotropically the same total power. This factor G is called the *gain* of the antenna in the direction in question. By our definition, the gain of the hypothetical isotropic radiator is 1 in every direction. For any other antenna, G will be greater than 1 in some directions and less than 1 in others. It is clear that G could not be greater than 1 in every direction, and in fact the average of G taken over the whole sphere must be just 1.

Usually we are interested in antennas for which G has a very pronounced maximum in one direction, that is to say, antennas which radiate a well-defined beam. This maximum value of G we shall denote by G_0. The

---

[8] Adapted from L. Ridenour, *loc. cit.* p. 19.

narrow, concentrated beams which are characteristic of microwave radar require antennas large compared to a wavelength. In nearly every case the radiating system amounts to an aperture of large area over which a substantially plane wave is excited. For such a system, a fundamental relation connects the maximum gain G_0, the area of the aperture A, and the wavelength λ:

$$G_0 = \frac{4\pi A K_0}{\lambda^2} \qquad (10\text{-}24)$$

The dimensionless factor K_0 is equal to 1 if the excitation is uniform in phase and intensity over the whole aperture; in actual antennas K_0 is often as large as 0.6 or 0.7 and is rarely less than 0.5. An antenna formed by a paraboloidal mirror 100 cm in diameter, for a wavelength of 10 cm, would have a gain of 986 according to Eq. (10-24) with $K_0 = 1$, and in practice might be designed to attain $G_0 = 640$, where $K_0 = 0.65$.

The connection between gain and beamwidth is easily seen. With the use of an aperture of dimensions d in both x and y directions, a beam may be formed whose angular width, determined by diffraction, is about λ/d radians. The radiated power is then mainly concentrated in a solid angle of λ^2/d^2. An isotropic radiator would spread the same power over a solid angle of 4π. Therefore, we expect the gain to be approximately $4\pi d^2/\lambda^2$, which is consistent with Eq. (10-24) since the area of the aperture is about d^2.

A complementary property of an antenna, which is of importance equal to that of the gain, is the effective receiving cross section. This quantity has the dimensions of an area and, when multiplied by the power density (power per unit area) of an incident plane wave, yields the total signal power available at the terminals of the antenna. The effective receiving cross section A_r is related to the gains as follows:

$$A_r = \frac{G\lambda^2}{4\pi} \qquad (10\text{-}25)$$

Note that G and not G_0 has been written in Eq. (10-25). The applicability of this equation is not restricted to the direction of maximum gain or to beams of any special shape. Once the gain of the antenna in a particular direction is specified, its effective receiving cross section for plane waves incident from that direction is fixed. Equation (10-25) can be based rigorously on the Reciprocity Theorem. Comparing Eq. (10-24) and (10-25) we observe that, if the factor K_0 is unity, the effective receiving cross section of an antenna in the principal direction is precisely the area of the aperture; in other words, all the energy incident on the aperture is absorbed. Quite generally, A_r will depend on the area of the antenna aperture and not on λ, whereas G_0 will depend on A/λ^2.

(b) *In general, uniform illumination produces maximum gain, a maximum value of K_0, minimum beamwidth, and a large quantity of high level side lobes.*

Consider Fig. 10-17; it can be seen that the practical necessity for uniform illumination of the parabola results in some energy spilling past the edge of the parabola. This energy results in side lobes.

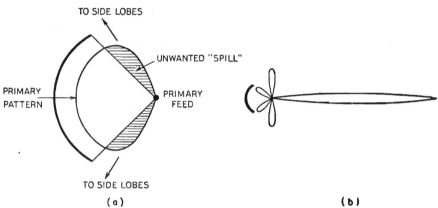

Fig. 10-17 Uniform Illumination: (a) Uniform Illumination of a Parabolic Reflector Showing a Source of Side Lobe Generation; (b) Resultant Secondary Pattern with High Level Side Lobes but Narrow Main Lobe.

(c) *In general, tapered or graded illumination produces less than maximum gain, greater than minimum beamwidth and lower side lobes than uniform illumination produces.*

Figure 10-18 shows a combination illustrative of the effect. Note that areas near the edges of the reflector receive less energy causing lower

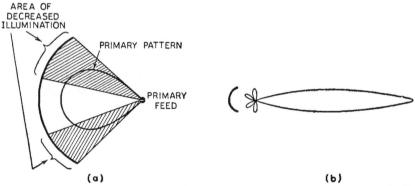

Fig. 10-18 Tapered Illumination: (a) Tapered Illumination of a Parabolic Reflector; (b) Resultant Secondary Pattern with Low-Level Side Lobes but Wide Main Lobe.

effective use of the reflector area (less gain). This is equivalent to reducing the value of the factor K_0 in preceding paragraphs. Note also that the side lobes do not disappear completely. Other causes of side lobes are nonoptimum reflector contour, feed system radiation directly away from the reflector, and feed system interference or shadowing.

Antennas large compared to a wavelength (area $> 10^4 \lambda^2$) are used for tracking targets at missile control stations, where space is not at a premium as it is in the missile itself. Control stations (either airborne or ground-based) may be located near the surface of the earth. It is desirable to direct as little energy as possible toward the earth so as to reduce the

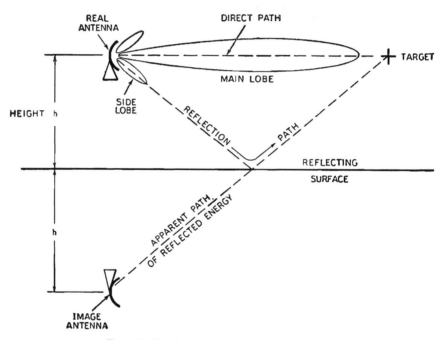

FIG. 10-19 Low-angle Antenna Problem.

interferometer action of the real antenna and its image. Reference to Fig. 10-19 should clarify this picture. If a target is directly illuminated by the main lobe or beam of an antenna, and energy also arrives at the target by a reflected path as shown, the apparent sources of the energy are the real antenna and its image. The resultant energy received at the target depends upon the vector addition of the energy propagated via the two paths, as previously discussed in Chap. 4.

If the target now moves along the direct path, it will be seen that the resultant energy at the target will be amplitude-modulated as the path length changes to cause reinforcement or cancellation. Also, if the relative velocity between the target and the antenna is such as to cause reinforcement and cancellation at a frequency nearly equal to one of the system information frequencies, the information gathering system can become noisy enough to be useless.

Interferometer effects can be caused either, as shown, by side lobe radiation or by a reflected path in the main lobe. The importance of reducing all radiation toward the reflecting surface can be appreciated.

Within this framework it is possible to distribute the parameters, in some cases, to obtain the most for the least. Several possible solutions present themselves:

a. It may be practical to reduce side lobes toward the earth at the expense of those skyward. This approach is called "beam shaping" and must nearly always be done empirically.

b. By properly tapering the illumination of the secondary radiator toward the edges, it appears possible in some cases to design an optimum balance between important side lobes and the widening of the main lobe so that the minimum interference effect is produced. It is, of course, necessary to consider how wide the main lobe must be and how high a side lobe level is tolerable to the system from other standpoints than that of interferometer effects. The discussion of the effects of the interferometer action will be continued later in this chapter.

The development of antennas small compared to a wavelength (area $< 10^4 \lambda^2$) is still an art and, as such, requires a rule-of-thumb technique. Small antennas must, unfortunately, be used in missiles. It appears possible to derive considerable design assistance from analogy. One analogy which has been helpful is the propagation of water waves from two-dimensional scaled antennas in shallow tanks.[9,10] It has been possible to simulate a number of simple antennas to a high degree of accuracy. The design of small antennas is usually accomplished by application of theory available for large antennas. Empirical corrections for design deficiencies are made on the basis of tests of prototype models.

The discussion of interferometer effects as applied to large antennas is equally applicable to smaller antennas except that, usually, less can be done to proportion the main lobe and the side lobes and so reduce the problem. Remedial measures must be taken elsewhere in the system.

10-21 RADAR R-F COMPONENTS

There is little in the design of r-f components which is peculiar to the field of missile guidance. In general, well-designed components as used in modern radar sets will suffice as well for missile guidance. There are,

---

[9] Cf. Chap. 19.

[10] Walbridge, Smith, and Woodward, "Water Ripple Analogue of Electromagnetic Propagation," *1952 University of Vermont Technical Report to Office of Naval Research.*

however, several rather obvious precautions which must be observed. The precautions are also partially applicable for other uses of radar. These concern the design of transmission lines, mixers, and local oscillator automatic frequency control circuits.

a. When a radar set is used in a missile guidance system, a number of the parameters such as p.r.f. (Pulse Repetition Frequency), radio frequency carrier, scan frequency, and the like, are available as carriers for guidance intelligence. The radar set must be designed so that the guidance intelligence, once impressed upon these carriers, is not altered by the radar. For instance, if the guidance intelligence is to be impressed upon the radio frequency carrier as frequency modulation, the transmission line must have the proper bandwidth or the frequency modulation may be accompanied by amplitude modulation. Problems of this nature arise in guidance techniques and usually require only a refinement in the design used in modern radar.

b. Much "to-do" has been made of local-oscillator-noise cancelling schemes in microwave mixers. While such schemes have some merit in improving the range of search sets, they have less merit in fire control sets where maximum range is not always a consideration. In airborne radars, in view of size, weight, and adjustment problems, the low-noise mixers presently used are of questionable value. The reasoning behind these statements is as follows. Receiver noise, of which local oscillator noise is but one component, becomes the important contributor to total noise only when the target being tracked approaches the maximum range for a given target-radar combination. Many missile systems are designed to use their radar components in the near and medium range regions where, for a given target-radar combination, the received signal is large compared to receiver noise. In these situations (there are, of course, exceptions) the balanced mixer and any other complex low-noise mixers are not useful. As an example, a ground-based laboratory radar system on X-band was adjusted through the use of component selection and elaborate test techniques to have a noise figure of approximately 12 db. The day-to-day noise figure over a period of months has been found to be as high as 20 db. A comparison of the balanced mixer used in this equipment against a well-designed unbalanced mixer with no complicated adjustments and no component selections showed a variation in noise figure of about 3 db. The variation of 3 db favored the unbalanced mixer about 50 percent of the times that the measurement was repeated.

c. A standard type of automatic frequency control (a.f.c.) for radar local oscillators is one which uses a stabilized cavity as a reference or discriminator element. To simplify the design of the frequency controlling servo system it is common to frequency-modulate the local oscillator at an audio rate to provide a carrier upon which the low frequency stabilizing corrections are modulated. The a.f.c. servo system cannot correct the intentional frequency modulation and still perform its low frequency corrective function, for if it does so it will remove the a.f.c. information carrier and its sidebands. It is very important that the intentional frequency modulation be at a rate which does not cause beats which can be passed by the other portions of the guidance system.

The design of the automatic frequency control can affect the ability of a system to overcome transmitter load impedance changes caused by a radome. In this instance the a.f.c. system must be made compatible with the rate of change of frequency as determined by the rate of change of antenna direction and rate of change of radome reflection coefficient with direction.

10-22 RADAR TRANSMITTERS

The design of a radar transmitter which is part of a guidance system differs from other applications only in detail. The choice of a frequency is based on many factors, two of which can be the avoidance of transmission difficulties, as discussed in Chap. 4, or the availability of components. The choice of a tube such as magnetron, klystron, triode, and the like is based mostly on the desired method of transmitting guidance intelligence. If the chosen method is frequency modulation, it would be unwise to use a magnetron because these devices are inherently difficult to frequency-modulate in a controllable fashion. In such a case, the use of a klystron would be more suitable. As another example, if a system were chosen which demanded the use of short pulses of a critically controlled length, the choice of a cavity oscillator using a triode vacuum tube would be unwise. The triode, to oscillate satisfactorily, requires a cavity which does not lend itself to short pulse operation with sharply defined pulse edges. A magnetron or klystron system could be designed for the application with little difficulty.

Another problem which is almost exclusive to airborne and missile systems is that transmitter load impedance changes, because of the variation of reflection coefficient of the radome which must be used. *Microwave Antenna Theory and Design* by Silver and *Radar Scanners and Radomes* by Cody et al.[11] give a thorough theoretical and design treatment of the problem. The theory and design data, however, cannot generally be used as other than an aid in the design of a usable radome. Only the empirical approach in combination with theory can aid the designer in producing a radome in which the impedance changes are reduced to a usable minimum. The technique involves the calculation and/or estimation of the reflection coefficient and its phase for a proposed radome. This informa-

---

[11] McGraw-Hill Book Co., Inc., New York.

tion used on the Rieke diagram[12] of the transmitter allows one to minimize the effect of impedance change on transmitter operation. However, the accuracy of estimation and calculation of the reflection coefficient is poor because of the complex nature of the physics and of the irregular shape of the radome required for aerodynamic or mechanical reasons. The only recourse is to experiment and test.

10-23 PULSE MODULATORS

The pulse modulator is a switch which applies a relatively short pulse to some element of the transmitter and causes it to emit a burst of radio frequency energy of suitable length to satisfy the problem requirements. Under these conditions the transmitter emits a power called the *peak power*. Over a long period of time this power has some average value which is determined by the peak power, the time duration of the pulse, and the time between pulses. The ratio of average power to peak power is called the *duty cycle*. It will be shown in Chap. 16 that the maximum range of a radar set depends upon the average power. It is also the average power which largely determines the size and weight of the pulse modulator.

Although earlier search radars used low-level grid modulation of triode tubes with attendant low power demand upon the switch, even simple modern radar sets use high-level (high-power) plate modulation because of the greater efficiency and ease of control thus obtained. High-level modulation requires that the switch handle tens of amperes at tens of thousands of volts. Either mechanical or electronic switches can be designed to meet these requirements. In a very simple radar used to obtain an echo from the moon, the switch was a hand-operated mechanical one. One form of mechanical switch is a rotary spark gap wherein a disk mounting a number of electrodes is rotated near a stationary electrode. Sufficient voltage is impressed between the disk and the stationary electrode to make the intervening air space ionize. The ionized space supports an arc through a small angle of disk rotation when a rotating electrode makes its closest approach to the stationary electrode. The arc thus formed is used to connect the high-voltage source to the transmitter. The time duration of the arc is usually controlled by the discharge of an artificial transmission line so that all pulses are of uniform time duration.

Electronic modulators employ either thyratron tubes in place of the rotary spark gap or use vacuum tubes to amplify a low-power pulse to the power level required.

If the radar guidance equipment utilizes pulse modulation as a subcarrier of information it is desirable to design the modulator to fit the particular situation. Several typical situations will be explored here.

---

[12] Reich, Ordung, Krauss, and Skalnik, *Microwave Theory and Techniques*, p. 554, D. Van Nostrand Co., Inc., New York, 1953.

When it is desired to use the pulse repetition frequency of the radar set as a subcarrier, the simpler pulse modulators will not operate satisfactorily.

The rotary spark gap has been useful as a switch in modulator application but it has a high rotational inertia. The inertia precludes the modulation of the radar p.r.f. at a rate suitable for use as a guidance link. The thyratron and vacuum tube modulators can, however, be successfully used for this purpose. The vacuum tube modulator is a power amplifier which can be designed to have a useful bandwidth, if a low-power input signal having the proper characteristics can be supplied.

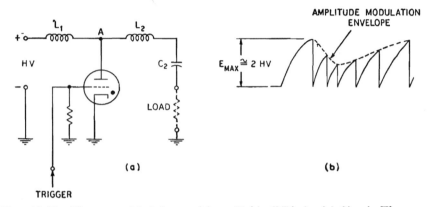

Fig. 10-20 Thyratron Modulator without Hold-off Diode: (a) Simple Thyratron Modulator Circuit; (b) Charging Waveform at "A" Showing Amplitude Modulation as a Result of Varying p.r.f.

The vacuum tube modulator is an inefficient device, at best, because of the large voltage drop across the switch tubes. The efficiency of a thyratron modulator is appreciably higher because the tubes act similarly to mechanical switches, in that they pass large currents with low voltage drop. Figure 10-20 shows one type of simple thyratron modulator circuit. In the period between the times when high-voltage pulses are delivered to the load, the resonant circuit L_1, L_2, and C_2 charges along a curve determined by the resonant frequency, $f = \frac{1}{2}\pi \sqrt{L_1 C_2}$. The inductance L_2 is usually small enough by comparison to L_1 that it may be neglected. When the voltage amplitude at the plate of the thyratron is near its peak, the trigger input, synchronized to the charge frequency, causes the thyratron to conduct heavily. This action causes the artificial transmission line L_1, C_2 to discharge a nearly rectangular pulse of current into the load. The artificial transmission line, sometimes called the *pulse network*, is usually comprised of more than the one section shown, though one section will suffice if the output pulse need not be very rectangular. The p.r.f.

of the radar and, of course, the trigger input must be nearly four times the resonant frequency of L_1, L_2, and C_2. If this condition were allowed to prevail, this modulator would be of no use in a system where the p.r.f. is to be used as a carrier of guidance information because the p.r.f. could not be varied without causing amplitude modulation of the output pulses. Figure 10-21 shows the same circuit except that a "hold-off" diode has been added. The purpose of the diode is to allow the voltage attained at the peak of the resonant charging action to be retained for some time after the peak, so that the input trigger may "fire" the modulator at any reasonable time after the peak. This basic circuit is the one most commonly used as a modulator in systems using modulation of the p.r.f. as a guidance link.

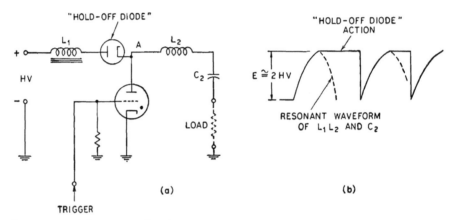

Fig. 10-21 Thyratron Modulator with Hold-off Diode: (a) Simple Thyratron Modulator Using a Hold-off Diode to Permit Variation of p.r.f. without Amplitude Modulation; (b) Charging Waveform at "A" Showing Diode Action.

For other guidance systems the designer must choose the modulator which best fits his needs (see Beacon Modulators). Guidance information may, for instance, be transmitted by using as a carrier the width, slope, or other shape factors of the radar pulse such as a series of pulses (pulse code). For such applications, the hard tube or power amplifier modulator seems the most suitable. In this type of modulator the guidance information may easily be impressed upon the pulse shape at low-power level and then amplified to the power level required by the transmitter.

10-24 TRACKING RADAR

The foregoing paragraphs have general application to radar whether the system is used for search or tracking. We now will deal mostly with parameters of tracking radar. The principal differences between search radar and tracking radar are as follows:

In a search radar, the dynamic operation of tracking is carried out with only nominal accuracy and a human operator is usually employed to track. In the tracking radar the dynamic operation is usually performed by automatic circuitry, because the required accuracy is high and operator time delays would be prohibitive. It might then be expected that the tracking radar requires more complex and precise equipment in those portions of the circuit where dynamic signal conditions result from some motion of the target which it is desired to follow or track.

The portions of the circuit of particular interest are the receiver and a.g.c., the range tracking circuit, the angle tracking circuit, the servo system, and the associated power supplies. Servo system theory is treated in Chap. 7 and elsewhere in this volume.

10-25 THE RADAR RECEIVER

Although radar receivers may be divided into several classifications, in each the ultimate purpose is to detect target-reflected radio frequency energy originally emitted by a radar transmitter and to furnish a usable output signal to viewing devices or automatic tracking circuits. This treatment will be limited to conical scanning microwave pulse radar receivers which are used in fire control or missile guidance systems. Emphasis will be placed on features of primary importance in obtaining accurate angle and range tracking. Receivers for other types of emission or for other specific applications, although employing some of the same techniques and engineering principles, will not be discussed.

Receivers with which we are concerned are almost universally of the superheterodyne type, employing a microwave local oscillator and mixer to convert the input signal to a much lower frequency for ease of handling. The converted signal is amplified by a very-high-gain intermediate frequency amplifier and rectified by a diode i-f detector. The output of this detector consists of video pulses which are approximate replicas of the envelopes of the received microwave signals. They are usually amplified by suitable video amplifiers, which are followed by a special video detector called a *pulse stretcher*. This device converts the train of video pulses into a d-c voltage upon which is superimposed an a-c signal proportional to the modulation envelope of the pulse train. The a-c component contains the angle information. The d-c component is a function of average pulse amplitude and is used to control the receiver gain. In either the i-f amplifier or the video amplifier, range gating is provided in order that the remaining circuits may track only desired targets. Gating is accomplished by drastically reducing the receiver sensitivity except for a brief interval of time during which the desired signal is expected to be present.

10-26 MIXERS AND LOCAL OSCILLATORS

The mixer combines the signal voltage received by the antenna system and a much-higher-amplitude, locally generated voltage. The frequency of the local oscillator is different from the signal by the frequency of the i-f amplifier. In the region near 3000 mc per sec crystal mixers are of either coaxial or waveguide type. At higher frequencies waveguide mixers are universally used since coaxial transmission lines are unsuitable. Figure 10-22a shows in cross section a 3000 mc per sec broadband coaxial mixer, and a simple waveguide mixer is shown in Fig. 10-22b.

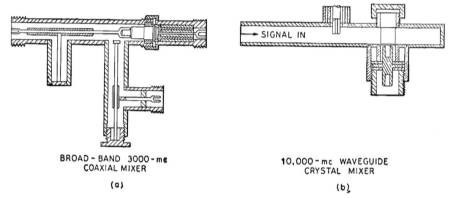

Fig. 10-22 Microwave Mixers. (By permission from *Microwave Receivers*, by Van Voorhis. Copyright 1948, McGraw-Hill Book Co., Inc.)

Local oscillators for microwave radar receivers may be of the usual low-frequency, negative-grid type with the tuning circuits consisting of coaxial elements; or, more often, velocity modulation tubes are used. The latter type is practically the only suitable oscillator for receiver use above 4000 mc per sec. The reflex klystron is the most popular velocity modulation tube. Two general types exist, one having the tuned chamber partly external to the evacuated envelope, the other having the tuning cavity entirely within the envelope. With external cavity types the frequency of oscillation is usually controlled by the depth of penetration of metallic screws. Tubes having the cavity integral with the envelope are mechanically tuned by distorting the cavity, thus changing the spacing of the grids. There are several narrow ranges of operating voltages in which a tube will oscillate, and between these regions no output is available. Within each mode of oscillation the frequency increases with increasing negative reflector voltage, and the power output rises from zero to a maximum and falls to zero again. Fine control of frequency of a reflex klystron is accomplished by varying the reflector voltage over a small range centered at the maximum power point of a selected mode. The useful electronic tuning range is usually considered to be the frequency range within which the power output drops to one half of the maximum value. When automatic frequency control is to be applied, the control voltage is usually applied to the reflector. Hence the slope of the frequency versus reflector voltage in the useful electronic tuning range and the spread between the zero power points are factors affecting the a.f.c. design. Generally speaking it is desirable to regulate the operating voltages. Tubes using external cavities and regulated power on all tube elements can be frequency-stabilized against temperature and pressure changes by using very heavy cavities made of low temperature coefficient metal. The internal cavity types usually are very poor in this respect and must be enclosed in a container in which temperature and pressure are carefully maintained if unattended operation without a.f.c. is required.

10-27 NOISE FIGURE CONSIDERATIONS

Any resistor at a temperature above absolute zero generates noise power in direct proportion to the absolute temperature and to the bandwidth under consideration. This noise is known as *Johnson noise* and its value is given by

$$N = KTB \qquad (10\text{-}26)$$

where N = noise power in watts
K = Boltzmann's constant
T = absolute temperature in degrees Kelvin
B = the bandwidth in cycles per second

Johnson noise is developed not only by physical resistors, but by the resistive component of the internal impedance of any generator, including antennas. Thus a receiver, even if it had no noise sources within itself, would have noise output when connected to an antenna. Such a receiver would have the same ratio of signal to noise at its output as existed at its input, and the figure of merit, known as noise figure, would be unity.

All receivers add noise to the input signal, and hence the output signal-to-noise ratio is inferior to that at the input. The degradation of output signal-to-noise ratio is a measure of the *noise figure*, which is given by

$$F = \frac{(S)}{(S_o)} \frac{(N_o)}{(KTB)} \qquad (10\text{-}27)$$

where F = the noise figure
S = signal power supplied by the signal source
S_o = the signal power output of the device
N_o = the noise power output of the device
K = Boltzmann's constant
T = the absolute temperature of the signal source in degrees Kelvin
B = the noise bandwidth of the device

The ratio S/S_o is the reciprocal of the power gain. The noise bandwidth B is very close to the half-power bandwidth if the frequency determining networks are three or more synchronously tuned simple L-C circuits.

In a radar receiver two major components control the overall noise figure, namely, the mixer and the i-f amplifier. Denoting mixer and i-f amplifier noise figures as F_m and F_{if} respectively, and calling the mixer gain G, the overall noise figure is

$$F = F_m + \frac{F_{if} - 1}{G} \qquad (10\text{-}28)$$

The value of F_{if} is the noise figure measured when the amplifier is driven by a source impedance equal to the i-f output impedance of the mixer and associated coupling circuits.

The noise output N_o of Eq. (10-27) is equivalent to Johnson noise from a resistor at some temperature T_1; thus

$$N_o = KT_1 B \qquad (10\text{-}29)$$

Equation (10-27) may then be written

$$F = \frac{T_1/T}{G} \qquad (10\text{-}30)$$

The ratio T_1/T may be considered as an "equivalent noise temperature." By making this substitution, Eq. (10-28) appears in a form particularly adapted to discussion of crystal mixers.

$$F = \frac{T_1/T + F_{if} - 1}{G} \qquad (10\text{-}31)$$

We can disregard the quantity F_{if} for the moment; it is important to see how mixer operation can be optimized so that the ratio T_1/T is made small. The conversion gain (always less than unity) of a mixer crystal is dependent upon the amount of local oscillator power it is absorbing, especially for very small amounts of power. The equivalent noise temperature of a crystal increases directly with the local oscillator power absorbed. There is an optimum compromise between conversion gain and equivalent temperature. The overall noise figure increases rapidly if the crystal excitation power is decreased below optimum. Degradation is much less rapid when local oscillator power is increased with respect to the optimum value. The local oscillator must be capable of supplying several times the power required by the crystal itself in order to permit considerable isolation between the local oscillator and the actual mixing section of the mixer assembly. Such isolation permits the local oscillator to be loaded for highest stability and prevents appreciable loss of desired signal toward the local oscillator. In practice, the power capability of the local oscillator should not be less than 20 db greater than that required by the crystal.

10-27]　　　NOISE FIGURE CONSIDERATIONS　　　397

The noise temperature of a crystal is in effect increased if the local oscillator signal contains modulation sidebands at frequencies removed from the carrier by the value of the receiver's intermediate frequency. Such noise is generated by "shot effect" [13] and allied phenomena in velocity modulation local oscillators. This noise is detected by the mixer and appears in its i-f output. In general, radar receivers use fairly high intermediate frequencies and local oscillator circuits have relatively small bandwidth. Both of these effects are beneficial, and at frequencies

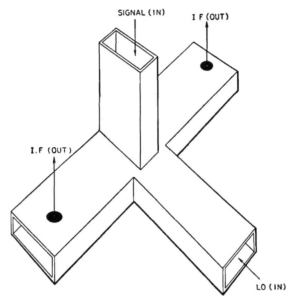

Fig. 10-23　Magic T Balanced Mixer. (By permission from *Microwave Receivers*, by Van Voorhis. Copyright 1948, McGraw-Hill Book Co., Inc.)

corresponding to S-band and lower, local oscillator noise is usually unimportant. At X-band, local oscillator noise becomes significant. A practical solution of the problem is the use of a mixer in which local oscillator power is fed to two mixing crystals in the same phase while the signal is supplied to them in phase opposition. The i-f outputs of the two crystals are fed to a balanced input circuit of the i-f amplifier. This causes detected local oscillator noise to be cancelled without affecting the desired signal. A "magic T," [14] shown diagrammatically in Fig. 10-23, may be used as such a balanced mixer. Proper operation of this device requires careful matching of the crystals. Aging of the crystals usually

[13] Brown, *Electronics*, p. 510, John Wiley & Sons, New York, 1954.
[14] Reich, Ordung, Krauss, and Skalnik, *Microwave Theory and Techniques*, p. 348, D. Van Nostrand Co., Inc., New York, 1953.

results in differing characteristics, so that even at X-band it is not always advantageous to use balanced mixers in equipments for military service.

10-28 I-f SYSTEMS

The i-f system of a radar receiver may be considered as comprising the preamplifier, main amplifier, and i-f detector. The preamplifier is usually located very near the transmitter plumbing so that unavoidable shunt capacitances across the mixer crystal i-f output will be small. The preamplifier is coupled to the main amplifier by coaxial cable which can be of considerable length, thus enabling the radar transmitter to be separated from the remainder of the equipment.

Equation (10-28) shows that, even with a low noise figure for a crystal mixer, the fact that its gain is less than unity causes the noise figure of the i-f amplifier to be of considerable concern. Similarly, the i-f amplifier may be considered to have two parts, the first stage and the remainder of the stages. If the gain of the first stage is high, the rest of the amplifier is unable to affect the noise figure appreciably. In radar receivers this is not entirely the case, and the effect of the second stage, although small, must be considered.

Once the designer has obtained an input stage with low noise figure and reasonable gain, the amplifier design is based upon obtaining adequate gain and optimum bandwidth, choosing a suitable operating frequency, and selecting the best interstage coupling method. In general, the i-f amplifier has at least enough gain to cause the noise to drive the i-f detector into the region of linearity. If the amplifier gain is made high enough so that noise actuates the a.g.c. loop, the amplifier will be gain-stabilized and aging of tubes will not seriously alter the overall gain. The usual radar receiver input noise dictates a gain of 100 to 120 db in the i-f amplifier for bandwidths of about 1 to 4 mc per sec.

If a rectangular pulse is applied to the input of a network, the rate at which the leading edge of the output pulse rises is directly proportional to the bandwidth of the network. Accordingly the i-f amplifier must have sufficient bandpass to allow the rectangular radar pulse to reach its peak value. Once this peak value is reached the signal amplitude remains constant, but the r.m.s. noise continues to increase directly with the one half power of the bandwidth. The best ratio of peak signal to r.m.s. noise occurs when the bandwidth of the i-f amplifier is the reciprocal of the pulse length. This relationship calls for bandwidths of 1.0 mc per sec for a 1.0-microsec pulse, 2.0 mc per sec for a 0.5-microsec pulse, etc. In practice the i-f bandwidth is made up to twice the optimum value. By so doing the faithfulness of reproduction is enhanced and the need for exact tuning of the local oscillator is lessened.

A number of factors relating the center frequency of an i-f amplifier with its performance are considered by a designer. Low center frequencies result in some improvement in noise figure, more freedom from input loading and Miller effect, and less critical tuning for a given bandwidth than do high frequencies. Among the relative benefits of high intermediate frequencies are better image rejection, smaller size of components, and greater freedom from various ills associated with automatic frequency control. These considerations have led to use of the spectrum between 30 and 60 mc per sec as the intermediate frequency in most modern pulsed fire control radar equipment. There are excellent texts devoted to the subject of i-f amplifier design[15] and the reader is referred to these for additional detail.

There is some advantage to range gating at intermediate frequency. It is possible to design a gating circuit which presents few problems with respect to gate residue because the coupling circuits of an i-f amplifier can be designed to discriminate against the video gating pulse. This advantage is purchased at the expense of having to supply an additional ungated i-f amplifier for displayed signals.

Diodes operated as half-wave rectifiers are by far the most popular i-f detectors used in pulsed radars. In general, vacuum tube diodes require the minimum input signal to be higher than about one volt in order to operate with good linearity. This means the r.m.s. i-f signal applied must be about 7 volts if linearity is required with modulation factors as high as 0.9. In a missile control system good detector linearity is required in order to prevent generation of harmonics of information-bearing signals. Such a signal might be the conical scan signal, harmonics of which bear no particular relationship to target position. The detector must reproduce the envelopes of the i-f pulses with reasonable fidelity in order to aid in range discrimination. Rise time of the video pulse is only slightly dependent upon the value of load resistance, depending principally on the values of i-f bypass capacitance and diode internal resistance. The load resistance must be determined on the basis of allowable pulse stretching. Desirable attributes of a diode for pulsed i-f detection are low resistance compared with the load resistance and driving source impedance, and low capacitance compared with the input capacitance of the next stage.

10-29 VIDEO AMPLIFIERS AND DETECTORS

The video amplifier delivers fairly-high-amplitude pulses of the desired polarity to the video detector and to any tracking or indicating devices which require a video signal. If range gating has not been accomplished in the i-f system, it is introduced in the video amplifier. This amplifier should introduce small rise and fall times, small overshoot and negligible droop to a rectangular input pulse of the greatest duration to be used.

[15] S. N. Van Voorhis, *Microwave Receivers*, McGraw-Hill Book Co., Inc., New York, 1948.

Suitable inductances in the plate circuit are often added, and by this means the cutoff frequency may be extended without introducing signal overshoot. The low frequency response required of a video amplifier depends upon how much "droop" is allowable on the top of the longest pulse to be handled. The reference level immediately following a rectangular pulse which has droop due to insufficient low frequency response is depressed by the amount of droop present. The low frequency response is determined by the time constants of the input coupling circuit, the plate and screen supply, and the cathode biasing arrangement. Overshoots, regardless of the origin, are detrimental to precise operation of range tracking circuits.

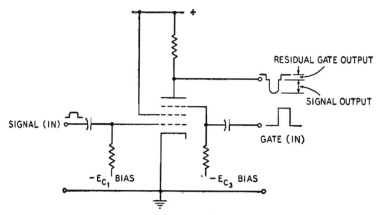

Fig. 10-24 Video Gating.

Gating of a video amplifier may be accomplished in several different ways. A very simple and easily adjusted method suitable for small positive signals is shown in basic form in Fig. 10-24. It is best suited for use with tubes like the 6AS6 and 6CS6 which have two grids of about the same transconductance. Plate current flow due to the gating pulse alone causes a pedestal to appear in the plate circuit output, and on this constant-amplitude pedestal the video signal appears. If it is objectionable, the pedestal may be removed by mixing a small percentage of the original gating pulse with the signal and pedestal applied to the next stage. The dynamic range of such a gated amplifier is not large, and it is advisable to restrict the input signal amplitude to a value just greater than that equivalent to 100 percent modulation of the a.g.c. regulated signal. A simple series diode type limiter is satisfactory.

The amplitude modulation on the pulse train introduced by the beam lobing process contains information about the amplitude and direction of antenna pointing error. The video detector recovers this amplitude variation, producing an a-c signal which contains the desired intelligence. The average energy per pulse cycle in a pulsed radar is usually very low, since the time between pulses is very large compared with the duration of one pulse. Video detectors, therefore, stretch each pulse and greatly increase the average energy per pulse. The most satisfactory detectors are the "boxcar" or 100 percent pulse stretchers. One form of this detector is the so-called infinite impedance pulse stretcher shown in Fig. 10-25. A positive pulse applied to the grid of V_1 places a charge on the storage capacitor, C. Immediately preceding the occurrence of the next signal pulse a clamping pulse is applied to V_2 which substantially discharges the

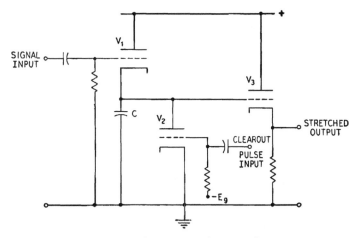

Fig. 10-25 100% Pulse Stretcher.

capacitor. A third tube V_3 is a cathode follower which offers very light loading of C and at the same time has a low output impedance. The clamping pulse may be obtained by differentiating the positive gating pulse. If the clearing pulses which appear at the output are objectionable, they may be eliminated by a simple low-pass filter. The theoretical transfer characteristic of this type of video detector is given by

$$\alpha = \frac{\sin \frac{\omega T_p}{2}}{\frac{\omega T_p}{2}} e^{-j\frac{\omega T_p}{2}} \qquad (10\text{-}32)[16]$$

where α = the complex transmission factor
       ω = the frequency of interest, in radians per second
       T_p = the repetition period in seconds

[16] Oliver, "Automatic Volume Control as a Feedback Problem," *Proc. IRE*, April 1948.

As an example: if the pulse repetition frequency is 500 pulses per sec, α will have the value $0.999 \underline{/-18°}$ at a modulation frequency of 50 cps. In practice α will have a lower magnitude and greater phase angle than the theoretical values. These quantities are factors which must be considered in the design of the receiver a.g.c. loop.

10-30 AUTOMATIC GAIN CONTROL [17]

The radar receiver is only one, although a very important, component of a servo system which produces information concerning instantaneous target range and angle. Operation of angle tracking and range tracking servo systems is discussed in Chap. 7. In order that the angle system may operate according to design, the receiver must furnish signals which are true indications of angular pointing error only. To this end the average

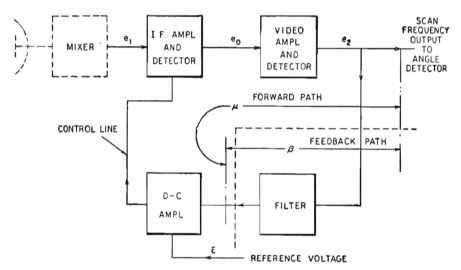

FIG. 10-26 A.g.c. System.

pulse level applied to the video detector must be held at a predetermined value regardless of distance to the target. If this is not done, the loop gain of the angle tracking system will depend upon the average amplitude of the received signals. Automatic gain control (a.g.c.) is used to accomplish this regulation of the output signal.

Figure 10-26 is a block diagram of the a.g.c. loop in a fire control or missile guidance radar receiver. The i-f pulses supplied by the mixer have a voltage amplitude e_1, which will vary as the inverse second power of range to the target if transmitter and receiver are at the same location. Superimposed upon it will be an a-c component, $m_1 e_1$, due to lobing of

[17] Oliver, *loc. cit.*

the antenna beam. The output of the video detector is a d-c signal of value e_2, which will be held within specified limits so that the lobing frequency-modulation voltage $m_2 e_2$ will not be dependent upon the target size or range. The filters have 100 percent transmission at zero frequency and are designed to produce stable operation of the loop. The d-c signal from the video detector and filter is compared with a reference voltage, E, and when the reference value is reached the d-c amplifier begins to produce a control voltage which decreases the i-f amplifier gain and thus opposes the effects of increasing e_1. Input signal e_1 has a-c components other than those due to target position in the beam. These are caused by variations in range to the target, varying target aspect and hence reflectivity as a function of time, interference patterns due to multipath transmission, and noise due to target dimensions itself when the target subtends an appreciable angle as seen by the antenna. Only the component of $m_1 e_1$ caused by the target position is of value. All others are considered to be noise as they result in degradation of tracking performance if allowed to reach the antenna positioning servos. The well-designed a.g.c. system has the following characteristics:

(a) It holds the zero frequency variation of the output signal within acceptable limits.
(b) It removes as much of the noise as possible by feeding it back as a degenerative control signal to some element in the μ, or forward, path.
(c) It leaves the desired modulation unimpaired in phase and amplitude.

It can be shown that, if $\mu\beta$ is large compared with unity,

$$e_2 \cong \frac{1}{\beta} E \qquad (10\text{-}33)$$

and that

$$\frac{de_2}{e_2} = \frac{1}{1 - \mu\beta} \frac{d\mu}{\mu} \qquad (10\text{-}34)$$

Equation (10-33) shows that, when $\beta = -1$, the output voltage will be nearly equal to the reference voltage and opposite in polarity. It also shows that an undelayed a.g.c. system ($E = 0$) should have an output which is almost zero. In practice this does not occur because, at very low values of e_1, $\mu\beta$ is not generally very large and hence Eq. (10-33) does not apply. Equation (10-34) indicates that any disturbance in the μ path will reduce by a factor $1/(1 - \mu\beta)$ as far as the output voltage is concerned. This can be shown to apply to variations in e_1, so that Eq. (10-34) may be extended to read directly:

$$\frac{de_2}{e_2} = \frac{1}{1 - \mu\beta} \frac{de_1}{e_1} \qquad (10\text{-}35)$$

"Loop gain," the product $\mu\beta$, is the ratio of the incremental output of the d-c amplifier in Fig. 10-26 to a very small input signal applied to the control line, the loop first being opened at the d-c amplifier output terminal. With no modulation present, the video amplifier and detector have a gain constant which is simply the gain of the amplifier times the gain of the detector, the phase angle being zero. The filters in the β, or feedback, path normally have a d-c gain of unity, and the d-c amplifier has a gain which, although not constant, may be assumed so for design purposes. Oliver[18] has shown that the modulation gain of the i-f amplifier is given by

$$g = 0.11514 \frac{dG}{dV} e_0 \qquad (10\text{-}36)$$

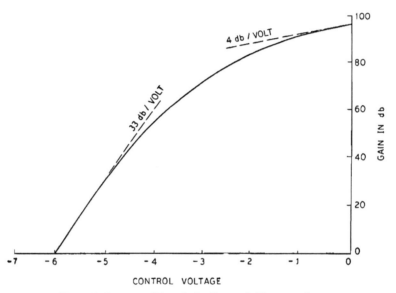

Fig. 10-27 Amplifier Gain Control Characteristic.

where dG/dV is the slope of the amplifier gain in db versus the control voltage, and e_0 is the i-f detector output pulse level. A typical G versus V curve for an i-f amplifier using grid control is shown in Fig. 10-27. In practice a truer idea of the variation in modulation gain with control voltage may be obtained if the d-c amplifier and i-f amplifier are measured as a unit. This is especially true when the d-c amplifier is operated at cutoff for signals below threshold, since the gain starts at zero, and varies with the input signal.

Figure 10-28 illustrates the advantages of using delayed a.g.c. whether or not there is d-c amplification in the control voltage path. The solid

[18] Oliver, *loc. cit.*

curve at the top shows the regulation obtained with the i-f amplifier whose characteristics are shown in Fig. 10-27 when the video and d-c amplifier gains are unity. Increasing this gain to 10 produces no effect below the threshold value, but reduces the variation above that point by a factor of 10. The center curve shows the action with no delay, unity gain; and the bottom curve shows the effect of a gain of 10 in the d-c amplifier. The only effect is to decrease the output level everywhere by a factor of 10 without improving the regulation percentage-wise. This illustrates the theoretical deduction that, with zero delay, the a.g.c. regulation is con-

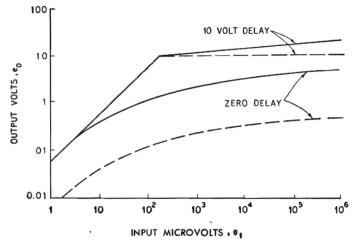

Fig. 10-28 A.g.c. Regulation Characteristics. (From Oliver, *loc cit*.)

trolled entirely by the modulation characteristics of the i-f amplifier and the operating control voltage.

In the usual case the a.g.c. system is inoperative for very small signals, since the output produced is below the desired level. This condition coincides with maximum gain of the i-f amplifier, which occurs at a control voltage of zero. As the input signal is increased the output rises, and at some predetermined level, the loop begins to close and holds the output within specified limits. If the operation is as described, the maximum loop gain required is:

$$\mu\beta_{(0)\max} = \frac{V_m g}{1 - \dfrac{e_{\min}}{e_{\max}}} \qquad (10\text{-}37)$$

where $\mu\beta_{(0)\max}$ = the maximum zero frequency loop gain needed

V_m = the control voltage needed to reduce the gain to the required value

g = the modulation gain of the i-f amplifier corresponding to V_m.

$e_{\min}$ = the i-f detector output level at which regulation starts

$e_{\max}$ = the greatest allowable value for the i-f detector output

As an example, suppose the amplifier of Fig. 10-27 must handle an input signal variation of 96 db and the output must be held between 10.0 and 11.0 volts. The control voltage begins at zero and must be -6.1 to effect the required gain reduction. The maximum modulation gain is $0.1154 \times 33 = 3.8$.

Substituting these values in Eq. (10-37), we have

$$\mu\beta_{(0)\max} = \frac{6.1 \times 3.8}{1 - \frac{10}{11}} = 255 = 48.1 \text{ db}$$

The loop gain needed is far below the actual reduction in gain required. In this case, an output variation of slightly less than 1 db for an input variation of 96 db was obtained with only 48 db of loop gain.

The filter shown in Fig. 10-26 determines the amplitude-frequency characteristics of the β path, and since μ is relatively large, the filter largely determines the closed loop frequency response of the a.g.c. system. It is desirable that this filter perform the following functions:

(a) transmit frequencies from d-c to just below the modulation frequency of interest;
(b) reduce the loop gain at the modulation frequency so that the modulation may not be washed out;
(c) cause the phase and gain margins of the loop to have suitable values in order to assure closed loop stability.

In radar receivers the i-f bandwidth is so great compared with the center frequency that there is no discrimination against sidebands which affect a.g.c. operation. Under these conditions, the effect of a.g.c. on signals of small modulation percentage is given by

$$m_0(\omega) = \frac{m_1(\omega)}{1 - \mu\beta(\omega)} \tag{10-38}$$

where m_0 and m_1 are the output and input modulation indices respectively. Thus at all frequencies where $\mu\beta$ is large, modulation appearing on the input signal will be attenuated in the output signal. It is evident that if 100 percent of the input modulation is to be recovered, the loop gain at that frequency must be zero. For practical reasons the a.g.c. design will attempt to recover only 90 percent or so of the input modulation. The filter usually is a low-pass or a double low-pass filter. Figure 10-29 shows the relative effects of the two types of filters. An arbitrary case of 40 db of loop gain at zero frequency and a corner frequency of 1.0 cps for the low-pass filter is assumed. For the 2-section case each low-pass filter has a corner of approximately 1.6 cps.

The usual closed loop stability requirements must be met in an a.g.c. system. To accomplish this, the open loop transfer characteristic is allowed to go through unity gain with slopes of 9 db per octave or less in order to insure 45 deg or more of phase margin. The need for high percentage recovery of scan modulation requires the loop gain to be very low at this frequency. Since in radar work the scan frequency usually is 10 percent or less of the repetition frequency, the foregoing requirement guarantees ample gain margin when the filter is a simple low-pass one. This follows from the fact that the pulse stretcher introduces a -90-deg phase shift at one half of the repetition frequency, making this the approximate frequency at which the overall phase shift becomes zero.

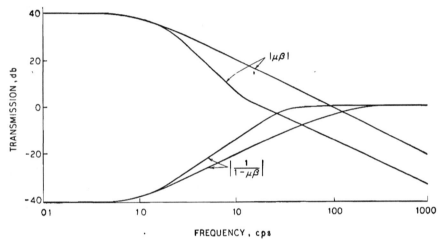

FIG. 10-29 Open and Closed Loop Response. (From Oliver, *loc cit.*)

It should be noted (see Fig. 10-27) that the modulation characteristic of the i-f amplifier is dependent upon the control voltage. The value of dG/dV varies from 33 to 4 db per volt. The loop gain consequently has a variation of 18 db for an input signal variation of 96 db. The i-f amplifier is the only element in the loop whose gain is dependent on signal amplitude. Whereas only the amplitude of $\mu\beta$ is dependent upon signal level, both *amplitude and phase* of $1-\mu\beta$ are dependent. This means that Eq. (10-38) implies a rotation of the scan modulation phase as a function of signal strength. In an automatic tracking radar this is very undesirable. Normally the angle detector reference signal phase is adjusted so that an error introduced in only one coordinate does not produce an output in the other coordinate. In other words, "crosstalk" between coordinates is removed.

If the signal containing angle information has a phase which varies, crosstalk will have been removed only at the signal level used in making the adjustment. Only a small amount of phase change is tolerable before the tracking noise increases markedly, taking the form of a nutating motion of the antenna.

Inspection will show that, if the gain in db versus control voltage could be made a straight line, the modulation gain would be constant. This might be done by special tube design. The variation between maximum and minimum slope may be minimized for a given range of signal handling capability by gain-controlling as large a number of stages as possible. For this reason, and because of the enormous range of amplitudes encountered, missile guidance and fire control radar receivers should control all i-f stages except the final one which feeds the detector. By setting the filter corner frequency back toward zero, the attenuation may be made so great that $\mu\beta(\omega)$ at the modulation frequency is low enough so that the phase variation of $1 - \mu\beta(\omega)$ is within acceptable limits. It is also possible to make $1 - \mu\beta(\omega)$ phase invariant at the scan frequency by designing the a.g.c. loop so that the phase crossover frequency (filter plus incidental phase shifts totaling 180 deg) is also the scan modulation frequency. This causes $1 - \mu\beta$ to have zero phase angle, a condition which is independent of the magnitude of $\mu\beta$, as well as of signal strength.

In attempts at making $\mu\beta(\omega)$ very small at the scan frequency, bridged T's or some form of parallel-T, R-C networks have been used. Such methods must be approached with caution, since the rapid phase shift with change in frequency and rising amplitude characteristic at frequencies higher than the null easily lead to oscillation of the loop at half the repetition frequency. Another disadvantage is that gain enhancement may occur. If $1 - \mu\beta(\omega)$ falls below unity at any frequency, modulation enhancement will result. This may be expected in the case of a radar receiver which uses a bridged-T type of network in the β path. Considerable gain enhancement may occur near the scan frequency.

10-31 AUTOMATIC RANGE TRACKING

Most of the weapons control systems of World War II made use of radar systems utilizing manual range tracking by an operator whose duty it was to position a marker in time (range) coincidence with the echo from the desired target. The positioning of the marker caused range data to be generated within the radar. The data could be extracted and used by other parts of the weapons system.

With the advent of high-performance aircraft and guided missiles, the inability of a human operator, aided by simple equipment, to range-track accurately for long periods of time caused the weapon system performance to be compromised. This need forced the development of automatic equipment to perform the range tracking function.

A typical automatic range tracking system is shown in the block diagram of Fig. 10-30. The relationship to a servo system is evident. The time discriminator corresponds to the comparator or error detector of the servo system; the shaping unit is recognized as the equalizer and amplifier and the time modulator is the motor.

If the automatic range tracker is electromechanical, it includes, in addition to the electronic parts, an electromechanical converter consisting of a motor and gear train which turn the input shaft of an electromechanical time modulator.

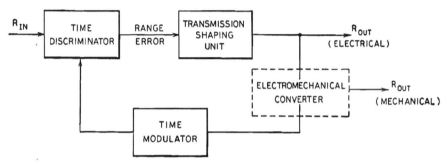

Fig. 10-30 Range Tracking Circuit.

The following paragraphs describe the design and operation of the time modulator and time discriminator as they affect system performance.

Early techniques in the design of time discriminators were based on several physical principles as shown in the literature.[19,20] In modern design, however, one basic physical principle has come to be acknowledged as superior. This principle is one wherein the video signal to be tracked is divided into an early part and a late part. The energies in these parts are compared in a differential circuit to develop a voltage proportional to range position error. The dividing line of the video signal is the center of a locally generated reference signal or gate.

Two basic variations of this method are in common use. Figure 10-31 shows the detailed difference. The theoretical difference between the methods can be shown to be zero. Figure 10-31a shows the waveforms of the inputs to the "doubled signal" type of time discriminator. The original video signal is delivered to a circuit which delays the signal by approximately its time duration. The delayed and inverted signal is combined

[19] Chance, Hulsizer, MacNichol and Williams, *Electronic Time Measurements*, McGraw-Hill Book Co.
[20] Starr, *loc. cit*.

with the original signal shown in (3) of Figure 10-31a. The original signal of (1) of Figure 10-31a may be either raw or range-gated video. Raw video may be used; however, the pre-gating is usually helpful in excluding chance spurious signals of large amplitude. A simplified circuit for accomplishing the signal doubling is shown on Fig. 10-32. An unterminated delay line whose time delay is approximately equal to one half of the pulse duration, Δ, is shunted across the plate load of a video amplifier. The positive output pulse of the video amplifier is reflected out of phase at the shorted end

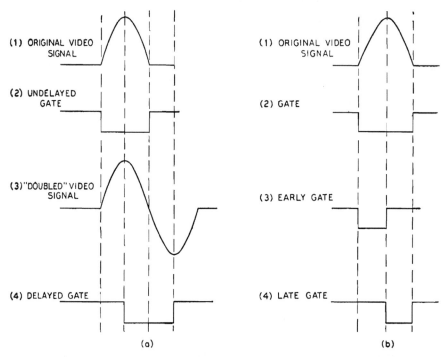

FIG. 10-31 Waveforms in a Time Discriminator: (a) "Double Signal" Type; (b) "Split Gate" Type.

of the line and appears at the amplifier plate as a negative-going replica of the original signal. A disadvantage of this circuit is that the delay line, which is actually a multisection low-pass filter, band-limits in the late half of the "doubled signal." This would not be serious if the video signal were always of constant amplitude and noise-free. The band-limiting that attends the use of the delay line causes the energy in the two halves of the doubled signal to be unequal to a degree dependent upon signal amplitude and noise amplitude. If the delay line is not of suitable design, the time discriminator may operate correctly at only one amplitude and

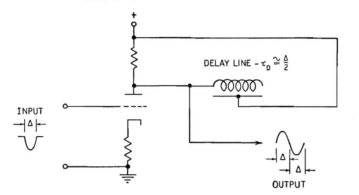

Fig. 10-32 Video Signal "Doubling" Circuit.

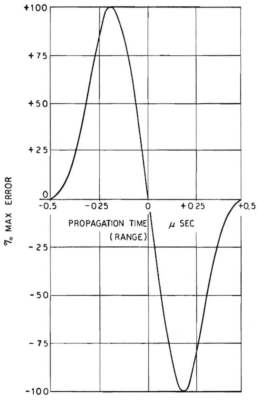

Fig. 10-33 Time Discriminator Characteristic.

may exhibit other than zero output for an input which is largely receiver noise. If the delay line can be designed to have a much greater bandwidth than the spectrum of its input pulse, the effect can be minimized. The local time reference generated by the range unit is delayed sufficiently (approximately one pulse duration) to cause its center, when zero range error is present, to coincide in time with the axis crossing of the "doubled signal" of waveform (3) of Fig. 10-31a.

If the waveforms of (3) and (4) of Fig. 10-31a are inputs to an integrating time discriminator, the output as a function of gate position with respect to the echo center is of the shape shown in Fig. 10-33. A typical time discriminator capable of working with these inputs is shown in Fig. 10-34.

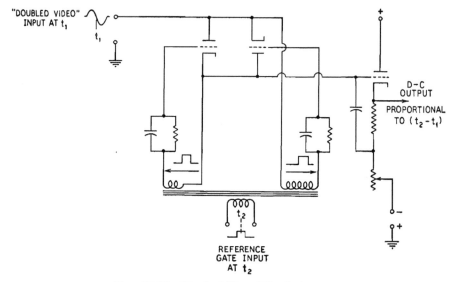

Fig. 10-34 Typical Time Discriminator.

The time discriminator appears to the range servo system as a low-pass filter. The low-pass characteristic must be designed so that sufficient integration of the pulse wave form is accomplished while at the same time appreciable phase shift, in the servo pass band, must be avoided. Analysis of the range tracking loop is simple if the time discriminator is considered as a voltage generator whose internal impedance is relatively high but certainly not infinite. This approach avoids the problem of what to do with the transconductance which appears when the time discriminator is considered as a current source.

A careful mathematical analysis of the time discriminator for the inputs of Fig. 10-31b will yield the same discriminator characteristic as shown in Fig. 10-33. From this point on, the comments made about the system of Fig. 10-31a hold for the system of Fig. 10-31b. At first appearance, the system of Fig. 10-31a has poorer range definition than that of Fig. 10-31b. This is not the case, however, because the same signal selection (gating) process, requiring the same pulse and gate lengths, must be used for both systems. This selection process determines range definition. The system of Fig. 10-31b, although it is less troubled with bandwidth variation in the comparison intervals, is very sensitive to the equality of the gate lengths. There seems to be little choice between the two methods.

If the time discriminator characteristic of Fig. 10-33 has the time axis multiplied by an inverse function of real time such as the output of a range search generator, the resulting curve and its derivatives may be used as an input function for the design of the servo system needed to acquire the target.

10-32 RANGE UNITS

The range unit is that part of a radar system which supplies the time discriminator with a local time reference against which range is reckoned. Basically the unit consists of a source of time signals and a mechanism for interpolating between them. Depending upon the accuracy required, the unit can be simple or complex.

A simple unit designed to measure range might consist of a linear sawtooth generator, a time modulator (the interpolator) to read out the amplitude, and shaping circuits to convert the sawtooth amplitude at a particular time to a pulse whose time displacement depends upon the amplitude. Such a unit is diagrammed in Fig. 10-35. The range accuracy of this unit can approach about ±1 percent of the maximum range to be measured.

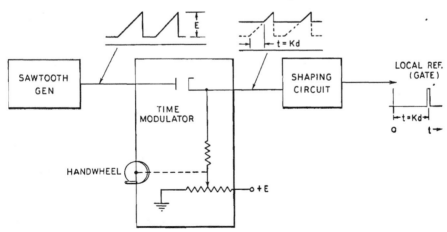

Fig. 10-35 Low-accuracy Range Unit.

If greater accuracy is required it is necessary to utilize a basic timing signal with higher accuracy than that of a so-called "linear sawtooth." The ultimate accuracy which can be achieved then begins to depend also upon the time modulator. One unit of high accuracy used in many fire control radar sets is the "Meacham" range unit. The basic time signal can be a crystal oscillator and the time modulator is usually a capacitor-type phase shifter. Such a unit is shown in Fig. 10-36. The crystal oscillator operates in the frequency range below 200 kc per sec. The phase shifter (which could also be 2- or 3-phase) is designed so that the rotor signal has a phase which is a continuous linear function of shaft angular rotation. Capacitors of this type are available. Such capacitors have a phase error of 0.7 deg in the kilocycle region. In order to make the phase error a small percentage of full-scale range it is necessary to have the time modulator recycle many times in attaining full-scale range. To avoid ambiguities it

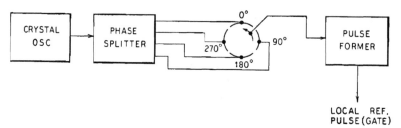

Fig. 10-36 High-accuracy Range Unit.

is usual to operate the unit in conjunction with a lower accuracy range unit of the sawtooth type as described previously. The accuracy of this auxiliary range unit need be only great enough to select the proper cycle of operation of the high accuracy unit, an end easily attained. The high accuracy or "fine" unit as shown is usually a continuous wave device. If it were desired to use the unit with a pulsed radar, it would be difficult, without additional equipment, to start the oscillator in the correct phase to have readings repeat for each pulse cycle.

To make operation with pulsed radar possible, it becomes necessary either to pulse the oscillator or to derive the radar p.r.f. from the oscillator frequency by means of frequency dividers.

The oscillator frequency can be controlled to almost any accuracy needed to make errors from this source negligible. The specification for the accuracy of the unit should read $\pm X\%$ of the range (caused by oscillator frequency) and $\pm Y$ yd (caused by error of a cyclic nature in the phase shifter at the frequency of use).

A range unit of high accuracy using a phase capacitor as described has one important disadvantage: that of high mechanical rotational inertia.

10-33 ANGLE ERROR DETECTORS

The design of a servo system to make use of the unit in an automatic tracking mode is made more difficult as a result of the inertia.

In a conical scanning fire control radar the target position data are modulated upon the scan frequency as was explained in Par. 10-7. The function of the angle error detector is to demodulate the data from the scan carrier and deliver them in the most usable form to the circuits which position the antenna.

Since the demodulator is a part of the forward path of the positioning servo system, it is desirable to use a balanced circuit that automatically eliminates the scan carrier frequency; thus the phase shift in a filter which would otherwise be necessary to reject the carrier is avoided. The scan

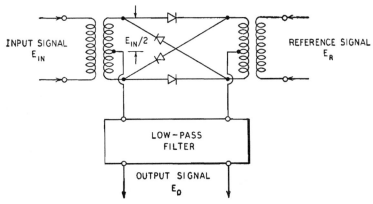

FIG. 10-37 Ring Demodulator.

frequency is the only frequency having sidebands representing true target motion (assuming sinusoidal scanning). It is then desirable to discriminate against all other signals since they carry only noise as sidebands.

Figure 10-37 shows the circuit for a "ring demodulator," one of the circuits which is capable of accomplishing these results. This circuit is sometimes called a "correlator" or a "product detector" in modern literature. The reference input signal E_R is the scan frequency sample with which it is desired to correlate the input signal E_{in}. E_R is usually obtained from a drag cup generator mechanically connected to the scanner. The generator output is made to be in phase (usually by mechanically rotating the generator frame) with the expected input signal.

For a high load impedance, the circuit output voltage may be written in terms of the input as follows:

$$E_o = E_i \frac{1}{\pi} \Big\{ \{\cos[(\omega_1 - \omega_2)t + \phi] - \cos[(\omega_1 + \omega_2)t + \phi]\}$$
$$+ \tfrac{1}{3}\{\cos[(\omega_1 - 3\omega_2)t + \phi] - \cos[(\omega_1 + 3\omega_2)t + \phi]\}$$
$$+ \tfrac{1}{5}\{\cos[(\omega_1 - 5\omega_2)t + \phi] - \cos[(\omega_1 + 5\omega_2)t + \phi]\}$$
$$+ \tfrac{1}{7} \cdots \Big\} \qquad (10\text{-}39)$$

where ω_1 = input signal angular frequency in radians per second
ω_2 = reference or switching angular frequency in radians per second
t = time in seconds
ϕ = relative phase in radians of the input signal with respect to the reference signal
E_o = output voltage
E_i = input voltage, maximum value

If ω_1 and ω_2 are equal and E_i contains no harmonic terms, the first term of Eq. (10-39) determines a d-c output signal as follows:

$$E_o = E_i \frac{1}{\pi} \cos \phi \qquad (10\text{-}40)$$

This relationship is the simple cosine curve plotted in Fig. 10-38. It is interesting to note that no output is obtained when ϕ is equal to either $\pi/2$ or $3\pi/2$ radians. It is this fact which makes the circuit useful for separating the up-down and right-left coordinates of a tracking radar. A fixed target observed by a radar using this device would then generate a

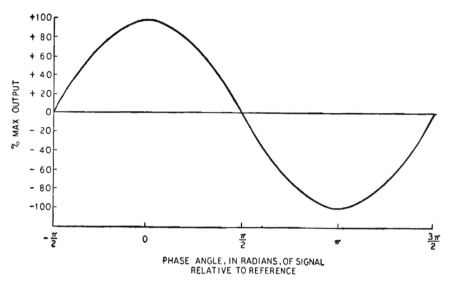

Fig. 10-38 Fundamental Frequency Phase Characteristic of Ring Modulator.

d-c voltage in each coordinate proportional to the target's displacement from the antenna axis in each coordinate.

If it is now assumed that the target performs a horizontal sinusoidal maneuver about the antenna axis, ω_1 becomes a carrier and the maneuver becomes evident as sidebands about ω_1. The output voltages from the left-right detector consist of a low frequency sinusoid at the same rate as the maneuver with an amplitude proportional to the maximum displacement of the target about the antenna axis. It was assumed for purposes of this discussion that the antenna was a linear modulator at the scan frequency.

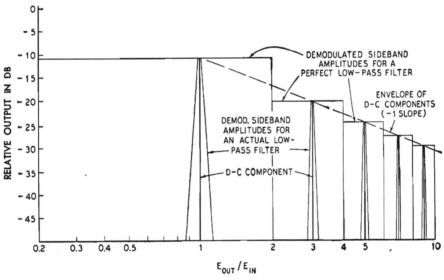

Fig. 10-39 Ring Demodulator Characteristic.

If the antenna is not a linear modulator or if the target fades so as to produce an apparent motion, it is important to examine other than the first term of Eq. (10-39). These terms can represent spurious outputs for a noisy input signal.

The relative output is plotted in Fig. 10-39 as a function of a constant-amplitude, variable-frequency input signal. The effects of both a perfect and an actual low-pass filter are shown. It can be seen that the inherent characteristics of the detector discriminate against noise components of the signal. The integrated output voltage is zero for inputs at all even harmonics of the reference signal and the output at odd harmonics is enclosed by a line of minus one slope. The output voltage without filtering is shown in Fig. 10-40 for various harmonic input conditions. Notice that, for the fundamental and its first few harmonics, the ratio of peak to average value of the output voltage is low. This makes it possible to accomplish low-pass filtering in some existing circuit element such as a servo motor without danger of system overload on peaks. The detector is

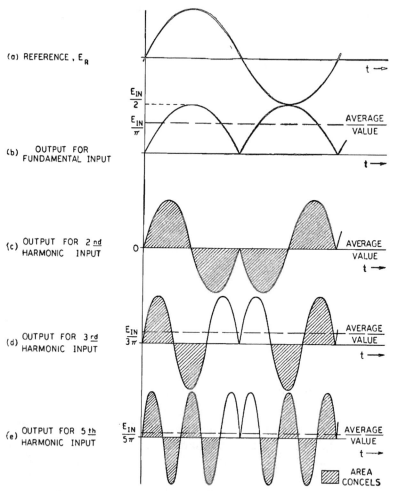

FIG. 10-40 Switching Analysis of Ring Demodulator.

actually a full-wave commutator in which the reference signal controls the switching sequence. It is of practical importance that the reference signal be at least twice the maximum expected input signal if the switching sequence is to remain under control.

10-34 POWER SOURCES

An important link in the radar guidance circuit is the power source. Although it is good practice to design radar circuits to operate over a wide range of plate supply voltages, this is frequently impossible. The alternative is to regulate the supply voltages to the required tolerance. The tendency in modern radar sets is to supply all plate power from one or several central sources. When this practice is followed, it becomes important to consider the regulation required as a function of circuit frequency. The designer is beset with the problem of connecting numerous circuits to the common power supply in a way that causes a minimum of crosstalk between units.

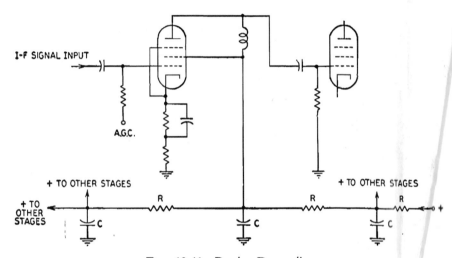

FIG. 10-41 Passive Decoupling.

Fortunately it is possible to reduce the crosstalk economically by a number of methods. Passive decoupling filters may be used or the problem can be solved by rather simple electronic voltage regulators.

In the design of passive decoupling networks for circuit operation, the designer must consider the application of the signals in the circuit. If one signal is used as a carrier for another signal, as is frequently the case, the decoupling network must be an effective integrator of the carrier and its sidebands. The decoupling circuit must also be examined as part of the vacuum tube plate load. It is possible, for example, to design decoupling networks for the plate circuits of an i-f amplifier which, although they effectively isolate the circuits at the intermediate frequency, enable the amplifier to become an efficient video or audio amplifier. Suppose that an i-f amplifier has been designed and connected to a power source through decoupling circuits which operate effectively at the intermediate frequency. The circuit is as shown in Fig. 10-41. When an a.g.c. system is used, the low frequency control signal impressed on the i-f amplifier grid may be amplified in the stage if the R-C decoupling networks are not properly designed. If the decoupling is not effective at a.g.c. frequencies, the a.g.c. system may oscillate or otherwise operate improperly. Even if no appreciable gain is realized at the a.g.c. frequency due to this cause, exsessive phase shift through the a.g.c. loop may result. It is possible to visualize other examples of this situation, but we will not discuss them here.

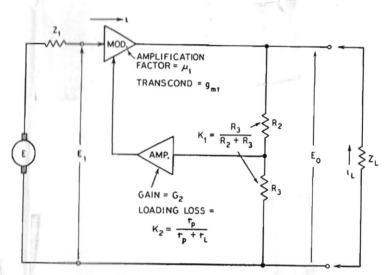

Fig. 10-42 Regulated Power System.

A simple electronic voltage regulator is the gaseous shunt tube such as the OD3, which has been available for a number of years. The average effective internal impedance of these tubes approximates 1000 ohms at frequencies between d-c and several megacycles. Frequently, this is not low enough to reduce circuit crosstalk to a usable value. It then becomes necessary to consider the use of an electronic regulator which operates on the principles of a servo system. Such a regulator can reduce the power source internal impedance to a very low value, depending on the servo system loop gain. A simple diagram of an electronic regulator is shown in Fig. 10-42. The design of an electronic regulator revolves about two important factors: (a) the required series regulation, $\Delta E_i/\Delta E_o$ and (b) the required internal impedance, Z_o.

10-34] POWER SOURCES

Series Regulation. The series regulation of an electronic regulator system is given by Seely[21] as

$$\frac{\Delta E_i}{\Delta E_o} = \frac{1 + \mu_1 + K_1 G_2 \mu_1}{1 + K_2 \mu_1} \qquad (10\text{-}40)$$

neglecting the effect of regulation of the source. The source regulation may be readily included as follows:

$$E_i = E - iZ_1 \qquad (10\text{-}41)$$

If the ratio of load current i_L to regulator internal current is very large, then

$$i \approx i_L = \frac{E_o}{Z_L} \qquad (10\text{-}42)$$

Substituting Eq. (10-42) into (10-41) we obtain

$$E_i = E - E_o \frac{Z_1}{Z_L} \qquad (10\text{-}43)$$

$$\Delta E_i = \Delta E - \Delta E_o \frac{Z_1}{Z_L} \qquad (10\text{-}44)$$

$$\frac{\Delta E_i}{\Delta E_o} = \frac{\Delta E}{\Delta E_o} - \frac{Z_1}{Z_L} \qquad (10\text{-}45)$$

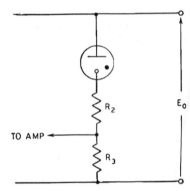

Fig. 10-43 Reducing Divider Loss by Use of Gas Tube.

This modifies Eq. (10-40) to include the effect of source regulation thusly:

$$\frac{\Delta E}{\Delta E_o} = \frac{1 + \mu_1 + K_1 G_2 \mu_1}{1 + K_2 \mu_1} + \frac{Z_1}{Z_L} \qquad (10\text{-}46)$$

One can readily see the advantage of reducing Z_1 as much as possible. Equation (10-46) can be further simplified by approximation. Let the modulator tube of Fig. 10-42 be a 6AS7-G, where $\mu_1 = 2.1$. A d-c amplifier gain G_2 of 100 can be readily obtained. K_1 can be made to approximate unity if a gaseous regulator tube is used to buck some of E_o as shown in Fig. 10-43.

In this case,

$$\frac{\Delta E}{\Delta E_o} \approx 70 + \frac{Z_1}{Z_L} \qquad (10\text{-}47)$$

If Z_1/Z_L were made to be approximately 35, the effect of source regulation would begin to be noticeable.

Internal Impedance. The internal impedance Z_0 of an electronic regulator is given by Seely[22] as,

---

[21] Seely, *Electron Tube Circuits*, McGraw-Hill Book Co., 1950.
[22] Seely, *loc. cit.*

$$Z_0 = \frac{1}{g_{m_1}K_1G_2} + \frac{Z_1}{(\Delta E/\Delta E_o)} \qquad (10\text{-}48)$$

Here the importance of a low source internal resistance is again evident. It is practical to reduce Z_0 by using a number of modulator tubes in parallel. This causes the factor g_{m_1} to be multiplied by the number of tubes used. As an example of what can be done, consider a regulator using 10-6AS7-G dual modulator tubes where $g_m = 7500 \times 10^{-6}$ mho per tube half. Also, let the amplifier gain $G_2 = 100$, $K_1 = 1$, and $Z_1 = 0$.

$$Z_0 = 0.0667\underline{/0°} \text{ ohm}$$

at low frequencies.

10-35 RADAR TRACKING AT LOW ELEVATION ANGLES [23]

One of the sources of noise in a tracking radar is the inability of the radar to determine accurately the elevation angle of arrival of an echo at an angle lower than approximately the antenna beamwidth above the horizon. The difficulty is caused by interference between energy propagated over direct and reflected paths to the target. This problem receives excellent treatment in Volume 13 of the *Radiation Laboratory Series*, part of which will be reviewed here.

The presence of the earth complicates the free-space concept of the propagation of energy. The earth reflects and scatters incident energy in such a way as to produce an interference pattern. It is convenient to introduce a *pattern propagation factor*, Γ, to take care of the disturbance. Γ is defined as the ratio of the amplitude of the electric field at a given point under specified conditions to the amplitude of the electric field under free-space conditions with the beam of the antenna directed toward the point in question. Symbolically,

$$\Gamma = \frac{\xi}{\xi_0} \qquad (10\text{-}49)$$

where ξ_0 is the free-space field magnitude and ξ is the disturbed field magnitude. In the special case of free-space propagation, $\Gamma = |f(\theta)|$, the normalized antenna pattern. θ is the angle off the beam axis.

The conically scanning tracking radar, in the elevation coordinate, attempts to null the energy in the upper scan semicircle against that in the lower scan semicircle. In free space this occurs when a line can be drawn between the effective source of radiation, the pattern crossover, and the target. Ideally this linear condition happens because the pattern propagation function $\Gamma = f(\theta)$ is a constant throughout a scan cycle.

Although this reflection problem can be studied in a plane normal to the surface and including the antenna beam axis, it is more difficult to

---

[23] After *Radiation Laboratory Series*, Vol. 13, Chap. 5.

study it throughout the scan cycle. If the scan frequency is sufficiently removed from the frequency generated by a target passing through the lobe structure (as is usually the case), it does not become important to conduct the study in other than the vertical plane. Such an assumption is tantamount to assuming that the value of Γ does not vary appreciably from scan to scan. The value of Γ actually does vary slowly from scan to scan.

Confining the problem only to the vertical plane means that the conical scanning radar, for purposes of this discussion, is equivalent to a lobe switching radar. A number of early radars, such as the U.S. Navy Mk.4, used the lobe switching method, wherein four discrete antenna beam

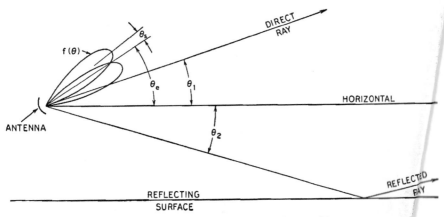

FIG. 10-44 Geometry of the Interference Region.

directions—namely, up, left, down, right—were used to improve angular resolution. Information regarding the direction to the target was obtained by comparing the echo received from the up-down or right-left lobes. The comparison, if accurately made, develops in the radar circuits an error voltage which positions the antenna in such a way as to make the Γ associated with the upper beam equal to Γ associated with the lower beam.

$$\Gamma = |f(\theta_1 - \theta_e - \theta_s) + \rho f(-\theta_2 - \theta_e - \theta_s)| \qquad (10\text{-}50)$$

and for the lower beam

$$\Gamma = |f(\theta_1 - \theta_e + \theta_s) + \rho f(-\theta_2 - \theta_e + \theta_s)| \qquad (10\text{-}51)$$

where the terminology is shown in Fig. 10-44 and where ρ is the effective reflection coefficient including the effect of divergence due to earth's curvature. The first term of the sum is the direct ray magnitude and the second term is the reflected ray magnitude. The direct and reflected rays are actually vectors, and the phase angle between them is proportional to the path length difference at the frequency of interest.

Solutions for Eq. (10-50) and (10-51) are shown on the envelopes of Fig. 10-45. The actual indicated angles between the envelope lines must be arrived at by taking account of the vectorial nature of the sum.

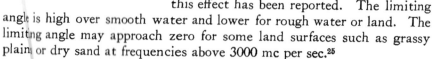

Fig. 10-45 Indicated Height as a Function of True Height at Constant Range.

Figure 10-46 shows the theoretical and experimental solutions for a radar sited at 100 ft above the water for a target at 600 ft altitude. The range at which the perturbations occur checks quite well, although the amplitude does not. This is to be expected because it was impossible to use instantaneous measured values of the reflection coefficient in the calculated curves.

Theoretical [24] and experimental evaluation of the limiting elevation angles shows that, for angles equal to or greater than about a single lobe beamwidth above the horizontal, the tracking noise is nearly as low as in free space. This condition exists for low side-lobe levels. If the side lobes are high in level, the expected limiting angle should be increased, although no study of this effect has been reported. The limiting angle is high over smooth water and lower for rough water or land. The limiting angle may approach zero for some land surfaces such as grassy plains or dry sand at frequencies above 3000 mc per sec.[25]

10-36 CORRELATION TECHNIQUES

In post World War II years the mathematical principle of "correlation" has become popular because of its possible application to the improvement in signal demodulation. The mathematics of the principle are not new[26] and receive further treatment in Chap. 6 of this volume. It is sufficient to state here that, if two functions of time are to be correlated, it is necessary to multiply one by the other and integrate the product over a long interval of time. The particular correlation processes of interest in electronics circuitry are known as "autocorrelation" and "cross correlation."

The autocorrelation function $H_{11}(\tau)$, is defined as

[24] R. A. Huner et al., "Radar Height Finding," *R. L. Report No. 21*, April 6, 1943.
[25] *Radiation Laboratory Series*, Vol. 13, p. 418 and p. 430.
[26] *Proc. Mat. Soc. (London)*, Vol. 20, 1922, p. 196.

$$H_{11}(\tau) = \lim_{t_1 \to \infty} \frac{1}{2t_1} \int_{-t_1}^{t_1} f_1(t) f_1(t - \tau) \, dt \qquad (10\text{-}52)$$

where $f_1(t)$ may be a continuous member function of a stationary random process such as broadband noise, or a periodic function; $f_1(t - \tau)$ is the same function delayed by an increment of time, τ. The cross correlation function, $H_{12}(\tau)$ is defined as

$$H_{12}(\tau) = \lim_{t_1 \to \infty} \frac{1}{2t_1} \int_{-t_1}^{t_1} f_1(t) f_2(t - \tau) \, dt \qquad (10\text{-}53)$$

where the functions $f_1(t)$ and $f_2(t - \tau)$ are not the same but are in some manner related to each other. The time delay between the functions remains as τ. Although the autocorrelation technique has theoretical possibilities for detecting signals deeply imbedded in noise,[27] the long observation time required makes this impractical in many cases. Most of

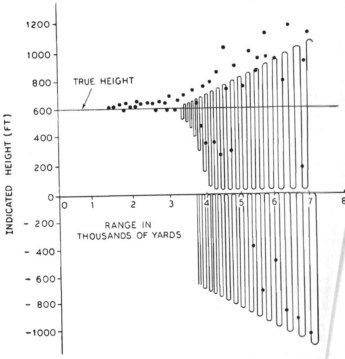

FIG. 10-46 Comparison of Theoretical and Observed Heights.

[27] Lee, Cheatham, and Wiesner, "Detection of Periodic Signals in Noise," *Proc. of IRE*, October 1950.

the presently used detectors or demodulators utilize the cross correlation technique.

Consider the situation where a radar operator using an "A" type presentation is searching for a signal nearly equal to noise. He is expecting an echo to have a particular shape, namely, that of the transmitted pulse. This is representative of the first function $f_1(t)$ in Eq. (10-53). An echo occurring at $t = (t - \tau)$ is the second function, $f_2(t - \tau)$. The operator's eye, aided by the cathode-ray tube phosphor, performs the integrating and averaging function. Since the eye and cathode-ray tube phosphor are not capable of performing this function over wide limits of time, the system is not capable of detection of signals appreciably below noise level. Isolated cases have, however, been reported of operators who, under very special conditions, could detect signals several decibels below noise.

The range time discriminator of Par. 10-31 is actually a cross correlator. A noise-free local gate is correlated with a noisy echo signal. The signals fit the definition, in that they are not the same but are related through their "parent," the transmitted pulse. As can be expected, the two signals correlate, but the noise and the gate do not. This is the basis for the observation of many experimenters that radar signals can be detected by appropriate circuitry at levels somewhat below noise level. It is to be noted, however, that, although the ability of some circuits to detect the weak nonmoving target is high, the ability is low for a moving target. This is caused by the need for appreciable integration time to make a cross correlator effective. Expressed in another way, a tracking system has zero bandwidth for a weak signal and does not develop the design information bandwidth until the signal is somewhat greater than the noise level.

The angular error detector of Par. 10-33 is a cross correlator. The scanning beam modulates the echo (if the target is off antenna axis but still within the tracking beam.) A noise-free replica of the modulating signal is derived in the equipment and sent to the angle error detector, where it is correlated with the noisy error signal. Over a long integration time the noise does not correlate, but the true signal does. Again, the long integration time results in a system with zero information bandwidth.

A moving-target indication system is a modified form of autocorrelator in which the correlated fixed targets are rejected and the noisy signal (noise being represented by target motion) is retained.

10-37 TRAVELING WAVE TUBES

A recent development in the field of vacuum tubes is a device called the "traveling wave" tube. Figure 10-47 is a simple diagram of the tube. An electron stream is made to traverse the field generated by an r-f wave

[28] Kompfer, Hatton, and Ashcroft, *British Admiralty Report C.V.D. C2.* Misc. 40, January 1945.

traveling in a low-velocity propagator. A helix is commonly used as the propagator; however, many other configurations are possible and several others have been used. An interchange of energy takes place between the radio frequency field and the electron stream. If the velocity of the electrons is slightly greater than the velocity of propagation of the r-f wave, the wave amplitude grows as the distance from the input terminal increases. It is difficult to give any more "practical" description than this of the amplification process. It can, however, be expressed more or less precisely in mathematical terms.[29]

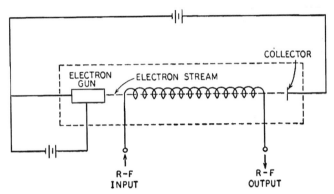

FIG. 10-47 Traveling Wave Tube.

The characteristics of this device are of interest to the radar guidance designer. Traveling wave tube amplifiers can be built to have high gain, low internal noise, and almost phenomenal bandwidth compared to other vacuum tube amplifiers. Gain as high as 39 db has been reported.[30] An amplifier with a noise figure as low as 10 db at 3000 mc per sec has been reported.[31] This competes more than favorably with the IN2IC crystal whose noise figure when used in an appropriate receiver is about 12 db. Another important characteristic of the traveling wave tube is its performance when overloaded. The tubes will withstand, without damage, much higher input signals than will crystals, and recovery after overload is instantaneous. The rapid recovery is apparently a result of the use of completely nonresonant components (this is also one of the causes of the wide bandwidth). During overload the output of the tube limits at some value which makes it possible to protect later stages of a radar receiver. The favorable overload characteristic could result in less stringent require-

[29] Pierce, *Proc. IRE*, Vol. 35, pp. 111-123, February 1947.
[30] Cutler, *Proc. IRE*, Vol. 39, pp. 914-917, August 1951.
[31] Watkins, *Proc. IRE*, Vol. 40, pp. 65-70, January 1952.

ments upon the *T-R* system of a pulsed radar, if a traveling wave tube were used in the receiver.

10-38 BEACONRY*

A beacon is defined as a device which serves as a signal for use as a guidance or warning aid. Radar beacons aid the radar set in locating and identifying special targets which may be difficult or impossible to sense otherwise. Radar beacons held only minor interest until the radar set became important as an operational military tool.

When a beacon is used in conjunction with a radar, the signal from the radar is detected by the beacon receiver and used to initiate a new transmission. The radar is often referred to as the "interrogator" and the beacon as the "transponder" or "responder." A block diagram of a simple radar-beacon system is shown in Fig. 10-48.

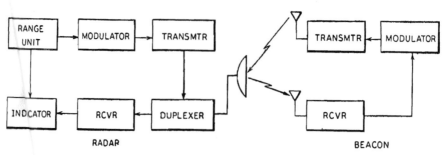

Fig. 10-48 Radar-Beacon System.

The transponder is normally a quiescent device, remaining passive until "triggered" by a suitable received signal. The received signal level does not affect the beacon transmitter output power.

A beacon reply is similiar to, but differs from, a radar echo in several respects:

(a) The received signal at the radar is not dependent upon radar output power or the reflecting characteristics of objects under surveillance.
(b) The output frequency of the transponder is usually different from that of the radar transmitter.
(c) Signals from the beacon may be coded regardless of the nature of the interrogation.
(d) There always exists an additional radar range delay because of the elapse of time in the beacon between reception of a signal and the transmission of a reply.

* Paragraphs 10-38 to 10-43 inclusive were written by John P. Kirwan, Radar Division, Naval Research Laboratory.

10-39 RELIABLE BEACON RANGE

At frequencies useful for beacon work, propagation is considered dependable only to the horizon. Under unusual and unpredictable conditions the horizontal range may be extended considerably at times by refraction. Because the r-f field intensity falls off rapidly below the radio horizon, it is impractical to increase the transmitter power output to offset this loss. Over water, multipath propagation may effect large fluctuations of the r-f field, relative to free-space propagation. The successful operation of a given system under conditions of multipath propagation is dependent primarily upon the margin of power available.

There are many variables which must be considered before any reasonable measure of reliable range can be calculated. Reliable range is the maximum range over which the system may be expected to operate under tactical conditions. Some of the factors which influence the reliable range of the radar-beacon combination are:

(a) The type of visual display utilized.
(b) Signal level requirements of the radar tracking circuits.
(c) Radar antenna scanning losses.
(d) Operator skill.
(e) Maximum number of missing responses from the beacon which may be tolerated by the radar.
(f) Radar receiver sensitivity and r-f line losses.
(g) Quality of equipment maintenance.

10-40 BEACON RECEIVERS

Superheterodyne, crystal video, tuned radio frequency, and superregenerative receivers have been used in beacon applications. Since r-f amplification by ordinary grid control tubes is impractical above 1500 mc per sec, the last two types mentioned find little use above this frequency. Because most radars used for missile guidance systems operate above 1500 mc per sec, only the superheterodyne and crystal video receiver will be discussed in this section.

The type of receiver used for a particular application is dependent upon the functions it will be required to perform. The fundamental operational characteristics of any receiver are sensitivity, fidelity, and selectivity. In some cases either the superheterodyne or the crystal video receiver may perform satisfactorily and the final choice may be determined primarily by weight, size, power requirements, or cost. It may be said generally that crystal video receivers are used where weight, size, and cost are of primary consideration as compared to the possible superior sensitivity, fidelity, and selectivity of the superheterodyne.

The sensitivity of a receiver may be defined most conveniently as the least r-f power required at a receiver input terminal to permit satisfactory operation of circuits following the receiver output terminals. If the beacon is to be used solely for extended radar range tracking, then the only sensitivity requirement may be that the receiver supply a signal of sufficient amplitude to trip a biased trigger circuit for a certain percentage of the incoming interrogations. If this is the case, signals near the noise level may be sufficient to operate circuits following the beacon receiver. On the other hand, if coded interrogation or command intelligence is being conveyed and interpreted by the receiver-decoder, signal-to-noise ratios greater than one at the receiver output terminals will be required. A pulse width decoder, for example, will require a signal in the order of 8 db above r.m.s. noise.[32] Where the satisfactory operation of a guidance system demands that each transmission be decoded and interpreted, the receiver output signal-to-noise level must exceed this value.

The sensitivity of the best superheterodyne receiver is in the order of 10^{-13} watt, whereas that of a crystal video is about 10^{-8} watt. The power output of the superheterodyne is proportional to the average power received. The power output from a crystal video receiver, because of the square-law, weak-signal characteristics of the crystal, is proportional to the square of the average power received. As a result, the improvement in signal-to-noise ratio as a function of signal strength is faster for a crystal video receiver.

Fidelity of a receiver is considered as the degree to which a receiver is capable of reproducing the r-f envelope at the video output terminals. Where the receiver output is used only to trigger a simple biased circuit, good fidelity may not be of primary concern. If the receiver output is used to operate a decoding device which depends upon good reproduction of the original transmitted r-f envelope, the receiver must exhibit good fidelity characteristics. Often this fidelity must be preserved over a wide dynamic range of received power levels. To guarantee good fidelity, the receiver must pass a band of frequencies which includes all important frequency components of the r-f envelope. However, the usual criterion of bandwidth equal to one or two times the reciprocal of the pulse width will suffice for most uses.

Superheterodyne and Crystal Video Receiver Comparison. A crystal video receiver is composed of an r-f crystal diode detector and a video amplifier, usually followed by a cathode follower. The superheterodyne consists of an r-f local oscillator and crystal mixer, an i-f amplifier, second detector, and a video amplifier with cathode follower output.

Over a wide range of receiver power levels, the superheterodyne receiver exhibits superior fidelity characteristics as compared to a crystal

---

[32] Roberts *Radar Beacons*, McGraw-Hill Book Co.

video receiver, primarily because the superheterodyne employs a linear detector and the crystal video a square-law detector. For n db variation of input signal level, there exists a variation of n db in signal power following the superheterodyne first detector and $2n$ db following the crystal video detector. The dynamic range of the crystal video receiver therefore must be extended to compensate for this difference if good fidelity is to be expected.

Crystal video receivers exhibit wide-band frequency coverage because of the inability of the crystal detector to detect changes in frequency. Limited r-f selectivity may be accomplished by the use of r-f line filter cavities, tuned crystal holders, and other r-f plumbing techniques. The superheterodyne is inherently a selective receiver, and its overall bandwidth is determined primarily by the design of the i-f amplifier.

For a given frequency response, because of the double sideband nature of the i-f signal, the superheterodyne i-f amplifier requires twice the bandwidth required of a video amplifier. Experience has shown that for low gain, higher gain-bandwidth product can be more easily attained with crystal video receivers than with superheterodyne receivers. However, it is difficult to design a wide-dynamic-range, high-gain video amplifier which exhibits good pulse reproduction. This difficulty arises from:

(a) The required dynamic range of the video amplifier following a crystal detector is twice the dynamic range of the input signal level in db.
(b) The voltage across the large number of coupling and by-pass capacitors in the amplifier tend to charge and discharge during or after the pulse, resulting in voltage overshoots and long recovery times.
(c) Extraneous signals may result from microphonics, stray electrical or magnetic fields, and hum pick-up from the power supply voltages.

10-41 BEACON MODULATORS

Beacon modulators are similar to radar modulators in that they supply high pulse power to an oscillator tube. Many of the requirements are identical since each is required to develop a voltage pulse which exhibits a flat top and steep leading and trailing edges. Often these characteristics must be maintained even though the pulse spacing or pulse width may be changed intentionally. A flat-top pulse is desired because the oscillator may shift frequency if the voltage is allowed to change during the pulse or from pulse to pulse. A well-shaped and adequately controlled waveform must therefore be applied to the transmitter oscillator if a satisfactory r-f frequency spectrum is to be developed.

The modulator input signal is usually taken from the beacon receiver cathode follower output terminal. If intelligence is conveyed back to the radar, coding action generally originates in a separate coder unit. A fixed coded reply may be developed prior to or in the modulator proper.

Present-day beacon modulators are usually of either the "hard tube" or "line type" design. The line type modulator, as described in Par. 10-23, consists of a pulse-forming network, a gas tube switch, and a pulse transformer which matches the impedance of the network to the oscillator tube. A circuit diagram of a simple line type modulator is shown in Fig. 10-21. This type of modulator is not adaptable to handling multipulse codes. It is also seriously affected by changes in load impedance and power supply voltage.

Hard tube modulators consist of a blocking oscillator, a biased isolation amplifier, and a final driver. A circuit diagram of a typical hard tube modulator is shown in Fig. 10-49. Upon arrival of a trigger pulse, blocking

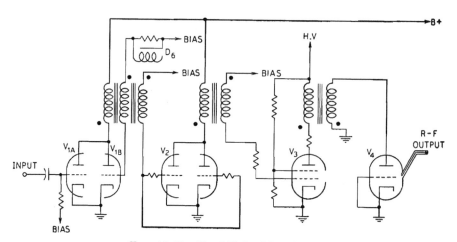

FIG. 10-49 Hard Tube Modulator.

oscillator action is initiated through the plate winding of the pulse transformer. The delay line DL is used to control the pulse duration. The pulse is then amplified and further shaped through the amplifier driver V_2 and the final driver, V_3. Hard tube modulators have been developed which have extremely short recovery time and are therefore capable of handling pulse code groups which are closely spaced.

The hard tube modulator has the advantage of producing well-shaped pulses, being easily adaptable to handling varying repetition rates and multipulse codes, and not being affected seriously by changes in load impedance or high-voltage supply. It does have the disadvantage of being more complex and larger than the line type modulator. In addition, two low-voltage and one high-voltage power supplies are usually required in the hard tube modulator.

10-42 BEACON ANTENNA CONSIDERATIONS

The type antenna used by the interrogator or the responder will depend upon the requirements of gain, coverage, polarization, and aerodynamic factors. "Coverage" is that region in space within which the system will operate satisfactorily, i.e., the region where the beacon can receive an interrogation and the interrogator can sense the reply. This overall volume coverage is determined by the antenna patterns of both the interrogator and responder. The antenna pattern must be sufficiently broad to allow complete manueverability of the aircraft or missile without sacrificing the performance of the system. If command intelligence is being handled by the interrogator-responder r-f link or if the interrogator is an automatic tracking radar, adequate coverage must be maintained at all times.

Free-space antenna patterns are usually altered and impossible to predict when the antenna is installed on an aircraft or missile. The difficulty is caused by reflection and diffraction from the metal surfaces near by. To minimize this problem, antennas are mounted as far from the interfering surfaces as possible. Actually, every antenna installation should be determined from exact scale models. Increased gain of the antenna results in decreased angular coverage. Thus, there is always a compromise in the antenna design between gain and coverage.

Polarization of the responder antenna is usually dictated by the polarization of the interrogating radar. Vertical polarization is usually preferred for most systems since propagation interference nulls are less pronounced. Circular polarization is often used when the polarization of one of the antennas may change during operation.

10-43 USE OF THE BEACON IN MISSILE GUIDANCE SYSTEMS

Probably the most important use of a beacon is to extend the useful range of radar. Since the radar set operates on a two-way transmission principle, the signal level at the receiver varies inversely as the fourth power of the distance between the radar and the target. The fourth power propagation loss, plus the fact that many missiles exhibit small and relatively poor reflecting surfaces, limits the reliable range of the radar in tracking missiles. On the other hand, the radar-beacon link is not dependent upon missile reflecting area and involves only one-way propagation losses. The signal at the radar or at the beacon receiver varies inversely as the square of the distance separating them. An r-f signal level of the order of 10^{-8} watt or less at the beacon antenna may be raised to a level of several hundred watts by the combined action of the beacon receiver and transmitter. The practical result is that radar-beacon ranges are generally limited only by the radar horizon.

The fact that a beacon transmitter may be operated on a frequency different from the radar transmitter permits an operator to track a missile without radar echo interference from objects in the vicinity of the missile or near the radar site.

Since both the interrogation and reply signals may be separately coded, a two-way communication link may be operated between the radar and the missile. In addition, coding may be used to interrogate only a specific beacon. This function is particularly important where the local area may have a high density of equipment operating at or near the same frequency.

System Requirements. The type of interrogator-transponder used for any particular missile guidance problem will depend upon the overall requirements of the system. Attempts have been made to design "universal" beacons and "universal" radar equipments, but actual results have proved that even these units are extremely limited in their versatility. In many cases, where the requirements of the system are not complex, an existing interrogator-responder may be modified to function satisfactorily as a unit. This is particularly true where the beacon is used only to extend radar tracking range. On the other hand, if the beacon is required to respond only to special coded interrogations, transmit a coded output, interpret the command guidance intelligence, or perform other functions, the radar and the beacon should be designed for the specific application. In summary, the following factors guide the design of a radar-beacon system:

(a) The purpose of the interrogating radar other than beacon operation.
(b) Limitations of weight, size, power, and cost.
(c) Interference of all types to be expected.
(d) Maximum reliable range and the degree of reliability required.
(e) Minimum range.
(f) Propagation coverage desired.
(g) Degree of fidelity required to handle all intelligence.
(h) Frequency and selectivity coverage required.
(i) Type and quantity of data to be conveyed.
(j) Requirements of selective interrogation and reply.
(k) Stability of "turn-around" time in responder.

CHAPTER 11

TARGET CONSIDERATIONS

Missile targets are generally classified into two broad groups: air targets, usually aircraft or other missiles; and surface targets, which include ships and built-up areas on the ground. Subclasses of various types are often established for convenience, and some of these have previously been discussed. In all instances, the target must be detected, identified, and tracked by the missile or associated equipment, and the tracking information used for at least the final phase of missile guidance. Some exceptions exist; for example, the tracking point might be some object other than the target but at a known position relative to it, and a proper offset injected into the guidance system. This might be done if the target had no identifiable characteristics relative to its surroundings. However, it is the intent of this chapter to describe target characteristics which make tracking possible, so that the target return is the input information to the guidance mechanism. For all-weather operation the information is usually obtained by radio waves, and this discussion will be limited to target characteristics associated with short radio waves.

11-1 REFLECTION OF RADIO WAVES

The mechanism of reflection of electromagnetic waves is covered adequately in the literature and will not be repeated. Basically, any material body having dielectric properties differing from its surroundings will cause reflection, refraction, or absorption of an incident wave. For simple geometrical shapes such as flat plates, cylinders, spheres, etc., the magnitude and phase of the reflected wave can be computed. The reflected signal from complex objects cannot be computed and can be described only in statistical terms. Area extensive targets, such as natural terrain or built-up areas, are further complicated by multiple reflections and the necessity for including the directivity effects of the receiving or transmitting antennas. Data of this nature must be obtained by experimental methods.

11-2 AIRCRAFT AS TARGETS

An isolated aircraft or missile can be considered in a special subclass if it is located remotely from the radar antenna. It then subtends a small angle at the antenna and is often considered to be a geometrical point. However, finite power cannot be reflected from a point and so an effective scattering cross section is determined by experimental methods. This cross section, along with the system parameters, provides a measure of maximum detection range. The elementary design of a radar detection system requires no further information about the target reflectivity characteristics.

If more than one target is present in the same general region of space, the problem of *resolution* is presented. In a pulse system, if the range differs by more than the product of the pulse duration and velocity of propagation, the targets can be resolved in range even though their angular coordinates are identical. Otherwise, they can be resolved only if their angular separation exceeds some fraction of the antenna beam width. This is a radar design problem involving the choice of beamwidth, which is closely interrelated with other system parameters. C-w systems do not provide range resolution, but can resolve in range rate because of the Doppler frequency shift. If two aircraft targets are flying a close formation and cannot be resolved in angle or range with a pulse system, they cannot be resolved in range rate with a c-w system either, since in formation their range rates are identical. If their range rates differ by a sufficient amount to be resolved by the Doppler difference, then, in a very short time, their ranges will differ sufficiently to obtain range resolution with a pulse system. On the other hand, if a single aircraft target is flying in close proximity to ground clutter, range resolution provided by pulse systems is of no value, whereas range rate resolution is effective, except for a short interval of time when the target is moving normal to the line of sight. Resolution in the c-w case is due to the difference in target return from clutter as compared to the moving aircraft. Although the difference is due to relative speed, it is important to note that the target characteristics and the wavelength of the incident illumination are involved to the extent that the Doppler shift must be detectable. In the present state of the art, angular resolution beyond that provided by the antenna radiation pattern is impossible.

11-3 STATISTICAL CHARACTERISTICS OF AIRCRAFT TARGETS

More detailed studies of target reflectivity reveal factors in addition to the usual concept of a scattering cross section. The figure quoted for various target types is an average value, subject to considerable fluctuation. The fluctuation appears to be quite random and thus can be defined only in a statistical sense. The scattering cross section can then be considered as some sort of central measure, e.g., the mean, the median, or the mode. Additional information would be useful to the designer of a detection system since it might be possible to make use of peak values in increasing the effective detection range.

A random function or, in this case, a random time series can be defined by an infinite sequence of probability functions. All of the useful information regarding a random series can be obtained from the first probability density and from certain moments of the second probability density. The first probability density gives the frequency of occurrence of various amplitudes. Its integral, or cumulative distribution, defines the percentage of the total time the signal exceeds any selected amplitude. The 50 percent point is often used to define the scattering cross section, although the first moment of the probability density is equally useful and is the value which would be indicated by a d-c meter if the random function were a voltage or current. For the type of time function resulting from target echoes, these values are nearly equal and the choice depends upon the experimental technique used to reduce the data. A knowledge of the shape of the distribution function permits the system designer to judge his optimism (or pessimism) in quoting detection ranges.

No information regarding the fluctuation rate is contained in the first probability density, and it is important to have this information since scanning speeds and other system parameters are related to it. This is contained in the second mixed moment of the second probability density, which for a random time series, is called the "autocorrelation function." The Fourier Cosine Transform of the autocorrelation function gives the power spectrum, which generally means more to the electronic engineer and which is more readily adaptable to steady-state system analysis and synthesis. Thus, knowing these functions, all of the useful information regarding the target is available. Of course, it is known that these functions can differ for different targets as well as for different radar wavelengths and must be evaluated experimentally over a variety of target types and conditions.

11-4 DETERMINATION OF ANGULAR COORDINATES

The position of an isolated target in space is usually defined in spherical coordinates and with various orders of precision. At long ranges only moderate precision is required since here the principal problem is that of detection and identification. A search-type radar scans in angle, and the presence and angular position of the target are indicated on a scope which is intensity-modulated. For a constant echo return from a small target the intensity pattern on the scope is that of the antenna radiation pattern. This will not be true if the echo is fluctuating with time, and an error in position is possible amounting to an appreciable fraction of the antenna beamwidth. If the scanning rate is sufficiently low, this type of error tends to be averaged out and, in any case, the resulting error is of minor importance. A serious problem, however, exists in a precision tracking system used for gunfire or missile control in which high position accuracy is required.

The direction-finding technique used in conventional search radars is inadequate for the precision tracking application. Continuous information is needed (or at least a sampling rate which is high compared with the rate of change of target position) and this is best obtained in null type systems. A scanning arrangement, called *lobing*, is used in which the axis of the antenna radiation pattern is offset from the bore-sight axis and is rotated in a conical fashion. For an on-axis point target, the receiver output is independent of the angle of rotation. Otherwise the output is amplitude-modulated at the scan frequency. The depth of modulation is a measure of the angle off-axis, whereas the phase of the modulation indicates the direction of the error. This polar indication is resolved into a pair of orthogonal components, usually traverse and elevation, by phase comparison with a reference signal at the scan frequency with known phase. Variations of this arrangement are numerous, such as those called *lobe switching* in which synchronous pulse repetition rate and scan rate schemes are used, but the basic system is unchanged. In any case, the system output is a signal in each axis whose magnitude and phase (or polarity in the d-c case) are measures of the pointing error. These error signals may be presented on indicators for manual control or used in a feedback system for automatic control.

In the design of a tracking system of this type many additional factors must be considered such as optimum offset or "squint angle," lobe symmetry, side lobes, etc., which are described elsewhere. These are engineering design problems and, in principle, their effects in degradation of tracking performance can be reduced to negligible proportions. There still remain the effects of the reflectivity characteristics of the target which were ignored in the simple description of system operation.

11-5 DETERMINATION OF THE RANGE COORDINATE

Range determination or tracking is also subject to varying degrees of precision, depending upon the application. Search radars using intensity-modulated scopes provide relatively crude range accuracy by comparison of target echo with internally generated range rings. More precise range can be indicated by expanded sweeps. In precision tracking applications continuous information is required, and for automatic tracking a null type indication is essential. This is accomplished by generating a pair of adjacent range gates controlled by a delay device which is set to bracket the received echo. The signal energy in the gates is compared in a time discriminator producing an error signal whose magnitude and phase (or polarity) indicate deviation from the null position. This error signal is used for automatic range tracking just as in the angle tracking case. One fundamental difference exists between the range and angle tracking problems. The range tracking system derives its information from each pulse rather than from pulses separated in time, although some range tracking systems have been built using a single gate with time modulation. The relative merits of these types will be discussed later in connection with target reflectivity characteristics.

11-6 DETERMINATION OF TRACKING NOISE

The analysis of precision tracking radars is quite simple when the ideal target is considered. In practice, with actual complex targets, it is known that tracking is not smooth but contains considerable "jitter" or noise. This can and has been evaluated experimentally, but it has been found to be extremely difficult to relate the measured noise to the target type and to system parameters and imperfections. System noise can be evaluated by using a noise-free artificial target such as a beacon or sphere. If the system is linear, the target noise might be evaluated by measuring total noise, using a specified target and taking differences in an r.m.s. sense. This assumes no correlation between target-induced noise and system noise, an assumption which appears reasonable but which has not been proved. The major difficulty with this procedure is in the experimental technique, the statistical fluctuations resulting from small samples, and in system nonlinearity at small amplitudes. An alternative approach is to measure the error signal generated in an open loop condition, calibrate the error signal as a function of angular error, and compare the result with the optical boresight. It is then assumed that the open loop noise, modified by the transfer characteristic of the closed loop, is a true measure of the closed loop response. This method appears to be valid, within the experimental error, at least for isolated targets. Again it assumes linearity, no correlation, and an input noise function which is statistically stationary.

11-7 ORIGIN OF TARGET NOISE

The statistical characteristics of target reflectivity were described in Par. 11-3 in terms of the output signal from a receiver. For a better understanding of the phenomenon it would be desirable to define or explain the cause. A complex target consists of a number of reflecting elements, randomly oriented in space. When illuminated by a plane wave each element reflects a portion of the incident energy. A reflecting element, small compared to the wavelength, tends to act as an isotropic reflector; large areas which are flat or have large radii of curvature will have directive reflection patterns. If an aircraft is considered to be a rigid body made up of a large number of such elements in combination, the echo signal will consist of the summation of these randomly phased reflections. As the aircraft rotates relative to the line-of-sight, the individual reflected signals are phase-modulated because of the changing path length. This summation is the input function to the tracking radar.

11-8 ANALYSIS OF A TWO-ELEMENT TARGET

A simple analysis of the tracking response of a system can be made if the multielement target is replaced by one consisting of only two reflectors. It is not expected that such a simple model will be realistic, but it is the first step beyond the idealized case and can be very informative. Figure 11-1 shows the antenna radiation pattern in two sequential positions in one tracking coordinate. At a given instant the target is viewed with the pattern at A and some time later at B. The displacement or squint angle is set to produce crossover about 2 db down from peak response. The total signal intercepted at position A is amplified and detected and compared with that obtained from position B. The difference (ideally the ratio) of these two signals is the off-axis error. For analytical purposes the shape of each lobe may be described by some function such as $\frac{\sin \theta}{\theta}$, $\frac{J_1(\theta)}{\theta}$, $1 - \theta^2$, etc., or it may be experimentally determined. The function may be expanded in a Taylor series about the crossover point θ_o, or

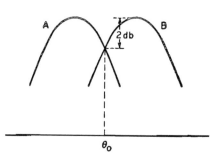

Fig. 11-1 Tracking Radar Lobe Patterns.

$$f(\theta) = f(\theta_o) + f'(\theta - \theta_o) + \tfrac{1}{2}!f''(\theta - \theta_o)^2 + \cdots$$

For small angles off-axis, only the first two terms may be retained, which is equivalent to the assumption that the response is a linear function of the error angle. The amplitude response may then be written

$$e = E_o[1 \pm p(\theta - \theta_o)]$$

For a single element target the signal from lobe A is

$$e_A = G[1 - p(\theta_T - \theta_o)] \cos \omega t$$

and from lobe B

$$e_B = G[1 + p(\theta_T - \theta_o)] \cos \omega t$$

where G is a factor lumping together target size, system gain, etc. The detector squares e_A and e_B and a low-pass filter rejects all but the d-c and low frequency terms. The error signal is $\overline{e_B^2} - \overline{e_A^2}$ which reduces to

$$\epsilon = 2G^2 p(\theta_T - \theta_o)$$

For on-target conditions $\epsilon = 0$ and $\theta_T = \theta_o$. There are no noise terms.

If the target consists of two reflecting elements, each will contribute to the received signal. They will have the same frequency but any phase depending upon the relative range. Then the lobe voltages are

$$e_A = G[1 - p(\theta_{T1} - \theta_o)] \cos \omega t + aG[1 - p(\theta_{T2} - \theta_o)] \cos (\omega t + \alpha)$$
$$e_B = G[1 + p(\theta_{T1} - \theta_o)] \cos \omega t + aG[1 + p(\theta_{T2} - \theta_o)] \cos (\omega t + \alpha)$$

where a is the amplitude ratio of the two elements. After detection the error signal is given by

$$\epsilon = 2G^2 p\{(\theta_{T1} - \theta_o) + a^2(\theta_{T2} - \theta_o) + a \cos \alpha [(\theta_{T1} - \theta_o) + (\theta_{T2} - \theta_o)]\}$$

which reduces to

$$\epsilon = 2G^2 p\{\theta_{T1}(1 + a \cos \alpha) + \theta_{T2}(a^2 + a \cos \alpha) - \theta_o(1 + a^2 + 2a \cos \alpha)\}$$

For an on-target indication $\epsilon = 0$ and

$$\theta_o = \frac{\theta_{T1}(1 + a \cos \alpha) + \theta_{T2}(a^2 + a \cos \alpha)}{1 + a^2 + 2a \cos \alpha}$$

If θ_{T2} is set equal to $\theta_{T1} + \theta_D$ where θ_D is the angular spacing between elements,

$$\theta_o = \theta_{T1} + \theta_D \frac{a^2 + a \cos \alpha}{1 + a^2 + 2a \cos \alpha}$$

For both signals in phase $\alpha = 0$ and $\cos \alpha = 1$. Then the coefficient of θ_D reduces to $\frac{a}{a+1}$ and the system will indicate no error when the tracking axis is on the amplitude "center of gravity" of the two elements. If $\alpha = 180$ deg, then $\cos \alpha = -1$ and the coefficient reduces to $\frac{a}{a-1}$. The angle of zero error will then be outside the limits of the two elements. In neither case is there any indication that more than one element exists. In the latter case it is interesting to note that if $a = 1$ the coefficient goes to infinity. Actually this will not occur, since the linear antenna response limits will be exceeded, but the apparent target position can be many times its span.

A family of curves of the balance point as a function of phase difference for various values of the amplitude ratio a is shown in Fig. 11-2. If α is a linear function of time, such as would result from a constant relative range rate, then α becomes $\omega_M t$ and Fig. 11-2 may be considered a plot of apparent angle of arrival versus time, which in this case is periodic. The target has not changed its position, and so this effect is target-induced noise which for convenience is called *angle noise*. Obviously, for a multi-element target moving in a random fashion the angle noise will be a random function, as has been observed experimentally.

It is apparent from this elementary analysis that angle noise is a result of the existence of a number of coherent waves summed in space and received by a system which is sensitive to r-f phase. If the signal were completely noncoherent, such as infrared or visible light, this effect would be nonexistent.

It is also important to note that the noise, expressed in angular units, is proportional to the angular spacing of the target-reflecting elements. Since the actual spacing is fixed, the noise will be inversely proportional to target range, becoming negligible at extreme ranges. Conversely, at short ranges, it may well be the limiting factor in tracking precision.

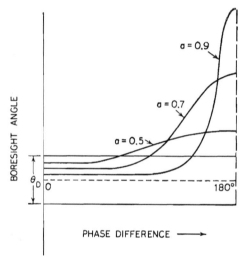

FIG. 11-2 Tracking Error for the Two-Element Target.

Care should be exercised in extrapolating to very short ranges, however, since the analysis is valid only in the far zone of the antenna system.

11-9 EFFECTS OF AMPLITUDE FLUCTUATION

The basic method of angle tracking has been described in Par. 11-4. It has been shown that the information regarding the deviation of the target from the tracking axis is carried by the lobing frequency as a subcarrier frequency. As a result, any signal modulation at this frequency constitutes an error signal to the radar. Amplitude fluctuations caused by a complex target may contain energy at this frequency and, if so, additional tracking noise is produced. Since the magnitude of this factor is related to the modulation depth it will be independent of target range in contrast to angle noise which varies inversely with range. It will be uncorrelated with angle noise so that it will add in an r.m.s. manner. Figure 11-3 is a qualitative plot of the two noise terms and their sum. The magnitude of "amplitude noise" is a function of the target but is under partial control of the system designer. With normal antenna design, the angle corresponding to a given fractional modulation is directly proportional to the beamwidth and hence narrow beams are desirable. Another choice available to the system designer is the lobing frequency. It should be set, if possible, at a frequency where the amplitude noise spectrum has its smallest magnitude. Ordinary reasoning would indicate that this would occur at high lobing frequencies, but this is not always the case. A pulse system has an upper limit of one quarter the p.r.f. since at least one pulse must

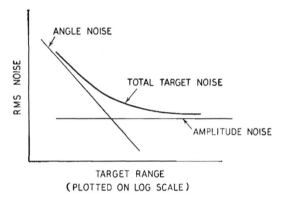

FIG. 11-3 Target Noise as a Function of Range.

be used in each quadrant. This may be difficult to obtain by mechanical methods. Aircraft targets using propellers produce spectral peaks at the blade frequency and harmonics which should be avoided. The final choice requires a knowledge of the amplitude spectrum expected.

Even though the precise value of the target-induced noise is unknown it does indicate that there is a limit to tracking precision obtainable regardless of the perfection of manufacture, and this should be recognized by the specification writer, as well as the system designer.

11-10 LARGE TARGET TRACKING

All of the preceding discussion relates to targets which subtend an angle at the radar which is small compared to the beamwidth. If this is not the case the problem is much more complicated. Analytical methods are impossibly complex because of the curvature of the antenna pattern and because a tracking system tends to be unstable. It appears, in most cases of this nature, to be more advantageous to use rapid scan techniques in preference to sequential lobing. The same is true for discrete targets

11-11 LOW-ANGLE TRACKING

The low-angle problem is in many ways similar to the two-target one. If the target and its surface-reflected image are not resolved by the antenna pattern, the tracking radar suffers from excessive noise in the elevation coordinate. By making use of certain known facts it is possible to reduce the noise, even though the actual target position is not defined. First, it is known that the target is in the range between zero and roughly one half the beamwidth so that limiting might successfully be applied. Second, the target maneuverability has known maxima, and any indication by the radar of a more rapid climb or dive is in error. Tracking bandwidth reduction in the elevation coordinate offers a possible noise reduction scheme. These methods are most effective in noise reduction but do not necessarily provide data on the true target elevation. However, for offensive action by guns or missiles, they have possibilities. The best solution to the low-angle problem seems to be to eliminate it by a change in tactics if at all possible.

CHAPTER 12

THE ANALYSIS OF FLIGHT PATHS

Symbols Used in Chapter 12

a = navigation constant
A_M = transverse or lateral acceleration of missile
c = constant of trajectory
  = $km^{-2}(1 + m^2)$
g = acceleration of gravity = 32.2 ft per sec^2
k = constant factor = pR
m = initial slope of beam-rider trajectory
p = ratio of missile speed to target speed = V_M/V_T
r = instantaneous slant range from point of control to missile; also instantaneous distance between missile and targets
r_0 = initial slant range to missile
r_f = final slant range at impact
R = constant target altitude
s = length of arc along trajectory
t_f = time of flight
V_M = speed of missile
V_T = speed of target
x, y = rectangular coordinates corresponding to r and θ

δ = fixed lead angle or missile heading relative to the line-of-sight
α_0 = constant initial angle
  = $\gamma_0 + \phi_0$
γ = missile heading relative to the line-of-sight
γ_M = fixed angle between missile heading and line-of-sight
γ_T = fixed angle between target heading and line-of-sight
θ = instantaneous elevation angle from point of control to missile
θ_0 = initial launching angle
θ_f = impact elevation angle
φ = angle between target velocity vector and the line-of-sight; also inclination angle of trajectory
φ_0 = initial value of φ
φ_M = missile heading from horizontal
φ_n = final value of φ at impact
ω = angular frequency
$G(\omega)$ = frequency spectrum

The material in this chapter treats the characteristics of trajectories arising from various methods of missile guidance. Among the most significant features in the design of an over-all guidance system, in addition to the trajectory itself, are the time of flight, maximum rate of turn, maximum lateral acceleration, and frequency demand required for control. The time of flight is important in determining parameters in computer design as well as in ascertaining tactical requirements. The maximum turning rate and the maximum lateral acceleration are of significance in the determination of the proper type of guidance to employ for a given tactical situation. These factors are also important in designing the missile airframe and control devices. The frequency demand necessary for guidance and control is implicit in the design of the control servos and associated networks.

In order to illustrate the method of analysis of flight paths, these salient features of the trajectories will be discussed in considerable detail for the line-of-sight course followed by a beam-rider missile. Following this detailed analysis, the pertinent broader aspects will be outlined as a foundation for more comprehensive analysis for the following flight paths: pure pursuit course, deviated pursuit course, constant-bearing course, and proportional navigation. These paths are, of course, applicable principally to homing missiles.

12-1 LINE-OF-SIGHT COURSE (BEAM-RIDER MISSILE)

The first course to be considered is the line-of-sight course which a beam-rider missile follows.

> A *line-of-sight* course is a course in which the missile is guided so as to remain on the line joining the target and the point of control.

In order to determine the pertinent facts required in guidance system design, the beam-rider trajectory must be determined.

Differential Equation for Line-of-sight Trajectory. In developing the beam-rider trajectory the following conditions are imposed in order to facilitate the handling of the mathematics:

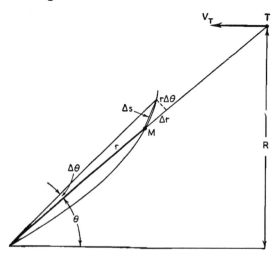

Fig. 12-1 Line-of-Sight Geometry.

12-1] LINE-OF-SIGHT COURSE (BEAM-RIDER MISSILE)

(a) A nonmaneuvering straight-line target course* is assumed.
(b) Both the missile and target speeds are considered constant.
(c) The point of control is established as a stationary reference.
(d) A two-dimensional coordinate system is set up in a plane determined by the target velocity vector and the line joining this vector with the origin or point of control.

The geometry of the line-of-sight trajectory is shown in Fig. 12-1 where the following symbols are employed:

s = length of arc along trajectory
r = instantaneous slant range from point of control to missile
θ = instantaneous elevation angle from point of control to missile
V_M = speed of missile
V_T = speed of target
R = constant target altitude
m = initial slope of trajectory

Referring to Fig. 12-1, we have

$$(\Delta s)^2 = (\Delta r)^2 + r^2(\Delta \theta)^2 \tag{12-1}$$

which becomes in the limit

$$\left(\frac{dr}{d\theta}\right)^2 + r^2 = \left(\frac{ds}{d\theta}\right)^2 \tag{12-2}$$

Now the distance the target travels in time t is given by

$$V_T t = R \cot \theta_0 - R \cot \theta \tag{12-3}$$

where θ_0 is the initial launching angle or the elevation angle of the target at time $t = 0$. Differentiating Eq. (12-3) we have

$$V_T \frac{dt}{d\theta} = R \csc^2 \theta \tag{12-4}$$

and by definition

$$V_M = \frac{ds}{dt} \tag{12-5}$$

Hence from Eq. (12-4) and (12-5)

$$\frac{ds}{d\theta} = \frac{ds}{dt} \cdot \frac{dt}{d\theta} = V_M \cdot \frac{R}{V_T} \csc^2 \theta \tag{12-6}$$

which combined with Eq. (12-2) yields

$$\left(\frac{dr}{d\theta}\right)^2 + r^2 = \left(\frac{V_M}{V_T}\right)^2 R^2 \csc^4 \theta \tag{12-7}$$

---
* A constant-altitude target is used in setting up the geometry; however, this is not an essential requirement.

If we define
$$p = \frac{V_M}{V_T} \qquad (12\text{-}8)$$
and
$$k = pR \qquad (12\text{-}9)$$
then the differential equation for the line-of-sight course is
$$\left(\frac{dr}{d\theta}\right)^2 + r^2 = k^2 \csc^4 \theta \qquad (12\text{-}10)$$

Solution of Differential Equation. The differential equation (12-10) for the beam-rider trajectory is of the first order, but is *nonlinear* and not solvable in closed form by ordinary methods. Although the solution may be exhibited in the form of quadratures, more useful for this particular equation is an infinite-series solution. Let us expand r in a Taylor series as follows:

$$r = r_0 + r_0'(\theta - \theta_0) + \frac{r_0''(\theta - \theta_0)^2}{2!} + \frac{r_0'''(\theta - \theta_0)^3}{3!} + \cdots \qquad (12\text{-}11)$$

where r_0 is the initial launching slant range from the control point to the missile and the subsequent derivatives of r are taken with respect to θ and evaluated at $\theta = \theta_0$. To obtain r explicitly it is necessary to evaluate the coefficients r_0, r_0', r_0'', etc., in terms of the initial boundary conditions

$$\left.\begin{array}{l} r_0 = 0 \\ \theta_0 = \tan^{-1} m \end{array}\right\} \qquad (12\text{-}12)$$

where m is the initial slope of the trajectory. From Eq. (12-10)

$$(r_0')^2 + r_0^2 = k^2 \csc^4 \theta_0 \qquad (12\text{-}13)$$

which by use of the first boundary condition in Eq. (12-12) reduces to

$$r_0' = k \csc^2 \theta_0 \qquad (12\text{-}14)$$

The second boundary condition of Eq. (12-12) yields

$$\csc^2 \theta_0 = 1 + \cot^2 \theta_0 = m^{-2}(1 + m^2) \qquad (12\text{-}15)$$

so that Eq. (12-14) can be written as

$$r_0' = km^{-2}(1 + m^2) \qquad (12\text{-}16)$$

In order to obtain r_0'' it is necessary to differentiate Eq. (12-10), giving

$$r'r'' + rr' = -2k^2 \csc^4 \theta \cot \theta \qquad (12\text{-}17)$$

At $\theta = \theta_0$, $\csc^4 \theta = m^{-4}(1 + m^2)^2$, and hence Eq. (12-17) becomes

$$r_0'' = -2km^{-3}(1 + m^2) \qquad (12\text{-}18)$$

This procedure is repeated to obtain successive coefficients. The coefficients through the tenth-power term are

$r_0 = 0$
$r_0' = C$
$r_0'' = -2Cm^{-1}$
$r_0''' = Cm^{-2}(6 + m^2)$
$r_0^{\text{iv}} = -Cm^{-3}(24 + 16m^2)$
$r_0^{\text{v}} = Cm^{-4}(120 + 120m^2 + 21m^4)$
$r_0^{\text{vi}} = -Cm^{-5}(720 + 960m^2 + 282m^4)$
$r_0^{\text{vii}} = Cm^{-6}(5040 + 8400m^2 + 3606m^4 + 301m^6)$
$r_0^{\text{viii}} = -Cm^{-7}(40{,}320 + 80{,}640m^2 + 48{,}384m^4 + 6816m^6)$
$r_0^{\text{ix}} = Cm^{-8}(362{,}880 + 846{,}720m^2 + 645{,}120m^4 + 169{,}680m^6 + 4681m^8)$
$r_0^{\text{x}} = -Cm^{-9}(3{,}628{,}800 + 9{,}676{,}800m^2 + 8{,}951{,}040m^4 + 3{,}310{,}320m^6 + 352{,}562m^8)$

where $C = km^{-2}(1 + m^2)$. The series solution is then

$$r = km^{-2}(1 + m^2)\left[(\theta - \theta_0) - m^{-1}(\theta - \theta_0)^2 + \frac{m^{-2}(6 + m^2)(\theta - \theta_0)^3}{3!} - \cdots\right] \quad (12\text{-}19)$$

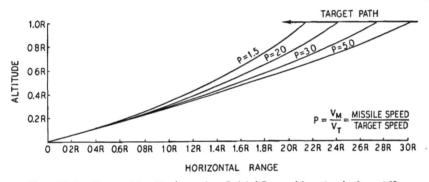

Fig. 12-2 Beam-rider Trajectories; Initial Launching Angle $\theta_0 = 15°$.

The line-of-sight trajectories are given by Eq. (12-19). Figures 12-2 through 12-4 show some sample beam-rider trajectories for initial launching angles $\theta_0 = 15°$, $30°$, and $45°$ and for missile-to-target speed ratios $p = 1.5, 2, 3$ and 5. It should be noted that these trajectories are plotted in rectangular coordinates with the radar dish at the origin. Both coordinates are expressed in terms of the target altitude R.

Time of Flight. The *time of flight* is the total elapsed time of the missile from launching to impact with the target. From Eq. (12-3) we have

$$V_T t_f = R \cot \theta_0 - R \cot \theta_f \quad (12\text{-}20)$$

where t_f is the time of flight and θ_f is the impact or final elevation angle. The time of flight is thus given by

$$t_f = \frac{R}{V_T}(\cot \theta_0 - \cot \theta_f) \quad (12\text{-}21)$$

450   THE ANALYSIS OF FLIGHT PATHS

The time of flight may also be expressed in terms of the slant range, r_f, at impact as follows. From Fig. 12-1

$$\sin \theta_f = \frac{R}{r_f} \qquad (12\text{-}22)$$

hence

$$\cot \theta_f = \frac{1}{R} \sqrt{r_f^2 - R^2} \qquad (12\text{-}23)$$

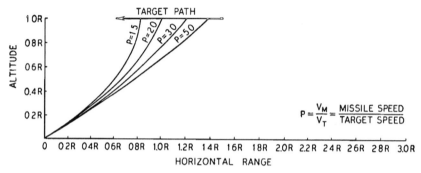

Fig. 12-3 Beam-rider Trajectories; Initial Launching Angle $\theta_0 = 30°$.

From Eq. (12-23), the time of flight in Eq. (12-21) becomes

$$t_f = \frac{1}{V_T}(R \cot \theta_0 - \sqrt{r_f^2 - R^2}) \qquad (12\text{-}24)$$

Either Eq. (12-21) or (12-24) may be used to determine the time of flight. If trajectories have already been plotted, then θ_f and/or r_f can be obtained graphically. The alternative is to obtain them by interpolation from the series solution, Eq. (12-19). The following example will illustrate the method.

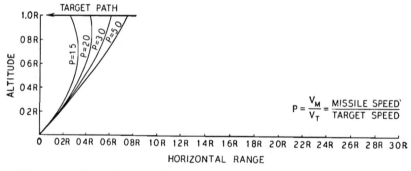

Fig. 12-4 Beam-rider Trajectories; Initial Launching Angle $\theta_0 = 45°$.

Example 1. From Eq. (12-19) the following values result for the case of $\theta_0 = 15°$ and $p = 2$.

	θ	r	x	y
	16°	0.4892	0.4702	0.1348
	18°	1.3080	1.2440	0.4042
	20°	1.9648	1.8463	0.6720
$\theta_f\begin{cases}\\ \end{cases}$	22°	2.5037	2.3214	0.9379 $\Big\} y_f$
	23°	2.7340	2.5166	1.0683

Here x and y are the rectangular coordinates corresponding to the polar coordinates r and θ. Now impact occurs at $y_f = 1$. Interpolation in the x, y columns gives (x_f, y_f) from which θ_f and r_f can be obtained. In the case here $x_f = 2.424$ and $\theta_f = 22.42°$. Using Eq. (12-21), we obtain

$$t_f = \frac{R}{V_T}(3.732 - 2.424)$$

$$= 1.308 \frac{R}{V_T}$$

For a target at 30,000 ft altitude traveling at Mach 0.66

$$t_f = \frac{1.308(30,000)}{656.7} = 59.8 \text{ sec}$$

At the time of missile launching the slant range to the target is 22.0 miles.

Beam-rider Turning Rate. The only control over a missile after it is launched may be the power to move the flaps in the direction and amount desired. To a good approximation the flap deflection is proportional to the rate of turn of the missile. The beam-rider turning rate is hence of considerable interest.

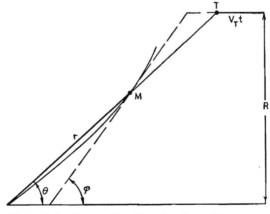

FIG. 12-5 Beam-rider Turning Rate Geometry.

In Fig. 12-5 the angle φ is the inclination of the trajectory; hence

$$\tan \varphi = \frac{dy}{dx} = \frac{d(r \sin \theta)/d\theta}{d(r \cos \theta)/d\theta} = \frac{r' \sin \theta + r \cos \theta}{r' \cos \theta - r \sin \theta} \qquad (12\text{-}25)$$

Differentiating Eq. (12-25) with respect to θ yields

$$\sec^2 \varphi \frac{d\varphi}{d\theta} = \frac{r^2 + 2r'^2 - rr''}{(r' \cos \theta - r \sin \theta)^2} \qquad (12\text{-}26)$$

In order to evaluate $\dot{\varphi} \equiv \frac{d\varphi}{dt}$ we must find $\dot{\theta}$ since

$$\dot{\varphi} = \dot{\theta} \frac{d\varphi}{d\theta} \qquad (12\text{-}27)$$

From Eq. (12-3)

$$\tan \theta = \frac{R}{R \cot \theta_0 - V_T t} \qquad (12\text{-}28)$$

Therefore, differentiating, we have

$$\sec^2 \theta \frac{d\theta}{dt} = \frac{V_T R}{(R \cot \theta_0 - V_T t)^2}$$

$$= \frac{V_T}{R} \tan^2 \theta$$

or

$$\frac{d\theta}{dt} = \frac{V_T}{R} \sin^2 \theta \qquad (12\text{-}29)$$

From Eq. (12-25) and the identity $\sec^2 \varphi = 1 + \tan^2 \varphi$ we have

$$\sec^2 \varphi = \frac{r^2 + r'^2}{(r' \cos \theta - r \sin \theta)^2} \qquad (12\text{-}30)$$

which, when substituted into Eq. (12-26), yields

$$\frac{d\varphi}{d\theta} = \frac{r^2 + 2r'^2 - rr''}{r^2 + r'^2} \qquad (12\text{-}31)$$

Using Eq. (12-10) in (12-17), we have

$$r'' = -\frac{2k^2 \csc^4 \theta \cot \theta}{\sqrt{k^2 \csc^4 \theta - r^2}} - r \qquad (12\text{-}32)$$

and thus Eq. (12-31) becomes

$$\frac{d\varphi}{d\theta} = 2\left(1 + \frac{r \cot \theta}{\sqrt{k^2 \csc^4 \theta - r^2}}\right) \qquad (12\text{-}33)$$

Finally, from Eq. (12-27), (12-29), and (12-33), the turning rate is

$$\dot{\varphi} = \frac{2V_T \sin^2 \theta}{R}\left(1 + \frac{r \cot \theta}{\sqrt{k^2 \csc^4 \theta - r^2}}\right) \qquad (12\text{-}34)$$

From Eq. (12-3) the time is given by

$$t = \frac{R}{V_T} (\cot \theta_0 - \cot \theta) \tag{12-35}$$

A few examples of the turning rate from Eq. (12-34) plotted against the time from Eq. (12-35) are shown in Figs. 12-6 to 12-9. These plots are normalized in such a manner that, if unity on the ordinate scale represents the maximum turning rate in radians per second at the time of impact, then the maximum value on the abscissa scale represents the time of flight in seconds, t_f.

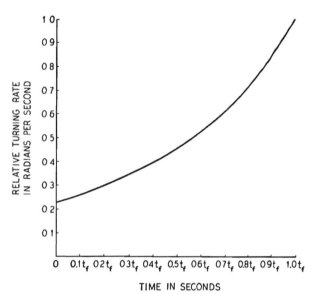

Fig. 12-6 Beam-rider Turning Rate; $\theta_0 = 15°, p = 1.5$.

It will now be shown that the turning rate for a beam-rider missile is always finite for $p = \frac{V_M}{V_T} > 1$. It can be seen from Eq. (12-34) that, in order for $\dot{\varphi}$ to be infinite, it must be true that

$$r^2 = k^2 \csc^4 \theta \tag{12-36}$$

or

$$r = k \csc^2 \theta$$

From Fig. 12-5 it is clear that the maximum value which r can attain is

$$r_{\max} = R \csc \theta_f \tag{12-37}$$

For any smaller θ, the missile will not have reached the target, and hence

$$r \leq R \csc \theta \tag{12-38}$$

454   THE ANALYSIS OF FLIGHT PATHS

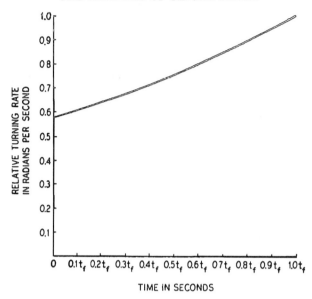

FIG. 12-7 Beam-rider Turning Rate; $\theta_0 = 15°$, $p = 5$.

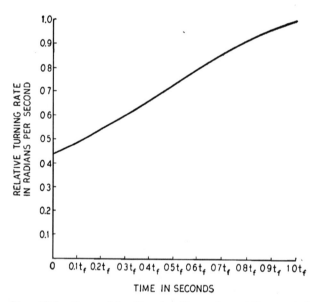

FIG. 12-8 Beam-rider Turning Rate; $\theta_0 = 45°$, $p = 1.5$.

which combined with Eq. (12-36) gives

$$k \csc^2 \theta \leq R \csc \theta \tag{12-39}$$

Since θ must lie in the interval $0 \leq \theta \leq \pi$, we have from Eq. (12-39)

$$k \csc \theta \leq R; \quad p \leq \sin \theta \tag{12-40}$$

This is impossible for $p > 1$; hence $\dot\varphi$ is always finite for $p > 1$.

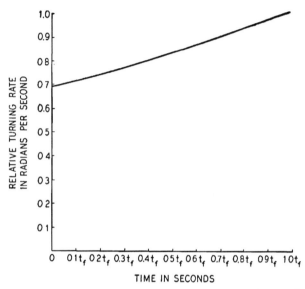

Fig. 12-9 Beam-rider Turning Rate; $\theta_0 = 45°$, $p = 5$.

Acceleration of Beam-rider Missile. The turning rate $\dot\varphi$ from Eq. (12-34) can readily be converted into the lateral or transverse acceleration of the missile by multiplying by the missile speed. The magnitude of the acceleration is given by

$$A_M = |V_M \dot\varphi| \tag{12-41}$$

The generalized turning-rate curves of Figs. 12-6 to 12-9 can readily be converted into acceleration curves showing the number of g turn required by the missile as a function of time elapsed since launching. This is accomplished by multiplying $\dot\varphi$ by the speed of the missile in feet per second and dividing by $g = 32.2$ ft per sec.^{2} Two examples of g-turn curves are given in Figs. 12-10 and 12-11 for missile speeds of Mach 1, 2, 3, and 4. The missile speeds are constant, the Mach number being taken at 30,000 ft altitude.

Frequency Spectrum of Turning-rate Curve. The *frequency spectrum* of the beam-rider turning rate is given by the Fourier transform of the turning-rate function. It is clear by inspection that the Fourier transform of a function as complicated as that given in Eq. (12-34) would be difficult, if not impossible, to obtain. The curves for turning rate suggest that a polynomial approximation* can be obtained to represent Eq. (12-34) from $t = 0$ to $t = t_f$. By the methods of curve fitting discussed in Par. 6-15 of Chap. 6 it is found that all of the curves of Figs. 12-6 through 12-9 can be well fitted by a cubic polynomial of the form

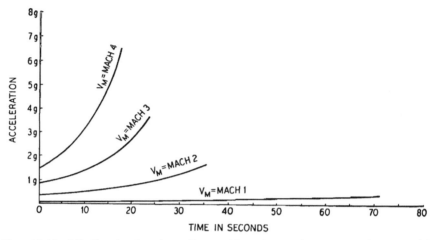

Fig. 12-10 Missile Acceleration—Beam-rider; $\theta_0 = 15°$, $p = 1.5$, Target Altitude = 30,000 ft.

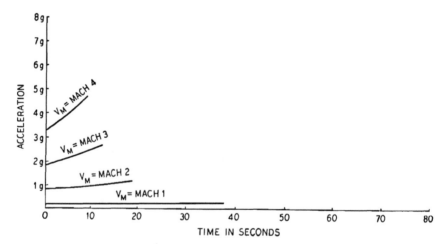

Fig. 12-11 Missile Acceleration—Beam-rider; $\theta_0 = 45°$, $p = 5$, Target Altitude = 30,000 ft.

* It is important to note that the approximation here assumes that the turning rate returns to zero after impact. Other assumptions could be made: e.g., that the turning rate remain constant at its final value after impact.

12-1]   LINE-OF-SIGHT COURSE (BEAM-RIDER MISSILE)   457

$$\dot{\varphi} = y(t) = at^3 + bt^2 + ct + d \qquad (12\text{-}42)$$

The frequency spectrum is given by the Fourier transform

$$G(\omega) = \int_{-\infty}^{\infty} y(t)e^{-j\omega t}\,dt = \int_{0}^{t_f} y(t)e^{-j\omega t}\,dt \qquad (12\text{-}43)$$

where $y(t) = 0$ for $t < 0$ and $t > t_f$. Each term of Eq. (12-42) must be evaluated in Eq. (12-43). For example, the evaluation of the bt^2 term by parts is

$$\begin{aligned}
\int_0^{t_f} bt^2 e^{-j\omega t}\,dt &= \frac{jbt^2}{\omega} e^{-j\omega t}\Big|_0^{t_f} - \frac{2bj}{\omega}\int_0^{t_f} t e^{-j\omega t}\,dt \\
&= \frac{jbt_f^2 e^{-j\omega t_f}}{\omega} + \frac{2bt}{\omega^2} e^{-j\omega t}\Big|_0^{t_f} - \frac{2b}{\omega^2}\int_0^{t_f} e^{-j\omega t}\,dt \\
&= \frac{jbt_f^2 e^{-j\omega t_f}}{\omega} + \frac{2bt_f e^{-j\omega t_f}}{\omega^2} + \frac{2bj(1 - e^{-j\omega t_f})}{\omega^3} \qquad (12\text{-}44)
\end{aligned}$$

Each term of the polynomial Eq. (12-42) will yield a similar result. In order to obtain the amplitudes of the frequency components, without regard to phase angle, it is necessary to determine the absolute value of

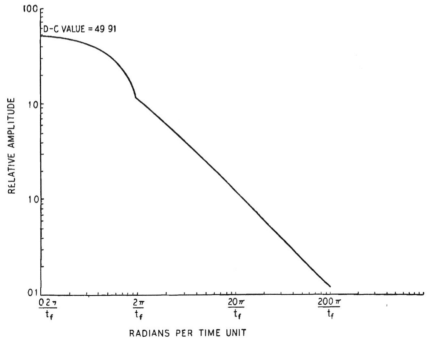

FIG. 12-12 Frequency Spectrum of Beam-rider Turning Rate; $\theta_0 = 15°$, $p = 1.5$.

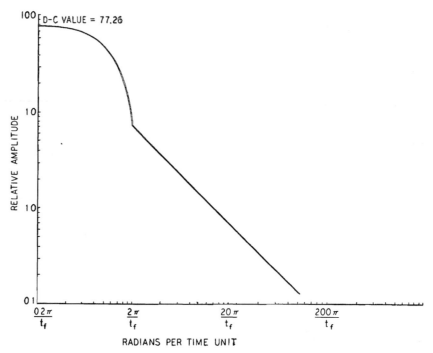

Fig. 12-13 Frequency Spectrum of Beam-rider Turning Rate; $\theta_0 = 15°$, $p = 5$

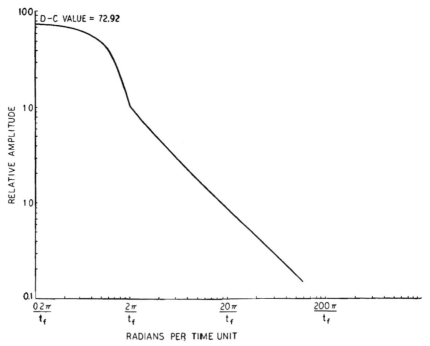

Fig. 12-14 Frequency Spectrum of Beam-rider Turning Rate; $\theta_0 = 45°$, $p = 1.5$.

$G(\omega)$. This gives the amplitude frequency spectrum of the missile turning rate. Figures 12-12 through 12-15 show frequency spectra for the turning rate curves in Figs. 12-6 through 12-9. The ordinates represent relative amplitude and the abscissas represent frequency in radians per second if the time of flight is normalized to the value t_f. The break in these curves at the reciprocal of the time of flight results from the assumption of zero turning rate after impact.

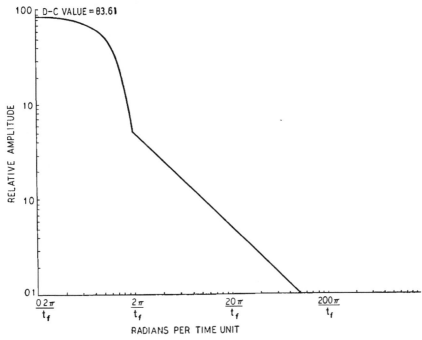

FIG. 12-15 Frequency Spectrum of Beam-rider Turning Rate; $\theta_0 = 45°$, $p = 5$.

The case discussed here is essentially the surface-to-air problem in which we assume that the missile is launched in the beam. The capture problem is discussed in Chap. 13 and 16. Obviously, the air-to-air case is considerably more difficult to handle, since the geometry would, in general, require a three-dimensional setup. Consideration of maneuvering targets is beyond the scope of this chapter. The complexity of the problem is almost always such as to prohibit the solution in closed form.

12-2 PURE PURSUIT COURSE

Perhaps the oldest and simplest type of flight path is that of the pure pursuit course, the "hound-and-hare" course. There are two kinds of pursuit courses: (1) pure or ordinary, in which the lead angle is zero and

(2) deviated or fixed-lead, in which there is a finite fixed lead angle. The pure pursuit course will be studied first.

A *pure pursuit course* is a course in which the missile velocity vector is always directed toward the instantaneous target position.

The Equations of Motion. In deriving the equations of motion the following assumptions are made:

(a) The target follows a nonmaneuvering straight-line course.
(b) Both the missile and target speeds are constant.
(c) A two-dimensional coordinate system is set up in a plane determined by the target and missile velocity vectors.

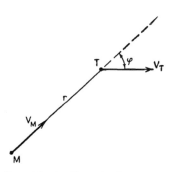

FIG. 12-16 Pursuit Geometry.

The geometry required for the derivation of the pursuit course equations of motion in polar coordinates is given in Fig. 12-16, where the following symbols are employed:

r = instantaneous distance MT between missile and target
φ = angle between target velocity vector and the line of sight

For an outgoing target as illustrated in Fig. 12-16 the equations of motion are obtained by taking components along r and normal to r:

$$\dot{r} = V_T \cos \varphi - V_M \qquad (12\text{-}45)$$

$$r\dot{\varphi} = -V_T \sin \varphi \qquad (12\text{-}46)$$

where the dot again represents differentiation with respect to time. The solution of these equations of motion is straightforward. Dividing Eq. (12-45) by Eq. (12-46), we obtain

$$\frac{\dot{r}}{r} = (p \csc \varphi - \cot \varphi)\dot{\varphi} \qquad (12\text{-}47)$$

where $p = V_M/V_T$ as previously defined. This can be integrated directly, giving

$$r = K \frac{(\sin \varphi)^{p-1}}{(1 + \cos \varphi)^p} \qquad (12\text{-}48)$$

where, for the initial values r_0 and φ_0,

$$K = \frac{r_0(1 + \cos \varphi_0)^p}{(\sin \varphi_0)^{p-1}} \qquad (12\text{-}49)$$

For an incoming target, the target and missile motions both tend to decrease r as long as φ is acute. Here φ is monotonic increasing and hence

12-2]   PURE PURSUIT COURSE

the equations of motion are

$$\dot{r} = -V_T \cos\varphi - V_M \quad (12\text{-}50)$$
$$r\dot{\varphi} = V_T \sin\varphi \quad (12\text{-}51)$$

Again dividing Eq. (12-50) by Eq. (12-51), we have

$$\frac{\dot{r}}{r} = -(p\csc\varphi + \cot\varphi)\dot{\varphi} \quad (12\text{-}52)$$

The solution by direct integration is

$$r = K' \frac{(1+\cos\varphi)^p}{(\sin\varphi)^{p+1}} \quad (12\text{-}53)$$

where the initial values r_0 and φ_0 give

$$K' = \frac{r_0 (\sin\varphi_0)^{p+1}}{(1+\cos\varphi_0)^p} \quad (12\text{-}54)$$

It is difficult to plot trajectories from Eq. (12-48) and (12-53) without having an explicit relationship between r, φ, and the time t. For the outgoing target from Eq. (12-45) we have

$$\dot{r}\cos\varphi = V_T \cos^2\varphi - V_M \cos\varphi \quad (12\text{-}55)$$

and from Eq. (12-46) we have

$$r\dot{\varphi}\sin\varphi = -V_T \sin^2\varphi \quad (12\text{-}56)$$

Subtracting Eq. (12-56) from Eq. (12-55), we have

$$\dot{r}\cos\varphi - r\dot{\varphi}\sin\varphi = V_T - V_M \cos\varphi$$
$$= V_T - V_M \frac{\dot{r} + V_M}{V_T} \quad (12\text{-}57)$$
$$= V_T - p\dot{r} - pV_M$$

which can be written as

$$\dot{r}(\cos\varphi + p) - r\dot{\varphi}\sin\varphi = V_T - pV_M \quad (12\text{-}58)$$

The differential equation (12-58) is easily solved as follows:

$$(\cos\varphi + p)\,dr - r\sin\varphi\,d\varphi = (V_T - pV_M)\,dt$$

$$\int_{r_0}^{r} \underbrace{(\cos\varphi + p)}_{u}\,\underbrace{dr}_{dv} - \int_{\varphi_0}^{\varphi} \underbrace{r}_{v}\underbrace{\sin\varphi\,d\varphi}_{du} = \int_0^t (V_T - pV_M)\,dt$$

$$r(\cos\varphi + p)\Big|_{r_0,\varphi_0}^{r,\varphi} = (V_T - pV_M)t$$

$$\therefore\ r(\cos\varphi + p) - r_0(\cos\varphi_0 + p) = (V_T - pV_M)t \quad (12\text{-}59)$$

The elapsed time in flight for the outgoing target is, from (12-59),

$$t = \frac{r_0(\cos\varphi_0 + p) - r(\cos\varphi + p)}{pV_M - V_T} \quad (12\text{-}60)$$

The incoming target can be treated in the same manner. The differential equation becomes

$$\dot{r}(\cos\varphi - p) - r\dot{\varphi}\sin\varphi = pV_M - V_T \qquad (12\text{-}61)$$

which has the solution

$$r(\cos\varphi - p) - r_0(\cos\varphi_0 - p) = (pV_M - V_T)t \qquad (12\text{-}62)$$

Hence, the elapsed time of flight for the incoming target, from Eq. (12-62), is

$$t = \frac{r(\cos\varphi - p) - r_0(\cos\varphi_0 - p)}{pV_M - V_T} \qquad (12\text{-}63)$$

From the equations already developed we are able to plot the trajectory for any particular case desired. For example, for an incoming target Eq. (12-53) and (12-63) are used. Here V_M, V_T, p, r_0, and φ_0 are specified and hence the initial relative positions are known. From the missile starting point successive points can be obtained as follows. Take a new

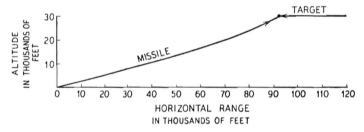

Fig. 12-17 Pursuit Trajectory.

angle $\varphi + \Delta\varphi$ and compute the new r from Eq. (12-53). Next compute elapsed time t from Eq. (12-63); from this t and V_T the distance traveled by the target are determined. The line-of-sight can be drawn through this new target position at angle $\varphi + \Delta\varphi$. The new missile position is found by laying off the new r along this line-of-sight.

Example 1. Plot a pursuit course from the following data for an incoming target:

$V_M = 4V_T$
V_T = Mach 0.66
Target initial horizontal range = 117,000 ft
Target altitude = 30,000 ft

Assume Mach 1 = 995 ft per sec at 30,000 ft, and $p = 4$.

Here $r_0 = 120{,}785$ ft and $\varphi_0 = 14.4°$. From Eq. (12-54), $K' = 7.60$. The pursuit course is plotted as described above and is shown in Fig. 12-17.

A brief explanation of this trajectory is in order. The initial distance from missile to target is 120,785 ft, and interception ultimately occurs at $\varphi = 180°$. However, when the missile heading is only 60°, the distance between the missile and target has already been cut to 79 ft after an elapsed time of 37.14 sec out of a total time of flight of 37.17 sec. This means that in the remaining 0.03 sec until interception the missile must turn 120°. This is a very high average turning rate; as a matter of fact, it is shown later that the turning rate is monotonic increasing and approaches infinity at interception. The scale used in Fig. 12-17 is such as to preclude accuracy of the trajectory near interception.

Time of Flight. The time of flight for an outgoing target is given by Eq. (12-60) for $r = 0$. It is

$$t_f = \frac{r_0 (\cos \varphi_0 + p)}{pV_M - V_T} \tag{12-64}$$

For an incoming target the time of flight from Eq. (12-63) is

$$t_f = \frac{-r_0 (\cos \varphi_0 - p)}{pV_M - V_T} \tag{12-65}$$

It is readily seen that for $p > 1$ the time of flight is always finite.

Example 2. Using the data of Example 1, find the times of flight for both incoming and outgoing targets.

Incoming from Eq. (12-65):

$$t_f = 37.2 \text{ sec}$$

Outgoing from Eq. (12-64):

$$t_f = 60.9 \text{ sec}$$

Pursuit Course Turning Rate. For an outgoing target the turning rate is given by Eq. (12-46) and (12-48) as

$$\dot{\varphi} = -\frac{V_T}{r} \sin \varphi = \frac{-V_T(1 + \cos \varphi)^p}{K (\sin \varphi)^{p-2}} \tag{12-66}$$

It is clear from Eq. (12-48) that $r \to 0$ as $\sin \varphi \to 0$. Hence for an outgoing target $\varphi \to 0$ as the missile approaches the target. For an incoming target the turning rate is given by Eq. (12-51) and (12-53) as

$$\dot{\varphi} = \frac{V_T}{r} \sin \varphi = \frac{V_T (\sin \varphi)^{p+2}}{K'(1 + \cos \varphi)^p} \tag{12-67}$$

Here $r \to 0$ as $\varphi \to \pi$ and hence the missile approaches the target as $\varphi \to \pi$ for an incoming target.

It is of interest to evaluate the limiting value of the turning rate as the missile approaches the target. This limit will be a function of the missile-to-target speed ratio p and may be different for the outgoing and incoming target cases.

Outgoing Target:

$$1 < p < 2: \lim_{\varphi \to 0} \dot{\varphi} = \frac{-V_T}{K} \lim_{\varphi \to 0} (\sin \varphi)^{2-p}(1 + \cos \varphi)^p = 0 \quad (12\text{-}68)$$

$$p = 2: \lim_{\varphi \to 0} \dot{\varphi} = \frac{-V_T}{K} \lim_{\varphi \to 0} (1 + \cos \varphi)^2 = -\frac{4V_T}{K} \quad (12\text{-}69)$$

$$p > 2: \lim_{\varphi \to 0} \dot{\varphi} = \frac{-V_T}{K} \lim_{\varphi \to 0} \frac{(1 + \cos \varphi)^p}{(\sin \varphi)^{p-2}} = -\infty \quad (12\text{-}70)$$

Incoming Target:

$$1 < p < 2: \lim_{\varphi \to \pi} \dot{\varphi} = \frac{V_T}{K'} \lim_{\varphi \to \pi} \frac{(\sin \varphi)^{p+2}}{(1 + \cos \varphi)^p} = 0 \quad (12\text{-}71)$$

$$p = 2: \lim_{\varphi \to \pi} \dot{\varphi} = \frac{V_T}{K'} \lim_{\varphi \to \pi} \frac{(\sin \varphi)^4}{(1 + \cos \varphi)^2} = \frac{4V_T}{K'} \quad (12\text{-}72)$$

$$p > 2: \lim_{\varphi \to \pi} \dot{\varphi} = \frac{V_T}{K'} \lim_{\varphi \to \pi} \frac{(\sin \varphi)^{p+2}}{(1 + \cos \varphi)^p} = \infty \quad (12\text{-}73)$$

Evaluation of the limits for the outgoing target are straightforward. The following proofs are used to evaluate the limits for the incoming target. For $1 < p < 2$, discarding the constant factor,

$$\lim_{\varphi \to \pi} \frac{(\sin \varphi)^{p+2}}{(1 + \cos \varphi)^p} = \frac{0}{0}$$

By l'Hospital's rule

$$\lim_{\varphi \to \pi} \frac{(\sin \varphi)^{p+2}}{(1 + \cos \varphi)^p} = -\frac{p+2}{p} \lim_{\varphi \to \pi} \frac{\sin^p \varphi \cos \varphi}{(1 + \cos \varphi)^{p-1}} = \frac{0}{0}$$

$$= \frac{p+2}{p(p-1)} \lim_{\varphi \to \pi} \frac{p \sin^{p-2} \varphi - (p+1) \sin^p \varphi}{(1 + \cos \varphi)^{p-2}} = \frac{0}{0}$$

$$= \frac{p+2}{p(p-1)} \left\{ \lim_{\varphi \to \pi} \frac{p \sin^{p-2} \varphi}{(1 + \cos \varphi)^{p-2}} - \lim_{\varphi \to \pi} \frac{(p+1) \sin^p \varphi}{(1 + \cos \varphi)^{p-2}} \right\}$$

$$= \frac{p+2}{p-1} \lim_{\varphi \to \pi} \frac{\sin^{p-2} \varphi}{(1 + \cos \varphi)^{p-2}} \quad (12\text{-}74)$$

since $p - 2 < 0$ for this case. Now since

$$\lim_{\varphi \to \pi} \frac{\sin \varphi}{1 + \cos \varphi} = \frac{0}{0} = \lim_{\varphi \to \pi} \frac{\cos \varphi}{-\sin \varphi} = \infty$$

then for $p - 2 < 0$ we have from Eq. (12-74) that

$$\lim_{\varphi \to \pi} \frac{(\sin \varphi)^{p+2}}{(1 + \cos \varphi)^p} = \frac{p+2}{p-1} \lim_{\varphi \to \pi} \left(\frac{\sin \varphi}{1 + \cos \varphi} \right)^{p-2} = 0 \quad (12\text{-}75)$$

This proves Eq. (12-71).

Next consider the case of $2 < p < 3$, again discarding the constant factor. Again

$$\lim_{\varphi \to \pi} \frac{(\sin \varphi)^{p+2}}{(1 + \cos \varphi)^p} = \frac{0}{0}$$

so that by applying l'Hospital's rule we have

$$\lim_{\varphi \to \pi} \frac{(\sin \varphi)^{p+2}}{(1 + \cos \varphi)^p} = -\frac{p+2}{p} \lim_{\varphi \to \pi} \frac{\sin^p \varphi \cos \varphi}{(1 + \cos \varphi)^{p-1}} = \frac{0}{0}$$

$$= \frac{p+2}{p(p-1)} \lim_{\varphi \to \pi} \frac{p (\sin \varphi)^{p-2} \cos^2 \varphi - \sin^p \varphi}{(1 + \cos \varphi)^{p-2}}$$

$$= \frac{p+2}{p(p-1)} (\lim 1 - \lim 2)$$

$$\lim 1 = p \lim_{\varphi \to \pi} \frac{(\sin \varphi)^{p-2} \cos^2 \varphi}{(1 + \cos \varphi)^{p-2}} = p \lim_{\varphi \to \pi} \left(\frac{\sin \varphi}{1 + \cos \varphi} \right)^{p-2} \lim_{\varphi \to \pi} \cos^2 \varphi$$

$$= p \cdot \infty \cdot 1 = \infty, \quad \text{since} \quad \lim_{\varphi \to \pi} \frac{\sin \varphi}{1 + \cos \varphi} = \infty$$

$$\lim 2 = \lim_{\varphi \to \pi} \frac{(\sin \varphi)^p}{(1 + \cos \varphi)^{p-2}} = \frac{0}{0}$$

$$= \frac{-p}{p-2} \lim_{\varphi \to \pi} \frac{(\sin \varphi)^{p-2} \cos \varphi}{(1 + \cos \varphi)^{p-3}}$$

$$= \frac{-p}{p-2} \lim_{\varphi \to \pi} \frac{(\sin \varphi)^{p-2}}{(1 + \cos \varphi)^{p-3}} \lim_{\varphi \to \pi} \cos \varphi$$

$$= \frac{-p}{p-2} \cdot 0 \cdot (-1) = 0, \quad \text{since} \quad p < 3$$

Thus,

$$\lim_{\varphi \to \pi} \frac{(\sin \varphi)^{p+2}}{(1 + \cos \varphi)^p} = \frac{p+2}{p(p-1)} (\infty - 0) = \infty \qquad (12\text{-}76)$$

which means that $\lim_{\varphi \to \pi} \dot{\varphi} = \infty$ for $2 < p < 3$. Now for $3 < p < 4$, p has increased by 1 and $\dot{\varphi}$ is multiplied by $\frac{\sin \varphi}{1 + \cos \varphi}$, whose limit as $\varphi \to \pi$ is ∞. Hence by mathematical induction

$$\lim_{\varphi \to \pi} \dot{\varphi} = \infty \qquad (12\text{-}77)$$

for all nonintegral values of $p > 2$.

Next let us consider integral values of p starting at $p = 2$. By applying l'Hospital's rule Eq. (12-72) is easily established; for

$$\lim_{\varphi \to \pi} \dot{\varphi} = \frac{V_T}{K'} \lim_{\varphi \to \pi} \frac{\sin^4 \varphi}{(1 + \cos \varphi)^2} = \frac{0}{0}$$

$$= \frac{V_T}{K'} \lim_{\varphi \to \pi} \frac{-2 \sin^2 \varphi \cos \varphi}{(1 + \cos \varphi)} = \frac{0}{0}$$

$$= 2 \frac{V_T}{K'} \lim_{\varphi \to \pi} \frac{-2 \sin \varphi \cos^2 \varphi + \sin^3 \varphi}{-\sin \varphi}$$

$$= \frac{4 V_T}{K'} \lim_{\varphi \to \pi} \cos^2 \varphi - 0$$

$$= \frac{4 V_T}{K'}$$

This proves Eq. (12-72). By the same inductive reasoning as before, since each integral increase in p multiplies $\dot{\varphi}$ by $\dfrac{\sin \varphi}{1 + \cos \varphi}$ which goes to ∞ as $\varphi \to \pi$, then $\lim_{\varphi \to \pi} \dot{\varphi} = \infty$ for $p = 3$ and so on. Hence $\lim_{\varphi \to \pi} \dot{\varphi} = \infty$ for all integral values of $p > 2$. This completes the proof of Eq. (12-73).

It can be shown that the maximum absolute value of the turning rate occurs at the impact point whenever $p \geq 2$, for both outgoing and incoming targets. However, for $1 < p < 2$ the turning rate has a maximum absolute value at $\varphi = \cos^{-1} p/2$ for the outgoing target and $\varphi = \cos^{-1}(-p/2)$ for the incoming target. This can be demonstrated by taking the first and second derivatives of $\dot{\varphi}$ with respect to φ. Hence for the outgoing target with $1 < p < 2$ we have

$$|\dot{\varphi}|_{\max} = \frac{V_T}{K}(1 + p/2)^p [1 - (p/2)^2]^{1-(p/2)} \qquad (12\text{-}78)$$

and for the incoming target with $1 < p < 2$ we have

$$|\dot{\varphi}|_{\max} = \frac{V_T}{K'} \frac{[1 - (p/2)^2]^{1+(p/2)}}{(1 - p/2)^p} \qquad (12\text{-}79)$$

Pursuit course turning-rate curves can be plotted from Eq. (12-66) and (12-60) for the outgoing target and from Eq. (12-67) and (12-63) for the incoming target. The procedure would be somewhat as follows. Starting at $\varphi = \varphi_0$ incremental values of φ could be assumed and the corresponding values of r could be determined from Eq. (12-48) or (12-53). From each value of (r, φ) a $\dot{\varphi}$ could be obtained from Eq. (12-66) or (12-67) and a corresponding t could be obtained from Eq. (12-60) or (12-63). Then $\dot{\varphi}$ could be plotted vs. t.

Example 3. Using the data of Example 1 plot a turning-rate curve in terms of g.

Fig. 12-18 is the required plot up to a maximum turn of $10g$. Note that in this case $p = 4$ means that the turning rate increases to infinity as the missile approaches the point of intercept. The curve therefore is plotted only up to $10g$.

It is obvious that in practice the maximum missile turning rate cannot be infinite. In courses where a turning rate is called for which is in excess of the capabilities of the missile, it is logical to assume that the missile will stay in its maximum turn until it is again heading along the line-of-sight. In general this will mean that the missile will cross the line of flight of the target and approach the target from the opposite side. It might be assumed that if and when the missile again sights the target it will again follow a pursuit course.

Acceleration in Pursuit Course. The lateral missile acceleration which a pursuit course demands is given by

$$A_M = |V_M \dot{\varphi}| \tag{12-80}$$

where $\dot{\varphi}$ is given by Eq. (12-66) or (12-67). It is seen from the preceding section that as the missile approaches the target infinite accelerations will be demanded for $p > 2$. For $p = 2$ the finite accelerations exist which are given by

$$A_M = \frac{4V_M V_T}{K} \tag{12-81}$$

for the outgoing target and

$$A_M = \frac{4V_M V_T}{K'} \tag{12-82}$$

for the incoming target. For $1 < p < 2$ no acceleration will be required as the missile strikes the target; however, the maximum acceleration during flight can be found by multiplying Eq. (12-78) or (12-79) by V_M.

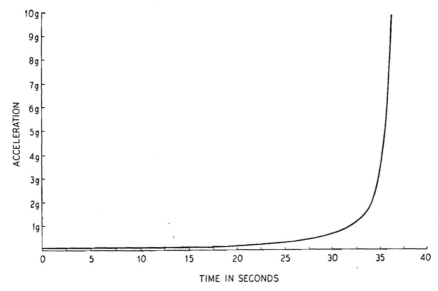

FIG. 12-18 Missile Acceleration—Pursuit Course; Target Altitude = 30,000 ft, $\varphi_0 = 14.4°, p = 4$.

Turning-rate Spectrum. The turning-rate spectrum can be determined in the same way as that for the beam rider in Par. 12-1. The procedure would be as follows: starting with the plot of the turning-rate curve, we can use the methods of Chap. 6 to fit a polynomial to the desired accuracy. The Fourier transform of this polynomial will provide the required turning-rate spectrum. In case the turning rate becomes infinite at interception some practical assumption must be made in order to obtain a reasonable spectrum.

12-3 DEVIATED PURSUIT COURSE

The second type of pursuit course to be considered is the deviated pursuit course, also known as *fixed-lead navigation* or *constant navigation*.

A *deviated pursuit course* is a course in which the angle between the missile velocity vector and the line of sight from the missile to the target is fixed.

If this fixed *lead angle* is zero a pure pursuit course results.

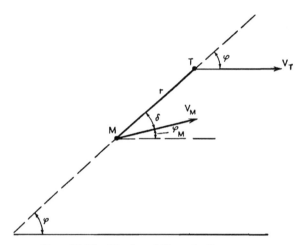

Fig. 12-19 Deviated Pursuit Geometry.

The Equations of Motion. The same assumptions apply here as in the previous case of a pure pursuit course. The geometry required to set up the equations of motion is given in Fig. 12-19, where the following new symbols are employed:

φ_M = missile heading from horizontal
δ = fixed lead angle or missile heading relative to the line-of-sight

The equations of motion are

$$\dot{r} = V_T \cos \varphi - V_M \cos \delta \qquad (12\text{-}83)$$

$$r\dot{\varphi} = -V_T \sin \varphi + V_M \sin \delta \qquad (12\text{-}84)$$

Dividing Eq. (12-83) by (12-84) we have

$$\frac{\dot{r}}{r} = \frac{\cos \varphi - p \cos \delta}{-\sin \varphi + p \sin \delta} \dot{\varphi} \qquad (12\text{-}85)$$

This can be integrated directly as follows:

$$\int_{r_0}^{r} \frac{dr}{r} = \int_{\varphi_0}^{\varphi} \frac{\cos \varphi \, d\varphi}{-\sin \varphi + p \sin \delta} + p \int_{\varphi_0}^{\varphi} \frac{\cos \delta \, d\varphi}{-p \sin \delta + \sin \varphi}$$

$$\ln \frac{r}{r_0} = \ln \frac{\sin \varphi_0 - p \sin \delta}{\sin \varphi - p \sin \delta}$$
$$+ \frac{-p \cos \delta}{\sqrt{1 - p^2 \sin^2 \delta}} \ln \frac{1 - p \sin \delta \sin \varphi + \cos \varphi \sqrt{1 - p^2 \sin^2 \delta}}{-p \sin \delta + \sin \varphi} \bigg|_{\varphi_0}^{\varphi}$$
(12-86)

where it is assumed in the third integration that

$$p^2 \sin^2 \delta < 1 \quad (12\text{-}87)$$

The formula for the trajectory of a missile following a deviated pursuit course is therefore given by

$$r = r_0 \left(\frac{\sin \varphi - p \sin \delta}{\sin \varphi_0 - p \sin \delta} \right)^{\frac{p \cos \delta}{\sqrt{1-p^2 \sin^2 \delta}} - 1}$$
$$\left(\frac{1 - p \sin \delta \sin \varphi_0 + \cos \varphi_0 \sqrt{1 - p^2 \sin^2 \delta}}{1 - p \sin \delta \sin \varphi + \cos \varphi \sqrt{1 - p^2 \sin^2 \delta}} \right)^{\frac{p \cos \delta}{\sqrt{1-p^2 \sin^2 \delta}}} \quad (12\text{-}88)$$

It should be noted that it has been assumed in deriving (12-88) that $p^2 \sin^2 \delta < 1$, which is a practical assumption. In case $p \sin \delta = 1$ the solution of the equations of motion takes the following form:

$$\frac{\dot r}{r} = \frac{\cos \varphi - p \cos \delta}{1 - \sin \varphi} \dot\varphi \quad (12\text{-}89)$$

which by direct integration becomes

$$\int_{r_0}^{r} \frac{dr}{r} = \int_{\varphi_0}^{\varphi} \frac{\cos \varphi \, d\varphi}{1 - \sin \varphi} - p \cos \delta \int_{\varphi_0}^{\varphi} \frac{d\varphi}{1 - \sin \varphi}$$

$$\ln \frac{r}{r_0} = \ln \frac{1 - \sin \varphi_0}{1 - \sin \varphi} - p \cos \delta \tan(\pi/4 + \varphi/2) \bigg|_{\varphi_0}^{\varphi}$$

$$\ln \frac{r}{r_0} = \ln \frac{1 - \sin \varphi_0}{1 - \sin \varphi} + p \cos \delta [\tan(\pi/4 + \varphi_0/2) - \tan(\pi/4 + \varphi/2)]$$
(12-90)

The trajectory for $p \sin \delta = 1$ is therefore

$$r = r_0 \left(\frac{1 - \sin \varphi_0}{1 - \sin \varphi} \right) e^{p \cos \delta [\tan(\pi/4 + \varphi_0/2) - \tan(\pi/4 + \varphi/2)]} \quad (12\text{-}91)$$

It can be shown that the solution for $p^2 \sin^2 \delta > 1$ leads to a trajectory which spirals about the target an infinite number of times and the missile does not intercept the target; hence this case will not be considered here. Both courses, Eq. (12-88) and (12-91), lead to an intercept in a finite time.

Unless time in flight is specified as a function of r and φ it is not possible to plot actual trajectories but only relative trajectories. In order to plot real trajectories, the time in flight will now be determined. From the equations of motion (12-83) and (12-84) we have

$$V_T \, dt = \frac{dr}{\cos \varphi - p \cos \delta} = \frac{r \, d\varphi}{-\sin \varphi + p \sin \delta} \qquad (12\text{-}92)$$

which can be expressed according to a well-known theorem[1] in algebra as

$$V_T \, dt = \frac{A \, dr + Br \, d\varphi}{A(\cos \varphi - p \cos \delta) + B(-\sin \varphi + p \sin \delta)} \qquad (12\text{-}93)$$

where A and B are completely arbitrary quantities. It is observed that Eq. (12-93) can be integrated if we let

$$\left. \begin{array}{l} A = p + \cos (\varphi + \delta) \\ B = -\sin (\varphi + \delta) \end{array} \right\} \qquad (12\text{-}94)$$

whence we have for the denominator of Eq. (12-93)

$$A(\cos \varphi - p \cos \delta) + B(-\sin \varphi + p \sin \delta)$$
$$= [p + \cos (\varphi + \delta)](\cos \varphi - p \cos \delta) - \sin (\varphi + \delta)(-\sin \varphi + p \sin \delta)$$
$$= (1 - p^2) \cos \delta$$

Equation (12-93) then becomes

$$V_T \, dt = \frac{1}{(1 - p^2) \cos \delta} [p \, dr + \cos (\varphi + \delta) \, dr - r \sin (\varphi + \delta) \, d\varphi] \qquad (12\text{-}95)$$

which is of the form

$$V_T \, dt = \frac{1}{(1 - p^2) \cos \delta} \{p \, dr + d[r \cos (\varphi + \delta)]\} \qquad (12\text{-}96)$$

This can be integrated directly into

$$t = \frac{\sec \delta}{V_T(p^2 - 1)} [r_0\{p + \cos (\varphi_0 + \delta)\} - r\{p + \cos (\varphi + \delta)\}] \qquad (12\text{-}97)$$

Deviated-pursuit trajectories can now be computed from Eq. (12-88) or (12-91), and (12-97).

Example 1. Using the data of Example 1 in Par. 12-2 plot trajectories for a lead-angle of $\delta = 10°$.

For $\delta = 10°$, Eq. (12-88) and (12-97) are used. Fig. 12-20 shows this trajectory. The plot is inaccurate near interception since it will be shown later that for $p = 4$ the turning rate becomes infinite at the point of impact.

[1] Hall, H. S., and Knight, S. R., *Higher Algebra*, pp. 3-4, Macmillan and Co., Limited, London, 1936.

12-3] DEVIATED PURSUIT COURSE

Time of Flight. The time of flight is easily obtained from Eq. (12-97) by letting $r = 0$. Then

$$t_f = \frac{r_0[p + \cos(\varphi_0 + \delta)] \sec \delta}{V_T(1 - p^2)} \quad (12\text{-}98)$$

It is seen that the time of flight is finite as long as $p > 1$ and $\delta < \pi/2$.

Example 2. Based on the data from Example 1, what is the total time of flight of the missile for $\delta = 10°$?

From Eq. (12-98) for

$$\delta = 10°, \quad t_f = 61.14 \text{ sec}$$

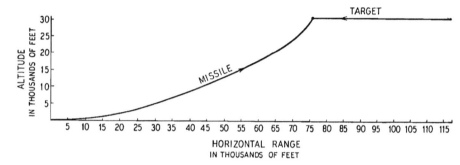

FIG. 12-20 Deviated Pursuit Trajectory; $\varphi_0 = 14.4°$, $\delta = 10°$, $p = 4$.

Deviated Pursuit Course Turning Rate. The turning rate is given by Eq. (12-84) as

$$\dot{\varphi} = V_T \frac{p \sin \delta - \sin \varphi}{r} \quad (12\text{-}99)$$

which expressed in terms of φ from Eq. (12-88) becomes

$$\dot{\varphi} = F(\varphi_0) \cdot \frac{[1 - p \sin \delta \sin \varphi + \cos \varphi \sqrt{1 - p^2 \sin^2 \delta}]^{\frac{p \cos \delta}{\sqrt{1 - p^2 \sin^2 \delta}}}}{[\sin \varphi - p \sin \delta]^{\frac{p \cos \delta}{\sqrt{1 - p^2 \sin^2 \delta}} - 2}} \quad (12\text{-}100)$$

where $F(\varphi_0)$ is given by

$$F(\varphi_0) = \frac{-V_T}{r_0} \cdot \frac{[\sin \varphi_0 - p \sin \delta]^{\frac{p \cos \delta}{\sqrt{1 - p^2 \sin^2 \delta}} - 1}}{[1 - p \sin \delta \sin \varphi_0 + \cos \varphi_0 \sqrt{1 - p^2 \sin^2 \delta}]} \left(\frac{p \cos \delta}{\sqrt{1 - p^2 \sin^2 \delta}} \right) \quad (12\text{-}101)$$

An examination of Eq. (12-100) shows that the turning rate cannot be infinite unless $\sin \varphi = p \sin \delta$. Let φ_n be the angle at which this is true, or

$$\varphi_n = \sin^{-1}(p \sin \delta) \quad (12\text{-}102)$$

It will be assumed that $F(\varphi_0)$ is finite; hence we have

$$\dot\varphi = F(\varphi_0)[2(1 - p^2 \sin^2 \delta)]^{\frac{p \cos \delta}{\sqrt{1-p^2 \sin^2 \delta}}} \lim_{\epsilon \to 0} \epsilon^{2 - \frac{p \cos \delta}{\sqrt{1-p^2 \sin^2 \delta}}} \quad (12\text{-}103)$$

It is seen that

$$\dot\varphi = 0 \quad \text{at} \quad \varphi = \varphi_n \quad \text{for} \quad 2 > \frac{p \cos \delta}{\sqrt{1 - p^2 \sin^2 \delta}} \quad (12\text{-}104)$$

and

$$\dot\varphi = \infty \quad \text{at} \quad \varphi = \varphi_n \quad \text{for} \quad 2 < \frac{p \cos \delta}{\sqrt{1 - p^2 \sin^2 \delta}} \quad (12\text{-}105)$$

If $p \cos \delta = 2\sqrt{1 - p^2 \sin^2 \delta}$ then we have

$$\dot\varphi = F(\varphi_0) p^4 \cos^4 \delta \quad \text{at} \quad \varphi = \varphi_n \quad (12\text{-}106)$$

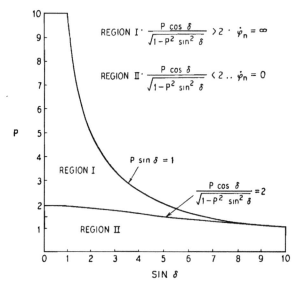

Fig. 12-21 Turning-Rate Criterion for Deviated Pursuit.

Fig. 12-21 shows a plot of the relationship between p and $\sin \delta$ which must exist in order that $\dot\varphi$ remain finite or zero. Values in Region I yield infinite turning rate whereas those in Region II do not. This means that only for $1 < p \leq 2$ will it be possible to select a δ which does not yield an infinite turning rate. Of course, in practice, the maximum turning rate of the missile is limited, and hence, when rates in excess of this maximum are called for, the missile will remain in its maximum turn until it cuts across the line of the target path and then either re-enters the proper course or is lost.

Turning-rate curves of $\dot\varphi$ vs. t can be plotted for any given parameters from Eq. (12-97) and (12-99) or (12-100). The frequency spectrum of the turning-rate curve can be found in the same manner as explained in discussing the pure pursuit course.

Acceleration in Deviated Pursuit Course. As in the pure pursuit course the lateral missile acceleration will be

$$A_M = |V_M \dot\varphi| \qquad (12\text{-}107)$$

where $\dot\varphi$ is given by Eq. (12-99) or (12-100). The acceleration can be made to remain finite as long as $1 < p \leq 2$, but for $p > 2$ infinite accelerations are demanded.

12-4 CONSTANT-BEARING COURSE

The next flight path to be discussed is that of a constant-bearing course.

> A *constant-bearing course* is a course in which the line-of-sight from the missile to the target maintains a constant direction in space.

This means that the line-of-sight from the missile to the target always remains parallel to itself. Since the assumption made throughout this chapter is that both missile and target speeds are constant, the constant-bearing course is rectilinear and results in the so-called *collision course*.

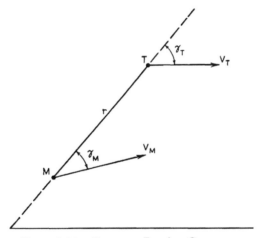

FIG. 12-22 Constant-Bearing Geometry.

As in the courses previously considered, a nonmaneuvering straight-line target course will be assumed and the analysis will be confined to the plane determined by the missile and target velocity vectors. The geometry of the constant-bearing course is shown in Fig. 12-22 where the following new symbols have been used:

γ_M = angle between missile heading and line-of-sight
γ_T = angle between target heading and line-of-sight

THE ANALYSIS OF FLIGHT PATHS

The definition for a constant-bearing course requires that the bearing angle φ remains fixed; hence $\dot\varphi = 0$. The equations of motion are then

$$\dot r = V_T \cos \gamma_T - V_M \cos \gamma_M \qquad (12\text{-}108)$$
$$0 = V_T \sin \gamma_T - V_M \sin \gamma_M \qquad (12\text{-}109)$$

For the case at hand Eq. (12-108) can be integrated directly, giving

$$r = r_0 + (V_T \cos \gamma_T - V_M \cos \gamma_M)t \qquad (12\text{-}110)$$

where r_0 is the initial distance between the missile and target at time $t = 0$. It is seen in Eq. (12-110) that the missile follows a straight-line path or collision course. This is the same trajectory as the deviated pursuit course for a fixed lead angle given from Eq. (12-109)

$$\gamma_M = \sin^{-1}\left(\frac{\sin \gamma_T}{p}\right) \qquad (12\text{-}111)$$

where p, as defined before, is $p = V_M/V_T$. For a target flying a straight-line course, the constant-bearing course is a particular case of a deviated pursuit course.

Using the following result from Eq. (12-109),

$$\cos \gamma_M = \sqrt{1 - p^{-2} \sin^2 \gamma_T} \qquad (12\text{-}112)$$

we can write Eq. (12-110) in terms of γ_T only:

$$r = r_0 + (V_T \cos \gamma_T - V_M\sqrt{1 - p^{-2} \sin^2 \gamma_T})t \qquad (12\text{-}113)$$

The time of flight can be found from Eq. (12-110) to be

$$t_f = \frac{r_0}{V_M \cos \gamma_M - V_T \cos \gamma_T} \qquad (12\text{-}114)$$

Example 1. Find the time of flight for a constant-bearing missile launched at an incoming target whose altitude is 30,000 ft, slant range is 120,785 ft, and speed is Mach 0.66. Assume $p = 4$.

Here $r_0 = 120{,}785$ ft and $\gamma_T = \sin^{-1}\dfrac{30{,}000}{120{,}785} = 165.6°$. (See Fig. 12-22). From Eq. (12-111) we have

$$\gamma_M = \sin^{-1}\left(\frac{0.24838}{4}\right) = \sin^{-1} 0.06209 = 3.55°$$

Also, $V_M = 2626.8$ ft per sec and $V_T = -656.7$ ft per sec. Hence from Eq. (12-114)

$$t_f = \frac{120{,}785}{(2626.8)(0.99808) + (656.7)(0.96858)}$$
$$= \frac{120{,}785}{3257.82} = 37.1$$
$$\therefore t_f = 37.1 \text{ sec}$$

It is evident from the definition of a constant-bearing course that both the turning rate and acceleration of a missile attacking a target flying a straight-line course are zero. Hence here

$$\left.\begin{aligned} \dot{\varphi} &= \dot{\gamma}_M = 0 \\ A_M &= 0 \end{aligned}\right\} \quad (12\text{-}115)$$

In the case of a maneuvering target it has been shown that, for constant speed missile and target, the missile acceleration cannot exceed the target acceleration.[2]

12-5 PROPORTIONAL NAVIGATION

The proportional or partial navigation course will be considered next.

A *proportional-navigation course* is a course in which the rate of change of missile heading is directly proportional to the rate of rotation of the line-of-sight from the missile to the target.

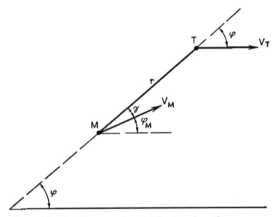

Fig. 12-23   Proportional-Navigation Geometry.

The purpose of such a course is to counter the tendency for the line-of-sight to rotate and hence to approximate a constant-bearing course. As in the previous discussions, the missile and target speeds will be assumed constant and a straight-line target course will be considered.

The Equations of Motion. The geometry of the proportional-navigation course will be confined to the plane containing the missile and target velocity vectors and is shown in Fig. 12-23. Here the newly introduced angle φ_M is the missile heading.

The equations of motion are readily obtained from Fig. 12-23 to be

[2] H. E. Newell, Jr., "Guided Missile Kinematics," *Naval Research Laboratory Report No. R-2538*, May 22, 1945, pp. 49-52.

$$\dot{r} = V_T \cos \varphi - V_M \cos (\varphi - \varphi_M) \tag{12-116}$$

$$r\dot{\varphi} = -V_T \sin \varphi + V_M \sin (\varphi - \varphi_M) \tag{12-117}$$

$$\dot{\varphi}_M = a\dot{\varphi} \tag{12-118}$$

The third equation (12-118) represents the proportionality mentioned in the definition where the constant a is called the *navigation constant* or the *navigational correction*. Direct integration of (12-118) yields

$$\varphi_M = a\varphi + \varphi_0 \tag{12-119}$$

If $a = 1$ and $\varphi_0 = 0$ a pure pursuit course results, and if $a = 1$ and φ_0 is fixed then a deviated pursuit course results. If $\dot{\varphi} = 0$, we have the constant-bearing course just discussed.

The equations of motion cannot be solved in closed form except for the case where $a = 2$. Numerical methods can be used for values of $a \neq 2$. The equations will now be solved for $a = 2$. It will be more practical to write the equations in terms of γ, the missile heading relative to the line-of-sight. For $a = 2$ the equations of motion become

$$\dot{r} = V_T \cos (\gamma + \varphi_M) - V_M \cos \gamma \tag{12-120}$$

$$r\dot{\varphi} = -V_T \sin (\gamma + \varphi_M) + V_M \sin \gamma \tag{12-121}$$

$$\dot{\varphi}_M = 2\dot{\varphi} = -2\dot{\gamma} \tag{12-122}$$

The third relation (12-122) integrates directly to

$$\gamma = -\varphi + \alpha_0 = \alpha_0 - (\gamma + \varphi_M) \tag{12-123}$$

where $\alpha_0 = \gamma_0 + \varphi_0$; hence the two equations of motion are

$$\dot{r} = V_T \cos (\alpha_0 - \gamma) - V_M \cos \gamma \tag{12-124}$$

$$r\dot{\varphi} = -V_T \sin (\alpha_0 - \gamma) + V_M \sin \gamma \tag{12-125}$$

Dividing Eq. (12-124) by (12-125) and using $\dot{\varphi}$ from Eq. (12-122) we have

$$\frac{\dot{r}}{r} = \frac{V_T \cos (\alpha_0 - \gamma) - V_M \cos \gamma}{V_T \sin (\alpha_0 - \gamma) - V_M \sin \gamma} \dot{\gamma} \tag{12-126}$$

Using $p = V_M/V_T$ as before, this can be rewritten as

$$\frac{\dot{r}}{r} = \frac{(p - \cos \alpha_0) \cos \gamma - \sin \alpha_0 \sin \gamma}{(p + \cos \alpha_0) \sin \gamma - \sin \alpha_0 \cos \gamma} \dot{\gamma} \tag{12-127}$$

The expression Eq. (12-127) can be integrated directly into

$$r = r_0 \left[\frac{p \sin \gamma + \sin (\gamma - \alpha_0)}{p \sin \gamma_0 + \sin (\gamma_0 - \alpha_0)} \right]^{\frac{p^2 - 1}{p^2 + 2p \cos \alpha_0 + 1}} e^{\frac{2p(\gamma_0 - \gamma) \sin \alpha_0}{p^2 + 2p \cos \alpha_0 + 1}} \tag{12-128}$$

It is not possible to obtain an expression in closed form relating r and γ to the time t. For this reason it is not simple to plot the trajectories for proportional-navigation courses. Two methods are available: (1) solve the equations of motion by numerical integration using continuous corrections or (2) approximate a solution from (12-128) by using incremental corrections. Fig. 12-24 shows a few typical trajectories[3] for $a = 2$ obtained by numerical methods. An arbitrary initial target bearing angle of $\varphi_0 = 60°$ is assumed. In curve C the initial lead angle γ_0 has been chosen so that a constant-bearing course results.

The time of flight cannot be obtained in closed form; however, it can be determined graphically from the trajectory or integrated numerically.

The Turning Rate for Proportional Navigation. Using Eq. (12-125) and (12-128), we find the turning rate for a proportional navigation course with $a = 2$ to be

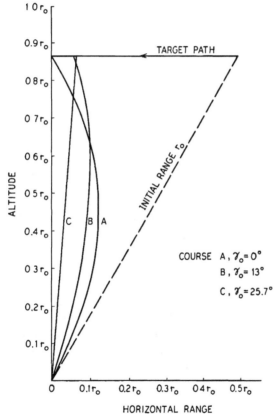

Fig 12-24 Proportional-Navigation Courses; $\varphi_0 = 60°$, $p = 2$.

[3] Spitz, Hillel, "Partial Navigation Courses for a Guided Missile Attacking a Constant Velocity Target," *Naval Research Laboratory Report No. R-2790*, March 25, 1946.

$$\dot{\varphi} = -\dot{\gamma} = \frac{V_T}{r_0}(p\sin\gamma_0 - \sin\varphi_0)\left[\frac{r}{r_0}\right]^{\frac{2(1+p\cos\alpha_0)}{p^2-1}} e^{\frac{2p(\gamma-\gamma_0)\sin\alpha_0}{p^2-1}} \quad (12\text{-}129)$$

As $r \to 0$ it is seen from Eq. (12-129) that, as long as $p > 1$,

$$\left.\begin{array}{ll} \dot{\varphi}_n = 0 & \text{for } p\cos\alpha_0 > -1 \\ \dot{\varphi}_n = \infty & \text{for } p\cos\alpha_0 < -1 \end{array}\right\} \quad (12\text{-}130)$$

It can be shown that the turning rate[4] remains finite at $p\cos\alpha_0 = -1$.

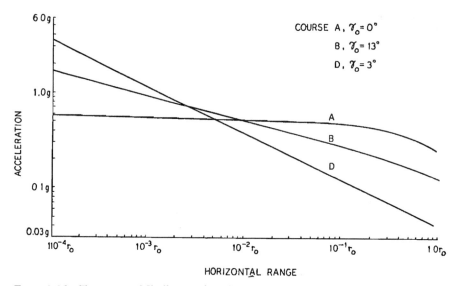

FIG. 12-25 Transverse Missile Acceleration—Proportional Navigation; $\varphi_0 = 60°$, $p = 2$.

Turning-rate spectra can be obtained in the manner previously outlined.

Acceleration for Proportional Navigation. The lateral acceleration of the missile for a proportional navigation course is given by

$$A_M = |V_M\dot{\varphi}_M| = |2V_M\dot{\gamma}| \quad (12\text{-}131)$$

The acceleration is finite as long as $p\cos\alpha_0 \geq -1$. Figure 12-25 shows the transverse acceleration for the same case as in Fig. 12-24, assuming the constant missile speed to be Mach 1 at 30,000 ft.

[4] *Ibid.*, pp. 15-17.

CHAPTER 13

PRELAUNCHING AND LAUNCHING

The purpose of this chapter is to discuss the field operations required by the guidance equipment in the forward tactical area during the prelaunching stage, and the guidance problems during the launching phase of the flight. The prelaunching operations are herein considered to include only the handling and testing of the guidance equipment from the time it is delivered to the tactical unit which will use the missile, until the missile is on the launcher, ready to be fired. The launching phase of the missile flight was previously defined as that portion of the flight between the time of firing and the time when the missile has reached a velocity at which it responds normally to control. When launching guidance is employed, the launching guidance phase is that portion of the missile flight between firing and the time when the midcourse guidance system assumes control of the missile. In order to discuss the various categories of missiles, the guidance systems and hypothetical missiles used illustratively in Chap. 8 will be reviewed for the launching phase.

13-1 PRELAUNCHING OPERATIONS, GENERAL

It is assumed that the guided missile, complete with the guidance system and necessary spares, will be delivered to the tactical unit which will use it, still packaged for storage and handling. The tactical unit may be a guided missile ship in the case of a Navy surface-to-surface missile; or an airfield in the theater of operations in the case of an Air Force air-to-surface or air-to-air missile; or a guided missile battalion, in the case of an Army surface-to-surface missile. The following general sequence of operations would logically be expected to develop:

a. *Tactical Unit Storage*. The missile will be delivered to the tactical unit from some forward storage area. The missile, upon receipt by the tactical unit, will be stored, the duration of the storage depending upon normal or expected tactical consumption.

b. *Testing*. The missile will be uncrated and tested to be sure it is ready for operational use. The testing must include the operation of the guidance system, the setting of critical frequencies, etc., to be sure it will operate with the particular guidance equipment of the tactical unit. The type of tests and the test equipment employed must be as simple as possible in order to establish that the missile system is in proper working order and that it is prepared to function with the particular equipment used by the tactical unit. In order to obtain maximum utilization of equipment transported to the forward area, replacement parts (or spares) must be provided so that the tactical unit can replace any deficient parts, within its capability. The degree of replacement may be expected to be limited to whole assemblies or major subassemblies, and the tests limited to "go" and "no-go" tests.

c. *Ready Storage.* The missile, after testing, is placed in ready storage, adjacent to the launcher or in such location that it is available to the handling equipment which will place it on the launcher. Tactical storage, testing, and ready storage may conceivably be in a single confined area and comprise one general operation if the circumstances so warrant.

d. *Handling and Loading.* These are the operations which must be accomplished in removing the missile from ready storage and placing it on the launcher. The handling equipment must be compatible with the missile, the stowage arrangement, and the launcher. When rapid loading is essential to the tactical use of the missile, the handling and loading equipment is largely automatic.

e. *Prelaunching Checks.* When the missile is on the launcher it is necessary to be sure that the missile and its subsidiary equipment are in operational readiness. The safety of the personnel may be involved in the event of a failure in the process of launching. The degree of detail involved in the final checking procedure will depend partly upon the hazard potential of failure at this point in the operations and partly upon the value of the missile that is being fired. For an intercontinental missile, the prelaunching checks will be extremely detailed and thorough. For an air-to-air missile, the pilot need only be assured, by some simple indication, that the missile and its equipment are functioning.

f. *Launcher.* The launcher must be designed in accordance with the demands of tactical use, the launching characteristics of the missile, and the requirements of the guidance system. When the missile is on the launcher, the guidance and other missile-borne electronic equipment is energized prior to launching, at least to the degree that tube filaments and other heating devices are on. The electric power is supplied by a source other than the missile. This power must be available for operational checks.

13-2 PRELAUNCHING OPERATION, GUIDANCE EQUIPMENT

The principles of design of launching and handling equipments and the operational procedures in this area of interest is treated fully in the *Launching* Section of this series of volumes. A review of the operations discussed in general above indicates that the designer of the guidance system has two major concerns during the prelaunching phase: (a) the testing of the guidance equipment prior to placing the missile in ready storage, and (b) the prelaunching checks of the guidance equipment when the missile is on the launcher immediately prior to being fired.

a. *Testing.* The degree of detail in the testing of the missile guidance equipment prior to putting the missile in ready storage is dependent upon the cost of the missile and the location of the tactical unit.

If, as an example, we consider the intercontinental missile of Case One, Chap. 8, any element of the system that is important to the success of the flight will be continually tested while the missile is being readied for flight. Because of the continued testing the components must be designed so as to accept many hours of operation prior to the flight, without detriment to successful operation during the flight. This imposes the necessity for a high degree of quality control and emphasizes the need for component reliability. In a missile of this type, it becomes difficult to isolate the testing and checking of the guidance equipments to unique phases of the prelaunching operations. As an example of the kind of test that might be employed with this missile, a flight simulator might be used with the actual missile guidance components to accomplish (and repeat, if need be) a precise simulation of the impending flight. The use of a simulator for this purpose is analogous to similar devices employed during the last war to train human pilots to navigate under adverse conditions. The complete navigation problem may be developed and the behavior of the guidance equipment noted for future correction. The details of the test equipment used are intimately associated with the precise details of the guidance system employed. The designer of the guidance system will be closely involved in the development of the testing equipment.

With missiles of lesser cost and as the separation between the point of manufacture and location of the tactical unit increases, the tests of the guidance system will be simplified. The tests must determine all phases of missile readiness: the performance of the servomechanisms which actuate the aerodynamic surfaces, the response characteristics of the many control loops, the operability of the missile-borne guidance equipment, and its compatibility with the external elements of the guidance system. The tests must be simple in concept but thorough in the ability to define clearly and quickly any possible deficiencies of the missile-borne equipment. There is a direct relationship between the simplicity and effectiveness of the tests and the probable reliability of the missile in service use. The ease with which the test equipment may be properly employed will determine the amount of training required to obtain efficient handling personnel.

The tests must be largely of the "go," "no-go" type. When a deficiency is discovered, the replacement will be limited to an assembly or a subassembly. Such replacement items will be delivered with the equipment as spares. The rejected items will be returned to a storage area for repair by more qualified personnel. The guidance system designer must be prepared to design, or at the very least to specify, the test equipment that is used by the tactical unit. During the development of the guidance equipment statistics must be gathered in order to predict the proper proportion of spares to guidance equipments as well as the kind of spares most likely to be required.

b. *Prelaunching Checks.* The prelaunching checks are simple indications that the system is functioning in readiness to fire. The checks may always be more thorough for an offensive missile than they are for a defensive missile. In the use of an offensive missile (surface-to-surface or air-to-surface), the time of launch may be accurately determined. In the case of a defensive missile (surface-to-air or air-to-air), it must be ready for instant use and the time between firing individual missiles or missile salvos is not under the ready control of the user.

The guidance system designer must specify the checks that indicate the operability of the guidance equipment. The checks must be kept to a minimum and preferably accomplished automatically, with the results indicated by some simple method such as an array of indicating lights visible to the officer who fires the missile. The exact criteria that will be employed to demonstrate the operability of the guidance system are dependent upon the type of guidance system under consideration.

When a defensive missile is employed, a failure on the launcher during enemy action usually necessitates clearing the launcher, if at all possible, consistent with personnel safety. The missile will therefore be fired even if the prelaunching checks indicate it is not functioning correctly. An offensive missile flight will be aborted until the difficulty is corrected. The missile may be removed from the launcher in this latter case.

13-3 LAUNCHING, GENERAL

The *Launching* Section of this series of volumes treats the launching problem in detail. The designer of the guidance equipment must, however, be aware of the facets of the problem which directly affect his work. For discussion purposes, let it be assumed that the guided missile is on the launcher with all prelaunching checks complete and in readiness to fire. It is further assumed that the location of the target is known and that the portions of the guidance equipment exterior to the missile are functioning. The following are the general areas of interest which will be expected to develop:

a. *Firing.* The missile may be fired either by an operation on the part of a human in control of the system or automatically by a computer or other device. The physical act of firing is usually the closure of an electric switch which energizes a circuit that causes the ignition of the propelling motor. The time of firing is frequently developed as part of the guidance problem. The act of firing activates many components within the missile, some of which are: (1) propelling motor and/or booster started; (2) internal electrical power supply activated; (3) power source for aerodynamic control activated; (4) gyros essential to stabilization activated. The missile-borne guidance equipment may or may not have already been in operation, depending upon the specific system design. Although activation of the power sources within the missile is initiated simultaneously with firing, in some instances the control surfaces will be kept locked until after the launching phase is complete, in order to avoid serious dispersions.

b. *Booster*. When a booster is employed to give the missile an initial impulse during the launching phase, the booster is usually separated from the missile after its energy is depleted. The aerodynamic characteristics of the combined missile and booster will vary radically from those of the missile alone. Separable boosters may cause damage when they fall, and their use is limited to tactical situations where they will not present a major hazard.

c. *Separation*. The separation of the booster from the missile is usually accomplished by the motor of the missile. When the missile motor operates, it thrusts backward against the booster, causing separation. Separation must be obtained before initiation of midcourse guidance because of the difference in the control characteristics of the missile before and after separation.

d. *Electrical Power Supply*. The missile in flight must obtain its electric power from an internal power supply. The power supply must be: (1) capable of remaining in storage for years, yet quickly ready for activation; (2) capable of being checked prior to launching, to be sure it will function at the proper time and in the proper manner; and (3) activated without causing either a voltage surge or a voltage drop as compared to the pre-launching electrical power.

e. *Hydraulic Or Pneumatic Power Supply*. In many missiles, hydraulic or pneumatic power is used as the direct source for the control of the aerodynamic surfaces. This power must be kept stored at high pressure and must be capable of being checked prior to the flight to be sure that sufficient power is available. When this power is activated at firing, it must not impose undue transients or shocks coincident with its application.

f. *Guidance Initiation*. In some cases the guidance system internal to the missile may be operative before launching; in others, the system is made operative after launching. Because of the many possibilities for transient shocks resulting both from the high accelerations of launching, and the activation of the power supplies, the commands from the guidance system are not acted upon for a period of time after firing, usually not until after the separation of the booster. If a launching guidance system is required, this system may be totally independent of midcourse guidance, including separate power supplies, controls, and possibly even different control surfaces, since the problems involved are so radically different.

g. *Launching Trajectories.* When a missile is fired from a stationary launcher the trajectory of its motion is determined by the acceleration of gravity, the acceleration of its propelling motor, the reactions of the aerodynamic surfaces with the air, and the temporary influence of the launcher rails (if such are employed). The control surfaces of a missile are designed to develop a given missile response to a given order when the missile is moving at design speed. Until the missile is flying at a speed which permits the application of normal control, the prediction of its trajectory is essentially a statistical ballistic problem. In order to have the trajectory statistically repeatable for any number of missiles of a type, quality control during both airframe and propellant manufacture is essential. When a missile is launched in a forward direction from a rapidly moving aircraft, it has already available to it the speed of the aircraft and can reach a controllable velocity that much more rapidly. In either case, it is to the advantage of the missile guidance problem to reach the design velocity as rapidly as possible. It is readily seen, however, that the trajectory of the missile before control is initiated is dependent upon the individual airframe and launching system design.

h. *Launching Dispersions.* No two missiles can be made exactly alike, nor will the thrust from the motors of two missiles be exactly the same. If a group of missiles is fired and the trajectories are plotted, it will be found that they will be distributed about some statistical mean trajectory. The distribution is usually normal, barring the influence of external forces, such as wind. The mean trajectory is employed in predicting the probable trajectory of any single missile.

Most guidance methods require that a finite limiting value of dispersion be maintained in order that the missile not be lost from system control. In specific cases, such as in a beam-riding system, the dispersion must be maintained at an extremely low value in order that a sufficiently great percentage of the missiles may be captured by the radar beam. The minimum launching angle must be great enough that there is little probability of a missile striking the ground.

i. *Launching Transients.* Upon the initiation of midcourse guidance, which occurs after the launching phase is complete, the missile is likely to have the greatest error of heading that will occur during the flight. At the instant the guidance system is activated, a large transient may be imposed upon the system to correct the heading of the missile and the direction of missile flight. In terms of bandwidth requirements for the guidance and control systems, the greatest bandwidth demand is likely to occur as a result of launching dispersions. The rapidity with which

13-4 LAUNCHING, SURFACE-TO-SURFACE MISSILE GUIDANCE

the launching error is corrected is usually the determining factor in establishing the minimum effective range of the guided missile.

Case One. This is the case of an intercontinental guided missile of 3000 miles maximum range, guided by a combined celestial and inertial navigation system. The missile is aerodynamic in character rather than of a ballistic type. The launching considerations for this case involve two fundamental problems for the designer of the guidance system: (a) the manner of take-off and (b) the launching guidance system.

The missile may be launched from a runway, as in the manner of conventional aircraft; it may be catapulted, i.e., boosted along a short railway; or it may be boosted upward at any angle up to vertical by a propelling booster which will separate from the missile after it has spent its force. If the missile is launched in the manner of a conventional aircraft, then a runway must be made available for its use and the missile must carry sufficient fuel to permit take-off as well as flight. The runway located in a forward area requires the expenditure of considerable manpower and materials to construct; it is easily visible from the air; and it offers a large target for enemy action. A catapult launcher is, compared to a runway, small in size. At the end of the catapult run the missile will be traveling at such speed as to assure its becoming airborne, but the amount of energy imparted will be limited by the parameters of the catapult design. There is no hazard from falling boosters to any surrounding populated areas when a catapult is used. The catapult may be used over and over again. The dissipation of its energy may be closely controlled. Boosters may supply more total energy than is possible in a catapult. The space required for booster launching will be less than for either of the previously discussed methods of launching. The boosters do present a hazard when they fall. Although it is possible to conceive of the recovering and reusing of boosters, it does not seem likely that such a practice would be successful under tactical conditions.

When the decision has been reached as to the method of launching the missile, only then is it possible to set down the exact parameters of the launching guidance system. Earlier in this text, it was pointed out that the inertial system employed for dead-reckoning navigation could also be adapted for launching guidance. The function of this system is to bring the missile to altitude in straight and level flight, with sufficient memory that the celestial navigation system may acquire the proper stars, despite the accelerations of launching. If the missile is launched vertically, or nearly so, the missile may be turned in flight, as in the case of the German missiles, by use of a gyroscope which is precessed to turn the missile in the correct direction during the launching phase of the flight. The precession is accomplished as a function of time of flight after launching. The inertial elements of the dead-reckoning system will integrate the motions of the missile and thus establish the memory required for the celestial navigation system. A discussion of inertial systems will be found in Chap. 16.

13-5 LAUNCHING, SURFACE-TO-AIR MISSILE GUIDANCE

Case Two. This case is that of a ship-launched surface-to-air guided missile, employing a beam-rider guidance system. Two missiles are to be launched in salvo. This case involves the launching of the missiles into a radar beam which they will ride to eventual detonation at the target. The problem of the designer is to determine whether or not the missiles launched from the deck of a ship will predictably enter the radar beam at the termination of the launching phase. If the missile trajectories are not statistically consistent in the launching phase, then some means of launching guidance must be provided.

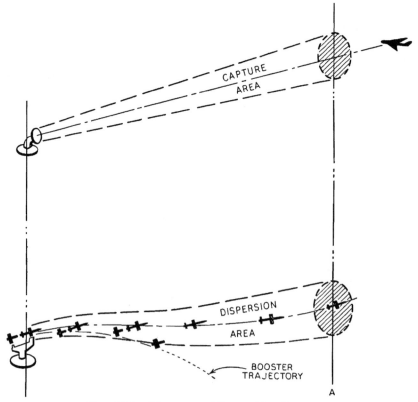

Fig. 13-1 Elements of Beam-rider Capture.

Figure 13-1 presents some of the elements of the beam-rider capture problem. Figure 13-1a shows the radar beam tracking a target. A volume around the center of that beam will be assumed to represent the area in which missiles may be captured. If the missile trajectory is outside of this space when the guidance system is activated, the missile will be lost. Figure 13-1b shows the launching trajectory of a missile. We shall assume the volume indicated around this trajectory represents the maximum deviation from the mean trajectory for 99 percent of the total number of missiles launched. Then, under static conditions, it may be assumed that, if the shaded areas are equal and coincident at range A, as indicated on the diagram, 99 percent of the missiles will be captured by the beam.

However, the situation is not a static one. The target is in motion, and it is necessary to predict its future position. The missiles will be launched at some lead angle as related to the line-of-sight to the target, so that they will be within the radar beam at the end of the launching phase when the beam-riding guidance is initiated. This is essentially the same ballistic problem that must be solved for gunfire. The methods of computation employed for the ballistic period of the missile flight are completely analogous to the gunfire control problem and knowledge of the problems of this field is applicable to the launching problem. Corrections are required for the motion of the ship, the wind, etc.

The only way to acquire knowledge of the trajectory of the missile during the launching phase is by test. The statistics of missile behavior during the launching phase must be collected in order to predict its position for varying flight times and so establish the prediction of interception with the guiding beam. The probability of capture will enter directly into the probable effectiveness of the guided missile system, so that if the statistics indicate the behavior of the missile cannot be accurately predicted, then some auxiliary method of assuring capture of the missile by the beam must be employed. Every effort to avoid the employment of a special guidance system for launching must be exerted, from the viewpoint of both simplicity and economy. This may necessitate precision manufacture in the elements most likely to affect the ballistic behavior of the missile. It is far less expensive to solve the launching problem by quality control in manufacture than to correct these deficiencies by adding a complex guidance system.

Some of the guidance problems involved in the launching phase are indicated by inspection of Fig. 13-2. Figure 13-2 shows a missile with a booster, which will separate from it in flight. It will be observed that the center of gravity of the combined missile and booster is at point A when the missile is on the launcher. During the launching phase of the flight, the booster weight is depreciated by the burning of the fuel. The center of gravity shifts forward. When the booster is separated from the missile the center of gravity shifts radically forward to the normal flight location. The major shift of the c.g. occurs when the booster is separated. Both the effectiveness of the aerodynamic control surfaces and the sense of the applied aerodynamic moments may change because of the shift of the center of gravity. The problem of guiding a missile both before and after separation becomes apparent.

Not only does the center of gravity change to such a degree that the effect of the aerodynamic moments of the controlling surfaces may be reversed in sense, but the missile during this period of the flight also passes through the transonic flight velocity. The response of any airborne vehicle

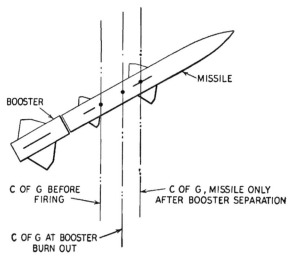

FIG. 13-2 Change in Location of the Center of Gravity during Launching Phase of Flight.

to control in the transonic flight region is not susceptible to ready analysis. It is highly desirable, then, that the statistical behavior of the missile and the volume encompassed by the guiding beam be so related that the system may be employed without the necessity for a separate guidance system.

13-6 LAUNCHING, AIR-TO-SURFACE MISSILE GUIDANCE

Case Three. This case involves the launching of a missile into a radar beam which will track its position so that appropriate commands may be issued to guide it to a target which is simultaneously being tracked visually by the pilot of the airplane. The radar is not inhibited (as in the case of the beam rider) by the necessity that it track the target. The statistics of the behavior of the missile must be known as in the beam-rider case, but the radar may pursue an automatic search, to be assured of capturing the missile. Further, the missile will employ a beacon to assist in the capture.

The missile is subsonic so that no booster will be required and the uncertainties of transonic behavior do not enter the guidance problem. The guidance system designer must have control over the parameters of the radar which is tracking the missile and must obtain by flight test the statistics of missile behavior during the launching phase of the flight.

13-9 LAUNCHING, AIR-TO-AIR MISSILE GUIDANCE

Case Four. This is the case of the air-to-air missile guided by a semi-active homing system. There are two design choices: (a) the pilot of the aircraft may acquire the target with the missile guidance system before launching the missile or (b) the guidance system may be so designed as to acquire the target automatically. If the pilot must perform the acquisition, his operations are made more complex. He must first acquire the target with the aircraft radar; then, by a coordinated presentation from the radar of the guidance system, again engage the target. When more than one missile is to be fired simultaneously, as in this case, the problem of inspecting multiple presentations becomes even more difficult. If the missile guidance system is to acquire the target automatically from information presented by the radar of the aircraft, the pilot need only be presented with an indication that it has acquired a target, before firing.

When reliance is placed on the missile guidance system to acquire the target automatically, there is always a chance that the pilot may engage one target and the missile equipment may engage another. The possibility of this must be considered, and the design of the equipment so ordered that the opportunity for this condition to arise is minimized.

If the missile guidance equipment is to acquire the target automatically, there still remain two choices to be considered. The missile may acquire the target either before launching or after the launching phase is completed. Either possibility may be considered if statistics indicate the probability of acquisition of the proper target is sufficiently high, so that the effectiveness of the system is not prejudiced. A corollary advantage of the latter choice is that of relieving the pilot of additional operations at a time when all of his judgment and skill are required to fly the aircraft.

CHAPTER 14

THE MISSILE AIRFRAME

The designer of missile guidance equipment has two basic interests in the missile airframe. First, the airframe is the structure in which the missile-borne guidance equipment is carried. The airframe dictates the environmental conditions for the missile-borne guidance equipment. The size and weight limitations for the internal guidance equipment are determined by the structure and character of the airframe. Second, the airframe in flight is an active element in the missile guidance system. As an element in the guidance system, the airframe has complex, but predictable, transfer characteristics. The contrasting needs between the design of the airframe as a structure and the design of the airframe as an element of the guidance system frequently require compromise in order to optimize both.

It is the purpose of this chapter to review the structural and environmental conditions as they affect the guidance system and to discuss the transfer characteristics of airframes.

14-1 AIRFRAME ENVIRONMENT

The missile-borne guidance equipment is looked upon as an integral part of the completed missile. It is, therefore, subject to any of the general environmental conditions to which the missile itself will be exposed. In addition, the airframe, by reason of its motion through space, the design of its structure, and the heat of its propulsion unit will create an internal environment which must be accepted by the missile-borne guidance equipment.

General Environmental Conditions. The various conditions of temperature, humidity, atmospheric pressure, degree of water resistance, etc., that must be withstood by the airframe and the internal guidance equipment are specified by the military services. A missile may be stored for long periods of time in the tropics where the sun can raise the temperature of a metal body to the boiling point; it may be stored in arctic regions where the temperature will be many degrees below freezing. The missile may be transported by any of many ways to the operating theaters of war; it will be handled roughly and subjected to many shocks in the process. The military services, with many years of experience and background in the handling of weapon equipment, are best able to specify the environmental conditions to which the missile will be subjected prior to its use. This experience is translated into specifications which outline the environmental tests for all service equipment.

Internal Airframe Environment. The environmental conditions imposed upon a missile-borne guidance equipment are generated by the behavior of the airframe during the various phases of its flight. The airframe during the launching phase is subjected to severe accelerations. If a booster is employed there may be severe transient forces imposed upon the airframe at the time of booster separation. The missile maneuvers may exert many gravities of acceleration. The propelling motor may have resonances and thus initiate vibrations within the missile structure. Under certain conditions some of the missile airfoils may flutter and induce vibrations. The internal structure of the missile may have different resonances in different sections. Such resonances may develop severe internal vibrations without appreciably affecting the behavior of the airframe in flight. The airframe structure may have compliance, i.e., distortion due to aerodynamic loads. Thus, the elements of the guidance system which measure motion of the missile must therefore be correctly located within the structure or they may measure values which are incorrect.

All of these conditions, and such others as may be pertinent, must be considered in establishing the environment of the missile-borne guidance equipment. The only adequate means of obtaining knowledge of this environment is by making statistical tests during missile flights. Such tests are usually accomplished by the contractor as part of the design of the airframe and the guidance equipment. The data developed are unique to the specific missile and cannot be applied generally, as in the case of the environment which is governed by the theater of operations.

In addition to the shock, vibration, and other accelerations imposed upon the guidance equipment, the interior of the missile may be subjected to heat from three independent sources:

a. The missile in high-speed flight may create high surface temperatures by reason of the air friction. This will affect radome design (if the guidance system employs such).

b. The propelling motor generates heat in copious quantities. If the guidance equipment is arranged around or near the motor, this will affect the operating temperature of the equipment.

c. The guidance equipment itself will generate heat. The amount of heat generated depends upon the specific equipment employed.

The internal temperature created by the guidance equipment, the propelling motor, and the missile in its flight must be considered as being imposed beyond the normal using conditions. These extra impositions can be determined only by test.

Environmental Specifications and Tests. As a result of the environmental tests of a specific missile, the contractor must prepare specifications and tests for the missile-borne equipment. These specifications will normally employ a safety factor to take care of any variations in the tolerance of production equipment. Tests must be developed to disclose fully that the equipment is satisfactory when subjected to the environment of the airframe. This subject is discussed in greater detail in Chap. 15 of this volume. The physical structure of the missile airframe is detailed in the *Structures and Design Practice Section* of this series of volumes.

14-2 THE AIRFRAME AS AN ELEMENT IN CONTROL LOOPS

Aerodynamic engineers conventionally express the stability of airframes in classical stability derivative form. The resulting mathematical expressions describe the parameters of the airframes by integrodifferential equations relating the airframe outputs to transient inputs. Integrodifferential equations are tedious to solve and do not lend themselves readily to design work in the field of servomechanisms. The classical expressions are in the

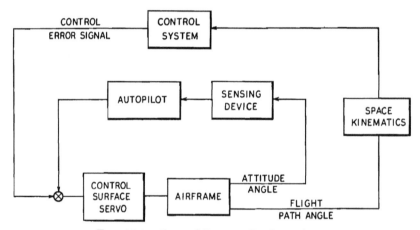

FIG. 14-1 Control System Configuration.

time domain. As hitherto discussed, the conventional servomechanism expressions are in the frequency domain. It is necessary, then, to convert the classical stability and control parameters into transfer or frequency characteristic form. A complete analysis of this subject is covered in an excellent treatise entitled "Dynamics of the Airframe,"[1] compiled by a group at Northrop Aircraft Corporation, which is drawn upon occasionally in this chapter.

---

[1] "Dynamics of the Airframe," *BuAer Report AE-61-4 II*, prepared under contract NOas 51-514 (C).

This discussion will be limited to the consideration of a cruciform airframe which must be controlled in pitch, yaw, and roll. The airframe, because of the necessity for control in different coordinates, performs as an element of many control loops of the guidance system. The mathematical processes of developing transfer functions of the airframe will here be limited to the pitch coordinate. The method employed in going from the classical expressions to the transfer functions is similar, however, in the other coordinates.

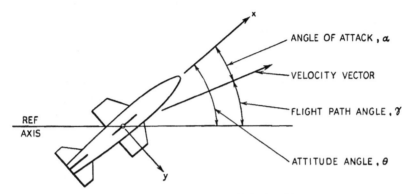

Fig. 14-2 Pitch Angle Relationships.

Figure 14-1 shows a simplified block diagram of a path angle configuration for a missile guidance system. This figure demonstrates that more than one function of the airframe response must be developed for a single coordinate. This diagram shows that two outputs from the airframe in pitch are employed: the pitch attitude and the flight path angle in the vertical coordinate.

Figure 14-2 illustrates the relationship between the attitude angle θ of the airframe, its flight path vector angle γ, and the angle of attack α.

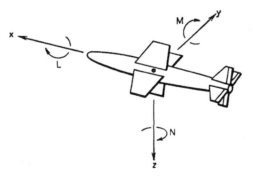

Fig. 14-3 Coordinate Nomenclature.

Any measuring device attached to the airframe measures the attitude of the airframe and/or the changes of the attitude angle. On the other hand, the output flight path vector, when integrated over a period of time, becomes the trajectory of the missile. The motion of the missile, when measured externally to the missile, is seen as the instantaneous heading of the missile along its trajectory and is therefore the flight path vector. These relationships are pointed out primarily to indicate the type of information obtained when examining the behavior of the missiles: (a) from within the missile itself and (b) from outside the missile.

14-3 CLASSICAL EXPRESSIONS FOR THE AIRFRAME

The designer is faced with the necessity of expressing the transfer characteristics of the airframe in a manner such that he can readily use them in analysis. In going from the classical expressions to the transfer characteristic of the airframe, it is assumed that the missile is in normal unstalled flight. In this case, relatively small aerodynamic surface deflections and relatively small angles of attack exist. While these assumptions hold good, the lift is proportional to the angle of attack and the control force or moment is proportional to the surface deflection of the controlling airfoil.

The initial step in analysis of airframe motion in the normal transfer characteristic form is the statement of the classical equations of motion of the airframe. The NACA list of symbols for the designations of coordinates and for the various parameters is used. Figure 14-3 gives the configuration to the airframe axes. The velocities along these axes and moments about them are normally defined as follows:

Axis	Linear Velocity	Angular Velocity	Summation of Moment	Summation of Forces	Disp. Angles	Moment of Momentum	Moments of Inertia
X	U	P Rolling Vel.	ΣL	ΣF_x	ϕ	h_x	I_{xx}
Y	V	Q Pitching Vel.	ΣM	ΣF_y	θ	h_y	I_{yy}
Z	W	R Yawing Vel.	ΣN	ΣF_z	ψ	h_z	I_{zz}

The study of the action of the airframe in pitch only leads us to be interested in those equations which describe the variation of the velocity along the x and z axes and for the angular motion about the y axis. To study the action of yaw and roll will require use of other appropriate equations concerning the appropriate axes.

The equation of lift of the airframe involves the use of the aerodynamic forces which are conventionally expressed as

$$L = \frac{\rho C_L V^2 S}{2} \qquad (14\text{-}1)$$

where L = the lift or force normal to the velocity vector
 ρ = the density of the air
 V = the velocity of the air past the aircraft
 S = a characteristic area of the airframe, in this case, the wing area
 C_L = the coefficient of lift, a dimensionless parameter whose value can be derived from wind tunnel tests

The lift of an airframe changes as a result of a change in the angle of attack, since the angle of flow of the air impinging on the wing also changes. In this case

$$C_{L\alpha} = \frac{dC_L}{d\alpha} \qquad (14\text{-}2)$$

where $C_{L\alpha}$ is the change in the lift coefficient with angle of attack. Similarly, the lift of the airframe changes when the control surface is deflected through the angle δ_E

$$C_{L\delta E} = \frac{dC_L}{d\delta_E} \qquad (14\text{-}3)$$

Similar expressions may be shown to apply for the drag forces, which, although not developed, are used later in the chapter.

The moments about the y axis may also be expressed in terms of the aerodynamic coefficients as

$$M = \frac{\rho C_M V^2 S c}{2} \qquad (14\text{-}4)$$

where M = a moment about the y axis
 C_M = the moment coefficient
 c = a characteristic length of the airframe, in this case the wing chord

The change in the moment coefficient caused by a change in the angle of attack is

$$C_{M\alpha} = \frac{dC_M}{d\alpha} \qquad (14\text{-}5)$$

where $C_{M\alpha}$ is the change in moment coefficient with angle of attack.

Correspondingly, a change in the control flap deflection affects the moment coefficient also, as shown by

$$C_{M\delta E} = \frac{dC_M}{d\delta_E} \qquad (14\text{-}6)$$

where $C_{M\delta E}$ is the change in moment coefficient with control flap deflection.

The effect of a change in the pitching velocity on the moment coefficient may be written

$$C_{MQ} = \frac{dC_M}{dQ} \qquad (14\text{-}7)$$

where Q = the pitching velocity
C_{MQ} = the change in moment coefficient with pitching velocity

14-4 DERIVATION OF TRANSFER FUNCTIONS IN PITCH

Let it be assumed that the cruciform missile under consideration is controlled in pitch by deflection of some control surface or surfaces. Further, it is assumed that the missile is controlled in roll and that the angles of roll of the missile are held to values sufficiently small that there are no significant interactions between roll and other motions of the airframe. Finally, it is assumed that the forward velocity of the missile is constant along the x axis. The first two assumptions are elective in character and are therefore valid. The effects of variation of the forward velocity will be the subject of later discussion.

Let us consider the cruciform airframe as a single-degree-of-freedom system (refer to Par. 9-5). With the foregoing assumptions, a simplified differential equation of motion of the missile in the pitch plane may be written as

$$I\frac{d^2\theta}{dt^2} + c'\frac{d\theta}{dt} + k\theta = \text{Summation of aerodynamic moments} \qquad (14\text{-}8)$$

Since the missile is not constrained to any particular angle θ, the term $k\theta$ may be omitted. The damping constant c' is $\dfrac{-\rho C_{MQ} V^2 S c}{2}$ since this term is resistive to the change in pitch velocity. The principal aerodynamic moments are those caused by changes in the angle of attack and by deflection of the wing flaps. Equation (14-8) may then be rearranged and written as

$$I_{yy}\frac{d^2\theta}{dt^2} - \frac{\rho C_{MQ} V^2 S c}{2}\frac{d\theta}{dt} - \frac{\rho C_{M\alpha}\alpha V^2 S c}{2} - \frac{\rho C_{M\delta E}\delta_E V^2 S c}{2} = 0 \qquad (14\text{-}9)$$

This equation may be written in operational form $\left(s = \dfrac{d}{dt} = j\omega\right)$ as

$$s^2\theta I_{yy} - s\theta\frac{\rho C_{MQ} V^2 S c}{2} - \frac{\rho C_{M\alpha}\alpha V^2 S c}{2} - \frac{\rho C_{M\delta E}\delta_E V^2 S c}{2} = 0 \qquad (14\text{-}10)$$

The summation of forces perpendicular to the flight path may be equated as

$$ma - \frac{\rho C_{L\alpha}\alpha V^2 S}{2} - \frac{\rho C_{L\delta E}\delta_E V^2 S}{2} = 0 \qquad (14\text{-}11)$$

14-4] DERIVATION OF TRANSFER FUNCTIONS IN PITCH

where m = the mass of the missile
a = the acceleration normal to the flight path = $\dot{\gamma}V$

Remembering that $\alpha = \theta - \gamma$, from Fig. 14-2, if that and the following substitutions

$$\omega_1{}^2 = \frac{\rho V^2 S c}{2 I_{yy}}$$

$$\omega_2 = \frac{1}{C_{MQ}}$$

$$\omega_3 = \frac{\rho V S}{2m}$$

are made, then Eq. (14-10) and (14-11) respectively may be rewritten in the following simplified manner:

$$\frac{s^2}{\omega_1{}^2}\theta - \frac{s}{\omega_2}\theta - C_{M\alpha}\alpha - C_{M\delta E}\delta_E = 0 \qquad (14\text{-}12)$$

$$\frac{s}{\omega_3}\gamma - C_{L\alpha}\alpha - C_{L\delta E}\delta_E = 0 \qquad (14\text{-}13)$$

Pitch Attitude Angle Response. To find the transfer function of this airframe in pitch angle we shall solve for the output pitch angle θ as a function of an input control surface deflection δ_E. In order to simplify the handling of the equations, these substitutions are employed

$$\omega_4 = -\frac{\omega_3 K_1}{C_{M\delta E}}$$

$$K_1 = C_{M\alpha}C_{L\delta E} - C_{M\delta E}C_{L\alpha}$$

$$K_2 = \frac{K_1}{\left(\frac{\omega_3}{\omega_2}\right)C_{L\alpha} + C_{M\alpha}}$$

$$A = -\frac{1}{\omega_1{}^2[(\omega_3/\omega_2)C_{L\alpha} + C_{M\alpha}]}$$

$$B = \frac{1}{[(\omega_3/\omega_2)C_{L\alpha} + C_{M\alpha}]}\left(\frac{1}{\omega_2} - \frac{C_{L\alpha}\omega_3}{\omega_1{}^2}\right)$$

The resulting ratio of output pitch angle to input control surface deflection is

$$\frac{\text{Output}}{\text{Input}} = \frac{\theta}{\delta_E} = \left(\frac{1}{As^2 + Bs + 1}\right)\left(\frac{\omega_4 + s}{\omega_4}\right)\left(\frac{K_2 \omega_3}{s}\right) \qquad (14\text{-}14)$$

This is the transfer characteristic of the cruciform airframe in pitch and represents that output of the airframe which might be measured by a rate gyroscope in an autopilot due to a deflection of the control surface.

The quadratic expression

$$\frac{1}{As^2 + Bs + 1} \qquad (14\text{-}15)$$

has been met before in this book (see Par. 7-6, Fig. 7-25). When plotted logarithmically, the asymptotes have a slope of zero, to the point of resonant frequency which occurs at $\sqrt{1/A}$, then a slope of -2, as shown in Fig. 14-4. The accompanying phase relationships are also indicated. The resonant rise has a magnitude of $\sqrt{A/B}$. The damping ratio ξ becomes

$$\xi = \frac{B}{2\sqrt{A}} \quad (14\text{-}16)$$

The expression

$$\frac{\omega_4 + s}{\omega_4} \quad (14\text{-}17)$$

is analogous to the high-pass filter transfer characteristic discussed in Chap. 7. This expression may be plotted with asymptotes of zero slope at unity gain to a frequency of ω_4, thence with an asymptote of slope of $+1$. The asymptotic characteristics and phase relationships are shown in Fig. 14-5.

The remaining expression from Eq. (14-14)

$$\frac{K_2\omega_3}{s} \quad (14\text{-}18)$$

is an integrator, which is characterized on a logarithmic plot by having a slope of -1 which passes through unity gain at a frequency corresponding to $K_2\omega_3$, as shown in Fig. 14-6. The accompanying phase relationship is also indicated on this figure.

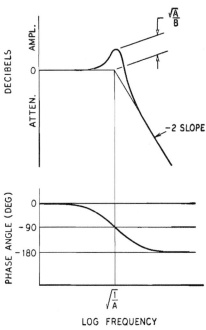

Fig. 14-4 Characteristics of Term $\dfrac{1}{As^2 + Bs + 1}$.

The pitch angle response to control surface deflections is of importance to the design of an autopilot in which the airframe pitch angle is measured by internal instrumentation such as a rate gyroscope. The measurement of the attitude angle may be used to obtain consistent pitch performance from the airframe, despite changing environmental conditions. An example of autopilot stabilization is given in Chap. 18.

Flight Path Vector Angle Response. Equally important in the design of a missile guidance system is the response of the flight path vector angle γ to control surface deflections δ_E. The velocity vector, when integrated with time, yields the trajectory of the missile. In some guidance systems, the error of the position of the missile with respect to a desired trajectory

14-4] DERIVATION OF TRANSFER FUNCTIONS IN PITCH

is measured, and the measurement is employed as a guidance signal to correct the trajectory of the missile. If we employ the following substitutions

$$H = -\frac{C_{L\delta E}}{\omega_1^2 K_1}$$

$$D = \frac{C_{L\delta E}}{\omega_2 K_1}$$

and solve Eq. (14-12) and (14-13) simultaneously for the ratio γ/δ_E we obtain

$$\frac{\text{Output}}{\text{Input}} = \frac{\gamma}{\delta_E} = \left(\frac{1}{As^2 + Bs + 1}\right)\left(\frac{K_2\omega_3}{s}\right)\left(Hs^2 + Ds + 1\right) \quad (14\text{-}19)$$

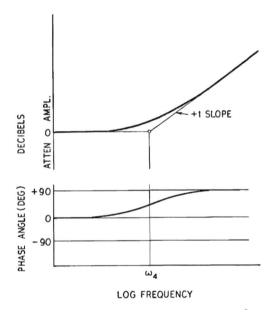

FIG. 14-5 Characteristics of the Term $\dfrac{\omega_4 + s}{\omega_4}$.

The first two terms on the right-hand side of Eq. (14-19) are the same as Eq. (14-15) and (14-17) and appeared previously as terms of Eq. (14-14). The asymptotic characteristics and phase relationships have been discussed and illustrated.

The quadratic expression

$$Hs^2 + Ds + 1 \quad (14\text{-}20)$$

is of the general form of the reciprocal of Eq. (14-15), but having different coefficients. This equation is plotted, as to its general form, in Fig. 14-7.

The response of this expression is asymptotic to unity gain (slope of zero) to a frequency of $1/\sqrt{H}$. At this point of discontinuity the curve becomes asymptotic to a slope of -2. At the point of discontinuity there is an attenuation of the magnitude of $D/\sqrt{H}$. The term ξ, which appeared in the discussion of Eq. (14-15), here has no real physical equivalent.

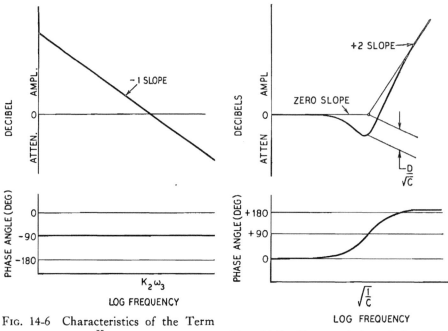

Fig. 14-6 Characteristics of the Term $\dfrac{K_2\omega_3}{s}$.

Fig. 14-7 Characteristics of the Term $Hs^2 + Ds + 1$.

Angle of Attack Response to Control Surface Deflection. The transfer function for the flight path angle, Eq. (14-19), has two terms which appear in the pitch angle response expression, Eq. (14-14). The dissimilar terms in these equations are

$$\frac{\omega_4 + s}{\omega_4} \quad \text{and} \quad Hs^2 + Ds + 1 \qquad (14\text{-}17), (14\text{-}20)$$

At low input frequencies both of these expressions have gains approaching unity. Thus it is apparent that for low input frequencies the difference between them is small. It is to be expected, therefore, that the angle of attack, which is the difference between the two, will be small at low frequencies.

The transfer function for the output of the angle of attack α, in response to an input of control surface deflection δ_E, may be obtained by simultaneously solving Eq. (14-12) and (14-13) for the ratio α/δ_E. In order to simplify the solution, the following substitutions are employed.

$$K_3 = -\frac{C_{L\delta E}(\omega_3/\omega_2) + C_{M\delta E}}{C_{M\alpha} + C_{L\alpha}(\omega_3/\omega_2)}$$

$$\omega_5 = -\omega_1^2\left[\frac{1}{\omega_2} + \frac{C_{M\delta E}}{\omega_3 C_{L\delta E}}\right]$$

The transfer function for the angle of attack may now be written

$$\frac{\text{Output}}{\text{Input}} = \frac{\alpha}{\delta_E} = \left(\frac{1}{As^2 + Bs + 1}\right)\left(\frac{K_3(\omega_5 + s)}{\omega_5}\right) \quad (14\text{-}21)$$

The first term of Eq. (14-21), $\frac{1}{As^2 + Bs + 1}$, is the familiar quadratic expression which has appeared in the previous transfer functions and has already been discussed. The second term

$$\frac{K_3(\omega_5 + s)}{\omega_5} \quad (14\text{-}22)$$

is analogous to a high-pass filter with a value of attenuation K_3. The logarithmic asymptotic characteristics and the phase relationships are shown in Fig. 14-8. It will be noted that the asymptotes have slopes of zero and

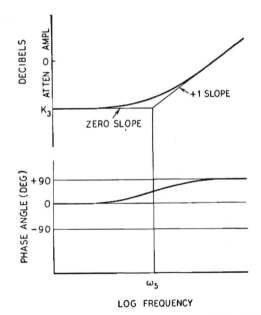

Fig. 14-8 Characteristics of the Term $\frac{K_3(\omega_5 + s)}{\omega_5}$.

+1, with the corner frequency occurring at ω_4, similar to the case of Eq. (14-17). The gain is, however, at K_3 instead of unity.

Forward Velocity Variations. One of the initial assumptions, prior to the discussion of the transfer characteristics of a cruciform airframe in pitch, was that of constant forward velocity. It is obvious that when a deflection of a control surface occurs, the drag of the missile is increased and the forward velocity undergoes a change. As a result of the velocity change, there is induced a low frequency oscillatory mode known as a *phugoid oscillation*. Accompanying the phugoid oscillation is a corresponding decrease of gain at the low frequency. Since at low frequencies the angle of attack is small, the effect of the phugoid oscillation on the angle of attack response characteristics is negligible. Since the effect on the angle of attack approaches zero (and since the angle of attack is the difference between the flight path vector angle and the pitch angle), it is readily evident that any effect induced by the phugoid oscillation will appear

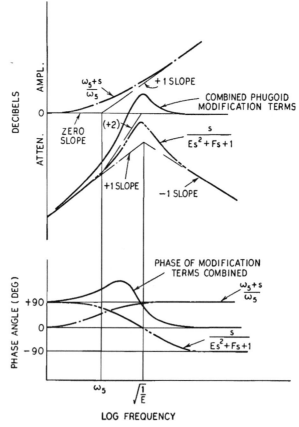

Fig. 14-9 Characteristics of the Phugoid Terms.

simultaneously and with equal effect in both the pitch angle and the flight path vector angle response characteristics.

A complete discussion of the derivation of the phugoid oscillatory terms requires the introduction of considerable aerodynamic theory beyond the scope of this book.[2] The effect of the phugoid oscillation may be illustrated by the addition of terms to Eq. (14-14). Without the assumption of constant forward velocity the transfer function for the pitch angle output θ in response to a control surface deflection δ_E may be written

$$\frac{\text{Output}}{\text{Input}} = \frac{\theta}{\delta_E}$$

$$= \left(\frac{1}{As^2 + Bs + 1}\right)\left(\frac{\omega_4 + s}{\omega_4}\right)\left(\frac{K_2\omega_3}{s}\right)\left(\frac{s}{Es^2 + Fs + 1}\right)\left(\frac{\omega_6 + s}{\omega_6}\right)$$

(14-23)

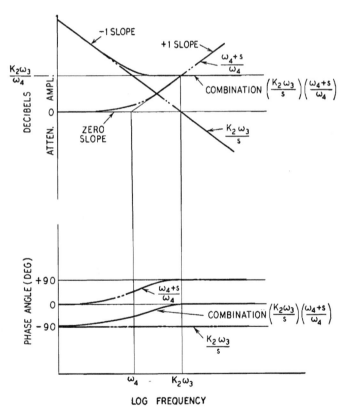

FIG. 14-10 Characteristics of the Combined Terms $\left(\dfrac{K_2\omega_3}{s}\right)\left(\dfrac{\omega_4 + s}{\omega_4}\right)$.

[2] For the interested reader, see "Dynamics of the Airframe," *BuAer Report AE-61-4 II* prepared under contract NOas 51-514(C), and the *Aerodynamics* section of this series of volumes.

504 THE MISSILE AIRFRAME

The additional terms contributed by the phugoid oscillation are

$$\frac{s}{Es^2 + Fs + 1} \quad \text{and} \quad \frac{\omega_6 + s}{\omega_6} \qquad (14\text{-}24)$$

The symbols E, F, and ω_6 will not be herein defined. They are derived from classical stability derivatives in the same manner as the previously discussed similar quantities. The important qualities of the terms are that the corner frequencies defined by $\sqrt{1/E}$ and ω_6 are low as compared to the corner frequencies defined by the remaining terms of Eq. (14-23), and that they are in character amenable to being plotted on a gain-phase basis. Figure 14-9 shows the general gain and phase plots of the complex terms of Eq. (14-24). The asymptotic slope relationships are self-explanatory. Associated with the phugoid oscillation is a sharp resonant rise accompanied by a rapid phase shift.

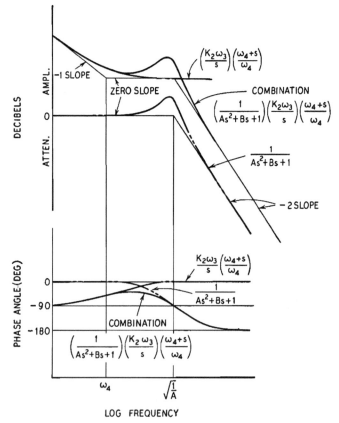

FIG. 14-11 Characteristics of the Combined Terms
$\left(\dfrac{1}{As^2 + Bs + 1}\right)\left(\dfrac{K_2\omega_3}{s}\right)\left(\dfrac{\omega_4 + s}{\omega_4}\right)$.

14-4] DERIVATION OF TRANSFER FUNCTIONS IN PITCH

Graphic Display of Airframe Transfer Characteristics. We have shown that the transfer function for the pitch attitude angle output as related to a control surface input is defined by at least five terms which have been independently plotted. Each of these expressions has been shown to have a corner frequency, the discrete value of which is related to the design and environmental parameters. On the general basis that $\omega_5 < \sqrt{1/E} \ll \omega_4 < K_2\omega_3 < \sqrt{1/A}$ the complete transfer function of the airframe in pitch may be displayed graphically.

Figure 14-10 shows the combination of the terms $(\omega_4 + s)/\omega_4$ from Fig. 14-5 and $(K_2\omega_3)/s$ from Fig. 14-6. Figure 14-11 displays graphically the combination of these terms from Fig. 14-10 and the expression $\dfrac{1}{As^2 + Bs + 1}$ from Fig. 14-4. Figure 14-11 is the graphic display of the

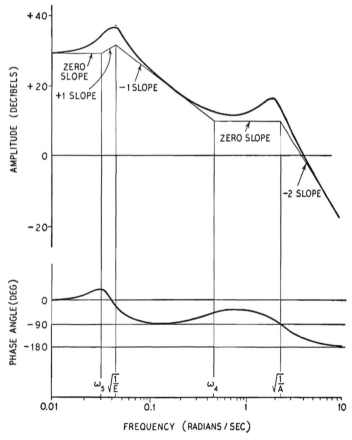

FIG. 14-12 Output Pitch Angle θ Due to an Input Control Surface Deflection δ_E.

general transfer function for pitch attitude angle in response to a control surface input, assuming that the forward velocity of the missile is constant, as in the derivation of Eq. (14-14).

The final step to the complete display of the transfer function of Eq. (14-23) is the combination of the terms $\left(\dfrac{1}{As^2 + Bs + 1}\right)\left(\dfrac{\omega_4 + s}{\omega_4}\right)\left(\dfrac{K_2\omega_3}{s}\right)$ as shown in Fig. 14-11 and the terms of the phugoid oscillation $\left(\dfrac{s}{Es^2 + Fs + 1}\right)\left(\dfrac{\omega_6 + s}{\omega_6}\right)$ as shown in Fig. 14-9. The graphic display of the complete transfer function is shown in Fig. 14-13. Figures 14-14 and 14-15 respectively show the transfer functions for the flight path vector angle and the angle of attack as related to an input of control surface

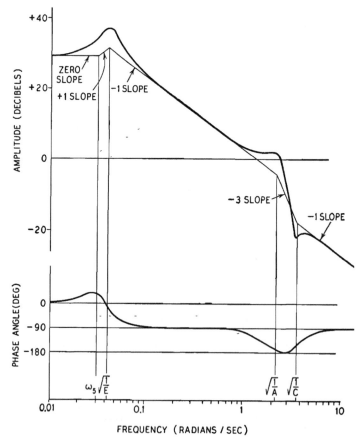

FIG. 14-13 Output Flight Path Vector Angle γ Due to an Input Control Surface Deflection δ_E.

14-5] EFFECT OF CHANGE OF ENVIRONMENTAL PARAMETERS

deflection. These figures include the phugoid oscillatory terms. Arbitrary quantitative values of gain and frequency are shown on the ordinates in the latter three figures in order that they may be employed in a later discussion.

14-5 EFFECT OF CHANGE OF ENVIRONMENTAL PARAMETERS

The transfer characteristics of a cruciform airframe for pitch angle, flight path vector angle, and angle of attack, each as a function of control surface deflections, have been shown in Fig. 14-12, 14-13, and 14-14. The performance of such an airframe may be changed either by altering the design of the stability parameters or by changes in the environmental or operating parameters. The following environmental parameters are those most likely to change during a missile flight:

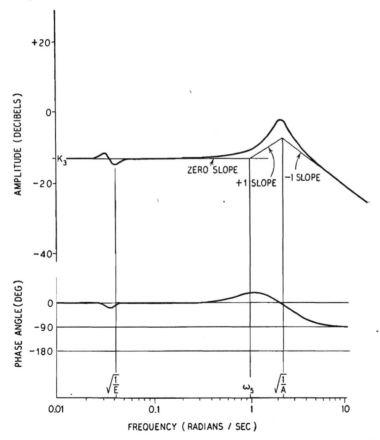

FIG. 14-14 Output Angle of Attack α Due to an Input Control Surface Deflection δ_E.

(a) The density of the air, since the missile is not usually constrained to a constant altitude.
(b) The mass of the missile and consequently the moment of inertia, since fuel must be expended and the mass changed accordingly.
(c) The forward velocity of missiles, since a missile may accelerate while the propelling motor is in operation and/or decelerate after the fuel is exhausted.

In considering the effect of the variation of the environmental parameters, the following substitutions will be recalled from the solution of the transfer functions

$$\omega_1 = \frac{\rho V^2 S c}{2 I_{vv}}$$

$$\omega_3 = \frac{\rho V S}{2}$$

It can be observed that a variation of the environmental parameters will cause a change in the corner frequencies of the transfer characteristics which will result, in effect, in a change in gain of the airframe as a system element. Under certain circumstances, however, the changing parameters tend to cancel their effect one upon the other. For example, in a surface-to-air missile fired at a high-altitude target, as the missile gains altitude the density of the air decreases. However, the moment of inertia and the mass of the missile also decrease and the effects tend to cancel each other. In the case of an air-to-surface missile, this compensating characteristic does not exist. In general, a change in the density of the air ρ causes a variation of the value of the frequency $\sqrt{1/A}$ at which the resonant rise occurs. This variation is proportional to the three-halves power of the density change. However, the magnitude of the resonant rise $\sqrt{A/B}$ changes only in proportion to the square root of the density change.

Missiles are normally designed so that the radius of gyration remains substantially constant with or without fuel. Therefore, the change in the moment of inertia by reason of fuel expenditure is nearly proportional to the change in mass.

If we consider the case of an air-to-surface missile, launched at 30,000 ft, the density of the air at the sea level terminus of the missile is 2.66 times the density of the air at the point of launching. If half of the initial weight of the missile were fuel, and the fuel were completely expended in flight, then the change in ω_1 would be 2.3 to 1 and ω_3 would vary 5.3 to 1, considering both the air density change and the fuel expenditure. On the other hand, if the example were a surface-to-air missile launched at sea level against a target at 30,000 ft altitude, then ω_1 would vary only 1.15 to 1 and ω_3 would vary only 1.33 to 1 during the flight. Thus, the compensating effects of the interacting parameters are demonstrated for the latter case.

There is also a change in the transfer characteristic by reason of a change in forward velocity, since the velocity appears as a squared term in both the ω_1 and the ω_2 expressions. The stability derivatives are essentially independent of velocity up through a velocity of Mach number of about 0.6. The nature of the variation from 0.6 to the transonic region depends upon the particular airframe configuration. Through the transonic range, the variations of the stability derivatives are liable to be both large and erratic.

At very low speeds or at high altitudes the airframe may require high angles of attack in order to obtain lift. Extreme angles of attack may lead to drastic changes in some of the stability derivatives, resulting in unpredictable nonlinearities and consequent instability of the control system.

Aerodynamic Range. The maximum aerodynamic range of a guided missile is frequently one of the most important operational parameters. The drag forces which restrain the forward motion of the missile are directly proportional to the density of the air. An air-to-air missile fired at 30,000 ft altitude at a target at approximately the same altitude will have roughly twice the maximum aerodynamic range of the same missile fired close to sea level against a target at like altitude (density ratio 2.66 to 1). For the same reason, a surface-to-air missile which is launched vertically against a high-altitude target and is turned to horizontal flight at the target altitude will have about twice the maximum aerodynamic range of a similar missile which is flown along a direct trajectory between the launching point and the same target.

14-6 EFFECT OF VARIATION OF STABILITY PARAMETERS

Lift Coefficient, C_L. Minor variation of the lift coefficient is of little importance in the airframe dynamics. An increase in C_L increases the damping of the phugoid mode, while reducing the frequency at which the phugoid resonance occurs.

Change in Lift with Angle of Attack. This parameter is of importance in the short-period oscillatory mode designated in previous discussion as the corner frequency $\sqrt{1/A}$. An increase in $C_{L\alpha}$ decreases the resonant rise of this oscillatory mode. However, a high value of $C_{L\alpha}$ requires a high aspect ratio and unswept airfoil, which conditions are not consistent with modern practice.

Coefficient of Lift Change Due to Control Surface Deflection. On the conventional airframe the control surface is at the end of a long moment arm (the distance from the center of gravity of the airframe to the control surface) and the area of the control surface is relatively small with respect to the area of the wing. On tailless aircraft the area is relatively large;

hence the change in lift with control surface deflection is more significant than on aircraft with elevator tail controls.

Change in Pitch Moment Coefficient with Angle of Attack. The stability of an airframe is more affected by variations in $C_{M\alpha}$ than by any other of the aerodynamic coefficients. A large value of $C_{M\alpha}$ results in a high degree of static stability in the airframe. However, if $C_{M\alpha}$ is too large, then, for proper control, $C_{M\delta E}$ must also be disproportionately large.

The burning of the propelling fuel, in addition to changing the total mass of the missile and its moment of inertia, will cause a shift in the location of the center of gravity of the missile. The moment arm of $C_{M\alpha}$ is the distance between the center of lift (known to the aerodynamicist as the *mean aerodynamic center*) and the center of gravity of the missile. When an airframe in flight has a large shift of the center of gravity by reason of fuel burnout, careful attention must be paid to evaluating the effects of the c.g. shift upon $C_{M\alpha}$ and the corresponding effects upon the dynamic stability of the airframe. As $C_{M\alpha}$ increases, the value of the frequency of the asymptotic corner $\sqrt{1/A}$ also increases. As the center of gravity approaches a limit, a rapid change may occur in the value of $C_{M\alpha}$ and the magnitude of the oscillatory mode may change rapidly. Instability in airframe control may result.

Change in Pitch Moment Coefficient with Pitching Velocity. The change in moment coefficient with pitching velocity, C_{MQ} is caused principally by a change in the angle of attack of the horizontal tail surfaces. The angle of attack causes a lift force to be applied to the tail. The coefficient C_{MQ} provides most of the damping for the resonance having a corner frequency at $\sqrt{1/A}$. This coefficient is also involved, to a minor degree, in damping the phugoid resonance. Usually a high value of C_{MQ} is desired. In certain airframe types, notably a tailless airframe, this coefficient becomes a critical factor in the design.

Change in Pitch Moment Coefficient with Control Surface Deflection. The change in pitch moment coefficient with control surface deflection $C_{M\delta E}$ is frequently called *elevator effectiveness*, although the basic considerations apply to any control surface. When a horizontal control surface is deflected, a change in pitch moment about the center of gravity of the missile is produced. The magnitude of $C_{M\delta E}$ is specified principally by the requirements resulting from the shift of the center of gravity and the magnitude of $C_{M\alpha}$. Limitation of the magnitude of the shift of the center of gravity is necessary in order to keep the size of the control surface within reasonable limits.

Drag Coefficient C_D. Although it is not usually referred to as a stability derivative, the coefficient of drag C_D is the main source of damping for the phugoid mode of oscillation. A large value of drag coefficient aids in damping the phugoid oscillation, but, in order to obtain optimum missile performance, a low value is desirable. Since the phugoid oscillation causes little angle of attack build-up, little drag increase occurs due thereto.

14-7 DERIVATION OF TRANSFER FUNCTION IN ROLL

The moment in roll about the x axis may be expressed in terms of aerodynamic coefficients as

$$M = C_l \frac{\rho V^2 S c}{2} \qquad (14\text{-}25)$$

where M = a moment about the x axis
C_l = the rolling moment coefficient
ρ = the density of the air
V = the forward velocity
S = a characteristic control area of the airframe
c = a characteristic control length of the airframe

The change in rolling moment caused by a change in roll control surface deflections is

$$C_{l\delta A} = \frac{dC_l}{d\delta_A} \qquad (14\text{-}26)$$

where $C_{l\delta A}$ is the change in roll moment coefficient with roll control surface deflection. Similarly, C_{lp}, the change in rolling moment caused by the rate of roll, is

$$C_{lp} = \frac{dC_l}{dp} \qquad (14\text{-}27)$$

As in Par. 14-4, considering the airframe in roll as a single degree of freedom system, a differential equation of motion in roll may be written as

$$I_{xx}\frac{d^2\phi}{dt^2} - \left(\frac{C_{lp}\rho V^2 S c}{2}\right)\frac{d\phi}{dt} - C_{l\delta A}\frac{\delta_A \rho V^2 S c}{2} = 0 \qquad (14\text{-}28)$$

If we substitute

$$\omega_a = \frac{C_{lp}\rho V^2 S c}{2 I_{xx}}$$

$$\omega_b = \frac{C_{l\delta A}}{C_{lp}}$$

then Eq. (14-28) may be simplified to read

$$s^2\phi - \omega_a s\phi - \delta_A \omega_a \omega_b = 0 \qquad (14\text{-}29)$$

Solving for the ratio of the roll output angle ϕ to the roll control surface deflection δ_A, we have

$$\frac{\text{Output}}{\text{Input}} = \frac{\phi}{\delta_A} = \left(\frac{\omega_b}{s}\right)\left(\frac{\omega_a}{\omega_a + s}\right) \qquad (14\text{-}30)$$

which is the transfer characteristic of the airframe in roll with respect to the deflection of the roll control surface. Figure 14-15 is the gain-phase plot of the general characteristics of this transfer function. It will be observed that the asymptotic slopes are, with increasing frequency, a slope of -1 breaking into a slope of -2 at a corner frequency of ω_a.

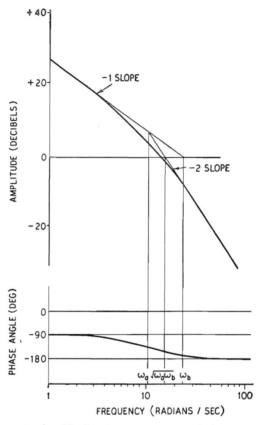

FIG. 14-15 Output Angle of Roll ϕ Due to an Input Roll Control Surface Deflection δ_A.

14-8 EXPERIMENTAL CONFIRMATION OF THE FREQUENCY RESPONSE OF AN AIRFRAME

The frequency response of system components is usually determined theoretically; then, when the components become available in physical form, the characteristics of the components are confirmed experimentally. The usual method of measuring the frequency response of a system or component of a system is to measure its steady-state response to different input sinusoidal frequencies.[3] This method of experimentation does not

[3] Charles F. White, "Some Sinusoidal System Studies," *NRL Report R-3303*, June 22, 1948.

lend itself readily to the determination of the performance of a missile airframe in flight, although it has been employed in piloted aircraft.[4] The development of considerable special experimental equipment, both for inserting the sinusoidal input signals and measuring the output response of the aircraft, is required. Insofar as guided missiles are concerned, in many missiles the time of flight is too short to permit the economic employment of this method of experimentally confirming the theoretical frequency response.

A more practical experimental method is to impose a pulse or step deflection on the control surface of the missile in one coordinate and measure the transient response of the missile in flight.[5] Theoretically, a single transient will contain the entire frequency spectrum, and the imposition of the transient function and observation of the resulting missile response require only a few seconds of flight time. A transient wave shape may be considered to be made up of a sum of sinusoidal wave shapes of varying magnitude covering the entire frequency spectrum. The response of a linear system to a transient input may then be viewed as its response to the sum of the sinusoidal waves contained in the transient input. The Fourier integral

$$F(j\omega) = \int_{-\infty}^{\infty} f(t) e^{-j\omega t}\, dt \qquad (6\text{-}56)$$

enables a time function $f(t)$ to be transformed into a complex frequency function $F(j\omega)$. The integral must be evaluated for each frequency at which $F(j\omega)$ is desired.

The reduction of flight test data to form usable for graphical analysis, and thence to the derivation of the transfer response equations, is arduous and time-consuming, but the experimental confirmation of the frequency response of the missile airframe is a necessary process in the design of the missile guidance system. The input transient deflection of the control surface in the tests should be as large as possible over the frequency range of interest in order to optimize the test data accuracy. In the case of an airframe, however, the response is linear only over relatively small values of control motion. The practical usable transient pulse in the tests becomes, necessarily, a compromise.

It must also be remembered that the response of the airframe is valid only for the air density and velocity at which the experimental work is accomplished. By the theoretical processes previously discussed, however,

---

[4] G. F. Campbell, D. W. Whitcomb and W. O. Breuhaus, "Dynamic Longitudinal Stability and Control Flight Tests of a B-25J Airplane—Forced Oscillation and Step Function Response Methods, Utilizing A-12 Autopilot," *Cornell Aero. Lab. Report No. TB-405-F-3*, April 1947 (*USAF Tech. Rep. 5688*).

[5] G. A. Smith and W. C. Triplett, "Experimental Flight Methods for Evaluating Frequency-Response Characteristics of Aircraft," *ASME Paper No. 54-SA-3*, February 1954.

it is possible to extrapolate the results to cover a wider variation of the environmental parameters.

Theoretically, it is apparent from Eq. (6-56) that an infinite amount of time must be allowed for the response to the transient input to become steady. From a practical point of view, a test flight for the purpose of experimentally verifying the theoretical frequency response characteristics of the missile might comprise a series of transient inputs of different magnitudes, with sufficient time between the pulses for the output to become steady. The presence of external forces, such as wind gusts, may distort the experimental data. Sufficient statistical information must be obtained that the results may be considered valid.

14-9 USE OF AIRFRAME CHARACTERISTICS BY THE CONTROL DESIGNER

This simplified discussion of airframe stability and control problems has ignored many of the more thorny problems with which the missile aerodynamicist is beset. A brief discussion of some of these problems is in order.

Stability in a Skewed Plane. If a cruciform airframe is used, where yaw characteristics and pitch characteristics differ because of a selection of airframe proportions (a condition wherein stability and controllability may be achieved in each of these two coordinates) it is still possible that in some intermediate plane instability may exist. When a large angle of attack may occur in each coordinate, the summation of these into an additional intermediate plane may cause an uncontrolled oscillation to build up. Attention should be paid to this when stability limits are approached in any plane. The evaluation of this phenomenon usually requires a complete three-dimensional study of the airframe on an analog computer. The techniques for setting up analog solutions on such a computer are discussed in Chap. 19.

Coordinated Turns. Conventional airframes differ in design from cruciform airframes in that they use coordinated turns wherein the aircraft is rolled and turned simultaneously, so that the acceleration remains in vertical airplane coordinates. This adds an integration in the yaw channel which requires consideration in guidance system design. It is usually impossible to make an airframe requiring a coordinated turn to have identical pitch and yaw response characteristics. Thus, when a roll is experienced, anticipatory to a turn, the feed-through into the pitch channel, sometimes referred to as *cross coupling*, requires pitch corrections. The design of the airframe for a coordinated turn is amenable to analysis and is discussed in "Dynamics of the Airframe" previously referenced. Final simulation and careful adjustment of control parameters are required to

14-9] AIRFRAME CHARACTERISTICS AND THE CONTROL DESIGNER

ascertain that the complete and extremely complex system is optimized in consideration of its tactical usage. Often such an airframe is considered for surface-to-surface missiles wherein the attitude or pitch control may be from an altimeter and the yaw control requires only mild turns at very low frequencies. In this way cross feeding of information from channel to channel is minimized, because the bank angles are minimized.

CHAPTER 15

ECONOMIC CONSIDERATIONS

There are three major areas to be considered in discussing the costs of a guided missile program: (a) *research and development*, (b) *production*, and (c) *maintenance*. The problems associated with the research and development of a weapon system do not differ in principle from the problems of research and development of any complex system required for civilian use, except as the requirements of environment and military reliability are concerned. Also, the economic problems of production, distribution, and maintenance are similar, except that in order to keep a weapon system "in being," long periods of storage may be required between production and delivery to the user. Guided missile programs, and hence missile guidance programs, may be initiated under either of two conditions of national economy: a wartime economy or a peacetime economy. It is the purpose of this chapter to discuss the magnitude of a guidance equipment program and some of the cost or economic factors which must be considered.

15-1 PEACETIME ECONOMY *vs.* WARTIME ECONOMY

The unit by which cost is measured is different in a peacetime economy from that in a wartime economy. When a nation is at war, the determining unit is that of time. If a known threat exists, a counter weapon must be put into action against it in the shortest possible time. The cost in dollars becomes unimportant; the cost in time becomes all important. In peacetime, the cost of the weapon program in units of dollars becomes the governing factor between competitive weapon systems.

Research and Development. In wartime the "shotgun," or multiple equipment development, approach is frequently employed to meet an existing threat. Many possible avenues of development may be explored simultaneously; programs are started in duplicate to put a counter weapon into tactical use as quickly as possible. In consequence, the development cost for a given weapon will be many times higher in wartime than in peacetime.

In peacetime, since competitive bidding is employed by the government, the dollar cost of research and development is the important criterion. Time is still important if there is a threat of war acting as the forcing function for the development of a specific weapon. There is no easy way to discuss the costs of a research and development program, since so much is dependent upon the ability of the personnel available to the contractor. There are other factors equally difficult to equate as items of cost: the amount of invention required to develop a given weapon, the probability of successful conclusion of research investigations, familiarity by the contractor with federal contracting and inspection processes, and the willingness of the contractor to accept the contract in view of existing work load. The cost figures for research and development reflect factors which are individual with each specific contractor; generalities become difficult to state and impossible to apply.

Production Costs. Production costs are partially measured by the man hours required to produce a given equipment. Production costs are greater in wartime than in peacetime, but the percentage variance is not, as a rule, as great as the difference in research and development costs. The reasons for the increased costs of production in wartime are: lack of available manpower, manpower turnover, training of new personnel, and the necessity for overtime work. The total number of units manufactured of a given missile or projectile will be greater in wartime than in peacetime. The production costs drop as a function of the total number of a given item produced, so that this factor tends to ameliorate the cost per unit of a given equipment.

Maintenance Costs. The maintenance cost per unit of a given expendable equipment such as a missile will decrease in wartime because of the accelerated use of such equipments. The distribution of the expendable units is made as direct as possible between the manufacturer and the tactical unit. In peacetime, the equipment is stored and the stored units are drawn upon only as replacements for those expended in training practice. When a considerable amount of equipment is placed in storage in preparation for the eventuality of a war, the equipment deteriorates during the period of storage and the maintenance required to keep it in working operation becomes costly. Equipment placed in storage will have a life expectancy of some given duration, after which it must be replaced. The life expectancy may be determined by many factors, two of which are: the degree of deterioration in storage and obsolescence due to technical advances or other causes.

Those parts of the missile guidance system, external to the missile, such as radar equipments, computers, guidance links, etc., also depreciate in value with time, since they are employed continually by tactical units. The life expectancy of equipment which is in constant use is increased by vigilant maintenance. The cost of maintaining equipment in use in the tactical unit should not vary appreciably between wartime and peacetime, but the life expectancy of the equipment in peacetime is probably greater.

518　ECONOMIC CONSIDERATIONS

15-2 MISSILE GUIDANCE EQUIPMENT RESEARCH AND DEVELOPMENT PROGRAM

Figure 15-1 shows the flow chart of the planning and progress for a guidance system research and development program. It is assumed that the contractor has been awarded a contract for a guided missile system to accomplish certain specified operational directions. Figure 15-1 is not illustrative of the program for any one specific method of guidance; rather, it is indicative of the program planning that may be required for the development of any guidance system equipment. A Navy guidance

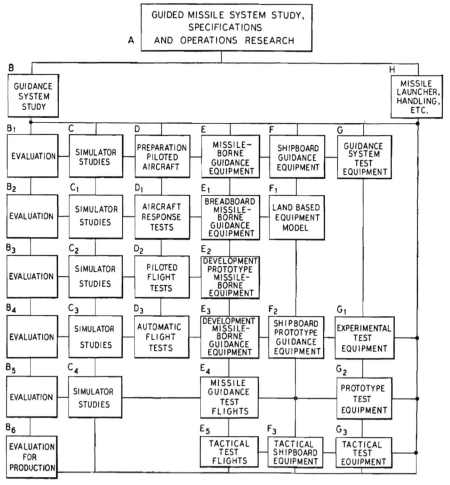

FIG. 15-1　Block Diagram of Research and Development Program for Missile Guidance System.

system has been used in the example in order to admit the additional steps required for the development of shipborne equipment.

Guided Missile System Study. Block *A* of Fig. 15-1 represents the complete program study for the guided missile system. Such a study is initially made by the contractor following the request to submit a bid for the research and development of a missile guidance system. After the award of the contract is made, detailed study work begins. The study continues throughout the life of the development program, coordinating the efforts of company engineers and subcontractors as detailed information on specific equipments becomes available to replace earlier estimates.

A theoretical synthesis of the guided missile system must be made on the basis of the tactical operational requirements. Specifications must be developed for the major portions of the system. It is the purpose of such specifications to develop the operational dynamic characteristics and accuracy requirements. The size, weight, and other physical characteristics must be delineated, tentatively at first but with increasing definitiveness as the program advances. These specifications are necessary to permit the design of the many portions of the missile guidance system to proceed simultaneously.

The specifications will include those for the missile, the handling equipment, and the launcher, as well as those of direct interest to the designer of the missile guidance system. Such specifications are seldom static, but must continually be coordinated with test information, and the information imparted to the succeeding blocks on the flow diagram. The important specifications to the designer of the guidance equipment are those for the ground-based and missile-borne guidance equipment, the dynamic characteristics of the missile, and the demands of the trajectory in all phases of flight. Within the group of engineers concerned principally with the guidance system, these specifications are reviewed to establish the research and development program necessary to implement them.

Guidance System Study and Synthesis. Block *B* represents the work of the coordinating group for the design of the missile guidance system. In turn, it is necessary to break down the specifications presented to the guidance system engineers so that these may be translated into component specifications for elements of the guidance system. On the basis of these specifications detailed engineering of the guidance system may be started. The necessity for basic research studies will here be determined and this work initiated. The areas of known design will be separated from the areas of work which require new development or invention. As the design proceeds and is translated into equipment, the tests of the components must be compared to the specified requirements continually. Changes may be made in either the specifications or the equipment to maintain the operational needs inviolate.

Blocks B_1 to B_5 represent the continuing evaluation of the elements of the guidance system as the design of the system progresses from the initial concept to the production prototype equipment. The results of the evaluation are reported back for the continuing guided missile system analysis, since information developed in the tests and the evaluation of them may reflect necessary changes on system elements not under the direct control of the guidance system group.

Simulator Studies. As an aid to the design of a missile guidance system, the engineers so involved will normally have at their command some type of analog simulator. The functions of such a device are: (a) to permit the engineer, on the basis of an assumed mathematical model of the missile and guidance system, to predict the behavior of the missile in flight and the probable accuracy of the guidance system; (b) to test components of the system in conjunction with the assumed mathematical model of the remainder of the system. The analog simulator is an extremely powerful tool when used in the design of complex system equipment. It may be used, of course, not only as a simulator for the entire system, but also for portions of the system.

The blocks of C_1 to C_5 indicate the continuing character of the simulator work throughout the entire research and development program. Chapter 19 deals in more detail with the use of analog simulators as aids to design of missile guidance equipment.

Piloted Aircraft Simulation. In addition to the analog simulator as an aid to the design of a missile guidance system, piloted aircraft may be used for captive flight tests of the system. This permits direct observation of the behavior of the equipment in flight and the exploration of many facets of development problems that may be accomplished in no other manner. The characteristics of the autopilot and of the piloted aircraft may be made to simulate the missile in flight. Chapter 19 deals with this type of simulation in greater detail.

Block D indicates the preparation of the aircraft for the tests of the guidance equipment. Block D_1 indicates the accomplishment of frequency response tests of the aircraft to develop its transfer characteristic. Block D_2 indicates the tests of the guidance equipment, with the aircraft under the physical control of a human pilot. During this phase of the tests, it is determined that the equipment is functioning correctly and that the outputs of the system will safely guide the aircraft in the desired manner. Block D_3 indicates the simulation of the missile flight by the piloted aircraft, with all elements of the guidance system functioning to guide the aircraft automatically as if it were the missile. The usefulness of captive flight tests is, of course, limited by the exactness of the simulation of the missile response characteristics by the piloted aircraft.

Missile-borne Guidance Equipment. The development of the missile-borne guidance equipment is represented by the E series of blocks in Fig. 15-1. The first step is that of translating the specifications for the equipment into circuitry by the processes of analysis and design, block E. "Breadboard" equipment, i.e., circuits and equipment on open chassis, are developed for test and evaluation, block E_1. The initial tests on breadboard equipment are made with test equipment simulating external portions of the system. As the components external to the missile are similarly developed these are included in the test set-up. During the testing of the breadboard equipment, the design of prototype equipment for the missile is proceeding on paper. When the correct circuit constants and design of mechanical components have been demonstrated by the breadboard tests, the construction of the test prototype equipment is initiated, block E_2. This equipment, after ground-based tests, is installed in the piloted aircraft for flight testing. Similar equipment is installed in the analog simulator so that results of both the analog tests and the flight tests may be compared and evaluated.

These tests may indicate the necessity for revisions in the design of the equipment. Such changes are continued throughout the development. Similarly, the results of the tests of the missile may force changes in the design concepts and specifications for the guidance equipment. The environmental conditions for the guidance equipment are developed. Integration of the results of the design and testing of all components and system elements is necessary. The design of the missile-borne prototype equipment then proceeds on the basis of full knowledge of the tests, which have elicited new specifications and performance requirements for the equipment. This phase of the work is indicated in block E_3.

The missile-borne equipment prototype is next tested by missile flight, block E_4. The results of these flights are evaluated and changes made in the equipment as required. The missile flight tests in this stage of the program are designed to evaluate specific items pertaining to the guidance equipment or missile design and are not in the nature of tactical tests. When the missile flight tests indicate satisfactory performance of the equipment, the tests flights move into the final phase, block E_5. The flight tests are here made under simulated tactical conditions, employing a real target and warhead, and with the equipment and test under the complete control of a tactical military unit. The engineers and designers are now in the role of observers. The introduction of military personnel into the program is gradual rather than sudden in aspect, with the military playing the role of observers during the earlier tests.

Shipborne Guidance Equipment. Block F represents the translation of the specifications into circuit and component design for the portions of the guidance system external to the missile, herein called the shipborne guidance equipment. The use of shipboard equipment was chosen in this example to show the necessity for additional steps in the equipment design. Because the early tests must be conducted on land, the design of this equipment will be expected to have two distinct phases, a land-based phase and a shipborne phase. The land-based equipment may be designed to be housed in mobile trailers, if this accelerates the testing program, or it may be designed for permanent mounting for the duration of the tests. The land-based equipment, block F_1, is employed during the piloted aircraft tests and the initial missile guidance tests, with the design of the shipborne prototype, block F_2, proceeding on the basis of the test results and evaluations. Since the piloted flight tests may be made in proximity to the contractor's manufacturing plant and the missile flight tests are made on a government test facility, the desirability of making the equipment mobile becomes evident.

By the time the missile tests have progressed to the degree that the tactical tests may be started, the shipborne equipment will be installed upon the ship that is to be used in the tactical tests. The final tactical testing proceeds only after all elements of the system have successfully passed the prior tests.

Test Equipment. The test equipment referred to in the G series of blocks, Fig. 15-1, is that equipment which is used to determine the operability of the guidance system for use under tactical conditions. The necessity for such equipment and the manner of its use was discussed in Chap. 13. In the fashion usual with electronic equipment, the equipment must be designed in accordance with specifications, block G; put into hardware form for use with the missile prototype equipment, block G_1; redesigned, if necessary, in accordance with guidance system changes, block G_2; and, finally, put in form for tactical shipborne use, block G_3.

In the event that the missiles, complete with guidance systems, will be stored for protracted periods of time, it will be necessary to develop other test equipment for the principal use of detecting deterioration in storage and for indicating the maintenance necessary on the stored equipment.

Missile Airframe, Handling and Launching Equipment. The programs required to develop these elements of the guided missile system are discussed in the *Systems Engineering*, *Structures and Design Practice*, and *Launching* sections of this series of volumes. For the purposes of the guidance system designer, it is necessary that the development of the entire guided missile system be integrated so that the elements of the system required in the process of the testing are available in proper form when required.

Evaluation for Production. The entire research and development program is pointed to the accomplishment indicated by block B_6, evaluation for production. This represents the successful culmination of the design, research, development, and testing of the guided missile system. When the system has been demonstrated to fulfill the tactical use for which it was conceived, the design of all components may be frozen and a contract for the production of the system in quantity may be let. Extreme care and careful judgment must be exercised to be sure that the major parameters of the system have been carefully explored and that the operational limitations have been fully delineated, before the final decision is made to produce the system in quantity for tactical use. The cost of the research and development of a weapon is only a fraction of the cost involved in the mass production of that weapon.

It should be noted that the sequential steps indicated in Fig. 15-1 are frequently telescoped into concurrent operations when time becomes important. Experimental prototypes are built while testing of the breadboard equipment is going forward; the design of production prototypes is in process while the tests of the experimental models are being made; and the production design is underway while the production prototypes are being tested. The shorter the available time, the greater becomes the amount of telescoping of successive steps in the development program. Since changes are almost inevitably indicated by the tests of the equipment, the changes tend to become of the "haywire" variety instead of being carefully integrated into succeeding designs. Failures of equipments undergoing tests tend to increase. Design changes may be required in the production equipments after many have already been produced, necessitating field changes in the early models of the equipment. This type of operation is extremely expensive and the question of whether or not the time saved by this means is justified becomes difficult to answer. Careful planning of the research and development program is the least costly and most effective means of saving both time and money.

15-3 PRODUCTION AND DISTRIBUTION OF EQUIPMENT EXTERNAL TO THE MISSILE

Production. Under this heading is included the shipborne guidance and test equipments and, in addition, the launching and handling equipments. These equipments were tabulated as part of the research and development program indicated in Fig. 15-1. As a general rule, the cost of these equipments is high per unit (considering the complete system as the basic unit), but the number of units which must be manufactured is relatively small. A guided missile system for Fleet use is designed to be put upon a certain class (or classes) of ships. The number of ships to be equipped determines the number of units which must be produced.

The exact equipment which goes to make up the system depends upon the method of guidance used. The specialized equipments for a guided missile which might be installed upon a ship could include the following, as an example:

(a) One search radar.
(b) One target tracking radar.
(c) One computer.
(d) Two sets of handling equipment.
(e) Two sets of launching equipment.
(f) Test equipment.
(g) Communication equipment.
(h) Spares for all equipments.

In addition to the cost of all equipment, the ship wherein it is to be installed must be prepared to accept it. Existing equipment must be removed. The structure of the ship may have to be changed to support the weight of the new equipment. New cables must be laid between com-

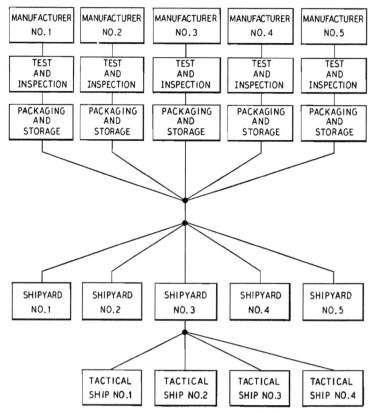

FIG. 15-2 Distribution of Shipborne Guidance Equipment.

ponents of the system; existing cabling may have to be removed or rerouted. Internal space changes must be made to accommodate the below-decks equipment and to provide for stowage of the missiles.

The cost to equip a ship with a guided missile system is considerable. The cost not only includes the purchase price of the missile system, but also the alteration of the ship to receive it. The ship will be unavailable for sea duty during the period of time that the work proceeds. The cost of the system must be amortized over a period of time since either technological development or use will make it obsolete within some definable period.

Distribution. The distribution of shipborne missile guidance system components is complex only in that different components of the system may be made by contractors and all components must be in hand, in storage, when a ship is available for their installation. Figure 15-2 indicates the flow of the distribution of the shipborne missile guidance system components. Many shipyards may be used for the installation of the equipment. Considerable planning is required so that all of the system components are available coincidentally with the ship. No maintenance is required during this period of storage.

15-4 PRODUCTION AND DISTRIBUTION OF MISSILE-BORNE GUIDANCE EQUIPMENT

Production. In planning for the production of a guided missile, there are two basic estimates which must be made: (a) in the event of war, the probable rate of expenditure of the missiles; (b) to be prepared for war, the number of missiles required to supply the tactical units until wartime production equals wartime demand. The first estimate determines the maximum rate of production which may be called for, and thus goes to establish the size and tooling of the production facility. The second estimate determines the peacetime production rate. The determination of an estimate in either case is a difficult procedure and is composed of equal parts of "crystal-ball" assumptions, common sense, and detailed logistic studies.

Some of the factors involved in estimating the probable rate of expenditures of the missiles in wartime are: the number of guided missile systems in tactical units, the distribution of the tactical units, probable attrition rate of the tactical units, the reliability of the missiles, intelligence or estimates of enemy tactics, probable intentions and disposition of the enemy force, etc. From an assessment of these and other factors is determined the maximum rate of production required.

Some of the factors involved in estimating the peacetime production rate are: the number of guided missile systems installed in active tactical units, the expenditure rate of missiles for practice use, the urgency in building up the tactical units for preparedness, the time required to go from some minimum economical production rate to the maximum production rate, the cost per year to maintain the missiles and tactical units in readiness, etc. From these and many other factors may be determined the rate of production in peacetime in order to be prepared for war.

After an estimate of the maximum production rate of missiles has been made, it is possible to design a production plant and the tooling to meet the needs for the maximum production rate. The production facility may be owned and built by the government and operated by a contractor. The production plant may be built complete with all necessary machine

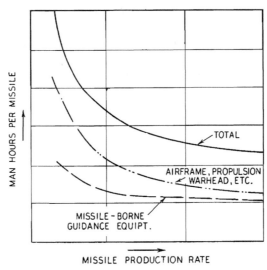

Fig. 15-3 General Relationship between Man Hours per Missile and Missile Production Rate.

tools, housing and other facilities, needing only manpower to bring it to maximum production. A compromise may be made by building the plant proper for the maximum rate and equipping it only for partial production. Any compromise such as this must be underwritten by having sufficient missiles available in storage for the period between the outbreak of hostilities and maximum missile production. Such compromises are dictated by the permissible annual expenditures for the guided missile program.

When the number of missiles required for preparedness has been estimated, it is possible to examine the general relationship between the cost per missile, the production rate, and some of the items which are involved. Figure 15-3 shows the general relationship between man hours per missile and the missile production rate. No significance should be attached to the units of the ordinates or the relationship between guidance equipment and airframe man hour requirements; the curves serve to indicate the fact that small production rates are extremely costly in man-hour requirements and that the man hours per missile tend to level off when the production rate approaches the design maximum of the plant. Similarly, the cost of materials per missile is indicated in the generalized curves of Fig. 15-4. Again the cost of materials per missile is high when the production rate is low and tends to level off when the maximum rate of the production facility is approached. The total cost per missile follows the same general pattern since it is the summation of the material and labor costs plus overhead charges. This relationship is indicated in Fig. 15-5. In choosing

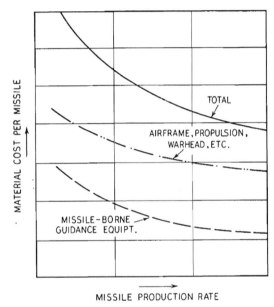

FIG. 15-4 General Relationship between Material Cost per Missile and Missile Production Rate.

a production rate for preparedness, the most missiles may be obtained for the least cost per missile after the break in the cost curve, as the price per missile tends to level off. This concept must be balanced against the total annual cost of maintaining the weapon in being. The total annual cost will be discussed subsequently.

Estimates of missile cost are frequently made on the basis of cost per pound. This is usually done for comparisons between missiles and missile guidance systems. The cost of the missile-borne guidance equipment per pound is usually arbitrarily estimated to be several times the cost per pound of the airframe structure, propulsion unit, and warhead. The total cost of the missile guidance equipment is usually small compared to the total cost of the missile, since the weight of the missile-borne guidance equipment is only a small part of the total weight. Exact cost relationships for a specific missile can be obtained only from statistical data of actual production.

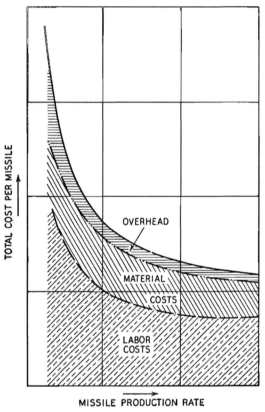

Fig. 15-5 General Relationship between Total Cost per Missile and Production Rate.

Distribution. Figure 15-6 indicates the flow of missiles, not in time of war, to keep the tactical units in a state of preparedness for hostilities. After production of the missile and its guidance equipment, it must be tested, inspected, and approved. It may then be packaged for shipment and perhaps temporarily stored at the terminal point of the production assembly plant. The missiles are then transported to suitably located storage depots. This storage represents a build-up of the missiles in preparation of war to have the weapon in being. Other than those employed for target practice by the tactical units, the missiles will remain in storage for an undetermined period. However, they must be ready, with a minimum of delay, for tactical use. This will necessitate continued maintenance to insure the readiness of the missiles.

These missiles which are required by the tactical units of the Fleet will be transported by supply ships and transferred to the tactical units wherever they might be. This portion of the distribution problem is also indicated in Fig. 15-6. No additional maintenance is required until the missiles are aboard the tactical ships.

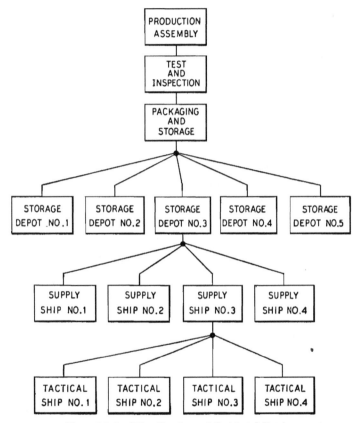

Fig. 15-6 Distribution of Guided Missiles.

In time of war or in the event that the threat of war is increased the missiles may be shipped to advanced bases in the critical operational areas for storage. Maintenance facilities may also be provided at the advance base depot, so that a minimum of effort is needed in the Fleet prior to tactical use.

15-5 MAINTENANCE OF SHIPBORNE GUIDANCE EQUIPMENT

The tactical unit requires a group of trained personnel to man the guided missile system. A portion of this group is also charged with the responsibility of maintaining the equipment aboard ship. The cost of training, feeding, and quartering the personnel required by reason of the guided missile system is chargeable to the annual cost of maintaining the weapon in readiness.

15-6 MAINTENANCE OF MISSILE-BORNE GUIDANCE EQUIPMENT

Maintenance of the missile-borne guidance equipment is necessary during the period of depot storage and when the missiles are aboard ship in ready condition for firing. In each case both personnel and test equipment will be required. The cost of the special maintenance personnel and test equipment must be charged in considering the annual cost of maintaining the weapon systems in readiness.

15-7 GUIDED MISSILE SYSTEM COSTS

The initial cost of developing, producing, and distributing a guided missile system for use in the Fleet may be equated as

$$C_0 = C_r + C_f + N_m C_m + N_s C_s + N_m C_{dm} + N_s C_{ds} \qquad (15\text{-}1)$$

where
C_0 = the total initial cost
C_r = the cost of research and development
C_f = the cost of the production facility
C_m = the cost per missile
C_s = the cost of shipborne equipment and installing in tactical ship
C_{dm} = the cost of distributing and storing the missiles per missile
C_{ds} = the cost of distributing and storing the shipborne equipment per system
N_m = the number of missiles produced
N_s = the number of systems manufactured

The cost of the research and development of the guided missile system, C_r, is made up from two principal items, the contractual cost of the development and the cost of the services supplied by the government in the form of test facilities, administration, and so forth.

The cost of the government-owned production facility, C_f, is comprised principally of the cost of the land, the plant buildings, housing, and machine tools.

The cost per missile, C_m, depends largely upon the production rate, as discussed in detail previously, and is composed principally of the contributing costs of the airframe, propulsion, warhead, fuel, guidance equipment, spares, and packaging.

The cost of the shipborne components, C_s, is the summation of the costs of the components and spares plus the cost of installation. In the cost of installation should be included the cost of keeping the ship out of active duty while the work is being performed, if the time required is in addition to standard overhaul requirements.

The cost of distribution and storage of the missiles, C_{dm}, is dependent upon transportation costs and the cost of any storage facilities which may have to be constructed specially for this purpose.

The cost of distribution and storage of the shipborne components, C_{ds}, is principally the cost of transportation to the site of the installation.

There are many other detailed costs in the overall initial cost of a guided missile system, but the foregoing discussion and equation cover the principal ones.

The yearly cost of supporting a guided missile system in being may be equated as

$$C_y = \frac{C_r}{a_1} + \frac{C_f}{a_2} + \frac{N_m(C_m + C_{dm})}{a_3} + \frac{N_s(C_s + C_{ds})}{a_4} + N_p C_p \quad (15\text{-}2)$$

where C_y = annual cost of maintaining the system in readiness
N_p = number of personnel required for maintenance of equipment
C_p = average cost per year per man of maintenance personnel
a_1 = amortization period of research and development costs
a_2 = amortization period of production facility costs
a_3 = amortization period of missile costs
a_4 = amortization period of shipborne equipment cost

All other notation is the same as that for Eq. (15-1). If the same period of amortization is used for all of the cost-contributing elements, the annual cost becomes:

$$C_y = C_0/a + N_p C_p \quad (15\text{-}3)$$

We may make a few assumptions in order to indicate the comparative cost between the various phases of a guided missile program. The figures chosen are not to be considered indicative of actual costs, since these will vary greatly between missile types and operational requirements, but will serve as an index of the possible magnitude of such a program.

In this hypothetical case, it is obvious that the cost of the research and development of the missile system is small relative to the missile system production costs. The system should be fully tested before production is initiated. Changes after production has started are extremely costly as compared to the same changes during the development work. It is equally obvious that the initial cost of a guided missile program, and the missile guidance program pertaining thereto, may be of sufficient magnitude as to have a significant effect upon the national economy.

Cost of research and development, C_r.	$ 20,000,000
Cost of production facility, C_f.	40,000,000
Number of tactical units equipped, $N_s = 50$	
Cost of shipborne equipment per tactical unit, $C_s = \$5,000,000$	
Total cost of shipborne equipment, $N_s C_s$	250,000,000
If it be assumed that 150 missiles per tactical unit will both satisfy the requirements of practice and keep the tactical units fully prepared for war, the total number of missiles, N_m, is then 7500	
Cost of per missile, $C_m = \$20,000$	
Total cost of missiles, $N_m C_m$	150,000,000
Cost per missile for distribution and storage facilities, $C_{dm} = \$200$	
Total cost of missile distribution, $N_m C_{dm}$	1,500,000
Cost per unit of shipborne equipment for distribution, $C_{ds} = \$500$	
Total cost of shipborne equipment distribution, $N_s C_{ds}$	25,000
Initial cost of guided missile program	$461,525,000
If we assume that the cost of the guidance equipment is approximately one-quarter of the total cost of the guided missile program, then the total cost for the guidance equipment only is	$115,381,250

15-8 ENVIRONMENTAL SPECIFICATIONS

It is the purpose of environmental specifications to define the most adverse conditions under which military equipment must operate. By so doing, they define many parameters of the design. The accuracy of estimating the adverse conditions and specifying the tests which clearly illustrate the ability of the equipment to operate under the adverse conditions constitute the greatest insurance of the reliability of service equipment. Entirely aside from the economic aspects, there is no greater weakener of morale in time of battle than an unreliable weapon.

The military services are best able to specify the adverse conditions to be met in the operational theaters in which the guided missile system will be used. Such conditions include the extremes of atmospheric pressure, temperature, and humidity; the shocks and vibrations of battle action, field handling, and transport; and the period and conditions of storage between manufacture and use. These general specifications are imposed upon all components of the guided missile system.

The environmental conditions within the missile itself are peculiar to the specific design and use of the missile. In order to develop the environmental specifications for missile-borne equipment, it is necessary to perform flight tests that will show the most adverse conditions probable. The instrumentation must indicate the shocks and vibrations to which the equipment will be subjected at the actual location of the equipment (see Chap. 9). The flights made to obtain these data must be of such character that any probable adverse conditions may be developed for all flight phases. The test information must be augmented by calculations to show the probable maximum accelerations under operational use. When sufficient data, both by test and computation, are available, specifications may be written. A suitable safety factor must be included in order to be sure that there will be adequate insurance against production tolerances. In addition, the specification should indicate the tests which shall be performed on components, subassemblies, and assemblies in order to prove the equipment that will be accepted by the military. If the missile test flights of the guidance equipment indicate continued failure of components (and the exact component failure is frequently difficult to ascertain), then the safety factor in the design must be increased and the tests of the equipment made more stringent before any production of the guidance equipment may be undertaken.

15-9 EQUIPMENT ENVIRONMENTAL RESEARCH

This field of research and testing is coming into greater prominence with the development of guided missiles and other complex automatic systems. When a human is in charge of the operation of complex equipment, he usually observes danger signs before the point of maximum stress is reached and, by anticipatory action, prevents the prolonged existence of an adverse condition likely to cause failure. In a complex automatic device, such as a missile, the point of destruction may be reached in response to transient demands without any attempt of the system to correct or compensate for them. When a failure occurs in missile flight, the cause of failure is frequently unknown and exact remedial measures to the design are impossible to apply. Instead of determining the exact point of failure (which may be a minor one) and correcting it, because of the uncertainty an entire assembly may be "beefed up" at considerable cost.

It is virtually impossible to design, by rigorous calculation, for the effects of shock and vibration on complex electronic and mechanical equipment. The difficulty is primarily due to the fact that these applied accelerations are seldom found in a pure or steady state and there are so many components of different types. Shocks, which are pulses of acceleration, vary widely both in amplitude and pulse shape. Vibrations imposed on the equipment vary both in magnitude and frequency. These adverse conditions change from flight to flight and between the various phases of missile handling, launching, and flight. Research in the field of shock and vibration, then, is essentially an empirical study, statistical in character.

The engineer charged with the responsibility of shepherding the guidance equipment through the environment design phase is presented with the following: General environmental specifications from the military, data from tests indicating the missile's internal environmental conditions, the safety factor required, information on military equipment standards, and one or more operating samples of the equipment. Tests are made, starting with adverse conditions well below those which will be met in use. The conditions are increased in severity until a failure occurs. The cause of the failure is corrected and the tests continue with increasing severity, developing failures and correcting them, until the equipment satisfies the environmental conditions with an adequate safety factor. The equipment is maintained in operation during the tests. The final tests frequently are more severe than called for in the specifications, for the express purpose of indicating probable points of weakness in the equipment. An engineer, competent in this field, can usually make corrective "fixes" by surprisingly small changes in the equipment.

Since the changes may be small to correct failures, it follows that small changes in the design of equipment that has successfully passed the environmental requirements can cause new sources of difficulty. For this reason, the shock and vibration tests continue throughout the duration of the development program. Whenever a change occurs, particularly in the change between prototype and production models of equipment, these tests must be carefully repeated.

The equipment required for an environmental testing laboratory is frequently sufficiently specialized that it must be designed for the specific missile and guidance system components undergoing investigation. The test equipment usually includes hot and cold rooms where the atmospheric conditions may be made to simulate the extremes specified by the military as to pressure, temperature, and humidity. Shock and vibration equipment may include shock test equipment of both the drop and hammer types, vibration tables capable of applying the large range of frequencies and amplitude required, and centrifuges for applying accelerations.

15-10 ENVIRONMENTAL ACCEPTANCE TESTS

Research work in the environmental field is sometimes confused with the environmental tests required as a necessary prior condition to acceptance of the equipment by the military. The equipment environmental research must be done by the contractor, at his instance, to develop his design to the point where it will reliably meet or surpass the requirements of the environmental specifications. Environmental acceptance tests are those tests performed by the contractor at the instance of the military in order to prove that the equipment does meet the specifications. The research work constitutes a design tool; the acceptances tests prove the design correctness.

Acceptance tests in the environmental realm are developed from the environmental specifications. Care must be exercised to be sure that the tests do accomplish this purpose completely. The environmental tests constitute the greatest single safeguard to assure reliability of the equipment in tactical use.

15-11 RELIABILITY

Reliability was earlier defined as the probability that a guided missile or its system components will not fail and thus cause failure of its mission. A guided missile is composed of several hundred components, the correct operation of each being essential to a successful flight. The guided missile system, including the missile and its components, consists of perhaps more than a thousand components; the correct operation of each may be essential to success of the missile flight. The missile guidance system encompasses the majority of the components which must operate without fail if the missile is to accomplish its mission. In addition to the components themselves, there are many thousands of soldered connections within the missile guidance system which are essential to the integrity of system operation.

The overall reliability (or probability of successful operation) of the guidance system is equal to the product of the reliabilities of each of the vital components. This may be equated as

$$p = p_1 \cdot p_2 \cdot p_3 \cdot p_4 \cdots p_n \qquad (15\text{-}4)$$

where p = the overall probable reliability
p_1, etc., = the probable reliabilities of the individual components

Let us assume that each of the components of a missile guidance system has an equal reliability. For convenience, let us assume that a hypothetical missile guidance system has five hundred components, each of which must operate correctly in order to obtain a successful missile flight. If a reliability of 99.5 percent were assigned to each component, then the overall reliability is 0.995^{500}, or 8.13 percent. A reliability of 99.5 percent (or a failure rate of 1 in 200 components) is considered excellent by most commercial standards. However, a guided missile system may be required to have a reliability of 90 percent. The missile guidance system may be required to have a reliability of 95 percent, or even greater (see Chap. 8), in order that the guided missile system may meet its requirements. For this reason the reliability of 99.5 percent for each component, as given in the previous example, is unsatisfactory for missile guidance use.

On the basis that the guidance system reliability shall be 95 percent, with 500 components of equal reliability, the reliability of each must be $\sqrt[500]{0.95}$, or 99.99 percent. The rate of permissible component failure is 1 for each 10,000 components. Special quality control and inspection are required to obtain component reliability as great as this.

Figure 15-7 shows the relationship between the reliability of a missile guidance system and the average reliability of its components. These curves are based upon one adverse condition that might cause failure. If more than one such condition arises during the flight of the missile, then the probability of success is diminished accordingly.

Reliability of missile guidance equipment is an extremely important economic factor. Let us take an extreme, but completely possible, example to illustrate how important. A surface-to-air guided missile system is developed, produced, and put into service. A tactical unit comprising personnel, equipment, and living facilities is put into being as a special unit to employ the weapon. The personnel are trained, paid, fed, and quartered for a period of years for one purpose only—to use the weapon in battle when the enemy is sighted. The enemy appears, the missile is fired, but a failure occurs. The lack of reliability has cost many hundreds of thousands of dollars and years of time. When a missile fails, the cost

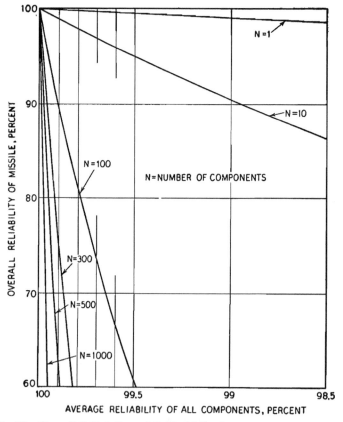

FIG. 15-7 The Overall Reliability of Guided Missiles as a Function of the Average Reliability of Their Components for a Single Adverse Condition.

is not just that of the missile alone but a proportionate share of the entire cost of the missile program, the training and cost of operating personnel, and the tactical installation. Wars may have a long duration, but the use of any weapon in battle by a single tactical unit is usually confined to an extremely short time, sometimes only a matter of minutes. The weapon *must* be reliable when that time comes.

The following are some of the considerations, which may assist to insure reliability in the tactical use of a guided missile system:

a. *Choice of guidance method.* The environmental and adverse conditions to which the portions of the guidance equipment external to the missile may be subjected are much less severe than the environmental and adverse conditions of missile-borne guidance equipment. Therefore, a guidance method that minimizes the amount of equipment located in the missile should, all other factors being equal, tend to be a more reliable method than one which employs a greater portion of the guidance system components in the missile.

b. *System simplicity.* As shown in Fig. 15-7, the fewer components there are in a given system, the less critical is the reliability of each component. It follows that, for two systems, each having components of the same average reliability, the system with the fewest number of components should have the higher reliability, all other factors being equal. There are other advantages to simplicity in addition to that of increased reliability. Training of both maintenance and using personnel is made easier; the costs of equipment and spares is reduced. The concept of using the most simple system and circuitry, consistent with the objectives, should always be maintained in design.

c. *Environmental specifications.* Environmental specifications should be based upon statistical tests augmented by such computations as may be required, to present a thoroughly realistic documentation of the probable maximum adverse conditions likely to be encountered in use.

d. *Design.* The responsibility for reliability or lack of it lies chiefly within the area of design of missile guidance systems:

(1) Adequate safety factors must be employed to take into account production tolerances on components and some deterioration in the use given the equipment by the military as compared to that accorded the equipment when in the hands of company engineers. (2) The specifications for the components must include tolerances which are compatible with reliability requirements. (3) The choice of circuit design must be such that the components employed will be reliable not only on the bench, but in rigorous field use. (4) Lastly, environmental research should be used intensely as a design tool.

e. *New techniques.* New techniques both of design and of production should be explored and employed if it can be irrefutably demonstrated by statistical tests that use of the techniques will improve reliability, consistent with high performance. Transistors and printed circuits, while not particularly new, are indicative of the type of developments which, when applicable, may improve reliability. The Navy-sponsored project Tinkertoy[1] of the National Bureau of Standards is a technique for automatic production and inspection of electronic components and circuits. Starting from raw or semiprocessed materials, machines automatically manufacture ceramic materials and adhesive carbon resistors, print conducting circuits, and mount resistors, capacitors, and other miniaturized component parts on standard, uniform steatite wafers. The wafers are stacked very much like building blocks to form a module that performs all of the functions of one or more electronic stages. The complete module is a standardized, interchangeable subassembly combining all of the requirements of an electronic circuit with ruggedness, reliability, and extreme compactness. Each module, in general, consists of some 4 to 6 thin ceramic wafers, bearing various circuits associated with an electronic stage. A number of individual modules are combined to form a major subassembly. The composition of modules into major subassemblies of electronic equipment is possible because there is great similarity between circuits and parts of circuits in modern electronic equipment. During each stage in the mechanized production of electronics, provision is made for completely automatic inspection. This is both a physical gaging and an electrical comparison. Printed circuits, resistors, and capacitors are compared with their electronic equivalents both before and after assembly. This is accomplished by use of electronic computers, bridge circuits, and other comparison devices. After the final assembly of the module the whole circuit is again tested to see that it meets specifications within set tolerances.

f. *Production.* Production purchases must adhere rigorously to the specifications, particularly with regard to tolerances and selection processes. Quality control must be instituted and carefully employed in all phases of the assembly and manufacture.

g. *Acceptance tests.* The acceptance tests are developed from the environmental tests and other sources. The tests should be carefully analyzed to be sure they will disclose properly the factors they are supposed to indicate.

h. *Prelaunching checks.* The checks made immediately prior to launching represent the last possible time to be sure that the equipment is operating satisfactorily. The checks must be simple, yet they must be effective. If they fail to indicate the unsatisfactory operation of a component, the missile will be listed statistically as an operational failure when it actually may be a failure attributable to maintenance.

[1] *Summary Technical Report 1824-A*, National Bureau of Standards, Washington, D. C., dated September 1953.

CHAPTER 16

MISSILE GUIDANCE SYSTEMS

Symbols Used in Chapter 16

A = Area of radar antenna
A_1 = Antilog$_{10}$ (propagation power losses in db)/10
G = Gain of the radar antenna
G_r = Gain of missile receiving antenna
G_t = Gain of transmitting antenna
H_1 = Altitude of one station (receiver or transmitter) in feet
H = Altitude of second station in feet
K = Constant of proportionality
P_a = Transmitted power for the active system
P_r = Power received in watts at the receiver input
P_{r1} = Required receiver sensitivity in watts for satisfactory overall operation
P_S = Transmitted power for the semiactive system

P_t = Peak transmitted power
P_{t1} = Required transmitter power output in watts
P_{min} = Minimum power required for detection
R = Range in nautical miles
R_a = Reliable all-the-way tracking range of the active system
R_r = Range from missile receiver to target
R_S = Reliable all-the-way tracking range of the semiactive system
R_t = Range from transmitter to target
R_{max} = Maximum radar range
λ = Wavelength
σ = Effective radar area of the target

In the previous chapters of this text we have shown that missile guidance systems involve the propagation and transmission of energy containing or communicating intelligence for guidance use; that guidance intelligence may be obtained from terrestrial and celestial references; and that the guidance and control of a missile constitute basically a servomechanism system problem. The manner by which the guidance intelligence may be detected and employed has been indicated. The principles and considerations the guidance system designer must utilize in the major areas of design have been discussed. Where pertinent, the elements which are involved in the system design have been mathematically treated in the frequency domain.

There has been no attempt made to illustrate the detailed design or circuitry of specific components. There are many texts available in the special fields of interest for isolated component design. The system concept—the outlining parameters of the component and its contribution to the system—has herein been kept paramount.

This chapter will illustrate and define the missile guidance systems which result from different combinations of components. These systems must be regarded only as illustrative of commonly considered combinations. There is an almost endless number of possible combinations. The systems will be detailed in block diagrams with sufficient information to illustrate the contributions of the separate components to the system as a whole. The control and guidance loops involved will be considered. Each system will be examined superficially in the light of the considerations of the foregoing chapters. Each guidance method will be considered in the light of its possible application to the four general categories of guided missiles.

16-1 SYSTEM DESIGN CONSIDERATIONS

The basic design considerations for a missile guidance system are these: that the system be stable, accurate, and reliable under both the steady-state and the dynamic conditions imposed by the tactical environment. The system concept is the consideration of each functional component of the system as a contributing and reacting element of the over-all system. Proper component design must consider the system stability, accuracy and reliability needs. System stability, accuracy, and reliability requirements have been treated in prior chapters of this text.

In system design the steady-state conditions are usually considered first. As an example, in an air-to-air system, the equations that a computer must solve will be determined mathematically, and means for mechanizing these equations will be explored. A steady-state solution of these equations alone is, however, not sufficient. The computer must also solve the equations within the specified accuracy when all of the inputs are undergoing change. The parent aircraft may be in accelerating motion; simultaneously the target aircraft may also be manuevering. The system components which deliver input functions to the computer (such as range, angular measurements, and derivatives of the same) may be generating not only correct and rapidly changing inputs, but also extraneous noise contributions. A computer which can correctly solve the equations using steady-state inputs is not suitable unless it is also capable of their solution under the dynamic conditions of tactical use.

Examination of the tactical conditions will frequently contribute to gainful compromises of the steady-state design. To continue the same example, by examining the character of the inputs to the computer it may be determined that the quality of the inputs is the determining factor in the system accuracy. The computer may then be redesigned so that it solves simplified approximations instead of the rigorous mathematical equations initially employed. In such a case, the result is a system that is simpler, lighter, and more reliable without sacrifice of over-all system accuracy.

16-2 HOMING GUIDANCE SYSTEMS

A *homing guidance system* may be defined as a guidance system by which a missile steers itself toward a target by means of a self-contained mechanism which is activated by some distinguishing characteristic of the target.[1] The homing guidance systems fall under one of the three general types: active homing, semiactive homing, and passive homing. There are possible permutations and combinations of the three basic types, depending upon intended application. The basic homing types also may be employed in conjunction with other guidance techniques. For example,

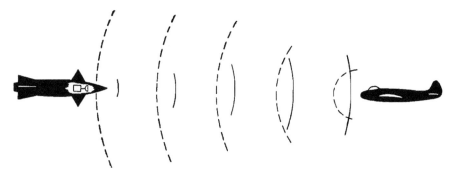

FIG. 16-1 Active Homing Guidance.

the control of a missile may involve several guidance phases each using a different guidance technique. Some of the possible combinations of guidance techniques are illustrated in this chapter under Par. 16-8.

An *active homing guidance system* is one in which both the source of energy to illuminate the target and the receiver of the energy reflected from the target are carried in the missile. Such a system is illustrated by Fig. 16-1.

The active homing guidance system, in its simplest form, consists of a transmitter and receiver of energy, which enable the missile to detect the presence of the target, a computer which predicts from the received energy the future position of the target, and missile control surfaces which respond

---

[1] *Glossary of Guided Missile Terms*, prepared by the Committee on Guided Missiles, 20 September 1949, p. 50.

to computed signals in such a fashion as to direct the missile to impact with the target. The energy used to illuminate the target may be in the form of radio, light, heat, or sound waves. A missile which uses active homing guidance is completely independent once homing starts; the missile does not require energy transmitted from an external source or externally derived guidance intelligence.

A *semiactive homing guidance* system is one wherein the receiver in the missile receives energy reflected from the target, the energy having been transmitted from a point external to the missile. This method of homing guidance is illustrated by Fig. 16-2. The semiactive homing guidance

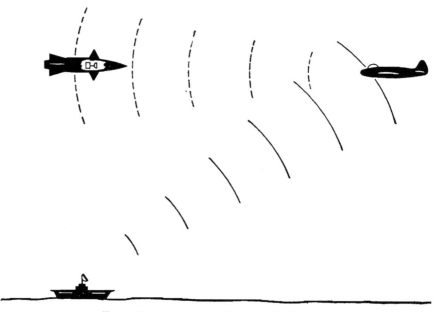

Fig. 16-2 Semiactive Homing Guidance.

system consists of a receiver in the missile which detects the presence of the target, a computer (also in the missile) which predicts from the received energy the future position of the target, missile control surfaces which direct the missile along the correct flight path for impact with the target, and an externally located transmitter which illuminates the target. This external transmitter may be located at the missile launching station, or at a point separated from the missile launching station. The transmitter may be a surface installation, as illustrated by Fig. 16-2, or it may be airborne. As in the case of active homing guidance, the transmitted energy may be in the form of radio, light, heat, or sound waves. The principal difference in the basic operation of an active and a semiactive guidance system is that the semiactive system is not independent of external sources. Its guidance intelligence is derived from energy transmitted from a point external to the missile. The reasons governing a choice between the two techniques will become apparent later in the chapter.

A modified version of this semiactive technique has the transmitter located in the missile and the receiver of the reflected energy at some remote point. Computation of the desired flight path takes place at a remote point and suitable commands are sent to the missile. This system is known as a *quasi-active homing guidance* system. Since the technique is analogous for both cases, the quasi-active guidance system will not be considered separately.

A *passive homing guidance* system is a guidance system wherein the receiver in the missile utilizes energy emanating from the target. A passive homing system is illustrated by Fig. 16-3. The basic difference between the passive homing technique and the two preceding techniques

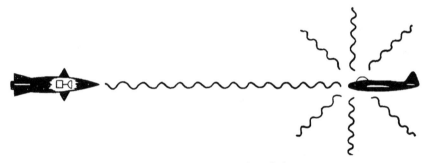

Fig. 16-3 Passive Homing Guidance.

is that energy from which the guidance intelligence is derived in the passive homing system is generated in the target; thus no other transmitter is required. In this system, the receiver, computer, and missile control surfaces serve the same functions as described for the previous systems. The energy emanating from the target may be in the form of heat, light, sound, or radio waves.

It is now of interest to investigate specific system considerations and applications of these three basic homing guidance techniques.

General Homing Guidance System. Before investigating specific guidance techniques, it is useful to analyze the basic essentials required to make any homing guidance system perform satisfactorily. A block diagram of a general homing guidance system is illustrated by Fig. 16-4. Basically, all homing guidance systems are alike. Information about target and missile positions and motions is collected within the missile and from this information the desired flight path of the missile is generated.

For this example, consider that the sensing device illustrated in Fig. 16-4 is a radar dish which is tracking the target. The dish angle in space is fed into a homing computer. Depending upon the type of computer employed, either angle or angular rate information may be used. This information may be obtained by measuring the dish position or changes in dish position or utilizing the output of the radar receiver. The tracking angle information is operated upon in the homing computer in such a fashion as to generate the flight path orders. The computational operations will vary for different missile systems, depending upon the desired flight path trajectory and the tactical use of the missile.

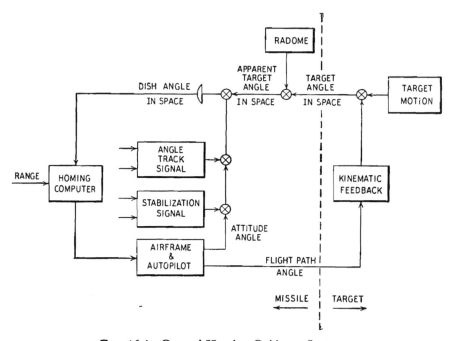

FIG. 16-4 General Homing Guidance System.

Outputs from the homing computer are fed into the autopilot as signals to control the angle of the flight path vector of the missile. When the missile changes heading in response to the autopilot output, the antenna must also be made to turn an equal and opposite angle so that it continues pointing at the target despite the motion of the missile. A change in missile heading may also occur from external disturbances, such as air currents or gusts. The correction of the sensing device for missile heading changes is known as *stabilization*. The stabilization information may be obtained from the antenna (e.g., measuring dish position in space coordinates) or from measurement of airframe attitude changes (autopilot rate-gyro). The stabilization signal is compared with the attitude angle. The difference is compared with the angle track signal. (It is assumed that the missile is roll-stabilized. If it is not, correction for roll must be introduced into the system.) Thus, regardless of missile maneuvers, either intentional or unintentional, the antenna continues to point at the target.

The kinematic feedback term represents changes in the missile-target space relationship as they affect the line-of-sight from missile to the target. This signal is compared with the target motion to give the target angle in space. Two channels similar to the one described above are necessary—one for pitch and one for yaw.

In many of the missile homing guidance systems it is necessary to provide a housing for the energy-collecting device. This housing is usually referred to as a *radome* when radio energy is employed or as an *irdome* when infrared energy is used. The effects of the radome on the transmission of energy are discussed in Chap. 4. The radome may introduce an erroneous signal to the missile system in the process of energy transmission. Such an error, as may be seen from examination of Fig. 16-4, might cause a shift of the apparent target angle in space. In a fast-moving vehicle, such as a missile, it is necessary to streamline the radome (see Fig. 4-17b). The shift of the target angle in space will vary and will depend upon the angle of the line-of-sight of the collecting device (antenna) with respect to the radome axis of symmetry in both azimuth and elevation. Any error contributed by the radome to the missile system is usually referred to as *boresight slope* (slope of a plot of degrees shift of target angle versus antenna angle). The effect is to cause the observed rate of rotation of the line-of-sight to the target to be different from the true rate. If the error is in the positive sense, the gain of the control loop will increase and, if it is negative, the gain will decrease. The radome must be designed with a boresight slope which can be tolerated by the system.

Additional refinements are necessary. For example, because of interference and other phenomena there may be periods of *target fade* (decrease or loss of signal). The tracking loop should include circuitry which will cause the radar to continue tracking at the same rate during these periods of fade. This "flywheel" characteristic is called *memory*.

The nature of all inputs to the guidance system and its many internal loops must be analyzed. As in conventional amplifier design, it is desirable to minimize the bandwidths of each loop, consistent with the use and the accuracy requirements thereof, to minimize the effects of noise on the system. Chapters 17 and 18 are illustrative of the bandwidth studies required.

Choice of Electromagnetic Frequency for Homing Guidance Systems. Frequencies from radio to ultraviolet might conceivably be used for homing guidance systems. Let us consider the transmission of such frequencies through the atmosphere. Figure 5-12 (Chap. 5) indicates that the attenuation is high in the ultraviolet region (wavelength less than 0.4 micron). There are available windows both in the infrared and optical wavelength regions. Figure 4-13 (Chap. 4) shows the attenuation of radio frequencies transmitted through the atmosphere and indicates wide bands of usable frequencies. It is obvious from this information that frequencies in the infrared and in the visible light, as well as commonly used radio frequencies, may be employed as intelligence carriers for guidance systems.

In addition to the transmission characteristics for a particular wavelength the problem of background noise must be considered. If the background of the target is such that it independently emits or returns energy in the band of frequencies being considered, the target may be indistinguishable from the background and no information of value about the target may be obtained.

Since homing systems are contained within the missile, available space for the equipment is always critical. Weight must be maintained at a minimum. As a general rule, space and weight requirements for an information-gathering system tend to be a direct function of the wavelength employed. This would indicate that high radio frequencies or available frequencies in the infrared and optical regions are to be desired for missile-borne equipment.

When the missile designer chooses the type of electromagnetic energy to be employed in the homing guidance system, he must consider system complexity. For example, in those systems which act both as a transmitter and receiver of the electromagnetic energy (i.e., active and semiactive systems), the transmitter may be extremely complex for one type of electromagnetic energy and relatively simple for another type.

Basic Radar Types Used in Homing Guidance Systems. The theory of design of radars employing velocity measuring techniques (Doppler) and for those employing range measuring techniques is discussed in Chap. 10. In those missile guidance systems which employ radar for detection of the presence of a target, the selection of the type of radar to be used will be dependent upon the tactical situation in which the missile is to be employed. Some of the factors involved in this selection are number and spacing of targets, target behavior, contrast, noise and attitude, and equipment size and complexity.

Equipment size and complexity may often dictate the type of radar used in the homing guidance system. For example, the C-W radar has the inherent problem of keeping out of the receiver the transmitted energy except for that reflected from the target. Because of the nature of the technique, the receiver and the transmitter must be on at the same time. This means that the transmitting and receiving antennas must be physically or electrically separated. The ideal C-W system is one wherein the transmitting and receiving antennas are separated physically by a great enough distance that coupling between them is no longer a problem. In active missile guidance systems it may be impossible to obtain great enough physical separation of the two antennas. Electrical separation can be used, but the resulting equipment is more complex than that of an equivalent pulse system. Another problem in the C-W active system is the reflection from the radome. Since the receiver is open at all times and since the reflected energy from the radome is much greater than the reflected energy from the target, a major interference problem results. These two examples suggest that for the *active* homing guidance system, the use of a pulse type radar may be more desirable.

There are many considerations involved in determining the type of radar most suitable for a specific missile application. For a given situation, one type of radar may have both advantages and disadvantages, as compared with the other. Throughout the remainder of this chapter, for purpose of convenience only, it will be assumed that all missile systems using radar employ a pulse type radar.

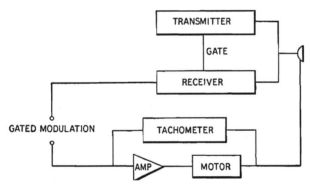

Fig. 16-5 Tracking Loop of an Active Homing System.

Active Homing Guidance. The basic block diagram for a missile homing guidance system applies equally to the three general types of homing guidance. The following sections will be devoted to a description of the fundamental differences between the homing guidance methods. The basic difference between the homing types lies in the tracking loop. Figure 16-5 is a block diagram for the tracking loop of an active system. This loop consists of a transmitter and receiver, a beam-forming and -collecting device such as a radar antenna, and a drive unit which keeps the collecting device continually pointed at the target. The illuminating energy originates in the missile. The received energy will contain extraneous information such as ground clutter and targets in the area other than the target of interest. A gate is generated in the system which eliminates all returned signals except those lying within the gate. The target of interest is *gated*, i.e., kept within that gate. The azimuth and elevation error signals for driving the tracking servomechanisms are then derived from the gated signal.

The gating or target lock-on process in the missile may be made to occur in many different ways. For example, in an air-to-air active system using a radar, the antenna may be slaved to that of an external radar located in the launching airplane. The range gate in the missile radar will then automatically search until the target toward which the antenna has been directed is gated. To ensure that the missile radar has selected the correct target, the gated signal can be compared with that of the aircraft's radar. Once the target is gated, the necessary target tracking information is derived within the missile.

A severe problem which confronts the designer of any active homing guidance system is available space for the guidance system in the missile. This is especially true in an active air-to-air system where the missile must be small in size. The importance of this problem can be shown by a manipulation of the standard radar range equation as follows:

$$R_{max} = \left(\frac{P_t G^2 \sigma \lambda^2}{64\pi^3 P_{min}}\right)^{\frac{1}{4}} \qquad (16\text{-}1)$$

where R_{max} = maximum radar range
P_t = peak transmitted power
σ = effective radar area of the target
G = gain of the radar antenna
λ = wavelength
P_{min} = minimum power required for detection

The gain of the radar antenna is

$$G = K\frac{A}{\lambda^2} \qquad (16\text{-}2)$$

where K = constant of proportionality
A = area of radar antenna

Thus

$$R_{max} = \left(\frac{P_t A^2 \sigma K^2}{64\pi^3 P_{min}\lambda^2}\right)^{\frac{1}{4}} \qquad (16\text{-}3)$$

For a given wavelength λ and target size σ, the maximum range is a function of the minimum power required for detection, the area of the radar antenna, and the transmitted power. The minimum power required for detection is a function of the receiver noise. Reduction in receiver noise is limited by noise generated in the input circuits of the receiver. In a missile, space and weight are very important factors in homing guidance systems design. A limit is soon reached on the size of antenna that can be used. Increasing the power output results in larger and heavier equipment; thus a practical limit is soon reached. In addition, it is necessary to increase the transmitted peak power sixteen times to double the maximum range. For these reasons, it is obvious that active radar missile guidance systems will be comparatively short-range devices.

Tactical Application of the Air-to-Air Active Homing Guidance System. The preceding section has described the general manner in which an active homing guidance system functions. It is of interest to investigate the use of active homing guidance systems in each of the four basic missile categories. The first to be considered is the air-to-air missile. The missile will be launched from an aircraft, either interceptor or bomber, against a target which may be an aircraft or another missile. (Throughout the remainder of the discussion on homing guidance the parent aircraft will be called an interceptor). Once the missile guidance system has obtained a target lock-on, the missile system is capable of independently generating a fire control solution. Thus, as soon as the missile is launched, the interceptor is free to break contact with the target under attack.

Figure 16-6 illustrates one possible application of the active homing guidance technique in the air-to-air missile field. The interceptor, having launched the missile which is actively homing on the bomber target, is breaking away. Prior to launch, a sequence of events must take place.

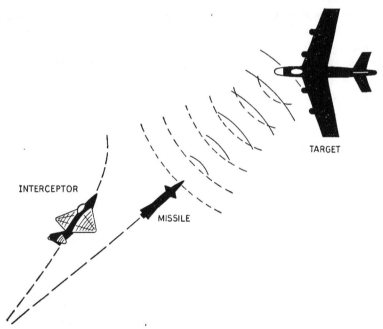

Fig. 16-6 Air-to-Air Application of the Active Homing Technique.

Theoretically, the target detection and lock-on process could occur in several different ways: (a) *Missile Radar:* The active air-to-air missile system may operate independently. The missile radar will automatically search for and lock-on the target. The missile radar information can be presented on a scope to the pilot who will determine if the correct target has been selected. (b) *Optical:* A second detection and lock-on process for the active air-to-air missile guidance system is one wherein all targets are first detected optically by the pilot. The missile radar antenna will be controlled by or slaved to an optical sight. The gate in the missile radar will automatically search until a target is gated. The pilot will determine if the homing system has selected the correct target. (c) *Interceptor Radar:* The active homing guidance system may be used in conjunction with an external radar. The interceptor will be able to carry a bigger radar, both in terms of antenna size and transmitted power, than could be housed in the missile. Thus the interceptor's own radar will have a much greater range capability than the missile radar. A visual system will not have as large a range capability as the system which operates in conjunction with the external radar. In addition, a visual system is handicapped by foul weather or night operating conditions.

To further the discussion of the air-to-air missile application of active homing guidance, we will assume that the interceptor pilot will use the aircraft's fire control system for detecting and tracking the target and for computing a fire control solution. The pilot will then fly the interceptor to the correct heading for missile launching. The required accuracy of interceptor heading at the time the missile is launched will be determined by the physical limitations of the missile (maximum rate of turn, launching error due to boresight misalignment and expected dispersion, beamwidth of the missile radar, and angle through which the missile radar antenna is free to turn). The pilot must then fly the interceptor until the missile radar acquires, or has a high probability of acquiring, the target. The pilot then launches the missile, after which time he is free to break away or launch another missile.

The traffic-handling capacity of the active air-to-air homing guidance system is limited only by the number of missiles carried by the interceptor aircraft and the time available for launching the missiles. For example, it is theoretically possible for the interceptor aircraft to launch more than one missile against the same target. In addition it is possible for the interceptor aircraft to launch one missile against a target, break away, and launch another missile against a different target.

It is apparent that the number of targets which can be engaged or the number of missiles which can be launched against a single target is dependent upon the time required for detection, lock-on, and a computer solution for the interceptor radar, the time required to detect and lock-on with the missile radar, and the time required to launch the missile. The steps in this attack procedure require time and should be kept to a minimum.

The number of attacks which can be made is dependent upon the number of missiles which can be carried by the interceptor aircraft. This number is determined by aerodynamic factors such as drag on the interceptor, weight, and space. Not only is the number of missiles which can be launched against a given target limited by the number which can be carried by the interceptor aircraft and by launching complexity, but it may also be limited by radar interference. This radar interference may be the result of mutual interference between the missile radars or interference between missile radars and the interceptor aircraft radar. This interference problem may be relieved by operating the missile radars at slightly different frequencies.

The conditions of the tactical situation (target and interceptor aircraft speeds, altitudes, and approach aspects) will play a predominant role in determining the number of attacks which can be made against the same or different targets. It is necessary that information be available to the interceptor concerning target position and behavior in time to allow the interceptor to engage the enemy before the enemy completes his mission.

It is apparent that because of the space and load limitations on the interceptor aircraft the missile must be small in size and light in weight. In general, the air-to-air missile which employs an active guidance system will be a comparatively short-range system. For this reason the designer should carefully examine the expected tactical situation to determine the possible effective launching zones about the given target in which the missile can be utilized and provide means for getting the missile out to this useful launching area (see *Operations Research* section of this series of volumes).

The air-to-air missile may be carried in pods mounted under the wings of the interceptor aircraft or within the fuselage (when the interceptor aircraft is a bomber). If the missile be carried externally on a launching rack, the designer must insure that provisions are made to maintain the required operating temperature of the missile regardless of ambient temperature.

Tactical Application of the Air-to-Surface Active Homing Guidance System. Figure 16-7 illustrates a typical air-to-surface missile employing active homing guidance. In the example shown, the missile, which is launched from an interceptor aircraft, is actively homing on a ship. Actually, the target may vary from something as large as a city to something as small as a bridge or dam.

The steps in the attack phase would be similar to those discussed for the active air-to-air case. The major difference is that the targets of interest in air-to-surface application will be much slower targets than those encountered in the air-to-air application. In this regard, time required for the operational procedures will not be as critical.

In most applications, the target will be detected by the interceptor aircraft's own radar. A fire control solution will be generated by the interceptor aircraft's fire control system and the pilot will fly the aircraft along the correct path until lock-on of the missile's own radar occurs. Once the target is gated by the missile's radar the missile can be launched. The interceptor aircraft is then free to break away and start a new attack against another target or continue the attack against the same target.

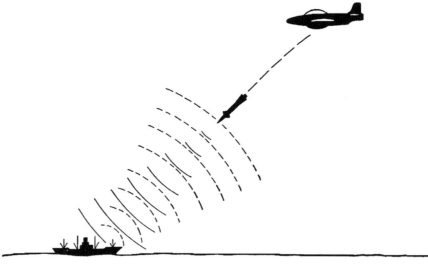

FIG. 16-7 Air-to-Surface Application of the Active Homing Technique.

The choice of an active homing guidance system for an air-to-surface missile will be determined by the target of interest and the type warhead carried by the missile. In general, there must be some distinguishing characteristic of the target with respect to its background, either in size or motion, before such an active system will be technically feasible. This type of system might be useful against an isolated target such as a ship at sea. If the missile carried a warhead powerful enough to destroy a large area, then extreme accuracy would not be required.

Other guidance techniques which are described in this chapter are probably more suited for the guidance of an air-to-surface missile. Because of the extreme difficulty in maintaining target lock-on after missile launch, a system wherein the pilot of the launching aircraft can retain control of the missile after launch is probably more suitable. Such systems are discussed later in this chapter.

Tactical Application of the Surface-to-Surface Active Homing Guidance System. Figure 16-8 illustrates a surface-to-surface missile using an active homing guidance system. In this illustration, the missile has been launched from a ship and is actively homing against another ship. In general the same considerations described for the air-to-surface missile that uses active homing guidance apply equally well to the surface-to-surface missile using active homing guidance. Once the missile is launched it becomes essentially an air-to-surface missile.

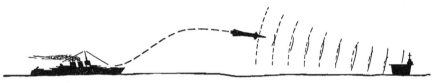

FIG. 16-8 Surface-to-Surface Application of the Active Homing Technique.

Even though the space and weight limitation is not as stringent as in an air-to-air or air-to-surface missile, the surface-to-surface missile, employing all-the-way active homing guidance only, will still be a comparatively short-range device. It is obvious that a long-range surface-to-surface missile must employ some other means of guidance (midcourse guidance) to bring the missile to the position where active homing guidance (terminal guidance) can begin. If the terminal guidance phase is to utilize the active homing technique, the target must have some distinguishing characteristic which will allow the radar of the active system to separate it from its surroundings since it is necessary for the missile radar to lock-on the target after launch. Further, it is evident that the acquisition capabilities of the missile radar must be carefully matched to the accuracy of the midcourse guidance. To this end, the radar may require both search and track modes of operation.

For short-range application, the radar of the active homing guidance system may be directed by a fire control radar at the launching site which has initially detected the target. Once the target is gated by the active homing system the missile is entirely independent.

Tactical Application of the Surface-to-Air Active Homing Guidance System. An example of the use of a surface-to-air system employing active homing guidance is illustrated by Fig. 16-9. The missile may be launched from a land base or from a ship against aircraft or other missiles. For this application, the missile radar antenna would be slaved to the antenna of a shipborne tracking radar. Once target lock-on occurs in the missile radar, the missile may be launched. Even though the surface-launched missile will not have as stringent size and weight restrictions as the air-

554 MISSILE GUIDANCE SYSTEMS

borne missile, the use of active homing guidance exclusively will still be feasible for only comparatively short ranges.

Semiactive Homing Guidance. Figure 16-10 is a block diagram for the tracking loop of a semiactive homing guidance system. External to the missile is a tracking device which illuminates the target and supplies synchronizing information to the missile. It will be assumed that this tracking

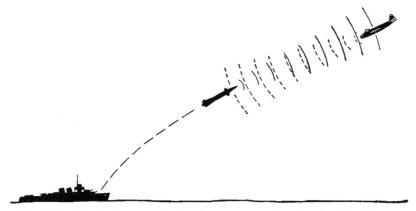

FIG. 16-9 Surface-to-Air Application of the Active Homing Technique.

device is a radar. In the missile, the tracking loop consists of a radar antenna and receiver, which are used to home on the energy reflected from the target, and a rearward looking antenna and receiver for energy received directly from the illuminating radar. The rear antenna and receiver are used to synchronize the missile guidance system with the illuminating

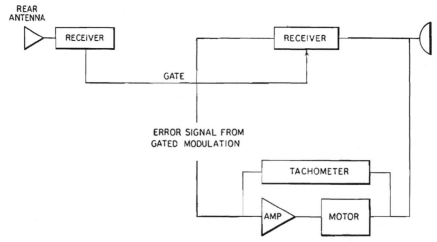

FIG. 16-10 Tracking Loop of a Semiactive Homing System.

radar in order that range, range rate, or Doppler may be measured in the missile. A gate is generated in the system which selects only the target of interest. The target may be gated in range (range gating) as in a pulse type system or in velocity (speed gating) as in a Doppler system. The gating techniques used are analogous to those described in the paragraphs on active homing guidance systems.

Range Comparison of Active and Semiactive Techniques. It was shown previously that missiles employing active homing guidance are comparatively short-range devices. This range restriction is imposed by the effective size of radar antenna that can be installed in the head of the missile and by the maximum power available because of space and weight limitations in the missile.

The maximum range restriction can be lessened somewhat if the radar transmitter is removed from the missile. This is precisely what is done in the semiactive guidance system. Since the launching station is capable of carrying a much heavier and larger load than could be carried by the missile, both the maximum transmitted power and the transmitting antenna size can be increased.

An examination of the basic radar equation will show the theoretical range improvement which can be realized for the semiactive system.

$$R_{\max} = \left(\frac{P_t G^2 \sigma \lambda^2}{64\pi^3 P_{\min}}\right)^{\frac{1}{4}} \tag{16-1}$$

Since the transmitted power and the antenna gain are the only variables, we will let

$$\frac{\sigma \lambda^2}{64\pi^3 P_{\min}} = \text{Constant} = C \tag{16-4}$$

then

$$R_{\max} = (P_t G^2 C)^{\frac{1}{4}} \tag{16-5}$$

For the active system, $R_{\max}$ is the range from the transmitter to the target. In a semiactive system we are also interested in the maximum range. However, the range performance can best be defined as

$$R_t R_r = (P_t G_t G_r C)^{\frac{1}{2}} \tag{16-6}$$

where R_t = range from transmitter to target
R_r = range from missile receiver to target
P_t = transmitted power
G_t = gain of transmitting antenna
G_r = gain of missile receiving antenna

The term $R_t R_r$ is defined as the *range product* of a semiactive system and is illustrated in Fig. 16-11. Here the tracking and illuminating radar is located on board a ship. Within the tracking limits of illuminating radar the ranges R_t and R_r may vary as long as the range product is kept constant. For example, consider that the range product for the system is 200 nautical miles squared. Then if the missile is required to home from the launching station,

$$R_t = R_r = \sqrt{200} = 14.14 \text{ nautical miles}$$

However, if the missile can be guided to such a point that homing starts when the target is 20 nautical miles from the launching station,

$$R_t = 20 \text{ nautical miles}$$
$$R_r = 200 \div 20 = 10 \text{ nautical miles}$$

This principle could be used in systems employing successive steps in guidance wherein semiactive homing is used for the terminal guidance phase.

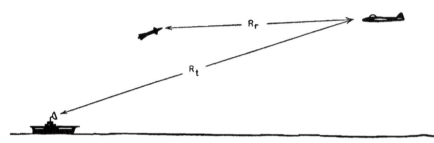

Fig. 16-11 Geometry of Semiactive Homing Guidance.

To compare the range capabilities of two systems, one using active homing guidance and the other using semiactive homing guidance, which utilize guidance from the launching point, we will express Eq. (16-5) as

$$R_a = (P_a G_r^2 C)^{\frac{1}{4}} \qquad (16\text{-}7)$$

where P_a = transmitted power for the active system
R_a = reliable all-the-way tracking range of the active system
G_r = gain of the common transmitting and receiving antenna

and

$$R_S = (P_S G_t G_r C)^{\frac{1}{4}} \qquad (16\text{-}8)$$

where R_S = reliable all-the-way tracking range of the semiactive system
P_S = transmitted power for the semiactive system
G_t = gain of the transmitting antenna
G_r = gain of the receiving antenna (same as that of the active system)

The ratio of the two ranges is

$$\frac{R_S}{R_a} = \left(\frac{P_S G_t}{P_a G_r}\right)^{\frac{1}{4}} \qquad (16\text{-}9)$$

If the transmitted power for the semiactive system can be made five times that of the active system

$$\frac{R_S}{R_a} = 1.495 \left(\frac{G_t}{G_r}\right)^{\frac{1}{4}}$$

If the power gain of the transmitting antenna of the semiactive system can be made twenty times that of the active system,

$$R_S = 3.16 R_a \tag{16-10}$$

An improvement in range of the general magnitude given above is possible. Thus, one of the major advantages of a semiactive system is that of obtaining an increased all-the-way homing range as compared to an active system.

Air-to-Air Missile System Utilizing Semiactive Homing Guidance. An air-to-air missile system which uses semiactive homing guidance is illustrated by Fig. 16-12. The missile is launched from an interceptor whose radar continues to illuminate the target until impact of the missile on the target. The target may be an aircraft or another missile.

Fig. 16-12 Air-to-Air Application of Semiactive Homing Techniques.

The semiactive system must receive intelligence from energy reflected from the target. Therefore, the illuminating radar, assumed to be a tracking radar, must be continuously pointed at the target. Obviously only one target can be handled by the system at a time, but any number of missiles (within the missile-carrying capacity of the interceptor) can be launched against this one target. The advantage of such a system over the previously described active system is that longer missile guidance ranges are possible since a larger transmitter and transmitting antenna can be mounted on the aircraft than could be carried in the missile.

The steps in acquiring the target and launching the missile will be identical with those of the active system. However, the demands of the missile on the interceptor aircraft after launch will be quite different. In the active system, once the missile is launched the parent aircraft is free to break away to avoid counterattacks or to attack another target. This is not true for the semiactive case. The illuminating radar must be pointed at the target continuously until missile impact and must simultaneously supply a rear signal to the missile. This obviously places very definite limits on the maneuvering of the interceptor aircraft. These limits will be established by the maneuverability of the missile, the beamwidth and *look angle* (angle between line-of-flight and the line-of-sight to the target) of the illuminating radar, and the number of missiles launched against the target.

The type of attack approach chosen for the air-to-air semiactive homing guided missile may be quite different than that chosen for the active homing case. Since the illuminating radar must continue pointing at the target after missile launch, serious consideration must be given to the maneuvers demanded of the interceptor. These maneuvers must be compatible with all the components of the system. Obviously, some degree of maneuverability is desirable to avoid enemy defensive fire.

Air-to-Surface Missile System Utilizing Semiactive Homing Guidance. Figure 16-13 illustrates the use of semiactive homing guidance for an air-to-surface missile. In this system the missile is launched from an aircraft which continues to illuminate the target until missile and target collide. The targets may range in size from a bridge up to a city. In the illustration of Fig. 16-13, the missile has been launched from an interceptor and is semiactively homing against a ship.

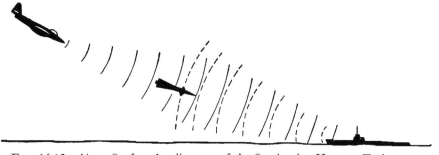

Fig. 16-13 Air-to-Surface Application of the Semiactive Homing Technique.

In general the same target considerations apply to the use of a semiactive system as were described for the active system when used in an air-to-surface missile. The target of interest must have some characteristic which distinguishes it from its background so that gating and tracking are possible. There is one major difference between the two techniques. In the semiactive system the radar operator can continuously monitor the tracking radar to ensure that it is illuminating the correct target.

Since the targets of interest will be, in general, relatively slow moving, time may not be as critical as in the air-to-air case. Thus the limited traffic-handling capacity of the system will probably not be as serious a restriction. The system is still only capable of handling one target during the flight time of any one missile. However, repeated attacks can be made since the speed advantage usually will greatly favor the interceptor.

Surface-to-Air Missile System Utilizing Semiactive Homing Guidance.
The missile is launched from a surface installation and homes on a target which is illuminated by the surface installation radar. The launching site may be on shipboard or land. The target may be an aircraft or another missile. This technique is illustrated by Fig. 16-14.

It has been shown previously that the active homing systems are comparatively short-range devices. The ability to take advantage of the increased range performance of a semiactive system is very pronounced in the surface-to-air application. It is possible to have high-power illumi-

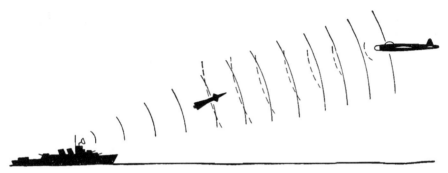

FIG. 16-14 Surface-to-Air Application of the Semiactive Homing Technique.

nating radars with large antennas on either a shipboard or land-based installation. Thus, comparatively large all-the-way homing ranges are possible.

In the surface-to-air application of the semiactive guidance technique, the missile may be guided by some midcourse technique out to a range where semiactive homing guidance can commence. Thus the flexibility of the technique, as illustrated by Fig. 16-11, and the accompanying derivation can be utilized.

As in the two preceding types of semiactive homing guidance, the system's traffic-handling capacity is limited. The illuminating radar must continue to track the same target until the missile arrives at the target. Multiple missile launchings against the same target are possible, but only one target can be engaged at a time.

Surface-to-Surface Missile System Utilizing Semiactive Homing Guidance.
A surface-to-surface missile utilizing semiactive homing guidance is illustrated by Fig. 16-15. In this illustration the missile has been launched from a ship and is semiactively homing against another ship. In general, the target may be any of a variety of surface targets. The missile may be launched from a ship or from a land base.

As in the air-to-surface semiactive application, the target must have some distinguishing radar characteristic. The traffic-handling capacity will be the same.

Passive Homing Guidance. The block diagram for the tracking loop of a passive homing guidance system is illustrated by Fig. 16-16. Of the three basic guidance systems, the passive system requires the least equipment in the missile proper. Since the target is the source of the energy used for guidance, no transmitter is necessary. This energy may be

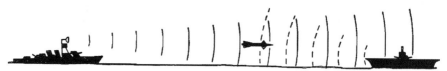

Fig. 16-15 Surface-to-Surface Application of the Semiactive Homing Technique.

sound, light, heat, or radio frequency waves. Sound systems are discussed in Par. 16-7 and will not be considered here. Since the general guidance technique for light or heat homing guidance is the same, it will be treated as a single system. The tracking loop consists of a collecting device (i.e., tracking head) receiver and drive unit. The error signal is derived from ungated modulation and is used by the drive unit to keep the collecting device pointed at the target.

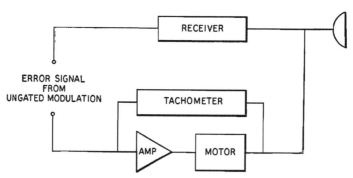

Fig. 16-16 Tracking Loop of a Passive Homing System.

Heat (Infrared) Passive Homing Guidance. In the system illustrated in Fig. 16-16, the receiver will be a heat-sensitive device such as a bolometer or other detector discussed in Chap. 5. Scanning techniques may be used to provide an information-gathering carrier for tracking the target, as discussed in Chap. 10. As in radar, the basic concepts of intelligence transmission apply, but the specific techniques differ because of the frequencies employed. The greatest single difference between the use of infrared and higher optical frequencies as compared to radio frequencies is that the techniques of heterodyning, and the sensitivity concomitant thereto, cannot be employed for infrared frequencies.

By suitable commutation the amplitude of the received infrared signals from four quadrants can be compared, and left-right, up-down guidance signals can be generated. These signals may be used to drive the tracking head. Since it is necessary to have a vertical reference in order that tracking information can be obtained, the tracking head must be space-stabilized.

Radio Frequency Passive Homing Guidance. One of the most commonly employed passive homing devices using radio frequency intelligence is the direction finder. The same general technique can be used in a missile guidance system. The intelligence may be derived from phase comparison techniques (such as an interferometer) if the energy transmitted by the target is of such a form as to make this possible. For example, if the target is operating a pulse type radar, phase comparison techniques would be possible. Another means of deriving intelligence from the energy transmitted by the target is by the comparison of the amplitude of the received signal during the scan cycle. The use of such techniques is based upon the premise that information is available concerning the frequency band in which the target is transmitting. In addition, it is necessary that provisions be incorporated for tuning the missile receiver over this frequency band.

Tactical Application of Passive Homing Guidance. One example of passive homing guidance is illustrated by Fig. 16-17. In this case the missile is of the air-to-air variety. Prior to launch, the procedure is essentially the same as described for the previous air-to-air systems. The presence of the target may be detected by an external device in the interceptor or may be detected by the receiver in the missile. The interceptor will then fly to the correct position for missile launching. Since the passive homing guidance system does not require transmitted energy from the

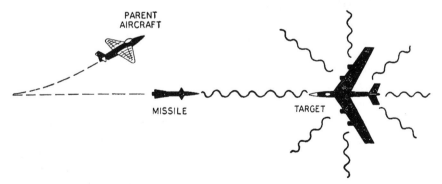

FIG. 16-17 Air-to-Air Application of the Passive Homing Technique.

interceptor, once the missile is launched the parent aircraft is free to break away.

Figure 16-17 illustrates only one possible application of passive homing guidance. This form of guidance also may be used in air-to-surface, surface-to-surface, or surface-to-air missiles. One main advantage of a passive system is missile equipment simplicity. No transmitter is needed in the missile. The missile tracking equipment can be very small and compact. A second advantage has been discussed in connection with Fig. 16-16, namely, that the passive system is an independent system once the target is acquired.

The use of any passive homing guidance system requires that the target of interest radiate energy from which guidance intelligence can be derived and that sufficient information is available about the radiated energy that it may be used. For example, a passive homing guidance system designed to home on radio frequency energy transmitted from the target is based upon the premise that the enemy will transmit such information at the desired time. Obviously, if the target maintains radio silence during the period of attack, this form of passive homing guidance cannot be used.

Passive homing guidance systems deriving guidance intelligence from either light or infrared energy require that the target have some characteristic which distinguishes it from its background. Weather conditions, target type, target aspect, and target background may greatly influence the success or failure of such systems. Both systems may have their homing range reduced drastically by fog or haze. If the target does not emit light or heat sufficiently different in intensity from that of its background, these systems may be useless. In general, the basic considerations described above apply equally to all types of missile systems utilizing passive homing. Some of the individual effects will be more pronounced for one type than for another.

16-3 COMMAND GUIDANCE SYSTEMS

A *command guidance system* is defined as one wherein intelligence transmitted to the missile from an outside source causes the missile to traverse a directed path in space. Command missile guidance systems in general require that the behavior of the missile (and of the target, if it is in motion) be monitored externally, that any deviation from a prescribed collision course be computed, and that the deviation be communicated to the missile and interpreted by its control system so as to realign the missile flight path toward an intercept with the target. As in the case of other guidance techniques, applied command systems vary from simple to complex. Inherently, however, command systems can be the simplest to instrument of all of the techniques considered. Command guidance was therefore the first guidance system to be demonstrated both on the surface with remote control of boats, tanks, and cars; and in the air, with remote control of drone aircraft and glide bombs. Command guidance is the most broadly applied of the techniques discussed and is used for control of many mechanisms other than missiles. Its most serious general limitation for missile use is low traffic-handling capacity. The typical command system can solve only one problem at a time; that is, it can guide only one missile against one target during a given time interval. The period during which a command system must be committed for each problem is important in considering this guidance method.

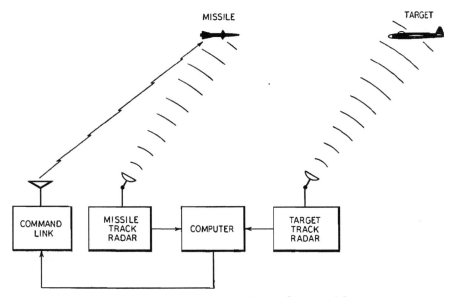

Fig. 16-18 Generalized Radar Track Command System.

Applied command guidance systems can be divided into two general categories: those wherein relative target and missile position and motion are derived from radar tracking information, called *radar track command;* and those wherein the monitoring is accomplished optically, called *optical track command.* Figure 16-18 illustrates a generalized radar track command system.

The system of Fig. 16-18 provides separately for the tracking of missile and target in range and angle. From these data, missile deviation from a prescribed trajectory is computed, and flight path error intelligence is communicated to a receiver in the missile via a communication link. Error magnitude and direction information is used by a control system in the missile, which is equivalent to an automatic pilot, to correct missile flight path. System variations of this method, to be considered later, include single-beam tracking of both target and missile, base-line missile tracking, and the stationary target case.

In the air-to-ground system illustrated by Fig. 16-19, the relative position of target and missile is optically monitored through a sighting system in the aircraft. Missile deviation from the desired flight path is observed optically, and this error intelligence communicated usually in rectangular coordinates to the missile receiver and control system via a radio link. System variations of this method are determined by the tactical situation for which the system is designed and result from performance requirements prescribed by the situation. Means for mechanizing functions common

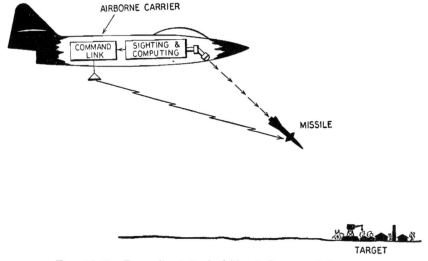

Fig. 16-19 Generalized Optical Track Command System.

to command guidance systems (sighting, computing, communication, and missile control) will thus vary with the tactical problem, the state of the art, and the whim of the designer.

Generalized Command Guidance System. Preceding discussions in Chap. 9 have shown how the performance of a missile system is specified from tactical requirements. Insofar as guidance is concerned the principal functions to be prescribed for command systems are the sighting and tracking means, computation of flight path error, communication of this intelligence to the missile, and a sensing and responding mechanism in the missile to effect a flight path correction. Figure 16-20 shows in block diagram form how these functions can be interconnected in a generalized command guidance system. Comparison of this guidance loop with the generalized loop illustrating homing guidance will show that the control requirements of both systems are analogous. The command guidance system of Fig. 16-20 differs basically in that relative position and motion measurement is accomplished at a location outside the missile. Additional problems thereby imposed are the establishment of a compatible coordinate system and the remote communication of error correction commands to the missile. This is somewhat compensated for by the fact that more space is available for control equipment outside of the missile than within it.

Typical parameters and characteristics of the following system elements will be discussed: missile flight guidance and control loop, sensing and tracking means, coordinate conversion, guidance intelligence generation (computing), and guidance intelligence communication.

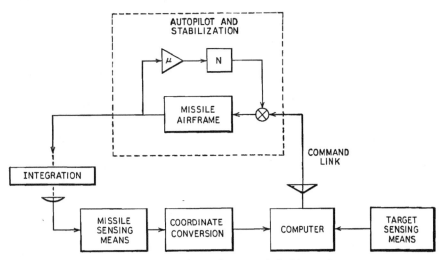

Fig. 16-20 Generalized Command Guidance System.

The missile flight guidance loop is in many respects comparable to a conventional automatic pilot having provision for operator overriding. Since the missile "operator" is displaced from the missile itself, a common reference direction such as "up" must be established for the control loop as a whole and be maintained throughout the control period. This is the N block of Fig. 16-20. Techniques to accomplish this include use of pendulous devices with the earth's gravity as the reference; prealignment of missile gyro(s) with the guidance station reference; or, where time of flight is very short, design for aerodynamic stability. Typically, common reference is obtained by prealignment of missile gyros which become a part of the missile control and guidance loops. The state of the art in the autopilot control field is sufficiently advanced and reported as not to need detailing here. Guidance intelligence, when transmitted by radio link, is derived in the missile by demodulation of the modulated radio frequency carrier. Information transmitted should produce the required rate, quantity, and direction of missile flight path correction. This electrical information is converted to mechanical displacement of airframe control surfaces. The local missile guidance system is then principally comprised of: receiver-demodulator, servo drive for airframe control members, the airframe itself, and autopilot feedback for stabilization and reference. Design parameters for this loop include its performance as an element of the overall guidance system, whose response characteristics are in turn partially prescribed by the type of trajectory tactically required, and certain constants such as airframe flight speed and response. Transfer characteristics of the local missile loop can be thus specified and its elements designed from this premise.

Missile sensing and tracking means are required for locating the missile and measuring its position and motion. This device, in ground-to-air command systems, is conventionally a tracking radar. Information from this source necessary for computation of guidance commands includes missile range and angle and their time derivatives. Radar tracking of the missile provides integrated range and angle information which will usually require coordinate conversion before delivery to the computer.

Target and missile sensing requirements are analogous. The nature of the target and its state of motion will determine the target sensing means to be employed. For surface targets, where target motion rates are low, a simple single sighting (or sensing) means may be used to provide relative missile-to-target position and rate information. If target coordinates are fixed, continuous observation of target position may be unnecessary. The motion of an aircraft target will require continuous monitoring, conventionally with a tracking radar. Detection, lock-on, and track are again the normal sequence. Detection may now additionally involve search, identification, designation, and acquisition. Where applicable these factors are discussed in later sections describing specific systems. A target coordinate system compatible for use with missile tracking intelligence is required for the computation process. The selection of a common coordinate reference for target and missile will be affected by the nature and functions of the command system.

The function of the computer is to generate command signals which, ideally, result in missile collision with the target. Input intelligence is processed to generate a radio-relayed signal which is a function of missile deviation from the desired flight path. Since the geometric problem is comparable in most guidance systems, the general computer requirements for such systems tend to be similar.

The computer receives position and rate information (together with noise), predicts optimum point of impact, and generates steering orders to cause the missile to fly a desired course to collision. A typical requirement for many systems is conversion of tracking data to rate of change of target bearing relative to missile line-of-flight. If the missile is guided so as to "zero" this rate of change, a constant true bearing trajectory results. Commands for this case are such as to minimize change in target angle as seen from the missile. This is only one of an infinite number of possible flight path solutions. The computer may, moreover, have numerous functions in addition to generation of guidance commands, such as pointing a movable launching platform, computing ballistics and parallax, or developing the timing sequence of necessary procedures prior to launch. Command computing systems thus can vary considerably in complexity, and their performance parameters can best be determined from particular system and application requirements.

Communication of guidance intelligence to the missile is ordinarily accomplished by radio link. This assembly is perhaps the least difficult to design of all the elements of the guidance and control loop. Bandwidth requirements, frequency, number of channels, carrier frequency, output power, etc., are determined in a straightforward manner and are not likely to be compromised by the present state of the art or to require new techniques. Conversely, the radio-link is a contributing component in the system loop and the design problem is not so simple as to permit its being drawn from stock.

Command Links. All command guidance systems require a communications link between the guidance station and the missile. This link is used to relay remotely generated steering orders and other commands to the missile. Practically, command links are limited to communication by radio or wire. The use of a wire command link for supersonic missiles has sufficiently obvious limitations so that only the radio technique will be discussed. Important design considerations include: information transfer quantity, quality and rate requirements; range; reliability; security; carrier frequency; and physical parameters relating to component size, power requirements, and weight.

Information Transfer. In addition to steering information the command link may be required to communicate other orders to the missile. These are determined by particular system requirements and may include arming, receiver gain setting, detonation of warhead near the target, self-destruction when flight is hazarding friendly forces, or other intelligence. An initial problem is the determination of system-imposed information transfer requirements in terms of type (off-on or proportional), quantity, rate, and accuracy. From this premise the number of channels, time-sharing indications, and required channel bandwidths can be established. Coding, time-sharing and carrier-modulation methods for the transmitter, as well as compatible carrier demodulation, decoding and time-sharing methods for the receiver, are design details the specifications of which logically follow.

Range, Carrier Frequency, and Power. Carrier frequency and power requirements are dictated practically by the effective range within which the missile system is to be applied and by receiver and transmitter elevation above the earth's surface. In general, since physical component size tends to vary inversely with carrier frequency, the carrier frequency should be high. Carrier frequency and power quantities then tend to be controlled by system design range, the nature of the path between transmitter and receiver, and availability of space within the missile.

Radio communication frequency bands of interest are popularly termed *HF* (high frequency 3-30 mc per sec) *VHF* (very high frequency 30-300 mc per sec), and *UHF* (ultra high frequency 300-3000 mc per sec). Transmission at frequencies above approximately 50 mc per sec tends to follow a direct path without reflection (sky wave) from ionized layers above the earth and thus maximum useful range is limited to line-of-sight between transmitter and receiver. Figure 16-21 gives approximate range limits for the *VHF* and *UHF* bands (frequencies above 50 mc per sec) as a function of the elevation of receiver above the earth for a transmitter at 100 ft. This figure was calculated by using a rule-of-thumb approximation:

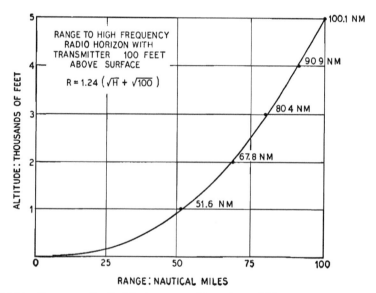

Fig. 16-21 Range to Radio Horizon as a Function of VHF-UHF Receiver Altitude.

$$R = 1.24(\sqrt{H} + \sqrt{H_1}) \qquad (16\text{-}11)*$$

where R = range in nautical miles
H = altitude of one station (receiver or transmitter) in feet
H_1 = altitude of second station in feet

It can be seen that frequency does not limit range when one or both stations are high above the surface of the earth. For an example of range limitation by high carrier frequency where elevations are small, assume that, in elevation, the transmitter is at 50 ft and receiver (missile) at 100 ft:

$$R = 1.24(\sqrt{100} + \sqrt{50})$$
$$R = 1.24(10 + 7.07)$$
$$R = 21.2 \text{ nautical miles range}$$

In addition to carrier frequency effects, useful range is determined by transmitter power, the directivity and size of receiving and transmitting antennas, the sensitivity of the missile receiver, the electrical noise level at the receiver, and the nature of the radio transmission path between transmitter and receiver.

Reliability. This parameter, again, is to be specified by system requirements and should not arbitrarily be considered as requiring performance at as high a level of reliability as the state of the art permits. Thus the degree of reliability within which the system can perform satisfactorily needs to be determined. A system requiring light-duty continuous control via the command link requires a higher degree of link reliability than is necessary for the case where command signals may be intermittent. Receiver sensitivity being ignored for the moment, the parameter having greatest effect upon link reliability is the signal-to-noise level at the receiving station. Transmitter power, antenna directivity, propagation factors, and range are the principal determinants of the receiver signal-to-noise level. Except for propagation factors (conditions of interference and noise through which the r-f carrier passes) those elements are under the control of the designer and will be determined in part by the degree of reliability required.

Security. Command link security is a design consideration of primary importance. It is usually the most fallible element of the system from the point of view of countermeasures. Introduction of a new weapon immediately challenges the opponent to develop countermeasures for its control or defeat. It can therefore be presumed that the opponent will attempt to detect and analyze the control signals with the intent of developing means for jamming or confusing them. The command link designer thus attempts to make detection and analysis of the command signals as diffi-

---

* See Eq. (4-6) for expression of range in *statute* miles.

cult as practicable. Ease of detection is affected by directivity of the signal, the duration of its use, and its amplitude.

Physical Size. Command receiver size, weight, and power consumption limitations are prescribed by such factors as missile diameter and space available. Size and weight are always paramount considerations in the design of airborne electronic equipment. For obvious reasons space conservation at the receiver is more important than at the transmitter. Design of the command link loop should therefore attempt to accomplish as many of the communication functions as practicable at the transmitting station.

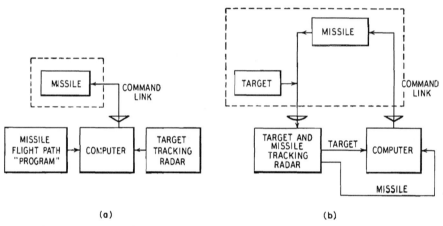

FIG. 16-22 Single-Beam Radar Track Command, Moving Target.

Missile design range and the complexity of the command signal required for a particular case (i.e., the number of control channels, signal continuity and accuracy) are frequently beyond the direct control of the command link designer. These tend to be specified by the overall system and represent parameters the command link shall satisfy. Techniques for reducing receiver size include time sharing, which may be applied within limits permitted by signal continuity requirements, and the simultaneous subcarrier transmission of several functions.

Single-beam Radar Track Command Guidance. **1.** *Moving Target Case.* Figure 16-22a illustrates a general block diagram for a system of single-beam radar track command guidance. In this case, the target position and motion are sensed by radar; the position and motion of the missile are not measured, but predicted on the basis of statistical ballistic data. For the system illustrated, target position and motion are continuously monitored by radar. Relative missile position may be estimated rather accurately since most of the factors which have caused it to arrive at its present position are known at the directing point. For the ballistic case the most important factors are velocity, drift (wind), angle of launch in two coordinates, and time. From these data missile trajectory can be continuously, though not precisely, computed as a function of time. Thus "canned" ballistic data defining a desired missile path can be examined with respect to the radar-derived target track. Deviation of the target from the predicted future path can be sensed and corresponding commands can be signaled to the missile for flight path correction. It is evident that uncertainty of missile present position will introduce solution error equivalent to that inherent in dead reckoning navigation.

Figure 16-22b illustrates a single-beam command guidance case where the missile is equipped with a beacon to facilitate simultaneous radar tracking of both target and missile motion. The single relatively narrow beam must illuminate both the missile and the target. The missile is

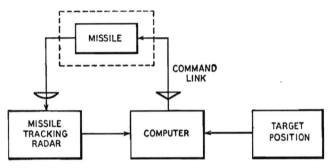

FIG. 16-23 Single-Beam Radar Track Command, Stationary Target.

thus committed to a trajectory wherein it is always along the line-of-sight from the radar to the target. With several important exceptions, the system's design problems are analogous to those for the beam-rider guided missile. Launch, boost, capture, and trajectory problems are comparable in both techniques. Certain disadvantages are imposed relative to the beam rider. The missile must carry both the command receiver and a beacon transponder. Flight path error computation, occurring at a position displaced from the missile, is more complex and will tend to be less precise. The tracking radar must separately include missile and target receivers, and only one missile at a time may be practically guided in the single beam.

2. *Stationary Target Case.* Figure 16-23 shows a simple block diagram of a single-beam radar track command guidance system where missile motion is sensed by radar and target position is constant and known.

For this case missile motion is continuously monitored by radar. Missile deviation (error) from a predetermined path to intercept is sensed and path correction orders are communicated to the missile via a radio link. This constitutes a relatively simple system, the principal uncertainty of which lies in the determination of the target position with respect to the missile launching site. In order to compute accurately a path from the missile launch point to the target the relative position of these two points must be known precisely. When the target cannot be observed from the guidance position, its location is necessarily estimated, and potential missile guidance accuracy is reduced by the estimation error.

Two-beam Radar Track Command Guidance. Figure 16-24 illustrates a simplified block diagram of a two-beam radar track command guidance system. Essential elements include the missile, target tracking radar, missile tracking radar, computer, and command link.

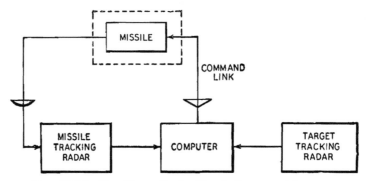

FIG. 16-24 Two-Beam Radar Track Command System.

The two-beam system is potentially more flexible and, for moving targets, more accurate than the single-beam system. From a systems point of view the principal addition is a requirement for continuous separate surveillance of target and missile motion. Design problems are analogous for both systems.

Optical Track Command Guidance. Optical track command systems are those wherein relative missile and target positions are continuously monitored by a human operator who transmits commands to the missile via a radio link to direct the missile along a desired path to collision. Such systems are obviously limited in range to optical line-of-sight. From the designer's point of view the least controllable functional element in the optical track command system control loop is the operator. System parameters are thus in part initially defined by operator capabilities and limitations. The optical track command technique is analogous to the single-beam radar track command system previously described. Figure 16-25 illustrates the functional control loop of a single optical track command system.

Relative target and missile motion is optically sensed by the operator from a point which may also be in motion (as the air launch case). Mental computation, in this complex dynamic situation, of the most efficient collision course for the missile is beyond operator capability. A more feasible sighting routine requires that the missile be maintained continuously along the operator's line-of-sight to the target. The operator observes misalignment of missile and signals two-coordinate flight path correction orders to the missile via a radio link. The internal missile control loop design problem is comparable to that of other command systems.

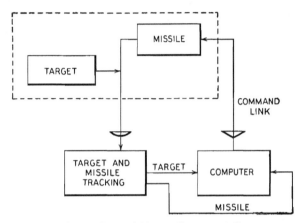

Fig. 16-25 Optical Track Command System.

Limitations imposed by operator capabilities upon optical track command systems are the requirements that target and missile both be visible, and that relative missile, target, and observer angular velocities be low. Application is thus restricted to short range and good visibility conditions and is further limited by the guidance capability of the operator. Certain important compensating advantages in system simplicity result from the use of this system. If we assume a well-trained operator, control loop complexity and cost are minimized with a resultant relative increase in reliability. For these reasons systems of this type had early application by the Germans.

Optical Track Command Guidance with Target Sensing in the Missile. This system, a special case of optical track command, displaces target sensing—and sometimes sighting—from the operator position to the missile. Figure 16-26 is a functional schematic.

The generalized optical track command system previously discussed imposes an inefficient, and for some applications impractical, trajectory upon the missile wherein the rate of required flight path correction tends to increase as range to target decreases. This trajectory results from the practical requirement that the missile be guided along a line-of-sight path between the operator and the target and is a beam-rider trajectory. If target sighting can be accomplished from the missile position and relayed to the operator (e.g., by television), several potential advantages accrue. Target position and motion are now observed relative to the missile. It is no longer necessary to monitor missile position with respect to the operator, and the generation of an efficient collision course for the missile becomes more practical. However, target sensing means in the missile and a missile-to-operator communications link add appreciably to the complexity of missile-borne equipment. Design of the command communication link and of the missile receiver and the control system presents the same problems as were discussed for the single- and two-beam command systems.

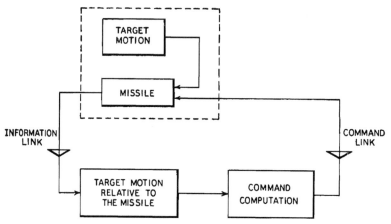

FIG. 16-26 Optical Track Command with Target Motion Sensing in the Missile.

16-4 BEAM-RIDER GUIDANCE SYSTEMS

A *beam-rider guidance system* is defined as a system for guiding missiles which utilize a beam directed into space, such that the center of the beam axis forms a line along which it is desired to direct a missile.[2] The beam, which may be either fixed or moving in elevation and azimuth, may be a radar beam or a light beam. Equipment is contained in the missile that can determine when the missile is in the center of the beam, as well as the direction and magnitude of the error when the missile has deviated from the center of the beam. Also in the missile are suitable electronic circuits, servo mechanisms coupled to aerodynamic control surfaces, and other equipment such that the missile will be caused by its own initiative

[2] *Glossary of Guided Missile Terms*, prepared by the Committee on Guided Missiles, 20 September 1949, p. 49.

to return toward the center of the beam when it has deviated therefrom for any reason.

Figure 16-27 shows a simple diagram of a beam-riding missile guidance system which includes the required basic elements when a radar beam is used as the guiding beam. The example shown is a surface-to-air application; however, this is in no way a fundamental requirement.

In view of the definition given, the diagram is almost self-explanatory. The radar is used to develop the beam along which the missile is to travel. Its antenna is directed so that the center of the beam is on the target. The missile launcher, if trainable, is used to point the missile in such a manner

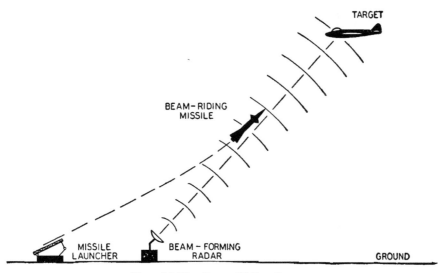

Fig. 16-27 Beam-Riding System.

that it will enter the beam after launching. The beam-riding missile contains a mechanism, which will be described later in this chapter, that permits it to measure its position with respect to the center of the radar beam and to move in such a direction as to reduce this measured error toward zero. These conditions fulfil the basic requirements specified in the definition of a beam-riding missile guidance system.

General Component Requirements and Limitations. It is seen in Fig. 16-27 that the four general components of a surface-to-air beam-riding guidance system are the tracking and guiding radar, the launcher, the missile, and the target. The individual requirements for these are interrelated and are further defined by the tactical application. A surface-to-air system will have different requirements than those of an air-to-air, an air-to-surface, or a surface-to-surface system. Certain of the requirements are independent of the specific tactical application. For example, there must be a line-of-sight path between the radar, the missile, and the target at all times regardless of the tactical application, whereas the possible range of missile guidance may vary widely, depending upon whether the radar is airborne or ground-based.

Figure 16-28 shows in block form one of the possible types of beam-rider guidance radar. Two general specifications must be met. First, the radar must contain provisions for continuously tracking the target in both elevation and train, regardless of any relative motion of the radar and the

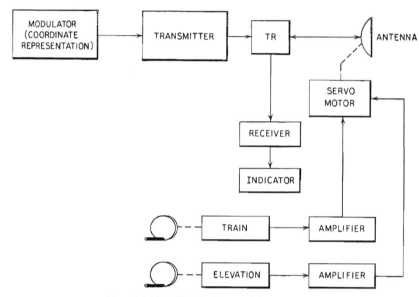

FIG. 16-28 Simple Beam-Rider Radar.

target. Second, the beam must contain coordinate information which can be used by the guidance receiver within the missile in order that it may guide itself along the center of the beam.

If the target being tracked is in free space, the principal problems involved in tracking it are that the radar system be sufficiently sensitive and have sufficient accuracy. Accuracy of tracking, as used here, means the angular accuracy of the tracking and guiding radar. Precision tracking radars, such as used for fire control, have narrow beams because high angular accuracy is necessary. In general, they meet the requirements of beam-rider missile guidance. Free space, in this case, means that the target is far enough from all other objects, including the earth, so that the transmitted beam is acted upon only by the target. These conditions are met by a single aircraft flying at several radar beamwidths above the surface of the earth within the range capabilities of the radar employed.

In many tactical situations the target will not be in free space as defined above. It may be close to the earth's surface or there may be other objects near it. The problems involved in tracking it may become extremely difficult as discussed in Par. 10-35. The effect of noise as a degradation of tracking accuracy was discussed in Chap. 11. The seriousness of these tracking problems will depend to a considerable extent upon the tactical employment of the guidance system.

So long as the beam-forming radar is on the earth's surface, its range is limited by the radar horizon. The antenna may be made almost any desired size. When the radar is to be airborne, severe restrictions are immediately imposed. The size of the antenna is restricted to that which the aircraft can accommodate and will be smaller than for a ground-based radar. Once the antenna size and the desired beamwidth are fixed the frequency is also fixed. The greater the ratio of antenna diameter to wavelength, the smaller the beamwidth. Another limitation is that of available power. In contrast with ground equipment, airborne radars are severely restricted in terms of primary power to drive them. This restriction limits the effective range of the airborne radar. Unfortunately these restrictions are generally beyond the control of the guidance system designer. For air-to-air or air-to-surface applications of beam-rider missile guidance techniques, one must recognize the restriction in range and plan the tactical use of the missile accordingly.

Missile Launchers. The launcher must be capable of being orientated so that the missile will be launched as nearly along and into the axis of the radar beam as possible. There are two reasons why this is desirable. There is an interval from the beginning of launch until the missile reaches some minimum velocity during which the aerodynamic surfaces have little or no effect in controlling the flight path of the missile because the surfaces are designed to be effective at the operating speed of the missile. During this time, dependency must be placed upon the inertial stability of the missile to keep it on the correct trajectory. If the angle of entry of the missile into the beam is too great the missile may pass completely through the beam and be lost to it. Unless the missile is captured by the beam it cannot be guided.

Another reason for launching as nearly along the axis of the beam as possible is that a transient will be developed in the missile flight path when the control surfaces become effective and begin to control the missile. The better the physical alignment of the missile axis and the radar beam axis, the smaller will be the transient and the more quickly the missile can settle at the center of the guidance beam. Moreover, the side-lobe polarity reversal would tend to guide a badly misaligned missile away from the axis of the beam.

If the launcher and the beam-forming radar are ground-based, a movable launcher is desirable to permit better alignment of the missile and the guidance beam during launching. If the launcher and the radar are airborne, the launcher must point along the line-of-flight of the aircraft. At the time that the missile attains sufficient speed for beam guidance, the launching aircraft must be in such a position that the missile and the target will be within the beam and it must maintain this status until impact of the missile on the target.

Missiles, Beam-rider Type. Figure 16-29 shows, in block diagram, the essential components of a beam-rider guided missile. The beam is re-

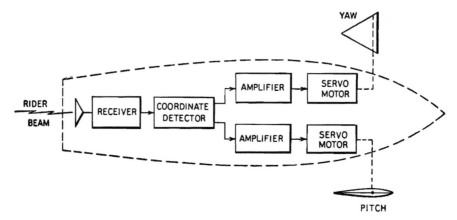

Fig. 16-29 Beam-Rider Guided Missile.

ceived by the rearward looking antenna, is passed through the receiver, and has the train and elevation coordinates separated in the coordinate detector. These separate signals are amplified and drive servo motors which actuate aerodynamic surfaces to change the train and/or elevation heading of the missile to cause it to move toward the center of the beam. The coordinate detector as shown here includes all the necessary circuitry to separate the train and elevation error signals contained in the output of the receiver.

It may not be evident at first that the missile guidance system is in the form of a closed loop servomechanism. This fact can perhaps be explained more clearly than it can be shown in block diagram form. The dotted lines of Fig. 16-29 represent the physical connection between the control surfaces of the missile and the antenna. The magnitude of the error signals received by the antenna will depend upon its physical position with respect to the center of the guidance beam. Error signals resulting from this misalignment will cause a movement of the control surfaces which will change the heading of the missile in such a way as to cause it to travel toward the center of the beam. This physical movement of the missile with the attached, fixed position antenna will cause the error signals to decrease because the antenna has been moved closer to the center of the beam. Thus one has a closed loop system in which the input is received from the guidance beam containing coordinate information and the output changes the heading of the missile with a consequent movement of the missile in such a direction as to reduce the magnitude of the error signals.

There is an additional problem which must be considered in the case of a missile traveling through the air. Because of air currents, mechanical unbalance, transients, or noise in the electrical control system the missile

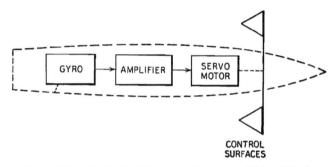

Fig. 16-30 Roll Stabilization of a Beam-Rider Missile.

may roll. If the magnitude of the roll approaches 90 deg the effect of the control surfaces becomes reversed and a signal which originally changed elevation now changes the train. Therefore it becomes necessary to roll-stabilize the missile. This can be accomplished by placing a gyroscope inside the missile with its axis of rotation orientated in such a way that it has an output if the missile tends to roll. A possible mechanization is indicated in Fig. 16-30. The output of the gyroscope is amplified and used to operate a pair of control surfaces having opposite deflections. These aerodynamic surfaces neutralize the tendency of the missile to roll. If the dynamic characteristics of the missile are such that there is a tendency for the missile to roll continuously in a particular direction, there must be a continuous trim correction of the roll-stabilizing surfaces.

Some stability of trajectory may be obtained if one deliberately causes the missile to roll. This will require some form of commutation in the guidance system. A reference point between the radar and the missile guidance system must be maintained at all times so that the error signals measured within the missile will have the proper sense when compared to the coordinate information being transmitted by the guidance radar.

The Germans employed spin stabilization of this type. Before using such a system, one should determine whether the additional complications are justified.

Targets. The target for any guided missile must have some unique characteristic as seen by the guidance radar. This characteristic is often the reflective property of the target compared to its surroundings. For example, an airplane flying in a free space has high radar reflectivity as compared to its surroundings and hence is a good radar target.

Beam-rider Guidance Intelligence. Mention has been made of the necessity for the beam to contain coordinate information in order to guide a missile. Some methods of getting such information onto the beam and some methods of detecting such information will be considered.

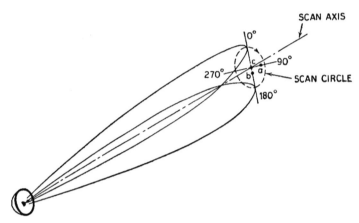

Fig. 16-31 Conical Scan.

The guidance intelligence must make available to the missile two facts. These are the amplitude of the error and the sense, or direction, of the error. With this information the missile can correct its error in position measured from the center of the beam within the limits of the guidance mechanism.

Let us consider the conventional scanning radar beam, as shown in Fig. 16-31. The center of the radar beam is pointed at an angle from the scan axis, and the beam is nutated so that the center of the beam follows the scan circle as it nutates. If a receiver were placed on the scan axis, the signal strength measured by the receiver would be constant as the beam circles the axis in its scan. If the receiver were displaced slightly from the axis, the amplitude of the received signal would be modulated at the scan frequency of the scanning antenna.

Figure 16-32 shows the varying amplitude modulation which results from placing the antenna of the receiver at three different points with

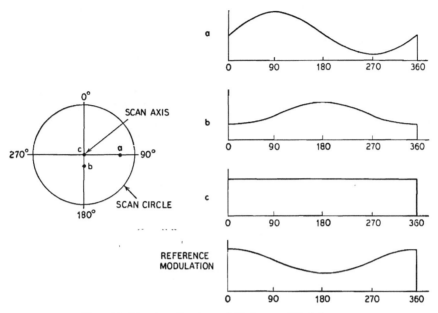

Fig. 16-32 Amplitude and Reference Modulations.

respect to the scan axis of the radar. When the receiver antenna is displaced from the scan axis at point *a*, a sine wave modulation is observed in the amplitude of the received signal, with the phase of the modulation such that the maximum signal amplitude is at 90 deg. Correspondingly, with the receiver antenna at point *b* we find the modulation reduced in amplitude and the phase of the modulation has changed so that the maximum amplitude of the received signal is at 180 deg. At point *c*, with the receiver antenna at the scan axis, the received signal is constant and no modulation exists.

The general relationship between the signal amplitude modulation and the displacement of the receiver antenna from the center of the scan axis is shown in Fig. 16-33. It will be observed that the relationship tends to be linear near the scan axis, but departs from the linear relationship

Fig. 16-33 Modulation Amplitude Related to Receiver Displacement from Antenna Axis.

as the receiver antenna goes out of the beam. This means that when the receiver is maintained near the scan axis of the beam, the signal amplitude modulation is directly proportional to the angular displacement (or error) of the receiver antenna from the beam center. By employing the amplitude modulation, which already exists as part of the radar transmission, a beam-rider receiver therefore has a measure of the amplitude of error of its departure from the scanning axis of the radar.

However, knowledge of the amount of error is not enough; the direction of error also must be obtained. In Fig. 16-32, a reference modulation is indicated for comparison with the amplitude modulations illustrating different locations of the beam-rider receiver antenna. It has been assumed in the figure that the reference modulation is at the same frequency as the scan frequency and that the peak of the modulation is at zero degrees. By comparing the phase relationships between each of the amplitude modulations with the reference modulation (since we know that the peak of the amplitude modulation discloses the location of the receiver antenna), the directions of the errors may readily be observed.

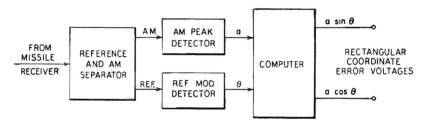

Fig. 16-34 Coordinate Detector.

The reference modulation must be in synchronism with the scanning frequency of the radar and must be transmitted in some manner to the beam-rider receiver. This may be accomplished in many differing ways. Since the radar itself employs a reference generator for precisely the same purpose (developing a reference modulation that may be used to indicate direction of error in polar coordinates), it is logical to employ the same generator to develop a reference which may then be transmitted to the receiver. Any method of transmission is satisfactory so long as the method employed lends itself to easy separation of the amplitude modulation and the reference modulation.

Figure 16-34 indicates in rudimentary form the separation of the reference and amplitude modulation signals and the transformation of them into the proper coordinate form. After the signals have been separated into usable form, they are passed through the amplitude and reference detectors. The output of the amplitude frequency detector is a voltage proportional to the displacement of the beam-rider receiver antenna from the scan axis of the radar. The output of the reference frequency detector is a voltage proportional to the angular position of the missile in the radar beam as measured from some arbitrarily fixed zero angular position. The combination of the two signals represents the error, expressed in polar coordinates, of the beam-rider antenna and, hence, of the missile from the center of the beam. In order to use this information for the control of the missile in pitch and yaw, it is necessary to convert the error information into rectangular coordinates.

This polar information is readily converted into rectangular form by multiplying the amplitude of the error by the sine of the angle for one coordinate and by the cosine of the angle for the other coordinate. This is accomplished by the indicated computer. The missile may thus be controlled by the information contained within the beam.

Some Tactical Considerations. The equipment carried by the missile is less complex in concept with beam-rider guidance than that required by most other missile guidance systems. It is considerably less complex than the equipment carried in those missiles which contain both a radar transmitter and receiver. The simplicity of the missile-borne equipment is a factor toward system reliability.

The tracking and guiding radar beam must be pointed at the target at all times during the flight of the missile after its initial capture by the beam. In air-to-air applications this requirement may restrict the maneuvers of the guiding aircraft. The flight path of the launching aircraft should ideally be one which produces a minimum of lateral motion of the missile. However, a missile can be guided by a radar-carrying aircraft which does not follow an ideal path. The requirement of having the missile and the target within the beam at all times after the initial capture of the missile by the beam must be met.

A beam-rider guidance radar is required for each target being attacked, although more than one missile may be guided simultaneously by the beam. The radar is committed from the beginning of the initial tracking to the impact of the missile and target. If several similar beam-rider guidance systems are being used in a small operational area, there may be mutual interference so that the tracking accuracy and hence the probability of successful interception may be greatly reduced.

16-5 INERTIAL, TERRESTRIAL, AND CELESTIAL GUIDANCE SYSTEMS

Inertial-gravitational System. An *inertial guidance system* is one which is independent of information, other than gravitational effects, obtained from outside the missile. The sensitive elements of the system make use of the principle of Newton's second law of motion.[3] In any weapons system wherein guidance intelligence is not derived from energy transmitted from the origin or from the target, the system must possess the ability to relate target and weapon motion with respect to a common

[3] *Glossary of Guided Missile Terms*, prepared by the Committee on Guided Missiles, 20 September 1949, p. 51.

reference. A simple inertial guidance system may be devised wherein the missile is controlled in azimuth along a predetermined course by a gyro. The trajectory in elevation to be followed by the missile is computed at the origin. The elevation trajectory is programmed in such a fashion that the missile's end of flight is at the target. The pitch angle of the missile is changed by a programmed precession of a gyro, thus causing the missile to fly the desired trajectory. This is, in effect, the mechanization of the German V-2 system. A more detailed description of this system can be found in Chap. 2.

Another example of an inertial system is a missile controlled in altitude by an altimeter and in azimuth by a gyro. The range traversed is measured by a simple milage counting device (e.g., an air log). The gyro axis is manually set to the desired heading and its output used to control the missile in azimuth.

Missile guidance, wherein the predetermined path set into the control system of a missile can be followed by a device in the missile which reacts to some property (field) of the earth such as magnetic or gravitational effects, is known as *terrestrial reference guidance*.[4]

A missile system whose guidance information is obtained from the earth's gravitational field and from acceleration data relative to inertial space, by virtue of Newton's laws of motion, is defined as an *inertial-gravitational* guidance system.

Basic Inertial-gravitational Guidance System. In the foregoing inertial systems, missile motion with respect to the earth is controlled by presetting into the system the missile heading and gravitational and wind corrections. Once the missile is in flight, several factors may cause error. For example, over long ranges it may be difficult to predetermine accurately wind conditions. For a long-range missile system to be accurate it is necessary to relate the missile's spatial motion to some reference which in turn can be related to the target's position.

The direction of the specific force of gravity is unique at any point on the surface of the earth as related to a spatial reference. This direction will be referred to throughout the remainder of this section as the *vertical*. Since the vertical at any point does possess unique features, a sensing mechanism that can measure the vertical at the position of the missile and relate this measurement to the vertical at the target position can be used to guide a missile. A missile system that performs such an operation is classed as an inertial-gravitational system. A plumb bob fixed with respect to the earth's surface may be used to determine the vertical at any point. The longitude and latitude of the point on the earth may be established very accurately by celestial observation.

Geometry of the Inertial-gravitational Guidance Problem. The use of

[4] *Ibid.*

inertial-gravitational guidance involves two major problems. The first is that of relating the geographical locations of two points: target and origin. The second problem is that of measuring the spatial motion of the missile with respect to the earth. For the moment it will be assumed that the earth is a stationary sphere and one in which the direction of gravity is always toward its center. Figure 16-35 illustrates the basic geometry of the inertial-gravitational guidance problem. The missile of interest is assumed to be capable of several thousand miles of flight. It was previously pointed out that the vertical at any point on the earth is unique, and it is this uniqueness which is the basis for establishing the geographical location of a point. From the simple sphere of Fig. 16-35

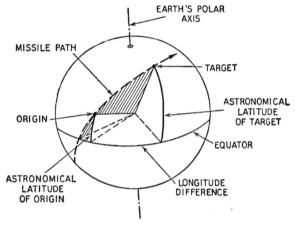

FIG. 16-35 Geometry of Inertial-gravitational Guidance.

it is apparent that the flight path along which the missile travels (a great circle on the assumed sphere) may be generated if the *astronomical latitude* (angle between the vertical and the plane of the equator) of the two points and the longitudinal difference between the two points are known.

The earth is actually in motion, and its shape is more of an oblate spheroid than a sphere, such as we have assumed. It is of interest to determine the errors and corrections resulting from these simplifying assumptions. In Fig. 16-36 two representations of the earth's shape are shown. The solid line represents the assumed guidance sphere and the dashed line represents the supposedly true shape of the earth. It is exaggerated for purposes of illustration. The vertical at point A does not go through the earth's center because of the centrifugal force of the earth's rotation and the oblateness of the earth. When the vertical is reconstructed on the guidance sphere there is a latitude error. A great circle flight path between two points on the surface of the assumed sphere must be translated toward the equator on the actual earth, because of this latitude error. The flat plane developing the great circle on the assumed sphere is warped in the translation and develops a slight curvature when applied to an oblate spheroid. This means that, as the missile flies between the target and origin, it will not fly along a great circle path but rather on a slightly curved path. The latitude error in radians is equal to the sine of twice the latitude multiplied by the oblateness of the earth. It was shown in Chap. 3 that the oblateness of the earth is approximately 0.339 percent. The radius of curvature of such a guidance path plane is extremely large (e.g., approximately one million miles) and the resulting acceleration will have only a very slight effect on the direction indicated by a vertical indicating device. Thus, if the exact vertical can be measured at the origin and the astronomical latitude and longitude differences for the target are known, the guidance path may be generated.

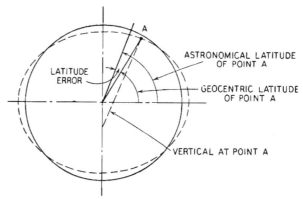

Fig. 16-36 Errors Resulting from Assumption of a Spherically Shaped Earth.

The second major problem in the construction of an inertial-gravitational guidance system is the development of mechanisms in the missile which will relate the missile's motion to the earth's motion. The plane cut through the earth along the great circle containing the verticals is the *track plane*. It is necessary to mechanize a guidance system which will fly the missile along this great circle path. When the problem of controlling the ground track of the missile in such a fashion that the center of gravity of the missile lies in the track plane is solved, then the remaining problem in the inertial-gravitational guidance technique becomes one of measuring the range traversed by the missile. Any deviation from the desired track will be fed as error signals to the autopilot to correct the missile's heading.

Once the guidance technique is established it is necessary to choose a suitable reference or coordinate system upon which the guidance system can be based. Convenient points on the earth's surface are illustrated in Fig. 16-37. The earth's polar axis, target vertical, and origin vertical are known and the vertical in the track plane at the equator and the vertical to the track plane may be readily obtained. The coordinate system may be established by the use of a suitable gyro gimballing arrangement if a stable platform as a reference can be established.

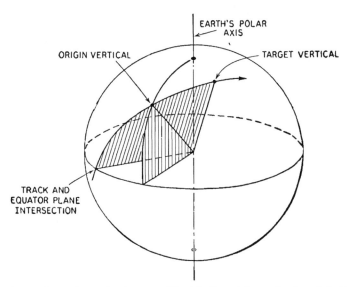

FIG. 16-37 Coordinate References Used in Inertial-gravitational Guidance.

A General Inertial-gravitational Guidance System. Figure 16-38 is a generalized block diagram of an inertial-gravitational guidance system. The *specific force of gravity*, i.e., the instantaneous direction of the vertical while the missile is in flight, is measured by the vertical sensing unit. The *range vertical* (an output from the vertical sensing unit) is the instantaneous vertical measured in the track plane. This is compared (via the computer) in the range angle indicator with the *range angle reference* which is the vertical, in the track plane, at the target. When the range vertical and the range angle reference coincide, the missile is at the target, or at a predetermined range from it if terminal guidance is to be employed. In this case, terminal guidance is initiated by the range angle indicator on the basis of range-to-go to the target.

The track vertical output from the vertical sensing unit is an error signal which represents the lateral displacement of the missile from the predetermined track plane. This error signal is employed by the computer, with airspeed and wind data, to develop the correct heading for the missile flight. When a flight error exists, appropriate changes in missile heading are initiated through the computer, airframe, and autopilot loop, resulting in a feedback to the vertical sensing unit to zero the error.

An altimeter is here indicated to cause the missile to fly at a predetermined constant altitude. Deviations in altitude as measured by the altimeter are used as signals to the autopilot to maintain the desired flight altitude of the missile.

Corrections may be applied to the vertical sensing unit to compensate for the motions of the earth. Consideration must be given to the rotation of the earth, particularly as it is related to Coriolis accelerations as discussed in Chap. 3.

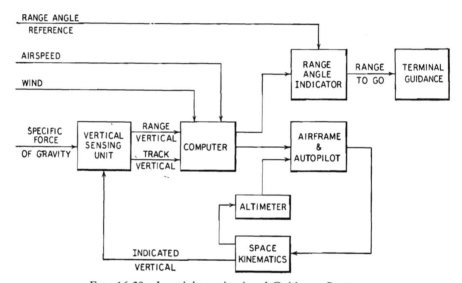

Fig. 16-38 Inertial-gravitational Guidance System.

Tactical Application of Inertial-gravitational Guidance. The complexity of system design will depend upon the range of the missile. For missiles of short range, several simplifications may be made. For example, the relative wind can be estimated and preset corrections can be made. For a long-range missile such corrections probably will be important.

Inertial-gravitational guidance systems have the main advantage of operational freedom. Such a system does not depend upon any transmitted energy from the source or from the target. It is not impaired by weather conditions and can operate at night as well as in the daytime. It is not susceptible to man-made interference. However, the magnitude of the errors tends to increase with the time of flight of the missile. Further, local anomalies (see Chap. 3) can cause variations in the vertical which cannot be predicted accurately. The targets of interest must be restricted to those which are fixed with respect to the earth's surface during the time of flight of the missile.

Inertial-celestial Guidance Systems. A system wherein a missile, suitably instrumented and containing all necessary guidance equipment, may follow a predetermined course in space with reference primarily to the relative positions of the missile and certain preselected celestial bodies is called an *inertial-celestial* guidance system.[5] An inertial-celestial guidance system may be thought of as an inertial-gravitational guidance system wherein the stars furnish the space reference. Some of the basic features discussed in the section on intertial-gravitational guidance apply equally well to inertial-celestial guidance. Because of this, only those parts which are unique to the inertial-celestial guidance system will be discussed in detail.

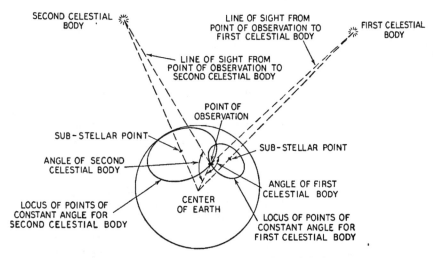

FIG. 16-39 Geometry of Inertial-celestial Guidance.

Geometry of the Inertial-celestial Guidance Problem. In inertial-celestial guidance systems, it is necessary to measure the vertical as was done in the inertial-gravitational system. The basic difference in the inertial-gravitational and inertial-celestial guidance systems is the manner in which space coordinates are related to earth coordinates. In an inertial-celestial guidance system, lines-of-sight to celestial bodies and astronomical data, when corrected for time, provide in the missile an earth reference to which the instantaneous measurement of the vertical can be compared and guidance information can be generated. In Chap. 3, navigation by

[5] *Ibid.*

celestial means has been discussed. For the purposes of the present discussion it will be assumed that the system derives reference information from the observation of two celestial bodies. Figure 16-39 illustrates the geometry of inertial-celestial guidance. The angles between the vertical at the point of observation and the lines-of-sight to two fixed stars are observed. Actually for each of the fixed stars this measurement defines a locus of points on the earth's surface where measurements would give the same celestial angle. There will be two intersections of the two locus of points, one of which can be readily eliminated if the approximate location of the target is known. The other intersection defines the astronomical latitude and longitude of the point of observation. The points on the earth where the line-of-sight to the celestial body is parallel to the vertical is called the *substellar point*. The lines-of-sight are *stellar lines*. Any substellar point is located astronomically by almanac data as a function of time, in terms of the celestial coordinates of the stars. In celestial coordinates the latitude is called *declination* and the longitude is called *Greenwich hour angle*. The line-of-sight to a star is essentially fixed in space, that is, because of the stellar distances the stars can be referred to as fixed stars. Thus the almanac provides a ready means for converting from spatial position to earth's position. The stellar line which is parallel to the vertical and the stellar line which goes through the point of observation are parallel because of the extreme distance to the celestial body. The distance in nautical miles from a substellar point to the point of observation is represented by the angle in minutes of arc between the vertical at the point and the line-of-sight to the star. This angle is the *complement* of the star's altitude, or the *co-altitude* of the star.

It is evident that the position of a point on the surface of the earth can be determined by celestial observation. The remaining problem is that of guiding a missile between two such points: namely, the origin and the target. The functions of controlling the missile along the desired course and the indication of arrival at the target can be handled in a manner similar to that of the previously described inertial-gravitational system. The basic difference between two such systems is the method of maintaining a stable platform. If a stable platform can be mechanized so that it is continuously perpendicular to the verticals along the desired track, then the angle between the line-of-sight to a fixed star (or stars) and the platform will indicate the true altitude of the star along the desired tracks. If the angle between the line-of-sight to a fixed star and a vertical sensing device is measured during the flight of the missile, it will be an indication of the actual altitude of the fixed star. If these two are compared, an azimuth error signal can be generated which will cause the missile to turn to the desired flight path. A second vertical sensing device orientated in such a fashion as to measure change of angle along the flight path, as described under the inertial-gravitational guidance technique, can be used to measure the range along the desired path and will indicate the range to the target. By observing two stars simultaneously no ambiguity will exist in the flight path of the missile. If in addition to the star trackers the system has gyros mounted on the stable platform it will be capable of performing satisfactorily as an inertial-gravitational system during periods when the trackers are unable to track the stars.

If in addition to the altitude the *azimuth* (angle between the meridian through the located point and the great circle from the located point to the substellar point) of the celestial body is measured, a guidance system can be employed which uses only one star tracker. This is true because the altitude of the star defines a locus of points and the azimuth defines one point on this locus.

A General Inertial-celestial Guidance System. Figure 16-40 illustrates the generalized block diagram for the inertial-celestial guidance system described in the preceding section. A major portion of this diagram is the same as that of Fig. 16-38. It is obvious that such a system can perform satisfactorily as an inertial guidance system, at least for short periods of time the length of which is determined by system drifts.

The star trackers and drive units should be space-stabilized with a suitable platform. The star trackers are essentially light-sensitive ele-

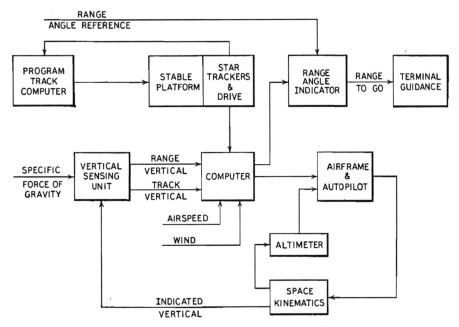

Fig. 16-40 Inertial-celestial Guidance System.

ments. Initially the star trackers should be driven by a memory device until the stars are captured, at which time automatic tracking commences. Generated signals represent the instantaneous angles between the star trackers and the verticals along the programmed missile flight path. These signals are used to cause the angle between the stable platform and the star trackers to change to agree with the predetermined angles along the desired flight path. The stable platform will always be at right angles to the verticals along the programmed missile flight path. The *specific force of gravity*, i.e., the instantaneous direction of the vertical while the missile is in flight, is measured by the vertical sensing unit. The track vertical output from the vertical sensing unit is a signal which represents the angle between the stable platform and the actual verticals (lateral displacement from the predetermined track plane). In the computer the track vertical signal is compared with the signal from the star trackers. The resultant signal, corrected for airspeed and wind, represents an error in missile heading. When an error exists, appropriate changes in missile heading are initiated through the computer, airframe, and autopilot loop, resulting in a feedback to the vertical sensing unit to zero the error.

The method of measuring range-to-go to the target is the same as that described for the inertial-gravitational system. The range vertical is a signal which represents the instantaneous measure of the vertical in the track plane. After suitable corrections in the computer, this signal is compared in the range angle indicator with the range angle reference signal which represents the vertical at the target. When these two verticals agree, the missile is at the proper range from the target. Terminal guidance, if employed, is initiated by the range angle indicator on the basis of range-to-go to the target.

An altimeter is used to cause the missile to fly at a predetermined altitude. The altimeter measures deviations in altitude from the predetermined value. These deviations are used as signals to the autopilot to cause the missile to make a correction in altitude.

Tactical Application of Inertial-celestial Guidance. The targets of interest obviously must be restricted to those which are fixed with respect to the earth's surface during the time of flight of the missile. The complexity of system design will depend upon the range of operation of the system. For example, in a long-range system corrections for the earth's rotation and relative wind may be necessary. In addition, it may be desirable to mount gyros on the stable platform to enable the system to operate as an inertial-gravitational system during periods when the stars are not visible to the star trackers. For short-range application the corrections for wind and earth's rotation probably can be ignored. The ability of the system to operate inertial-gravitational as well as inertial-celestial may not be needed.

An inertial-celestial system as described has the advantage over the inertial-gravitational system in that a constantly corrected stable platform is available. Thus system drifts will not play as important a part in ultimate guidance accuracy. Since the star trackers must be mounted in a protective dome, refraction problems similar to those encountered in airborne radomes may exist.

Terrestrial-magnetic Guidance System. The character of the earth's magnetic field was discussed in Chap. 3. The use of this field as a reference is so widespread for navigational purposes that its possible application to missile guidance was early explored.

Positions on the surface of the earth are determined by use of an arbitrary geographical coordinate system consisting of latitude, longitude, and a prime meridian. Distances north and south (latitude) are measured with respect to the equator, which is halfway between the north and south geographical poles; distances east and west (longitude) are measured from some specified meridian, commonly the Greenwich prime meridian.

The magnetic field of the earth has comparable reference coordinates. The location of the magnetic reference lines are determined by actual measurement rather than by arbitrarily locating a line as is the case in the geographical coordinate system. Three quantities must be measured to establish completely the magnetic field of the earth. These are: (1) the magnitude of the horizontal component of the total magnetic intensity; (2) the angle that the horizontal magnetic intensity makes with the geographical meridian (called *declination*); (3) the angle between the total intensity and horizontal component of the total intensity, called the *dip angle* or the *inclination*. These quantities are measured with magnetometers.

Lines which connect points having equal declination are called *isogonic lines* and are the counterpart of longitude lines in the geographical system. There will be two lines along which the magnetic declination will be zero. These are called *agonic lines* and are the counterpart of the zero meridian and the 180th meridian. A line connecting points having zero vertical magnetic component, that is zero dip angle, is the *magnetic equator*. Lines through points having equal dip will be roughly parallel to the equator and are called *isoclinic lines*. These are the counterpart of latitude lines. Finally lines having equal horizontal intensity are called *isodynamic lines*. The isoclinic lines and the isodynamic lines may not coincide because the total magnetic intensity is not uniform over the surface of the earth.

The locations of the magnetic poles are less clearly defined than the locations of the geographical poles. If the criterion that the poles are located where there is zero horizontal magnetic intensity be used, there are two general areas in each hemisphere which satisfy. However, if the criterion that the pole is located where the isogonic lines converge is employed only one general area is defined in each hemisphere. This latter has come to be the correct definition of the *earth's magnetic poles*. The exact location of the magnetic poles is indeterminate as compared to the location of the geographical poles.

All of the magnetic lines discussed are irregular in both intensity and direction. They are greatly modified by local conditions such as deposits of ferrous ores. In fact, the position of a line can be determined only by making point-by-point measurements. This may become an almost impossible task because of the large number of measurements necessary if a detailed plot of a given area is desired. Generally, the irregularities increase as one approaches either magnetic pole.

In addition to the irregularity of direction of the magnetic lines there are several different types of variation in total intensity. There is a daily variation in both intensity and direction, a yearly variation, and a continuous variation in declination extending over centuries. Superimposed upon these variations are erratic and unpredictable variations which are called *magnetic storms*. In some cases these are coincident with sun spots.

It should be apparent that any attempt to use terrestrial magnetism as the sole guiding reference for a missile system will be difficult. In fact, all the components of the magnetic field which might be used for guidance are quite unpredictable. Despite this there are possible mechanizations in which terrestrial magnetism is used as one of the guiding elements.

Missile Guidance Mechanisms, Magnetic. One of the first devices that might be considered is a magnetic compass. It may be suspended so that it is free to move in a horizontal plane. The magnetic bearing to the target must be known. This is introduced into the missile guidance system so that any deviation of the missile trajectory from this direction will produce an error signal. The error signal may then be used to cause the missile to change its direction to reduce the error to zero.

The German V-1 used a magnetic compass as part of its guidance system. The system (described in Chap. 2) was designed so that the magnetic compass controlled the missile in azimuth only. The missile was controlled in altitude by a barometric altimeter and in range by an air log.

If a compass needle is suspended so that it has two degrees of freedom, both declination and dip can be measured. If the desired declination and dip are calculated and stored on magnetic tape, the difference in what these values should be and what they are at any given time can be measured. The resulting error signals can be used to control the missile and any desired flight path can be followed if sufficient information is available in regard to magnetic field along the line-of-flight.

The magnetic field of the earth can be used as the field for a d-c generator. If the axis of rotation of the armature points along the line of the total magnetic intensity, there will be a zero output voltage. If an angle exists between the axis of rotation and the total magnetic intensity, a voltage will be developed. It would be possible to use such a system to control a missile along the line of the total magnetic intensity. By use of a programmed system as described above, the missile might be guided. Other magnetic mechanisms used in combination with stabilizing gyroscopes are described in Chap. 9.

Any system of magnetic guidance for missiles will be a relatively inaccurate system because of the irregularities and variations in the magnetic field of the earth. Unless augmented by some form of terminal guidance, the targets against which it could be used would have to encompass relatively large areas. On the other hand, the use of the earth's magnetic field results in a relatively simple guidance system which is difficult to influence by external countermeasures.

16-6 APPLICATION OF RADIO NAVIGATION TECHNIQUES TO MISSILE GUIDANCE

Radio navigation systems most commonly in use fall under one of three general categories; radial, circular, and hyperbolic. Before World War II radio navigation was essentially limited to direction-finding techniques. This is the familiar method in which the navigator of a ship takes a bearing on two transmitters of known location. By plotting the reverse bearings from the transmitters the ship's location can be determined. Systems operating on this principle fall under the *radial* classification. During the war the Germans developed a much more complex radial system called *Sonne*. By properly spacing, keying, and phasing of three fixed vertical antennas, a radiation pattern consisting of approximately a dozen sectors in which successions of dots are heard that alternate with sectors in which dashes are heard is produced. Along the radius boundary sectors a steady tone (equisignal) will be heard. The dots and dashes are emitted, one a second, for a minute, during which the radiation pattern is slowly rotated by shifting the phases of the two outside antennas, and hence at the end of a minute each dot sector has moved into the place of the adjacent dash sector and vice versa. During the next minute a steady omnidirectional tone is emitted by the central antenna. Then the procedure is repeated. The operator determines his radial line of position within his sector simply by counting the number of dots and dashes from the start of the period until the equisignal sweeps pass him. Having determined his radial line within the zone the operator can determine his zone by simple direction finding.[6]

The position of a ship or aircraft can be determined by finding the location on a circle or circles about known locations. This is the *circular*

[6] Pierce, McKenzie, and Woodward, *Loran*, pp. 4, 5, Radiation Laboratory Series, Vol. 4, McGraw-Hill.

method of radio navigation. Several such systems are in use among which are *Oboe, Micro-H,* and *Shoran*. The Oboe system was much used during the war for blind bombing. The distance to the aircraft is measured by two ground stations (radars) and signals transmitted instructing the aircraft to fly along a predetermined circle about one of the stations. When the distances from the stations correspond to the distances from station to target a signal to release bombs is transmitted. This system is complex and has limited traffic-handling capabilities. Micro-H and Shoran both operate on the same principle except that the requirement for detailed coordination between ground radar operators and aircraft is eliminated by placing the range measuring device in the aircraft and two beacons at fixed ground locations. In the Micro-H system a radar is used for range measurement. In Shoran the range is determined by a simple distance measuring set rather than a radar.

Hyperbolic navigation is a general method for determining lines of position by measuring the difference in distance of the navigation apparatus from two or more stations whose positions are known. By measuring the difference of time of arrival of signals transmitted from the two or more stations the difference in distance can be determined. A line of constant difference in distance will be a hyperbola. Some of the systems now in use are *Decca,* which employs continuous wave signals, *Loran* and *Gee,* both of which employ pulse transmission. The fundamental characteristics of these systems are the same.

Since beacons are used in many radio navigation systems it is of interest to consider the beacon range equation. The power received for a one-way transmission path may be calculated by the range equation

$$P_r = \frac{P_t G_t G_r \lambda^2}{(4\pi R)^2} - A_1 \qquad (16\text{-}12)$$

or the power required of a transmitter as

$$P_{t1} = \frac{(P_{r1} + A_1)(4\pi R)^2}{G_t G_r \lambda^2} \qquad (16\text{-}13)$$

where P_r = power received in watts at the receiver input
P_{r1} = required receiver sensitivity in watts for satisfactory overall operation
P_t = transmitter power output in watts
P_{t1} = required transmitter power output in watts
G_r = effective gain of the receiving antenna over an isotropic radiator
G_t = effective gain of the transmitting antenna over an isotropic radiator
R = range in any units
λ = wavelength in the same units as R
A_1 = antilog$_{10}$ (propagation power losses in db)/10

Considerable care must be exercised in handling, modifying, or measuring the quantities involved in the range equation if calculated values are to agree with actual test results. For example, if the radar automatically tracks a beacon target at a beam crossover point 3 db down on the antenna pattern, then the known gain of the antenna must be reduced by 3 db. Where either of the antennas may be operated off axis during a portion of a flight, the loss in gain must be considered. In all cases G_t and G_r must represent useful gain of the antennas. The propagation power losses contained in A must include all losses that exist between the transmitter output and receiver input. Further details on beaconry are to be found in Par. 10-38 through 10-42 of Chap. 10.

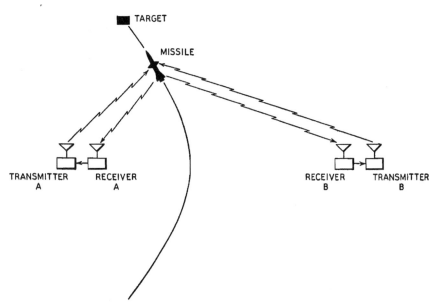

Fig. 16-41 Application of Hyperbolic Navigation to Missile Guidance.

Both circular and hyperbolic navigation techniques are applicable to missile control. Discussion of these two techniques has been given in preceding chapters; further and complete details may be found in any navigation textbook. However, a brief description of basic geometry of each as it applies to missile guidance is in order.

The Geometry of Hyperbolic Navigation. The basic geometry of any hyperbolic navigation system is illustrated by Fig. 10-5. The lines of constant differences in distance between transmitters A and B are hyperbolas. This is true because by definition a hyperbola is the locus of points all of which are farther from one fixed point than they are from another fixed point by the same distance. The two fixed points, in this case transmitters *A* and *B*, are the foci. The line which is equidistant from *A* and *B* is a hyperbola of zero curvature. The other lines will be concave toward the nearer station. These lines represent a family generated by the two stations. In practice one transmitting station is the master station and the other station or stations are slave stations. The cycle of transmission always begins at the master station. The Loran system has a master station and one slave station in each Loran pair. The Decca and Gee systems each have two slave stations operating in conjunction with the master station.

Application of the Hyperbolic Navigation Technique to Missile Guidance. The hyperbolic navigation technique can be used for two-dimensional guidance of missiles. One possible technique is illustrated in Fig. 16-41. In this system the missile carries the master transmitter. Basically the guidance action is as follows: A signal is transmitted from the missile and is received at each of the two slave stations. Each of the slave stations then transmits a signal which is received at the missile. A time comparison of the two signals received at the missile is made and, from this, guidance

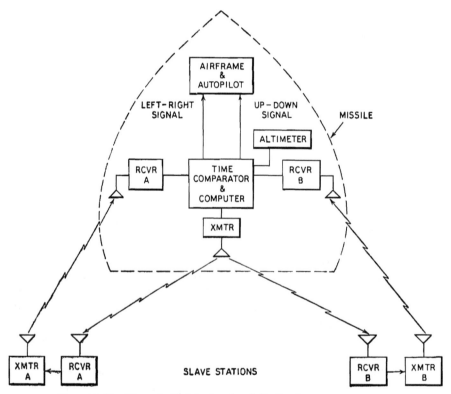

FIG. 16-42 Hyperbolic Navigation Missile Guidance System.

information is derived. The missile then flies a course of constant-distance difference, which passes through the target.

Figure 16-42 is a more detailed block diagram of the entire system. The missile equipment consists of the master transmitter, two receivers, a time comparator and computer, control unit (airframe and autopilot), and an altimeter. Each of the slave stations consists of a transmitter and a receiver. In addition one station will have a range computer. When the signal, which is transmitted from the missile is received at the slave station the two transmitters are keyed. To avoid confusion in the missile, these transmitters (A and B) must be operating on different frequencies. Therefore, two receivers are needed in the missile. The signals from the slave stations are received in the missile where they are compared. If the time difference (range difference) is not the same as the value required for the missile to be flying along the correct hyperbola, a left or right signal is generated which causes the missile to turn to the correct course. Some means must be incorporated to keep the missile flying at the correct altitude. This may be done by the use of an altimeter. The output of the altimeter is fed into the computer where up-down signals are generated to keep the missile flying at a predetermined altitude.

So far the indicated system has the capability of flying the missile along the correct course at the predetermined altitude. This is not enough. It is necessary to determine when the missile is over the target. This may be done by means of the computer in the missile. The range of the missile may be determined from the slave stations by time-comparing the transmitted signal from the missile with the signal received from one of the slave stations. When this agrees with a preset time, which represents the distance from the slave station to the target, terminal guidance, if employed, begins. The terminal guidance phase may use one of the homing techniques previously described or the missile may simply be caused to go into a dive.

Advantages of a Hyperbolic Guidance System. A hyperbolically controlled flight of missiles can be operated without close control between the launching crews and the controlling groups and without saturation of the guiding facilities. Under inertial control or other midcourse guidance the missiles may be launched into the hyperbolic field in any quantity. With a system of this sort, missiles could be launched from many points into a large area. Many launching sites could independently send off missiles sensitive to a single line of position, without any requirements for coordination. These missiles would follow their independent courses until they came within the zone of influence of the hyperbolic line, whereupon each would change its course and come about exponentially to ride the line to the objective.[7]

[7] *Ibid.*, pp. 116, 117.

The missile equipment can be very simple and compact in form. In Fig. 16-42 three antennas are shown in the missile. The slave station frequencies can be very close together so that a common antenna might be used. The slave station equipment consists of a simple transmitter and receiver. Since all parameters are preset in the missile, no knowledge of missile trajectory is required at the slave stations or at the launching station.

Tactical Considerations. It is obvious that the target's location with respect to the two slave stations must be known with a fair degree of accuracy. The degree of accuracy required will vary with warhead lethal area, target size, and knowledge of target and beacon station locations on

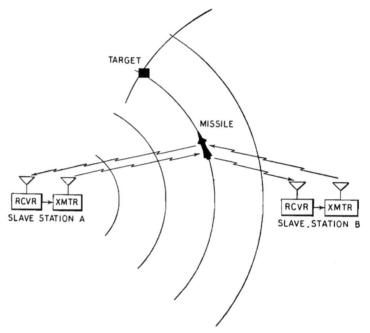

Fig. 16-43 Basic Geometry of Circular Navigation.

the earth's surface. Since the target must be fixed with respect to the slave stations, obviously this system will have utility against only those targets which are stationary during the time of flight of the missile.

Application of Circular Navigation Techniques to Missile Guidance. Figure 16-43 illustrates one possible application of circular navigation techniques to missile guidance. The missile flies along a line of constant distance from the transmitter. The lines of constant distance from the transmitter will be circles. Thus the missile must be guided along a circle which passes through the target. One such possible missile guidance system is illustrated by Fig. 16-44. In this system the master station is in the missile. A signal transmitted from the missile is received at the slave station A and triggers the transmitter at this station. The signal transmitted from this slave station is received in the missile. By measuring the time for the signal to go from missile to station A and back less the time for delays in the system, the distance from the missile to this slave station can be determined. By comparing this with a fixed range in the range comparator, left-right signals can be generated which will cause the

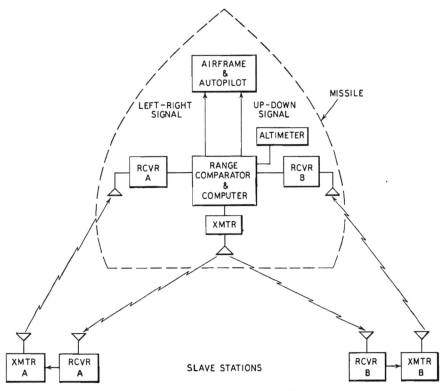

Fig. 16-44 Circular Navigation Missile Guidance System.

missile to fly along the correct circle which goes through the target. Altitude information is derived from altimeter signals which are compared with a fixed altitude in the computer. Thus the missile flies at a predetermined altitude. Slave station B is necessary in the system to determine when terminal guidance should begin. When the range from this station to the missile agrees with a preset range in the missile computer, which is equal to the range from station B to the target, terminal guidance may begin. This terminal phase may utilize one of the homing guidance techniques previously discussed or the missile may be caused to go into a dive. The two slave station transmitters must operate at slightly different frequencies and two different receivers are needed in the missile. To avoid possible ambiguity in the range at which terminal guidance begins, no transmission from the missile occurs until the missile is approximately over the line between the slave stations.

The advantages of such a system are that it requires very little coordination between ground facilities, has high-traffic handling capacity, has very simple missile equipment, and has very simple external equipment.

Obviously the same tactical considerations apply to the circular navigation technique as were discussed for the hyperbolic technique. The target must be stationary during the flight of the missile. The location of the target with respect to the slave stations must be known with a fair degree of accuracy.

16-7 MISSILE GUIDANCE BY ACOUSTIC MEANS *

The sharp acoustic differentiation between an aircraft and its surroundings and the fact that its propulsion is inextricably related to the radiation of acoustic energy have led to speculation on the possible application of acoustics to guided missiles. As in infrared applications, the target provides its own signal so that a relatively simple passive system may be used against it.

Target Signal Characteristics. The target signal can range from about 100 db (where reference level is 10^{-16} watts/sq cm) for a reciprocating engine converting 10 percent of the mechanical power to acoustic power to a level of 140 db for a turbojet with after-burner and a 1 percent conversion efficiency.[8] While these are sound levels found very near the aircraft, it is common experience for one to distinguish the presence of an aircraft while it is a considerable distance away, even in the presence of normal 80-90 db ambient street noises. The frequency spectrum characteristic of propeller targets is peaked at frequencies around 150-200 cps and decays in the higher frequency range. For jets, the sound is more evenly distributed. Aircraft noise radiates in a directional pattern, the overall static pattern of a reciprocating engine airplane being predominantly to the sides whereas the jet airplane pattern is mostly to the rear (see Fig. 16-45).

In flight, there is theoretical evidence to indicate that the sound will shift somewhat forward as a function of the source's speed.[9] Without

---

* Par. 16-7 has been prepared by Martin H. Paiss, Aeronautical Electronic and Electrical Laboratory, U. S. Naval Air Development Center, Johnsville, Pa.

[8] H. E. VonGierke, *The Journal of the Acoustic Society of America*, Vol. 25, No. 3, May 1953, pp. 367-380.

[9] M. J. Lighthill, *Proceedings of the Royal Society of London*, A211, pp. 564-587 (1953); and Hans L. Oestreicher, *CADO Technical Data Digest*, September 1951, pp. 16-22.

delving into the theoretical details, such a shift becomes plausible when one thinks in terms of the shock wave generated in front of a body as it approaches sonic speed. Looked at another way, the forward motion of a sound source increases the frequency of the sound in the direction of motion (Doppler effect). If we assume constant amplitude of displacement of the particles in the medium, the frequency shift upward increases the root mean square distribution of the velocity of the particles about the mean point. Since the intensity is directly proportional to this velocity, and the divergence of the sound flux is less in unit time in the forward direction than in other directions, a net increase in intensity results. Figure 16-46 shows the characteristics of an omnidirectional sound source

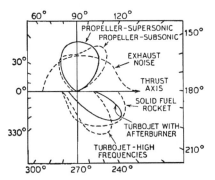

FIG. 16-45 Directivity Patterns of the Overall Sound Pressure Amplitude around Various Aircraft Noise Sources.

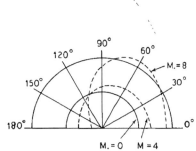

FIG. 16-46 Directivity Pattern of a Sound Source of Zero Order in Uniform Rectilinear Motion.

moving at various speeds. As a target passes sonic speed, the sound no longer precedes the target and, although the sound intensity is strongest in the forward quadrants, it is still received after the target passes.

Tactical Considerations. The foregoing discussion reveals that homing against supersonic targets is restricted to the rear quadrants and, specifically, to a solid angle defined by the Mach cone. A further complication arising from the low sonic velocity compared to usual missile-target relative speeds is the large separation between the actual and the virtual target (the apparent source of the sound disturbance created by the aircraft). Consider, for example, a target moving at sonic speed as illustrated in Fig. 16-47. Here the sound front will diverge spherically and, for an impulse generated at any instant, the aircraft moves away from the center of the disturbance as rapidly as the sound front. By the time the sound front reaches the homing missile, the target is an equal distance from the virtual target. Figure 16-47 shows that, except in direct tail-chase, the homing device will not point a missile at the actual target except at small ranges where the virtual target is close to the actual target. It is obvious that the ratio of the target-to-virtual target distance to the missile-to-virtual target distance is equal to the Mach number of the target and is independent of the approach angle of the homing missile. While the existence of the virtual target complicates the trajectory of an acoustic homing missile, it does not appear to be an insurmountable obstacle to the design of a practical missile.

A distinct advantage of the acoustic homing missile lies in the relative impossibility of jamming its receiver. The large amount of power re-

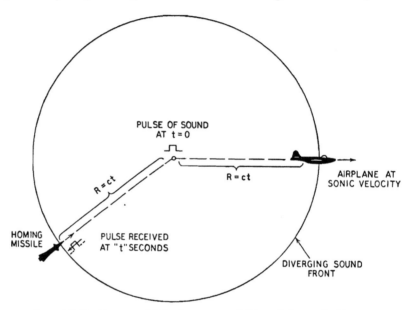

FIG. 16-47 Rearward Displacement of Virtual Acoustic Target.

quired to provide sufficient acoustic energy to decoy the missile from an aircraft would necessitate power plants equivalent to aircraft engines themselves; thus effective countermeasures using decoy devices released by pursued aircraft are hardly practical. The only effective countermeasure against this type of sensor would be momentarily to silence the engines. This type of countermeasure has obvious tactical drawbacks.

Self-noise and Propagation Considerations. There are other problems that qualify the advantages of homing on an acoustic target. One problem is that of the noise from the sensor's own propulsive system. This cannot be easily shielded; therefore the missile must be supersonic. This means that tactical utility against slow targets is limited where high closing velocities might require excessive missile maneuvering. Furthermore, the supersonic velocity of the sensor can result in aerodynamic buffeting which might generate sufficient acoustic noise to blanket the target signal.

Propagation anomalies and the fact that high acoustic frequencies are attenuated directly as the square of the frequency also limit the types of targets that may be attacked. There are other limitations, beyond the scope of this text, that render the development of an acoustic homing missile difficult and problematical.

German Development. During World War II, the Germans were engaged in the development of acoustic homing devices. Two such devices were designed as guidance for the *X*-4 missile. Both methods coupled sounds from two separate entrance ports, comparing the phase of the incident sound front and thus determining the direction of the target. Phase comparison circuits were used to command the missile to maneuver such that the phase angles were made equal. The missile was thus made to point directly at the virtual target and a pursuit trajectory was achieved.

16-8 GUIDANCE SYSTEM COMBINATIONS

In the preceding paragraphs of this chaper the guidance techniques in general have been considered for separate and unique systems. In the practical case, control of the missile may require a combination of guidance techniques. The applied missile guidance problem can be divided into three phases: launching guidance, midcourse guidance, and terminal guidance. In certain applications the latter two may be combined. The manner by which specific guidance system combinations are chosen for particular missile applications is discussed in Chap. 8. The following is intended as a general discourse on some possible combinations of guidance techniques in the four general categories of guided missile systems.

Combined Systems in Air-to-air Missile Application. Since the air-to-air missile is transported to the vicinity of the target and will be of the short-range variety, only one guidance method need be employed. The guidance technique employed may be of the beam-rider, passive, active, semiactive, or command types. For situations where passive, active, or semiactive guidance is employed, the missile guidance equipment may be locked-on the target before launching. Thus, the launching guidance phase requires that the missile be aerodynamically stable in order that it will fly toward the target along a trajectory which does not introduce a launching error beyond the capability of the guidance system until a missile speed is reached where the control surfaces can function properly. In a command system the missile obviously must be sufficiently stable so that it stays within the limits of the equipment from which command information is generated (optical or radar) during the period when the missile has not yet reached control speed. In a system employing beam-rider guidance, it is necessary to compute the proper launch angle which will insure beam-capture of the missile. Aerodynamic stability must maintain the missile along the correct flight path until control speed is reached.

Combined Systems in Air-to-surface Missile Application. The types of guidance combinations employed in air-to-surface missile application will depend upon the intended range of operation of the missile. If the missile is intended for short-range application, the midcourse and terminal guidance phases will be combined into a single guidance method. Examples of possible techniques useful for short-range air-to-surface missiles are beam-rider, command, and active, passive and semiactive homing guidance.

If the missile is intended for long-range application, distinct midcourse and terminal guidance phases using two or more guidance methods may be employed. Beam-rider or command guidance are examples of the techniques which may be employed for the midcourse guidance phase. As the range of the missile system increases, the missile-to-target miss distance for both the beam-rider and command techniques tends to increase. This miss distance may become excessive and a more accurate terminal guidance phase may become necessary. The terminal guidance phase may utilize active homing by a radar in the missile or passive homing if energy of sufficient level is transmitted from the target.

The launching guidance phase, as in the case of the air-to-air missile systems, will be short in nature and may be handled as a matter of airframe stability.

Combined Systems in Surface-to-air Missile Application. Since it is desirable to shoot down the invading aircraft beyond the limits of the target's armament, the missile range will, in general, be greater than that which can be obtained by optical guidance techniques. Thus, the surface-to-air missile system may use semiactive homing, radar beam-rider, or radar command midcourse guidance. Active and passive homing guidance may be used, but the resulting system will be limited in range. If any of the homing techniques are employed, no terminal guidance phase is necessary. However, for systems employing beam-rider or radar command midcourse guidance a separate terminal guidance phase may be desirable if the system accuracy requirements so dictate. This terminal guidance phase may use active or passive homing techniques.

Because the time available between detection of the target and missile impact is limited, the missile will probably be launched from the close proximity of the surface guidance equipment. Thus, the launching guidance problems are similar to those of the air-to-air or air-to-surface missile systems. The launching problems will be less stringent for the surface-to-air missile because the launching site will be stationary or relatively slow moving.

Combined Systems in Surface-to-surface Missile Application. It is in the long-range surface-to-surface missile field that combined systems will be most useful. A wide variety of such systems, limited partially by the target type and warhead lethality, is possible.

In the application of surface-to-surface missiles it is often desirable to have the missile launching site and the point from which midcourse guidance starts widely separated. For example, in the systems previously discussed which employ radar navigation guidance techniques, it may be desirable to launch the missile from a ship at sea while the beacons, from which midcourse guidance information is derived, may be land-based. In this case a launching guidance phase of long duration is conceivable. It is necessary to place the missile in the vicinity of the beacons. This might be accomplished in a variety of ways, examples of which are magnetic and command guidance.

The midcourse guidance phase may utilize magnetic, gravitational, or celestial references or radio navigation techniques. The necessity for a terminal guidance phase will be dictated by the accuracy of the midcourse guidance phase and the missile warhead lethality. This terminal phase may use passive or active homing guidance or a programmed missile maneuver, depending upon the nature of the target.

Fusing. Maximum effectiveness of any missile warhead depends upon its detonation or "fusing" at an optimum time; this is particularly true for aircraft targets. Thus, information as to closing velocity, range, and direction of the target is useful in fusing techniques. Guidance systems produce some or all of this information in such form that it can be used directly or with modifications for this purpose.

BIBLIOGRAPHY

1. *Glossary of Guided Missile Terms*, Prepared by the Committee on Guided Missiles Department of Defense, Washington, D. C., 1949.
2. J. N. Ridenour, *Radar System Engineering*, McGraw-Hill Book Co., Inc., New York, 1947.
3. MIT Radar School Staff, *Principles of Radar*, 2nd Ed., McGraw-Hill Book Co., Inc., New York, 1946.
4. J. A. Pierce, A. A. McKenzie, and R. H. Woodward (Eds.), *Loran*, Vol. 4, Radiation Laboratory Series, McGraw-Hill Book Co., Inc., New York, 1948.
5. V. A. Suydam, *Fundamentals of Electricity and Electromagnetism*, D. Van Nostrand Co., Inc., New York, 1940.
6. H. E. Von Gierke, *The Journal of the Acoustic Society of America*, Vol. 25 No. 3, pp. 367–385, May 1953.
7. M. J. Lighthill, *Proceedings of the Royal Society of London*, pp. 564–587, 1952.
8. H. L. Oestreicher, *CADO Technical Data Digest*, pp. 16–22, September 1951.

CHAPTER 17

BANDWIDTH STUDIES

Symbols Used in Chapter 17

a = a constant relating actual beamwidth to the general case
A_E = effective back scattering area of target, square meters
C_1 = capacitance in first section
C_2 = capacitance in second section
E_o = output voltage
$\mathcal{E}(t)$ = error quantity = $\theta_i - \theta_o$, a function of time
F = pulse repetition rate, recurrences per second
G = ratio, antenna gain over isotropic
G_R = receiving antenna gain
G_T = transmitting antenna gain
i_1 = current in first section
K = gain factor
N = numerical factor
$\overline{NF}$ = receiver noise factor, ratio
P_{ax} = power at the angle ax
P_{fmax} = maximum power
P_T = transmitted peak power, watts
R_0 = slant range to target at crossover

R_1 = resistance in first section
R_2 = resistance in second section
$R_{\max}$ = maximum radar range
$s = \sigma + j\omega$ (see Chaps. 6 and 7)
t = time
t_{coast} = velocity memory time
V = target horizontal speed, knots
x = angle from center of main lobe
θ = angle, train
θ_s = squint angle, angular distance between opposite extreme positions of nutated beam
$\dot{\theta}_i$ = input train angle velocity
$\ddot{\theta}_i$ = input train angle acceleration
$\dddot{\theta}$ = rate of change of $\ddot{\theta}$
λ = r-f operation wavelength, meters
μ_1, μ_2 = gain factors
τ = pulse duration, sec
ϕ_0 = target elevation angle, at crossover
$\omega_1 = 1/R_1 C_1$
$\omega_2 = 1/R_2 C_2$

In anything but a superficial discussion of a guided missile, the ancillary launchers, missile ready service and storage arrangements, search radars, tracking radars, guidance radars, and computers must be considered. The entire aggregation is recognized as a guided missile system composed of equipments that reflect in their design the demands imposed upon the weapon system by the targets and the dynamics of their flight paths. This is to say that all things stem from the tactical problem. Operational requirements are developed for a proposed missile system from such considerations. Feasibility studies are based upon the presumed target tactics. Engineering specifications for many parts of the weapons system are established by determining control system response characteristics required to combat a specific type of target.

In the present chapter, missile system design considerations related to a specific hypothetical tactical problem are examined to show the deliberations involved in developing complete system specifications. In the hypothetical example, one of the military services provides a contractor with a statement of the tactical requirements and the desired missile system performance specifications. This chapter contains a discussion of the tactical problem, performance demands upon the ground-based equipment including the search radar, the tracking radar with the ship-roll stabilization problem, the launcher servo system, and the launcher lead computer. The missile-borne radar considerations are also discussed. To complete the guided missile system specifications, the subject is continued in Chap. 18, in which an analysis of the required characteristics for the outside missile control loop is given together with the performance requirements of loops such as the missile-roll control system and the missile wing-flap servo system.

17-1 TACTICAL PROBLEM

A complete specification of the tactical problem must include statements regarding the launching point, the type of target and the presumed target tactics to be used as a design basis, the type of guidance intelligence to be employed and the type of missile control system desired, the missile range and accuracy requirements, the system overall reliability demanded, and a specification of the kill probability expected. Ordinarily, many of these factors are established by the contractor, but for the purposes of the present treatment the foregoing is assumed. As provided by the government bureau, in the hypothetical example, in which the figures used are intentionally unrealistic, these are as follows:

Launching point
  The launching point will be from shipboard (a cruiser converted to a guided missile ship).

Target
  The target shall be considered to be a nonmaneuvering medium bomber, i.e., with presumed tactics that of a constant-altitude, straight-line, constant-speed course: (altitude = 30,000 ft, speed = 400 knots, horizontal crossover range = 4000 yd).

Missile
  The missile shall have a maximum range of 40,000 yd, be capable of cruising at a 30,000 ft altitude with a Mach 2.64 speed, contain receiv-

ing and control equipment for a semiactive homing system, carry a warhead such that the accuracy requirements are that the missile shall pass within 800 ft of target 80 percent of the time.

Effectiveness

A single missile shall be capable of inflicting a damage probability of at least 50 per cent at maximum range.

Reliability

The reliability of the overall system shall be at least 90 percent.

The foregoing is meant to be an abstract from the specifications of all information initially supplied that is pertinent to the scope of the planned discussion. Such a specification is normally the result of an operations research study by the government bureau. After study of the specifications, the contractor decides that information regarding the search radar and the tracking radar performance characteristics against the medium bomber is needed. Subsequent conferences with the bureau develops the following facts and desired parameters:

Search Radar

Maximum search radar detection range is 100 nautical miles and experience shows a 90 percent probability of detection at 38-mile target range and that a 30-sec delay from instant of detection until identification, evaluation, and assignment (to a particular tracking radar) must be permissible.

Tracking Radar

Type: Pulse
Frequency: X-band
Peak power: 200 kw
Pulse length: 1μ sec
Pulse repetition rate: 400 pulses per sec
Scan rate: 30 cps
Antenna dish diameter: 5 ft
Delay time (from assignment to lock-on): 20 sec

Target

Target effective area: 40 sq meters

The contractor is now in a position to verify the actual feasibility of the proposed development. Figure 16-11 illustrates the geometry of the guidance system. Figure 17-1 shows the results of a study establishing the timewise relationships. The detection range (with 90 percent probability) is shown at 38-nautical mile range. During the 30-sec delay before assignment to a particular tracking radar, the bomber target covers a distance

$$400 \text{ knots} \cdot \frac{1}{3600} \frac{\text{hr}}{\text{sec}} \cdot 30 \text{ sec} = 3.33 \text{ nautical miles} \qquad (17\text{-}1)$$

to reach a range of 34.7 miles. The additional delay due to the time for the tracking radar to lock-on (20 sec) brings the target to the 32.4-mile range ($t = 0$) point. The missile will accelerate rapidly from an assumed zero velocity at the launcher to reach cruising speed quickly. The determination of the exact manner in which a missile reaches full speed is a major study in itself. For present purposes, it will be assumed that the missile accelerates to reach a speed of 995 ft per sec (the velocity of sound at a 30,000-ft altitude under standard conditions) at a range of

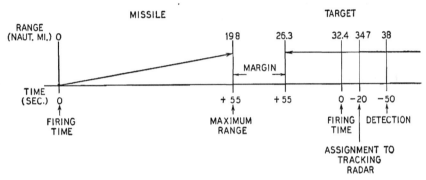

Fig. 17-1 Timewise Feasibility.

$\frac{1}{2}$ nautical mile (6 sec after launching). Further, that acceleration to a velocity of 2627 ft per sec (Mach 2.64 at 30,000-ft altitude) is reached 20 sec after launching. Assume that a simple average of 995 and 2627 ft per sec or an average velocity of 1811 ft per sec during an interval of 14 sec exists to cover an additional 4.2 miles to a range of 4.7 miles (+20 sec). To reach the maximum range of 40,000 yd, an additional time of

$$(19.8 - 4.7)\frac{6080.2}{2627} = 35 \text{ sec} \qquad (17-2)$$

is required. The missile is at a range of 19.8 nautical miles at time +55 sec. During the 55-sec period, the bomber target traverses an additional 6.1 miles to a range of 26.3 miles. From a timewise feasibility viewpoint, the margin of 26.3 minus 19.8 or 6.5 nautical miles permits an additional allowable dead time of 58 sec to cause no range limitation on the missile. Alternately, there is margin for a slightly later target detection. The margin calculated is sufficient to eliminate any necessity for refinement in the calculations and to establish the timewise feasibility of the development insofar as no inconsistency in the specifications is concerned, provided the tracking radars involved are capable of the ranges required.

17-2 RADAR RANGE CALCULATIONS

The customary procedure in determining radar ranges is to use a radar-range slide rule computer based upon the equation

$$R_{\max \atop (\text{naut. mi})} = 5.44 \sqrt[4]{\frac{P_T \cdot G^2 \cdot \lambda^2 \cdot \tau \cdot F^{\frac{1}{3}}}{\overline{NF}} A_E} \qquad (17\text{-}3)$$

which appears as Eq. (16) in the "M-12 Radar Range Computer",[1] where

$R_{\max}$ = maximum radar range
P_T = transmitted peak power, watts
G = ratio, antenna gain over isotropic
λ = r-f operation wavelength, meters
τ = pulse duration, seconds
F = pulse repetition rate, recurrences per second
$\overline{NF}$ = receiver noise factor, ratio
A_E = effective back scattering area of target, square meters

In the example under consideration,

P_T = 200,000 watts
$G = \dfrac{G_t + G_r}{2} = \dfrac{41.5 + 27.4}{2} = 34.5$ db
λ = 0.03 meters
$\tau = 1 \cdot 10^{-6}$ sec
F = 400 pulses per sec
$\overline{NF}$ = 15 db
A_E = 40 sq meters

Substitution into Eq. (17-3) gives a value of $R_{\max}$ = 58 nautical miles which is based upon 50 percent probability of detection by illuminating and missile radars combined. For the two radars side-by-side we have a range product of $(58)^2 = 3364$. When the target is at a range of 34.7 nautical miles, the missile radar should have a range of $3364 \div 34.7 = 97$ miles. This figure may be converted to a 90 percent probability figure by use of a curve like Fig. 8-3, for the particular radar system. If Fig. 8-3 is used, we have a reduction from 50 to 38 in going from 50 percent to 90 percent probability or, in the case being studied, $50 \div 38 = 97 \div R$, or $R = 74$ miles, which is greatly in excess of the system demands of 34.7-mile range.

17-3 MISSILE SYSTEM

The missile system requires coordinated performance of a search radar, an evaluation and designation system, illuminating radar with fire control radar characteristics, further evaluation and finally designation to a particular missile launcher, a computer to provide proper firing angle information, a missile launcher capable of following the computer information,

[1] J. W. Nelson, Jr., General Electric Company, 1951.

and the missile handling system with its storage, assembly, and ready-service system. The missile itself contains a semiactive homing radar capable of automatically searching in range and locking on target. The tracking head is fixed with respect to the missile axis. For the purposes of the present discussion and to avoid extension of the treatment beyond what may be properly associated with a book on principles, the assumption will be made that a pure homing system is employed in the missile. The relative significance of such factors as target flight path demands upon the missile servo systems, initial transients at the start of the missile flight due to launching inaccuracies, and variability in control surface effectiveness as a function of speed and altitude are all subjects treated in Chap. 18. In order to have a definite basis for determination of ground-based radar servo bandwidths, it is assumed that a minimum missile range of 10 nautical miles is desired.

17-4 ILLUMINATING RADAR AND LAUNCHER

The illuminating radar servo system performance requirements may be evaluated by using the pass-course theory derived in Chap. 7. The maximum demands occur at the minimum range end. The range at firing for a minimum range of 10 nautical miles (assumed equal to 20,000 yd) is found for a target at an altitude of 30,000 ft and a horizontal crossover range of 4000 yd by simple geometry and the aid of Fig. 17-2.

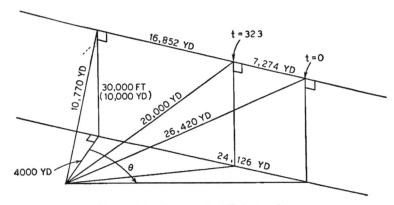

FIG. 17-2 Geometrical Relationships.

The missile has reached a range of 4.7 miles in 20 sec. The remaining 5.3 miles at Mach 2.64 requires $5.3(6080.2 \div 2627) = 12.3$ sec. In $20 + 12.3 = 32.3$ sec, the bomber travels $32.3(6080.2 \div 3)(400 \div 3600) = 7274$ yd to the 10-nautical mile slant range point. The slant range at crossover is (refer to Fig. 7-6 and Fig. 17-2) $R_0 = (H^2 + R_{h0}{}^2)^{\frac{1}{2}} = \overline{(10,000^2}$

$+ \overline{4000^2})^{\frac{1}{2}} = 10{,}770$ yd. The flight path distance at a slant range of 20,000 yd equals $(\overline{20{,}000^2} - \overline{10{,}770^2})^{\frac{1}{2}} = 16{,}852$ yd. When added to the bomber travel the resultant distance is $7274 + 16{,}852 = 24{,}126$ yd. The range at time of firing is $R = (\overline{10{,}770^2} + \overline{24{,}126^2})^{\frac{1}{2}} = 26{,}420$ yd. The angle $\theta = \tan^{-1}(24{,}126 \div 4000) = \tan^{-1} 6.0315 = 80.59$ deg.

Figure 7-7 is not accurate enough in the region of $\theta = 80°$ to permit a system design directly from the curves. However, Eq. (7-47) and (7-48) may be used to determine the velocity and acceleration components of the input signal due to target motion. Accordingly, for

$K_1 = 0.5630$
$V = 400$
$R_0 = 10{,}770$
$\cos \phi_0 = \dfrac{4000}{10{,}770} = 0.3717$
$\theta = -80.59°$, $\cos \theta = +0.16361$

we have at time of firing, using Eq. (7-47),

$$\dot{\theta} = 57.296 \left[\dfrac{0.5630 \cdot 400}{10{,}770 \cdot \dfrac{4000}{10{,}770}} \right] (+0.16361)^2 = 0.086 \text{ deg per sec} \quad (17\text{-}4)$$

and, using Eq. (7-48),

$$\ddot{\theta} = -57.296(0.0563)^2(0.16361)^2(-0.32254) = 0.016 \text{ deg per sec}^2 \quad (17\text{-}5)$$

As established in Chap. 7, a suitable servo characteristic for the angle circuits of a ground-based radar operating against the tactics considered here is the "improved type 1" system specified by the asymptotic gain characteristic slopes of $-1, -2, -1$ as shown in Fig. 7-10. The error equation for this system, using the first terms of Eq. (7-69), is

$$\varepsilon(t) = \dfrac{\dot{\theta}_i}{K\omega_1} + \dfrac{\ddot{\theta}_i}{K\omega_1^2}\left(1 - \dfrac{1}{N}\right) \quad (17\text{-}6)$$

If we specify K and N on the basis of the study in Chap. 7, suitable values for illustrative purposes are $K = 200$ and $N = 10$.

Before a specific answer to the question of required bandwidth (now resolved into a determination of the value of ω_1 in Eq. (17-6)) can be obtained, a suitable value for the maximum allowable error ε must be established. An X-band (3-cm wavelength) radar with a 5-ft diameter dish has a beamwidth in the neighborhood[2] of 1.6 deg. The launcher angular

---

[2] The value 1.6 deg was found by using a G. E. Radar Range Computer M-12. In Ridenour, L.N., *Radar System Engineering*, McGraw-Hill Book Co., 1947, p. 271, the formula $\theta \cong 70\lambda/D$ is given which gives a beamwidth of 1.4 deg. In Silver, Samuel, *Microwave Antenna Theory and Design*, McGraw-Hill Book Co., 1949, p. 437, differentiation between horizontal and vertical polarization is made and the values $\theta_H \cong 72\lambda/D$ and $\theta_E \cong 80\lambda/D$ are given. The variability is due to aperture illumination nonuniformity, and beamwidth is more properly determined by measurement of the specific antenna.

position accuracy requirements are low because of a possible launching dispersion considerably in excess of the radar beamwidth due to missile thrust misalignment, aerodynamic asymmetry, wind gusts, etc., as discussed in the *Launching* section of this series of volumes. A desirable condition for the missile-borne radar is a constant level r-f signal. Changing aspects of the target as viewed from both the illuminator and the missile receiving radar account for large variations. In order that additional signal strength variations due to illuminating radar tracking inaccuracies be minimized, a specification limiting such variation to some amount, say, 3 db, could be made. If this is taken as the basis for allowable error, the equivalent allowable *angular* tracking error must be found. The nature of radar beams is discussed in Chap. 10. In general, a search radar beam may be represented reasonably accurately (for main lobe) as an angular power variation defined by

$$\frac{P_{ax}}{P_{\max}} = \left| \frac{\sin ax}{ax} \right|^2 \qquad (17\text{-}7)$$

where P_{ax} = power at the angle ax
$P_{\max}$ = maximum power at $ax = 0$
a = a constant relating actual beamwidth to general case
x = angle from center of main lobe

Determination of direction by maximizing signal return is a very poor technique because of the relatively blunt nose of the main lobe; it is better to take the difference of signal amplitudes between two slightly displaced beams. Displacement is accomplished by nutating (or lobe switching). The customary definition of beamwidth is the angle between half-power points ($b - b'$ of Fig. 17-3) or two times the ax of Eq. (17-7) determined by setting the power ratio to one-half as follows:

$$\frac{1}{2} = \left| \frac{\sin ax}{ax} \right|^2 \qquad (17\text{-}8)$$

$$ax \cong 79.73 \text{ deg} \qquad (17\text{-}9)$$

Since the antenna under consideration has a beamwidth of 1.6 deg, the constant

$$a = \frac{79.73 \cdot 2}{1.6} = 99.66 \qquad (17\text{-}10)$$

When used as a tracking radar, the nutation angle is usually selected to result in a 1.5-db decrease in one-way signal power as shown in Fig. 17-3 by the point p. If we let θ represent the actual antenna angular position with respect to the line-of-sight to the target, then $\theta = 0$ as shown in Fig. 17-3 in which an extreme left and an extreme right position during nutation of the radar beam are depicted. The nutation or squint angle θ_s is determined as follows:

616   BANDWIDTH STUDIES

$$0.707 = \left| \frac{\sin ax}{ax} \right|^2$$

$$ax = 57.41 \text{ deg}$$

$$\theta_s = 2x = \frac{2 \cdot 57.41}{99.66} = 1.15 \text{ deg} \tag{17-11}$$

Of interest here is the angular position corresponding to an average power from left and right extreme positions that is one-half that of $\theta = 0$. If the left position is represented by Eq. (17-7), then the right position may be written as

$$\frac{P_{ax}}{P_{\max}} = \left| \frac{\sin (ax - 2 \cdot 57.41°)}{(ax - 2 \cdot 57.41°)} \right|^2 \tag{17-12}$$

If we write

$$Average = \frac{\text{left} + \text{right}}{2},$$

then

$$2 \cdot Average = \left| \frac{\sin ax}{ax} \right|^2 + \left| \frac{\sin (ax - 114.8°)}{(ax - 114.8°)} \right|^2 \tag{17-13}$$

Two times the average power at $\theta = 0$ is 1.414 times the maximum of the main lobe. At the limiting angular misalignment, the average is to be one-

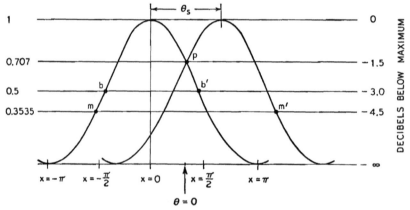

FIG. 17-3 Tracking Antenna Patterns.

half that for $\theta = 0$ or one-half of 0.707 (i.e., 0.3535). Two times the desired average is 0.707. Accordingly, substituting in Eq. (17-13), with an eye to Fig. 17-3, we obtain

$$0.707 = \left| \frac{\sin ax}{ax} \right|^2 + \left| \frac{\sin (ax - 114.8°)}{(ax - 114.8°)} \right|^2 \tag{17-14}$$

$$ax \cong 172.5° \tag{17-15}$$

$$\frac{172.5° - 57.4°}{99.66} = \frac{115.1°}{99.66} = 1.155° \tag{17-16}$$

17-4] ILLUMINATING RADAR AND LAUNCHER

Thus, the allowable tracking radar misalignment is $\pm 1.155°$ ($m - m'$ of Fig. 17-3) as compared with $\pm 0.8°$, had the radar been used as a search or non-nutating radar.

Returning to Eq. (17-6), we may now substitute $\varepsilon = 1.155°$, $K = 200$, $N = 10$, $\dot{\theta}_i = 0.086$, and $\ddot{\theta}_i = 0.0016$ and solve for ω_1 to determine a required value of $\omega_1 = 0.0004$ radian per sec. The foregoing result shows an extremely small servo system demand. Clearly, considerations other than target tracking prior to missile launching will dictate the tracking radar servo system bandwidth specification.

In a half-ship conversion to guided missile installations, the tracking radars may alternatively function as an information source for a gunfire control system. Thus, it is not sufficient that a specific component design be based upon a given system. Consideration must be given to its performance requirements in other systems as well. We have a concept of systems within systems that further emphasizes the importance of the system concept.

The same straight-line pass-course used previously may be employed as the basis for exploring radar servo system bandwidth requirements by considering conditions at crossover together with a realistic figure for tracking accuracy. Such a figure may be taken as ± 0.25 milliradians allowable error due to target motion effects. For $V = 400$ knots, $R_0 = 10{,}770$ yd, and $\phi_0 = \tan^{-1}(10{,}000 \div 4000) = \tan^{-1} 2.5 = 68.2°$, Fig. 7-8 shows at $V \div R_0 \cos \phi_0 = 400 \div (10{,}770)(0.37137) = 0.1$, the value $\dot{\theta}_{max} \cong 3$ deg per sec and essentially zero $\ddot{\theta}$ and $\dddot{\theta}$ values. Figure 7-7 shows $\dot{\theta}$ to be a maximum at crossover ($\theta = 0$). Again returning to Eq. (17-6), substitute $\varepsilon = 0.25 \cdot 10^{-3} \cdot 57.296 = 0.014$ deg, $K = 200$, $N = 10$, $\dot{\theta}_i = 3$ deg per sec, $\ddot{\theta}_i = 0$, and solve for ω_1 to determine the required value of $\omega_1 = 1.1$ radians per sec.

The foregoing has served to indicate the nature of the studies necessary before the tracking radar servo bandwidth specification can be written. In an actual problem, many additional considerations are involved such that a typical system bandwidth greatly in excess of that computed above would be employed. In addition to angle servos there is, of course, a radar-range servo system. The same procedure may be used as shown in Chap. 7 in a study of this problem.

The launcher servo bandwidth specification is not revealed by a study of target motion effects. Its actual performance will be dictated almost entirely by the acquisition phase and slew rates desired. In order that the majority of the delay time of 20 sec from assignment to lock-on be allowed the tracking radar, the launcher should be able to follow the radar director without excessive additional errors. Comparable bandwidths are indicated as a first estimate.

17-5 LAUNCHER COMPUTER

The launcher computer will not be required to provide more than a simple lead-angle computation based upon a straight-line constant-velocity target; the information bandwidth requirements are almost precisely identical with that of the radar servo system.

This is a simple fire control problem, discussed in Chap. 2, in which lead angle is developed as an integration of the angular rate of turn of the line-of-sight times a constant determined by the time of flight before the missile guidance control becomes effective at which time the missile heading should be such that the target is dead ahead.

In the event that investigation shows the magnitude of the lead angle to be small as compared with realizable launching errors, no computer may be needed.

17-6 STABILIZATION AGAINST SHIP MOTION

Since the hypothetical missile system is shipborne, a problem of ship motion exists. The radar tracking error signal will be correspondingly larger due to ship roll and pitch unless a stabilization system is incorporated. These systems use gyroscopes as a reference and may be designed to eliminate effectively ship motion results under any conditions that would otherwise permit missile firing. Specification for the system bandwidth will be modified only in the event that the spectrum of ship motion contains high frequency components. The problem is mentioned here only as an example of the considerations involved in a study of the missile system.

17-7 MISSILE-BORNE RADAR

The missile-borne radar is, in the example under study, a radar receiver only (no transmitter) excited from signals received by the fixed antenna mounted in the nose of the missile behind a radome as discussed in Chap. 4. The antenna pattern has a main lobe which, by amplitude discrimination, tends to establish a volume in space, located ahead of the missile, as the volume of interest.

Range Discrimination. In order to localize further the point of interest, a range unit is employed. The volume is thus reduced to a space defined angularly in the left-right and in the up-down directions by the antenna pattern and in the direction of the missile line-of-sight to the target by the radar range gate width. The effects of interfering signals are thus minimized, but other means must be incorporated to insure further the reliability of tracking and the consequent accurate homing of the missile. One such means is the design of the radar range unit on the basis of the demands imposed by the signal, with its characteristics due to target motion, and in addition on the basis of desired performance *in the absence of the signal!* The allusion is to a design that endows the range unit with a "coast time," or "velocity memory" to permit continuation of tracking after an interruption due to signal fadeout. In the studies detailed in Chap. 7, servo system characteristics are related to bandwidths. It is desirable that the expression for velocity memory be given in terms of the corner or reference frequencies used in Chap. 7. Although evenness of treatment would preclude a detailed study of the subject, such consideration is ignored to give an example of the extent to which all factors should be examined.

Velocity Memory. In the design of any servo system it is important to consider the nature of the input signals in selecting the transfer characteristic for the system. This approach may be used in the case of a radar-range-unit servo system by specifying a typical tactical situation. A plot of range as a function of time may be made and, by successive graphical differentiations, plots of range rate and range acceleration may also be derived. Engineering approximations to the error expressions for the commonly employed servo system ordinarily involve only these three functions of the input signal, that is, position, velocity, and acceleration. The design problem is that of choosing the system that keeps the error within a specified allowable value and simultaneously demands the minimum in servo bandwidth.

A desirable characteristic of a radar range unit is that generated range continue to change at the rate existing at the instant the input signal is lost. Such a feature presents a possibility of uninterrupted tracking, provided the signal fadeouts are of short duration. This characteristic is variously called *velocity memory time* and *coast time*. It is desirable to be able to determine the effects on velocity memory time resulting from modifications of the open-loop frequency response characteristic.

Figure 17-4 shows the equivalent circuit for a range unit under consideration in a form suitable for analysis of the system performance. This system is not recommended as a practical system but is chosen for the purposes of the present discussion. The initial conditions indicated are

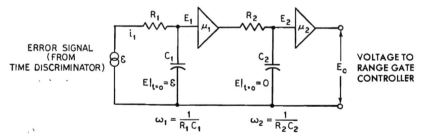

Fig. 17-4 Equivalent Circuit of a Range Unit.

based on the assumption that tracking at a constant velocity has persisted until steady-state conditions exist in the first section. Accordingly, the capacitor C_1 has charged to the full value of the error voltage ε at $t = 0$ (the instant that the echo in the range gate disappears). Since in practical operation of the system the voltage on the second capacitor C_2 never exceeds a few percent of the voltage $\mu_1 E_1$, the assumption of zero voltage on C_2 at $t = 0$ is made. The effect of an input transient (loss of echo) may be determined by making the usual transient analysis. Accordingly, for the first section we have

$$i_1 R_1 + \frac{1}{C_1} \int_0^t i_1 \, dt = \varepsilon \tag{17-17}$$

Transformed (remembering that initial conditions are not zero and that the direction of current i_1 reverses), Eq. (17-17) becomes

$$I_1 R_1 + \frac{1}{C_1} \frac{I_1}{s} = \frac{\varepsilon}{s} \tag{17-18}$$

where $s = d/dt = j\omega$ (for steady state). The input to the first amplifier is

$$E_1 = I_1 R_1 = \frac{\varepsilon}{s} \cdot \frac{1}{R_1 + 1/sC_1} \cdot R_1$$

$$= \frac{\varepsilon}{s + 1/C_1 R_1} = \left(\frac{1}{s + \omega_1}\right) \varepsilon \tag{17-19}$$

For the second section we have an input $\mu_1 E_1$ to the filter followed by an amplification μ_2. Accordingly,

$$E_o = \frac{\mu_1 E_1}{R_2 + \dfrac{1}{sC_2}} \cdot \frac{1}{sC_2} \cdot \mu_2$$

$$= \mu_1 \mu_2 E_1 \left(\frac{1}{1 + sC_2 R_2}\right)$$

$$= \frac{\mu_1 \mu_2 E_1}{C_2 R_2} \left(\frac{1}{s + \dfrac{1}{C_2 R_2}}\right) \tag{17-20}$$

Upon substitution of the expression for E_1 given by Eq. (17-19) and indicating $1/C_2 R_2$ as the frequency ω_2, we have

$$E_o = \mu_1 \mu_2 \left(\frac{1}{s + \omega_1}\right)\left(\frac{\omega_2}{s + \omega_2}\right) \varepsilon \tag{17-21}$$

Using transform pair No. 448 of "Fourier Integrals For Practical Applications" by Campbell and Foster, we have

$$E_o = \mu_1 \mu_2 \left(\frac{\omega_2}{\omega_2 - \omega_1}\right) (e^{-\omega_1 t} - e^{-\omega_2 t}) \varepsilon \tag{17-22}$$

Equation (17-22) shows that the output voltage E_o has the form of the difference of two exponentials. In the practical case, $\omega_1 \ll \omega_2$ and a plot of Eq. (17-22) takes the form of Fig. 17-5. The slope of the function is found by differentiation to be

$$\frac{dE_o}{dt} = \mu_1\mu_2\left(\frac{\omega_2}{\omega_2 - \omega_1}\right)(-\omega_1 e^{-\omega_1 t} + \omega_2 e^{-\omega_2 t})\mathcal{E} \qquad (17\text{-}23)$$

The maximum value of Eq. (17-22) occurs at

$$-\omega_1 e^{-\omega_1 t} + \omega_2 e^{-\omega_2 t} = 0$$

$$t\bigg|_{\max E_o} = \frac{1}{\omega_2 - \omega_1} \log_e \frac{\omega_2}{\omega_1}$$

$$t\bigg|_{\max E_o} = \frac{1}{\omega_2 - \omega_1} 2.3 \log_{10} \frac{\omega_2}{\omega_1} \qquad (17\text{-}24)$$

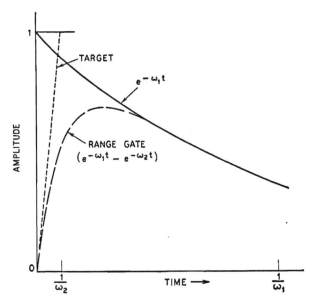

FIG. 17-5 Exponentials in Transient Analysis of Range Unit.

The magnitude of the maximum value is given by

$$E_o\bigg|_{\max} = \mathcal{E}\mu_1\mu_2\left(\frac{\omega_2}{\omega_2 - \omega_1}\right)\left(e^{-\frac{\omega_1}{\omega_2-\omega_1}2.3\log_{10}\frac{\omega_2}{\omega_1}} - e^{-\frac{\omega_2}{\omega_2-\omega_1}2.3\log_{10}\frac{\omega_2}{\omega_1}}\right) \qquad (17\text{-}25)$$

In a typical practical example $\omega_2 = 10\omega_1$. Thus,

$$t\bigg|_{\max E_o} = \frac{2.3}{9}\frac{1}{\omega_1} = \frac{0.256}{\omega_1} \qquad (17\text{-}26)$$

and

$$E_o\bigg|_{max} = \mathcal{E}\mu_1\mu_2 \left(\frac{\omega_2}{\omega_2 - \omega_1}\right)\left(e^{-\frac{2.3}{9}} - e^{-\frac{2.3}{0.9}}\right)$$

$$= \mathcal{E}\mu_1\mu_2\left(\frac{\omega_2}{\omega_2 - \omega_1}\right) \cdot (0.697) \qquad (17\text{-}27)$$

The initial slope is found by setting $t = 0$ in Eq. (17-23). Thus,

$$\frac{dE_o}{dt}\bigg|_{t=0} = \mu_1\mu_2\omega_2\mathcal{E} \qquad (17\text{-}28)$$

The constant velocity target being tracked immediately prior to loss of input signal is represented by the equation

$$\frac{dE_o}{dt}\bigg|_{t=0} \cdot t = \mu_1\mu_2\omega_2\mathcal{E}t \qquad (17\text{-}29)$$

and by the dotted line of Fig. 17-5.

With two integrations the range unit is described as having "velocity memory" as contrasted with the single integration type which has "position memory" only. The measure of velocity memory time, or "coast time," is the time elapsed before the difference between the constant velocity target position and the range gate position exceeds a preassigned allowable range error $\mathcal{E}'$. Using Eq. (17-29) and (17-22), we have

$$\mathcal{E}' = \mu_1\mu_2\omega_2\mathcal{E}t - \mu_1\mu_2\left(\frac{\omega_2}{\omega_2 - \omega_1}\right)\mathcal{E}(e^{-\omega_1 t} - e^{-\omega_2 t})$$

$$= \mu_1\mu_2\omega_2\mathcal{E}\left[t - \frac{1}{\omega_2 - \omega_1}(e^{-\omega_1 t} - e^{-\omega_2 t})\right] \qquad (17\text{-}30)$$

To solve Eq. (17-30) for time in explicit form, first substitute a series expansion for the exponentials. Thus

$$\mathcal{E}' = \mu_1\mu_2\omega_2\mathcal{E}\left[t - \left(\frac{1}{\omega_2 - \omega_1}\right)\left(1 - \omega_1 t + \frac{\omega_1^2 t^2}{2} + \cdots\right.\right.$$
$$\left.\left. - 1 + \omega_2 t - \frac{\omega_2^2 t^2}{2}\cdots\right)\right]$$

$$\mathcal{E}' \doteq \mu_1\mu_2\omega_2\mathcal{E}\left(\frac{1}{\omega_1 - \omega_2}\right)(\omega_1^2 - \omega_2^2)\frac{t^2}{2} \qquad (17\text{-}31)$$

Solving for t, we have

$$t_{\text{coast}} = \frac{1}{\omega_2}\sqrt{\frac{1}{1 + \omega_1/\omega_2}}\sqrt{\frac{2\mathcal{E}'}{\mu_1\mu_2\mathcal{E}}} \qquad (17\text{-}32)$$

where t = "coast time," or velocity memory time
ω_1 = 1st integrator corner frequency
ω_2 = 2nd integrator corner frequency
$\mathcal{E}'$ = range error beyond which constant velocity target is lost (often taken as equivalent to one-half gate width)

μ_1 = gain of 1st amplifier
μ_2 = gain of 2nd amplifier
ε = range error at instant of loss of signal of constant velocity target

For the previously used example ($\omega_2 = 10\omega_1$), less than 5 percent error is made in using the approximation

$$t_{\text{coast}} \cong \frac{1}{\omega_2} \sqrt{\frac{2\varepsilon'}{\mu_1 \mu_2 \varepsilon}} \qquad (17\text{-}33)$$

The performance of a double-integrator range unit may be studied from an open-loop log-gain versus log-frequency plot like Fig. 17-6 (in which only asymptotic segments are shown.)

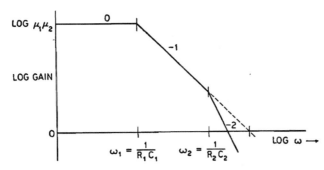

Fig. 17-6 Open Loop Log-Gain versus Log-Frequency Characteristic of the Particular Range Unit Considered.

Velocity memory time is seen to vary inversely with the magnitude of the frequency at which the -2 slope starts. The foregoing statement becomes more strictly exact as ω_1/ω_2 approaches zero. The exact expression is given by Eq. (17-32).

In the particular guided missile under consideration the factors of dynamic performance in the presence of the received signal and the effects of short duration fadeouts can thus be studied to arrive at a desirable design.

17-8 INTERPRETATION

The material in this chapter is not to be interpreted as definitive of the scope or exhaustiveness of the studies required to establish the specifications for a missile system. Rather, an effort has been made to give enough examples to suggest the type and range of considerations involved. In the next chapter, the considerations surrounding the missile of the same hypothetical system will be explored.

CHAPTER 18

MISSILE GUIDANCE BANDWIDTH STUDIES

This chapter takes the problem situation of the preceding chapter and, from it, develops the airborne control loops of the system. Chapter 17 defined the tactical problem, gave specifications for a hypothetical guided missile system, and indicated the nature of the missile guidance system. In this chapter, the tactical problem will be examined to establish the bandwidth of the missile control loop and the resulting accuracy of the guidance. The transients developed immediately subsequent to launching will be examined. The guidance loop for a homing missile, employing a pursuit trajectory, will be discussed. In considering the autopilot loop, bandwidth studies for the aerodynamic control surface system mechanization and the gyroscopic element will be made. The kinematics of the guidance method and missile will be considered. In addition, the study will encompass the bandwidth specifications for a roll control loop compatible with the remainder of the system.

18-1 GENERAL DISCUSSION

Here is the general tactical picture. The target is an aircraft, a bomber, having an equivalent reflecting area of 40 sq ft. The target is flying a straight course at a speed of 400 knots, such as to have a minimum horizontal range of 4000 yd to the missile ship at the point of closest approach. The altitude of the target is constant at 30,000 ft.

It is assumed that the target has been detected by a search radar, either on the missile ship or elsewhere in the task force, and that it has been acquired by the search radar of the missile ship and evaluated as to its probable intent. Having evaluated the target as an enemy bomber, the action against it has been assigned to the missile ship. The position and motion of the target have been designated to the missile guidance system, which now has illuminated the target with its missile guidance radar. The launcher containing the missile and its booster is positioned so as to point the missile directly at the target.

The guidance system employed in this hypothetical example is a semiactive homing system, in which the directive antenna of the radar is not movable, but is directed forward along the longitudinal axis of the missile. The homing radar receiver of the missile is activated while the missile is on the launcher. The signals developed by the radar receiver will not be transmitted to operate the control surfaces of the missile, however, until the missile has completed the boost phase of its flight. At the end of the boost phase, the missile will be misaligned in both heading and direction as a result of wind or other indeterminates in the ballistics of the missile during boost. When signals are transmitted to the missile control surfaces at the completion of the boost phase, the misalignments of the boost phase become transient errors which must be reduced so that the missile may fly the desired trajectory to the target. Since the radar reflector is fixed within the missile, the missile heading when under guidance system control will be, assuming perfect guidance, such that the missile always points toward the target. This defines the trajectory that the missile will follow as being a pursuit trajectory.

The radar receiver in the missile generates a signal which is proportional to the error of the heading of the missile from the line-of-sight to the target. While the missile is on the launcher with the target gated and during the boost phase of flight, this signal is not applied to the control loop of the guidance system. A timing device, or other switch mechanism, is operated to introduce the signal into the guidance loop at the termination of the boost phase. It is at this time that the system may be subjected to a large error (or transient) signal. This signal, proportional to the heading error, is fed into an autopilot control loop. This loop contains the control servomechanisms, aerodynamic control surfaces, the airframe, and a rate gyroscope or other motion measuring device. The output of the autopilot loop is the motion of the airframe. In the process of this discussion, only the motions of the airframe in pitch will be considered. The same operational considerations will apply to the yaw coordinate, since this is a cruciform airframe. The airframe output is the pitch angle of the airframe in space, i.e., the angle at which the radar antenna dish is looking into space, compared to some arbitrary reference.

Through appropriate mathematical modification of the pitch angle, we may obtain the flight path vector angle. Integration of the flight path vector with respect to time gives the trajectory of the missile. As the missile and target move through space, there will be a change in the angle of the line-of-sight in space between the missile and the target. This motion of the line-of-sight is the determinant of the transfer characteristic of the kinematics portion of the missile guidance loop. The transfer characteristic of each of the physical elements of the loops will be illustrated, using the airframe characteristic illustrated in Chapter 14 and the tactical problem of Chapter 17.

The definitions of the reference angles of the missile, in space, are shown by Fig. 18-1. The angle of the line-of-sight of the homing radar dish is the same as the pitch angle of the airframe, θ. The error angle measured by the fixed radar dish is proportional to the angle of missile heading off the line-of-sight to the target, ε. The airframe is moving along the flight path vector at an angle, γ, with the reference line. The angle γ is the *flight path vector angle*. The difference between the heading of the missile and the flight path vector angle is the angle of attack, α.

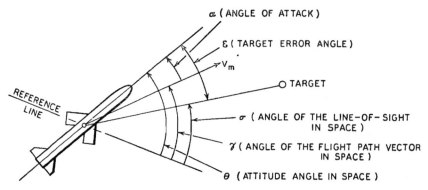

Fig. 18-1 Definition of Angles Utilized in the Missile Intercept Problem (Airframe Geometry).

A rudimentary block diagram of the system is shown in Fig. 18-2. It will be seen that the radar dish is looking to the target and is located along the longitudinal axis of the diagrammed missile. The effect of motion of the missile in space is indicated as a feedback from the space kinematics to the line-of-sight of the radar dish. The effect of target motion is shown as an input to the line-of-sight between the missile and target. The missile airframe outputs are changes to its pitch angle in space and to its flight path vector in space. The flight path vector angle, when integrated with

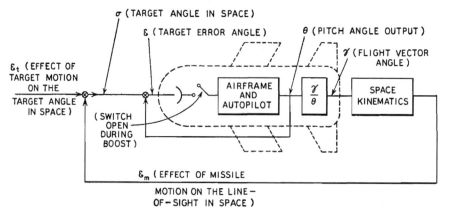

Fig. 18-2 Pursuit Navigation Loop.

18-2 SPACE GEOMETRY AND KINEMATIC TERMS

Figure 18-3 shows the missile and target velocity vectors and the line-of-sight in space. The rotation of the line-of-sight in space, utilizing both the missile and target components of velocity normal to this line becomes

$$-\dot\sigma = \frac{V_m \sin(\gamma - \sigma)}{R} + \frac{V_t \sin\beta}{R} \qquad (18\text{-}1)$$

The symbol R is the range between the missile and the target. Equation 18-1 is separable into two terms; the first involves the missile velocity,

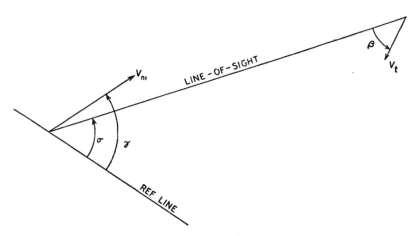

Fig. 18-3 Space Geometry.

V_m, and is the portion of the kinematic feedback due to the missile motion; the second term which involves target velocity, V_t, is the effect of target motion on the kinematic feedback.

Missile Motion Kinematics. The radar dish in the nose of the missile acts as the sensing element leading to a receiver output error which is proportional to the angle between present missile heading and the line-of-sight to the target. This error signal, or the corresponding error angle, is directly related in both magnitude and sense to the error in heading of the missile. To study the transfer characteristic of the kinematic elements of the loop (see Fig. 18-2) we shall assume that the loop is opened so that the radar receiver output does not influence the autopilot and airframe loop to correct this error. If the missile airframe is displaced through an angle, there is an instantaneous appearance of an error voltage at the receiver output terminals corresponding to this displacement. This may be expressed mathematically by $E = K_1(\gamma - \sigma)$. In addition, a rate of change of the angle $\mathcal{E}$ occurs which is proportional to the input displacement $\gamma - \sigma$. This may be expressed mathematically by $\dot{\mathcal{E}} = \omega_1(\gamma - \sigma)$. The parameter ω_1 is equal to the ratio of the missile velocity divided by the range between missile and target multiplied by a proportional constant K_2. Accordingly, the combined error signal becomes the sum of two terms. Letting $K_1 = 1$, $K_2 = 1$, and integrating both sides of the expression for the rate signal, we have for the error angle missile motion transfer function

$$\frac{\mathcal{E}_m}{\gamma - \sigma} = 1 + \frac{\omega_1}{s} \qquad (18\text{-}2)$$

where $\qquad \omega_1 = \dfrac{V_m}{R}$

$s =$ the Laplace transform variable

$\mathcal{E}_m/(\gamma - \sigma) =$ assumed constant

When the missile is at long range, ω_1 is small; hence ω_1/s is small with respect to 1. Thus we see that under these conditions the effect of the integration term is small. This is saying in effect that the rate of change of the angle of the line-of-sight is small. As the range decreases, the term ω_1/s increases in magnitude. The 90-deg phase shift associated with this term can cause instability at short range. As the range decreases, the phase of $\mathcal{E}_m$ lags the phase of the input disturbance by increasing amounts.

Target Motion Kinematics. Let us now consider the remaining term from Eq. (18-1), $\dfrac{V_t \sin \beta}{R}$. This is the expression for the effect of target motion on the line-of-sight angle in space, which is reflected as an error at the radar dish, herein called $\mathcal{E}_t$. We may write

$$\mathcal{E}_t = V_t \int_0^t \frac{\sin \beta}{R} \, dt \qquad (18\text{-}3)$$

Since we are interested in the transfer function where $\mathcal{E}_t$ is the output error and β is the input, we may write the expression as

$$\frac{\mathcal{E}_t}{\beta} = \frac{V_t}{\beta} \int_0^t \frac{\sin \beta}{R} \, dt \qquad (18\text{-}4)$$

If the assumption is made that, during an interval of time, the angle β and the range have particular values and are not functions of time, and since $\mathcal{E}_t$ may be taken to be constant, we may write Eq. (18-4) in the form

$$\frac{\mathcal{E}_t}{\beta} = \frac{\omega_2}{s} \qquad (18\text{-}5)$$

where $\omega_2 = V_t \sin \beta / R\beta$

It will be observed that the effect of target motion has the transfer characteristic of an integrator. In this case, however, there is no feedback, so that the integration effect remains unmodified. The value of ω_2 of the integrator term varies with target velocity, the angles of the space geometry, and range to the target. At long ranges, the value of ω_2 is low, so that target motion has little effect upon the rate of change of the line-of-sight angle in space. However, when the range decreases, small perturbations of target motion (or missile motion) may cause large variations of the target angle. In turn, this will demand large corrective actions by the guidance system and by the control surfaces of the airframe. As the range approaches zero, σ_t/β approaches infinity, and the required system bandwidth will also approach infinity, a condition which must lead to instability. A similar development of the mathematics for the space

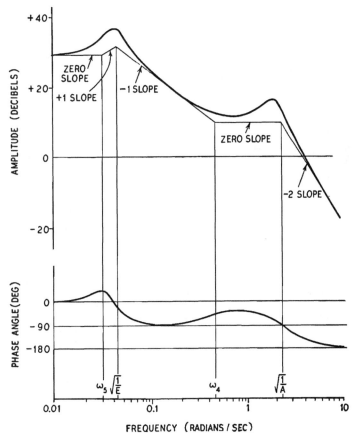

Fig. 18-4 Amplitude and Phase as a Function of Frequency for Output Pitch Angle θ Due to an Input Control Surface Deflection δ_E.

kinematic terms for a beam-rider guidance system is shown in Chap. 19, Par. 19-6. It will be noted that the beam-rider system also exhibits the same term

$$V_m \int_0^t \frac{1}{R} dt$$

which is, in general, typical of space feedback terms for missile guidance systems.

18-3 THE AUTOPILOT LOOP

The transfer characteristics for a cruciform airframe were developed in Chap. 14. Although Fig. 18-4 and 18-5 are the same as Fig. 14-12 and 14-13 used earlier in the text, they are reproduced here again for the convenience

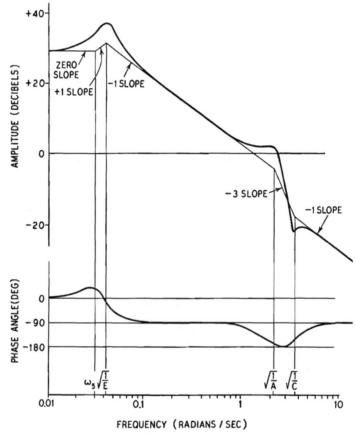

FIG. 18-5 Amplitude and Phase as a Function of Frequency for Output Flight Path Vector Angle γ, Due to Input Control Surface Deflection δ_E.

18-3] THE AUTOPILOT LOOP

of the reader. They illustrate the transfer characteristics in pitch angle and flight path vector angle in response to the deflection of a control surface. A -1 slope of the output flight path vector angle would indicate that the rate of change of the flight path vector angle would be proportional to the control flap deflection. It is desirable that this condition hold true over as great a bandwidth of frequencies as is utilized in the missile control loop. To do this it is often necessary to add feedback around the airframe in the form of an autopilot. An autopilot is, from a transfer function viewpoint, simply a device which either measures the airframe attitude or the flight path vector angle and with this quantity modifies the input to the control surfaces to give a more predictable performance between the output flight path vector and an input control signal.

Figure 18-5 shows a typical arrangement of an autopilot loop for the control of an airframe in flight. The signal from the guidance system is fed into the aerodynamic control surface mechanism. The behavior of the airframe in pitch is measured by a rate gyro, which is a feedback element, and its output is used to modify the signal input to the wingflap servomechanism.

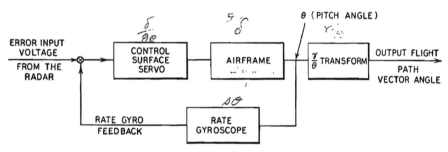

FIG. 18-6 Autopilot Loop Block Diagram.

The angle of the flight path vector γ is the input to the kinematic space geometry. It is this angle which is of importance in the control system analysis. The pitch angle θ is the attitude of the airframe in space. It is this angle which affects an autopilot gyro. The difference is the airframe angle of attack, the angle at which the air impinges on the airframe. As long as an oscillation occurs at a frequency in which the difference between the flight path vector angle γ and the pitch angle θ is small, stabilizing the oscillation of one angle will also stabilize the oscillation of the other. Without angle of attack measurement the autopilot cannot operate directly upon oscillation in the angular position of the flight path vector γ, but must function to influence the pitch angle, θ. Since θ is approximately equal to γ over the range of frequencies employed in the control system, a satisfactory solution is obtained in this indirect manner.

For the assumed airframe at extremely low frequencies (below 0.4 radian/sec) there is virtually no difference between the flight path vector angle output and the pitch angle output. This is to say that the angle of attack at low frequencies is negligible. Using Eq. (14-14) and (14-19) we can solve for

$$\frac{\gamma}{\theta} = (Hs^2 + Ds + 1)\left(\frac{\omega_4}{\omega_4 + s}\right) \tag{18-6}$$

Equation (18-6) shows the transfer function of the flight path vector angle of the airframe as related to the pitch angle. This transfer function occupies a place in Fig. 18-2. Figure 18-7 shows the gain phase plots for Eq. (18-6). From the phase curves, it may be seen that there is negative phase shift contribution by this term between the frequencies $\omega_4 = 0.45$ radian and the frequency corresponding to $\sqrt{1/H}$, 2.5 radians per sec.

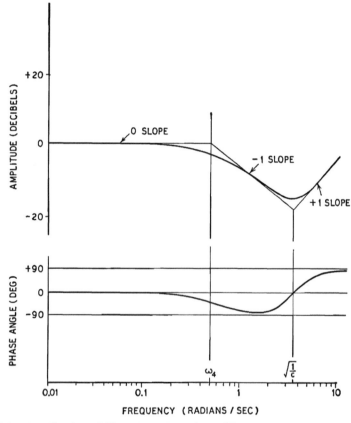

FIG. 18-7 Amplitude and Phase as a Function of Frequency for an Output Flight Path Vector Angle γ for an Input Pitch Angle θ.

This negative phase shift contributes difficulties to any attempt to stabilize the guidance loop above a frequency of 0.8 radian per sec. For this reason, it is uneconomical to attempt to design the autopilot airframe loop to a higher frequency than 2 radians per sec. The limiting factor in the stabilization in the autopilot airframe loop of this particular airframe, then, is not contained within the loop itself nor the demands of the trajectory, but one contributed by the kinematics of the guidance method.

Autopilot Rate Gyro. The autopilot-airframe loop will be designed with an open loop bandwidth of 2 radians per sec. The rate gyro should not contribute any appreciable phase change characteristic at this frequency. In order to fulfill this criterion, the rate gyro should be damped at approximately 0.6 of critical and have a resonant frequency at least one decade higher than the frequency to which the system must be operable. The

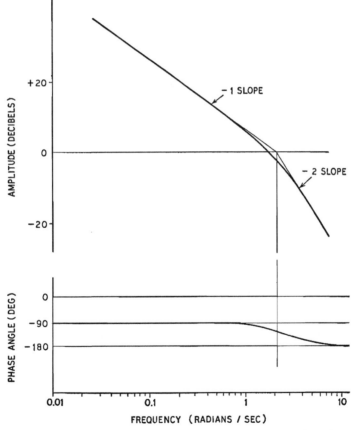

Fig. 18-8 Amplitude and Phase as a Function of Frequency of an Output Pitch Angle θ Resulting from Input Signal to the Autopilot.

resonant frequency of the rate gyro should, therefore, be higher than 20 radians per sec. Chapter 9 gives information on rate gyros, damping coefficients, and related phase characteristics. In a practical case, it is not difficult to obtain a rate gyro with a resonant frequency of 30 or more radians per sec. Figure 18-8 shows gain-phase plots of the airframe-rate gyro combination, using the pitch angle response of the cruciform airframe from Fig. 18-5. It will be observed that, when the rate gyro has been inserted in the feedback path of the autopilot loop, it causes the asymptote of the output in pitch to have a -1 slope out to the gain crossover frequency of the autopilot loop, which has been selected to be 2 radians per sec. At frequencies higher than 2 radians per sec the asymptote will have a slope of -2. This characteristic is different from the characteristic of the airframe alone in that the resonant terms no longer appear in the output. This is because the transfer characteristic of the autopilot loop now

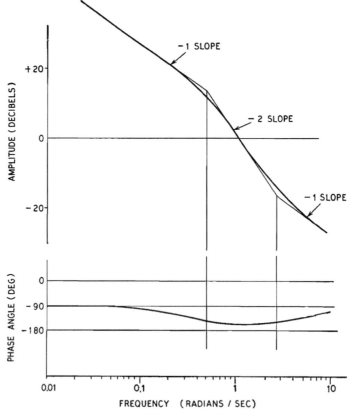

FIG. 18-9 Amplitude and Phase as a Function of Frequency of an Output Flight Path Vector Angle γ Resulting from Input Signal to the Autopilot.

follows the inverse of the characteristic of the rate gyro used in the feedback path. The characteristic low frequency phugoid oscillation has been eliminated. At high frequencies where the gain of the autopilot loop is low, the output will be similar to that of the unmodified airframe. The characteristic from the input of the autopilot loop to its output can be characterized as a single integrator throughout the useful range of frequencies. This allows the output pitch rate to be expressed as being directly proportional to an input control signal without reference to the normal disturbing oscillatory modes.

The change in the flight path vector which results from an input autopilot control signal is determined by combining the response described by Eq. (18-8) and Fig. 18-8 for relating pitch response and that of the flight path vector with the autopilot pitch angle response shown in Fig.

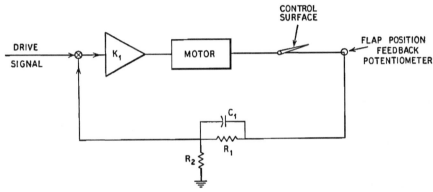

Fig. 18-10 Configuration of the Control Flap Servomechanism.

18-9. This is done in Fig. 18-10 and shows that at an input frequency of 2 radians per sec the phase angle between the input autopilot error signal and the output flight path vector is 170 deg.

Control Surface Flap Servomechanisms. The control loop for the control surface servomechanism is shown in Fig. 18-10. The fundamental consideration in the determination of the bandwidth of the wingflap servomechanism is that it faithfully pass all frequencies up to the design bandwidth of the autopilot and the loop in which it is employed and that it shall not contribute any undesirable characteristics. An input drive signal is amplified by amplifier K_1. The output from the amplifier drives a servo motor which in turn moves the aerodynamic control surface. The position of the surface is measured by a potentiometer to generate a feedback signal. After being fed through appropriate networks this is added to the input to the control amplifier. A characteristic of the feedback network is that it should provide a center position signal to the amplifier so that if no drive signal is present the flaps will remain on center. This is done by causing a d-c signal to be fed back through resistors R_1 and R_2 to maintain a center position reference. The corner frequencies of this network will be adjusted to 2 radians per sec and 20 radians per sec. The network will have a characteristic

$$\frac{E_{out}}{E_{in}} = \frac{\omega_3}{\omega_4}\left(\frac{\omega_3 + s}{\omega_3}\right)\left(\frac{\omega_4}{\omega_4 + s}\right) \qquad (18\text{-}7)$$

At low frequencies this network causes the system to provide gain, while the corner frequencies of the network provide system limitations to signal flow at high frequency. Thus, the servomechanism will not be subjected to high frequency noise, yet it will provide adequate gain at low frequency. The transfer characteristic for the complete wing flap servomechanism is illustrated in Fig. 18-11.

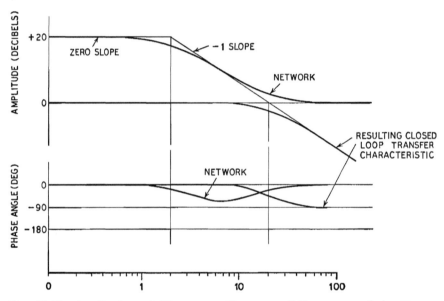

FIG. 18-11 Amplitude and Phase as a Function of Frequency of the Output Voltage from the Control Flap Compensation Network Due to a Network Input Voltage.

The gain crossover frequency will be adjusted to 20 radians per sec by variation in the gain of the controlling amplifier K_1. This servomechanism will contribute little phase shift at the gain crossover frequency of the autopilot control loop. The insertion of this transfer characteristic will not modify the transfer characteristic of the autopilot loop because its transfer characteristic is unity out to far in excess of the autopilot loop bandwidth.

18-4 PITCH GUIDANCE LOOP

An input error angle, ε, will cause an error voltage to be fed into the autopilot loop to generate a change in the output pitch angle in space. A pitch angle modifies the error angle measured by the dish in two ways: (a) since the dish is fixed to the missile, the angle of the dish in space—and hence its error angle—is directly affected by the pitch angle output; and (b) the pitch angle causes a rate of change of ε to exist. The sum of these is the input error angle voltage fed to the input of the autopilot. The gain and phase shift characteristics of the airframe-autopilot portion of the loop have been discussed in the preceding section. The space kinematic portion has also been discussed and shown to have phase and gain characteristics which are variable as range is varied.

At long ranges, the effect of the space kinematics is to modify the angle of the line-of-sight in space only very slightly. As the range between the missile and the target decreases, as it will prior to impact, the magnitude of the contribution of this term becomes large. The phase shift contribution of this term, as the gain of this term increases, becomes increasingly difficult for the system to cope with. The space kinematic term is given by Eq. (18-2) which is (repeating)

$$\frac{\varepsilon_m}{(\gamma - \sigma)} = 1 + \frac{\omega_1}{s} \qquad (18\text{-}2)$$

The parameter ω_1 which controls the characteristic of this expression varies inversely as range:

$$\omega_1 = \frac{V_M}{R} \qquad (18\text{-}8)$$

At the range between missile and target after completion of the boost when control is initiated with this system, ω_1 has a value of 0.023 radian per sec. At this time the range is 115,600 ft and the missile velocity is 2627 ft per sec.

$$\omega_1 = \frac{2627}{115,600} = 0.023$$

As the range to the target decreases, the rate of change of the line-of-sight which results from a missile maneuver increases. This is shown by an increase in ω_1. At 3290 ft range, ω_1 reaches a value of 0.8 radian per sec. At this range the combined phase shift from the kinematic term and the phase shift from the airframe and autopilot loop reaches −180 deg. This is the necessary condition for unstable oscillations to occur. Thus at a range of 3290 the control loop should be opened and the autopilot should be used to keep the straight-line flight. This occurs within 2 sec of impact so that the error will be small.

In Chap. 12, Par. 12-2, the required accelerations for this particular pursuit course were calculated. At a time approximately 2 sec before impact, which would correspond roughly to this range for the given missile velocity, the acceleration caused by the trajectory increases rapidly. Control beyond this point becomes impossible because of the acceleration limitations of the missile itself. The trajectory will call for approximately

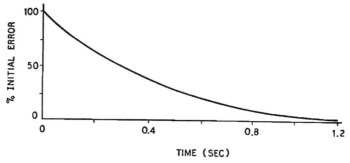

Fig. 18-12 Launching Transient Error.

3 g's acceleration at a 1000-ft range from the target. If, at this time, the missile accelerates in an incorrect direction at the maximum acceleration of which it is capable, the increase in miss will be negligible. It is apparent from these figures that a bandwidth of the entire control loop of 0.8 radian will develop satisfactory control over the complete usable range of the missile.

18-5 LAUNCHING TRANSIENTS

If the hypothetical missile is launched at its designed maximum range, control will be initiated at a range of 115,000 ft. Because of booster misalignment and aerodynamic asymmetry an input error will exist. When the switch initiating control completes the circuit, this error signal will act as a step function transient in the angle ε. Figure 18-12 shows the response of the system to a transient input when the airframe is at this range. It will be noted that the misalignment of the angle, ε, is reduced to 38 percent of its initial value in 0.4 sec. The contribution of the space kinematics which relates to line-of-sight change due to this misalignment is very small because of the range. The control characteristics are related primarily to the characteristics of the autopilot control loop. The gain of this loop is such that an error of 1 deg in ε will cause a change in the pitch angle θ at a rate of 2.5 deg per sec.

The tactical objective given in Chap. 17 called for minimum launching range of 20,000 yd from impact. The range from the missile to the target, at the end of the boost phase and at the time guidance is initiated, is 57,800 ft. The kinematic feedback critical frequency for this range is 0.045 radian per sec.

$$\omega_1 = \frac{2627}{57,800} = 0.045$$

At this range, the contribution of the line-of-sight change resulting from changes in the flight path vector is small, and control is limited by the airframe autopilot loop characteristics. Hence, the transient characteristic given in Fig. 18-12 is equally valid for this case.

18-6 ROLL CONTROL

It is necessary to limit the rate of roll of a missile to keep the signals which belong in the pitch coordinate from introducing errors into the yaw coordinate and vice versa. Unless oscillatory frequencies are kept high with respect to frequency utilized in the pitch and yaw channels, crosstalk between these channels will occur. It is not necessary to maintain the missile pitch coordinate vertical at all times. A slow roll of the missile will cause interchange of relationships between pitch and yaw channels, but will not necessarily introduce any significant errors into

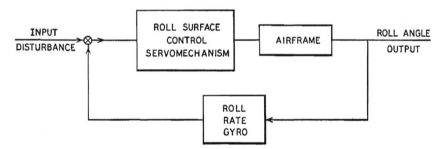

FIG. 18-13 Roll Control Block Diagram.

either channel if the frequencies of oscillation in the roll are higher than the frequencies to which the pitch channel can respond. The use of a roll rate gyro combined with miscellaneous unbalances in circuits associated with a rate gyro may result in a slow rotation of an airframe. However, with rather simple design techniques, the frequencies of oscillation of the roll can be kept above the frequencies utilized in the pitch and yaw channels.

Figure 18-13 shows a typical roll rate limiting servomechanism. Input roll disturbance will cause a signal to appear on the output of the rate gyroscope. This signal will be introduced into a roll control flap servomechanism to deflect the flap. This flap deflection will create an aerodynamic moment to correct the roll disturbance. The bandwidth of this loop must be in excess of the 2 radians per sec bandwidths of the yaw and pitch channels. A comfortable margin for this loop is a bandwidth 1 decade above the yaw and pitch control bandwidth, or 20 radians per sec. The gyro will be selected with a resonant frequency equal to 80 radians per sec. This gyro will be damped to 0.6 of critical. Thus, it will introduce no appreciable phase shift in the operating range of the roll control loop.

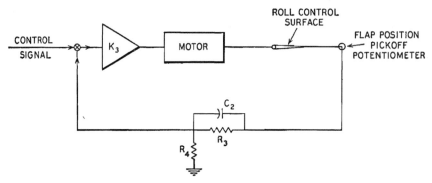

FIG. 18-14 Roll Surface Drive System.

Figure 18-14 shows the circuit to be used for controlling the roll control loop flap. A drive signal is introduced to the controlling amplifier K_3. After amplification it is introduced into the servomechanism motor for driving the flap. The output flap angle is measured by a potentiometer and fed back through the circuits shown to be added to the input control signal, thus closing the loop. The network in the feedback loop provides a centering signal for the flap so that in the absence of any large gyroscope output signals the flaps will remain centered. In the presence of a flap deflection, the characteristics of this network provide low frequency gain which allows transfer characteristics, as shown in Fig. 18-16, to exist. The feedback network will have the following characteristic:

$$\left(\frac{0.2}{0.2+9}\right)\left(\frac{8+9}{8}\right) = \frac{E_{\text{out}}}{E_{\text{in}}} \tag{18-9}$$

The airframe transfer characteristics in roll are:

$$\frac{\omega_x}{s}\left(\frac{\omega_s}{\omega_s+s}\right) = \frac{25}{s}\left(\frac{8}{8+s}\right) = \frac{\theta}{\delta_E} \tag{18-10}$$

The combination of these two expressions with the characteristic for the roll rate gyro, which is approximated by the expression:

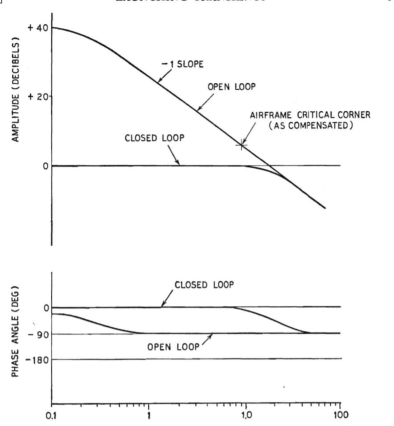

FIG. 18-15 Amplitude and Phase as a Function of Frequency of the Output Roll Angle Due to an Input Roll Disturbance.

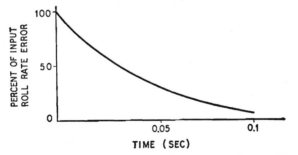

FIG. 18-16 The Transient in Roll Rate Due to a Roll Rate Disturbance.

$$\frac{\omega_x}{s} = \frac{\theta}{E_{in}},\quad \text{wherein}\quad \omega_x = 20 \text{ radians per sec}$$

gives the transfer characteristics shown in Fig. 18-15.

It will be noted that we have elected to modify the airframe transfer characteristic by the inclusion of a term tending to increase the frequency at which the airframe characteristic changes from a -1 to a -2 slope. This will give a roll control loop the characteristic transient response which is shown in Fig. 18-16. If an input disturbance occurs which applies a transient in roll, the roll rate will be diminished to 38 percent of its initial value in $\frac{1}{20}$ sec.

18-7 MISS DUE TO SYSTEM LIMITATIONS

The trajectory for a pursuit system, with the limitations assumed herein, was developed in Chap. 12. A miss will result with a pursuit system under any circumstances wherein the assumed missile and target

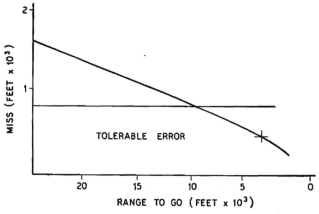

FIG. 18-17 The Magnitude of Miss of a Pursuit Missile if Control Is Removed.

velocities cause an infinite turning rate to be called for at the time of impact. Any missile system will be limited to a finite turning rate. Therefore, it is evident that the system should be made inoperative some time prior to the actual impact. This will result in a miss of the target. Figure 18-17 shows the miss that will occur for the particular assumed trajectory. If the system is cut off at 3.6 sec prior to impact (at a range of 9500 ft) a miss of 800 ft will occur. If it is cut off at 1000 ft prior to impact, with $\frac{1}{2}$ sec to go until impact, a 300-ft miss of the target will occur. Since instability will occur at 3290-ft range the system will be shut off at this range. A miss of 500 ft results.

In actuality system bandwidth limitations, as compared to trajectory demand, is only one of several causes for a miss. The actual system will be operating in the presence of noise and with a systematic tracking error at all times. The evaluation of the miss contributions due to these other causes requires a more complete analysis than may be permitted here. However, it is evident that with an inaccuracy due to the bandwidth limitations of about 500 ft, the tactical requirement of an 800-ft miss should be met. These approximations yield a good starting point for more elaborate computations.

18-8 INTERPRETATIONS

The material in this chapter has been developed from very elemental assumptions as to the character of both the guidance system and the elements which comprise it. It is obvious that the system proposed in this chapter will have little practical application. However, the principles disclosed in the mathematical operations are illustrative of principles which must be employed in exploring the bandwidth requirements for a more realistic application. The emphasis upon steady-state frequency conditions as a determinant in developing the transfer functions of the control and guidance loops is made for clarification. The studies do indicate the type and range of considerations which are necessarily employed in the preliminary stages of guidance system design.

In actual practice, as soon as the method of guidance has been determined and the general bandwidth specifications of the components have been developed, the analysis of the system then proceeds using an analog simulator. When a mechanical simulator is employed, the input parameters (such as target range, altitude, velocity of both missile and target, etc.) may be varied over a wide range. The stability of the system is developed over the probable range of input parameters. Further exploration is normally made of the ability of the system to handle transients, both of missile and target motion. All of these considerations, and many others, must be fully explored in a design of a guidance control system for a given tactical mission.

CHAPTER 19

SIMULATION, COMPUTATION, AND TELEMETRY

The first problem faced by the designer of a missile guidance system is that of translating the missile tactical problem into specifications for the guidance system design. A synthesis of the proposed system must be made in order to develop the specifications at a time when only the mathematical expressions which govern the behavior are known, and those are known only approximately. As an aid to the processes of design, simulation of the system by analog and digital computers is employed. As the design progresses, complete simulation may give way to partial simulation, by substituting some of the completed elements of the system for the mathematical expressions previously employed. Thus, simulation is a continuing aid to designer throughout the duration of the program.

When the guidance system has been developed, the behavior of the equipment is proved by flight tests. Data are collected from missiles in flight by the use of telemetry. These data, when evaluated, furnish an additional aid to the designer of the guidance system. In the process of the evaluation, computers again are usually employed.

Computers are employed as components of missile guidance systems. Such computers may be either external to the missile or a part of the missile-borne equipment, or both. The discussion in this chapter on analog and digital computers is generally confined to the use of such devices as simulators, but the principles disclosed apply equally to the design of computers as components of the missile guidance system.

19-1 SIMULATION *

Definitions. Simulation is the imitation of the behavior of the actual missile system by the behavior of some other device easier to construct; this other device can be made more flexible than the final "hardware," changes in it can be accomplished with relative ease and at low cost, and it can be subjected to performance tests under controlled conditions. In its most basic form this "device" may simply set up the set of equations governing the behavior of the guided missile.

The equations governing the behavior of a guided missile constitute

---

* Paragraph 19-1 has been written by Dr. Louis Bauer, Project Director of Project Cyclone, Reeves Instrument Co., N.Y.C., N.Y.

a set of complicated differential equations involving nonlinearities of many kinds. These nonlinearities may stem from the aerodynamic behavior or from such mechanical effects as limiting, dead-space, backlash, and hysteresis effects. These examples by no means exhaust the possibilities but serve merely as illustrations. In the solution of the guided missile equations two possibilities (not mutually exclusive) present themselves:

1. Reduction of the complexities by simplifying assumptions. Here one simply hopes that the behavior of the reduced system will be sufficiently similar to the full system for useful conclusions to be drawn from the simplified system.
2. Use of some automatic means of computation. Originally, it is for this specific purpose that most of the electronic and electromechanical analog computers now in use were developed.

For this reason one generally refers to such an analog computer when speaking of a *guided missile simulator*.

Stages of Simulation. Thus, in its basic function, any simulator is an equation solving device. According to the fashion in which the simulator is used, one may distinguish between two broad categories of simulation, so-called (1) *mathematical simulation* and (2) *test simulation*.

In mathematical simulation (or full simulation) the entire guided missile problem is represented mathematically and the resulting equations are set up on a computer and solved.

In test simulation (sometimes called *partial* or *physical simulation*), only part of the guided missile system is represented mathematically and set up on the simulator. Parts of the guided missile constituting actual "hardware" are inserted in the computing loop to complete the problem. In this case only part of the problem is simulated, and part of it is handled with complete realism without the necessity of mathematical representation or simplifying assumptions.

In the first type of simulation the usual procedure is to take simplified parts of the problem and solve them first; later the problem is brought closer to reality by gradually introducing the complicating factors of the full problem. Simplified phases which are thus analyzed first may constitute the following: longitudinal and lateral aerodynamic stability analyses without, and then with, consideration of the drag equation; stability analyses of the control system; two-dimensional trajectory analyses without aerodynamic consideration; three-dimensional stability analyses. Separate studies of launching, mid-course guidance, and homing phases are made. Finally, the complete three-dimensional trajectory analysis with full regard to aerodynamics and control system performance is set up and solved. In the last of these, all known complications are thrown into the problem in an attempt to discover which of them produce significant effects. The influence of noise is also studied in any of the foregoing phases so that a kill probability can be predicted. Different missile-target configurations are analyzed in order to discover the regions of missile effectiveness or, putting it another way, target vulnerability.

This type of simulation has the advantage that any convenient time scale may be used; i.e., the dynamic problems do not have to be solved on a "real-time" basis. It has the disadvantage that a full mathematical statement of the problem is required. Since the actual behavior of some of the guided missile equipment may not be known, a mathematical expression for it will have to be assumed. This assumption may lead to inaccuracies in the resulting predictions.

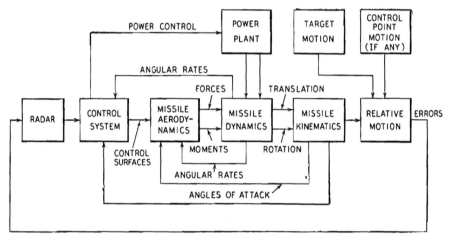

Fig. 19-1 Block Diagram Depicting Simulation of a Missile Guidance System.

In the second type of simulation (partial simulation) this disadvantage is avoided. On the other hand, real-time solutions will be required to accommodate any actual components in the loop being simulated. The real-time requirement places a greater burden on the performance of the simulating equipment. All electromechanical equipment will have to have very high performance characteristics to avoid the introduction of errors. This may necessitate the elimination of all mechanical devices, or a radical redesign, or the simulation of nonlinear effects by purely electronic means, often entailing a loss in accuracy or an increase in cost. The alternative is the simplification of those nonlinear expressions which have to be generated electronically in test simulation.

The foregoing points may be illustrated by means of a block diagram (Fig. 19-1) depicting the operation of a guided missile.

Starting, say, with the missile kinematics and given the motion of the target, a relative motion computer determines the errors from a desired course. These errors are detected by the missile radar and yield error signals which are applied to the control system. The control system, in turn, activates the control surfaces and also receives inputs from the actual missile motion in order to allow for maneuvers in progress. The control surface deflection will cause such aerodynamic forces as to lead to the desired course corrections. In the aerodynamics block there are other internal loops corresponding to the aerodynamic stability of the missile.

In the full simulation mentioned earlier every one of the blocks shown is replaced by the simulator. In test simulation it is the control system which is most frequently kept in its actual form, and the missile is "flown" in the laboratory by simulation of missile aerodynamics and kinematics.

Methods of Simulation. The methods used in missile guidance simulation differ according to the different stages of simulation above, and according to the complications encountered. The following are possible methods:

a. Analytic methods.
b. Numerical solutions of guided missile equations by hand computations.
c. Automatic computation. Here one may distinguish between digital and analog computers.

The following considerations apply to these methods:

a. *Analytic methods.* In the earliest stages of design the behavior of the servos and airframe in the complete loop is approximated by linear differential equations with constant coefficients. These equations can be solved by well-known analytic methods and the solutions found in this way. Servomechanism theory discussed in a previous chapter can be applied directly at this stage for determination of the basic designs.

In the solution of linear differential equations with constant coefficients it becomes necessary to find the roots of polynomials. When the polynomials are of a high degree (i.e., when the differential equations are of a high order) the necessary computations become very cumbersome. Automatic methods of computation have been developed for this type of problem and either digital or analog computers may be used to find the roots of these polynomials.

b. *Numerical solution of the guided missile equations by hand computation.* When the equations representing the guided missile are refined, so that they contain some nonlinearities, most analytic methods of solution fail. In that case, if the system of equations is still not very complex, some numerical method may be used and the solution carried out by hand computation, using a desk calculator.

c. *Automatic computation.* This method is used when the guided missile equations are so complicated that the effort involved in obtaining hand-computed solutions becomes prohibitive.

Analog computers are preferred whenever very many different solutions are required, as, for instance, in a systematic study of the effect of parameter variation. The accuracy of the solutions is generally not better than 0.1 percent. (In some of the lowest cost computers the accuracy may be of the order of several percent, or worse.)

Characteristic of analog computers is the ease with which problems may be programmed (in fact, the ease with which the operation of the computers may be learned), the speed with which solutions may be obtained (ranging from 1/60 sec on computers of the repetitive solution type, to a few seconds, or several minutes, for problems run on real-time, or an extended time scale), and the ease with which parameter changes may be made. The simulation of noise is also accomplished without any difficulty.

The chief limitation of analog computers is their accuracy. It is difficult to maintain consistently an accuracy of 0.1 percent or better, and when the accuracy requirements become higher than 0.01 percent it becomes impractical to use analog computers. Another drawback compared to digital computers is the fact that there do not exist such clearcut mathematical methods for error analysis and error prediction as in numerical analysis. A beginning has been made in this field for linear equations with constant coefficients.

For the most complex problems solved on analog computers one generally obtains one check solution by a numerical method, usually by means of a digital computer. After obtaining a match with the check solution all other desired solutions are run off on the analog computer. The number of these solutions may run into the thousands, and their correctness is established by continuity considerations.

Briefly, the advantages of analog computers are the speed of obtaining solutions and their cheapness and ease of operation. The limitation is one of accuracy.

19-2 MECHANIZATION OF EQUATIONS *

The procedure for synthesizing (called "mechanizing" the equations) a system of computing components, whose response corresponds to the solution of an equation, can be described most effectively by means of an example. Consider the sum of several quantities,

$$a + b + c = d \tag{19-1}$$

in which a, b, and c are computer inputs and d is the output. Writing Eq. (19-1) implicitly and admitting a negligible error from which the solu-

* Paragraph 19-2 has been written by William A. McCool, Mechanics Division, Naval Research Laboratory.

tion can be generated by a high-gain amplifier, we have

$$a + b + c - d = \varepsilon = d/A \approx 0 \qquad (19\text{-}2)$$

where A is a very large constant representing the amplifier gain. The system whose response simulates the solution of Eq. (19-2) is shown in Fig. 19-2. This example can be generalized by replacing the summing network with any circuit arrangement which properly simulates the given equation in implicit form. The solution, or any quantity from which the solution can be derived explicitly, is always generated from the error signal. For differential equations the highest order derivative is usually obtained directly as the output of the high-gain amplifier. The solution and the remaining derivatives are then obtained by successive integrations. It is important to note that *every mechanization of a single equation is characterized by a "closed loop" which might be described as a constraint by which the high-gain amplifier forces the system to simulate the equation and forces the response of the system to satisfy the equation.* In the literature, this is called the "implicit function technique."

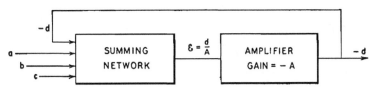

Fig. 19-2 Computer Circuit for Mechanizing the Equation $a + b + c = d$.

As another example, consider the differential equation,

$$\frac{d^2y}{dx^2} + a\frac{dy}{dx} + by = C(x) \qquad (19\text{-}3)$$

where a and b are constant coefficients. Writing Eq. (19-3) in implicit form and adding the usual error term, we have

$$\frac{d^2y}{dx^2} + a\frac{dy}{dx} + by - C(x) = \varepsilon = \frac{d^2y}{dx^2}/A \approx 0 \qquad (19\text{-}4)$$

The mechanizing circuit is easily established by beginning with *the error signal which will finally be generated*. The circuit is shown in Fig. 19-3. In both of the preceding examples as well as in the general case, the *error signal is always generated by the network summing the various terms of the equation*. Consequently, the mechanizing procedure can be simplified by combining the summing network and the high-gain amplifier (as shown inside the dashed block of Fig. 19-3) in a **single computing** component which is logically called a "summing amplifier." Thus, the first example shown in the design of Fig. 19-3 is nothing but a summing amplifier.

With this simplification, the initial step in the general mechanizing procedure consists of transposing the given equation so that the highest order derivative is given explicitly as the sum of all the other terms in the equation. In other words, the output of the summing amplifier is equated to the negative sum of its inputs. For example, from Eq. (19-3), we have

$$\frac{d^2y}{dx^2} = -a\frac{dy}{dx} - by + C(x) \qquad (19\text{-}4)$$

The concept of the error signal, which is actually developed internally in the summing operation, has been introduced and emphasized only to explain the basic philosophy of electronic analog computation.

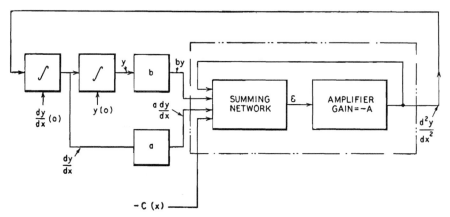

FIG. 19-3 Computer Circuit for Mechanizing the Equation
$$\frac{d^2y}{dx^2} + a\frac{dy}{dx} + by = C(x).$$

In solving a system of equations, each equation is designated to generate one of the unknowns. There is a summing amplifier and at least one closed loop for each equation. Each loop is appropriately interconnected with the others in order to simulate the given system. In general, these interconnections terminate at the summing amplifier inputs. The mechanization of a system of equations is illustrated later with an example.

In general, a given equation or system of equations has many possible mechanizations; i.e., the procedure is not unique. Since each one inherently provides only approximate solutions, considerable experience is required to synthesize one of the most accurate computing circuits.

The output voltage of a summing amplifier is the negative of the algebraic sum of its input voltages. The summing network is arranged so that each of the inputs can be individually amplified, i.e., multiplied by a constant. In particular, one manufacturer incorporates seven inputs, one having a multiplier of 10, two having a multiplier of 4, and four having a multiplier of 1. The mechanism of the summing operation is easily described with a summing amplifier with two inputs having multipliers A and B respectively. A diagram of the circuit is shown in Fig. 19-4. The d-c amplifier having a high-gain μ is assumed to have infinite input impedance and zero internal impedance at the output terminals. If the output voltage is E_o, then the input grid voltage E_g must necessarily

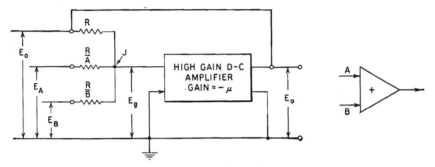

Fig. 19-4 Summing Amplifier Circuit and Symbol.

be $-E_o/\mu$. Since the sum of the currents at the network junction J must be zero,

$$\frac{E_A - E_g}{R/A} + \frac{E_B - E_g}{R/B} + \frac{E_o - E_g}{R} = 0 \tag{19-6}$$

Appropriately rearranging Eq. (19-6) we have

$$E_o = -(AE_A + BE_B) - E_o(A + B + 1)/\mu \tag{19-7}$$

If $\mu >> (A + B + 1)$ negligible error is incurred in simplifying Eq. (19-7) to

$$E_o = -(AE_A + BE_B) \tag{19-8}$$

According to Eq. (19-8) the summing amplifier output is the negative sum of the input voltages each multiplied by a constant factor determined by the ratio of the feedback resistance to the corresponding input resistance.

The output voltage of an integrating amplifier is the negative of the time integral of the algebraic sum of its input voltages. The basic integrating amplifier is identical to the summing amplifier except that the feedback resistance R is replaced with a capacitance C. This is indicated in Fig. 19-5. Again the sum of the currents at the junction J must be zero;

$$\frac{E_A - E_g}{R/A} + \frac{E_B - E_g}{R/B} + C\frac{d}{dt}(E_o - E_g) = 0 \tag{19-9}$$

Substituting the relation $E_o = -\mu E_g$ into differential Eq. (19-9), integrating each term with respect to t, and then rearranging in a form similar to that of Eq. (19-7), we have

$$E_o = +(E_o)_{IC} - \frac{1}{RC}\int_0^t (AE_A + BE_B)\,dt$$
$$- \frac{1}{\mu}\left[E_o + \frac{A+B}{RC}\int_0^t E_o\,dt - (E_o)_{IC}\right] \quad (19\text{-}10)$$

If μ is sufficiently large and if the period of integration is not too long, negligible error is incurred in simplifying Eq. (19-10) to

$$E_o = -\frac{A}{RC}\int_0^t E_A\,dt - \frac{B}{RC}\int_0^t E_B\,dt + (E_o)_{IC} \quad (19\text{-}11)$$

The initial condition of the output $(E_o)_{IC}$ is established by charging the capacitor C prior to the integration interval (i.e., $t < 0$). In a typical integrating amplifier the RC product has the value unity ($R = 1$ megohm, $C = 1$ microfarad). The inputs can have the same multiplier arrangement as that of the summing amplifiers.

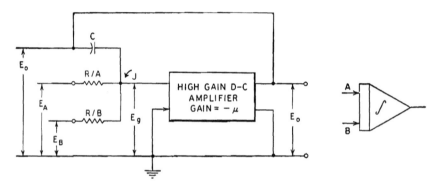

Fig. 19-5 Integrating Amplifier Circuit and Symbol.

Since integration is provided by the capacitor charging phenomenon, the computer independent variable is real time. The mathematical functions performed by all the other computing components are independent of time. When the mechanization of a differential equation is actually set into the computer, therefore, all the circuits may be completed except the integrating amplifier inputs, whose simultaneous connection constitutes the $t = 0$ condition.

The inverting amplifiers are simply summing amplifiers with only two inputs each having a unity multiplier. Changing the sign of a function is their primary purpose.

In all three types of amplifiers the sign reversal is an inherent consequence of the feedback arrangement. The dynamic gain of a typical d-c amplifier is about 75,000 (the gain for very slowly varying voltages is about 20,000,000 as a result of the drift compensation). Thus the errors in Eq. (19-8) and (19-11), incurred by assuming that μ is very large, are so small that large variations in tube constants can be tolerated. Actually, the computing accuracy is limited by the tolerance (± 0.1 percent) and stability of the computing capacitors and resistors, provided the computation interval is not too long and the drift of the d-c amplifiers is negligible.

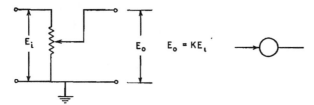

Fig. 19-6 Scale Factor Potentiometer and Symbol.

Numerical coefficients are mechanized by *scale-factor potentiometers* in conjunction with the amplifier input multipliers. For example, if it is desired to multiply an input by the coefficient 5.59, the input is fed into a potentiometer set at 0.559 whose output is then fed into a 10-input multiplier of an amplifier. These potentiometers have 10 turns and the dial calibration has 100 divisions per turn. They have a 0.1 percent linearity tolerance so that they can be accurately set within one division. The potentiometer circuit is shown in Fig. 19-6.

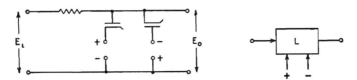

Fig. 19-7 Limiter and Symbol.

Variables represented by voltages can be limited to specified maximum and/or minimum values with *limiters*. This electronic operation is analogous to the function of a mechanical stop for shaft rotation. The schematic diagram of a limiter is shown in Fig. 19-7. Appropriate values of bias voltages establish the limits.

One type of multiplying device employs the principle that the output voltage of a linear potentiometer is proportional to the product of the voltage impressed across the total resistance and the angle of rotation of the potentiometer arm. Conversion of one of the input voltages to a corresponding angle of rotation is effected by a positioning type of servomechanism. Both input quantities, of course, are slowly varying d-c voltages.

The servomechanism proper (often abbreviated "servo") as shown in Fig. 19-8 consists of a summing network for developing the usual error signal from the sum of the input and feedback voltages and an amplifier to excite the servo motor which in turn drives a "follow-up" potentiometer, excited by a *fixed reference voltage*, for furnishing the feedback voltage. Without regard to the internal electromechanical conversions, the servo is similar to an inverting amplifier since the follow-up potentiometer output voltage is forced to be essentially the negative of the servo input voltage. It is easy to see, therefore, that the angular displacement of the

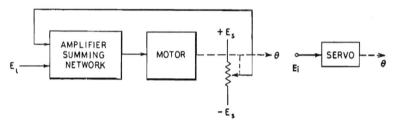

Fig. 19-8 Servomechanism and Symbol.

follow-up potentiometer O, for a constant value of excitation voltage E_s applied thereto, must be proportional to the servo input voltage E_i. If θ_o is the total angular displacement of the potentiometer, then

$$\frac{\theta}{\theta_o} = \frac{E_i}{E_s} \qquad (19\text{-}12)$$

The output E_o of a *multiplying potentiometer*, a duplicate of the follow-up potentiometer, which is coupled to the servo motor and is excited by a second variable E_2, is

$$E_o = \frac{\theta}{\theta_o} E_2 = \frac{E_i}{E_s} E_2 \qquad (19\text{-}13)$$

An additional product can be formed with each multiplying potentiometer coupled to the servo shaft. All the products have a common multiplier

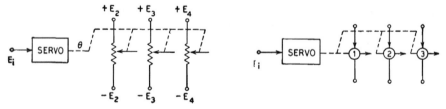

Fig. 19-9 Multiplying Servo and Symbol.

E_1/E_s. Since the servo "senses" both positive and negative inputs and since all the potentiometers have balanced positive-negative excitation (center-taps at zero-potential) the polarity of the products is preserved. Figure 19-9 is a diagram of a complete multiplier with several product outputs. According to Eq. (19-13), division can be performed by exciting the follow-up potentiometer with a fixed reference voltage. Unfortunately, this division scheme has rather severe limitations because the servo dynamic properties are critically affected by the follow-up potentiometer excitation.

One of the most satisfactory division methods utilizes the "implicit function technique." In this case, however, the high-gain amplifier does not become a summing amplifier with simple resistive feedback (see Fig. 19-4). Instead, the feedback resistor is replaced with a multiplier which

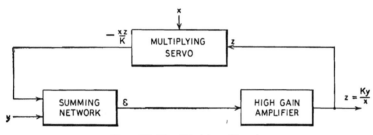

Fig. 19-10 Division Circuit.

functions exactly like a variable conductance whose magnitude is directly proportional to the divisor. The dividend is fed in as the normal amplifier input. The mechanization is shown in the diagram of Fig. 19-10. If the quotient Z is given by

$$Z = \frac{Ky}{x} \qquad (19\text{-}14)$$

then, in implicit form,

$$\frac{Zx}{K} - y = \varepsilon = Z/A \approx 0 \qquad (19\text{-}15)$$

where A is the amplifier gain.

The *resolving servos*, which are used also as multiplying servos, provide two-dimensional transformation of coordinates. In one mode of operation, the axes of the rectangular components of a vector (x, y) are rotated through an angle θ, the quantities x, y, θ being inputs. The new vector components, which are servo outputs, are

$$\begin{aligned} x' &= y \sin \theta + x \cos \theta \\ y' &= y \cos \theta - x \sin \theta \end{aligned} \qquad (19\text{-}16)$$

For the special case $x = 0$, Eq. (19-16) become the usual polar to rectangular coordinate transformation, which is the most frequently used function of the resolving servos. In the other mode of operation, the two inputs are rectangular components of a vector and are converted into polar coordinates. Resolving is usually performed with sine and cosine potentiometers whose angular position θ is established by a multiplying type of servo.

One of the most important factors affecting computing errors is the choice of *solution-recording* medium. In a typical analog computer installation, any one of three different types of recording devices may be used to present solutions in the most usable and accurate manner. The one with the greatest resolution is a "plotting board" whose available writing area is about 30 in. by 30 in. The coordinates of the pen position are established by servos whose respective inputs can be any two of the problem variables which appear explicitly in the computing circuit. Since both of the coordinate driving mechanisms of the plotting board have considerable inertia, solutions must be recorded sufficiently slowly to prevent "overshooting." Although this characteristic restricts the dynamic "frequency range" of the whole computing system, it is not usually objectionable, except in cases of physical simulation where real-time solutions are required.

A recording drum called an "input-output table" has an available writing area of about 9 in. by 15 in. Since the recording pen is driven by servos, the operation and limitations of these devices used as recorders are essentially the same as those of the plotting board. As the name implies, an input-output table is also an input device, i.e., one that converts graphical information into corresponding electrical signals to be fed into the computer. The "curve-following" is an automatic operation in which a wire graph is formed according to the desired function. Since the abscissa input remains "arbitrary" even when the ordinate output is controlled by the "following" procedure, functions of dependent variables as well as independent variables can be generated. Assuming that there is no overshooting, the recording error incurred by the input-output tables does not exceed $\pm\frac{1}{4}$ percent of full scale. The recording precision is much better and is on the order of $\frac{1}{2}$ mm (the width of a pen line).

Finally, a six-channel recorder may be used for less precise work. Since the recording paper must be run at one of two constant speeds, the abscissa for each channel is always proportional to time. As a consequence, solutions cannot be recorded as functions of a dependent variable. This recorder, however, has certain advantages. Since each channel has an amplifier with a stable gain from 0.1 to 10, quite a diversity of levels can be recorded without using additional computing components. Also, the solutions can be run off much faster without overshooting of the pens,

(The dynamic properties of the pen motor are far superior to the cumbersome servo arrangements in the other computing devices.) This six-channel recorder is especially useful for recording exploratory solutions where the problem parameters or initial conditions are varied over wide ranges.

Instead of actually recording solutions in some problems it is more accurate and convenient to read some maximum or final value from a servo dial (a servo is often used as a precision voltmeter).

In general, a given equation or system of equations cannot be mechanized without "scaling" the independent variable. Since time is necessarily the computer independent variable, the time scale-factor connecting the equations and the computer mechanization controls the "speed of solution." The choice of this factor is usually a compromise between too long a computing period and too short a computing period. In the former case, errors due to integrated drift voltages and other sources become excessive. When the computing period is too short, the "rise-time" of the computing amplifiers (poor response to the higher frequency components of solutions) introduces distortion of solutions. This latter limit becomes even more restrictive in computing circuits involving servos. It is particularly important to note that computation errors arising from a poor choice of time scale-factor can be detected readily from a comparison of solutions obtained with different choices of time scale-factor.

As a matter of experience it has been found that, after each equation is arranged to give the highest order derivative explicitly in terms of the equation's remaining terms, the time scale-factor should be chosen so that none of the coefficients is much greater than unity. If this selection makes the computing time too long, then a new mechanization involving special techniques may have to be devised.

A few examples will effectively demonstrate some of the important aspects of mechanizing equations with the computing components and the philosophy just described. Consider first the differential Eq. (19-3) rearranged as in Eq. (19-5). The mechanizing circuit, using the symbols already indicated for the various components, is shown in the diagram of Fig. 19-11. It is assumed that the summing amplifier output generates a voltage (from the internal error voltage ε) corresponding to the second derivative of the solution. Two successive integrations of the assumed voltage yield the first derivative and the solution itself from which the corresponding terms of Eq. (19-5) are formed. The function $C(x)$ is arbitrary and, therefore, can be obtained in any convenient manner. The differential Eq. (19-5) is mechanized when all the terms are summed in the summing amplifier whose output then supplies the assumed voltage, and thus the characteristic feedback loop is formed.

One of the simple forms of the well-known Van der Pol differential equation,

$$\frac{d^2y}{dx^2} - \mu(1 - y^2)\frac{dy}{dx} + \omega^2 y = 0 \qquad (19\text{-}17)$$

describes relaxation oscillations. This nonlinear differential equation is interesting because it is applicable to a number of physical systems. In the general case, μ and ω can have values which require independent variable scaling. Moreover, the coefficient of the first derivative term indi-

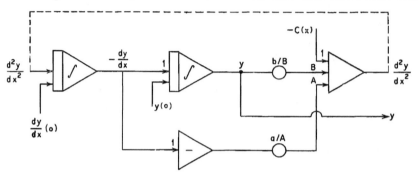

FIG. 19-11 Example Mechanizing Circuit for Eq. (19-3).

cates that the maximum amplitude of the solution will never be much greater than one because of the functional relationship between the damping and the solution magnitude. Improved accuracy and resolution are obtained when the maximum amplitude of any solution is almost as large as the dynamic range of the computer (± 100 volts) will permit. In the

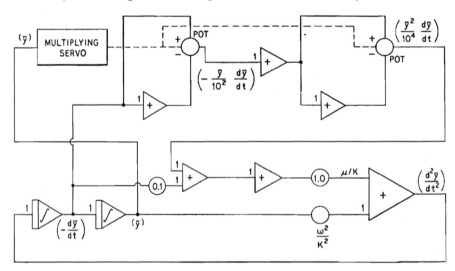

FIG. 19-12 Computer Schematic Diagram for Solution of a Van der Pol Equation.

mechanization, therefore, the solution itself must be scaled. The scaling can be accomplished by substituting the relations

$$y = 10^{\frac{3}{2}} \bar{y}$$
$$t = kx$$

into Eq. (19-17) which, after solving explicitly for the second derivative term with unity coefficient, then becomes

$$\frac{d^2\bar{y}}{dt^2} = \frac{\mu}{k}\left(1 - \frac{\bar{y}^2}{10^3}\right)\frac{d\bar{y}}{dt} - \frac{\omega^2}{k^2} \cdot \bar{y} \qquad (19\text{-}18)$$

It should be emphasized that this scaling is simply a linear change of variable.

Equation (19-18) with some slight modifications is mechanized as shown in the diagram of Fig. 19-12. The "major loop" is established in the same manner as the previous example. It is interesting to note that the particular way in which the damping term is formed requires only one multiplying servo. Expansion of the damping term into two separate

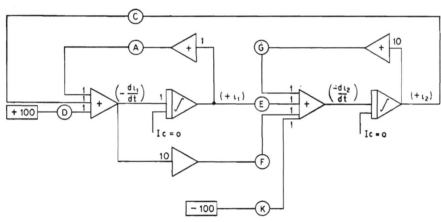

FIG. 19-13 Example: Mechanizing Circuit for Eq. (19-19).

terms permits successive multiplications by $\bar{y}$ which is on the servo shaft. It is also interesting to note that the possible range of time scale-factor, and hence μ and ω, would have been more restricted if it had been necessary to put $d\bar{y}/dt$ on a servo shaft because of the "speed of solution" considerations. The practical steady-state solution of this Van der Pol equation is independent of the initial conditions which influence only the transient response.

As a final example consider the system of differential equations describing an electrical circuit with both magnetic and conductive coupling.

$$di_1/dt + A\,i_1 - C\,i_2 = 100\,D$$
$$di_2/dt + 10\,G\,i_2 - E\,i_1 - 10\,F\,di_1/dt = -100\,K$$
$$i_1(0) = i_2(0) = 0$$
$$0 \leq A, C, E, D, F, G, K$$
(19-19)

The mechanization of Eq. (19-19) is shown in the diagram of Fig. 19-13. The major loop for each equation is evident. In the first equation "$-C\,i_2$" is the "coupling" term, i.e., i_2 is generated in the second equation and is then multiplied by the constant coefficient, $-C$, and the result is summed in with the terms of the first equation. The terms with the coefficients $-E$ and $-F$ are also coupling terms.

In this particular problem, as in many others, it is very simple to calculate the analytic solution. However, determination of the effects of varying the coefficients over wide ranges required so many numerical solutions that machine methods had to be employed.

19-3 ESSENTIALS OF THREE-DIMENSIONAL GUIDED MISSILE SIMULATION *

Operational Block Diagram. The fundamental aspects of a typical three-dimensional guided missile simulation problem are shown in block form in Fig. 19-14. Taking the aerodynamics computer as a starting

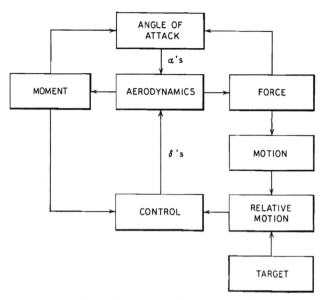

Fig. 19-14 Block Diagram of Typical Missile Problem

* Paragraph 19-3 has been written by Dr. Louis Bauer, Project Director of Project Cyclone, Reeves Instrument Company, N.Y.C.

point, the angles of attack, the angular rate components, and the control surface deflections of the missile are accepted as inputs, and the aerodynamic forces and moments are produced as outputs. In the force unit, the missile force equations are integrated, yielding the missile forward velocity and flight path angles or the linear components of the velocity vector in a suitable coordinate system. In the moment unit, the equations of missile rotation are integrated, yielding the components of the angular rate vector. A second integration yields the missile orientation angles. Finally, from the data describing the missile orientation and the missile velocity vector, the angles of attack in pitch and yaw are obtained. As shown in the block diagram, the last two steps are performed in the angle of attack computer, the output of which is used as input to the aerodynamics computer.

A different method of obtaining the angles of attack is sometimes found preferable. Instead of using flight path angles and missile orientation angles, one may compute the angles of attack directly from the velocity components expressed in the missile coordinate system.

The portion of the block diagram described above constitutes a closed system containing the aerodynamic stability characteristics of the missile in uncontrolled flight. This closed loop can also be applied to simulate the aerodynamic stability of conventional aircraft.

The remainder of the block diagram contains the units involved in determining the deviations of the missile from a desired course and in simulating the control action taken to correct these errors. Thus, this portion of the simulator represents the characteristics which determine the control system stability and performance.

By integration of the missile velocity components the coordinates of the missile trajectory are obtained in three-dimensional space. The coordinates of the target towards which the missile is aimed are generated independently; similarly, if required in the guidance problem, the coordinates of one or several control stations, which direct the flight of the missile, are generated. The relative motion computer accepts these data and determines the distances between missile, target, and control station, respectively. Furthermore, it computes such quantities as the horizontal and vertical error distances of the missile from the desired course or the error angles under which the target appears in the missile's target seeking equipment. The error distances or angles are then fed into the guidance and control equipment simulator. In this unit the response of the missile's guidance and control equipment to the detected error signals is simulated, and the control surface deflections in pitch, yaw, and roll are computed and fed back into the aerodynamics unit.

Additional Units. For a complete guided missile simulation study it may be necessary to set up the follow additional units: a power plant computer that yields the forward thrust as a function of velocity, altitude, and control action; an air properties unit that yields the pressure, density, and temperature of the atmosphere as functions of altitude; and a mass change unit, that takes into account the effects of a fuel consumption on force and moment equilibrium.

Some of the units mentioned involve complications of a particular kind. For example, the aerodynamics unit may be required to yield forces and moments over a wide variation of Mach numbers if the flight is to be simulated from the instant of launching until target interception. This requires a rapid variation through the subsonic and transonic range to high supersonic speed in a short period of time during which the aerodynamic forces and moments undergo critical changes, which may lead to unstable conditions during the boost phase.

As the missile carries out the maneuvers dictated by the guidance system in order to attain the desired flight path, its pitching and yawing motions undergo large transients. Under these conditions, which occur especially in the initial and terminal phases of the attack, the linearized aerodynamic theory customary in conventional aircraft analysis is no longer applicable. The simulation, therefore, must be extended to include strongly nonlinear influences in aerodynamic forces and moments.

Since the aerodynamic reactions vary with Mach number and altitude, the simulation program usually requires a representative number of flights in which the initial speed and altitude are varied as parameters. In order to facilitate these changes, the simulator setup should include provisions for convenient change of the function units which generate the empirical functions involved.

Special Networks. The guidance and control equipment simulator usually calls for elaborate computing circuits. For different missile simulation problems, radically different elements in this unit may be required. The following sub-units may have to be included in this portion of the simulator:

(a) Circuits representing the characteristics of the error signal detecting devices, involving the dynamic response of the seeker head and the nonlinear distortion and limiting of guidance signals.
(b) Seeker noise simulators and noise filter networks.
(c) Command shaping networks or guidance computer circuits.
(d) Acceleration command limiters, intended to protect the missile from dynamic overload.
(e) Wing deflection simulators including servo time lags and nonlinearities such as dead-space, rate and deflection limits.

The object of using a realistic representation of these equipment characteristics in some of the more advanced guidance studies is to evaluate the influence of the inherent imperfections of the guidance and control system upon the accuracy of target interception.

Achievement of Accuracy. In planning a large simulator facility, it is important to recognize the role of three-dimensional guided missile simulation as one of the last stages in guided missile design and development. In order to fulfill its function properly, any simulator must have the capacity and adaptability for handling the most complex relationships which describe equipment imperfections, nonlinearities, and cross-coupling effects present in the guidance problem. The separate influence of any one of these phenomena may be studied adequately on medium-sized or small simulators, or by analytical methods. The combined effects and the mutual interactions of these phenomena can be analyzed only on a large simulator. The results obtained have practical significance only if the phenomena of particular interest can be simulated in a highly realistic manner. It is hardly possible to assess in advance the relative importance of various complicating aspects of the problem when formulating the program for a complete three-dimensional guidance study. At this stage, therefore, certain complicating conditions, which at a less advanced stage are rarely taken into account, must not be ignored.

Consider, for example, the terms which complicate the missile dynamic and kinematic equations if the missile motion is not restricted to a horizontal or vertical plane. The number of degrees of freedom of the airframe increases from three to six. There is dynamic cross-coupling in the force and moment equations. It occurs in the accelerations of translation and rotation as well as in the aerodynamic forces and moments. There is kinematic cross-coupling in the equations which yield missile position and orientation in the earth coordinate system. In addition there is severe cross-coupling in error signal detection due to rotation of the seeker device in the missile, and to missile rolling motions. The steering commands given to the missile control system by the guidance equipment are also subject to cross-coupling errors due to roll. Finally the missile attitude control system may be affected by cross-coupling errors which originate in the sensing instruments. It is obvious that only an intimate knowledge of these effects can provide an indication as to where it is permissible to simplify the exact relationships. Therefore, a tendency to include all of these complications in the formulation of the complete problem can generally be observed among users of a simulation facility. Such considerations had to be kept in mind in the planning and design of the new simulation laboratory at Project Cyclone for the Bureau of Aeronautics, U. S. Navy.

19-4 COMPUTERS, ANALOG AND DIGITAL*

Very effective aids to the design of missile systems, and in no small part their control, are the automatic type of computers, either analog or digital. At present, the analog computing system is the principal device used for simulation of dynamic problems in the study of the control-loop and system performance associated with a missile's ability to respond to received signals. The digital computer system has, to date, been applied primarily for the purposes of delayed data reduction problems or for specific scientific calculations where long solutions of a repetitive nature with high precision were necessary. When used as a simulator the computer must produce, from the input functions, output signals that are defined by the transfer characteristics of the components being used in a missile control system. The most readily available and applicable device for this application has been the analog computing systems. In most instances the analog device can be made to reproduce directly the characteristics of the control element or missile system under test. This has proved to be a most economical method of obtaining information without actual flight of the costly missile. This is made possible because of the very close relation between the analog signals normally developed or available within a physical system and the signals required for the operation of the analog computing devices. Cost-wise, for small computational requirements of reasonable precisions, the analog computing elements are most ideal, since each element can, by itself, perform a mathematical operation. However, as the computational problem becomes more and more complicated, thereby demanding increasing numbers of computations to be performed upon a set of input data, the efficiency and precision of the analog computer decreases. It is at this point that the automatic, programmed, high-speed digital computer begins to offer overweighing advantages.

Application of the high-speed digital computer art began about 1946 and has since been growing rapidly. Speed has been increased many fold, but not without an increase in complexity. The precision possible in the digital computer is almost unlimited, but for practical purposes it is seldom over that of 10 decimal digits. More recently the size and complexity of these mammoth machines have been reduced while their capabilities have remained unchanged; this latter feature has also resulted in increased reliability. With all of the signs as indicated by these trends it appears that the digital computer will be capable of being a very practical competitor to the analog computer in many more medium-complexity com-

* Paragraphs 19-4 and 19-5 have been written by D. H. Gridley, Applications Research Division, Naval Research Laboratory.

puting applications as well as for the very complicated computations, as is now the case.

The significant differences are apparent between the analog and the digital computers in regard to their precision of operation. The analog device is, at the best, accurate to about 0.1 percent or about 3 to 4 decimal digits. When a number of these 0.1 percent elements are interconnected to perform the solution of a more complicated problem, each additional element has a tendency to reduce the overall precision of the final answer. That is why, as the complexity of the problems increase, the degrading effect of cascading analog elements reduces the effectiveness. However, in the digital type of computer, once a value of input data has been received by the computer, barring circuit malfunctioning, it will maintain the precision with which the data were received throughout the entire computation process. The accuracy of the computational process is a function of the skill exercised by the mathematician who programs the method of problem solution.

Another advantage offered by the digital type of computer is the freedom from computer down-time required for problem setup. In order to change a method of problem solution on an analog computer, a considerable amount of computer time is required to set up a new problem. With a digital computer, the setup time is transferred to the time spent by the mathematician and the programmer in setting up the form of solution and the final preparation of the instruction tapes used for control of the computer during problem solution. When the control tape is completed, the time required for the digital computer to be transferred from one problem to another is only that time required to read in the new control tape and its associated numerical data. This extreme versatility of the digital computer is one of its foremost assets.

19-5 DIGITAL COMPUTERS

A digital computer can be best described by the block diagram of Fig. 19-15. Here are illustrated the major elements of any programmed type of digital machine, composed of the Input, Arithmetic, Control, Storage, and Output elements. In the operation of a desk calculator the human operator serves in all capacities except that of the Arithmetic element. Communication between elements is either by parallel or serial transfer of the binary coded digits. In the parallel handling of internal data considerably higher speeds of operation are obtained and, when used in the computer design, offer increased overall speed without necessitating the high-speed computer components that would be required in a serial computer of the same overall speed. It is true, however, that the serial computer probably makes more efficient use of components and, in turn, requires fewer of the components in order to perform the same function. Nevertheless, it will be found that the highest-speed computers are of the parallel type, using the very-highest-speed components, but arranging them in a parallel design.

The Input-Output devices for use with the digital type computers are normally punched paper tape, punched cards, magnetic tape, or automatic typewriters for direct input or tabulation. These are used primarily for general-purpose computer applications, such as that required for delayed-time data reduction or the solution and evaluation of general scientific problems. When the computer is to be used in a simulation

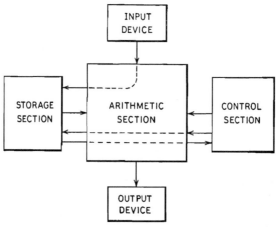

Fig. 19-15 Block Diagram; Program Controlled Digital Computers.

type of application the interconnecting analog-to-digital transducers must be used. The storage element can take a number of different forms, each selected for its particular merits as required by the overall computer design and/or access times. Higher-speed storage devices are the electrostatic type cathode-ray tube storage, and the new square-hysteresis-loop magnetic-core type of storage. Intermediate-speed storage systems are composed of the various forms of electrical or acoustic delay lines and magnetic drums. The magnetic tapes are often used for an intermediate storage where very high capacity is required but relatively slow access time is acceptable. The Arithmetic and Control elements of the digital machines cannot be listed in any specific categories; since they are usually a combination of features found most desirable by the designer for the particular plan of computer operation assumed.

In addition to the general-purpose computer and the digital computer used as a simulator there are numerous other special-purpose types of machines that will serve well in the field of design, control, and more efficient data handling. These computers are, in most instances, serial or serial-parallel in design and again conform closely with the diagram of Fig. 19-15. However, because of their special usage, various elements are in more or less prominence than seen in a general-purpose machine. These special computers are used as digital differential analyzers, automatic air traffic control systems, process control systems, and long-range navigation computers, just to state a few applications.

Real-time Computation. One of the principal advantages of the analog computer is its ability to perform "real-time" computation. The inputs to this type computer are supplied as continuous, but variable quantities, and a continuous solution appropriate to the input variables and their past history will be delivered at the output. The output solution function will undoubtedly have a lag, but only to the extent as governed by the bandwidth limitations within which the analog computer components had been designed to operate. When using the digital type of computer all of the inputs must be in a time-sampled form, each represented by a discrete digitally-coded-quantized value. The speed of computation for a particular problem by the computer usually determines the maximum rate of sampling. This rate of sampling, computation, and the precision of output data smoothing determine the ability of the digital type computer to perform as a real-time device. In many instances, especially in the slower punched card and relay type of digital computers, even a very simple problem cannot be performed in real time because the computer cannot keep up with the continuous flow of input data. However with the newer, very-high-speed computers, real-time computation for many problems has become an actuality. It is even proposed that time sharing of the computer may be possible, with a single machine performing several different solutions on unrelated input data. Like the analog computer, a similar limitation as to lag is possible in the output answers of a digital computer. Should the input data change at very high rates or frequencies, the computer will be required to sample the input data at a greater rate and also provide faster solutions to the problem. This must be done in order to produce a true and accurate answer without the unwanted lags in data which tend to diminish its usefulness for dynamic control.

Data Transducers. Following the above discussion on the requirements for a real-time solution, the need for analog-to-digital and digital-to-analog transducers is obvious if digital computers are to perform a function as part of a simulation system. Practically all measured quantities in nature are originally analog in form (length, weight, pressure, angles, velocity, etc.). This is why the analog computer has been so effective when performing the role of simulation on a true dynamic physical system. Only minor changes in the data have to be effected by the data transducers between the input data and the computer or the computer and the output data. This is not the case when the digital computer is to be used. Here the analog quantity must be measured and transformed into a discrete set of numbers or coded representative values. The transducers required must be adaptable to a considerable range of precision. Many quantities in their analog form are accurate to only a fraction of one percent or less (pressure, voltages, etc.); whereas other values such as length and velocity can be accurately determined and measured to accuracies greater than one part in several ten thousands. Specific transducers for transforming analog to digits and the reverse have recently been devised and are now available to provide practical instrumentation between nature's analog quantities and the high-speed digital-type of computer.

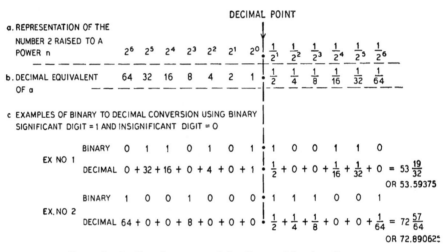

FIG. 19-16 Development of the Binary Number System.

Number Representation. The lower-speed types of digital computers more commonly associated with precision calculations are the desk calculator, punched card machines, and perhaps just the mathematician and his pencil. These all make use of the decimal number system in arriving at an answer. It is true that the human has learned this number system and continues to think more clearly in that system even though it is composed of ten different representative symbols. However, a digital computer does not easily recognize the decimal system and requires considerable extra equipment to handle it. Most ideally suited for mechanical, relay, or electronic circuits is the binary number system based on the radix (powers) of "2." This number system requires only two symbols, or a two condition representation, such as "on" and "off"—a situation quite adaptable to electronic circuitry. A sample representation of the binary-decimal comparison is illustrated in Fig. 19-16, with binary digit

SAMPLE OPERATIONAL INSTRUCTIONS*

Operation Code	Coding Symbol	Operational Instructions
10	LO s	Transfer the control to the left-hand order of the word at storage location s.
11	RO s	Transfer the control to the right-hand order of the word at storage location s.
12	CL s	If the number in the A register is greater than or equal to zero, transfer the control to the left-hand order of the word at storage location s; otherwise, proceed to the next order of the routine.
13	CR s	If the number in the A register is greater than or equal to zero, transfer the control to the right-hand order of the word at storage location s; otherwise, proceed to the next order of the routine.
20	LAL s	Replace digits 0 through 12 of the word at storage location s by digits 0 through 12 of the word in the A register.
21	LAR s	Replace digits 24 through 36 of the word at storage location s by digits 0 through 12 of the word in the A register.
22	IL s	Increase the storage-location designation of the left-hand order of the word at storage location s by one.
23	IR s	Increase the storage-location designation of the right-hand order of the word at storage location s by one.
30	AL(n)	Shift the contents of the A and U registers (excepting sign digits) n places to the left. The overflows on the left of the A register are successively placed in the vacated digital positions of the U register, while the vacated positions of the A register are made zero.
31	AR(n)	Shift the contents of the A register (excepting the sign digit) n places to the right. The vacated digital positions on the left take the same condition as the sign digit, and the overflow at the right is dropped. The contents of the U register remain unchanged during this operation.
32	RD s	Read the words between the "start" and "stop" indications from the magnetic tape of the magnetic-tape reader to consecutive storage locations beginning with storage location s.
33	RC s	Record the word at storage location s on the magnetic tape of the magnetic-tape recorder.
40	U A	Transfer the number in the U register to the A register.
41	A U	Transfer the number in the A register to the U register.
42	A s	Transfer the word in the A register to storage location s.
43	U s	Transfer the number in the U register to storage location s.
50	s A	Transfer the word at storage location s to the A register.
51	$-s$ A	Transfer the negative of the number at storage location s to the A register.
52	s A	Transfer the absolute value of the number at storage location s to the A register.
53	$-s$ A	Transfer the negative of the absolute value of the number at storage locations s to the A register.

* Operational instructions for the NRL Electronic Digital Computer (NAREC).

SAMPLE OPERATIONAL INSTRUCTIONS (Continued)

Operation Code	Coding Symbol	Operational Instructions
54	s Ad	Add the number at storage location s to the word in the A register and place the result in the A register.
55	$-s$ Ad	Add negatively the number at storage location s to the word in the A register and place the result in the A register.
56	s Ad	Add the absolute value of the number at storage location s to the number in the A register and place the result in the A register.
57	$-s$ Ad	Add negatively the absolute value of the number at storage location s to the number in the A register and place the result in the A register.
60	m s	Multiply the number at storage location s by the number in the A register and form the high-order product in the A register and the low-order product in the U register.
61	M s	Multiply the number at storage location s by the number in the A register and form the rounded-off high-order product in the A register.
70	D/s	Divide the number in the A register by the number at storage location s and form the rounded-off quotient in the A register.
71	X U	Reset the U register to zero.
80	X A	Reset the A register to zero.
81	$T(s_1, s_2, n)$	Transfer the n words at storage locations s_1 to $[s_1 + (n-1)]$ to storage locations s_2 to $[s_2 + (n-1)]$ respectively.
82	STOP	Stop machine operation.

FIG. 19-17 Sample Order List for Single Address Computer Code.

values illustrated both to the left and to the right of the decimal point. In addition to the case with which electronic circuitry can handle the "on"-"off" (1 or 0) symbol representation, mathematical calculations can easily be performed in this number system.

Computer Orders. A high-speed digital computer is directed through its operations by a series of commands developed within the control section of the machine. These commands are generated as a result of the sequence of orders provided by the prepared program. Each order has an indication of the operation to be performed along with single, double, or triple addresses, depending on the design of the computer being used. An address refers to a particular storage location within the computer storage section and can represent either a location where numerical data operands are to be found or it can be the location where the answer is to be placed after performing the specified operation. The single-address order is probably the simplest form, since the lone address associated with the operation order gives the storage location for either obtaining or recording information within the storage. That to be accomplished depends on the particular operation order being handled. The double-address order is not commonly used, but it contains two addresses, one designating the location of one operand whereas the other address specifies the location for recording the answer; the required second operand in either the single- or double-address code is usually found in the arithmetic section where it remains as a result of the previous operation. The triple-address order code has all three addresses of storage location possible involved in a particular order.

Sample operational orders for a single-address digital computer are listed in Fig. 19-17. Here a total of thirty-one orders are specified which, by being used separately or in combination, permit the solution to any mathematical problem that can be reduced to a method for numerical solution.

Coding of a Simple Function. To illustrate how a problem is coded for solution on a digital computer, the following simple example can be used. Suppose a coder came to a section of a program that called for the evaluation of the polynomial

$$f(x) = a_1 x^3 + a_2 x + a_3$$

The numerical coefficients, a_1, a_2, a_3, would have to be stored in three storage locations, say, address $c1$, $c2$, and $c3$. The value of x would have to be stored in some location, say address $w1$, and a location, say $w2$, would have to be designated to store the final result. Once this is done the instructions to the machine (in a single-address code—see Fig. 19-17) to find $f(x)$ could be written as follows:

Symbol		*Explanation*
$w1$	A	Bring the number x to the A register.
M	$w1$	Multiply by x, to form x^2
M	$w1$	Form x^3
M	$c1$	Form $a_1 x^3$
A	$w2$	Store $a_1 x^3$ temporarily in the location reserved for the final result.
$w1$	A	Bring x to the A register
M	$c2$	Multiply by a_2, the result $a_2 x$ will be left in the A register
$w2$	Ad	Add $a_1 x^3$ to $a_2 x$
$c3$	Ad	Add a_3 to $a_1 x^3 + a_2 x$
A	$w2$	Store the resulting $f(x)$ in location $w2$.

Each of the symbols above would then be replaced with a representative number which the computer could interpret, and the coding and numbers needed would be stored in the designated locations in the computer storage section. Other orders would obviously be needed to make this section of coding a useful part of a larger program.

19-6 SIMULATION OF MISSILE BY CONVENTIONAL AIRCRAFT *

In the development of a guided missile system, an urgent need exists for early information about the performance of components and of the entire guidance system under actual conditions. Short of a test firing, which, indeed, is the only way of testing under *actual* conditions, a considerable amount of useful data that closely parallel results from actual missile firings can be obtained by application of the principles of simulation. The missile environment cannot be accurately duplicated, except by another missile, but certain aspects pertinent to the guidance system and its performance can be adequately simulated.

Designed and built into a missile airframe are certain capabilities of flight maneuver. When made a part of a missile guidance system there

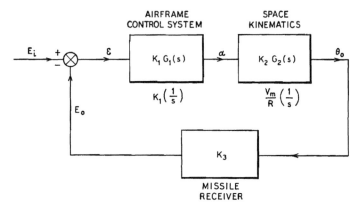

Fig. 19-18 Beam-rider Control Block Diagram.

is augmenting and compensating to achieve a desired control transfer function. The transfer function is selected on the basis of maximum performance against the presumed target tactics within servo system bandwidth limitations. To employ a conventional aircraft as a simulator of the missile, the control transfer function of the aircraft is determined and proper modifications are made to duplicate that of the missile control system. If we assume that the conventional aircraft cruising speed and maximum rate-of-turn capabilities are less than that of the missile, a trajectory simulation can be achieved only with a simulation scale factor other than unity. The control system requirements for trajectory simulation are established later. Desirability of trajectory simulation stems from the mathematical difficulties involved in a theoretical performance study

* Paragraph 19-6 has been written by C. F. White, based, in part, upon material originally prepared by R. E. Gaylord.

for any but a limited number of target flight paths and control system designs. As an example, consider a beam-rider missile with a pass-course target trajectory. The analytical determination of the missile trajectory for the restricted bandwidth and prescribed transfer function of the missile control system is of such an order of difficulty that some type of simulation is desirable, either by use of analog computers or by utilization of the "flying laboratory" to be discussed here. In the beam-rider missile mentioned, the scale factor concept allows control system performance development and verification, but the entire problem is not necessarily solved. For instance, in the beam-rider example many components, e.g., a rate gyro, cannot be fully tested unless the aircraft control system bandpass matches that of the missile. With some low performance missiles this is possible, but, in general, such is not the case.

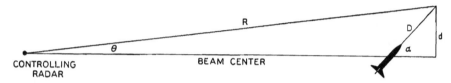

FIG. 19-19 Beam-rider Geometry.

Beam-rider Transfer Function. To make the discussion specific, consider a beam-rider missile. The system may be depicted by the block diagram of Fig. 19-18, in which a series combination of the missile receiver, which converts angle off desired trajectory to an equivalent voltage, the airframe-control system transfer function, and the space kinematics transfer function are depicted. The transfer functions are shown as the product of a frequency-invarient term, K, and a complex frequency function, $G(s)$. Figure 19-19 shows the geometry of a beam-rider in which, for a given angular misalignment in missile heading with respect to the radar beam axis α, the missile is depicted as traversing a distance

$$D = \int_0^t V_m \, dt \tag{19-20}$$

where D = distance traversed by missile in time t
V_m = missile speed
t = time

At the end of time t, the missile range from the controlling radar is R. The angular misalignment of the line of sight to the missile and the radar beam axis is θ, while the distance from the beam center is indicated as d. From Fig. 19-19 may be written the relationship

$$d = R \sin \theta = D \sin \alpha \tag{19-21}$$

Substituting D from Eq. (19-20) and rearranging, we obtain

$$\frac{\sin \theta}{\sin \alpha} = \frac{1}{R} \int_0^t V_m \, dt \tag{19-22}$$

For small angles, the approximation $\sin x = x$ may be made to obtain

$$\frac{\theta}{\alpha} = \frac{1}{R} \int_0^t V_m \, dt \tag{19-23}$$

Equation (19-23) shows the transfer function of the space kinematics block in Fig. 19-18 to be that of an integrator. Using Laplace transform notation (see Chap. 6 and Chap. 7), we have

$$\frac{\theta_o}{\alpha} = K_2 G_2(s) = \frac{V_m}{R}\left(\frac{1}{s}\right) \tag{19-24}$$

An idealized airframe control system transfer function is that of a perfect integrator. This fact can be appreciated from the concept of the missile rate of turn being proportional to the wing flap angle. Such a characteristic is realizable for low frequencies and constant velocity and may be indicated by

$$\frac{d\alpha}{dt} = K_1 \varepsilon(t)$$
$$s\alpha = K_1 \varepsilon(t) \tag{19-25}$$

The airframe-control system transfer function becomes

$$\frac{\alpha}{\varepsilon} = K_1 G_1(s) = K_1\left(\frac{1}{s}\right) \tag{19-26}$$

The foregoing establishes the fact of an inherent double-integrator or, in terms of the steady-state analysis of Chap. 7, a servo system open loop transfer function with a -2 slope. Such a characteristic is definitely unstable, and satisfactory beam-rider control is precluded unless something is introduced into the control loop to reduce the value of the slope. In common practice, a $0, +1, 0$ characteristic, obtained by the use of a resistance-capacitance shunted high-pass network, is employed to provide a frequency band with an asymptotic slope of -1. The overall loop transfer function becomes $-2, -1, -2$ and, for unity gain level within limits roughly defined by the limits of the -1 slope segment, satisfactory system operation becomes possible. In Fig. 19-20 the compensated transfer function for a beam-rider control system is shown by an asymptotic gain characteristic expressed mathematically by

$$\left.\frac{\theta_o}{E_1}\right|_{\substack{\text{open}\\\text{loop}}} = \underbrace{\left[\frac{\omega_m}{s}\right]^2}_{\substack{\text{basic } -2\\\text{slope term}}} \underbrace{\left[\left(\frac{s+\omega_1}{\omega_1}\right)\left(\frac{\omega_1}{\omega_2}\right)\left(\frac{\omega_2}{s+\omega_2}\right)\right]}_{\substack{\text{equalizer}\\\text{term}}} \underbrace{\left[\frac{\omega_2}{\omega_1}\right]}_{\substack{\text{gain}\\\text{term}}} \tag{19-27}$$

19-6] SIMULATION OF MISSILE BY CONVENTIONAL AIRCRAFT

The gain term in Eq. (19-27) is present to compensate for the attenuation inherent in use of the physical equalizer network. The relationship between the quantities of Fig. 19-18 and Eq. (19-27) can be recognized. The basic -2 slope term is equal to the product of the two integrator terms given by Eq. (19-24) and (19-26). Thus

$$\left[\frac{\omega_m}{s}\right]^2 = \frac{V_m}{R}\left(\frac{1}{s}\right) \cdot K_1\left(\frac{1}{s}\right) \tag{19-28}$$

The term given by Eq. (19-24) shows that the gain in the system varies directly with change in missile velocity and inversely with range from the controlling radar. In Fig. 19-20 higher gain can be visualized as a downward shifting of the unity gain line. Accordingly, there is a direct correspondence between the system gain as shown in Fig. 19-20 and the range to the target. That is to say, at closer ranges the unity gain line crosses the asymptotic characteristic near ω_2 and at far ranges near ω_1.

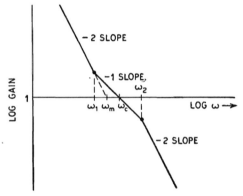

Fig. 19-20 Compensated Transfer Function for a Beam-rider Control System.

Simulant Transfer Function. A trajectory simulation is accomplished if the simulator traverses exactly the same positions in space traversed during the flight of the craft being simulated. Since, in general, the simulator travels at lower speed than the missile, the elapsed time for a given flight is greater than for the missile flight. The scale factor involved can be established as follows. Consider any servo system transfer characteristic (for instance, the $-2, -1, -2$ characteristic discussed here) and the system response for a position step input. The equation specifying the output as a function of time will, in all cases, contain a product of time and a factor proportional to the system bandwidth wherever the variable time occurs. If the product of bandwidth and time is held constant, the value of either may be changed without altering the result. Thus,

$$\omega_m \cdot t_m = \omega_s \cdot t_s$$

or
$$\frac{t_m}{t_s} = \frac{\omega_s}{\omega_m} \qquad (19\text{-}29)$$

where ω_m = quantity related to missile bandwidth
ω_s = corresponding simulator bandwidth quantity
t_m = time for missile maneuver
t_s = corresponding time for simulator maneuver

Designating this time scale factor by $\overline{\text{TSF}}$, and incorporating the equivalence given by Eq. (19-28), we have

$$\overline{\text{TSF}} = \frac{t_m}{t_s} = \frac{\omega_s}{\omega_m} = \frac{\sqrt{V_s K_{1s}}}{\sqrt{V_m K_{1m}}} \qquad (19\text{-}30)$$

where V_m = missile speed
K_{1m} = missile turning rate factor
V_s = simulator speed
K_{1s} = simulator turning rate factor

If the simulator has the same transfer characteristic (except for a bandwidth multiplier) as that of the missile, recordings of simulator response as a function of time become duplicates of similar missile tests, provided the time scale factor is applied to the simulator data.

The foregoing defines the necessary relationships for exact duplication of trajectories. In practice, the desire may be to achieve a unity scale factor. Such does not imply a system duplication factor by factor but means that the control system performance is made identical.

Design of Hypothetical Simulant. The missile guidance system to be simulated will be assumed to have the following pertinent characteristics:

(a) A ground-to-air beamrider with a guidance beamwidth of 3 deg.
(b) Missile speed of 800 knots.
(c) Operating midrange of 10,000 yd.
(d) Maximum maneuverability of 6 g (in both train and elevation).
(e) An open-loop system transfer function for airframe and autopilot combination together with the space kinematic term described as a simple -2 log-gain log-frequency characteristic.
(f) Stabilization to be accomplished by introduction into the control loop of an equalizer (plus amplifier to compensate for the equalizer d-c loss) having a $0, +1, 0$ characteristic (obtainable by use of a resistance-capacitance shunted high-pass network) to establish an overall system open loop characteristic specified by $-2, -1, -2$ slopes with the -1 asymptotic segment extending over a one-decade frequency span equally distributed with respect to the gain level corresponding to midrange.
(g) The beam-rider receiver (the only element common to both the missile and the simulant systems) is assumed to have a bandwidth sufficiently wide that the system response is not limited by it.

19-6] SIMULATION OF MISSILE BY CONVENTIONAL AIRCRAFT

The characteristics of the aircraft selected for the trajectory simulator system assumed are:

(a) Transport-utility type aircraft.
(b) Speed of 125 knots while climbing at a 3-deg elevation angle (low beam elevation angles are employed due to usual limitation of climb angle during sustained climb in transport or utility aircraft).
(c) A maximum desired maneuverability of 1 g (in both train and elevation).
(d) Open-loop transfer function (in coordinate of lowest performance) described as a -1 slope to $\omega = \omega_b = 2.5$ radians per sec followed at higher frequencies by a 6-db resonant rise before final response drop off at -2 slope at higher frequencies.

The foregoing includes one item, the aircraft open loop transfer characteristic, which limits the simulant system bandwidth (at $\omega = 2.5$ radians per sec) since extreme measures would be required to equalize beyond this frequency. In order that no contribution from autopilot servos and unequalized coupler be involved, it is assumed that their transfer characteristics are flat a decade above ω_b or to $\omega = 25$. Upon combining the autopilot and airframe and closing the control loop around the sensing devices, which in the example of a typical utility type autopilot is a rate gyroscope in the train or turn coordinate and a free vertical gyroscope in the elevation or pitch coordinate, the result obtained is as shown in Fig. 19-21. With the further addition of the necessary coupler and of the beam-rider receiver to complete the loop shown in Fig. 19-18, the characteristics shown in Fig. 19-21 are integrated once, i.e., the slope of each asymptotic segment is made one step more negative. The -1 slopes become -2 and so forth.

Comparison between the final result above and the missile idealized -2 slope discussed in connection with Fig. 19-18 reveals low frequency correspondence in the turn coordinate. An integration, accomplished by electromechanical or by electronic means, may be incorporated into the coupling device to make the pitch coordinate exhibit similar correspondence. In this connection, owing to the aerodynamics of the usual airframe and resulting system instability it is desirable that the static stability introduced by the vertical gyro of the aircraft autopilot be retained. Accordingly, replacement of the usual autopilot pitch gyroscope with a rate gyro is undesirable.

The final design problem is the design of the equalization network to provide corner frequencies (ω_1 and ω_2 of Fig. 19-20) at the proper values to duplicate the missile equalization. The first step is to determine the allowable maximum turning rate for the specified speed (125 knots) and the stated maximum load factor (1g). Since turning rate is found by dividing transverse acceleration by forward velocity, we have

678 SIMULATION, COMPUTATION, AND TELEMETRY

$$\alpha = \frac{\ddot{d}}{V_s} = \frac{n_g \cdot 32.2 \cdot 3600}{V_s \cdot 6080.2} = \frac{19.1 n_g}{V_s} \tag{19-31}$$

where $\alpha = d\alpha/dt$, the heading turning rate, radians per second
$\ddot{d}$ = lateral acceleration, feet per second^2
V_s = simulant speed in knots
n_g = load factor in "g" units

In the present case

$$\dot{\alpha} = \frac{19.1 \cdot 1}{125} = 0.153 \text{ radian per sec} \tag{19-32}$$

From Eq. (19-24), the space kinematics gain factor K_2 for $V_s = 125$ knots and midrange $R = 10{,}000$ yd becomes

$$K_2 = \frac{V_s}{R} = \frac{125 \cdot 6080.2}{3600 \cdot 10{,}000 \cdot 3} = 0.007 \text{ radian per sec} \tag{19-33}$$

For the specified 3-deg beam and the turning rate determined previously

$$K_1 K_3 = \frac{\dot{\alpha}}{\theta} = \frac{0.153 \cdot 57.296}{3} = 2.92 \text{ radians per sec} \tag{19-34}$$

The total loop gain equals $K_1 K_2 K_3 = 0.02$.

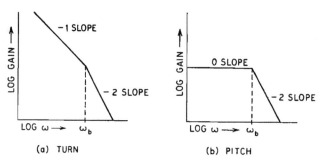

Fig. 19-21 Autopilot, Airframe, and Sensing Devices Combination Asymptotic Response.

To determine the frequency corresponding to unity gain in the midrange example,

$$\left| \frac{K_1 K_2 K_3}{s^2} \right| = \left| \frac{K_1 K_2 K_3}{\omega^2} \right| = 1$$

$$\omega_m = \sqrt{K_1 K_2 K_3} = \sqrt{0.02} = 0.143 \text{ radian per sec} \tag{19-35}$$

The ω_1 and ω_2 of the equalizer network becomes, for symmetrical distribution of the -1 slope segment around midrange and a ten-to-one frequency range,

$$\omega_1 = \frac{\omega_m}{\sqrt[4]{10}} = \frac{0.143}{1.778} = 0.08 \text{ radian per sec} \tag{19-36}$$

$$\omega_2 = 10\omega_1 = 0.80 \text{ radian per sec} \tag{19-37}$$

Unity gain at a level corresponding to ω_1 is equivalent to a simulant range of 31,600 yd, whereas a level corresponding to ω_2 is a range of 3160 yd. Optimum system performance at midrange of 10,000 yd is not maintained at the above extremes of range. The value of ω_2 is noted to be considerably lower than the $\omega = 2.5$ imposed by the airframe.

Derived Advantages. The use of the trajectory simulation described has the advantage of inexpensive (as compared to an actual missile firing) tests performed with scientific personnel in the aircraft observing system operation. Automatic data recording using standard laboratory apparatus (rather than the telemetering procedure required in actual missile testing) further simplifies development. Since all such systems are not strictly *linear* systems, simulation avoids the sometimes dubious approximations required for the usual analysis based upon linear theory. In actual practice, the system simulation using an aircraft is preceded by simulation on an analog computer. The modern analog computer is principally an assemblage of electronic operational amplifiers, computing components (resistances and capacitances), and arrangements for interconnection, introduction of initial conditions, servo multipliers, function generators for input signals, and output indicating and recording equipment. In the next subparagraph, the beam-rider system discussed earlier is translated into proper form for analog computer simulation.

Beam-rider Control System Simulation on an Electronic Analog Computer. With some computers the system is conveniently simulated as an open loop transfer function and then the system is converted into a closed loop system on the computer. With other computers, e.g., the REAC, the problem is manipulated from a closed loop expression. Both approaches are illustrated, in the order mentioned.

Equation (19-27) may be written in the form

$$\left.\frac{\theta_o}{E_i}\right|_{\substack{\text{open}\\\text{loop}}} = \left[\frac{\omega_m}{s}\right]^2 \left[\frac{s+\omega_1}{\omega_1}\right]\left[\frac{\omega_2}{s+\omega_2}\right] \qquad (19\text{-}38)$$

If the asymptotic characteristic frequency corresponding to unity gain is a frequency between ω_1 and ω_2 designated by ω_u, the substitution

$$\omega_m{}^2 = \omega_1 \cdot \omega_u \qquad (19\text{-}39)$$

may be made. Further the gain may be expressed by the parameter

$$K = \frac{\omega_u}{\omega_1} \qquad (19\text{-}40)$$

Finally, the upper equalizer corner frequency ω_2 may be normalized with respect to the lower corner ω_1 by defining a parameter

$$N = \frac{\omega_2}{\omega_1} \qquad (19\text{-}41)$$

Substitution of the foregoing into Eq. (19-38) gives the open loop transfer function

$$\left.\frac{\theta_o}{E_i}\right|_{\substack{\text{open} \\ \text{loop}}} = K \left[\frac{\omega_1}{s}\right]^2 \left[\frac{s + \omega_1}{\omega_1}\right] \left[\frac{N\omega_1}{N\omega_1 + s}\right] \qquad (19\text{-}42)$$

in the form desired for computer simulation.

Although some of the basic concepts of operational amplifiers arranged

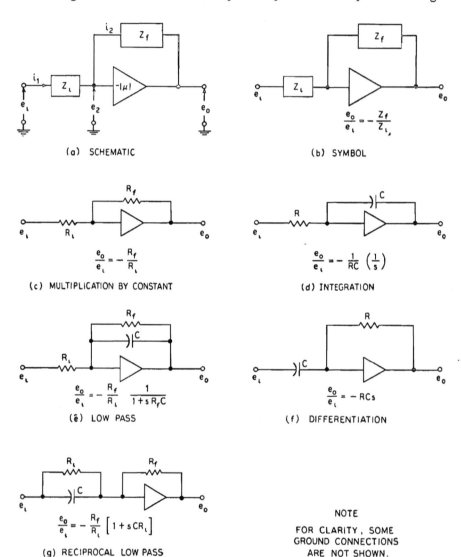

FIG. 19-22 Operational Amplifier Circuits.

for computation have been introduced earlier, more detail is in order for present purposes. An operational amplifier is basically a direct current or d-c amplifier with a very large gain. Gain in the order of 10,000 (from the d-c amplifier) times 500 (from the a-c drift stabilizing associated amplifier) or effectively *5 million* is involved in some computers. Resistances and capacitances are used either as input or as feedback impedances. Consider the circuit of Fig. 19-22a, in which the assumption of zero grid current is made (in view of the high gain the grid voltage never exceeds a few millivolts and the assumption of zero grid current corresponds very closely with fact). Writing equations

$$e_i - e_2 = i_1 Z_i \qquad (19\text{-}43)$$
$$e_2 - e_o = i_2 Z_f \qquad (19\text{-}44)$$
$$e_o = -|\mu|e_2 \qquad (19\text{-}45)$$

and, as a consequence of the statement regarding zero grid current,

$$i_1 = i_2 \qquad (19\text{-}46)$$

we may now derive the transfer function expression

$$\frac{e_o}{e_i} = -\frac{Z_f}{Z_i} \cdot \frac{1}{1 + \frac{1}{\mu}\left(1 + \frac{Z_f}{Z_i}\right)} \qquad (19\text{-}47)$$

where the absolute value sign on the gain has been dropped. For the usual case of $\mu >> \left(1 + \frac{Z_f}{Z_i}\right)$,

$$\frac{e_o}{e_i} \cong -\frac{Z_f}{Z_i} \qquad (19\text{-}48)$$

Equation (19-48) is the basic equation from which the computer functions are derived. Figure 19-22c shows the use of a resistance in both the Z_i and Z_f positions to perform the function of multiplication by a constant (with a change of sign).

$$\frac{e_o}{e_i} = -\frac{Z_f}{Z_i} = -\frac{R_f}{R_i} \qquad (19\text{-}49)$$

Figure 19-22d shows Z_i a resistance and Z_f a capacitance to obtain integration (with a change of sign).

$$\frac{e_o}{e_i} = -\frac{\frac{1}{sC}}{R} = -\frac{1}{RC}\left(\frac{1}{s}\right) \qquad (19\text{-}50)$$

Figure 19-22e shows a low-pass characteristic $\dfrac{e_o}{e_i} = -\dfrac{1}{R_i}\dfrac{R_f \cdot \frac{1}{sC}}{R_f + \frac{1}{sC}}$

$$\frac{e_o}{e_i} = -\frac{R_f}{R_i} \cdot \frac{1}{1 + sR_fC} \qquad (19\text{-}51)$$

$$= -\frac{R_f}{R_i} \cdot \frac{\frac{1}{R_fC}}{s + \frac{1}{R_fC}} \qquad (19\text{-}52)$$

with a multiplicative constant $(-R_f/R_i)$ which may, if desired, be made unity (again with a change of sign). The form given in Eq. (19-51) is that employed by computer operators as distinguished from the corner frequency form $\left(\omega_x = \frac{1}{R_fC}\right)$ of Eq. (19-52). Figures 19-22f and g show the method for producing differentiation and for producing reciprocal low-pass characteristics.

With the variety of functions shown on Fig. 19-22, the simulation of a closed loop system defined by the open loop expression given by Eq. (19-42) may be accomplished. Conveniently select $\omega_1 = 1$ (this selection is one aspect of "scaling"). Figure 19-23 shows introduction of the gain

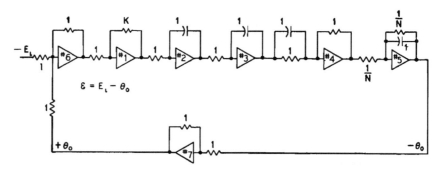

Fig. 19-23 Analog Computer for Beam-rider Control System.

parameter K by operational amplifier number 1. In common usage, resistances are expressed in megohms and capacitances in microfarads (so used in Fig. 19-23). Amplifiers number 2 and 3 are used to provide the double integration term. Amplifier number 4 is connected to provide a reciprocal low-pass with the corner at ω_1. In practical operation a small resistance in series with the capacitance avoids computer high frequency instability. Amplifier number 5 exhibits a low-pass characteristic at $N\omega_1$. Here the resistances are indicated as $1/N$ to allow use of a capacitance with a value of 1 microfarad (in some computers the *only* value available). Ignoring possible error in sign, the cascaded combination for numbers 1 through 5 simulates the system open loop transfer function. To set up a closed loop an error detector is needed. This takes the form of a multiplier with two inputs, amplifier number 6. The quantity $\varepsilon = E_i - \theta_o$ is desired at the outputs of number 6. Since a sign reversal is experienced through the amplifier, the inputs must be $-E_i$ and $+\theta_o$. Indicate the inputs and output accordingly. Focusing attention on the output of number 6 which is positive, we count sign reversals down the chain of numbers 1 through 5 to find that the output of number 5 has a negative sign. The feedback at the feedback point is for $+\theta_o$ instead of the $-\theta_o$ at the output of number 5. The loop is accordingly closed through another (unity gain) stage, number 7. The closed loop system is now complete with the input connection available to apply a forcing function. If one is concerned about the minus sign on the input and demands a plus input point, such may be provided by another inverter like number 7 connected ahead of the indicated input.

Note the direct correspondence between points in the actual system and in the analog. The closed loop system output and the system error may both be recorded for various inputs. For a ten-to-one equalization spread ($N = 10$) and the values of K from 1 to 10 which correspond to a ten-to-one decrease in range the system response to a step function input is shown in Fig. 19-24.

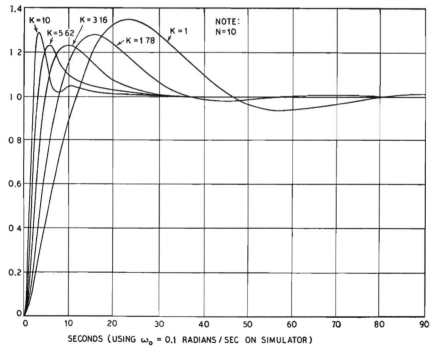

Fig. 19-24 Beam-rider Transient Response to Input Position Step.

684   SIMULATION, COMPUTATION, AND TELEMETRY

A frequently used alternative method of simulation starts with manipulation of the system open loop expression into the corresponding closed loop expression and follows with other steps shown for the same illustration as follows:

$$\left.\frac{\theta_o}{E_i}\right|_{\substack{\text{open}\\\text{loop}}} = \mu = K\left[\frac{\omega_1}{s}\right]^2\left[\frac{s+\omega_1}{\omega_1}\right]\left[\frac{N\omega_1}{N\omega_1+s}\right]$$

$$\left.\frac{\theta_o}{E_i}\right|_{\substack{\text{closed}\\\text{loop}}} = \frac{\mu}{\mu+1}$$

$$= \frac{NK\omega_1^2 s + NK\omega_1^3}{s^3 + N\omega_1 s^2 + NK\omega_1^2 s + NK\omega_1^3} \quad (19\text{-}53)$$

$$(s^3 + N\omega_1 s^2 + NK\omega_1^2 s + NK\omega_1^3)\theta_o = (NK\omega_1^2 s + NK\omega_1^3)E_i$$

$$\dddot{\theta}_o + N\omega_1 \ddot{\theta}_o + NK\omega_1^2(\dot{\theta}_o - \dot{E}_i) + NK\omega_1^3(\theta_o - E_i) = 0 \quad (19\text{-}54)$$

Inspection of Eq. (19-54) reveals that the time derivative of the input is involved. If the input is a position step function, the result would be the delta function—a spike. To avoid such a situation, take the integral

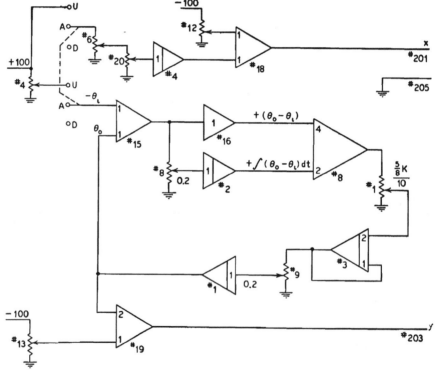

FIG. 19-25 Alternate Analog Computer Simulation.

of every term to get the equivalent expression

$$\ddot{\theta}_o + N\omega_1\dot{\theta}_o + NK\omega_1^2(\theta_o - E_i) + NK\omega_1^3\int(\theta_o - E_i)\,dt = 0$$

Finally, rewrite as follows:

$$\ddot{\theta}_o = -N\omega_1\dot{\theta}_o - NK\omega_1^2(\theta_o - E_i) - NK\omega_1^3\int(\theta_o - E_i)\,dt \quad (19\text{-}55)$$

Equation (19-55) is in the preferred form for many computers, e.g., the REAC. The remaining procedure involves assuming the availability of some of the quantities on the right side, performing indicated operations, summing, and finally equating to the left side. The assumed quantities startlingly appear (see Fig. 19-25 which uses the notation employed with REAC computers). The method of introducing the input step function (from potentiometer number 4) is shown together with an arrangement for setting the recorder (an x-y plotter) at the desired initial position (by adjustment of potentiometers numbers 13 and 12). The horizontal motion or time axis is established by applying a step function to an integrator (number 4). The slope of the ramp function determines the rate of motion in the x-coordinate.

19-7 THE USE OF RADIO TELEMETRY AS AN AID TO MISSILE GUIDANCE SYSTEM DESIGN *

Basic design, construction, and test of circuitry for missile guidance systems can be achieved for the most part in the laboratory where conventional test equipment can be utilized. However, the development of design improvements based upon system integration and environmental effects can be achieved only by performance testing under simulated or actual environmental conditions. In the case of missile guidance systems, simulated conditions can be represented most accurately and economically by flight testing in piloted aircraft before actual missile flight tests. It is very important that such tests be thorough and adequate before the vastly more complicated and costly missile flight tests are undertaken. Although flight testing in piloted aircraft can be accomplished using conventional test equipment and data recording devices, the problems encountered are quite formidable, to say the least. Hence, a requirement is generated for specialized test equipment suitable for determination of system performance under both simulated and actual environmental conditions. In addition to providing a means of gathering upper atmosphere research data, aerodynamical test data, rocket motor performance data, etc., radio telemetry has also provided the specialized test equipment so useful in simulated flight testing of missile guidance systems and so necessary in actual missile flight tests.

* Paragraph 19-7 has been written by P. T. Stine, Radar Division, Naval Research Laboratory.

Requirements for Radio Telemetry. The use of radio telemetry for instrumenting flight tests in piloted aircraft before missile flight testing is an important one indeed. The strongest advocates of this application of telemetering are those who have attempted to gather inflight data using conventional test equipment or recorders in the crowded quarters of a maneuvering aircraft. Some of the principal reasons for this support are summarized below.

a. Modern radio telemetering systems have a very large information capacity which can be defined as the product of the number of channels and the maximum frequency response per channel. In general, a large number of conventional test instruments and/or data recording devices would be required to provide equivalent information capacity in the aircraft.

b. Conventional test instruments and data recorders are usually much heavier and more bulky than telemetering equipment and thus create a weight and balance problem in the aircraft. Naturally this problem is more severe in small aircraft.

c. Conventional test equipment is not designed for installation in an aircraft and suffers from shock and vibration.

d. The use of conventional equipment which is not designed for operation in aircraft is conducive to "haywire" interconnections which are not only unreliable but create a safety problem as well.

e. Changes in atmospheric pressure, temperature, and humidity affect the calibration, performance, and longevity of delicate instruments unless specially designed for use under such environmental conditions.

f. The electrical power available in an aircraft for data gathering is extremely limited both in quantity and type. Present-day radio telemetering equipment is designed for use with typical aircraft power systems and requires only comparatively small amounts of power.

g. The performance of operating personnel is reduced tremendously under conditions of testing in which maneuvering of the aircraft sometimes becomes sufficient to cause airsickness.

h. Other methods of data gathering such as photographing or televising of instrument readings results in poor resolution, low frequency response, and decreased accuracy in spite of the fact that the equipment required is heavier and more bulky than radio telemetering equipment.

As a specialized test instrument, radio telemetry is called upon to measure a wide variety of information including position, velocity, acceleration, vibration, pressure, temperature, strain, fuel flow, cosmic ray counts, and voltage. Each type of information may be essentially constant or varying at a rapid rate. Accuracy requirements vary widely with the use of the information to be telemetered. Strictly qualitative data may require accuracies of only 10 to 30 percent, whereas 1 to 3 percent is desirable for most quantitative data. Occasional items of scientific research data may warrant special techniques directed toward achieving accuracies in the order of 0.1 to 0.3 percent. When used as an aid to missile guidance system design, the problems of radio telemetry are somewhat simplified in that all information items to be telemetered are voltages or may be readily converted to voltages. Although the frequency content of some data to be telemetered may be quite high, experience has shown that most data items are essentially constant or slow varying in nature and may be commutated.

The Basic Radio Telemetering System. As a result of the varied requirements for data telemetering and the large number of missile contracts which have been let, many types of radio telemetering systems have been developed. The basic elements of a radio telemetering system include the *pick-up devices* for detection and measurement of the information (sometimes referred to as transducers or end instruments), a device for multiplexing the various items of information, a radio frequency transmitter, transmitting and receiving antennas, a radio frequency receiver, a device for separating the items of information, and display devices for indicating and/or recording the data. Most of the various systems may use similar pick-up and display devices since their characteristics are primarily determined by the type of information to be measured and the type of record or display desired. Major differences exist in the methods of multiplexing, modulation, demodulation, and separation of the data channels. Amplitude modulation, frequency modulation, pulse position modulation, pulse width modulation, mechanical commutation, and electronic multiplexing have been used in various combinations, giving rise to as many different developments as there were missile programs.

In the interest of economy and coordination of usage, the various branches of the Armed Services cooperatively initiated and sponsored a standardization program which has done much to clarify the situation without closing the door to continued research and improvement in the field of radio telemetry. The primary approach was to standardize on certain well-defined specifications as determined by performance requirements rather than standardizing on specific equipments. It was realized that one standard telemeter could not fulfill the needs of all the many varied missile programs. As a result, the following three general systems were adopted wherein information handling capacity, Nf, is defined as the product of the number of information channels and the maximum frequency response per channel:

(a) A small, simple, low-capacity telemeter having only a few channels of limited frequency response.
(b) A medium-capacity telemeter providing a medium number of channels with wide range of frequency response available.

(c) A large, high-capacity telemeter having a large number of channels of relatively high frequency response.

The first system has been defined as a time-division system (information items sampled and transmitted sequentially) using pulse width modulation–frequency modulation, customarily abbreviated PWM-FM. A frequency-division system (information measured continuously and used to modulate subcarriers) of the frequency modulation–frequency modulation (FM-FM) type has been widely used and accepted as the medium telemeter with detailed standard specifications set by the standardization program. Because of the relationship of bandwidth to information capacity, it has also been generally accepted that the large telemeter should

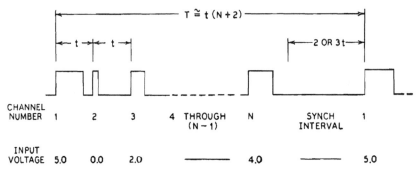

FIG. 19-26 Typical Pulse Train for Pulse Width Modulation.

be a time-division system using pulse position modulation–amplitude modulation (PPM-AM). Detailed specifications have not been standardized to date other than to designate the radio frequency band in which it shall operate. By cooperative effort on the part of all concerned, the advantages of telemetering standardization have been generally achieved and accepted by those working in the telemetering field.

Low-capacity Telemetering Systems. Pulse width modulation–frequency modulation (PWM-FM) telemetering systems provide for sequential sampling of information channels and hence are referred to as time-division systems. Because of the narrow bandwidth and wide pulses used in the present systems, they have relatively low information handling capacity. However, they may be quite small in size and simple in design. PWM-FM systems in use are designed to accept 0 to 5 volts d-c information inputs, each input being used to vary the width of a voltage pulse. Hence, if N represents the number of data channels to be telemetered, a train of N variable width pulses is generated as illustrated in Fig. 19-26. This train of pulses is then used to shift the frequency of the radio frequency carrier by a fixed amount. Synchronization is accomplished by the absence of pulses during a time interval equal to two or three channels.

Inspection of Fig. 19-26 reveals that each information channel occupies a time interval t and is sampled once in each frame represented by time interval T. Since T is directly proportional to the number of channels, the sampling rate of each information channel is inversely proportional to the number of channels. Hence, the user of such a system must strike a compromise between the number of information channels he wishes to telemeter and the frequency response or maximum rate of change of in-

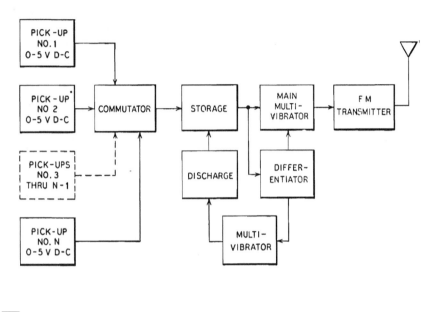

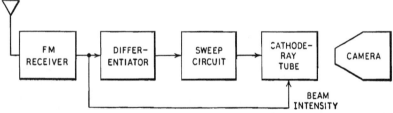

Fig. 19-27 Simplified PWM-FM Telemetering System.

formation. Although it is generally accepted that from five to six samples per cycle are required to reconstruct sine wave information "by eye" and keep uncertainties less than about 5 percent, high quality low-pass filters can be used to effect the same restoration with as few as about 2.5 samples per sine wave cycle. On this basis, $T \leq 1/2.5f$, wherein f represents the required frequency response. Conversely, $f \leq 1/2.5T$ is a maximum for the case, wherein $T = t$ which allows only one data channel.

The telemetering standardization program specifies that the minimum pulse width for PWM-FM systems shall be 90 microsec ±30 microsec and the maximum pulse width shall be 660 microsec ±50 microsec. Hence the time interval t must be of the order of 800 to 1000 microsec. On this basis, Nf, the product of the number of channels and the maximum frequency response per channel, is about 500. The radio frequency band is 216 to 220 mc with a carrier shift of 50 kc minimum and 125 kc maximum. The 225 to 230 mc band is available on a noninterference basis only. A block diagram of a typical PWM-FM telemetering system is shown in simplified form in Fig. 19-27. Pulse width modulation–phase modulation (PWM-PM) telemetering systems are quite similar in principle and offer additional radio frequency stability through the use of a crystal controlled transmitter oscillator.

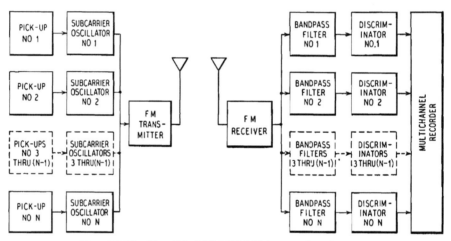

Fig. 19-28 Simplified FM-FM Telemetering System.

Medium-capacity Telemetering Systems. Frequency modulation–frequency modulation (FM-FM) telemetering systems are referred to as frequency-division systems since the modulation spectrum of the frequency modulated carrier is divided among several subcarriers, each of which is normally frequency-modulated by a single information input. Figure 19-28 is a simplified block diagram of a typical FM-FM telemetering system. Since the subcarrier oscillators may be frequency modulated by a change in voltage, inductance, resistance, or capacitance, this type of system is readily adaptable to use with a wide variety of pick-up devices.

Standardized subcarrier center frequencies (F_0), frequency deviation (ΔF_0), and typical subcarrier frequency responses (f_m) have been specified as shown in Table 19-1. The frequency responses given are based upon

TABLE 19-1 STANDARD SUBCARRIER BANDS FOR FM-FM TELEMETERING USE

Band No.	Center Frequency F_0 (cps)	Frequency Deviation ΔF_0 (percent)	Lower Limit of Band (cps)	Upper Limit of Band (cps)	Conservative Frequency Response (cps)	Maximum Frequency Response (cps)
1	400	± 7.5	370	430	6	30
2	560	"	518	602	8	42
3	730	"	675	785	11	55
4	960	"	888	1032	14	72
5	1300	"	1202	1398	20	98
6	1700	"	1572	1828	25	128
7	2300	"	2127	2473	35	173
8	3000	"	2775	3225	45	225
9	3900	"	3607	4193	60	293
10	5400	"	4995	5805	80	405
11	7350	"	6799	7901	110	551
12	10,500	"	9712	11,288	160	788
13	14,500	"	13,412	15,588	220	1088
14	22,000	"	20,350	23,650	330	1650
15	30,000	"	27,750	32,250	450	2250
16	40,000	"	37,000	43,000	600	3000
17	52,500	"	48,560	56,440	790	3940
18	70,000	"	64,750	75,250	1050	5250
A*	22,000	± 15	18,700	25,300	660	3300
B	30,000	"	25,500	34,500	900	4500
C	40,000	"	34,000	46,000	1200	6000
D	52,500	"	44,620	60,380	1600	7880
E	70,000	"	59,500	80,500	2100	10,500

* Note that no two adjacent wide bands may be used simultaneously. Bands A through E may only be used if other bands are omitted as indicated below:

Wide Band Used	Omit Band(s)
A	14 and 15
B	14, 15, and 16
C	15, 16, and 17
D	16, 17, and 18
E	17 and 18

use of a minimum modulation index (ratio of frequency deviation to maximum information frequency) of five to insure a high signal-to-noise ratio and high quality. Higher maximum frequency response may be achieved by reducing the frequency deviation and accepting a lower minimum modulation index. For example, if the modulation index is permitted to drop to the order of 0.5 to 1.0, a frequency response equal to the maximum frequency deviation ΔF_0 can be achieved, but with corresponding reductions in signal-to-noise ratio and accuracy. It becomes readily apparent that the user has a choice of high quality (low distortion and good accuracy) or high frequency response and must make a compromise based upon the final use of the data. It is possible, however, to use different maximum frequency deviations for the various subcarrier bands and have a wide range of quality and frequency response combinations. The primary reason for specification of the frequency responses of the various bands in Table 19-1 is to indicate the importance of selecting recording equipments having frequency response compatible with that obtainable from the telemetering system for the particular values of minimum modulation indices used. Of the subcarrier frequencies shown in Table 19-1, typical telemeter receiving stations are equipped to receive and demodulate as

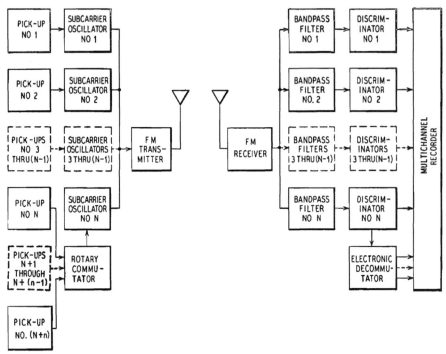

FIG. 19-29 Simplified PAM-FM-FM Telemetering System.

many as 12 to 14 simultaneously. Hence, typical FM-FM systems have a medium information handling capacity with Nf ranging from about 500 to 10,000.

As in the case of PWM-FM systems, the radio frequency band specified for FM-FM telemetering is 216 to 220 mc with the 225 to 230 mc band available on a noninterference basis. Standard frequency deviation of the radio frequency carrier is ±125 kc. Hence, FM-FM telemeter receiving stations are readily adaptable for receiving PWM-FM signals by the addition of synchronization and sweep circuits, oscilloscope, and photorecording equipment following the receiver.

In cases requiring a large number of low frequency response channels in combination with a few high frequency response channels, it is customary to use time-division multiplexing of one or more of the higher frequency subcarriers of an FM-FM system. This actually results in a form of triple modulation (PAM-FM-FM) and is usually accomplished by means of a rotary mechanical commutator. The telemetering standardization program has specified maximum and conservative sampling rates; conservative and minimum sample lengths; nature of synchronizing pulses; and frequency deviations for reference level, minimum information signal, and maximum information signal. With the advent of standardized commutation, some automatic decommutators have become available for use in standard FM-FM telemeter receiving stations. A typical PAM-FM-FM system is shown in Fig. 19-29.

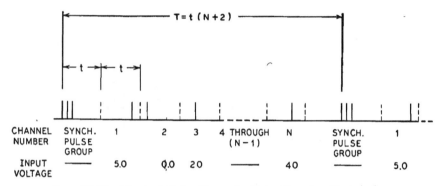

Fig. 19-30 Typical Pulse Train for Pulse Position Modulation.

High-capacity Telemetering Systems. The radio frequency band assigned for pulse type telemetering systems requiring wide bandwidths is 2200 to 2300 mc. Use of narrow pulses and wide bandwidths permits a corresponding increase in the information handling capacity since the time interval allowed per data channel can be decreased in the same proportion as the pulse width. Hence, more samples can be taken in a given amount of time. Most high-capacity telemetering systems in use at the present time are pulse position modulation–amplitude modulation (PPM-AM) systems with the product of the number of channels and the frequency response per channel ranging from about 4000 to 20,000. A typical pulse train is shown in Fig. 19-30. Typical PPM-AM systems, such as shown in the simplified block diagram of Fig. 19-31, provide about 30 to 35 data channels with frequency responses of about 120 to 540 cps based upon the requirement of 2.5 samples to reconstruct each sine wave cycle by use of high quality low-pass filters. As in all time-division systems, the Nf product remains constant after design, and the user has the option of increasing the frequency response at the expense of the number of data channels which may be telemetered. The basic accuracy depends upon the design of the equipment and is unaffected by the user's choice of number of channels versus frequency response per channel.

With regard to the typical pulse train of a PPM-AM system shown in Fig. 19-30, it should be pointed out that the pulses are of the order of 1 microsec or less in width, and the time interval t is much shorter than the time interval t of Fig. 19-26. Whereas the leading edges of the pulses in

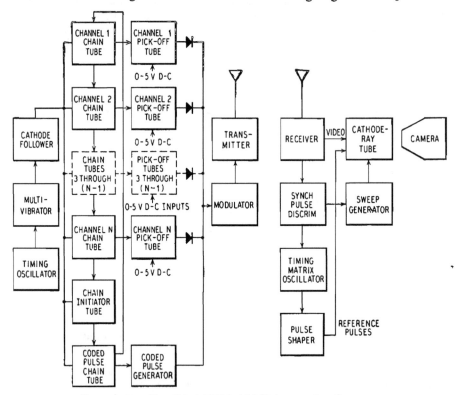

FIG. 19-31 Simplified PPM-AM Telemetering System.

Fig. 19-26 provide a reference from which the pulse width is measured, the channel references in Fig. 19-30 (as shown by the broken line pulses) are usually not transmitted but are reconstructed by a synchronized timing oscillator in the receiving equipment as shown in the simplified block diagram of Fig. 19-31. Recording methods are usually much more complex than shown in Fig. 19-31, providing for greater accuracy by recording only a few data channels on each of several cathode-ray tubes, or providing separation of channels and smoothing of data for recording on multichannel oscillographs.

Pick-up Devices. Transducers, end instruments, gages, and pick-ups are various terms which have been applied to the devices used to measure and convert data to be telemetered into a form suitable for modulation of the telemetering link. Such devices, when designed to measure a particular type of information, are more specifically called pressure gages, strain gages, vibration pick-ups, accelerometers, fuel flow meters, airspeed indicators, position potentiometers, gyroscope position indicators, cosmic ray counters, etc. Although much progress has been made in this phase of telemetering, pick-up devices are still the primary limitation on telemetering accuracy for certain types of data. This is understandable when one considers the fact that most laboratory instruments have accuracies of only 3 to 5 percent, whereas many users of telemetered data ask for accuracies of 1 percent or better. It should be borne in mind that even when such overall accuracies are achievable, the cost of achievement may be quite high. For this reason if for no other, the user of telemetered data should review his accuracy specifications with an eye to asking for no more than is actually required.

Data in the form of voltage measurements are probably the most convenient to telemeter since all standard telemetering systems can accept 0 to 5 volts d-c or 1.75 volts rms superimposed on 2.5 volts d-c. Pick-up devices are available for converting almost any type of data to a voltage measurement. In some cases, however, considerations of accuracy, calibration, frequency response, and environmental effects may dictate the use of other types of pick-up devices. As previously mentioned, FM-FM telemetering systems are extremely flexible in that they may be easily adapted for use with any type of pick-up device available. In any event, selection of the proper pick-up devices is dependent upon many factors determined by the application and as such constitutes a task for the experienced telemetering engineer. However, it may be generally stated that the use of radio telemetering as an aid to missile guidance system design seldom involves data which are not in voltage form or easily converted to voltage form.

Data Recording. Methods of recording the data outputs from a telemetering system vary widely, depending upon the use to be made of the data. Factors to be considered include frequency response, accuracy, permanency of record, and time availability of the record. Meters may be used to give a real-time indication to observers, and various types of pen recorders are available to present a permanent record in real time. Typical pen recorders make use of from four to six inking pens, electric stylii, or hot wire stylii to record on specially ruled paper. Such recorders have maximum frequency responses of the order of 50 to 100 cps and hence are limited to the recording of only low frequency information.

Multichannel recording oscillographs making use of electromagnetic galvanometers and photosensitive recording papers or films are extensively used because of their large information recording capacity. Typical oscillographs of this type may simultaneously record as many as 50 data channels with frequency responses as high as 3000 to 5000 cps. One disadvantage is that the photosensitive paper or film must be photoprocessed before the record is available. However, recent advances in photo-

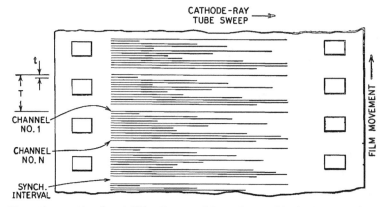

FIG. 19-32 Simulated Film Record Made from "Line" Presentation.

processing equipment have reduced the time delay between recording and the availability of the permanent record to about 30 min for a record 250 ft in length and 12 in. wide.

Another widely used method of recording is the direct photorecording of data displayed on cathode-ray tubes. Each channel output from the telemetering equipment may be used to deflect the cathode-ray beam of a

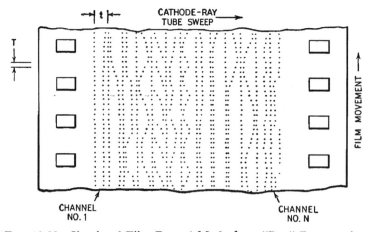

FIG. 19-33 Simulated Film Record Made from "Dot" Presentation.

single cathode-ray tube in the case of frequency-division telemetering systems. Various methods of cathode-ray tube presentation are used with time-division systems. In the case of either pulse width or pulse position modulation systems, all data channels may be displayed as a "line" presentation on a single cathode-ray tube as indicated in Fig. 19-27 by intensity modulating or gating the successive sweeps to lengths which are

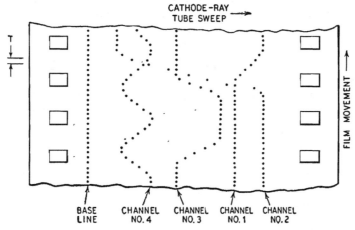

Fig. 19-34 Simulated Film Record Made from Gated "Dot" Presentation.

proportional to the time intervals of the individual data channels. An illustration of the appearance of such a film record is shown in Fig. 19-32.

Another method is to intensity-modulate the sweep for each channel reference and each channel data pulse as done in Fig. 19-31 to effect a "dot" presentation such as illustrated in Fig. 19-33. Accuracy is limited

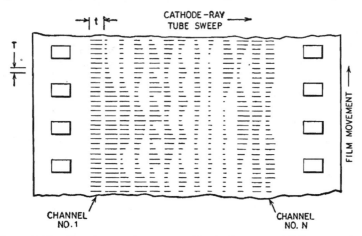

Fig. 19-35 Simulated Film Record Made from "Dash" Presentation.

by the reduced resolution due to the compression of the time scale in the "dot" presentation, whereas the "line" presentation is difficult to interpret unless reduced by a data reduction machine designed to handle this type of data record. Accuracy may be improved and interpretation made easier by electronically gating only a few data channels to each of several cathode-ray tubes to produce a record similar to the illustration shown in Fig. 19-34. If the cathode-ray beam is intensified during the entire time interval between each channel reference pulse and its respective channel pulse, a "dash" presentation results as illustrated in Fig. 19-35.

Recent advances in the design and performance of magnetic tape recorders have resulted in widespread use of tape recording for storage of multiplexed data from FM-FM or PWM-FM telemetering systems. This type of data storage is used primarily as a safeguard in the event of failure of demodulation or recording equipment during the telemetering operation. It is also useful where only a limited amount of equipment can be installed or transported to the receiving location. The magnetic tape record can then be "played back" through the demodulation equipment to data recorders at a later time or under more ideal operating conditions. In general, magnetic tape recorders are not usable with PPM-AM telemetering systems because of the high frequency response required to record the narrow pulses used in such systems.

Conclusions. Several types of radio telemetering systems are available to the guidance system designer. In general, the primary factor in determining which system to use is the information handling capacity required by the particular application. The method of recording the telemetered data is primarily dependent upon the characteristics of the data itself and the eventual use for which it is intended.

Radio telemetry is by far the most practical means of gathering data from the flight testing of guided missiles, their components, and their guidance systems. It is also an indispensable instrument in the field of upper atmosphere research. Because of its compactness, ruggedness, reliability, accuracy, and large data handling capacity, present-day radio telemetering is a very useful and important aid in the developmental flight testing of missile guidance systems under simulated conditions.

19-8 RADIO WAVE PROPAGATION SIMULATION *

Missile guidance systems frequently require the design of directive antennas wherein the phase of radiation should be constant or vary in a particular manner. Often, the beam tilt and the deviation from phase front linearity with various placements of the feed point are of interest. It may also be desirable to know how the phase fronts and beam shapes

---

* Paragraph 19-8 has been written in major portion by N. L. Walbridge, H. M. Smith, Jr., and L. A. Woodward, Engineering Experiment Station, University of Vermont and State Agricultural College.

are affected by changes in excitation frequency. Aerodynamic considerations usually restrict the size of antenna that can be accommodated within a guided missile and also put severe requirements on the radome designer.

Since the calculation or experimental determination of phase-front and beam patterns is usually a difficult, tedious, and expensive operation, there is a need for a simple analogous device to aid in determining the interrelationships among the many factors involved.

The *ripple tank* has long been used to demonstrate interesting properties of wave motion. The essential feature is a shallow tray of water with a glass bottom. By some means, very small waves, or ripples, are generated in the water surface, and, then, by transmitted light the motion of the waves is portrayed on a screen. The resulting two-dimensional pattern illustrates dramatically many of the mathematical theories of electromagnetic radiation which includes X-rays, light, infrared rays, and radio waves. Of especial interest are the short wavelength bands employed in radar.

For the electronics engineer to use the ripple tank intelligently, it is necessary to know some of the techniques and limitations of ripple-tank operation. It is usually disturbing to note that the velocity of water-ripple propagation is dependent on wavelength, which is not the case for electromagnetic waves. The theoretical ripple velocity (v) in centimeters per second may be calculated from the formula

$$v = \left(\frac{2\pi T}{\lambda d} + \frac{g\lambda}{2\pi}\right)^{\frac{1}{2}} \tag{19-56}$$

where surface tension (T) is expressed in dynes per centimeter; water density (d), in grams per centimeter; acceleration of gravity (g), in centimeters per second; and wavelength (λ), in centimeters.

This variation in velocity with wavelength turns out to be unimportant in most two-dimensional antenna model work because the basic scaling relationship that should be maintained is

$$\frac{d_m}{\lambda_m} = \frac{d_a}{\lambda_a} \tag{19-57}$$

where d_m and d_a are corresponding dimensions of the model and antenna respectively and λ_m and λ_a are the wavelengths for the model and the antenna respectively. Since most work requires the use of only one frequency at a time, it makes no difference what the velocity of propagation may be as long as the relationship in Eq. (19-57) is maintained. All measurements should be made in terms of wavelengths and not of frequency. It is interesting to note that the velocity of propagation of ripples is less than the velocity of electromagnetic waves by a factor[1] of the order of 10^9.

---

[1] A. H. Schooley, Supt. Electronics Division, NRL, *NRL Report No. 3559*. Also *Proceedings of the National Electronic Conference*, 1950.

700 SIMULATION, COMPUTATION, AND TELEMETRY

In 1949, Schooley described such a device to be used as an aid to phase front visualization, which was constructed at the Naval Research Laboratory. It was considered a possibility that such a device could be extended not only to demonstrate but to measure accurately the radiation from certain sources and reflectors. When light rays are directed vertically upward through the water surface, they are refracted differently at each point of the wave, as shown in Fig. 19-36. As a consequence, each small section of the wave crest acts as a lens with its own focal length and, like images of a point source, is distributed in space above the water surface.

Considering the coincidence of two images from corresponding sections of two different waves, very convenient equations may be derived which relate the amplitude directly to the distance between these waves, or the wavelength, and to the distance of the point of coincidence from the ripple lens. In Fig. 19-36, the rays were drawn according to calculations for slightly attenuated waves, and the points of coincidence, such as (a), are seen to be progressively farther from the water surface.

In practice, this coincidence is found on a ground-glass screen by moving it along a two-meter optical bench and using an auxiliary lens. The value of this method lies in the good definition of these images and the sensitivity

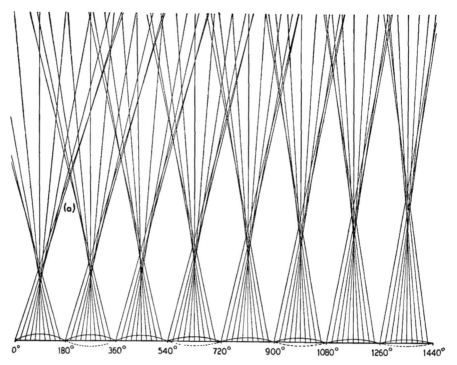

Fig. 19-36 Refraction of Light Rays by Attenuated Plane Ripples.

of this coincidence to small motions of the screen. An auxiliary lens is mounted on a rotating ring which helps map the field in degrees and increases the accuracy at low amplitudes. An amplitude scale, calculated for a single fixed frequency, is marked off on the optical bench so that the amplitude of the wave motion is read directly from the position of coincidence.

This method is accurate to 1 percent for the largest amplitudes measured, which are about 0.050 mm. The range of amplitudes usually extends down to about 0.001 mm where the accuracy has diminished to about 5 percent. The existence of waves as low as 0.0002 mm in amplitude can be detected. Their wavelength is about 11 mm.

A necessary condition for such accuracy as this is a light source strobed or chopped in exact synchronism with the waves emitted by the vibrator. This is accomplished by a master oscillator furnishing a signal to be shared by all the magnetic vibrators in the system. Two of these phonograph cutting heads vibrate the strobing flags. One flag, with a very small hole, passes twice through the light beam every cycle. The other flag is used to color images from alternate waves, which in complicated patterns is

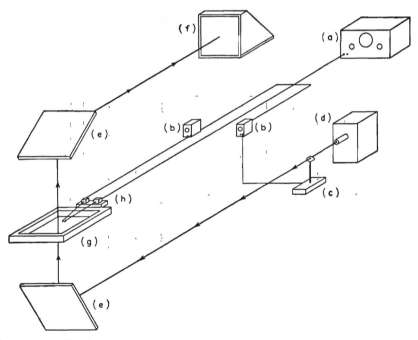

FIG. 19-37 Ripple Tank and Equipment: (a) Oscillator, set at 20 cps. (b) Phase Shifter and Amplifiers. (c) Strobing Flag. (d) Concentrated Arc 1.5 mm Source. (e) Front Surfaced Selected Glass Mirrors. (f) Ground Glass Screen. (g) Ripple Tank, 1" Water Layer. (h) Probes Mounted on Comparator.

702   SIMULATION, COMPUTATION, AND TELEMETRY

very helpful in noting phase relations. Similar cutting heads activate the supporting rods which hold the radiating points, these rods being carefully adjusted for mechanical resonance at the frequency being used. The frequency chosen was 20 cps, the resulting wavelength being approximately 11 mm, which allows the small parts within the tank to be constructed quite accurately to scale in terms of wavelength.

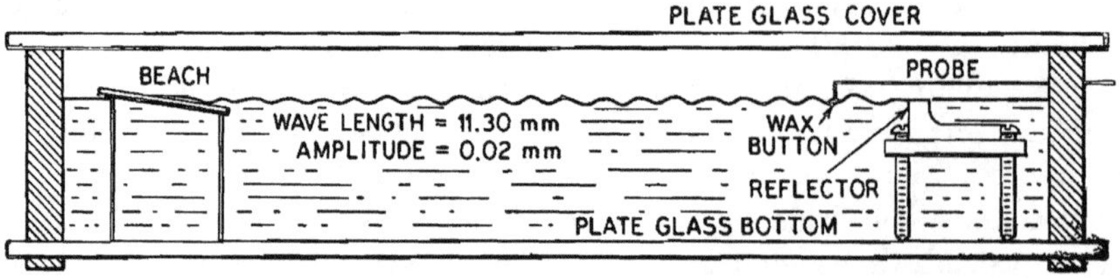

![Ripple tank diagram]

FIG. 19-38 Diagram of Ripple Tank Showing Waves Absorbed by the "Beaches."

The arrangement of the ripple tank and its equipment is shown in Fig. 19-37. The signal from the oscillator, set at a desired power level, is divided among the several vibrators, with a phase shifter in the lines to two of them. The phase of the flags is controlled so that a wave crest is always under the lens when a measurement is made; in addition, the variations in phase around a circle with the source as a center may be measured. A phase shifter is necessary for probe number 2 when particular phase relations are desired between the parts of an antenna simulator.

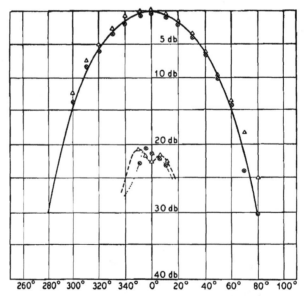

FIG. 19-39 Primary Radiation from "Double-H" Feed.

The details of the ripple tank itself are shown in the diagram of Fig. 19-38. Distilled water was found best for a medium to carry the waves after considerable investigation into the properties of various liquids. Clean ground-glass beaches were found to be the only satisfactory means of controlling reflection. These strips of ground glass about an inch wide and set at very small angles with the water surface will absorb practically all the energy of the small waves running up on them. In practice, when the beaches are not properly wet, the presence of disturbing reflections is quickly noticed; when they are correctly adjusted as to position and

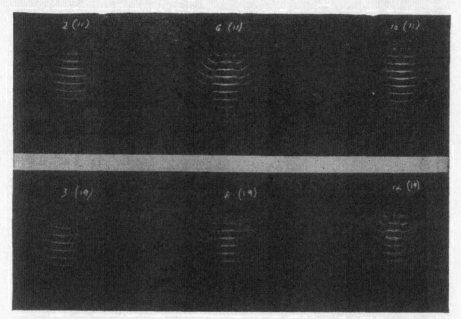

Fig. 19-40 Wave Patterns with Parabolic Reflector, $f = 11.1$ mm.

height, and with the water film upon them, no reflections can be detected.

Let us first investigate the beam from a small dish-type reflector. For this problem there is necessary a suitable source of primary radiation and a reflector of adjustable size and shape. The double-H type of radiator is chosen because of the directed beam it produces and because of the relatively small shadowing effect it has on the radiation coming back through it from the reflector. This radiator, as treated in theory, consists of one pair of points separated by one-half wavelength and vibrating in phase, and a second similar pair alongside the first at one-quater wavelength from it and vibrating 90 deg ahead of it in phase.

The theoretical curve for such a double-H antenna is shown in Fig. 19-39. Experimentally measured amplitudes are indicated by two series

704 SIMULATION, COMPUTATION, AND TELEMETRY

of points, one taken in the morning and the other at the end of the experimental work for the day. They can be seen to agree within 5 percent on the average.

For a general idea of the radiation from a given reflector, the views in Figure 19-40 have been reproduced. These are snapshots, taken with 3-sec exposure at F/4.5, of the pattern seen on the ground-glass screen.

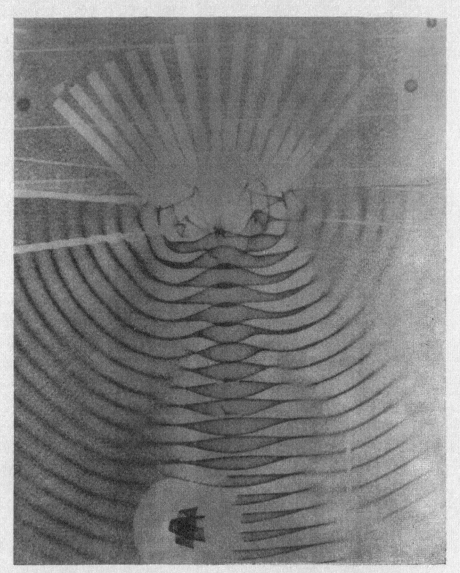

FIG. 19-41 Typical Patterns as Seen on Ground Glass Screen.

The general character of the radiation can be observed and in a qualitative way the effect of changing some parameter. In (a) the three feed points were 6, 10, and 14 mm from a parabola whose aperture-to-wavelength ratio was 2.9; (b) the same feed points were used with a parabola of same focal length but for which $a/f = 4.6$.

The value of this apparatus and the coincidence method of measurement lies, however, in accurate measurements of amplitudes and thereby of intensities. A typical pattern as seen on the screen is reproduced in Fig 19-41, the screen having been correctly adjusted for the one amplitude measurement that can be obtained at this setting. The point of coincidence can be seen in the center of the lens and over the crosshair. A reading of the angular position of the lens is made from the large ring with one-degree gradations which carries the lens and the crosshairs. Twice as many waves are shown in the pattern as are actually there, owing to the double strobing which yields greater accuracy.

The question of how closely these ripple waves do simulate electromagnetic radiation has been the subject of considerable study. The most comprehensive recent study was that of H. H. Alexander at Princeton University in 1950. In this report is shown the similarity between a set of equations applying to two-dimensional transverse waves and a set of equations for electromagnetic radiation. These equations, of course, are all derived from identical fundamental assumptions.

Another problem that suggests itself for possible simulation by a ripple tank is that of the radome, in which the refraction caused by the radiation passing through a medium of differing index can impose difficult design problems. A glass plate can be placed with its surface just under water in the described tank and the depth of the layer above may be carefully controlled. Since the speed of the water waves is dependent upon the depth and since the speed corresponds to the index of refraction, forms may be constructed and so placed that they are, to scale, models of actual radomes. It has been found that, by carefully varying the depth between 1.0 and 0.5 mm, refraction indices may be simulated from a value of 1 to over 1.5.

19-9 DISCUSSION

The major process in the design of missile guidance systems is, by broad definition, that of simulation. When, by logical analysis, based on experience and prior knowledge, we evaluate guidance methods in a specific tactical situation, we are, in essence, simulating mentally the flight of the missile. When, by use of transfer response functions we synthesize the proposed system, examine its stability, and estimate the required stabilizing networks, we are simulating the performance of the missile guidance and control loops. When we laboriously analyze by hand computation the response of the system to a transient input, simulation is again being employed. As the design of the system solidifies in concept, analog computers are used as simulators of the problem, in order that the labor of exploring the outputs of the equipment for widely varied input parameters may be used. As equipment elements become available, they are substituted for the equivalent mathematical expressions, and the process of simulation continues step-by-step through laboratory and field experimentation until the time arrives when the behavior of the missile becomes a statistic in tactical use.

This book has dealt principally with the process of manual simulation wherein the mathematical simulation is accomplished by the designer and the complexities of the problem are greatly reduced by the use of simplifying assumptions. The reasons for this are: (a) this type of simulation is the most flexible in the initial stages of design investigation and evaluation, and (b) unless this fundamental method of mathematical simulation is clearly understood by the designer, the nuances of the guidance problem will have no meaning to him. The value of the output of the simulation is dependent upon an appreciation of the meanings of the initial assumptions in the input to the simulation. The tools of simulation are relatively simple to use, but the correct adaptation of the tools to the problem is frequently found to be difficult.

This book, in emphasing the *principles* of missile guidance, has concentrated on mathematical simulation of components and systems under the conditions of steady-state frequency inputs. This is because a system must first be demonstrated to be stable under steady-state conditions before embarking on the more tedious investigation of its stability under conditions of transient inputs. It may be categorically stated that the behavior of all systems must be examined for transient inputs to which they may be subjected. It may be shown that systems which are stable under steady-state conditions may have a response to a transient input which makes the system unusable in the tactical situation in which it is designed to be employed. Furthermore, the transients introduced do not necessarily involve the missile *per se*, but may exist as a result of target behavior or other conditions not readily within the purview of the designer.

The assumptions made in the discussions in this text have been, perhaps, oversimplified. This is the result of practical necessity in the earlier stages of system evaluation and synthesis. When the selection of guidance method has been made, and the characteristics of the active system elements become firm by reason of increasing design inflexibility, the assumptions also become less generalized and more specific. When this stage of the design process is reached, the simulation changes from the hand operations of the engineer to problem mechanization on a computer-simulator.

At this stage of design a wider exploration of the effect of input parameter variations becomes possible and the stability of the system may be explored for its response in relation to nonlinear elements in the system. Thus the simulation proceeds step by step through the stages of design, with each successive step more closely approaching tactical realism.

CHAPTER 20

THE SYSTEM CONCEPT

The words "system concept" have been used many times in this text. This is the result of a continued and deliberate attempt to stress the mental image of the system to a degree above that of its component parts. The systems with which we have here concerned ourselves are called missile guidance systems and have been shown to be composed of elements concerned with sensory perception, communication, and control. These also define a general field of study called *cybernetics*. The employment of the principles discussed here is valid not only for a missile guidance system, but for any complex system, whether it be electrical, mechanical, or physiological. An automatic manufacturing process may employ all of the basic elements and generate extremely similar problems, in principle, to those delineated under the qualifying adjectives of "missile guidance."

The study of missile guidance systems embraces a wide scope of technologies and physical sciences. One of the difficulties most frequently encountered is that the fields and subfields of science are tending more and more toward obscure specialization. To quote Norbert Wiener, "A man may be a topologist or an acoustician or a coleopterist. He will be filled with the jargon of his field, and will know all its literature and all its ramifications, but, more frequently than not, he will regard the next subject as something belonging to his colleague three doors down the corridor, and will consider any interest in it on his own part as an unwarranted breach of privacy."[1]

The disposition of an individual to refuse to encroach on what he may feel to be another's field is often abetted by the language barrier which has grown up in the idioms of specialization. It is not uncommon to witness an argument between two men of differing specialties who require considerable time to recognize that they are arguing in complete agreement with each other, but are not understood because of the specialized jargon employed. Such confusion is not always lessened by the common language of mathematics because the symbols employed as standard by

[1] Norbert Wiener, *Cybernetics*, p. 8, The Technology Press, John Wiley & Sons, New York, 1948.

one specialty may have differing meanings in another and the habits formed in translating symbols are not easy to break.

This book has attempted to show that in complex systems there are common meeting grounds for discussion of components developed by different specialties, and that as an aid to the process of design it is possible to develop compatible analogs to the components that comprise the system. As a result, a missile may be guided in simulated flight and its probable accuracy and behavior under tactical conditions evaluated before it has even reached a drawing board. The specifications for the behavior of a component may be written by a mathematician who has no physical concept of the design of the component. But, in the final analysis, since compromise between component requirements is always a stark reality, the design of a working system requires that each of the specialists has some knowledge, however fundamental it may be, of the system and the problems involved in the construction of other components by other specialists.

There has been no attempt made in this book to describe the detailed processes of design for any specific component of a missile guidance system. There are many texts that cover the details of design of system elements. The function of this text has been to acquaint the reader, whether he be a worker in the field or a student of it, with general information about the many specialized areas so that the problems of each, as they pertain to the system, may be recognized. By examining the tactical requirements and their effect upon the development of the system, and observing, in turn, how the system specifications develop the characteristics for the components, it is hoped that a greater appreciation of the roles of the specialized fields may have been reached.

20-1 SCOPE OF SYSTEM STUDY

The scope of a system study for missile guidance must go beyond the study of the missile guidance system itself. For example, in the case of a surface-to-air guidance system for naval use, the missile guidance system forms a major element of the guided missile system. The guided missile system is but a part of the air defense system for a unit of the Fleet, which in turn is but a part of the air defense system of a task force, and so on. The minimum scope of a missile guidance system study is a study of the tactical employment of the guided missile system. For example, in the case of an air-to-air missile guidance system, the study must be concerned with the manner by which the aircraft is vectored to the target, the air craft performance, the sensing device in the airplane, the characteristics of the human pilot, and other armament carried by the aircraft, the performance of the target, and, lastly, the missile and its guidance system.

A study which thoroughly examines or simulates all of the portions of the overall system will frequently disclose methods of simplifying the missile guidance system. From this simplification may come a guided missile system which is cheaper, more reliable, yet capable of better tactical performance than one designed without the background of the study. Although these studies may seem to fall in the category of operational research, they differ in that operational research is dedicated to disclosing the need for or value of a weapon, whereas the system study determines the guidance needs as related to the tactical or operational problem.

20-2 THE HUMAN AS A SYSTEM ELEMENT

The human enters into the tactical employment of the guided missile system in two distinct roles. He has the function of decision in the use of the system, and he, in some instances, may be an active element of the guidance system. In the first instance his behavior will affect the effectiveness of the system; in the latter, his response characteristics must be considered.

Relation to System Effectiveness. Many so-called automatic systems employ a half dozen or more skilled human operators. The function of the human is primarily that of making the decisions necessary in the employment of the weapon systems. The human may never see the airborne target that is attacking his position, but he must decide that the sensing device has indicated a target and not some spurious signal. Having decided that the signal portrayed to him is indeed a target, he must evaluate the threat and decide what weapon system shall be used to defeat it. When the function of destroying the target is relegated to a specific weapon system, human operators are again brought into play for the purposes of detection, acquisition, evaluation, and firing. All of these operations require that a human be employed in order to make a decision.

Lack of proper training, ineptness, inability, fatigue, boredom, environmental conditions, or any reason that results in the failure of the man to perform properly his operations or decisions will affect the probability that the weapon system will succeed in destroying the target. The effectiveness of the weapon system, then, is directly affected by the human decisions.

It is entirely within the realm of feasibility, with the system techniques now available, to replace the human decision by a computed decision. A computer would be faster, and if the inputs to it were correct, it would make fewer errors of judgment than a man. Considering the momentary status of computer design, the human is still required for the following general reasons: (a) The man requires less space, at least insofar as the computational mechanism is concerned. Although the mechanized computer has the principal advantage of speed over the human, the human brain in mechanized form would be tremendous in size, using presently available techniques. (b) The human is more versatile in event of an emergency. In order to keep computers to a reasonable size, they are highly specialized in the memory elements and problem solutions. The computer is adapted or set up for the solution of a particular problem or problems and cannot be rapidly changed. (c) The man is required to maintain the computer in operation, and the training for this function is usually more specialized and time-consuming than the training required for the performance of the operational functions connected with the weapon system. The one element that will make it necessary that the man be displaced from his present role of decision making is that of time. When the time available becomes too small to permit the use of a man as part of the system (by reason of increased target speed or other), then he must be replaced by some mechanized device.

Environmental Design. The ability of a man to make a correct decision from an operational presentation of information depends upon both the proper design of the presentation and his environment. The presentation must be designed so that the pertinent information is available in the simplest and most readily understood manner. Confusion must be designed out of the equipment display. If it is necessary for the man to perform one or more operations, then the character of the operations must be simplified and the manner of the handling of the equipment be made such as to eliminate the possibility of error. Switches must be accessible to the hands which are employed to operate them; knobs or dials which are employed should be distinctively shaped and conveniently located.

Attention must be paid to the comfort of the operators. Operation of equipment tends to be a dull, routine, humdrum affair, even in wartime. An operator is on watch for a prescribed period of time. For optimum effectiveness of the system, he must be attentive over the entire period of the watch. Discomfort may keep him awake, but it will also tire him. Comfort must be maintained to the degree that the operator is relaxed and at ease, but not to the degree that sleep may readily overcome him.

The surrounding environment assists in maintaining both the operator's attention and his optimum performance. The equipment should not be designed so that the operator's eyes must be adapted to poor lighting on the display, under circumstances wherein the adaption may be easily lost. Airborne equipment is particularly susceptible to this problem; the sky may be bright and the cockpit presentation poorly lighted. An appreciable period of time may be required to adapt the pilot's eyes from a look at the sky until he can clearly see some of the instruments. The equipment must be designed to minimize this problem.

The operator's environment is frequently noisy. Reduction in the surrounding noise level assists the operator in staying more alert over the full period of his watch. Methods of optimizing the attention of the operator should be explored; it may be possible, for instance, that the operator will respond to audible signals in some instance more readily than to visible signals, or that combinations of sound and light may obtain the optimum response. This complete field of study of the optimum relationships between the operator and the equipment is called *human engineering*.

Human Response Characteristics. Man is sometimes an active element in a missile guidance system and, as such, his response to both steady-state frequency inputs and transient inputs is of interest. Man, speaking generally, is a nonlinear system. However, for low frequency inputs, and for operations within his performance ability, his output is linear. The characteristics between men also differ, but there is an area of operation wherein the human characteristics are sufficiently similar. This is the area that the designer of a system must employ.

Let us take a simple case. A man is assigned the problem of following a steady-state frequency input, such as a spot of light moving with a sinusoidal motion in a single plane. If the mechanism he is employing to track the moving spot is within his physical capabilities of handling, he will behave as a linear power amplifier to a frequency of one or more radians per second. When the frequency is increased so that he no longer can track the moving spot, his response becomes completely unpredictable. If high frequency noise is superimposed upon the fundamental signal frequency, the bandwidth of his linear operation is reduced. This would imply that noise should be removed from any presentation to the man, and that he may best be employed as an amplifier at low frequencies.

In the case where a man is tracking optically a target which is moving at constant velocity, the angular rate of the target motion, as seen by the man, is not constant, but changes gradually. If the tracking device employs a rate memory element, the input to the man becomes the difference between the angular rate of his tracking device and the observed angular rate of the target. This is called *rate aiding* or *aided tracking*. Under the condition of rate aiding, the bandwidth of the aiding device and the man combined becomes considerably greater than if the inputs to the man were the full target motion.

The bandwidth of the man may be reduced by his environment. If, in the process of his operation, he is subjected to noise, heat, shocks, or other disturbing influences, his bandwidth is reduced.

20-3 FUTURE MISSILE GUIDANCE SYSTEMS

Missile guidance systems represent one category of devices which are ushering in an age of automation. This is an era of servomechanisms, of eliminating man from operations in which he has always been a necessary part. The form of automaticity that is represented in missile guidance systems has been created by the deficiencies of man's sensor devices and the inability of man to speed up his mental processes in correspondence to the machines he has built for war. The necessity for the creation of automaticity in weapons stems from the urge of survival. When a moving weapon is built, a counter weapon must be constructed; when the range at which an enemy can destroy you is increased, your range of retaliation must increase, if you are to survive. As long as the technologies of war improve, then missile guidance systems must continue to increase in automaticity and in all of the combating parameters; of meeting new offense with new defense; of meeting new threat with promise of new retaliation.

There is a publicized school of thought which believes that the days of a human pilot in a high-speed offensive or defensive aircraft are numbered. There is no question that, with presently available techniques, it would be possible to send an aircraft to a predetermined point on the globe, have it drop its bombs, and return to the starting point without the assistance of a human pilot in the aircraft. Similarly, it seems technically feasible to intercept attacking aircraft with long-range unmanned interceptors. Indeed, these are the present-day requirements for missile guidance systems.

The practical question is: where do we start the automatic operations in the chain of offense or defense? The obvious answer is that when man becomes the weak link in the chain, for any reason, he must be replaced by a specialized automatic device. The future missile guidance systems will, therefore, be much more comprehensive in their automaticity than those of present conception.

INDEX

Absorption bands of molecules, 163
Absorption in a gaseous medium with a free charge, 121
Absorption of radio waves, 109
Aberration, 173
Accelerometers
    angular, 349ff
    linear, 339ff
Acceptance tests of missile guidance systems, 535, 538
Accuracy requirements of missile guidance systems, 302, 312, 318, 322
Acoustic guidance, tactical considerations, 603
Acoustic homing guidance, 602ff
    advantage of, 604
    German development, 605
    tactical considerations, 603
Acoustic target, signal characteristics, 602
Active homing guidance (*See* Homing guidance, active)
Adel, Arthur, 160
Aerodynamic missile, 57
Aerodynamic range, 509
Agonic lines, 593
Aided tracking, 712
Aircraft target noise (radar tracking), 439
Aircraft targets, statistical characteristics, 436
Aircraft autopilots, 52ff
Air Force, guidance systems for, 17
Airframe, angle of attack response to control surface detection, 500
    aerodynamic range, 509
    classical expressions for, 494
    coordinate nomenclature, 493
    coordinated turns, 514
    cross coupling, 514
    derivation of transfer functions in pitch, 496ff
    derivation of transfer function in roll, 511ff
    effect of variation of stability parameters, 509
    element in control loops, 492
    environment, 490, 491
    environmental parameters, effect of change of, 507
    experimental confirmation of frequency response, 512
    flight path vector angle response, 498
    forward velocity variations, 502
    performance, 305, 315
    phugoid oscillation, 502
    stability in a skewed plane, 514
    stability parameters, effect of variation of, 509
    transfer characteristics, graphic display of, 505
    transfer function in roll, derivation, 511
Alexander, H. H., 705
Altimeter, FM, 382
American Nautical Almanac, 77, 81
American Practical Navigator, 58
Amplitude modulation, carrier and two sidebands, 328
    single sideband, suppressed carrier, 359
    suppressed carrier, two sidebands, 358
Amplitude-modulated communication systems, comparison of, 360
Analog computation, basic philosophy of, 650
Analog computers, 664 (*see also* computers)
    accuracy of, 648
    division by, 655
    multiplication by, 654
    recording mediums, 656
Analog to digital converters, 668
Angle-of-attack response to control surface deflection, 500
Anomalies of the ionosphere, 93
    of terrestrial magnetism, 75

INDEX

Antennas, large compared to wave length, 386
  small compared to wave length, 387
Antiaircraft gunfire control, 23
Army, guidance systems for, 16
Astronomical latitude, 585
Asymptotic segment concept, extension of, 270
Atmosphere, 91
  attenuation, computation of, 162
  transmission, spectra of, 158ff
Atmospheric absorption bands, map of, 159
Atmospheric radiation, effect of, 168
Attenuation of radio waves by scattering, 160
Attenuation-phase diagrams for servo systems, 210
Aurora, 87
Autocorrelation function, 177, 197, 198, 424, 437
Automatic frequency control, 388
Automatic gain control, 402
Autopilot, from a transfer function viewpoint, 631
  loop, 630
    block diagram, 631
  rate gyro
    system, 354
Azimuth angle, 79, 591
Azimuthal equidistant chart, 61
Azon guided bomb, 43

B Kill, 294
Baka bomb, 3, 34
Ballistic missile, 37
Balwanz, William W., 119
Bat missile, 43
Beacons, 428ff
  antenna considerations, 433
  in missile guidance systems, 433
  modulators, 431
  omnidirectional, 51
  range, 429
  receivers, 429
  system requirements, 434
Beam rider, analysis of flight paths, 449ff
  component requirements and limitations, 575
  control block diagram, 672
  coordinate detector, 582
  design of hypothetical simulant, 676
  frequency spectrum of turning rate, 455ff
  geometry, 446, 673
  guidance intelligence, 580ff
  guidance systems, 312, 574ff
  launching, 577
  missiles, 578
    acceleration of, 454
    roll stabilization of, 579
    tactical considerations, 583
  optical, 317
  reference modulations, 581
  simulant transfer function, 675
  simulation by conventional aircraft, 672ff
  system simulation on an electronic analog computer, 679ff
  system transient response, 683
  trajectory, differential equation for, 446
    solution of differential equation, 448
    time of flight, 449
  trajectories, 449ff
  transfer function, 673
  turning rate, 451
  turning rate geometry, 451
Beam riding, 312, 313, 322
Beer's exponential law, 162
Binary number system, development of, 668
Black body, 128, 131, 138
Blout, E. R., 175
Blue stars, 77
Bolometers, 147 (*see also* Thermistor bolometers)
  sensitivity of, 148
Boltzmann's constant, 395
Boltzmann gas constant, 140
Boresight slope of radomes, 545
Booster, 483
Bouwers, A., 169
Burgund guidance system, 38
Buzz bomb (*see* V-1)

Carrier, spectrums of, 364
Cauchy-Riemann equations, 199
Celestial body, altitude of, 80, 84
  co-altitude of, 590
Celestial navigation, 87
  air, 82

automatic, 85, 307
  marine, 82
Celestial references for navigation, 76ff
Celestial sphere, 78
Charts, for navigational use, 68
Chemosphere, 91
Circles of equal altitudes, 82
Circular distribution of errors, 299
Circular navigation, application to missile guidance, 600
Circular probable error, 296, 299
Closed loop characteristics, 286ff
Closed loop relationship, 234ff
Coast time in radar range tracking, 619, 622
Compass, gyromagnetic, 336
  gyroscopic, 87
  gyrostabilized, 336ff
  magnetic, 335
Co-latitude in the navigational triangle, 78, 79
Collision course (*see* Constant-bearing course)
Combined guidance systems, air-to-air missile application, 605
  air-to-surface missile application, 606
  surface-to-air missile application, 606
  surface-to-surface missile application, 606
Command guidance, 311, 562ff
  command links, 567
  definition of, 562
  German World War II, 38ff
  information transfer in, 567
  in guided bombs, 43
  optical track, 563, 572ff
  radar track, 563
  range, carrier frequency and power, 568
  receiver, physical size, 570
  reliability of, 569
  security, 569
  single-beam, radar track, 570
  system, generalized, 564
  two-beam, radar track, 572
Communications systems, 357
Computers, analog and digital, 648, 664ff
  coding of a function, 671
  data transducers, 667
  input-output devices, 666
  operating instructions, 669

real time, 667
  storage devices, 666
Conductivity of a gaseous medium with a free charge, 120
Constant-bearing course, 473ff
  geometry of, 473
  time of flight, 474
Constant navigation course, 468
Control surface flap servomechanisms, 635
Converters, analog to digital, 668
Coordinate frames on earth, 69
Coordinated turns of airframe, 54
Coriolis, 84
  acceleration, 69, 87, 335
  deflection, 46
  effect, 69
Corner frequency in servo systems, 237
Correlation coefficient, 228
Correlation functions, 197
Correlation techniques, 424
Cross correlation, 424
  functions, 177, 197
Crystalline materials, transmission of, 174
Curve fitting, 211ff
  by finite differences, 217
  by least squares method, 212
Cybernetics, 708
Cyclone project, 663

D-layer, 91, 92, 370
Damped natural frequency, 287
Damping constant, 337, 341, 351
  critical, 192, 339
Damping, over, 192
  ratio, 253, 351
  under-, 192
Data transducer, 667
Dead reckoning, 83, 306, 308
Decade, use in transfer-function design technique, 267
Decca, navigation system, 51, 596
Declination, magnetic, 74, 590, 593
Design of missile guidance components, new techniques, 537
Design, system considerations in, 540
Detector, integrated response of, 166
Deviated pursuit course (*see* Pursuit course, deviated)
Differential equation of motion, 242
Digital computers, 648, 664, 665

Digital computers (*Cont.*)
  arithmetic and control elements, 666
  coding of a simple function, 671
  number representation, 668
  orders, 670
  sample operational instructions, 669
Dip angle, magnetic, 74, 593
Dip of the horizon, 84
Direction of a trajectory, 56
Dispersion of missiles, 222
Distance between points on earth's surface, 56
Distribution function, 226
Divergence factor, 99
Division circuit in computers, 655
Doppler effect, use of in missile velocity measurement, 38
Doppler principle, 362
Doppler radar, c-w, 377, 436
  pulsed, 380
  range-measuring, 379
Draper, J.W., 156
Driving function, unit ramp, 190
  unit step, 189
Driving transform, 189
Dortmund-Duisburg wire link guidance system, 41ff
Dual path transmission of r. f., 104
Duren-Detmold wire command link guidance system, 42
Duty cycle, 390

E layer, 91, 92, 370
  reflection, sporadic, 93
Early warning, 320
4/3 earth radius diagrams, 96
Earth, centrifugal force of rotation, 66
  errors resulting from assumption of a spherical shape, 586
  magnetic field of, 326, 357
  magnetic poles of, 594
  magnetism of, 74
  mass of, 65
  motions of, 64
  precession of, 73
  rotation of, 64
  revolution of, 73
  shape of, 64
  space motion of, 73
Ecliptic, plane of, 73
Effectiveness of missile, 610

Electromagnetic frequency, choice of for homing guidance systems, 545
Electron concentration in high temperature gases, 123
Elsass command guidance system, 41
Emissivity (*see* Thermal emissivity)
Environmental acceptance tests, 534
Environmental conditions, 305, 315, 490
Environmental research, 533, 534
Environmental specifications, 305, 315, 492, 532, 537
Equations, mechanization of, 648ff
Error characteristics, 254
Error expression, steady-state, 244
Error function, 227
Error, train tracking, 250, 255
Excitation function, 189
Exponential, damped, 180
External missile equipment, production and distribution of, 523

F layer, 370
F 1 layer, 91, 92
F 2 layer, 91, 92, 370
FX-1400 guided bomb, 43
Federal Communications Commission, 89
Feedback systems, negative, 252
  attenuation-phase diagrams, 210
  degree of stability, 209
  gain crossover, 211
  gain margin, 211
  phase angle, 209
  phase margin, 209
  relative stability, 209
  stability in, 200ff
Felix, 44
Filters, active, 286, 287
  infrared (*see* Infrared filters)
  low-pass, 272
  multisection low-pass, 410
  optical, 173
  single-section, high pass, 268
  single-section, low-pass, 265
Finite differences, method of curve fitting, 212
Fixed lead navigation course, 468
Fleming, J. J., 296
Flight path vector angle, response, 498, 626
  transfer function of, 632
Flux density, 129

Flux gate compass, 337
Forward velocity variations, 502
Four-thirds (4/3) earth radius diagrams, 96
Fourier transform, 193ff
   direct, 193
   inverse, 193
   operational form, 195
Frequency function, 226
   normal, 226, 227
Frequency modulation, 360, 688, 690, 693, 695
Frequency response of an airframe, experimental confirmation of the, 512
Frequency-response function, 179, 193, 194
Function-transform pairs, 180, 181
Fusing, 607

GB-1, guided bomb, 43
GB-4, guided bomb, 43
Gain crossover in servo systems, 211
Gain margin in servo systems, 211, 241
Gating in range, 548
Gauss error curve, 227
Gaussian distribution, 227, 295
Gee navigation system, 51, 596
Geographical position, 78, 80, 81
Geometric mean frequency, 237
German missiles, 34
Glasses, heat transmitting, 174
Gnomonic chart, polar, 61
Gnomonic projection, 61
Goddard, Robert H., 46
Golay cell, 149, 151
Gold, reflectivity of, 170
Gravitational flattening, 67
Gravitational force, 65ff
Gray body, 132
Grazing angle of radio waves, 98ff
Great circle, 55, 61
Greenwich Civil time, 72, 81
Greenwich hour angle, 81, 590
Gregory-Newton interpolation formula, 219
Ground direction finding, 49
Guidance initiation, 483
Guidance intelligence, nature of, 364
Guidance equipment, distribution of
   ship-borne, 524
   missile-borne, 520

   ship-borne, 520
Guidance method, choice of, 537
Guidance system combinations, 605ff
   in air-to-air missiles, 605
   in air-to-surface missiles, 606
   in surface-to-air missiles, 606
   in surface-to-surface missiles, 606
Guidance system study and synthesis, 519
Guided bombs, 42
Guided missiles, categories of, 4
   costs, 516ff
   definition of, 3
   distribution, 528
   firing, 482
   handling and loading, 480
   launcher, 480
   launching, 479ff
   launching trajectories, 484
   launching transients, 484
   power supplies, 483
   prelaunching checks, 480, 482
   production costs, 517
   ready storage, 480
   research and development, 516, 518
   separation from booster, 483
   simulator, 645
   simulator studies, 520
   system costs, 530
   system study, 519
   tactical unit storage, 479
   testing, 479, 481
   World War II types, 34
Guided missile system, definition of, 4
   yearly cost of supporting, 531
Gunfire control systems, airborne, 30
   antiaircraft, 23ff
   parallax computation for, 29, 39
   stabilization on shipboard, 28
   surface, 27
Gyro compass, 87
Gyromagnetic compass, 336
Gyroscope, 52, 327ff
   effect of Coriolis acceleration on, 335
   effect of earth's rotation on, 332
   effect of missile motions on, 333
   free, 327ff
   precession, 329
   rate, 350ff
   rate, for lead computing gun sights and fire control systems, 26, 328
   rate, transfer characteristic of, 352

Gyroscope (*Cont.*)
  rate, use in feedback path, 635
  response characteristics of, 335
  vertical, 330, 331
Gyrostabilized compass, 336, 337

Handling and loading, 480
Havens limit, 151, 152
Haze, 161, 162, 165
  spectral attenuation curve of, 163
Heading of moving vehicle, 56
Helicopter, 15
Homing guidance, 312, 317
  acoustic (*see* Acoustic homing guidance)
  air-to-air missile utilizing semi-active, 557
  choice of r-f for, 545
  comparison of range of active and semi-active, 555
  geometry of semi-active, 556
  kinematic terms, 627ff
  passive, 543, 560ff
    definition of, 543
    infrared, 560
    r-f, 561
    tactical application of, 561
  radar types, 546
  radio frequency passive, 561
  semi-active, 322, 554ff, 613
    definition of, 542
    example of use, 613
  space geometry, 627ff
  surface-to-air missile system utilizing semi-active, 559
  system, active, 322, 547ff
    definition of, 541
    quasi-active, definition of, 543
    tactical application of air-to-air active, 549
    tactical application of air-to-air semi-active, 557
    tactical application of air-to-surface active, 317, 551
    tactical application of air-to-surface semi-active, 558
    tactical application of surface-to-air active, 553
    tactical application of surface-to-air semi-active, 559
    tactical application of surface-to-surface active, 553
    tactical application of surface-to-surface semi-active, 559
  systems, 541ff
    definition of, 541
    general, 543ff
Howard, J. N., 165
Human, as a system element, 710
  environmental design, 711
  relation to system effectiveness, 710
  response characteristics, 712
Hutchins alloys, 145
Hyperbolic guidance system, advantages of, 599
Hyperbolic navigation, as applied to missile guidance, 598
Hyperbolic navigation, the geometry of, 597
Hyperbolical navigation, tactical consideration, 600
Hyperbolic navigation systems, 51, 596
Hyperbolic nets, 51

I-D equations, the solution of, 184, 185, 188
I-f systems, 398
Identification of aircraft targets, 308, 320
Inclination, 593
  magnetic, 74
Index of refraction, effect of, on radio wave transmission, 95
Inertial-celestial guidance, geometry of, 589
Inertial-celestial guidance systems, 589ff
  general, 591
  tactical application of, 592
Inertial-gravitational guidance, geometry of, 584
Inertial-gravitational guidance system, 583ff, 587
  definition of, 583
  tactical application of, 588
Infrared, 127ff
  absorption by the atmosphere, 156
  absorption bands, 157
  absorption by liquids, 157
  filters, dyed plastic, 175
    glass, 175
    powder, 173
  window regions in the, 164
Instrument landing systems, 54

Integrating amplifier, circuit and symbol, 652
Integro-differential equation, solution of, 184, 188ff
Intelligence transmission, modes, 357
  use of r-f carriers, 357
Interceptor radar, 323
Interceptor search, 321
Interference patterns, r-f transmission, 105
Interference phenomena, 99
Interferometer effects, 387
Interrogator, 428
Inverting amplifiers, 652
Ionosphere, 91ff
  anomalies of, 93
  critical frequencies of, 93
  effect of, on radio wave transmission, 93
  storms, 93
Ionization, regions of, 91
Ionized layers of the atmosphere, 90
Irdome, 545
Isoclinic lines, 593
Isodynamic lines, 593
Isogonic lines, 593
Isotropic radiator, 100

Johnson noise, 395
Jump, rocket fire control, 33
Jupiter, 76

K kill, 294
KRS 5 filter material, 171
Kehl radio transmitter, 39, 40
Kill probability, 293
  single shot, 313
Kinematic feedback, 545
Kirchhoff's Law, 169, 185
Klystron, 394
Knuppel joystick control, 38
Kran-Brigg radio command link, 41
Kroll, Wilhelmina D., 348

Lambert conformal projection, 61
Lambert cosine law, 129
Laplace transform, 179ff, 197, 241, 242, 253, 263
  basic theorems of, 182ff
  function-transform pairs, 180, 181
  inverse, 180, 241, 258
  inverse, of rational fractions, 186
  method, 179
  of rational fractions, 186
  operation-transform pairs, 184
Latitude, 56, 59
  magnetic, 75
Launcher, 480
  computer, 618
Launching, 304, 315, 324, 482
  air-to-air, missile guidance, 489
  air-to-surface, missile guidance, 488
  surface-to-air, missile guidance, 486
  surface-to-surface, missile guidance, 485
Launching dispersions, 484
Launching guidance, 18, 307, 315, 319
Launching phase of flight, change in location of the center of gravity during, 488
Launching transients, 484, 638
Launching trajectory, 484
Lead angle, computation of, 26, 31
Least squares, method of curve fitting, 212
Levy, Samuel, 348
Libration, 76
Limiters, employment in analog computers, 653
Linear network, 178
Linear systems, 177
Line-of-sight trajectory, 446 (*see also* Beam-rider trajectory)
  differential equation for, 446
  solution of, 448
Longitude, 56
Long wave lengths, materials transparent to, 170
Loop gain, 404
Loran, 51, 56, 365ff, 596
  computed time differences, 371
  effect of crossing angle, 372
  measured time differences, 371
  pairs, identification of, 367
  plane hyperbola generation, 366
  possible missile application, 373
  propagation effects on, 369
  service areas for, 365
  system accuracy, 371ff
Lossless material, in radomes, 115
Lossy material, in radomes, 115
Loxodromic curve, 59

Magic T balanced mixer, 397
Magnetic charts, 75
Magnetic compasses, airborne, 335
Magnetic declination of earth, 74
Magnetic equator, 593
Magnetic field of earth, effect on ionosphere, 93
Magnetic inclination of earth, 74
Magnetic latitude, 75
Magnetic missile guidance mechanisms, 594
Magnetic storms, 75, 87, 93, 594
Maintenance costs of guided missiles, 517
Maksutov, D.D., 169
Map, definition of, 64
Margin of stability in servo systems, 200
Mars, 76
Mathematical simulation, 645ff
Mean absolute error, 296, 297
Mean error, 296
Mean radial error, 299
Mean spherical radial error, 301
Mean sun, 72
Mechanization of equations, 648ff
Median error, 296
Mendenhall wedge, 128
Mercator chart, 58, 81
Mercator projection, 57
   inverse, 61
   transverse, 59
Meridian angle, 79
Meridian, prime, 56
Meridianal parts, 59
Meridians, 56
Mesosphere, 91
Metallic powder film transmission of infrared, 153
Micro-H, 596
Microwave radiometry, 144
Midcourse guidance, 18, 306
Minute of arc, length of, 56
Mirick, C.B., 52
Miss due to system limitations, 642
Missile (see Airframe)
Missile-borne guidance equipment, maintenance of, 530
   production and distribution, 525
Missile control flap servomechanisms, 635
Missile cost relative to production rate, 528

Missile firing, 482
Missile intercept problem, airframe geometry, 626
Missile guidance, air-to-air, 12ff, 320ff, 489
   air-to-air, choice of, 321
   air-to-surface, 10ff, 316ff, 488
   air-to-surface, choice of, 317
   application of circular navigation technique, 600
   application of hyperbolic navigation, 597
   Air Force requirements for, 17
   Army requirements for, 16
   autopilot loop, 630ff
   costs of equipment, 530ff
   distribution of equipment, 528
   Navy requirements for, 16
   system design considerations, 540
   surface-to-air, 8ff, 308ff, 486ff
   surface-to-air, choice of, 311
   surface-to-surface, 5ff, 301ff, 485
   test equipment, 522
   for underwater targets, 14ff
Missile guidance system, definition of, 4
Missile guidance systems, 539ff
   evaluation of for production, 522
Missile launchers, 577
Missile launching transient error, 638
Missile motion kinematics, 627
Missile pitch guidance loop, 637
Missile production rate, general relationship to material cost per missile, 527
   general relationship to man hours per missile, 526
Missile roll control, 639ff
   compensation of, 640
Missiles, piloted aircraft simulation of, 520
Mixers and local oscillators, 394
Modulation index, 361
Modulated r-f carrier, amplitude modulation, 358ff
   frequency modulation, 360ff
   spectrum of, 359
Modulator, hard tube, 432
Modulators, live type, 432
Moon, 73, 76
   axis of rotation, 76
Multipath transmission, 94
Multiplying potentiometer, 654

NRL electronic digital computer (NAR-EC), 669
Natural frequency, damped, 287
  undamped, 287
Natural rotational frequency, 338
  undamped, 341
Naval Observatory, Washington, D.C., 73
Navigation, airborne, 47
Navigation by recognition, 47
Navigation by triangulation, 48ff
Navigation constant, 476
Navigation by earth or space references, 51
Navigation in polar areas, 86ff
Navigational correction, 476
Navigational triangle, 78ff
Navy, guidance systems for, 16
Near infrared, materials useful in the, 173
Networks, application of transfer-function procedure to, 271
  assymptotic segment concept, 270
  feedback path, 284
  general two terminal-pair, 178
  impulse response of, 178
  L section, 264
  linear, electrical and mechanical analogies, 177
  RC, high-pass, 268ff, 276
  RC, low-pass, 265ff, 274
  RC, phase-lag, 275
  RC, phase-lead, 277
  RC, two-section shunted, high pass, 278
  series, 283
Newton's divided difference formula, 221
Noise figure considerations, 395ff
Noise bandwidth, 287
Normal distribution, single variable, 297
  three variables, 300
  two variables, 298
Normal distribution function, 227
Normal frequency function, 227, 228
Novae, 77
Number representation in computers, 668
Nutation angle in radars, 615
Nyquist's criterion, 200, 204, 205
Nyquist diagram, 203
Nyquist stability criterion, 203, 207

Oboe navigation system, 596
Omnidirectional beacon, 51
Open loop characteristic, 237
Operations research, 292
Operations-transform pairs, 184
Optical beam riding, 317 (*see also* Beam rider)
Optical materials, 169

Parallax in celestial navigation, 84
Parallax computation, 29, 39
Partial navigation course, 475
Partial simulation, 645
Pass-course, 248
  as range servo problem, 259
Passive homing guidance, 543
Peak power of radar transmitter, 390
Pelican missile, 44
Pfund, A. H., 153
Phase margin, 209, 241
Phase modulation, 362
Phase shift, 265
Photoconductive cells, 154
  choice of, 155
  relative spectral response curves of phs and phte cells, 156
  response of, 166
Photoconductive detectors, 168
Phugoid oscillation, 502
Physical simulation, 645
Pick-up devices, 687
Pitch, derivation of transfer functions in, 496
Pitch angle relationships, 493
Pitch attitude angle response, 497
Pitch control channel, autopilot, general, 53
Pitch control loop in Viking, 46
Pitch guidance loop, 637
Planetary motions, 76
Planck Distribution Law, 138, 143
Planck function, 169
Planck's constant, 140
Pneumatic cells, 152
Pneumatic, or Golay, detector, 149, 151
Polaris, 86
Polarization of radio waves, factors affecting choice of, 104, 105
Polar navigation, 86ff
Polar regions, 86

Polyconic projection, 63
Polyethylene, transmission spectra of, 172
Position angle, 79
Position memory, 622
Power source, series regulation, 421
Power supply electrical, 483
  hydraulic or pneumatic, 483
Power system, regulated, 420
Prelaunch testing, 479, 481
Prelaunching checks, 480, 482, 538
Probable effectiveness of a single missile, 294
Probable error, 297
Probable reliability, 295
Probability, basic concepts of, 222
  density, 226
  distribution, 225
  empirical, 225
  function, 225
  integral, 227
  relationships in missile system, 295
  theory, 222ff
Probability of acquisition, 310
Probability of kill, 293
Probability of missile survival, 295
Probability of successful operation, 295, 535
Probability of target damage, 295
Production costs, 517
Project Cyclone, 663
Proportional navigation course, 475ff
  acceleration for, 478
  equations of motion for, 475
  turning rate for, 477
Ptolemy, 77
Pulse modulators, 390
Pulse stretcher, 393
Pure pursuit course (*see* Pursuit course, pure)
Pursuit course, deviated, 468ff
  definition of, 468
  equations of motion for, 468
  missile acceleration, 467
  time of flight, 471
  trajectory, 471
    turning rate, 471
    turning rate criterion for, 472
Pursuit course, pure, 459
  acceleration in, 466
  definition of, 460
  equations of motion for, 460, 468
  maximum absolute value of the turning rate, 466
  time of flight, 463
  turning rate, 463
  turning rate spectrums, 467
Pursuit navigation loop, 626

Quartz, absorption of, 174

REAC computer, 684
Radar, analysis of a two-element target, 440ff
  angle error detectors, 415ff
  angle noise, 441
  antennas, 383ff
    diameter of reflector small compared to wave length, 387
    gain and beamwidth relationship, 384
    secondary pattern, 385
    tapered illumination, 385
  automatic frequency control, a.f.c., 388
  automatic gain control, a.g.c., 402ff
  automatic range tracking, 408ff
  beacon, 49, 428
  beam shaping, 387
  beamwidth, relation to reflector diameter, (see footnote) 614
  c-w Doppler, 377
  clutter, 378
  correlation techniques, 424
  determination of angular coordinates, 438
  determination of the range coordinate, 438
  determination of tracking noise, 439
  effects of amplitude fluctuation, 442
  i-f systems, 398
  illuminating, for semi-active homing guidance, 613ff
  gapless coverage, 106
  guidance, 375, 388
  homing guidance, first introduced, 43
  large target tracking, 443
  lobe patterns, 440
  lobe switching, 438
  look angle, 558

INDEX   725

low-angle tracking, 422ff, 444
Mark 4, U.S. Navy, 423
maximum range, 106
missile borne, 618ff, 624ff
in a missile guidance system, 388
power sources, 419ff
pulse modulators, 390ff
pulsed Doppler, 380
r-f components, 387
range calculations, 611
range measuring Doppler, 379
range units, 413ff
receiver, 393
regulated power supply, 421
resolution of, 436
search type, 437
scanning type, 363, 438
spectrum, conical scanning, 363
system parameters, pulsed, 382
systems, FM, 377
target noise, 439
target noise as a function of range, 443
tracking, 314, 321, 392
tracking antenna patterns, 616
tracking at low elevation angles, 422ff
tracking noise, 439
tracking response of a system, 440ff
transmitters, 389
types used in homing guidance systems, 546
video amplifiers and detectors, 399ff
video gating, 400
Radiation (*see* Thermal radiation)
Radio frequency, factors affecting choice of, 113
Radio frequency bands, allocation of, 89
Radio frequencies, classification of, 89
Radio horizon, approximate distance to, 96
Radiometer, 132
  calibration of, 135
Radiometry, 132ff
Radio navigation techniques, application of, to missile guidance, 595
Radio telemetry as an aid to missile guidance system design, 684
Radio waves, absorption of, 109
  absorption of in gaseous medium with free charge, 121
  attenuation by condensed water and other forms of precipitation, 111
  classification by frequencies and wave lengths, 90
  conductivity of gaseous medium with free charge, 120
  diffraction of, 106
  divergence factor, 99
  dual path transmission, 99
  ducting of, 97
  effect of flames on transmission of, 119
  effect of ionosphere on transmission of, 92ff
  electric field of, 97
  factors affecting choice of frequency, 113
  field strength curves, 107
  grazing angle, 98
  index of refraction of, 93, 106
  ionospheric refraction, 92
  magnetic field of, 97
  oxygen absorption of, 109
  plane of polarization of, 97
  propagation of, 89
  reflection of, 98, 122, 435
  reflection coefficient of, 98, 103
  refraction of, 95
  scattering of, 111
  transmission of, 89ff
  transmission through dielectric material, 115
  transmission through ionized gases, 119ff
  water vapor absorption of, 110
Radomes, 113ff, 545
  normal incidence, 113, 115
  other than normal incidence, 113, 117
Random variables, 225
Range angle reference, 587
Range discrimination, 618
Range product, 555
Range tracking, automatic, 408
Range unit, exponentials in transient analysis, 621
Range vertical, 587
Rate aiding, 712
Rate gyroscopes (*see* Gyroscope, rate)
Rayleigh distribution, 229
Rayleigh frequency function, 229
Rayleigh-Jeans equation, 143
Ready storage, 480
Real-time computation, 667
Recovery of instrumentation, Viking, 45
Red stars, 77

Refraction, for air, index of, 92
  in the ionosphere, 93
  of light, 84, 88
  layers of constant index of, 95
Reliability, 303, 314, 535ff, 569, 610
  relationship between the reliability of a missile guidance system and the average reliability of its components, 536
Research and development, "shotgun" approach, 516
Research and development program, missile guidance equipment, 518
Resonant frequency, 288
  natural undamped, 259
Responder, 428
Response transform, 189
Rheintocher missile, 41
Rhodium, reflectivity, 170
Rhumb line, 59
Ring demodulator, 417
  characteristics of, 417
  switching analysis of, 418
Ripple tank, 698ff
Robin, 44
Rocket impact point predictor, 46
Roll control, 53, 639
  block diagram, 639
Rosen, Milton W., 44ff
Rotating frame of reference, 69
Routh's array, 203
Routh's criterion, 201, 288
Royal Observatory, Greenwich, England, 56

Sapphire, window of, 155
Saturn, 76
Scale factor potentiometers, 653
Scattering, infrared frequencies, 160
  r-f, 111
Schmetterling guided missile, 38
Schmidt, B., 169
Schooley, A. H., 699
Search radar, 610
Semi-active homing guidance (*see* Homing, semi-active)
Semi-diameter of the sun or moon, 84
Separation of missile and booster, 483
Servomechanism, in analog computer, 654
  multiplying, 654
Servo motor, transfer function of, 279ff
  sample calculations of corner frequency, 281
  torque-speed characteristics, 281
Servo system, amplitude and phase relationships, 239ff
  application of stability criterion, 288
  bandwidth, 288
  basic type I, closed loop response of, 243
  basic type I (position control), 207ff, 236ff
  basic type I, steady-state error expression, 244ff
  basic type II, amplitude and phase characteristics, 256ff
  basic type II, error expression, 259
  basic type II, open loop characteristics, 256
  basic type II, steady-state sinusoidal performance, 257
  basic type II (velocity control), 208ff, 255ff
  closed loop relationships, 234ff
  closed loop response, 240
  corner frequencies, 237
  damped natural frequencies, 287
  definition of, 232
  design, RC networks in, 274
  error, 245
  error expression, 259
  frequency response in design of, 289
  fundamental design concepts, 233
  gain margin, 241
  geometric mean frequency, 237
  improved type I, 250ff
  improved type I, open loop asymptotic characteristics, 251, 256
  improved type I, steady-state response, 252
  improved type I, response to transient input, 254
  incorporation of elements in feedback path, 284
  linear, 231
  noise bandwidth, 287
  open loop characteristics, 237
  performance, improvement of, 282
  phase margin, 241
  response to transient input, 241, 289
  resonant frequency, 288
  steady-state error expressions, 235
  tactical problem, 246ff, 259ff

theory, 231ff
transfer-function design technique, 263
transient response of improved type I for position step input, 254
transient response of type II for position step input, 258
type II, sinusoidal steady-state performance, 257
undamped natural frequency, 287
use of active filters in, 286
Sextant, 82, 83, 86
 index correction, 84
Ship-borne guidance equipment, maintenance of, 530
Shoran navigation system, 51, 596
Shot effect, 397
Silver chloride, photosensitivity to blue light and the ultra violet, 171
Simulation, achievement of accuracy, 663
 analytic methods, 647
 automatic, 647
 by analog computer, 645, 647
 by digital computer, 665
 definition of, 644
 mathematical, 645
 methods of, 647
 numerical, 647
 of missile by conventional aircraft, 672
 of a missile guidance system, block diagram depicting, 646
 of radio wave propagation, 698
 partial, 645
 philosophy of, 705
 physical, 645
 stages of, 645
 test, 645
 three-dimensional guided missile problem, 660
Simulator studies, 520
Single-shot kill probability, 313
Sonne navigation system, 51, 595
Specific force of gravity, 587, 592
Spectral emissivity, 143
Spectral intensity, 139
Spherical probable error, 301
Squint angle, 615
Stability, absolute, 209, 236
 criterion, application of, 288
 degree of, 209

margin, 209
relative, 209, 236
of a system, degree of, 210
Stabilization, 544
 against ship motion, 618
Standard deviation, 222
Standard error, 296, 301
Stars, color of, 77
 magnitude of, 77
 number of, 78
 temperature of, 77
 visible, 77
Stefan-Boltzmann constant, 140
Stefan-Boltzmann Law, 129
Stellar lines, 590
Step-input, response, 253, 257
Steradiancy, 129
Stine, P. T., 684
Stratosphere, 91
Stellar lines, 590
Sterographic chart, 61
Strassburg radio receiver, 39
Subcarriers, r-f, 362
Submarine, detection of, 14
Substellar points, 590
Summing amplifier, 649
Summing amplifier circuit, 651
Sun, 73, 76
 rotation of, 77
Superheterodyne and crystal video receivers, comparison of, 430
Superposition, principle of, 178
Surface gunfire control, 27
System concept, 708

Tactical considerations, 292ff
Tactical problem, dynamics, 233
 specification of, 609
Tactical storage, 479
Tactical test equipment, 522
Target, aircraft as, 435
 assignment of, 309
 basic categories of, 1
 surface, 304
Target damage definitions, 293
Target fade, 545
Target lock-on, 548
Target motion kinematics, 628
Target noise, origin of, 439
Teflon, transmission spectra of, 173
Telemetry, radio, 684, 685, 698

Telemetry, radio (*Cont.*)
  accuracy of, 686, 687, 691, 694, 695, 697, 698
  band width, 688, 693
  carrier shift, 690
  channels, 686, 690, 693, 694, 696, 698
  channel separation, 687, 694
  commutation, 692, 693
  "dash" presentation, 697, 698
  demodulation, 687, 692, 698
  display devices, 687
  "dot" presentation, 696, 698
  end instruments, 687, 695
  frequency deviation, 690, 693
  frequency division, 688, 690, 697
  frequency response, 686, 696, 698
  FM-FM, 688, 690, 693, 695
  gated "dot" presentation, 697
  high capacity systems, 688, 693
  information capacity, 686, 688, 690, 692, 693, 698
  "line" presentation, 696, 698
  low capacity systems, 687, 688
  medium capacity systems, 687, 688, 692
  modulation, 687, 695
  modulation index, 691, 692
  multiplexing, 687, 693
  pick-up devices, 687, 690, 695
  PAM-FM-FM, 692, 693
  PPM-AM, 688, 693, 694, 698
  PWM-FM, 688, 690, 692
  radio frequency, 690, 692, 693
  recording, 685, 687, 692, 694, 698
  requirements for, 686, 687
  sampling rate, 689, 693
  standardization, 687, 688, 690, 693
  sub-carrier bands, 688, 690, 691, 692
  synchronization, 688, 692, 693
  time division, 688, 693, 697
  transducers, 687, 695
Temperature inversion, 97
Terminal guidance, 19, 307, 315, 319
Terrestrial-magnetic guidance system, 593ff
Terrestrial reference guidance, 584
Test simulation, 645
Thermal detectors, 130, 168
  blackening of, 152
  response of, 166ff
Thermal emissive power, 139, 141
Thermal emissivity, 128ff
  measurement of, 135
  of selected materials, 136
Thermal radiation, 127ff
  detectors of, 144
  exchange of, 131
  flux density of, 129
  intensity of, 129
  power exchange, 131ff
  pyrometry, 134
  response of a selective receiver to, 166
  spectral distribution of, 138
  total, 127ff
Thermistor bolometers, 148, 152
  characteristics of, 148
Thermistor materials, 154
Thermocouples, 133, 134, 135, 144, 145, 152
  for infrared spectrometers, 170
  resistance, 145
  characteristics of, 146
  loss of heat from, 146
Thermo electric voltage, 145
Thermopile, 145, 147
Thyratron modulators, 392
Time, 72
  sidereal, 72
Time of flight, 22, 449
Total emissive power, 128
Tracking radar, 314, 610
Traffic handling capacity, 550
Trajectory, air-to-air missiles, 314
  air-to-surface missiles, 319
  surface-to-air missiles, 314
  surface-to-surface missiles, 303
Transducers, 687
Transfer characteristic, 179, 196, 235, 266
  for wing flap servomechanisms, 636
Transfer function forms, 269ff
  differentiator function, 269
  integrator function, 269
  low-pass function, 269
  reciprocal low-pass function, 269
Transfer functions, 178, 189, 266, 268, 269, 288
  of airframe in roll, 511
  of airframe for the angle of attack, 501
  of airframe for the output of the angle of attack, 500
  closed loop, 238
  design technique, 263ff
  in pitch, 496

of servo motor, 279ff
  procedure applied to a network, 270
Transformation calculus, 179ff
Transient response, for position step input, 241
  system design based upon, 290
Transmission, computation of water vapor, 163
Transmission spectra of the atmosphere, 158
Transponder, 428
Traveling wave tubes, 426
Troposphere, 91

UHF radio range, 51
Ultraviolet, 160
Undamped natural frequency, 287
United States Marine Corp, guidance systems for, 17
Unit ramp function, 180
Unit step function, 180

V-1, 34, 35, 56, 57, 71, 76
V-2, 34, 36, 44, 45, 56
Van der Pol differential equation, 658
Van der Pol equation, computer schematic diagram for solution of, 658
Variance, 222, 296
Variations, 74
  annual, 75
  diurnal, 75
  magnetic, 74, 75
  secular, 75
Vectoring, 321
Velocity memory in radar range unit, 622
Velocity memory time, 619
Venus, 76
Video amplifiers and detectors, 399
Viking missile, 44ff, 56
Visual two-course range navigation system, 51

Wac Corporal missile, 44
Wasserfall missile, 41
Weary Willies, 52
Weems star altitude curves, 83
Weighting function, 178, 194
Wien distribution equation, 143
Wiener, Norbert, 708
Wien law, 143
Wind, use of for guidance, 76
Wire command link, 41
Wollaston wire, 147

X-4, air-to-air missile, 41, 42
X-7 missile, 41

Yates, Harold, 165
Yaw control channel, autopilot, general, 53
Yaw control loop, in Viking, 46

CPSIA information can be obtained
at www.ICGtesting.com
Printed in the USA
BVHW011555160619
550821BV00013B/146/P